Management
Total Quality in a Global Environment

Management
Total Quality in a Global Environment

Michael J. Stahl

The University of Tennessee

First published 1995

Blackwell Publishers, the publishing imprint of Basil Blackwell Inc.
238 Main Street
Cambridge, Massachusetts 02142
USA
Basil Blackwell Ltd.
108 Cowley Road
Oxford OX4 1JF
UK

Library of Congress Cataloging-in-Publication Data
Stahl, Michael J.
          Management: total quality in a global environment/Michael J. Stahl
                    p.   cm.
          Includes index.
          ISBN 1-55786-610-4 (hbk)
          ISBN 1-55786-611-2 (pbk)
          1.   Total quality management. 2.   Competition, International.
I. Title.
HD62.15.S734   1995

658.5'62--dc20   94-15348
A CIP catalogue record for this book is available from the British Library.

Typeset in 10/12 Garamond Light by Elm Street Publishing Services, Inc.

This book is printed on acid-free paper.
Cover source: Image courtesy of NASA.

To my wife Barbara . . . who has always understood and been supportive even when the journey is difficult and time consuming.

FOREWORD

In August 1991, six U.S. corporations with substantial global operations—American Express, Ford, IBM, Motorola, Procter & Gamble, and Xerox—sponsored the Total Quality Forum. The Forum was an annual gathering of academic leaders and corporate executives. Its purpose was to discuss the role of Total Quality Management in the United States and its role on campuses, especially in business and engineering schools.

The chief executive officers of the six sponsoring companies summarized the importance of Total Quality Management in "An Open Letter: TQM on Campus," published in the November–December 1991 issue of the *Harvard Business Review*: "We believe business and academia have a shared responsibility to learn, to teach, and to practice total quality management. If the United States expects to improve its global competitive performance, business and academic leaders must close ranks behind an agenda that stresses the importance and value of TQM . . . Our system of higher education is one of this country's most powerful competitive weapons. Working together, companies and institutions of higher education *must* accelerate the application of total quality management on our campuses if our education system and economy are to maintain and enhance their global positions."

In 1989, 14 leading European corporations founded the European Foundation for Quality Management. By 1993 its membership had grown to nearly 300 European organizations (corporations and universities). Its September 1993 membership information brochure included the following "Objective and Vision": "The European Foundation for Quality Management (E.F.Q.M.) believes that, through Total Quality Management, Western Europe will become a leading force in the world market. Our objective is to create conditions to enhance the position of European industry by strengthening the role of management in quality strategies. E.F.Q.M.'s vision is to become the leading organisation for promoting and facilitating Total Quality Management in Western Europe. This vision will be achieved when TQM has become an integrated value of the European society, and European management has achieved a global competitive advantage."

The commitment of the Japanese to quality management is legendary. Herein lies the theme of this book: As a system of management, whether in the Americas, the Pacific Rim, or Europe, TQM has become a significant factor in global competitive positioning.

This book has been designed, written, and produced for students taking their first course in management or organizations. Thus the book assumes no prior formal education in management. Its goal is to help educate students in a system of management by discussing a number of important topics in the theory and practice of management.

Intense global competition in recent years has caused managers and their organizations to experience, and to continue to experience, wrenching changes. Because of this fierce international competition, worldwide customers are now able to choose among several international competitors. As a result, customers have become increasingly demanding. Today they require high quality, low prices, and short delivery times, and tomorrow they may demand additional components of value from their chosen vendors.

Intense international competition has been the stimulus for the spread of Total Quality Management (TQM) throughout the world. In addressing that theme, this book is a comprehensive Principles of Management text whose primary focus is TQM in a global environment.

Total Quality Management is a systems approach to management that aims to enhance value to customers by designing and continually improving organizational processes and systems. This definition permeates all of the topics discussed in this book.

Managers of the 1990s are concerned with delivering value to customers. This concept of customer value underlies the external focus of today's managers, which contrasts with the internally focused way of managing that prevailed in earlier decades.

As the definition of Total Quality Management suggests, present-day managers are involved in the management of systems and processes, rather than in the supervision and control of people as they formerly were. Processes are groups of activities that take an input, add value to it, and provide an output to an internal or external customer. Systems are collections of processes and resources.

Managing processes and systems results in a horizontal focus, in contrast to the vertical focus of internally focused hierarchies. This explains the flatter organization structures and self-managed work teams of today, as compared to the tall, pyramidal organizations and narrow supervision of the past.

The process and system focus also allows managers to deal comprehensively with organizational ethics. Unethical managerial behavior can be described as a result of a defect in an organizational system. Such system or process defects could include inadequate training, vague organizational codes of ethics, or organizational reward systems that reinforce unethical managerial behavior.

Similarly, the process and system focus allows managers to deal comprehensively with a diverse workforce and with discrimination. Discrimination refers to human resource actions based on criteria that are not job relevant. As such, discrimination is a defect in an organizational system. Such process or system defects could include inadequate training, vague organizational policies on diversity, or organizational reward systems that do not reinforce diversity.

Consistent with the Total Quality Management theme of this book, there are at least seven major pedagogical features in each of the 18 chapters. The chapter opener is a three-part Quality Case (with discussion questions). A Quality Exhibit, an International Exhibit, an Ethics Exhibit (with questions), and a Diversity Exhibit present actual managerial and organizational situations in each chapter. At the end of each chapter, the Chapter Case (with discussion questions) applies the material in the chapter. An Experiential Exercise, also at the end of each chapter, helps students to experience some of the chapter's ideas.

These cases, exhibits, and exercises are an integral part of each chapter. They are meant to help students actualize real-world managerial and organizational situations, and students are advised to consider carefully the cases, exhibits, and exercises in each chapter.

To reinforce the learning process, there are additional pedagogical features common to all of the chapters. Each chapter starts with a list of behavior-based learning objectives. These objectives are meant to shape the students' behavior in studying the material, cases, exhibits, and exercises in the chapters. A chapter outline follows. It presents an overview of the chapter.

At the end of each major section within a chapter, two or three Critical Thinking Questions appear. These questions focus on the major discussion points of the section and ask students to critically evaluate or apply the points.

Key terms are defined in the text and highlighted with boldface. The definitions are repeated in the Key Terms list at the end of each chapter.

A Summary is presented at the end of the text discussion. Together with the Learning Objectives and the Chapter Outline at the beginning of the chapter, the Summary helps to provide an overview of the chapter.

Endnotes are provided to document the material in the chapter. They also provide references for students who wish to read further on issues covered in the text.

Two icons have been incorporated throughout the text as a learning tool for the students. 🌐 at the end of a paragraph means that there is an example of a U.S. firm conducting international operations, or that U.S. managers are involved in international business. ⬤ means that there is an example of a non-U.S. firm conducting international operations.

CORPORATE ACKNOWLEDGMENTS

Many managerial examples from real-world organizations are presented throughout the book. Because of space limitations, listing all of those organizations here is not possible.

The following organizations are covered in some detail in the cases, exhibits, exercises, and figures. I am grateful for the permissions extended to reprint the material in this text. The material from actual managerial situations is intended to enrich the learning experience for future managers as they study Total Quality Management in a global environment.

Chapter 1: Coca-Cola, Harley-Davidson, Johnson & Johnson, Levi Strauss, Liz Claiborne, Lutheran General Health Care System, Merck, 3M, Pepsico, J.C. Penney, Procter & Gamble, Rubbermaid, Sonoco, Wal-Mart, Withrow Cabinets.

Chapter 2: AT&T, Elton Textiles, Ford, Hoechst Celanese, Mercy Hospital, Sheet Metal Workers' International Association.

Chapter 3: Alcoa, Chrysler, Coca-Cola, Dresser Industries, Ford, Honda, General Motors, International Oil, McDonald's, Sing's Chinese Restaurant, SAI do Brazil, Tandy.

Chapter 4: Bluebird Smelter, Burroughs Wellcome, Johnson & Johnson, General Motors, Lincoln Savings and Loan, McDonnell Douglas, Pacific Lumber, Sloane Products, Westinghouse Electric.

Chapter 5: Acme Supply, Coca-Cola, Levi Strauss, Procter & Gamble, Pepsico, T.H. Sandy Sportswear.

Chapter 6: American Airlines, Braniff Airlines, Caterpillar, Continental Airlines, Delta Airlines, Eastern Airlines, Falls Church General Hospital, Komatsu, National Rubber and Tire, PanAm Airlines, Procter & Gamble, United Airlines, USAir, Xerox.

Chapter 7: Champion International Paper, Food and Drug Administration, Lands' End, Revlon, Old State University, Saturn, Sea Ray Boats.

Chapter 8: Dow Corning, KLM Airlines, Marlow Industries, Ohio Printing, Potlatch.

Chapter 9: Carnegie Mellon University, Equal Employment Opportunity Commission, NationsBank, Promus, Union Pacific Railroad.

Chapter 10: American Overseas, AT&T, Disney, Promus, Union Carbide, Velsicol Chemical.

Chapter 11: Loco Department Stores, Bendix, Heinz, Investment-U.S., Monroe County, Western Food Products.

Chapter 12: Drexel Burnham Lambert, Federal Express, IBM/Rochester, Coconut International.

Chapter 13: Chick-fil-A, City of San Jose, McDonald's, General Motors, New United Motors Manufacturing, Toyota.

Chapter 14: American Express/Benelux, Chrysler, Federal Express, Montgomery Construction, Motorola, Norwest Financial, Qualchem.

Chapter 15: BTR Hose, Capsugel, Eastman Chemical Company, Grace Dearborn, ICL, Royal Mail, Sea Ray Boats, Union Carbide.

Chapter 16: Delta Airlines, Fidelity Investments, Pitney Bowes, Sundstrand Data Control, United Parcel Service, USAir.

Chapter 17: Black & Decker, Corning Laboratories, Du Pont, Ford, Lockheed, OPCO, Personal Computer, Toyota.

Chapter 18: Asarco, Circuit City Stores, Digital Equipment, Ford, General Motors, Kaiser Aluminum, Motorola, Panasonic, Radio Shack, Sundstrand, Velcro, Xerox.

PERSONAL ACKNOWLEDGMENTS

In writing a book of this magnitude, it is nearly impossible to acknowledge all the people who were instrumental in its many phases. With a sense of gratitude, I acknowledge the following contributions with all due apologies if my memory is faulty.

Our three daughters, Lisa, Shelley, and Debbie, all word processed parts of the manuscript and understood the time their father spent on this book.

Our special friends Roy and Gloria helped us to persevere in this project and provided valuable marketing advice.

Tami Touchstone, my administrative assistant at The University of Tennessee, managed many of the administrative issues and word processed many of the cases.

Chris Carson and Doug Hof, my graduate research assistants, researched much of the material for the cases and exhibits.

My colleagues at The University of Tennessee offered valuable suggestions and references on the breadth and depth of the Total Quality Management model.

Rolf Janke, executive editor at Blackwell in the United States, believed in this project at a crucial time and was instrumental in its completion.

Richard Burton, executive editor at Blackwell in the United Kingdom, found some of the international cases and managed the international marketing.

Mary Riso and Jan Leahy at Blackwell in the United States handled many of the administrative, development, and production issues.

At Elm Street Publishing Services, Barbara Campbell coordinated the production services.

Several reviewers offered invaluable suggestions at crucial times during the development of the manuscript. They are:

Ivan Blanco, *Barry University*

Bonnie Daly, *New Mexico State University*

Stacey Nutt, *Georgia Institute of Technology*

Larry Siebers, *Utah State University*

Theodore O. Wallen, *Syracuse University*

Fred T. Whitman, *Mary Washington College*

There are approximately 130 cases and exhibits in this book. I am indebted to all who provided cases, exhibits, or material to help write them.

With gratitude,

Michael J. Stahl
Knoxville, Tennessee
October 1994

Michael J. Stahl, Ph.D., is Associate Dean and Professor of Management in the College of Business Administration at The University of Tennessee, Knoxville. Dr. Stahl received his B.S. in electrical engineering from the State University of New York at Buffalo and his Ph.D. in management from Rensselaer Polytechnic Institute. He was head of the Management Department at Clemson University, as well as program manager on the development and production of a communications satellite system at the Space and Missile Systems Organization in Los Angeles.

Professor Stahl is part of the Advisory Council for Total Quality Forums III–VI and was co-chair of a working council defining faculty development needs concerning Total Quality Management. He is a reviewer for the National Science Foundation's research program on Transformations to Quality Organizations. He is also on the Advisory Board to the Applied Technology Division at the Oak Ridge National Laboratory and is involved with a number of organizations concerning TQM and Strategy. In addition, Dr. Stahl has worked with the American Assembly of Collegiate Schools of Business on TQM in academia and has presented at national and international conferences on the subject.

Dr. Stahl has published more than 40 journal articles in a variety of areas including Strategic Management and Total Quality Management and eight books including *Competing Globally Through Customer Value* and *Strategic Management for Decision Making*. He is also TQM editor for a series of books in business and engineering. Currently, Dr. Stahl is teaching management courses with emphasis on TQM to undergraduates and executives.

CONTENTS IN BRIEF

CONTENTS

CONTENTS

Chapter 3

International Competition and Management, 56

Chapter 9

Managing Human Resource Systems, 244

Chapter 12

Motivation for Total Quality, *332*

Chapter 17

Managing Technology and Technological Change, 472

Chapter 18

Operations Management for Control and Improvement, 498

Management Today

Managers and Organizations Today

LEARNING OBJECTIVES

After reading this chapter, you should be able to accomplish the following:

- Define the terms *management* and *Total Quality* and discuss the relationship between them.
- Discuss the need for managers in organizations today.
- Describe the various levels of responsibility for managers.
- Discuss the responsibility of managers for the ethical conduct of their organizations.
- Discuss the responsibility of managers for the diversity of their workforces.
- List and describe the various skills required of managers.
- Explain the significance of Deming's 14 Points of Management.
- Explain the significance of the Malcolm Baldrige National Quality Award criteria.

CHAPTER OUTLINE

Total Quality and Management
  Total Quality
  Management Defined
  Deming's 14 Points of Management
  Other Pioneers in Total Quality
  Baldrige Quality Award Process
Organizations and the Need for Managers
  Keeping in Touch with the Environment
  Keeping in Touch with Customers
  Establishing Vision, Goals, and Objectives
  Ensuring Performance to Realize the Vision
Management Levels of Responsibility
  Strategic, Tactical, and Operational Control
  Top, Middle, First-line Levels
  Systems Responsibility
  Ethics Responsibility
  Diversity Responsibility
Management Skills
  Technical Skills
  Interpersonal Skills
  Conceptual Skills
  Diagnostic Skills
  Continuous Learning and Improvement

Cases and Exhibits
  Harley-Davidson
  Most Admired Corporations
  J.C. Penney
  Sonoco
  Withrow Cabinets
  Women Break Glass Ceiling
  TQM in Hospitals

Harley-Davidson's Near Death and Quality Rebirth

Harley-Davidson's President Teerlink rides to Harley Owner's Group (H.O.G.) weekend rallies on his bike to meet with customers and assess their needs. (Photo credit: Chris Sanders.)

Harley-Davidson is a remarkable story of a 90-year-old U.S. company that almost went bankrupt because its managers lost sight of its customers. The near bankruptcy was all the more remarkable considering that big, bad, loud, Harley "HOGS," as the bikes were known, are icons of Americana. The bankruptcy was avoided and many of Harley's customers returned after its managers refocused on customers by making a massive investment in quality.

In 1903 three brothers, William, Walter, and Arthur Davidson, along with their neighborhood friend, William Harley, fabricated the first Harley-Davidson motorcycle. In the ensuing years Harley survived two world wars and the Great Depression. Partly because the company focused on super-heavyweight bikes, HOGS personified "the American desire for power, speed, and per-

sonal freedom." Due to the popularity of "HOGS," by 1953 H-D was the sole domestic maker of motorcycles in the United States. Harley made its initial public stock offering in 1965.

The AMF Corporation acquired Harley-Davidson three years later partly on the basis of plans to invest in the company and help it grow. The irony is that AMF increased production dramatically and drove down quality. HOGS were failing final quality inspection more than 50 percent of the time and many defects were showing up in the hands of customers.

This was about the time that Japanese motorcycle companies—Honda, Suzuki, Yamaha, Kawasaki, and others—were invading the U.S. motorcycle market with high-quality bikes. Soichiro Honda, the founder of the Honda Company, described his strategy: "If you turn out a superior product, it will be patronized by the public. Our policy is not simply to turn out a product because there is demand, but to turn out a superior product and create a demand." Honda entered the United States by creating demand at the low end of the market with lightweight bikes.

Harley-Davidson's managers initially ignored the international competitors. The managers' attitude toward lightweight bikes was typified in 1973 by a comment of William H. Davidson, the firm's president and son of the founder: "Basically, we don't believe in the lightweight market." While Harley was disbelieving and ignoring the threat, international competitors first built substantial market share in the lightweight segment and then attacked Harley by selling super-heavyweight bikes.

continued

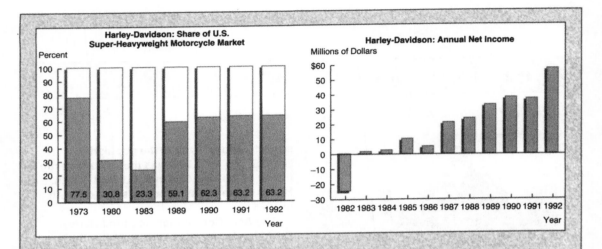

Harley-Davidson: Share of U.S. Super-Heavyweight Motorcycle Market

Harley-Davidson: Annual Net Income

Because of the attack with high-quality bikes by Japanese firms and Harley's quality problems, Harley's market share plummeted. As the first of the accompanying charts indicates, its domestic market share fell by over two-thirds in ten years, from more than three of every four bikes in 1973 to less than one of every four bikes in 1983.

Associated with the market share loss, Harley lost money in 1981, and as the second chart shows, it lost about $25 million in 1982. Based on those market and financial losses, bankruptcy seemed imminent. How could Harley's managers rescue the company and save an American institution from international assault?

TOTAL QUALITY AND MANAGEMENT

What do managers do? Why do they do what they do? Are the roles of managers changing due to intense international competition? Are managers' jobs changing because customers are more demanding? Should managers in other companies expect the kinds of demands that the Harley-Davidson managers faced?

Total Quality

How do we define management? To do so, we must first understand the concept of Total Quality Management (TQM), sometimes referred to simply as Total Quality (TQ). Throughout this book the terms TQM and TQ will be used interchangeably.

Total Quality Management (TQM) is a systems approach to management that aims to continuously increase value to customers by designing and continuously improving organizational processes and systems. TQ involves all employees and extends backward and forward to include the supply chain and the customer chain.[1] As the word *Total* implies, Total Quality Management is concerned with managing the entire system, and not only subsystems or functional departments. **Processes** are groups of activities that take an input, add value to it, and provide an output to an internal or external customer. **Systems** are collections of processes and resources.

After almost going bankrupt as the result of producing inferior-quality products in the face of high-quality products from international competitors, Xerox subsequently launched efforts toward Total Quality that earned the company a *Malcolm Baldrige National Quality Award* (see page 9). Xerox's efforts included continuously improving quality by working horizontally across departments, by working with suppliers to provide consistent quality, and by working closely with customers to deliver superior value. ◑

From this definition of TQ, we see the purpose of management as providing value for the customer. We also see the theme of integration of activities and processes across functions and departments. Armed with the definition of TQM, we are now positioned to offer a definition of management for this book.

Management Defined

Management is the creation and continuous improvement of organizational systems that when used by organizational members lead to increased value for the customers of its products or services.[2] Continuous improvement is required in an internationally competitive world characterized by rapidly changing technology and customer demand for higher levels of value. **Continuous improvement** refers to the constant refinement and improvement of products, services, and organizational systems to yield improved value to customers. The term *continuous improvement* is derived from the Japanese term *Kaizen,* meaning small but continuous improvement. ◑

Our definition of management does not refer to the behavior of a manager whose primary role is to maintain the status quo. Nor does it refer to managerial behavior that is focused primarily on planning, on organizing, on commanding, or on controlling the behavior of others. Such a traditional definition tells us what managers do without telling us for what purpose they engage in such activities.[3] To be sure, managers do serve such functions, and in Chapter 2 we discuss the reasons for their doing so. However, this classic definition misses the purpose of management in the 1990s, which is to provide increased value to customers. Our new definition is a pronounced shift away from the old "command and control" connotation of the "M" word (management).

The integration of Total Quality Management with the traditional functional approach to describing management needs to be explored. Figure 1.1 helps us to visualize the merger of two approaches to the study of management by combining the ideas of TQM with the ideas of employee involvement. **Employee involvement** refers to the participation and involvement of employees in their jobs in order to increase the value provided to customers. The figure shows how the classic managerial functions of planning, organizing, leading, and controlling are now shared with nonsupervisory employees in a TQM organization. Classic models of management segregated the four functions as strictly the purview of managers. In Figure 1.1 TQM is a model for deciding what is important to work on (customer value and system/process improvement), while employee involvement is a model for deciding how to go about working on these objectives.[4]

FIGURE 1.1   *Integrating Total Quality Management and Employee Involvement*

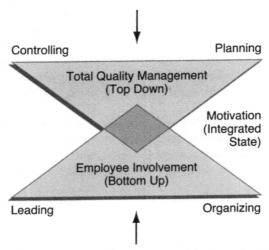

Source: L. Pace, "Moving Toward System Integration," Survey of Business (Summer 1989): 57–61. Reprinted with permission.

For example, in 1981 Milliken and Company implemented Milliken's Pursuit of Excellence (POE), a commitment to customer satisfaction for all company levels at all locations. In 1989 Milliken was awarded the Malcolm Baldrige National Quality Award for its leadership in the arena of Total Quality.

Milliken employs 14,300 workers, or what the company terms "associates." The company has achieved a flat management structure in which associates, working primarily in self-managed work teams, exercise considerable authority. **Self-managed work teams** are groups of employees who have the power to make operating decisions and operate the systems designed by managers. This approach has worked so well that Milliken has eliminated nearly 700 management positions since 1981, freeing that many individuals to serve as process-improvement specialists. There has been a 77 percent increase in the ratio of production to management associates. Since the early 1980s, productivity has increased 42 percent, and sales have risen significantly.[5]

In a Total Quality Forum in 1992, Roger Milliken, chairman of Milliken and Company, presented data showing that managers in well-run Japanese companies spent 60 percent of their time on continuous improvement of systems (see Figure 1.2). He also indicated that those Japanese managers spent little time on command and controlling people.[6] Figure 1.2 shows some of the dramatic differences between traditional Western management and the best Japanese management.

Managers in the most admired firms in the United States understand the importance of the quality of products and services and how to deliver quality to customers. These managers also understand that they are operating in a globally competitive marketplace and that they must compete globally in order to prosper. These two themes are apparent in the international exhibit.

FIGURE 1.2 *Differences between Western and Japanese Management*

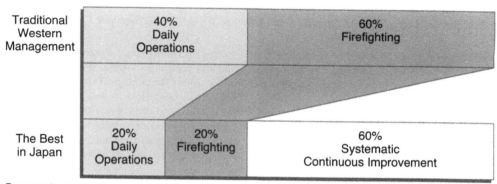

Source: Presentation by R. Milliken at Total Quality Forum IV, Cincinnati, OH (November 11, 1992).

Deming's 14 Points of Management

One way to understand the changes required of Western managers is to review the prescriptions of W. Edwards Deming, an influential American who is credited with remaking Japanese industry after World War II. Deming's 14 points (Table 1.1) are widely viewed as directives for a new way to manage. Deming described his 14 points as no less than a complete agenda for managerial action. "The 14 points are the basis for transformation of American industry. It will not suffice merely to solve

TABLE 1.1 *Deming's Revised 14 Points of Management*

1. Management must demonstrate constantly their commitment to a widely published statement of the purposes of the company.
2. Learn the new philosophy, top management and everybody.
3. Understand the purpose of inspection, for improvement of processes and reduction of cost.
4. End the practice of awarding business on the basis of price tag alone.
5. Improve constantly and forever the system of production and service.
6. Institute training.
7. Teach and institute leadership.
8. Drive out fear. Create trust. Create a climate for innovation.
9. Optimize toward the purposes of the company the efforts of teams, groups, staff areas.
10. Eliminate exhortations for the work force.
11a. Eliminate numerical quotas for production and institute methods for improvement.
11b. Eliminate Management by Objective and improve the capabilities of processes.
12. Remove barriers that rob people of pride of workmanship.
13. Encourage education and self-improvement for everyone.
14. Take action to accomplish the transformation.

Source: Author's adaptation of Dr. Deming's 14 Points, W. E. Deming, Out of the Crisis, Cambridge, MA: MIT Center for Advanced Engineering Study (1986): 23–24. (Revised January 10, 1990.)

INTERNATIONAL   EXHIBIT

Globalization and Total Quality at America's Most Admired Corporations

Over the last 11 years, *Fortune* magazine has ranked "America's most admired corporations." The rankings are the result of *Fortune's* Corporate Reputations Survey.

For the 1993 rankings 8,000 senior executives, outside directors, and financial analysts were asked to rate corporations on eight attributes. The attributes were quality of management; quality of products or services; innovativeness; long-term investment value; financial soundness; ability to attract, develop, and keep talented people; responsibility to the community and the environment; and wise use of corporate assets.

In defining overall corporate reputation, 82 percent of the polled executives, analysts, and directors cited quality of management as the primary attribute. Quality of products or services was rated as the second most important attribute by 62 percent of the voters.

The accompanying table contains the list of the most admired corporations in 1993. Two important characteristics of the firms in this list are worth discussing. The first is the quality of products and services. Indeed, the firms' commitments to quality go beyond today's products and services. Three of the top ten firms (Wal-Mart, 3M, and Procter & Gamble) have been actively disseminating TQ material to academia. All of the top ten firms are close to their customers—a key characteristic of Total Quality that will be emphasized throughout this book.

The second notable characteristic is the international presence evidenced in the table. Several of the firms (Merck in pharmaceuticals, Boeing in aerospace, Coca-Cola in soft drinks, 3M in scientific, photo, and control equipment, and Procter & Gamble in consumer products) receive about half of their sales from their international operations. The average amount of international sales as a percentage of total sales was about 30 percent. These data demonstrate that the most admired firms had adapted to the international business environment of the 1990s.

America's Most Admired Corporations: 1993

1. Merck (pharmaceuticals)
2. Rubbermaid (rubber and plastic products)
3. Wal-Mart Stores (retailing)
4. 3M (scientific, photo, and control equipment)
5. Coca-Cola (beverages)
6. Procter & Gamble (soaps, cosmetics)
7. Levi Strauss Associates (apparel)
8. Liz Claiborne (apparel)
9. J. P. Morgan (commercial banking)
10. Boeing (aerospace)

Sources: "America's Most Admired Corporations," *Fortune* (February 8, 1993): 40; *Value Line Investment Survey,* New York: Value Line Publishing (October 1992); and "America's Most Admired Corporations," *Fortune* (February 10, 1992): 43.

problems, big or little. Adoption and action on the 14 points are a signal that the management intends to stay in business and aims to protect investors and jobs."[7]

Deming's prescriptions are anything but business as usual. He stresses themes of quality, leadership, horizontal management, continuous improvement, employee involvement, and training. His model is substantially different from the old bureaucratic model of inward-looking administrators whose primary interest is in directing and controlling the behavior of others.

Deming's themes are used throughout this book and influence managerial activities throughout the world. The Japanese instituted a Deming Prize shortly after World War II to recognize substantial advancements in quality.

Deming was not the only pioneer in Total Quality. In some areas others made even greater contributions to the advancement of quality in organizations. They helped managers to realize that the practice of management had evolved in the twilight of the twentieth century.

Other Pioneers in Total Quality

Joseph Juran viewed quality as a cross-functional integration issue. His work began after World War II and has continued to today. Juran was concerned with processes that spanned at least two of the functions of design, production, marketing, or finance. His ideas are treated in detail in this book, especially in the areas of cross-functional processes and organizational design. His ideas have influenced the way managers structure organizations and teams today.

Kaoru Ishikawa, working through the 1950s and 1960s, was concerned with the prevention of defects before they occurred. Some of his work, which has much to do with the managerial emphasis on systems and process improvement today, will be reviewed in Chapter 15.

From 1970 to present day, Philip Crosby is noted for his ideas relating to the cost of quality. The **cost of quality** is the cost incurred as a result of producing poor-quality products and services. Crosby helped U.S. managers understand that improved quality can lead to lower costs if the product or service and the process that generated it are designed correctly.

Baldrige Quality Award Process

Another way to examine management and organizations in the 1990s is to review the Malcolm Baldrige National Quality Award criteria. The Baldrige was initiated on August 20, 1987, with the enactment of U.S. Public Law 100-17, for the purpose of recognizing firms that are leaders in providing increased quality and value to their customers in an internationally competitive era.[8] Although there have been some complaints about the amount of work required to satisfy all the Baldrige criteria (see Table 1.2), these criteria have been used by many managers as a guide for managerial and organizational improvement. For example, some companies require their suppliers to apply the Baldrige criteria to their firms to improve their operations.

To be sure, there has been some criticism of the Baldrige Award.[9] Nevertheless, the Baldrige criteria indicate how management has changed in the internationally competitive era of the 1990s, which is characterized by rapidly changing technology and demanding customers who have alternatives available to them. Many of the firms that have won the Baldrige are leaders in this new era and are providing new models of management for the twenty-first century. The emphasis in the Baldrige criteria on customer satisfaction and quality marks the areas at the very core of managerial attention and action in the 1990s.

There are other quality criteria and other quality awards that are also influencing present-day managerial action. The European Quality Award (a quality standard published by the International Standards Organization) and the ISO 9000 (a quality standard published by the European Community) will be discussed in Chapter 3, "International Competition and Management."

TABLE 1.2   *Malcolm Baldrige National Quality Award Criteria*

Examination Category/Item		Maximum Points
1.0	Leadership	95
2.0	Information and Analysis	75
3.0	Strategic Quality Planning	60
4.0	Human Resource Development and Management	150
5.0	Management of Process Quality	140
6.0	Quality and Operational Results	180
7.0	Customer Satisfaction	300
	Total Points	1,000

Source: Malcolm Baldrige National Quality Award: 1993 Application Guidelines, Washington, DC: U.S. Department of Commerce (1993): 15.

The Malcolm Baldrige National Quality Award symbolizes the importance of quality improvement in U.S. firms as an international competitive strategy. (Photo credit: U.S. Department of Commerce.)

Q U A L I T Y   E X H I B I T

The Penney Idea: Seven Principles Have Guided the Company Since 1913

In 1913, the year J.C. Penney was incorporated, the company also formulated and adopted "The Penney Idea," a set of seven principles that guide the retailer to this day.

Says chairman Bill Howell: "These are ideals that Mr. Penney set forth as an obligation, and that he was able to articulate in his own personal standards and lifestyle. These are the values that we try to maintain and sustain, even as we celebrate our 80th anniversary this year."

1. To serve the public, as nearly as we can, to its complete satisfaction.

2. To expect for the service we render a fair remuneration and not all the profit the traffic will bear.

3. To do all in our power to pack the customer's dollar full of value, quality, and satisfaction.

4. To continue to train ourselves and our associates so that the service we give will be more and more intelligently performed.

5. To improve constantly the human factor in our business.

6. To reward men and women in our organization through participation in what the business produces.

7. To test our every policy, method, and act in this wise: "Does it square with what is right and just?"

Source: *Stores* (January 1992): 73.

It should be noted that the concern for quality and delivering value to customers is not a new business philosophy. The quality exhibits from 1913 and 1931 demonstrate that quality and customer value are not new concepts. J. C. Penney is a large U.S. retailer and Sonoco is a worldwide manufacturer and distributor of packaging material based in South Carolina.

CRITICAL THINKING QUESTIONS

1. Compare and contrast the role of a manager in a Total Quality Management organization with that of a manager in an organization that does not subscribe to TQM.

2. Describe the significance of Deming's 14 Points of Management for the practice of managers in the 1990s.

3. Are the Malcolm Baldrige National Quality Award criteria applicable to a university? Why or why not?

ORGANIZATIONS AND THE NEED FOR MANAGERS

Managers of an organization must be prepared to anticipate and adapt to change by keeping in touch with the external environment and the organization's customers. For the firm to prosper and grow in a changing environment, managers must articulate a vision, as well as goals and objectives for the future.

QUALITY   EXHIBIT

Sonoco's Heritage of Quality

James L. Coker, Sonoco's president from 1931 to 1961, set the tone for Sonoco's dedication to quality with this 1931 summary of the company's quality philosophy:

> By quality products, I mean a product or service, or both, that fills the need better than any other product or service; a product that by its peculiar advantages and benefits to the user enables him to derive from its use more dollar value than from all other similar products; a product that justifies its purchase and use every time it is bought; a product that lives up to every promise of its maker and every expectancy of its user; a product backed by the faith, honor and integrity of its maker and manufactured with such painstaking care that it will be set apart from all other related products; a product that exacts from its user neither the penalty of cheapness nor the penance of costliness. These things, therefore, are what we are striving for when we say that we will manufacture quality products.

Source: Sonoco Products Company, Hartsville, SC (1993).

Keeping in Touch with the Environment

A principal function of managers is keeping the organization in touch with the external environment. By maintaining close contact, managers are prepared to structure the organization and its activities to capitalize on opportunities that the environment offers and to avoid threats inherent in that environment. Effective managers relate the organization to its environment and then guide internal activities to maximize the external opportunities and minimize the external threats.[10] Managers need to be externally focused in spite of the temptation to act solely in terms of the firm's internal organizational activities.

Change tends to be a natural part of organizational life, for both external organizational environments and customers change. Moreover, in the internationally competitive environment of the 1990s, change is virtually assured. It takes exceptional management to anticipate and to profit from change.

An analysis of the corporations ranked in 1983 (see Table 1.3) reveals some interesting changes relative to 1993. Only one firm that was on the "most admired" list in 1983 (Merck) was still among the "most admired" in 1993. In fact, three of the 1983 firms (Eastman Kodak, IBM, and Digital Equipment) were experiencing financial difficulty in the early 1990s. Eastman Kodak was slow to adapt to customer demands for electronic imaging in cameras. IBM had grown very large and inwardly focused. Digital Equipment had pursued technology and lost sight of its customers' requirements. All three saw the firing of their chief executive officers in the early 1990s for failure to adapt their organizations to change.

Keeping in Touch with Customers

Increasingly today the essence of management is being defined in terms of service to the customer.[11] One of the most popular management books published recently

TABLE 1.3 *America's Most Admired Corporations: 1983*

1. IBM	6. AT&T
2. Hewlett-Packard	7. Digital Equipment
3. Johnson & Johnson	8. SmithKline Beckman
4. Eastman Kodak	9. General Electric
5. Merck	10. General Mills

Source: "Ranking Corporate Reputations," Fortune (January 10, 1983): 35.

has been Peters and Waterman's book, *In Search of Excellence.* The authors define excellent companies in terms of several characteristics, including being "close to the customer. Excellent companies learn from the people they serve. They provide unparalleled quality, service, and reliability—things that work and last. They succeed in differentiating—à la Frito-Lay (potato chips), Maytag (washers), or Tupperware—the most commodity-like products."[12]

A pioneer in the quality movement in the United States since the 1950s, Armand Feigenbaum understood the primacy of the customer and the implications of quality for managerial behavior and systems. In 1989 he noted: "As the American consumer continues to place increasing demands on American products and services, business needs to be ready to respond. After all, quality is what the customer says it is. Before American business can effectively address these needs, the following must first take place: Consumers' needs are addressed as quality becomes a fundamental way of managing a company."[13]

Throughout this book we hold that the customer is the reason for the existence of the entire organization. The primacy of customer value under an umbrella of Total Quality will be discussed further in Chapter 7, "Customer Value Strategy."

Establishing Vision, Goals, and Objectives

Nearly all management scholars agree on the need for managers at all levels to envision and describe the future for the organization; the only difference of opinion may be in the length of the time horizon. As entire managerial levels disappear in many organizations, and as organizations become flatter and flatter, the remaining managers have become more involved with visions, goals, and objectives for the future.

An increasing number of firms understand that a dramatic commitment to their customers through Total Quality is a necessary part of survival in these internationally competitive times. This commitment to quality starts with managerial leaders.

One characteristic common to a number of TQ companies is strong leadership—a chief executive who leads the charge with a strong belief in quality. Leadership is the most important ingredient for launching and sustaining a quality-improvement process. Leaders of TQ companies establish clear, results-oriented goals for continuous improvement, and communicate their expectations.[14]

Peter Drucker, one of the most noted of all management theorists, summed it up rather succinctly: "The foundation of effective leadership is thinking through the organization's mission, defining it and establishing it, clearly and visibly. The leader sets the goals, sets the priorities, and sets and maintains the standards."[15]

Ensuring Performance to Realize the Vision

Once the vision has been established, managers take the lead to ensure that the vision is achieved. They do this by steering performance to make it consistent with the vision. Many refer to this managerial behavior as *controlling*.

Harold Geneen, the infamous tough boss who built ITT into one of the world's largest organizations in the 1970s and 1980s, described the responsibility of managers for performance in the following way: "I think it is an immutable law in business that words are words, explanations are explanations, promises are promises—but only performance is reality. Performance alone is the best measure of your confidence, competence, and courage. Only performance gives you the freedom to grow as yourself. Just remember that: *Performance is your reality.*"[16]

Fortune magazine ran a cover story on managing entitled "America's Toughest Bosses." In that article the editors described the role of the boss in ensuring performance under the label of toughness. Toughness was defined broadly as the condition of being demanding and hard to please, for whatever reason. A good toughness pushes people to the limits of their abilities, and no further, for constructive and legitimate purposes.[17]

CRITICAL THINKING QUESTIONS

1. Describe the need for managers in organizations today.
2. Do you expect the need for managers to stay in touch with the environment and customers to strengthen or weaken over the next decade? Explain.

MANAGEMENT LEVELS OF RESPONSIBILITY

In fulfilling their responsibilities, managers have different levels of responsibilities. These can be characterized in terms of the relative significance of the responsibilities, the organizational level, the systems breadth, and the values or ethics involved.

Strategic, Tactical, and Operational Control

The relative significance of the responsibilities is concerned with three kinds of control: strategic, tactical, and operational. **Strategic control** is the strategic direction of the organization over time in relation to its environment. Since strategic control deals with the most global of issues impacting the entire organization over time, this type of control is generally the province of the most senior executives at the top levels of the organization. **Tactical control** deals more with the implementation of the strategic

Q UALITY CASE

Back to the Harley-Davidson Case

Forecasting that the future contained bankruptcy given their dismal results under AMF, Harley's executives bought the company back from AMF. With their weakened market and financial conditions, the executives lobbied for and achieved substantial tariff protection from the U.S. Congress for five years against foreign motorcycles. This gave the executives five years to rescue the company as the tariffs raised the price of foreign bikes and thereby limited their market growth.

The executives tried a number of programs, including wage cuts and automation. However, nothing they tried seemed to work until they implemented quality improvement that emphasized employee involvement.

Harley's executives dared to rebuild the company and win back customers by making a massive commitment to improving the quality of H-D HOGS. As part of their commitment to the customer through Total Quality, Harley executives travel to H.O.G. (Harley Owner Group) rallies on their bikes on weekends to assess customer needs and customer satisfaction with current products. Partly as a result of those executive trips to assess customer needs, Harley's managers purposely designed their bikes with the motor and parts not covered with sheet metal as in the case of more aerodynamic-looking Japanese bikes.

Harley's efforts toward Total Quality also included supplier training and supplier partnerships. Harley cut the number of its suppliers from 320 to 120 and taught the remaining firms TQ concepts. In 1992 Gary E. Kirkham, Harley's manufacturing manager, said: "We buy 50 percent of the dollar value of our motorcycles from suppliers. So improvements we made (internally) only got us halfway."

Changes were made on several other fronts to improve quality. Massive worker training in TQ ideas and methods, and the active buy-in from the union were part of the quality-improvement change. The organization started using cross-functional quality teams with representatives from different functions such as manufacturing, purchasing, and marketing. A flatter organization structure was implemented with fewer layers of managers, since the employees were now better trained and working together across departmental boundaries. Statistical process control was implemented to control the manufacturing process before defects were produced. Just-In-Time (Materials as Needed) manufacturing also has become part of Harley's commitment to Total Quality.

plan. Tactical control is generally the province of general managers at the divisional level in the firm. **Operational control** deals with near-term achievement of goals.[18] Operational control is the concern of lower-level managers in the organization.

Top, Middle, First-Line Levels

Another way to examine managerial responsibilities is through the organizational hierarchy. The higher the manager is in the organization, the broader is the manager's responsibilities. As we have already indicated, top, middle, and first-line levels in the organizational hierarchy loosely correspond with strategic, tactical, and operational control.

E T H I C S   E X H I B I T

Shutdown at Withrow

Bill and Barbara Redding first met while working at Withrow Cabinets Company in their small hometown of Derwent. They subsequently fell in love, married, and began saving for their first home. Their future seemed assured.

But not any more. The grapevine has it that Withrow plans to move its operations to a state where labor is cheaper. The rumor has caused much concern and bitterness in Derwent, where Withrow Cabinets has been the town's main workplace for generations.

"I don't know what we're going to do," Bill tells his wife, who is expecting their third child in a few months. "You just start getting ahead of the game and they pull the rug out from under you."

In addition to the Reddings, about half of Derwent's 2,000 workers will lose their jobs if Withrow Cabinets relocates. What's more, residents not employed by Withrow are small-business people or self-employed contractors, mechanics, and plumbers; all are dependent on the presence of the plant for their livelihood. And to make matters worse, a local bank vice president has predicted that such a move would severely hamper local government, which is largely dependent on the sizable real estate tax that the company currently pays.

Company owner Gary Withrow knows there is one alternative to moving. It would involve laying off older workers who receive high wages and replacing them with cheap labor who would accept the minimum wage level or below. He realizes that few displaced employees could get jobs elsewhere in the town and would probably be forced to move. But it is an alternative. Since Withrow Cabinets is not a union shop, the owner could take such action without fearing reprisals from organized labor.

Discussion Questions

1. If Withrow moves, does it have any responsibilities to its workers and to the community at large? If it does, what are they?

2. Since costs and productivity seem to be the basic issues, are there alternatives other than the two mentioned? If so, what are they? Discuss the pros and cons.

Source: V. Barry, *Moral Issues in Business*, 2nd ed., Belmont, CA: Wadsworth (1983): 177–178.

Systems Responsibility

As more managers learn that critical organizational work is accomplished through horizontal systems and cross-functional processes, senior managers are assigning systems responsibilities to specific managers.[19] **Cross-functional processes** are activities linked to providing value to customers that span at least two of the functions of design, production, marketing, and finance. The new-product design and development process is a cross-functional process in that it involves activities in design, production (concerning manufacturability), marketing (concerning marketability), and finance (concerning the budgets and the profit projections). Managing cross-functional systems and processes is fundamentally different from managing vertical structures.

There are challenges associated with managing horizontal areas outside the manager's immediate vertical range of control and influence. We cover this important issue of systems responsibility in greater detail in Chapter 8, "Organizational Structure and Design."

FIGURE 1.3   *Number of Sexual Harassment Complaints Filed through the Equal Employment Opportunity Commission*

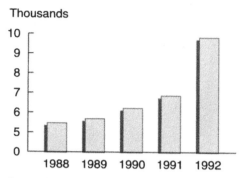

Source: Equal Employment Opportunity Commission.

Ethics Responsibility

There is a close link between Total Quality Management and managerial ethics. TQM is concerned with the continuous improvement of systems for the purpose of eliminating defects. Nearly all organizations claim that they want their managers and employees to act ethically in deciding business issues. Unethical business behavior, therefore, can be viewed as a result of a defect in an organizational system. Such system or process defects could include inadequate training, vague organizational codes of ethics, or organizational reward systems that reinforce unethical managerial behavior. **Ethics** can be described as doing the right things right the first time.

Managers assume responsibility for the ethical conduct of their organization. For example, it was reported that "Dow-Corning employees for several years falsified certain documents concerning the manufacture of silicone breast implants."[20] What kind of an ethical climate did some managers establish if such falsification continued to occur for years?

This issue of managers being accountable for the ethical behavior of employees is receiving increased attention today due in part to the increasing charges of sexual harassment in the workplace. In 1992 the Equal Employment Opportunity Commission reported a 50 percent increase in the number of sexual harassment charges filed (see Figure 1.3). An increasing number of managers are recognizing that it is management's responsibility to lead the fight to reduce this form of unethical behavior in the workplace.[21]

Many of the business ethics issues that managers face today are discussed in this book, and each chapter has its own ethics exhibit. In this chapter's ethics exhibit a firm proposes to shut down operations in a town that had grown to be dependent on the company.

Diversity Responsibility

In addition to business ethics issues, managers today deal with a diverse workforce and with discrimination laws. There are an increasing number of laws relating to

Today, managers must recognize the increased importance of a diverse workforce to fully capture the array of talent and to deal with a variety of customers. (Photo credit: Bruce Ayers/Tony Stone Worldwide.)

diversity issues, and an increasing number of organizations are training managers in the issues associated with a diverse workforce.

A process and system focus on Total Quality allows managers to deal comprehensively with a diverse workforce and with discrimination in the workplace. **Discrimination** refers to human resource actions based on criteria that are not job relevant. As such, discrimination is a defect in an organizational system. Such system or process defects could include inadequate training, vague organizational policies on diversity, or organizational reward systems that do not reinforce diversity. The diversity exhibit examines gender diversity among executives.

CRITICAL THINKING QUESTIONS

1. Describe the various levels of managerial responsibility.

2. Why has the responsibility of managers for the ethical conduct of their organizations received so much attention in the media in the last ten years? What is your forecast for the future?

3. Why has the responsibility of managers for the diversity of their workforce received so much attention in the media in the last ten years? What is your forecast for the future?

MANAGEMENT SKILLS

As business is recognizing the increased importance of skills to managerial performance, a number of business schools are emphasizing skill development in managerial education.[22] A comprehensive review of managerial behavior and performance views "key managerial skills" as critical to managerial performance.[23]

D I V E R S I T Y   E X H I B I T

An Increasing Number of Women Break the Glass Ceiling into the Executive Suite

The glass ceiling, a perceived invisible barrier keeping women and minorities out of executive ranks, is being broken by an increasing number of women. The U.S. Department of Labor published a report with some encouraging data on the upward mobility of women. The report showed that among 90,000 contractors who reported to the department, women accounted for 25 percent of the total officers and managers in 1991. This was up from 18 percent in 1981. Minority employees rose to 10 percent from 8 percent in the sample.

This progress is especially noteworthy at the very top of corporate America—in the boardroom. The presence of women is being increasingly noted on corporate boards of directors. *The Wall Street Journal* reported that the proportion of corporate boards appointing women in 1992 reached a record of 60 percent.

Since such boards are the pinnacle of power in most corporations, women's presence on such boards may lead the way to shattering the glass ceiling for other women. Especially since women are increasingly functioning on powerful committees of those boards, their ability to influence corporate practices is growing. "Token women on boards are dead. Today's women board members, armed with more business knowledge and experience, can be found heading powerful executive and audit committees. Others are influencing policy in finance, acquisitions and executive pay."

Progress is not uniform, however, as roadblocks remain. Many women's managerial experience is relatively short, narrow, and in areas that have not been associated with executive career paths—for example, in communications.

Many women are also finding that when conducting international business, they are not accepted as equals by managers in many other countries. In certain foreign countries, because business is still more of a man's world than in the United States, women face problems being accepted as professionals. US

To counter these roadblocks, women are increasingly seeking line managerial experience in marketing and in operations. As international experience is more and more in demand for executive careers, some women are placing more emphasis on international participation and assignments. Such international experience, combined with breadth in line managerial positions, should lead to further disintegration of the glass ceiling for women. US

Sources: "Once Male Enclaves, Corporate Boards Now Comb Executive Suites for Women," *The Wall Street Journal* (January 22, 1993): B1; "Gender Gap: Businesswomen Face Formidable Barriers When They Venture Overseas" *The Wall Street Journal* (October 16, 1992): R20; "Doors Still Closed to Women, CEO Survey Says," *USA Today* (September 3, 1992): 7B; "Progress Seen in Breaking 'Glass Ceilings,'" *The Wall Street Journal* (August 12, 1992): B1.

There are a variety of different skills associated with effective managerial performance. In this chapter we cover some of the more important ones. Many successful managers have strong combinations of technical, interpersonal, conceptual, and diagnostic skills.[24]

Technical Skills

Technical skills consist of the specific competencies to perform particular operational tasks. Technical skills include proficiency with the methods, procedures,

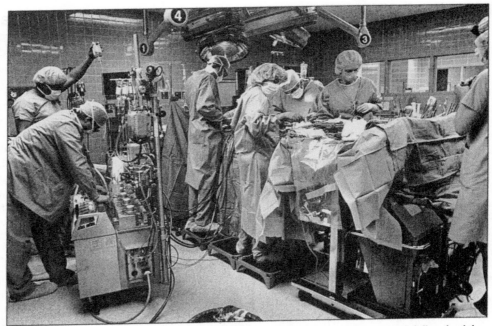

The head of this open heart surgery team must rely on both technical and interpersonal skills to lead the team to peak performance. (Photo credit: Jean-Claude Lejeune.)

techniques, knowledge, and equipment involved with the specific functions of, for example, manufacturing, sales, accounting, finance, or engineering.

The importance of technical skills to a manager is usually related to that manager's level in the organization. Many managers are promoted into an entry-level managerial position because of their excellent technical skills. As managers rise in the organization, human and conceptual skills assume increased importance, as indicated in Figure 1.4. For example, an entry-level production manager is expected to be knowledgeable about the firm's computerized manufacturing management system. The vice president for manufacturing is not expected to have the same degree of knowledge about the computerized system.

Interpersonal Skills

Interpersonal skills constitute the manager's ability to deal effectively with and through other people both inside and outside the organization and to work effectively as a team member. These skills are demonstrated in the ways the manager relates to other people—by leading, coordinating, motivating, and communicating.

For example, Roy Vagelos, chief executive officer of Merck and one of the most admired business leaders in America, leads the only firm included in all 11 years of the *Fortune* "most admired corporations" list from 1983 to 1993. Vagelos makes an effort to become acquainted with Merck's employees, treats them with respect, and is open when he talks with them. He makes it a point to meet with employees in the informal, nonthreatening setting of the firm's wellness center. [25]

FIGURE 1.4 *The Importance of Management Skills by Organizational Level*

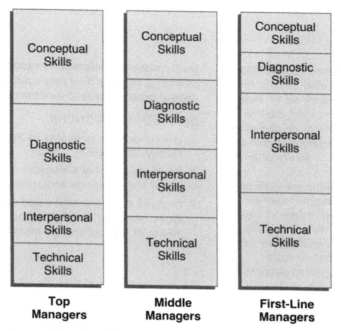

Source: Adapted from R. L. Katz, "The Skills of an Effective Administrator," Harvard Business Review (September-October 1987): 90–102.

Conversely, Frank Lorenzo, ex-chair of Texas Air Corporation, had acquired Eastern Airlines a few years prior to its bankruptcy and liquidation. Some charged he was responsible for the failure. Lorenzo was not presented as an interpersonal role model by *Fortune.* "Frank Lorenzo of Texas Air might be called many things. But to Lorenzo's subordinates, 'loose cannon' probably fits him best. For Lorenzo sometimes creates as much havoc among his crew as he creates among his competitors."[26]

Conceptual Skills

Conceptual skills involve the manager's abilities to think abstractly, to see the "big picture," and to comprehend the interrelationships among the various segments of the organization. Managers with conceptual skills "see" relationships and recognize opportunities where others do not. Michael Dell, founder and president of Dell Computer Company, seeing a need for direct marketing of low-priced personal computers, started a very successful computer company that marketed its computers over the phone and through the mail.

Conceptual skills are essential for managers at all levels in the organization. However, as shown in Figure 1.4, they are needed in increasing doses as managers ascend the organizational hierarchy.

QUALITY CASE

Conclusion to the Harley-Davidson Case

If Total Quality is to succeed, executives must "walk the talk" and lead the commitment to Total Quality, as they do at Harley-Davidson. The near bankruptcy, quality rebirth, and dramatic turnaround at Harley-Davidson prove the importance of managerial focus on the customer in an era of intense international competition.

As a result of its commitment to its customers and their quality requirements, Harley's market share had grown by 1993 to 63 percent and climbing. Its profitability had risen dramatically and its stock price had increased 24-fold from 1986 to 1993. International sales of HOGS (20 percent of total sales) were helping to fuel the profit and sales growth.

In the quality transformation, owning a HOG had become respectable. Jay Leno talked about his HOG on the "Tonight Show," and actors like Arnold Schwarzenegger were helping to make the bikes popular by driving around Hollywood on them. As a measure of the bike's respectability, one in three of Harley buyers in the early 1990s was a professional or a manager.

Harley's story is not unlike the Xerox story. Both firms lost dramatic market shares in markets where they had been dominant, and both almost went bankrupt. Both firms lost touch with their customers by delivering poor-quality products in the face of high-quality products from international competitors. In dramatic turnarounds, both recovered before it was too late by changing the way they managed in order to deliver greater value to customers.

DISCUSSION QUESTIONS

1. How important is quality to the rebirth of Harley-Davidson?

2. What were Harley's chances of surviving under the corporate structure of AMF?

3. Discuss the advantages and disadvantages of Harley's targeting other segments of the motorcycle market.

Sources: "Harley-Davidson," Value Line Investment Survey (September 3, 1993): 1763; "The Enduring Harley Mystique," Charlotte Observer (July 27, 1993): D1-2; S. Draper, A. Dundon, A. North, R. Smith, S. Adams, and A. Griffin, "Harley-Davidson, Inc.," in D. Grigsby and M. Stahl, Strategic Management Cases, Boston: PWS-Kent (1993): 352–377; "The Payoff from a Good Reputation," Fortune (February 10, 1992): 77; "Learning from Japan," Business Week (January 27, 1992): 59; D.T. Kearns and D.A. Nadler, Prophets in the Dark: How Xerox Reinvented Itself and Beat Back the Japanese, New York: Harper-Collins, 1992; R. Rose, "Vrooming Back," The Wall Street Journal (August 31, 1990): 1; P. Reid, Well Made in America: Lessons from Harley-Davidson on Being the Best, New York: McGraw-Hill (1990): 9, 25; Mark Marvel, "The Gentrified Hog," Esquire (July 1989): 25–26; R. Willis, "Harley-Davidson Comes Roaring Back," Management Review (March 1986): 20–27; T. Rowan, "Harley Sets New Drive to Boost Market Share," Advertising Age (January 29, 1973): 34; Journal of Commerce (November 6, 1965): 23. Figure Sources: R. L. Polk & Co. and Harley-Davidson Inc.; Harley-Davidson Inc.

Diagnostic Skills

Diagnostic skills involve the manager's ability to understand cause-and-effect relationships and to recognize acceptable solutions to problems. For example, if a manufacturing operation is producing repetitive defects, it cannot today afford to solve the problem through inspection and destruction of the costly scrap. Present-

Whether in Singapore or London, managers need to understand international markets in order to compete. (Photo credit: Singapore Tourist Promotion Board and The British Tourist Authority.)

day managers must diagnose the problem of poor quality and design and continuously improve the process to eliminate defects before they occur.

It is no longer acceptable to wait until an ethical breach such as sexual harassment occurs and then publish a policy on workplace ethics. Managers must take the lead in ethical issues and attempt to prevent infractions by diagnosing the situation before the cause-and-effect loop is complete.

These diagnostic skills are presently considered important, chiefly at upper levels in the organization. As the organizational hierarchy flattens and as more of the managerial function shifts to include systems management, diagnostic skills will take on increased importance at lower levels.

Continuous Learning and Improvement

As Figure 1.4 indicates, the relative importance of the four classes of skills changes as a function of level in the organization. If managers wish to advance in the organization, then they must be prepared to learn and improve upon skills as the demands of the job evolve. As managerial methods and styles change as a function of competitive challenges and evolving organizational life, managers must be prepared to continuously improve.

For example, conceptual and diagnostic skills are more important today than they were 20 years ago due to the flattening of organizations in response to competitive cost pressures and customer demands for quality. In the era of Total Quality, employees are becoming more empowered and better trained to perform many of the technical tasks performed by managers in an earlier era. Technical skills may therefore become less important for managers in the future.

CRITICAL THINKING QUESTIONS

1. Compare and contrast the various skills required of managers in the 1990s with those that will probably be required in the year 2005.

2. How will the trend toward self-managed teams impact the skills required by managers?

SUMMARY

Deming's 14 Points of Management are viewed as a new prescription for managing and doing business in a world in which intense international competition gives customers choices. The Baldrige Quality Award process provides a standard for organizations that heavily weights the customer. Deming, Juran, Ishikawa, Crosby, and the Baldrige combine with the practice of Total Quality to yield a definition of management that focuses on continuous improvement, organizational systems, and customer value.

International competition, rapidly changing technology, and demanding customers are the primary forces operating on managers today. These TQ themes are reviewed throughout this book as they shape the concepts and practices of management.

The foremost responsibility of managers today is to keep the organization in touch with the external environment and with the customers served by the organization. Managers must develop and communicate a vision for the future of the organization and set goals and objectives. Managers are also charged with guiding performance to ensure that this vision and these goals are reached.

Management operates at several levels of responsibility. The strategic level is concerned with the direction of the organization relative to its environment. The tactical level relates to the implementation of the strategic plan. The operational level deals with the near-term achievement of goals. Another way to view management's responsibilities is through the organizational levels of top, middle, and first-line.

Management also has responsibility for systems and processes. In the last ten years, managers have increasingly recognized that systems improvement is associated with sustainable quality improvement.

Managers also have responsibility for the ethical conduct of their organizations. Indeed, managers should take the lead in communicating ethical standards of conduct. In addition to business ethics, managers are also asked by the law and corporate policy to take the lead in issues relating to workforce diversity.

Managers need several skills in varying amounts as a function of their organizational level. These skills include technical, interpersonal, conceptual, and diagnostic skills. In the spirit of continuous learning, managers recognize that the mix of required skills changes during a managerial career.

EXPERIENTIAL EXERCISE

Ethical Problems and Attitudes

The following survey can reveal the patterns in your ethical system. Its purpose is not to discover faults or flaws, but to lead you to a better understanding of your standards and ethics. Because your instructor may wish to discuss how the class as a whole responded, please complete the survey without consulting your classmates.

Listed below are a number of statements that have been made by observers of the business scene. Please check the column that best corresponds to your opinion about each of these statements.

	Agree	Disagree
1. Sound ethics is good business in the long run.	—	—
2. Whatever is good business is good ethics.	—	—
3. Clergymen should not meddle in the social problems of business.	—	—
4. The American business executive tends to ignore the great ethical laws as they apply immediately to his work. He is preoccupied chiefly with gain.	—	—
5. For corporation executives to act in the interest of shareholders alone, and not also in the interest of employees and consumers, is unethical.	—	—
6. To get ahead in business, one must be willing to conform.	—	—

After you have completed the survey, the instructor will divide the class into groups of four or five students each for discussion purposes. Each group will discuss the statements and attempt to arrive at a consensus for each statement. After 30 minutes of discussion, each group should report its group answers to the class.

Source: R. Fulmer, *Supervision: Principles of Professional Management,* Encino, CA: Glencoe (1976): 125.

CHAPTER CASE

Total Quality Management in Hospitals

A number of companies with a reputation for excellence in quality have leveraged this reputation by organizing separate strategic business units (SBUs) to market consulting and training services. Such a company is 3M, whose Management Services Division has clients ranging from airlines to public-school districts. Labeled "masters of innovation" in a *Business Week* cover story, the company has been noted over time as a quality manufacturer of over 50,000 products worldwide.

A central idea of 3M's total quality system, called "Managing Total Quality" (MTQ), is the "Vision for Success," the key motivating force behind the MTQ process. Following the example of 3M, a number of hospital clients have drafted new mission statements as the basis for a quality-management system. Stephen Ummel, president and chief executive officer of the Park Ridge, Illinois, Lutheran General Health Care System, says, "Too many mission statements read alike. Many say, 'We're going to deliver high-quality health care at the lowest possible price.' It's a little corny and trite and doesn't tell you anything about the hospital's

mission in the market." Presented below is the mission statement of Lutheran General:

The purpose of Lutheran General Health Care System (LGHCS) is to provide quality health care and health-related services. We are committed to a comprehensive approach that effectively and efficiently meets the needs of individuals, families and the community, including those who are most vulnerable.

Our mission, which is an integral part of the healing and teaching ministry of the Evangelical Lutheran Church in America and an expression of our philosophy of Human Ecology, demands that our practices demonstrate concern for the whole person—body, mind, emotions, spirit and relationships—as fundamental to every human encounter. We encourage the adoption of this philosophy through services, research, charity, advocacy and example.

Chicago's Rush-Presbyterian-St. Luke's Medical Center and the South Carolina Baptist Hospitals are among those health care facilities that have adopted

Total Quality Management based on the MTQ process of 3M. Administrators at these hospitals are enthusiastic. Each admits that TQM is necessary in light of ever-increasing health care costs and steadily decreasing federal funding for Medicare and Medicaid.

Employee involvement is a primary characteristic of TQM and the 3M system. Because participation by all individuals—ranging from the nursing staff to administration to environmental services—is strongly encouraged, each employee is empowered to make decisions and initiate service goals without first having to pass ideas through several levels of authority. Because it is important to involve all constituents, steering committee members are composed of hospital volunteers and employees, patients, and physicians. This broad mix of input providers ensures that all constituents have a voice in the quality process.

Discussion Questions

1. Describe how the mission statement of Lutheran General can be implemented and made operational.
2. How can quality, as defined in the mission statement, be measured?
3. Would the Lutheran General mission be appropriate for a for-profit hospital? For a corporation not in the health care industry? Explain.
4. Will mounting pressure for reduction of health care costs make it more difficult to implement TQM? Explain.

Source: J. Ross, *Total Quality Management,* Delray Beach, FL: St. Lucie Press (1993): 124-125.

KEY TERMS

conceptual skills   Skills that involve the manager's abilities to think abstractly, to see the "big picture," and to comprehend the interrelationships among the various segments of the organization.

continuous improvement   Constant refinement and improvement of products, services, and organizational systems to yield improved value to customers.

cost of quality   Cost incurred in producing poor-quality products and services.

cross-functional processes   Activities linked to providing value to customers that span at least two of the functions of design, production, marketing, and finance.

diagnostic skills   Skills that reflect the manager's ability to understand cause-and-effect relationships and to recognize acceptable solutions to problems.

discrimination   In the workplace, human resource actions based on criteria that are not job relevant.

employee involvement   Participation and involvement of employees in their jobs in order to increase the value provided to customers.

ethics   Doing the right things right the first time.

interpersonal skills   Skills that reflect the manager's ability to deal effectively with and through other people both inside and outside the organization and to work effectively as a team member.

management   Creation and continuous improvement of organizational systems that when used by organizational members lead to increased value for the customers of its products or services.

operational control   Control related to near-term achievement of goals.

processes   Grouped activities that take an input, add value to it, and provide an output to an internal or external customer.

self-managed work teams   Groups of employees who have the power to make operating decisions and operate the systems designed by managers.

strategic control   Control concerned with the strategic direction of the organization over time in relation to its environment.

systems   Collections of processes and resources.

tactical control   Control related to the implementation of the organization's strategic plan.

technical skills   Specific competencies to perform particular operational tasks.

Total Quality Management (TQM)   Systems approach to management that aims to continuously increase value to customers by designing and continuously improving organizational processes and systems.

ENDNOTES

1. J. Rampey and H. Roberts, "Core Body of Knowledge Working Council: Perspectives on Total Quality," in Report of the Total Quality Leadership Steering Committee and Working Councils, Cincinnati, OH: Procter & Gamble (November 1992): 2-2.

2. G.H. Carothers, G.M. Bounds, and M.J. Stahl, "Managerial Leadership," in M.J. Stahl and G.M. Bounds (eds.), *Competing Globally Through Customer Value: The Management of Strategic Suprasystems,* Westport, CT: Quorum Books (1991): 80.

3. H. Fayol, *General and Industrial Management,* New York: Pitman (1949); S. Carroll and D. Gillen, "Are the Classical Management Functions Useful in Describing Managerial Work?" *Academy of Management Review* 12 (January 1987): 38–51.

4. L. Pace, "Moving Toward Systems Integration," *Survey of Business* (Summer 1989): 57–61.

5. J. Bowles and J. Hammond, *Beyond Quality: How 50 Winning Companies Use Continuous Improvement,* New York: Putnam (1991): 159.

6. R. Milliken, "Perspectives on TQ in Industry," presentation at Total Quality Forum IV, Cincinnati, OH, November 11, 1992.

7. W. E. Deming, *Out of the Crisis,* Cambridge, MA: MIT Press (1986): 23.

8. *Malcolm Baldrige National Quality Award: 1991 Application Guidelines,* Washington, D C: U.S. Department of Commerce (1991): 43.

9. "Does the Baldrige Award Really Work?" *Harvard Business Review* (January-February 1992): 126–147; "The Baldrige Boondoggle," *Machine Design* (August 6, 1992): 25–29.

10. M. J. Stahl and D. W. Grigsby, *Strategic Management for Decision Making,* Boston: PWS-Kent (1991): 4.

11. G. H. Carothers, G. M. Bounds and M. J. Stahl, "Managerial Leadership," in Stahl and Bounds (eds.), 80; W. A. Band, *Creating Value for Customers,* New York: Wiley (1991).

12. T. Peters and R. Waterman, *In Search of Excellence,* New York: Warner Books (1982): 14.

13. A. V. Feigenbaum, "How to Implement Total Quality Control," *Executive Excellence* (November 1989): 15.

14. J. Bowles and J. Hammond *Beyond Quality: How 50 Winning Companies Use Continuous Improvement,* New York: Putnam (1991): 119–121.

15. P. Drucker, "Leadership: More Doing Than Dash," *The Wall Street Journal* (January 6, 1988): 14.

16. H. Geneen and A. Moscow, *Managing,* Garden City, NY: Doubleday (1986): 285.

17. "America's Toughest Bosses," *Fortune* (February 27, 1989): 40.

18. P. Lorange, M. Morton, and S. Ghoshal, *Strategic Control Systems,* St. Paul: West Publishing (1986): 10.

19. G. M. Bounds, and G. H. Carothers, "The Role of Middle Management in Improving Competitiveness," in Stahl and Bounds, 146–188.

20. "Dow Corning Employees Falsified Data on Breast Implants, Counsel Concludes," *The Wall Street Journal* (November 3, 1992): A3.

21. "Getting Serious About Sexual Harassment," *Business Week* (November 9, 1992): 78-82.

22. "Responsiveness to Customers Drives Curriculum Changes," *Newsline,* American Assembly of Collegiate Schools of Business (Summer 1992): 15.

23. S. Carroll and D. Gillen, "Are the Classical Management Functions Useful in Describing Managerial Work? " *Academy of Management Review* (January 1987): 38–51.

24. R. L. Katz, "The Skills of an Effective Administrator," *Harvard Business Review* (September-October 1987): 90–102.

25. "Leaders of the Most Admired," *Fortune* (January 29, 1990): 40-54.

26. "America's Toughest Bosses," 40.

2

CHAPTER

The Evolution toward Total Quality Management

LEARNING OBJECTIVES

After reading this chapter, you should be able to accomplish the following:

- Compare and contrast Weber's ideas of bureaucracy with Taylor's ideas of scientific management.
- Compare and contrast the human relations school with the organizational behavior school.
- Compare and contrast the operations research school with the industrial statistics school.
- List the major tenets of the management function school.
- Describe Mintzberg's three primary managerial roles.
- Discuss the various schools' shortcomings in an era of international competition.
- Describe the forces associated with the emergence of Total Quality Management.
- Discuss the four primary themes of Total Quality.

CHAPTER OUTLINE

The Classical School
  Weber's Bureaucracy
  Taylor's Scientific Management
The Behavioral School
  Human Relations
  Organizational Behavior
  The Quantitative School
  Operations Research
  Industrial Statistics

The Management Function School
  Planning
  Organizing
  Commanding
  Coordinating
  Controlling
  Fayol's Principles of Management
Managerial Roles
  Interpersonal Roles
  Informational Roles
  Decisional Roles
School Shortcomings and International Competition
  Internal Focus
  Short-Term Profit Orientation
  Intensity of Global Competition
  Rapidly Changing Technology
  Japanese Lessons
  Crisis Management versus Systems Improvement
The Emergence of Total Quality
  Early Focus on Quality
  Commitment to Total Quality in the 1990s
  Total Quality Themes
  Managerial Work and Total Quality
  Shortcomings of Total Quality
Cases and Exhibits
  AT & T
  Elton Textiles
  Sheet Metal Workers
  Ford Taurus
  Hoechst Celanese
  Hospital Waste Disposal

AT&T Awakens to Compete Globally through Quality

As the telecommunications and information industries become more integrated, AT&T's Chairman, Bob Allen, recognizes the importance of the company broadening its areas of business to better serve its customers. (Photo credit: Ted Hardin.)

AT&T had been a very large, inwardly focused, tradition-bound, slow-to-respond symbol of corporate America prior to divestiture and deregulation in 1984. As a secure, lifetime employer of hundreds of thousands of managers and employees in the United States, AT&T had acquired the somewhat affectionate title of "Ma Bell." For most of this century, managers joining the firm expected to work for "The Phone Company" until they retired. Additionally, AT&T had the protection of the government, which treated AT&T as a monopoly in communications.

As a large, stable firm producing fat profits in a noncompetitive market, the firm received the approval of corporate America. Many financial advisers referred to AT&T as a "widow and orphans stock," since AT&T stock could be counted on to produce substantial dividends while maintaining price stability. As Table 1.3 on page 13 indicates, AT&T was one of the ten most admired corporations in America in 1983.

Much of this changed on January 1, 1984. The federal government ordered AT&T to divest itself of its local operating companies effective on that date. AT&T was allowed to retain 23 percent of the former firm's assets, including its long-distance lines, Bell Laboratories, and Western Electric, the manufacturer of telecommunications equipment. The divestiture also removed the monopoly from the long-distance market. Other long-distance carriers were allowed to form and compete with AT&T for long-distance services. Within a short period of time, MCI and Sprint were formed and began to compete with AT&T in the long-distance market. AT&T's long-distance market share shrank from over 90 percent in 1984 to 62 percent in 1992, and the company shed 140,000 employees within the same period of time.

For the first time in its corporate existence, AT&T managers were forced to compete in a deregulated marketplace. How would they compete in such a strange competitive market without the monopolistic protection of the government?

Throughout recorded history there have been various managerial and organizational practices in vogue to fit the demands of the times.[1] As indicated in the preceding quality case, managers must change managerial practices to fit the times.

Rather than review all models of management and organization throughout recorded history, in this chapter we shall review and analyze only the most popular schools of management in the twentieth century. We present this review as a means of understanding how Total Quality Management as a system of management evolved from earlier schools and why it is appropriate for managers in the 1990s.

THE CLASSICAL SCHOOL

The **classical school** of managerial thought is based in part on the hierarchical structure of both the Roman military, and the Catholic Church. In today's organizations there are many vestiges of those strict, vertical hierarchies.

Weber's Bureaucracy

Max Weber (pronounced *váy-ber*) (1864–1920) was a German sociologist who developed what he believed to be the ideal management approach for large organizations.[2] His ideas became the theoretical underpinnings of large-scale bureaucracies. Weber's key concepts are summarized in the following characteristics of an ideal bureaucracy:

1. Labor is divided among tasks with clear lines of authority and responsibility. These divisions are legitimized as official duties.
2. Positions are organized in a hierarchy of authority. Each position is under the authority of a higher one. The ordering results in a chain of command.
3. All organizational members are selected and promoted based upon technical qualifications. Such qualifications are measured by examination or by training and education.
4. Managerial decisions are recorded in writing. Written records provide organizational memory and continuity over time.
5. Management is separate from the ownership of the organization.
6. Managers are subject to rules and controls regarding the conduct of their official duties. Rules are impersonal and uniformly applied to all employees.[3]

Weber believed in the need for specialization, hierarchy, and rules in large organizations. As organizations grew larger and larger in the early and mid-1900s, his ideas became popular because they seemed to make sense in the absence of more efficient models of organization. He thought that rules and formal structure would ensure fair treatment for all workers, as well as the satisfactory performance of routine organizational tasks. Weber viewed bureaucracy as the best option that a large organization could employ to accomplish work fairly.

A serious drawback is that it is hard to coordinate work in bureaucracies. Moreover, bureaucracies change very slowly.

Taylor's Scientific Management

The American Frederick W. Taylor (1856–1915) is considered the father of scientific management.[4] He was interested in applying scientific methods of observation, data collection, and data analysis to improving managerial practice. Taylor conducted **time and motion studies** of employees in which he carefully observed workers' motions and the time it took to complete certain motions, broke down their activities into small repeatable steps, and determined the best way for workers to do their jobs. Such studies and analyses led to dramatic improvements in productivity.

Taylor also developed a **piece rate system** in which workers were paid for each item they produced. Thus workers could earn more money if they were more productive. This system was intended to counter workers' fears that they would work themselves out of a job if they completed the work too quickly.[5]

Taylor's philosophy is summarized in the following central ideas of scientific management:

1. The scientific selection of the worker
2. The scientific training of the worker
3. Job specialization
4. The importance of wage incentives
5. A fair division of responsibility between workers and management[6]

CRITICAL THINKING QUESTIONS

1. The organization of the Roman military and of the Catholic Church provided examples upon which many large bureaucracies are based today. Discuss the appropriateness of those examples for today's organizations.

2. Weber was concerned with specialization, formalization, and structure. How valid are those concerns in the rapidly changing business environment of the 1990s?

THE BEHAVIORAL SCHOOL

The impersonality, formalized structure, and specialization of the classical school produced some rigid organizations unable to fully use their human resources and unable to react to changes. The behavioral school flourished in the mid-1900s partly in reaction to the impersonal nature of Weber's bureaucracy and Taylor's scientific management. The **behavioral school** considers the needs of the worker as an individual and as a group member, as well as the organization of the work.

Human Relations

The human relations movement started early in the twentieth century. This movement was based on the "contented cow theory," which held that contented cows deliver more milk. The logic was extended to human beings to suggest that satisfied employees are productive employees.

TABLE 2.1   *McGregor's Assumptions about People at Work*

Theory X Assumptions	Theory Y Assumptions
1. People do not like work and try to avoid it.	1. People do not dislike work; work is a natural part of their lives.
2. People do not like work, so managers must control, direct, coerce, and threaten employees to get them to work toward organizational goals.	2. People are internally motivated to reach objectives to which they are committed.
3. People prefer to be directed, to avoid responsibility, to want security; they have little ambition.	3. People are committed to goals to the degree they receive personal rewards when they reach their objectives.
	4. People will both seek and accept responsibility under favorable conditions.
	5. People have the capacity to be innovative in solving organizational problems.
	6. People are bright, but under most organizations their potentials are

Source: Adapted from D. McGregor, *The Human Side of Enterprise,* New York: McGraw-Hill (1960): 33–34. Copyright 1960 McGraw-Hill. Reproduced with permission.

There are two popular models proposed by the human relations school. One model is **Maslow's hierarchy of human needs,** which states that people are motivated by five groups of needs and that these needs exist in a hierarchical order. If managers help to satisfy the needs of workers, then the workers will be productive. Maslow's model, along with other motivational models, is explored in detail in Chapter 12.

Another noteworthy model in the human relations movement is based on the assumptions of Douglas McGregor, labeled Theory X and Theory Y, about the nature of people at work.[7] Table 2.1 describes McGregor's theories.

A manager who held Theory X assumptions would logically treat subordinates in a very controlling, sometimes harsh manner. Alternatively, a Theory Y manager would be more enlightened toward subordinates and try to maximize their contributions to the organization in a variety of ways.

Organizational Behavior

The human relations movement, with its assumption that happy workers are productive workers, gave rise to the organizational behavior school. This school is based on scientific investigation of individual and group behavior in the workplace. Studies in psychology and sociology have created a body of knowledge in this area, and many of these findings are reviewed in Chapters 11–14, which deal with the behavioral processes.

The behavioral school led to a more humanistic approach to dealing with people. In many organizations, such as Elton Textiles in the ethics exhibit, the needs of workers are considered in depth.

E T H I C S   E X H I B I T

A Snag at Elton Textiles

"The point I'm trying to make," said Betty Farnsworth, production supervisor with Elton Textiles, "is that we simply can't afford to carry Barney Riles for another three years."

Farnsworth was referring to a 62-year-old, 30-year employee in her charge. In her view Barney Riles, although still exhibiting the same degree of competence he always had, in recent years had shown a marked decline in productivity. As Farnsworth put it, "In many cases Barney takes twice as long as necessary to do a task, twice as long as he took five years ago." She was pointing out to Elton's president that such a decline in productivity not only hurt the firm, but also was undermining morale in her division. The president asked her to be specific.

"Well," she began, "as you know, we have a considerable complement of young, bright, ambitious people. I'm thinking of one in particular, Bill Matson, who's been with us seven years. He came to us right out of college. Bill shows considerable promise. But his morale recently has plummeted, primarily because of Riles. For one thing, Bill finds himself spending too much time doing Barney's job as well as his own so that the division can meet production goals. What's more, Matson is eager for and deserving of advancement."

"Matson would like to be quality control engineer?" the president asked with pointed reference to Barney Riles' position.

"He's next in line for it," Farnsworth replied.

"Can't Bill be patient for a few more years?" suggested the president.

"I don't think so," Farnsworth said. "He's already alluded to offers he's had elsewhere, and I'm convinced they're genuine. Any firm would love to have him, and I can see why."

The president sat silently for a moment before saying, "As you know, Betty, our voluntary retirement age is 65."

"But Barney's not going to retire voluntarily," Farnsworth said adamantly.

"You know that for a fact?" queried the president.

"He's said as much."

"Do you mean Barney wants to stay on till he's 70?" the president asked.

Farnsworth said he did. Then she added, "But even if Barney were going to retire at 65, in my professional judgment we can ill afford to indulge him for another three years."

The president reminded Farnsworth of how much the company prided itself on its compassionate treatment of its senior members. He emphasized that this stemmed from the company's recognition of the invaluable contributions these employees had made to Elton's currently attractive profit picture. But he was quick to add, "Of course, that doesn't justify featherbedding."

Farnsworth acknowledged that forcing someone to retire presented delicate legal and moral problems. "I know," she said, "that Barney would suffer financially."

"In fact," the president pointed out, "he stands to lose about 50 percent in retirement benefits against mandatory retirement at 70."

"But is that consideration enough to justify productivity losses?" Farnsworth asked him. "Is it enough to jeopardize losing a highly qualified person like Bill Matson?"

"You've put the choice I face starkly," the president said, "but most accurately."

Discussion Questions

1. Describe the decision and the alternatives facing the president.

2. Suppose the president summons Riles for a conference at which he explains the situation to him. Upon reflection, Riles agrees that he's not as productive as he once was, that he is a liability to the firm. Do you think Riles would then have a moral obligation to retire? What ideals would he have to consider? What effects?

Source: V. Barry, *Moral Issues in Business*, 2nd ed., Belmont, CA: Wadsworth (1983): 147–148.

CRITICAL THINKING QUESTIONS

1. Describe the kinds of situations in which Theory X might be appropriate.

2. Describe the kinds of situations in which Theory Y might be appropriate.

THE QUANTITATIVE SCHOOL

The quantitative school was formed on the belief that there are principles underlying organizations and activities that can be described in mathematical terms. Operations-research/management science adherents, for example, use precise equations, and industrial statisticians recognize and analyze variation in organizational activities.

Operations Research

The operations research approach had its beginnings in World War II when the military applied large-scale, powerful mathematical models of supplies and of movements of troops and armaments to facilitate military operations.[8] **Operations research** is the application of the scientific method to operational problems of a system and the solution of mathematical models representing these problems. Many refer to operations research as management science. In Chapter 18, "Operations Management," we explore some of the results of operations-research/management science studies.

Industrial Statistics

The operations-research/management science approach to organizations is based on assumed cause-and-effect relationships. However, many organizational processes contain some unexplained variation or randomness. Thus industrial statistics attempts to analyze this variation so that managers can reduce the variation and consistently produce high-quality products and services. Statistical quality control and other statistical tools, which are reviewed in detail in Chapter 15, enable managers to understand variation, reduce variation, and improve processes to yield higher quality.

THE MANAGEMENT FUNCTION SCHOOL

A popular concept that describes what managers do in their daily managerial activities was offered by Henri Fayol. He stated that managers perform the following five functions or processes: planning, organizing, commanding, coordinating, and controlling.[9] These managerial processes have been widely used to describe the managerial job.[10]

Planning

Planning is deciding in advance what the organization's objectives ought to be and what its members ought to do to attain these objectives. As such, planning is future-oriented. To reach the future goals, managers must attend to three important issues.

— *Where is the organization now?* Managers must be aware of the strengths and weaknesses of the organization. They need to understand how these strengths and weaknesses position the firm relative to customers' demands and to competitors' positions.

— *Where does the organization want to go?* With knowledge of where the organization is now, managers need to decide the appropriate future goals for the organization. They also need to determine factors that could hinder attainment of these goals, in order to anticipate and work around those factors.

— *How will the organization reach the goals?* Strategies, policies, and procedures that will enable the organization to reach its goals need to be developed in detail. These three planning questions are explored in detail in Part 2 of this book.

Recognizing that the future is uncertain, managers must be ready to change plans to reflect changes in the external environment of the firm. For example, the Persian Gulf War in 1991 caused firms to revise their plans and objectives for sales in that year.

Organizing

Organizing involves structuring work relationships. People, resources, and tasks need to be structured and grouped for efficient performance of the organization's goals. Part 3 of this book examines organizing in detail.

Commanding

Some do not like the militaristic connotation of the word **commanding** and prefer words like **directing, motivating,** or **leading.** All four terms refer to managerial behavior aimed at causing employees to accomplish the tasks assigned to them. Attempts at motivation have ranged from the use of threats and whips in ancient times to the use of money in more recent times. Today many managers recognize that motivation is a complex individual and group process. An important motivational task for today's managers is to determine the needs of individuals and groups, and to design ways to satisfy their needs through effective job performance. Part 4 of this book deals with these behavioral issues in detail.

Coordinating

Coordinating is the process of integrating the activities of individuals and units so as to provide unity of action in the pursuit of the organization's goals. Many view coordinating as the very essence of management.[11] Thus it is an activity that should underlie all managerial activities, rather than be described as a separate managerial function.

Controlling

Controlling means ensuring that the organization is actually achieving its planned objectives. Some discuss planning and control together and describe "planning and control systems" because controlling involves comparing actual performance with planned performance.[12] An example of control activity is measuring production output for the day, comparing the output to the objective, and then if the output falls short, assigning more people or authorizing overtime to increase the output to match the objective. Part 5 of this book is concerned with control.

A drawback of the management function school is that it does not describe *why* managers perform the functions. Is it to improve internal efficiency, or to increase profits, or to serve customers? With no indication of purpose, managerial activity can be misdirected. The management function school also segregated the five functions—planning, organizing, commanding, coordinating, and controlling—as strictly the purview of managers. In many organizations today these functions are shared with highly trained workers in self-managed work teams.

Fayol's Principles of Management

In addition to the five managerial functions, Fayol also described 14 principles of management for more efficient managerial behavior and more logical organizations. These 14 principles are summarized as follows:

1. *Division of labor.* The more people specialize, the more efficiently they can perform their work. Fayol described work specialization as the best way to use the human resources in an organization. Division of labor increases total production by simplifying the tasks required of each worker. The assembly line, which permits mass production to flourish, is a good example.

2. *Authority and responsibility.* Authority was defined by Fayol as "the right to give orders and the power to exact obedience." Responsibility means being accountable and goes hand in hand with authority in organizations.

3. *Discipline.* Discipline implies that members follow the rules and regulations that govern the organization. Discipline results from good leadership at all levels in the organization. In includes fairness, rewarding superior performance, and willingness to penalize employees promptly for breaking the rules.

4. *Unity of command.* Each organizational member receives orders from only one superior. If an employee reported to more than one boss, the employee would be confused.

5. *Unity of direction.* In order to avoid having different policies and procedures, those activities within the organization that have the same objective should be directed by only one manager using one plan.

6. *Subordination of individual interest to the common good.* The interest of one employee or group of employees should not prevail over that of the organization as a whole.

7. *Remuneration.* Compensation should be fair both to employees and to the organization.

8. *Centralization.* Centralization is the process of lessening the importance of the role of subordinates, especially in decision making and planning. Power and authority tend to be concentrated at the upper levels in an organization. Managers must retain final responsibility but they should delegate enough authority to subordinates to enable them to do their jobs.

9. *Scalar chain.* There should be a clear chain of command from the top to the bottom of an organization. All employees should follow this chain of command. This helps to ensure the orderly flow of information and is consistent with the unity of command principle.

10. *Order.* Materials and people should be in the right place at the right time.

11. *Equity.* Managers should treat subordinates equally and fairly.

12. *Stability of tenure of personnel.* High turnover of employees, which is not good for the efficient functioning of the organization, should be avoided.

13. *Initiative.* Managers should give subordinates the freedom to formulate and implement plans after the plans have been decided upon by management.

14. *Esprit de corps.* Management should encourage harmony, team spirit, and togetherness, thereby helping to give the organization a sense of unity.[13]

There are commonalities in Weber's concept of bureaucracy, Taylor's ideas of scientific management, and Fayol's principles of management. Some of Fayol's principles are practiced today. Others are in disfavor as they do not address today's challenges associated with intense international competition, rapidly changing technology, and customer demands for quality.

CRITICAL THINKING QUESTIONS

1. One drawback of the functional school of management is that it does not describe *why* managers conduct the managerial functions. Describe the organizational purposes that are consistent with the managerial functions.

2. Discuss the assumptions about employees that are consistent with the functional school of management.

MANAGERIAL ROLES

Henry Mintzberg, an often quoted managerial scholar, noted that managerial behavior can be described in terms of managerial roles.[14] A **managerial role** is a set of expectations for managerial behavior. Mintzberg listed three groups of managerial roles and ten specific managerial roles. These roles prepared a road map for expected managerial behavior in a variety of managerial situations.

Managers recognize the importance of diversity in cultural backgrounds throughout the workforce. (Photo credit: Jose Luis Pelaez/The Stock Market.)

Interpersonal Roles

Interpersonal roles are roles pertaining to relationships with others. Three subroles are assumed under interpersonal roles. (1) The **figurehead role** relates to symbolic or ceremonial activities within the organization. Presiding at graduation or distributing awards are examples of figurehead behavior. (2) The **leader role** pertains to relationships with subordinates. (3) The **liaison role** pertains to relationships with outside groups.

Informational Roles

Informational roles are roles relating to activities that develop and maintain an information network. There are three subordinate informational roles. (1) The **monitor role** pertains to activities of seeking and receiving information. (2) The **disseminator role** relates to activities of distributing information. (3) The **spokesperson role** pertains to informing people outside the organization of organizational issues.

Decisional Roles

Decisional roles are roles relating to activities associated with making managerial decisions. Four subroles are assumed under decisional roles. In the **entrepreneur role** the manager initiates change. The **disturbance handler role** relates to conflict resolution activities. The **resource allocator role** is concerned with distributing various resources in order to accomplish organizational goals. The **negotiator role** relates to bargaining activities.

An important class of managerial decisions concerns the hiring of personnel. Today's population is characterized by diversity, and managers must ensure that their hiring decisions reflect that diversity. Otherwise, the legal system might force such diversity, as illustrated in the diversity exhibit concerning a labor union and the city of New York.

D I V E R S I T Y   E X H I B I T

Quotas for Sheet Metal Workers

Local 28 of the Sheet Metal Workers' International Association was sued by the city of New York in 1971 for persistent exclusion of minorities from membership. A series of district court rulings established a long record of discriminatory practices in hiring by the union as well as staunch resistance to attempts by the city to end those practices. Nepotism was found to be the basic system of recruiting, training, admission, and advancement; this system established an impenetrable barrier to nonwhite employment that had never been passed by a nonwhite candidate. The union was ordered by the court to achieve a goal of 29 percent minority membership by the year 1981, later extended to 1982. The union was also fined enough money to set up a penalty fund to provide money for training and assistance for minority workers. In 1982 and again in 1983 the city and state charged that little had been done to achieve the mandated goal. The court found the union in contempt both times.

The union maintained that the membership goal and the fund exceeded the boundaries of a justifiable remedy because they extended race-conscious preferences to individuals who are not the identified victims of unlawful discrimination. The Solicitor General of the United States support-ed the union in this claim in arguments before the Supreme Court. However, the Supreme Court held in July 1986 that in circumstances of egregious discrimination of this sort, preferential treatment involving quotas could be justified even if it benefits individuals who are not the actual victims of discrimination, in order to remedy the discriminatory situation. It found the quotas "appropriate equitable relief" under the objective of equal employment opportunity. However, it maintained that quotas could not be justified in every case "simply to create a racially balanced workforce."

Discussion Questions

1. Does the filling of a 29 percent quota entail denial of equal employment opportunity to white applicants who have no history of discrimination? Explain.

2. Is reverse discrimination at work in this case? If so, is it justifiable?

3. Is the target goal of 29 percent appropriate equitable relief? Why or why not?

Source: T. L. Beauchamp and N. E. Bowie, *Ethical Theory and Business*, Englewood Cliffs, NJ: Prentice-Hall (1988): 394–395.

CRITICAL THINKING QUESTIONS

1. Compare and contrast Mintzberg's roles with Fayol's managerial functions.

2. How are Mintzberg's roles related to providing value to customers?

SCHOOL SHORTCOMINGS AND INTERNATIONAL COMPETITION

The schools of management thought discussed above have several shortcomings that had been masked prior to the advent of intense international competition with its menu of choices for customers. The intensity of this global competition has acted as a magnifying glass to reveal latent managerial and organizational problems that had always been beneath the surface.

Internal Focus

There is a tendency in the classical, behavioral, and management function schools of managerial thought to focus internally on the organization, its managers, and employees. This internal focus on how managers spend their time, how nonmanagers should be organized, how reporting relationships should be managed, and how organizations should be structured caused many managers to focus on the organization as an entity unto itself. The external customer seemed to take a back seat. Where is the customer in Weber's concepts of bureaucracy, or in Taylor's philosophy, or in McGregor's Theory X and Theory Y, or in Fayol's principles of management?

Internal focus is one of the common corporate practices that has been associated with the lagging performance of U.S. firms. As one author noted, "In recent years, executives have been mostly concerned about being the 'right size' or having the 'right technology' or becoming the 'lowest-cost producer,' all too often overlooking their most important competitive weapon—their customers. In other words, companies have been looking *in* instead of *out*."[15]

In many organizations this internal focus seemed to be compounded by size. As organizations grew larger, they became more isolated and more removed from their customers. Some large organizations, such as AT&T, Xerox, Motorola, Procter & Gamble, and Ford, recognized the dangers of this internal focus and embraced the mantle of Total Quality as a rallying cry for change and improvement.

In an earlier era many managers had thought of their careers in terms of lifetime employment spent advancing upward through the corporate structure within a single corporation. In a description of today's internationally competitive and customer-focused era, *Fortune* magazine noted that millions of managerial jobs had been eliminated in the restructuring and flattening of corporate America. The tall corporate structure had been eliminated in many organizations and success was now being measured in terms of the success or failure of a business in the external global marketplace.[16] For the first time in the memory of many managers, the standard of comparison was external to the firm.

The opposite of the internal-focus failing discussed above is a focus external to the organization—a focus on the customer and on providing customer value. Because international competition has offered the customer alternatives from which to choose, customers are demanding and expect to receive superior value. Today a top priority for managers is defining customer requirements, dealing with customer dissatisfaction, and ensuring continuous quality-improvement efforts.

Short-Term Profit Orientation

There have been several criticisms of the short-term profit orientation of many U.S. managers relative to their Japanese and European competitors. After a lengthy, highly visible study of the role of financing in international competitiveness, one researcher concluded that the short-term profit orientation of many U.S. firms and their managers was an international competitive disadvantage for the United States.[17]

Such a short-term profit orientation may cause some managers to do things that actually decrease value for customers. For example, short-term profits can be

In 1992 and 1993, the Ford Taurus was the best selling car in the United States. (Photo credit: Ford Motor Company.)

increased by deferring machine maintenance, worker training, process improvement, and new-product development. These steps can increase the number of defects and lengthen the time needed to deliver new products to customers. In today's internationally competitive world and its rapidly changing technology, demanding customers want the latest that technology has to offer. One need only look at the rapid spread of antilock brakes in automobiles to appreciate the importance of speedy new-product development. In Chapter 17 we shall discuss the importance of technology and of managing technological change.

This short-term profit orientation may be partly associated with the method of financing of most U.S. firms—that is, equity. The equity owners demand a certain visible return for their invested funds. These demands grow stronger in times of high inflation when the equity owners demand an inflation premium. In periods of low inflation, the owners will accept a smaller return. This may be one of the reasons why many U.S. firms were weak international competitors in the highly inflationary environment of the 1970s. Interestingly, many U.S. firms began to regain their competitiveness in the presence of the low inflation of the late 1980s and early 1990s.

Intensity of Global Competition

In the 1980s and 1990s, the United States has been part of the most intense international economic competition in the history of humanity. Studies of the forces associated with international competition indicate that this competition will continue to intensify in the future (see Chapter 3). Such international competition affords customers alternatives from which to choose. It is also forcing a reappraisal of the utility of some of the schools of management thought that do not explicitly deal with international competition and the customer.

One way to deal with intense international economic competition and even to benefit from it is through the Total Quality practice of competitive benchmarking. **Competitive benchmarking** is analyzing what the best competitor or leading companies in the industry are doing to discover the products, processes, and prac-

ＬＮＴＥＲＮＡＴＩＯＮＡＬ   ＥＸＨＩＢＩＴ

International Benchmarking at Taurus

Feature	Car	Feature	Car
Lowest ignition switch effort	Ford	Best oil filter accessibility	Nissan
Lowest air register operating	Audi 100		Maxima
Best accelerator pedal feel	Audi 100	Best transmission control	Opel
Best accelerator pedal location	Chevrolet	(travel/feet)	Senator
	Celebrity	Least transmission gear noise	Ford Escort,
Lowest effort to rotate sun visor	Honda		Supra
	Accord	Best steering wheel feel	Porsche 924
Lowest effort to adjust	Toyota	Best outside mirror	Mazda 626
rearview mirror	Cressida	remote control	
Best hand control ergonomics	Opel	Most effective sun visor	Honda
	Senator	(travel/feet)	Accord
Best visual ergonomics	Honda	Best trunk storage capacity	Chevrolet
	Accord		Celebrity
Best night-time illumination	Honda		
of switches	Accord		
Best clock readability	Audi 100		
Best fuel gauge accuracy	Toyota		
	Supra		

Source: Ford Motor Company, *Automotive Industry,* January, February, July 1986.

tices that satisfy customer needs. The international exhibit shows how Ford pays attention to global competition by internationally benchmarking competitors for the design and production of its Taurus model.

Rapidly Changing Technology

Prior to the Vietnam War era, technology changed slowly. In such an environment stable production processes that stressed internal efficiency through functional specialization were relevant. In today's environment where new technology is rapidly being introduced, manufacturers constantly incorporate the new technology in order to satisfy customers who demand the latest. In Chapter 17 we deal exclusively with the impact of technology and the management of technological change.

In Detroit in the 1950s and 1960s, the bodies of automobiles changed some from year to year to give the appearance of a *new* model, but the engine, transmission, brakes, suspension, and other critical components changed very slowly. Today automobile models often change significantly, inside and out, every three or four years. In 1992 the Ford Taurus and the Honda Accord competed for the title of the most popular car model. The Ford Taurus won partly because it was in the first year of a new model and offered airbags and antilock brakes, whereas the Accord, in the third year of the model, had neither.

FIGURE 2.1   *Frequency of Use of Quality Information to Evaluate Business Performance*

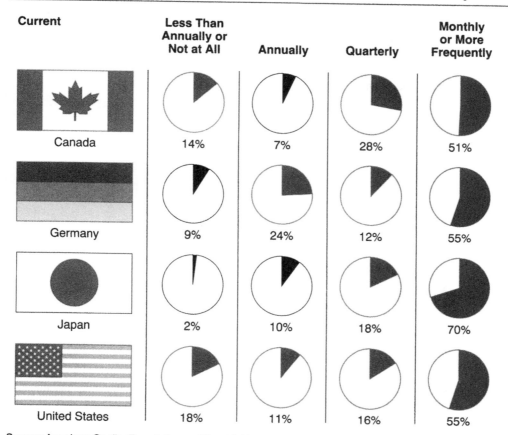

Current	Less Than Annually or Not at All	Annually	Quarterly	Monthly or More Frequently
Canada	14%	7%	28%	51%
Germany	9%	24%	12%	55%
Japan	2%	10%	18%	70%
United States	18%	11%	16%	55%

Source: American Quality Foundation and Ernst & Young, "International Quality Study: The Definitive Study of the Best International Quality Management Practices," Cleveland: Ernst & Young (1991): 16.

Japanese Lessons

After World War II many of the Japanese manufacturing industries, influenced by Deming and Juran, incorporated Total Quality into their organizations. The Japanese dedication to high quality *and* low cost is associated with its focus on customer requirements.[18]

Figures 2.1 and 2.2 present some of the lessons to be learned from Japanese industry. The Japanese focus on quality, customer satisfaction, time-based competition, and process simplification yields an external focus, in contrast to the internal focus inherent with some of the schools of management thought described earlier. Clearly, in the United States some changes are needed in management thought to reconcile the Japanese advances in a competitive world with the demands of today's customers. "One high-profile victim of such insights will be 'the traditional American bureaucratic command-and-control' style of management," says Paul H. O'Neill,

FIGURE 2.2   *Comparing Quality Cultures: U.S. and Japanese Commitment to Strategic Quality Elements*

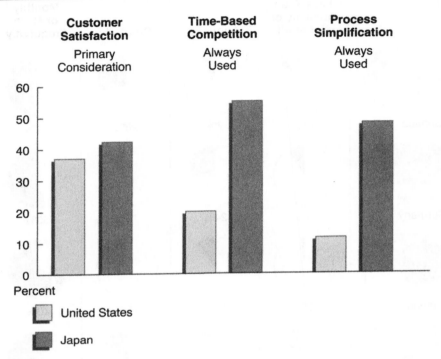

Source: Adapted from American Quality Foundation and Ernst & Young, "International Quality Study: The Definitive Study of the Best International Quality Management Practices," Cleveland: Ernst & Young (1991): 18–28.

chairman of Alcoa. "In the future, managers will have to cede power and responsibility to employees, the people who can do the most about quality."[19]

Crisis Management versus Systems Improvement

An unfortunate side effect of the classical and management-function schools is the idea that one of the main functions of a manager is to solve problems. In the United States managers' careers are sometimes highlighted by the crises they have resolved. This problem-solving/crisis mentality is in direct contrast to the Japanese mentality of continuous improvement.[20] As we learned in Chapter 1, continuous improvement is the constant refinement and improvement of products, services, and organizational systems to yield improved value to customers. The philosophy of continuous improvement holds that managers should continuously work on improving the systems and processes that yield the firm's products or services. Improving systems is associated with long-term quality improvement, rather than with the

Q UALITY CASE

Back to the AT&T Case

For a few years the new, deregulated AT&T floundered. It is hard to compete in a deregulated, internationally competitive market when the corporate history had been written around a monopoly. Between 1984 and 1988 AT&T lost dramatic market share and many employees.

In 1988 Bob Allen became chief executive officer with a vision of telecommunications "anytime, anywhere." Bob hired a number of outside executives to help breathe new life into the hidebound, internally focused culture at AT&T. The two new watchwords became *global* and *quality*.

In the telecommunications industry, consumer electronics, cable TV, communications (including wireless cellular communications), computing, and multimedia were all converging. To help make AT&T the master of the convergence of these industries and to help change its corporate culture, Allen engineered a number of mergers to position AT&T in areas where it had no historical strength. In 1991 AT&T acquired National Cash Register (NCR) for $7.5 billion, thereby rescuing AT&T's fledgling computer business. In 1993 AT&T acquired the foremost cellular phone company, McCaw Cellular, for $12.6 billion. These acquisitions and several lesser ones not only built strengths in areas where AT&T

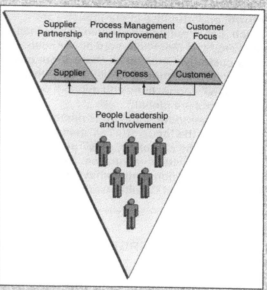

AT&T's Total Quality Approach. (Source: Courtesy of AT&T Archives, New York, 1992).

needed them, but they also helped turn the old AT&T's inward focus outward to the customer. The CEO of McCaw Cellular, Craig O. McCaw, remarked: "We've been invited to cause a little trouble within AT&T."

continued

short-term focus of after-the-fact inspection to catch and repair defective products. We shall explore in Chapter 15 this central tenet of TQM relating to continuous improvement of systems.

CRITICAL THINKING QUESTIONS

1. Explain how present-day international competition has magnified the shortcomings of an internal focus and a short-term profit orientation.

2. How does rapidly changing technology coupled with international competition challenge the classical school of management?

A number of the mergers helped improve AT&T's global reach. Allen was asked about his goal of 50 percent of the business being global. "Fifty-fifty is not magic. What is magic is that we be a global company. The growth opportunities in our industry are much higher outside the United States than they are here. More and more of our business customers are global. Many of our customers travel abroad as businesspeople and want AT&T connections and service. Our competitors are global." (U.S)

To deliver more value to its customers and to turn the focus of AT&T managers outward to the customer, AT&T pursued Total Quality with a vengeance. As of 1993 it was the only company to have won two Baldrige National Quality Awards for two different parts of the company. AT&T described its TQ approach with the accompanying figure and the following statement. "For more than a century, AT&T has stood for quality. Much has changed for AT&T —and the world—since our company was founded in 1885. But our commitment to quality has not. Our fundamental principles continue to guide us:

— The customer comes first.

— Quality happens through people.

— All work is part of a process.

— Suppliers are an integral part of our business.

— Prevention is achieved through planning.

— Quality improvement never ends."

THE EMERGENCE OF TOTAL QUALITY

Few managers in the United States and Europe immediately recognized the potential effects that international competition, rapidly changing technology, and demanding customers would have on firms and managerial behavior. It was decades before this belated awareness resulted in a serious commitment to Total Quality.

Early Focus on Quality

Throughout the 1970s quality efforts in this country focused on controlling the number of defects by inspection after the product or service had been generated. Most attempts at quality control were in the manufacturing industries.[21]

The 1980s witnessed the loss of market share, money, and jobs by many U.S. firms and even entire U.S. industries to fierce international competitors, especially Japan and Germany. There was considerable soul searching about the strengths and weaknesses of management in the United States; for example, a TV documentary on June 24, 1980, titled "If Japan Can . . . Why Can't We?"[22] This documentary was a widely cited wake-up call to U.S. managers to focus on quality and on customers' requirements.

Commitment to Total Quality in the 1990s

A commitment to Total Quality seemed to provide a rallying cry in the early 1990s to deal with a number of the international competitiveness issues.[23] As U.S. firms geared up to improve their systems in order to provide greater value to customers, their international competitors continued to do so. This caused J. Bowles, a noted writer in the field, to remark: "In this age of tough competition, TQM is the minimum requirement for staying in the game."[24]

How widespread is this commitment to TQM? A growing number of business leaders argue that TQM is critical to U.S. competitiveness. As a measure of this commitment, the chief executives of American Express, Ford, IBM, Motorola, Procter & Gamble, and Xerox published an open letter on TQM in the *Harvard Business Review.* "We are absolutely convinced that TQM is a fundamentally better way to conduct business and is necessary for the economic well-being of America. TQM results in higher-quality, lower-cost products and services that respond faster to the needs of the customer."[25]

Business leaders need to understand and implement TQ concepts and practices if businesses are to continuously improve their operations and to satisfy their customers in an internationally competitive era. Current students—as the nation's future business leaders and managers—need to understand TQ, for they will likely work for firms that have implemented TQ or for suppliers to TQ firms. Since these statements apply to both products and services, there are throughout this book both manufacturing and service examples from both large and small organizations.

Total Quality Themes

Several themes constitute the essence of Total Quality Management. We recall the definition from Chapter 1: *Total Quality Management* is a systems approach to management that aims to continuously increase value to customers by designing and continuously improving organizational processes and systems. In this section we discuss four themes that are crucial to understanding the essence of TQM and how it relates to the managerial task for the 1990s.

The Customer and Customer Value   Absolutely crucial to an understanding of Total Quality is the centrality of the customer and the necessity of providing value to the customer. Some authors describe the customer as the first principle of TQ from which all other TQ principles are derived.[26] This TQ theme pervades our discussion throughout this book; additionally, the concept of the customer and customer value is elevated to a business strategy in Chapter 7.

Continuous Improvement   As we saw in Chapter 1, W. Edwards Deming included the idea of continuous improvement as one of his 14 Points of Management: "Improve constantly." This idea of slowly, incrementally, and continuously improving systems to yield better products and services is different from the traditional notion of "If it isn't broken, don't fix it." The spirit of continuous improvement argues "If it isn't perfect, make it better," and it strives for a continuous stream of base hits, rather than waiting for the home run.

The System and the Process   Rather than focus on inspection of the product or service after it has been generated, Total Quality aims to design and improve the system or process that generated the product or service. Finding and eliminating the root cause of a defect can prevent a recurrence of that defect. Chapter 15 is devoted to a discussion of this issue. Such systems improvement work is the essence of managerial leadership when it is coupled with customer value.[27] Milliken and Company, in implementing its Pursuit of Excellence program that we discussed in Chapter 1, today refers to many former "managers" as "system improvement specialists."

Q U A L I T Y   E X H I B I T

Hoechst Celanese's Quality Policy

Quality leadership is vital to the long-term success of Hoechst Celanese in an increasingly competitive marketplace. Building quality into our workplace, products and services is essential to a successful future for our customers, employees, suppliers, communities and shareholders. Hoechst Celanese will work with customers to provide products and services that always meet or exceed their expectations. Management will commit the resources and create an environment in which each employee can contribute skills, talents and ideas to a never-ending process of improvement and innovation in all aspects of our business.

Quality is our way of doing business. Our values, along with these five core principles of our quality process, guide everything we do.

Customer-Driven Priorities

First and foremost, we focus on our customers' needs, defining our business goals through their eyes. Through close partnership relationships, we develop an understanding of our customers' businesses. Then we help them to succeed through the continuous improvement of our products and services. Our goal is total customer satisfaction, achieved by anticipating our customers' future requirements and exceeding their current expectations. We pursue opportunities for excellence throughout our supplier-customer chain—from our dealings with our own suppliers and internal customers to our customers' customers. We do this for the benefit of all the stakeholders who are touched by our business, including investors, communities, employees and governments.

Values-Based Leadership

When Hoechst Celanese was created, one of the first actions of the new company was the articulation of our Values, a comprehensive statement of shared beliefs which is the foundation of our quality tradition. The Values, developed with significant employee input, are our vision of the culture we want to achieve. They form the design criteria for all of our business systems. From the corporate level to individual work teams, leaders provide direction which results in strategic goals, short-term objectives and daily actions consistent with our Values. These shared Values help to keep us on course in a rapidly changing global business environment.

Continuous Process Improvement

Recognizing that process improvement is the avenue to long-term business improvement, we view all work as a process. Some processes cross organizational and functional boundaries, while others are performed within work groups or by individuals. In this approach, we identify core tasks that add value toward the implementation of our strategy and make sure that we have people with the competencies and skills to carry out those tasks. Supporting our people are systems for empowerment, information sharing, and performance recognition, along with basic tools such as statistical process control, self-directed work teams and group problem solving. We use these tools and methods to achieve continuous improvement and lasting change in the way our organization does its work.

Empowered People Working Together

"Empowered people working together" is our vision for the individual and collective behavior of all of us at Hoechst Celanese. Our corporate culture, expressed in the Values, is open and participative. Business units are encouraged to develop modes of operation suited to their needs, within the common framework which the Values provide. Groups and individuals take responsibility for the success of the business because it is *their* business. There is an emphasis on teamwork and continual learning. And individuals from diverse backgrounds are encouraged to contribute their ideas, perspectives and experiences toward a common goal—the best results for our customers.

continued

Excellent Performance

We measure our success in multiple dimensions—customers' satisfaction with the performance of our products and services; progress in environmental protection, health and safety; our stature as a preferred employer; and financial returns. In fact, we believe that sustainable financial success is the result of persistent excellence in all areas of the business. We believe that when our treatment of individuals is consistent with our *people* values, when our organization and utilization of our people are guided by our *process* values, and when their efforts are focused on our *performance* values, excellence will be the result.

Source: Hoechst Celanese Corporation, Somerville, NJ (1993).

By stressing all five core principles, Hoechst Celanese has produced an integrated Quality Policy. (Photo credit: Hoechst Celanese Corporation.)

Cross-Functional Teams and Processes We recall from Chapter 1 that one of Deming's 14 points is "Break down barriers between departments."[28] Thus processes and systems that span functions and departments are crucial. Chapter 1 defined cross-functional processes as activities linked to providing value to customers that span at least two of the functions of design, production, marketing, and finance. In Chapters 8 and 14 we shall examine cross-functional processes and teams in greater detail.

Many TQ efforts in industry recognize that the source of quality problems is found between groups and departments. Thus many firms are using teams with representatives from several areas to design and improve cross-functional operations. For example, Chrysler used "platform teams," consisting of representatives from design engineering, manufacturing, marketing, and finance, to design and build its new LH "cab forward" series of cars.

An example of TQ themes applied to a large organization is presented in the quality exhibit. Hoechst Celanese is a large German-based international chemical firm with extensive operations in the United States.

Managerial Work and Total Quality

A research study examined the functional school of management and questioned whether the management functions were useful in describing managerial work. By including the manager's "work agenda" of goals and tasks, the researchers found that they were and indicated that the manager's work agenda is influenced by several focused factors.[29] If international competition, changing technology, and customer requirements are recognized as principal drivers of the manager's work agenda, then there is utility in describing managerial work in terms of managerial

FIGURE 2.3   *A Model of Total Quality in Managerial Work*

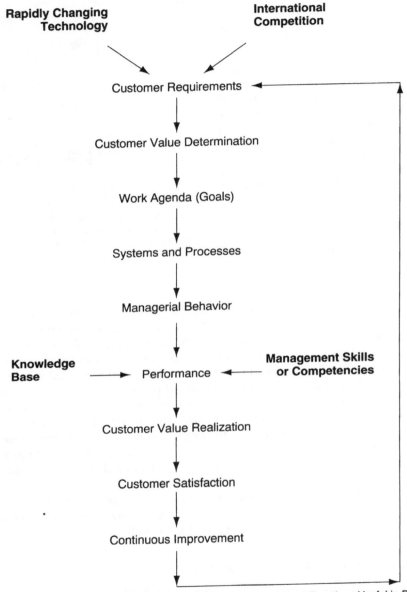

Source: S. Carroll and D. Gillen, "Are the Classical Management Functions Useful in Describing Managerial Work?" *Academy of Management Review* (January 1987): 47; G. Carothers, G. Bounds, and M. Stahl, "Managerial Leadership," and G. Bounds and G. Dobbins, "The Manager's Job: A Paradigm Shift to a New Agenda," both in M. Stahl and G. Bounds (eds.), *Competing Globally Through Customer Value,* Westport, CT: Quorum Books (1991): 83, 122.

Q UALITY CASE

Conclusion to the AT&T Case

In the mid 1990s AT&T was on a roll. Its stock had quadrupled since the divestiture of 1984. In 1993 the value of its stock ($79 billion) made it the fourth largest company in the world. With revenues of $65 billion in 1993, and a goal of doubling these revenues within about ten years, AT&T was clearly positioned for growth.

In less than ten years following the government-mandated divestiture, AT&T had come a long way. With acquisitions and outside executives changing its old, internally focused culture, a major TQ effort to focus on the customer, and a globalization program, AT&T managers were a new breed. They had awakened from a government-protected monopoly to compete globally through quality.

DISCUSSION QUESTIONS

1. How important was the globalization program to the change in management and in the culture at AT&T?

2. How important was the TQ effort with its focus on the customer to the change in management and in the culture at AT&T?

3. How important was bringing in several key outside executives to the change in management and in the culture at AT&T?

Sources: "AT&T's Bold Bet," *Business Week* (August 30, 1993): 29; "AT&T," *Value Line Investment Survey* (July 16, 1993): 749; "Could AT&T Rule the World," *Fortune* (May 17, 1993): 62; "AT&T's Total Quality Approach," New York: AT&T, 1992: 2; "Ranking Corporate Reputations," *Fortune* (January 10, 1983): 35.

functions.[30] Figure 2.3 presents a model of managerial work that includes international competition, changing technology, and focus on the customer.

Shortcomings of Total Quality

There are a growing number of criticisms of Total Quality in the 1990s.[31] Some dislike its vocabulary.[32] Some think the Baldrige Award is a cookbook and not a substitute for good management. Some contend that like any other new managerial model, TQ is just a fad. Some TQ failures have been documented, with a common reason for failure being the lack of sustained managerial commitment to TQ themes.[33]

Although the vocabulary of TQ may evolve over time, the Baldrige process may be altered over time, and the Baldrige award may even be eliminated in time, nevertheless the concept of managing systems with cross-functional teams to continuously provide greater value to customers will remain regardless of the labels appended to it.

CRITICAL THINKING QUESTIONS

1. Explain the forces associated with the emergence of Total Quality. Forecast the future of those forces and the future impact on TQ.

2. Compare and contrast the fundamental managerial changes associated with TQ with the faddish changes.

SUMMARY

The first of the prominent twentieth-century schools of management thought was the classical school. This school was concerned with Weber's concept of the division of labor and Taylor's scientific management theories that relied on time and motion studies.

The human relations and organizational behavior schools grew out of a desire to put the worker back into the picture. The operations-research/management science school uses mathematical models to understand complex organizational issues. The industrial statistics school applies industrial statistics to understanding and improving on the variance and randomness in systems.

The management function school argues that managers perform certain common functions of planning, organizing, commanding, coordinating, and controlling. Unfortunately, the purpose of the managerial activities has been ignored. Managerial roles indicate the expected behavior of managers.

All of these schools have several shortcomings. With their concern for structure and reporting relationships, some seem to ignore the customer. Their interest in efficiency is associated with a short-term profit orientation. Most of the schools are not responsive to conditions of intense international competition and rapidly changing technology coupled with demanding customers.

To overcome these shortcomings, many managers and organizations have made commitments to Total Quality in the 1990s. This system of management, which focuses on meeting customer requirements, is associated with a managerial rebirth.

EXPERIENTIAL EXERCISE

Budgeting Your Time

Make a list of everything you would like to accomplish in the coming week. Estimate the amount of time it will take to accomplish each goal. Now increase your total estimate by 40 percent to allow for unforeseen problems, interruptions, and other time wasters. Add in time for routine work, sleep, meals, recreation, club meetings, and the like. You may want to use a chart similar to the following:

1. Write the days of the week in a row across a wide sheet of paper, and below each day write your goals for that day.
2. Place your time estimate for accomplishing each goal to the right of the goal.
3. Add your time estimates for each day and place this figure in Row A below the day's column at the bottom of the sheet.
4. Multiply your estimated time needs by 40 percent and place the resultant figure in Row B for each day.
5. In Row C, write 24 hours as the total time available.
6. Subtract Row B from Row C and place this figure in Row D. If your time estimate exceeds the time available, the figure in Row D will have a minus sign. If you have time left over in a day, the figure in Row D should have a plus sign.

Now look at your time figures in Row D for each day, and answer the following questions:

1. Did you set too many or too few goals?
2. Do you need more than 24 hours time in a day? How much more?
3. How could you cut down some of your time-wasting activities to gain more time?
4. If you have time left over, how will you use it?

Source: Adapted from R. Fulmer, *Supervision: Principles of Professional Management,* Encino, CA: Glencoe (1976): 104–106.

CHAPTER CASE

Hospital Waste Disposal

Ann Kaufman, 33, an energetic divorced woman with an 8-year-old son, had just been promoted to administrator of a hospital. Mercy Hospital, a very large institution in an urban district, was one of many owned by the A. H. Corporation. The patients who used the facilities at Mercy Hospital were primarily blue-collar, semiskilled factory workers from several large industrial complexes located in and around the city. Mercy had a long-standing policy of accepting all patients who needed care, whether or not they had insurance or were able to pay their bills.

Ann was, of course, very excited about her new job. She had previously been administrator of a very small A. H. Corporation hospital in a small community. Thus this promotion was a signal that Ann was on the fast track at A. H. Corporation.

Six months after the promotion, however, the local economy collapsed. Several of the largest plants in the city closed; in some cases, the parent company moved production to other areas with more promising economies. Several thousand employees in the city were laid off or fired. In the first month after the plant closings, Mercy Hospital experienced a dramatic drop in billables (accounts on which the hospital actually expects to receive payment). A. H. Corporation executives sent Ann a memo reminding her that if billables did not increase, she would need to cut expenses if she wished to keep her position. Ann responded by reducing her office staff and the hospital's nursing staff, despite an already chronic shortage of nurses. Even though the quality of care might suffer, Ann firmly believed that these were only temporary measures.

In the second month after the plant closings, billables continued to decline. Ann tried to explain to her superiors that this trend reflected the plant closings, but her bosses believed otherwise. They suspected the problem was due to Ann's inadequate performance, perhaps to her lack of experience in managing a large urban hospital. Consequently, they directed her either to increase billables or to reduce costs. In response, Ann slowed down payments to the hospital's creditors and increased the pressure for collection of bills from insurance companies and patients. These actions helped, but only for a short while.

The next month was a disaster for Ann and Mercy Hospital. Billables continued to decline, and a new government regulation concerning the proper disposal of medical wastes came into force. To comply with the law, waste disposal companies were forced to raise their fees dramatically. Ann was now in a real bind. She took the problem to her superiors, who informed her they did not care what actions she took so long as the hospital remained profitable.

The following day, Ann met with John Macke, owner of Macke Disposal, which had been handling disposal of all the hospital's wastes. Macke informed Ann that he knew about the new regulation but that he would continue to dispose of the hospital's wastes at the same costs as before. Ann asked him if his company was going to obey the new federal law. Macke again replied that he would continue to dispose of the hospital's wastes for the same amount of money. Ann knew that what Macke really meant was that the wastes would not be disposed of properly in accordance with the new law. Later that day, the home office told Ann that she was dangerously close to losing her job because of the problems at Mercy.

Ann considered her options for making the hospital profitable and keeping her own job. She could obey the new law and face rising costs for waste disposal (and ultimately lose her job); she could disobey the law by employing Macke Disposal, which could have legal consequences for the hospital, and could hurt her own career, if the decision was later discovered; or she could cancel Mercy Hospital's policy of accepting indigent patients. The last option was extremely distasteful to Ann, who had been brought up to believe that the purpose of a hospital is to take care of all people with health needs. On the other hand, she also believed that the law of the land should be obeyed.

Discussion Questions

1. What should Ann do?
2. Describe the various conflicts that exist in this situation: personal-organizational, personal-societal, and organizational-societal.
3. How will the opportunity to dispose of the hospital's wastes improperly affect Ann's decision?

Source: O. C. Ferrell and J. Fraedrich, *Business Ethics: Ethical Decision Making and Cases,* 2nd edition, 1994. Copyright © 1994 by Houghton Mifflin Company. Reprinted with permission.

KEY TERMS

behavioral school   School of management that considers the needs of the worker as an individual and as a group member, as well as the organization of the work.

classical school   School of management that stresses hierarchy, impersonality, formalized structure, and specialization.

commanding (directing, motivating, or leading) Type of managerial behavior aimed at causing employees to accomplish the tasks assigned to them.

competitive benchmarking   Analyzing what the best competitor or leading companies in the industry are doing to discover the products, processes, and practices that satisfy customer needs.

controlling   Ensuring that the organization is actually achieving its planned objectives.

coordinating   Integrating the activities of individuals and units in order to provide unity of action in the pursuit of the organization's goals.

decisional role   Role relating to activities associated with making managerial decisions.

disseminator role   Role relating to activities of distributing information.

disturbance handler role   Role relating to conflict resolution activities.

entrepreneur role   Role in which the manager initiates change.

figurehead role   Role relating to symbolic or ceremonial activities in the organization.

informational role   Role relating to activities that develop and maintain an information network.

interpersonal role   Role pertaining to relationships with others.

leader role   Role pertaining to relationships with subordinates.

liaison role   Role pertaining to relationships with outside groups.

managerial role   Role based on a set of expectations for managerial behavior.

Maslow's hierarchy of human needs   Human relations model stating that people are motivated by five groups of needs and that these needs exist in a hierarchical order.

monitor role   Role relating to activities of seeking and receiving information.

negotiator role   Role relating to bargaining activities.

operations research   Application of the scientific method to operational problems of a system and solution of mathematical models representing these problems.

organizing   Structuring work relationships.

piece rate system   System that pays workers for each item they produce.

planning   Deciding in advance what the organization's objectives ought to be and what its members ought to do to attain these objectives.

resource allocator role   Role concerned with distributing various resources in order to accomplish organizational goals.

spokesperson role   Role pertaining to informing people outside the organization of organizational issues.

time and motion studies   Studies that observe workers' motions and the time it takes to complete certain motions, that break down their activities into small repeatable steps, and that determine the best way for the workers to do their jobs.

ENDNOTES

1. D. Wren, *The Evolution of Management Thought,* 4th ed., New York: Wiley (1994).
2. M. Weber, *The Theory of Social and Economic Organization,* New York: Oxford University Press (1947).
3. Ibid., 328–337.
4. A. Bluedorn, "Review of Scientific Management by F. W. Taylor," *Academy of Management Review* (April 1986): 443–447.
5. Bluedorn; and F. W. Taylor, *Scientific Management,* New York: Harper (1911).
6. Taylor.
7. D. McGregor, *The Human Side of Enterprise,* New York: McGraw-Hill (1960).
8. H. Taha, *Operations Research: An Introduction,* New York: Macmillan (1988): 1–2.
9. H. Fayol, H. *General and Industrial Management,* London: Pitman (1949).
10. S. Carroll and D. Gillen, "Are the Classical Management Functions Useful in Describing Managerial Work?" *Academy of Management Review* 12 (January 1987): 38–51.
11. B. Victor, "Coordinating Work in Complex Organizations," *Journal of Organizational Behavior* (1990): 187–199.
12. R. J. Mockler, ed., *Readings in Management Control,* New York: Appleton-Century-Crofts (1970): 14.
13. Adapted from Fayol, 19–42.
14. H. Mintzberg, *The Nature of Managerial Work,* New York: Harper & Row (1973): 92–93.
15. W. Band, *Creating Value for Customers: Designing and Implementing a Total Corporate Strategy,* New York: Wiley (1991): 8.
16. "Where Managers Will Go," *Fortune* (January 27, 1992): 51.
17. M. Porter, "Capital Disadvantage: America's Failing Capital Investment System," *Harvard Business Review* (September-October 1992): 65–83.
18. W. E. Deming, *Out of the Crisis,* Cambridge, MA: MIT Center for Advanced Engineering Study (1986).
19. "The Quality Imperative: Questing for the Best," *Business Week* (October 25, 1991): 10.
20. Masaaki Imai, *Kaizen: The Key to Japan's Competitive Success,* New York: Random House (1986).
21. W. Shewart, *Economic Control of Quality of Manufactured Products,* New York: Van Nostrand Reinhold (1931).
22. J. Bowles and J. Hammond, *Beyond Quality,* New York: Putnam Sons (1991).
23. D. Moore, "TQM—Not LBOs," *International Business Magazine* (September 1992): 1.
24. "The Cost of Quality," *Newsweek* (September 7, 1992): 48–49.
25. "An Open Letter: TQM on Campus," *Harvard Business Review* (November-December 1991): 94–95.
26. R. Schonberger, "Is Strategy Strategic? Impact of Total Quality Management on Strategy," *Academy of Management Executive* 6 (August 1992): 82.
27. G. Carothers, G. Bounds, and M. Stahl, "Managerial Leadership," in M. J. Stahl and G. M. Bounds (eds.), *Competing Globally Through Customer Value,* Westport, CT: Quorum Books (1991): 75-97.
28. W. E. Deming, *Out of the Crisis,* Cambridge, MA: MIT Center for Advanced Engineering Study (1986).
29. Carroll and Gillen.
30. G. M. Bounds and G. H. Dobbins, "The Manager's Job: A Paradigm Shift to a New Agenda," in M. J. Stahl and G. M. Bounds (eds.), *Competing Globally Through Customer Value,* Westport, CT: Quorum Books (1991): 117–145.
31. D. Niven, "When Times Get Tough, What Happens to TQM?" *Harvard Business Review* (May-June 1993): 20–34.
32. R. Zemke, "A Bluffer's Guide to TQM," *Training* (April 1993): 49–55.
33. S. Becker, "TQM Does Work: Ten Reasons Why Misguided Attempts Fail," *Management Review* (May 1993): 30–33; R. Cole, "Introduction," Special Issue on Total Quality Management, *California Management Review* 35, no. 3 (Spring 1993): 8; "TQM: More Than a Dying Fad?" *Fortune* (October 18, 1993): 66–72.

3
CHAPTER

International Competition and Management

LEARNING OBJECTIVES

After reading this chapter, you should be able to accomplish the following:

- Describe the role of increased global competition in the decline of U.S. industrial competitiveness.

- Discuss the forces at work shaping future global economic competition.

- Explain the role of declining international trade barriers in the growth of Japanese and European industries.

- Describe the forces favoring the formation of regional trading blocs.

- Discuss the role of patriotism and protectionism in international management.

- Compare and contrast the advantages and disadvantages of the North American Free Trade Agreement.

- Describe the options available for the development of international business.

- Discuss the impact on a firm's functional areas from a management decision to operate internationally.

- Explain the role of quality in global competition.

General Motors Suffers from International Competition and Demanding Customers

The Honda Accord, a high-quality, strong selling car, blurs the definition of a "foreign car" because it is built in Ohio by Americans with a majority of parts provided by U.S. suppliers. (Photo credit: Honda of America Manufacturing, Inc.)

Few companies have responded as slowly to global competition, and paid such a steep price, as General Motors. Perhaps the world's largest industrial organization had grown too big and too inwardly focused for it to be responsive to a changed world. As recently as 1974, some were comparing the power of GM to that of foreign governments. However, as the saying goes, "the bigger they are, the harder they fall."

In the early 1980s both Ford and Chrysler suffered huge losses and restructured themselves to become more responsive to cus-tomers. Their increased customer responsive-ness yielded increased profitability.

Despite intense Japanese competition and inroads in the North American car market, GM delayed its restructuring until it had realized some staggering losses. GM lost $2 billion in 1990, over $4 billion in 1991, and $23.5 billion in 1992. Although the 1992 loss was in part due to an accounting change, this loss was the largest loss ever reported by a Fortune 500 company. The losses at GM were so severe that ratings on its financial debt were downgraded by the debt-rating agencies.

In terms of both profitability and growth in sales, GM trailed competitors in the 1987-1991 period, as is shown in the following table. After considering inflation, GM's sales growth was flat in the five-year period.

Automakers' Profitability and Growth: 1987–1991

Company	Profitability[a]	Sales Growth
Ford	18.0	11.3
Chrysler	10.2	7.7
Honda	9.5	12.2
GM	6.2	3.3

[a]Profitability is the five-year average through 1991 of return on stockholders' equity expressed as a percentage. Sales growth is the five-year average of dollar volume of sales growth expressed as a percentage.

Source: "Detroit's Crisis: Too Many Competitors, Too Much Capacity, Too Few Buyers," *Forbes* (January 6, 1992): 120.

continued

GM's miserable profitability and sales growth performance were mirrored in customer satisfaction data and market share data. In the 1992 J. D. Power Customer Satisfaction Survey, only one GM car, the Saturn, placed in the top five. Of the top-selling cars for the first half of 1992, the top-selling GM car was fifth, behind the higher sales of Honda Accord, Ford Taurus, Toyota Camry, and Ford Escort. At 120,000 cars sold, the Pontiac Grand Am sold 70,000 less than the Honda Accord.

Not only were Ford, Honda, and Toyota beating GM in terms of the most popular individual models, but GM's North American market share had been in a persistent slide for over a decade. GM's market share slid from 44.5 percent in 1982 to near 35 percent in 1993.

Associated with GM's poor market share and profitability data are the successes of the Japanese automakers. In the 1960s and early 1970s a "Made in Japan" auto was synonymous with poor quality. By continuously improving their production processes, quality, and products, the Japanese automakers slowly but steadily improved their popularity with U.S. customers, who found GM's products lacking. Additionally, some German cars, such as the Mercedes and BMW, were selling as high-priced, well-engineered cars. What was GM to do in the face of such unrelenting international competition and demanding customers?

For most of the twentieth century, the United States was the world's premier industrial power. Its wartime enemies and many other combatant nations lost their industrial bases in World War II. The Japanese and the Germans had their industrial plants leveled by intense bombing campaigns conducted by the Allies in World War II.

Given the absence of international competition, U.S. firms produced for a worldwide market and the United States ran international trade surpluses for decades following the war. However, this once unchallenged position changed in the late 1970s as Japan and Germany brought their rebuilt economies, replete with new plant and equipment, to a competitive footing. In the 1980s the United States consistently ran trade deficits, particularly with Japan.

THE EXPLOSION OF GLOBAL COMPETITION

In the 1980s U.S. firm after U.S. firm in a variety of industries suffered from explosive global competition. Many U.S. firms were not prepared for the severity of the international competition, as GM would attest.

Decline of U.S. Competitiveness

Many industries were not prepared for the global competition. In some industries the international competitors were not taken seriously until several U.S. firms in those industries had been acquired by international competitors. In some industries several U.S. firms left the industry because they could not match the new international competitors.

Good examples of declining U.S. competitiveness are two industries in which U.S. firms' previously unchallenged positions are currently severely threatened—the tire industry and the aircraft industry. By 1989 all major domestic tire makers, except for Goodyear, had merged with or been acquired by international firms.[1]

The same global competition drastically altered the U.S. aircraft industry. Once unchallenged, Boeing has lost significant market share to Airbus Industries in Europe, which is partially subsidized by some European governments. Increasingly, the airlines are buying aircraft from Airbus Industries in Europe. The tough new global competition that Boeing faces has already virtually wrecked the airliner business of its domestic rival, McDonnell Douglas Corp.[2]

This decline in American competitiveness is reflected in a new body of thought called "declinism" as documented in a *Harvard Business Review* article. "Real wages are falling. Productivity growth is down. Companies aren't competitive in global markets. So pervasive is this preoccupation with decline that it has given birth to its own school of thought. Call it 'declinism.'"[3] Declinism was founded on the decline in American industrial competitiveness and a pessimism that international competition would remain so fierce that the United States would not recover its lost industrial preeminence.

In 1992 *Fortune* magazine analyzed the competitive stance of American industries. The magazine rated the competitiveness of 13 key U.S. industries relative to Japan and Europe. "The U.S. is still losing ground in many markets that promise the fastest growth."[4] Those data are contained in Table 3.1, where the grades assigned reflect production data, company performance, and expert opinion. The lower-scoring industries were losing ground in terms of U.S. competitiveness relative to Japan and Europe.

Associated with the decline of U.S. competitiveness are two important factors: (1) the emergence of the world economy and (2) short-term myopia (near-sightedness), which stressed attention to quarterly profits.[5] In a recent analysis of America's capital investment system, it was concluded that some changes are needed so that American managers can invest for the long term without interference from the investment markets demanding high short-term returns. Such a modification toward the long term would produce an investment system like that of Japan and Germany.[6] Without a long-term focus, Porter argues, the ability of U.S. firms to compete internationally is handicapped.

America's world market share shrank in several different products over the last 15 years. Market share data are important because they show relative changes in value to customers. Shrinking market share data indicate that customers are defecting to other firms to receive better value. The size of the market share declines depicted in Figure 3.1 are quite large except for hard disks. Such declines indicate that there were both absolute and relative declines in customer satisfaction relative to competitors. From their own observation and experience, many consumers are familiar with U.S. world market share declines in textiles, shoes, automobiles, and consumer electronics.

Figure 3.1 shows America's declining world market share for several high-technology industries over a ten-year period. *Fortune* magazine highlighted these industries because they are important for industrial competitiveness. These industries involve numerous industrial suppliers and in many cases are suppliers to other industries.[7]

TABLE 3.1   *U. S. Competitiveness Relative to Japan and Europe: Scorecard in 13 Key Industries*

Grade	Industry
A	Pharmaceuticals
A	Forest products
B+	Aerospace
B	Chemicals
B	Food
B	Scientific and photographic equipment
B	Petroleum refining
B–	Telecommunications equipment
C+	Computers
C	Industrial and farm equipment
C	Motor vehicles
C–	Metals
D	Electronics

Source: "How American Industry Stacks Up," *Fortune* (March 9, 1992): 30. © 1992 Time, Inc. All rights reserved.

GM is a highly visible example of an American firm's loss of significant market share, as we saw in the quality case at the beginning of this chapter. Nearly all of the loss in market share by GM was taken by Japanese automakers.

After over a decade of losses, some U.S. firms stabilized and started to regain worldwide market share. In the early and mid-1990s, the U.S. automakers were slowly winning back customers, one at a time, from Japanese automakers. The quality of some U.S. models was approaching the quality of Japanese models, whereas in the 1980s the average quality of U.S. models lagged far behind. As U.S. firms started to control their costs through improved processes, and as the Japanese yen increased in value, U.S. cars were more price competitive in the 1990s.

What caused GM and other large U.S. firms to lose market share in the first place in the 1980s? To be sure, there were many causes, some under the control of management and some under the control of the U.S. government and other governments. The short-term financial focus of many U.S. managers was part of the problem.[8] That short-term financial focus coincided with many large firms' losing sight of their customers and becoming inwardly focused.[9] Many large firms apparently forgot how to create and deliver value to their customers. They forgot about the customers' demands for quality in an era in which customers could find high-grade products from international suppliers. In addition to GM, Harley-Davidson and Xerox are two other large, previously dominant U.S. firms that lost substantial market share after falling into such an inward focus.

Although seemingly well intentioned, the U.S. government imposed substantial costs on U.S. industry during this time. Regulatory policies, including workplace standards, environmental standards, and product safety standards, added to the cost of business in the United States. Human resource policies, including discrimination

FIGURE 3.1   *America's Declining Market Share: U.S. Share of World Markets*

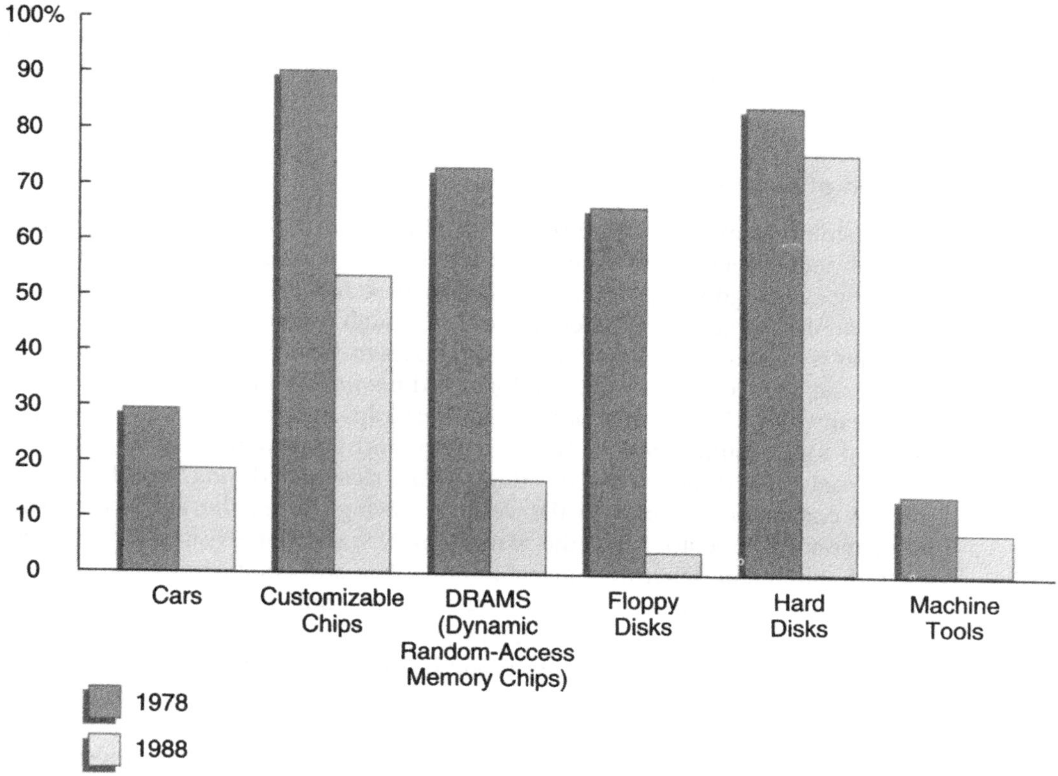

Source: *Fortune* (January 1, 1990): 74. © 1990 Time, Inc. All rights reserved.

policies and labor laws, also added to the costs of U.S. business. These costs and other government-imposed costs helped to make U.S. products and services more expensive than those of other countries.

U.S. Post–World War II Dominance

As the world returned to peacetime pursuits following World War II, the U.S. industrial machine was intact. That machine had performed very well during the war, producing planes, tanks, trucks, ships, guns, and other instruments of war in enormous numbers. The production of durable consumer goods like automobiles, refrigerators, washers, and dryers was at a low level throughout the war, as it had been in the 1930s due to the Great Depression.

After World War II consumers throughout the world were demanding such durable consumer goods, and U.S. industry was able to respond with an abundance of goods. The United States ran substantial trade surpluses for the decades immediately following the war. Since many buyers were first-time customers buying their first car, stereo, or washer and dryer, attention was focused on the quantity of standardized production and not on the quality or variety of the products.[10]

In the late 1970s many U.S. firms started to experience substantial international competition both from Japan and Europe. The Japanese competition is definitely worth reviewing because that competition has impacted U.S. industry more than that of any other single country in the 1980s and 1990s.

Growth of Japanese Industry

In rebuilding its manufacturing base after World War II, the Japanese concentrated on both technological and managerial advances. Since the devastation of the U.S. bombing campaign was so complete, the Japanese had to start from scratch with all-new manufacturing plants and equipment. Although it was a slow start, two decades after the war Japan had a new, large, ultramodern industrial base with plants containing the latest equipment, technology, and manufacturing processes.

Meanwhile, U.S. industry operated at near capacity, trying to satisfy worldwide demand for consumer goods. The U.S. plant and equipment base was dated and worn from years of heavy use meeting military demands during World War II and intense consumer demands in the years following. Given the absence of strong international competitors after the war, many U.S. companies simply continued to use old equipment rather than invest in new plant and equipment.

The first notable example of the aging U.S. technological and plant and equipment base contrasted with the new Japanese technological and plant and equipment base was in the steel industry. After rebuilding its war-ravaged cities with low-cost, high-quality steel made in its new steel plants, Japan turned its attention to the worldwide steel market. U.S. steelmakers were trying to compete against the Japanese with dated plant and equipment, high wages, and a limited understanding of quality manufacturing processes.[11]

While rebuilding its industrial base, Japan maintained restrictive trade barriers to protect its industries. Government trade barriers served to officially keep out imports. Cultural trade barriers, including a definite bias in favor of doing business with other Japanese, also helped to protect Japanese industries.

Besides developing new technologies and equipment that lowered their cost of production, the Japanese were learning about quality from W. Edwards Deming.[12] Although Deming had tried to preach his quality strategy to U.S. managers, most were too busy cranking out the product to satisfy unmet worldwide demand. In addition to Deming, Kaoru Ishikawa, Joseph Juran, and others were teaching the message of quality to the Japanese.[13] Many Japanese were culturally ready to implement quality improvement, because as an island nation with few natural resources, there was a built-in bias against waste.

Prior to World War II, "Made in Japan" was synonymous with inferior quality. In time Japanese managers came to understand the importance of quality to the customer, and they learned how to develop and continually improve systems and processes to achieve consistently high quality.[14] In the late 1970s American consumers and managers began to realize that the Japanese were consistently producing high-quality goods at low worldwide prices.

Q UALITY CASE

Back to the General Motors Case

For a long time GM seemed to ignore the Japanese automakers and continued to pay inadequate attention to customer demands for quality and improved value. Instead, GM focused on its profits and shareholders' demands. GM may have ignored customers too long. In an earlier era, when the only competitive choices available were Fords and Chryslers, GM was able to get away with its less than responsive attitude to customers' demands. But the Japanese willingness to meet customers' needs for quality and value translated into increased market share, and the competitive scene changed dramatically.

Partly because GM thought it "owned" the domestic market, its managers let the firm's costs get out of control. Of the world's major automobile companies in the early 1990s, GM had the dubious honor of being the highest-cost producer. GM paid $34.60 an hour in United Auto Workers (UAW) wages and benefits for work that rivals were doing for half those rates in nonunion shops. Additionally, GM's managers had agreed to some of the most restrictive work rules in the industry, which also increased its costs.

In trying to control its bloated payroll, GM planned to shrink its hourly workforce by nearly 150,000 from 1985 to 1995. However, the combative UAW members were determined to keep their high wages and jobs, and they demonstrated their resolve by using sporadic strikes in late 1992.

In this new era GM faced conflicting demands among its constituents. Customers demanded high-quality cars at reasonable prices, which Japanese competitors were willing and able to offer in their intense bid for more of the world's car market. Combative UAW workers demanded job security and above-market wages and benefits. And finally, stockholders demanded profits.

The world's largest corporation reconciled such conflicting demands by focusing on profits. In response to the question posed by Fortune magazine, "How much market share do you want to get back and how soon?" GM chairman Robert Stempel provided the following answer: "Our plan isn't based on regained market share; our plan is based on being profitable at whatever share of the market we get."

This financial focus in the early 1990s was consistent with the short-term financial focus observed at GM in 1989. "The finance men hold the high ground, but their analyses, which tend to follow trends rather than anticipate them, helped keep GM from deploying the minivan that its designers developed in the 1970s. Their caution has also delayed the four-door versions of the GM-10 cars and the Blazer sport utility vehicle. More recently, some GM product people say privately that the pressure to increase short-term profits is causing short-sighted scrimping on their programs." At a time when other firms under the banner of Total Quality Management were reinforcing relationships with suppliers on the basis of consistent quality, GM was squeezing its suppliers on the basis of cost.

An indication of how committed the Japanese are to quality is found in Figure 3.2. Relative to both the United States and Germany, Japanese firms are more committed to the four major quality themes of customer satisfaction, competitive benchmarking, time-based competition, and process simplification.[15] **Competitive**

FIGURE 3.2   *Comparing the Quality Cultures of Three Leading Trading Nations*

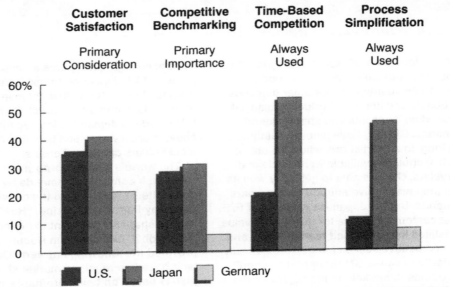

Source: Adapted from American Quality Foundation and Ernst & Young, "International Quality Study: The Definitive Study of the Best International Quality Management Practices," Cleveland: Ernst & Young (1991): 18–28.

benchmarking is analyzing what the best competitor or leading companies in the industry are doing to discover the products, processes, and practices that satisfy customer needs. **Time-based competition** is competition based on doing the job faster than others so that the customer receives the product or service faster. **Process simplification** is the simplification of systems and work flow to reduce both defects and time.

Japan's commitment to quality, combined with its relatively new technological plant and equipment base, caused it to become an economic powerhouse starting in the late 1970s. Japan ran substantial trade surpluses with the United States in the 1980s and early 1990s, as the data in Figure 3.3 show. A **trade surplus** exists when a country exports more than it imports. A **trade deficit** exists when a country imports more than it exports. The Japanese surpluses (U.S. deficits) seemed to be stuck at a high level—between $40 billion and $60 billion. This was occurring during a time in which the overall U.S. trade deficit with the rest of the world was being cut in half. Some even forecast that at current rates of growth of trade deficits between the United States and Japan, Japan would become the world's largest economic power by the year 2010.[16]

Although the competition with the Japanese was painful due to the loss of market share and loss of jobs in some industries (GM, for example, cut its workforce by 150,000), the intensity of the competition forced many U.S. managers to seek dramatic improvements in managing. This theme is discussed in greater detail later in this chapter.

FIGURE 3.3   *U.S. Trade Deficits with Japan: 1980–1992*

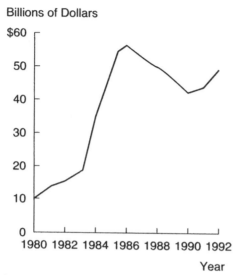

Billions of Dollars

Source: U.S. Department of Commerce.

Pacific Rim Countries

Japan has been the most formidable Asian competitor. However, there are a number of other Asian trading partners whose competitive presence is being felt in the world. Table 3.2 lists the economic sizes of these Pacific Rim countries in 1993. The map positions the countries. **Gross domestic product (GDP)** is the value of all goods and services produced domestically. Although in the early 1990s South Korea was only about one-tenth the economic size of Japan, it was using competition based on low price to compete with some Japanese firms. Some futurists were predicting that by the turn of the century China would be the next economic powerhouse in Asia.

The European Economic Area

Like Japan, Europe rebuilt its industrial base with new plant and equipment and new technologies following World War II. And as in Japan, the new plant and equipment and new technologies gave many European manufacturers a quality and cost edge over U.S. competitors. However, the political fragmentation of Europe, where some countries have fought each other on the battlefield for centuries, prevented Europe from being a single international competitive powerhouse. That changed with the formation of the European Community.

The **European Community (EC)** is a group of Western European countries that have agreed to eliminate trade barriers among themselves to encourage trade and improve economic development in Europe. Negotiations were held in the late 1980s and early 1990s about the possibility of forming a single currency. Some futurists had even discussed the possibility of political union, but that seemed far off.

TABLE 3.2   *Pacific Rim and Other Asian Trading Partners: Gross Domestic Products (GDP)*
(Billions of Dollars)

Country		GDP	Percentage of Total
Japan		$2,836	65.8%
China		368	8.5
South Korea		270	6.3
"7 Tigers"		545	12.6
Hong Kong	79		
Indonesia	126		
Malaysia	59		
Philippines	52		
Singapore	64		
Taiwan	71		
Thailand	94		
Australia, New Zealand		294	6.8
Total		$4,313	100%
U.S. GDP		$5,673	

Sources: *International Business Practices,* U.S. Department of Commerce, 1993; *National Trade Data Bank,* May 1993.

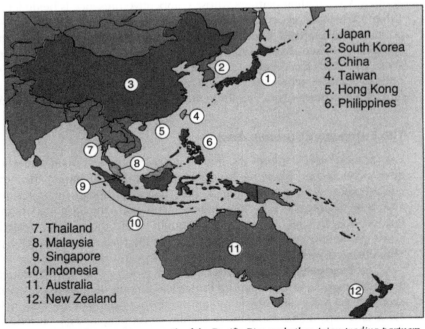

1. Japan
2. South Korea
3. China
4. Taiwan
5. Hong Kong
6. Philippines

7. Thailand
8. Malaysia
9. Singapore
10. Indonesia
11. Australia
12. New Zealand

The international competitive strength of the Pacific Rim and other Asian trading partners,
is underscored by their economic size.

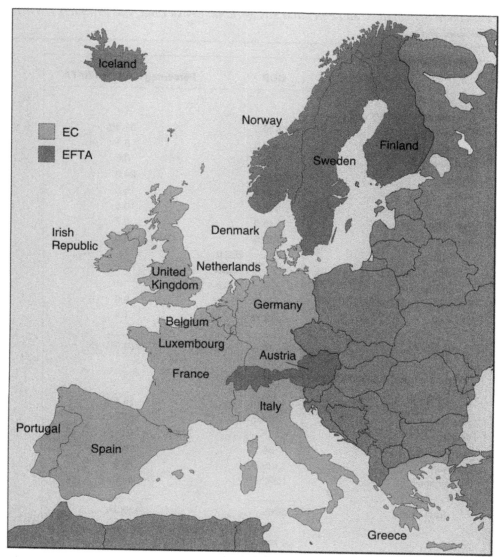

The economic size of the European Community and the European Free Trade Association underscores their international competitive strength.

Not as powerful or wealthy as the EC, the **European Free Trade Association (EFTA)** is a group of European countries that have agreed to cooperate among themselves to encourage trade. The hoped-for combination of the EC and the EFTA is referred to as the **European Economic Area (EEA).** The EEA was not a formal union in the early 1990s, unlike the EC and the EFTA, but rather a convenient way to refer to all of the countries in the EC and the EFTA. The EC was the most powerful of the three entities in the early 1990s. The map shows the countries in the

TABLE 3.3   *European Economic Area (EEA) and Switzerland: Gross Domestic Products (GDP)*
(Billions of Dollars)

	GDP		Percentage of EC or EFTA
European Community (EC):			
Germany	$1,570.0		31.4%
United Kingdom	408.3		8.1
Irish Republic	28.7		0.6
France	1,200.0		24.0
Italy	825.6		16.5
Spain	526.0		10.5
Portugal	35.0		0.7
Benelux	239.5		4.8
Belgium		203.0	
Netherlands		26.6	
Luxembourg		9.9	
Denmark	101.3		2.0
Greece	72.2		1.4
Total EC	$5,006.6		100.0%
European Free Trade Association (EFTA):			
Norway	$106.0		14.0%
Sweden	238.0		32.0
Iceland	a		—
Austria	64.1		8.0
Finland	125.0		16.0
Switzerland[b]	232.6		30.0
Total EFTA	$765.7		100.0%
Total EEA	$5,772.3 trillion		
U.S. GDP	$5,673.0 billion		

[a] Less than $5 million. [b] Withdrew in 1992.
Sources: *International Business Practices,* U.S. Department of Commerce, 1993; *National Trade Data Bank,* May 1993.

EC and in the EFTA. Table 3.3 lists the economic sizes of those countries and the economic size of the United States in 1993.

At midnight on December 31, 1992, the EC together with EFTA became the world's largest free-trade area. There is some concern about European ambitions to create an economic and political superstate.[17] Such a development would dramatically intensify international competition for U.S. firms trying to conduct business in the EEA.[18]

In some industries it is difficult for U.S. firms to compete in Europe because of International Standards Organization (ISO) 9000. **ISO 9000** is a comprehensive standard specifying the management systems and processes a firm must possess in order to market certain products in the EC. Without ISO 9000 certification, a firm with regulated products in the health, safety, or environmental sectors may be prohibited from marketing its products in Europe. A great many products have a health, safety, or environmental impact. Because of its quality theme, multiple comparisons have been made between the Baldrige Quality Award and ISO 9000. Many U.S. firms in the early 1990s were qualifying themselves under both criteria as a statement of their commitment to the quality of their products or services.

Just as there is a national award for exemplary quality in the United States—the Baldrige—there is an award for exemplary quality in Europe—The European Quality Award (EQA). The EQA is administered by the European Foundation for Quality Management (EFQM). The EFQM consisted of 330 European organizations (corporations and universities) in 1993. The EQA criteria shown in Figure 3.4 are similar to the Baldrige criteria discussed in Chapter 1. The EFQM and the EQA help underscore the importance given to Total Quality as a competitive weapon in Europe.

Decline of International Trade Barriers

A potent force favoring global economic competition has been the decline of international trade barriers. A **trade barrier** is an impediment, usually quotas on quantity or tariffs on price or technical specifications on trade items, to prevent free trade among countries. A study of international competitive strategy listed "falling tariff barriers" as one of the major forces favoring international trade since World War II.[19]

There are outright trade quotas on the amount of foreign-made textile products that can enter the United States. There are also tariffs on foreign-made trucks to discourage their importation to the United States. The Japanese have technical specifications on telecommunications products that have kept much U.S.-made telecommunications equipment out of Japan.

The Smoot-Hawley Tariff Act passed by the U.S. Congress in 1930 helped to contract world trade at the wrong time. The tariffs included in the act reinforced the business contraction of the Great Depression by making international trade expensive. After World War II most of the world showed that it did not wish to repeat that mistake and substantially lowered tariffs. In spite of repeated rumblings from some politicians scattered throughout the world calling for increased tariffs, it appears that the world is on the path of increased free international trade. Politicians and governments seem to be providing a more friendly international playing field for managers to expand international trade.

The General Agreement on Tariffs and Trade (GATT) was passed in late 1993. It cut tariffs on a variety of products and services and thereby promised to increase world trade. The combination of GATT and the North American Free Trade Agreement (NAFTA) will substantially lower international trade barriers and could lead to increased world trade and global prosperity.

FIGURE 3.4   *Framework of The European Quality Award*

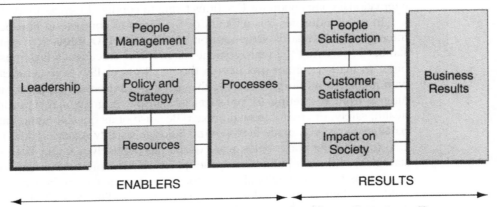

Source: *Total Quality Management: The European Model for Self-Appraisal,* Eindhoven, The Netherlands: The European Foundation for Quality Management (1993).

The European Quality Award symbolizes the importance of quality improvement in European firms. (Photo credit: European Foundation for Quality Management.)

FIGURE 3.5 *Trade Patterns in North America*

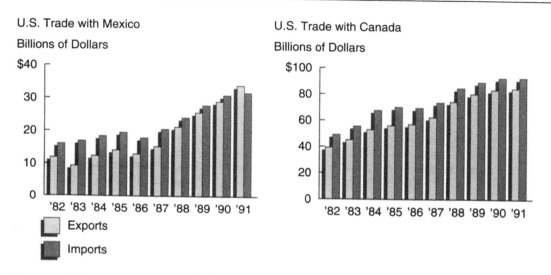

Sources: U.S. Department of Commerce; *Economic Report of the President* (1992).

North American Free Trade Agreement (NAFTA)

As Figure 3.5 shows, trade between the United States and Canada and between the United States and Mexico has been growing. Many politicians in North America have recognized the economic benefits to member countries of the EC from low tariffs agreed upon by the EC. The North American Free Trade Agreement was meant to create a large trading bloc among the three North American countries with low or nonexistent trade barriers among the three countries, as in the EC.

Such a trading bloc would be even larger than the EC. The data in Table 3.4 show a combined NAFTA GDP of $6.5 trillion, in comparison to the EC GDP of $5.0 trillion in Table 3.3.

NAFTA was meant to simplify trade among the three trading partners in North America. But the pact was not without controversy. The free traders argued that the pact would enrich all three countries by expanding trade and jobs. The protectionists countered that NAFTA would decimate jobs in the United States by exporting low-skilled jobs to Mexico for lower wages.[20] Some workers would be displaced from country to country. However, the history of tariffs has shown that lowering tariffs and thereby increasing international trade causes net economic gains for all involved countries through increased economic growth.

The debate over NAFTA was heightened by some bad experiences with maquiladoras. **Maquiladoras** are manufacturing plants in Mexico that perform low-wage operations, usually assembly of parts manufactured in the United States. Some maquiladoras paid such low wages that there were charges of exploitation of workers, and some maquiladoras polluted the environment more than their U.S. counterparts.

TABLE 3.4   *Size of U.S., Canadian, and Mexican Markets*

Country	Gross Domestic Product (Billions)	Population (Millions)
United States	$5,673	253
Canada	572	27
Mexico	283	83

Sources: "Mega Market," *Time* (August 10, 1992): 43; "Debate Rages over Trade Pact," *USA Today* (August 10, 1992): B1.

Regional Trading Blocs

The formation of the European Community and of the North American Free Trade Agreement, as well as the Japanese dominance in the Pacific Rim, present a troubling possibility. Three major global trading blocs might emerge. It would be easy and cheap to trade within those blocs, because of low or no trade barriers, including low tariffs. However, trade across the blocs might be difficult and costly, because of substantial trade barriers, including high tariffs. Only time will tell if these trading blocs and these barriers across the blocs will emerge.

Forecast for Global Economic Competition

As General Motors and many other U.S. corporations can testify, global economic competition has been intense in the 1980s and early 1990s. The same forces at work in the 1980s are at work in the 1990s, suggesting that the global economic competition will continue to intensify for the balance of the 1990s and the early part of the twenty-first century. Whereas Japanese firms were the nemesis of many U.S. firms in the 1980s, there will likely be increasing competition from several other international sources in the foreseeable future as well.

Now that the Berlin Wall is down and the Eastern European countries have gravitated toward market-based, deregulated economies, these countries are also entering the internationally competitive battle. *Fortune* magazine recently diagnosed Czechoslovakia, former East Germany, Hungary, and Poland as possessing promising economic potential because of their workforces and their bias toward private ownership of property.[21]

Although the domestic Japanese industry was in recession in 1994, Japan's basic industrial might remained intact. Japan's trade surplus was strong even in the face of domestic recession. Some forecast that Japan would emerge from its recession even stronger than before.[22] The strength of several Japanese manufacturing firms was well known. The world finance and banking communities had also come to recognize the strength of the Japanese in their industries. In 1992 seven of the world's ten largest banks, five of the world's ten largest insurers, and four of the world's ten largest securities firms were Japanese.[23]

E   T   H   I   C   S   E   X   H   I   B   I   T

Dresser Industries and South Africa

At its 1980 shareholders' meeting, Dresser Industries had defeated a shareholder resolution, which had received 11.2 percent of the shareholder votes cast, demanding that the company sign the Sullivan Principles. Dresser was one of the world's leading suppliers of technology, products, and services to industries involved in the development of energy and natural resources.

The Sullivan Principles—a set of norms for U.S. corporate operations in racially divided South Africa—were designed by the Reverend Leon Sullivan, a black Philadelphia minister. The principles covered such areas as nonsegregation of all facilities, equal pay for equal work, equal employment practices, and improved quality of life for employees outside of work in areas such as housing, education, and health care. By 1980, 135 corporations, representing 85 percent of U.S. investment in South Africa, had signed the principles. Dresser had not signed, nor had 163 other U.S. companies operating there.

Dresser was one of the nonsignatories that faced growing pressure to sign the principles. The company offered to sign, provided that it did not have to submit progress reports or permit on-site monitoring by a nongovernmental authority.

Soon after Dresser's top executives learned of the upcoming shareholder resolution on the principles, they also began receiving concerned letters from 25 institutional investors. Some institutional investors also divested stock in Dresser because of Dresser's refusal to sign the principles. Dresser's top executives had to decide what to do next.

Discussion Questions

1. Should Dresser's management sign the Sullivan Principles? Why or why not?

2. When a U.S. firm is operating in a foreign country, should the firm abide by that country's ethical standards or by U.S. ethical standards? Explain.

Sources: M. G. Velasquez, "A South African Investment," in M. W. Hoffman and J. M. Moore (eds.), *Business Ethics*, 2nd ed. New York: McGraw-Hill (1990): 597–603; and K. O. Hanson and P. Mintz, "Dresser Industries and South Africa," in Thomas Donaldson (ed.). *Case Studies in Business Ethics*, Englewood Cliffs, NJ: Prentice-Hall (1984): 123–128.

The North American Free Trade Agreement was passed by the U.S. Congress in late 1993. Some tariffs between the United States and Mexico were cut on January 1, 1994. The balance of the tariffs among Canada, Mexico, and the United States were scheduled to be eliminated over a 15-year period, leading to greater trade among the three countries.

As global competition continues to grow, and as more U.S. firms and managers operate in other countries, many managers will need to address an ethical issue. When a U.S. firm is operating in a foreign country, should the firm abide by that country's ethical standards or by U.S. ethical standards? Such was the issue addressed by Dresser Industries in South Africa, as indicated in the ethics exhibit.

CRITICAL THINKING QUESTIONS

1. Describe the role of increased global competition in the decline of U.S. industrial competitiveness.

2. Explain the forces at work shaping future global economic competition.

3. Describe the role of declining international trade barriers in the growth of Japanese and European industries.

4. Explain the forces favoring the formation of regional trading blocs.

5. How will the North American Free Trade Agreement aid economic development and political stability in Mexico?

INTERNATIONAL BUSINESS OPTIONS

In our discussion thus far we have documented the explosive growth in global economic competition and the international developments which suggest that worldwide economic competition will continue to intensify. Given this situation, there are specific options among which management must decide. These options range from not competing, under the banner of protectionism and patriotism, to the establishment of aggressive global and multinational businesses. Although the government is the organization that implements protectionism, it typically does so at the insistence of corporations and managers who choose to lobby for protectionism.

Protectionism and Patriotism

We have already discussed the negative effects on the world economy of the last major attempt by the U.S. Congress to halt free international trade (the Smoot-Hawley Tariff Act of 1930). Despite that bitter experience, there are some firms and politicians in this country, in Japan, and in the EC who pursue protectionism rather than competition.[24]

For example, in 1991 the three U.S. automakers in Detroit charged some Japanese automakers with selling minivans in this country at less than their cost of manufacture, that is, "dumping" the minivans at a loss in order to build market share in the United States. The U.S. automakers' attempt at protectionism was not upheld by the U.S. government, which ruled that the Japanese were not "dumping" the minivans.[25]

There appears to be a growing backlash in this country and in the EC against the Japanese, partly because the Japanese have used a variety of trade barriers to keep U.S. products from becoming too strong in Japan. In a recent survey 61 percent responded yes when asked: "Should the United States restrict Japanese imports?"[26] A danger of such protectionist sentiment is that it could draw attention away from the needed quality improvements in many U.S products and services.

To capitalize on a protectionist theme, some firms appeal to patriotism. Chevrolet was not at all reluctant to use a patriotic theme to sell cars. Its television ads referred to Chevrolet as "the heartbeat of America."

In the past few years several Japanese automakers have located manufacturing plants in this country, employing thousands of U.S. workers. This practice protects the Japanese firms from the risk of an appreciating currency, and it counters the growth of protectionist sentiment among U.S. consumers and politicians. Honda's television ad in the fall of 1992 touted: "Honda: Making Quality Cars in America." At more than 80 percent, the percentage of parts in the 1994 Honda Accord made in the United States was among the highest of any car built in the United States.[27] How can one argue with "quality" *and* a "Made in America" label? Such a practice of locating plants in the country where the sales are targeted is a strategy that seems to diffuse the patriotism and protectionist arguments. This international strategy is described in the following sections.

I N T E R N A T I O N A L   E X H I B I T

International Business Blunders

1. *Timing*. The Tandy Corporation scheduled its first Christmas promotion of Radio Shack stores in Holland around December 25. After realizing sales below their expectations, Tandy discovered that the Dutch trade gifts on December 6, which is St. Nicholas Day.

2. *Language*. An insurance company doing business in Brazil named its branch there "SAI do Brazil." The locals pronounced it "Saee do Brazil," which when translated meant "Get out of Brazil." McDonald's used the term "Gran Mac" when introducing the Big Mac in France. Only after the promotional literature had been printed did someone point out that "Gran Mac" in French translated into "master pimp." Chevrolet's "Nova" was spoken as "no va" in Spanish, which means "it doesn't go." Coca-Cola in Chinese characters became "bite the wax tadpole" or "a wax-flattened mare." Ford's "Fiera" meant "ugly old woman" in Spanish.

3. *Symbols*. The hand sign for perfection in the United States, making a circle of the index finger and the thumb while pointing the three other fingers skyward, is a hand sign meaning an obscenity in Australia. It is analogous to holding up the middle finger in this country.

4. *Color*. Black is associated with death in the United States and Europe, but in Japan white is associated with death, and in Latin America purple is associated with death. The choice of color in packaging can be very tricky.

Sources: I. Lowen, "Eyes on Europe," *Direct Marketing* (October 1990): 45; D. Ricks, *Blunders in International Business,* Cambridge, MA: Blackwell (1983): 30–36; "Radio Shack's Rough Trip," *Business Week* (May 30, 1977): 55.

Strategies for International Businesses

A way to characterize strategies for international businesses is to show the advantages of global business systems and the advantages of local adaptation. **Global business systems** are systems that use the same business processes and operations throughout the world. The advantages of global business systems arise primarily from global economic advantages like worldwide purchasing of parts and worldwide standardization of processes. **Local adaptation** is the modification of a multinational organization's business operations to fit the requirements of specific countries. Advantages of local adaptation arise from government requirements or cultural values. Figure 3.6 presents international strategies as a function of the global/local tradeoffs.

The strong advantages of global business systems and the weak advantages of local adaptation suggest "global businesses." **Global businesses** use the same business processes throughout the world and market a nearly identical line of products throughout the world. Examples of global businesses are IBM in computers, Sony in consumer electronics, and Coca-Cola in soft drinks. When there are strong advantages to or strong needs for local adaptation coupled with weak reasons for global business systems, then "local/national businesses" are recommended. **Local/national businesses** adapt their operations and products to specific countries. Food processing is an example. "'Blocked global businesses' form when there are economic advantages of global business, but the government or local culture prevents a global business. **"Blocked" global businesses** are businesses forced into local adaptation despite the advantages of global business systems. Examples include weapons man-

FIGURE 3.6   *International Business Strategies*

Advantages of/Need for Local Adaptation

		Low	High
Advantages of Global Business Systems	High	Global Businesses	"Blocked" Global Businesses
	Low	Mulltinational Businesses (Multimarket)	Local/National Businesses

Source: H. Henzler and W. Rall, "Facing Up to the Globalization Challenge," *McKinsey Quarterly* (Winter 1986): 52–68. Reprinted by permission of McKinsey and Co., Inc.

ufacturing and local telephone companies. It would be more efficient to manufacture weapons on a worldwide basis, yet some governments require that weapons be made to government specifications by domestic manufacturers. **Multinational/multimarket businesses** require some degree of local adaptation in situations where there is limited economic advantage of global business systems. One example is the manufacturing of electrical equipment, in which some adaptation is needed owing to the different voltages and frequencies of electricity in different countries.[28]

Cultural Factors

No matter what kind of international business strategy the firm uses, it must be careful to design its products and marketing with the country's language and customs in mind. Otherwise the company could face ridicule and risk a sales flop for committing an unintentional international blunder of the first order, as described in the international exhibit.

There are numerous examples in which well-intentioned U.S. managers were just not aware of local customs or language nuances. Careful planning and study of the potential international market, including hiring native citizens of the host country, are essential. Who can help the international firm understand customer requirements in the host country better than locals? Understanding customer requirements is the first priority of Total Quality Management, whether international or domestic. Errors in language translations and ignorance of local customs can destroy the best-positioned international product, just as ignorance of domestic customers can destroy a domestic product.

CRITICAL THINKING QUESTIONS

1. Describe the roles of patriotism and protectionism in international management. Why are they so often used?

2. Explain the strategies for international businesses.

3. What is the value of requiring business students to study a foreign language and foreign customs?

MANAGING INTERNATIONAL ACTIVITIES

Once a firm has decided to compete in the international arena, it must decide how to conduct its international activities. There are several considerations in the areas of international operations, marketing, finance, research and development, human resources, and information systems that need to be dealt with.

It is important to recognize that decisions made in one area of international activities impact activities in another area. For example, when Chrysler decided to reduce its domestic manufacturing activities and resell several Japanese models, Chrysler's R&D and its marketing activities were affected. The company had to deal with the fact that some of its models were not perceived as "American" models in spite of the nameplate. (See the experiential exercise at the end of this chapter.)

International Operations

U.S. manufacturing operations have received the greatest brunt of international challenges. Some U.S. firms have been making dramatic improvements in this area in order to remain competitive; those not able to improve the quality of their products or services have been severely threatened and in some cases have gone out of business.[29]

As the experiential exercise at the end of this chapter shows, many cars sold under a Detroit label were assembled in another country. The term **hollow corporation**, meaning a firm that contracts out most of its manufacturing, was coined to describe many U.S. manufacturing firms in the 1980s. Chrysler became essentially an assembler and marketer of Japanese cars in the 1980s. Most televisions, VCRs, stereos, and other consumer electronics bought in this country were produced in foreign countries. Shoes and textiles were subjected to intense global competition.

What drove many U.S. managers to move in the direction of offshore manufacturing and become hollow corporations? The important forces influencing a firm's decision to pursue global manufacturing operations—cost competitiveness, competitive markets, government policy, and manufacturing processes—are depicted in Figure 3.7.

Factors in cost competitiveness include the relative cost of labor, materials, transportation, and exchange rates. Some decisions to manufacture in Taiwan, South Korea, and the Caribbean countries have been associated with the relatively low labor costs in those countries. The more recent decisions by several Japanese firms to locate manufacturing facilities in this country are associated with the cost advantage resulting from the strength of the Japanese yen versus the U.S. dollar and with lower transportation costs to deliver the final product to the U.S. customer.

Competitive markets become a reason to pursue global manufacturing operations as foreign competitors enter U.S. markets and as international markets grow. The former may have been a reason for Goodyear to enter the European tire market and for Procter & Gamble to sell personal-care products in Japan. The latter may have been a reason for Whirlpool to enter the Latin American and Asian markets in its search for growth opportunities. Frequently, the best defense is a good offense.

Government policy that lowers trade barriers encourages global manufacturing operations. Sometimes fear of import restrictions from a host government causes a

FIGURE 3.7   *Factors Driving Global Manufacturers' Operations*

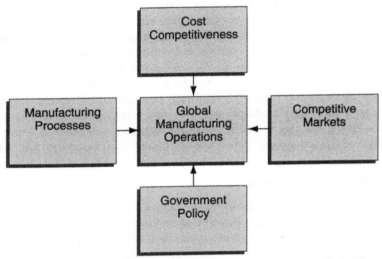

firm to decide to locate manufacturing facilities in the host country so that the manufactured items escape the import restrictions. This reasoning may explain the decisions of several Japanese firms to locate automobile plants in the United States. Motorola's recent decision to locate a cellular telephone plant in China appears to have been motivated in part by Chinese government policy.

Improved manufacturing technologies and processes have been associated with the decision to pursue global manufacturing operations. Automation, the extensive use of information technologies, and high-quality manufacturing systems permit many firms to pursue worldwide operations with efficiency.

Global manufacturing will be an international competitive battleground at least through the 1990s. There is hope for the U.S. manufacturing industry. A growing number of American firms have recognized the challenge and were in the process of implementing some of the needed changes in the early 1990s as the quality and cost of some awakened U.S. manufacturers were at world-class standards.[30]

U.S. managers operating in other countries must be sensitive to and adapt to local culture and the values of the populace. The diversity exhibit demonstrates the disastrous result of ignoring local religious beliefs.

International Marketing

International marketing has received almost as much attention as the area of international operations. The decision to market globally is typically a long-term, organization-survival decision impacting the entire organization.

There are several reasons why a firm may decide to launch international marketing activities. The most important reasons are summarized in Figure 3.8. The lack

FIGURE 3.8   *International Marketing Decisions*

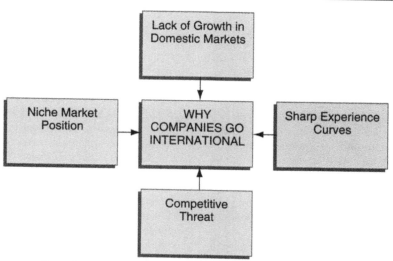

of growth in domestic markets, as, for example, in the U.S. appliance industry, is one of the most common reasons for pursuing international marketing activities.

Another reason to launch international marketing programs is that dramatically lowered unit production costs can be observed with high production volume. **Experience curves** cause the unit cost of production to decline at a constant rate as the cumulative production volume doubles. The electronics and semiconductor industries are two good examples in which the unit cost of production declines as the volume expands.

Competition is another reason to market internationally. Sometimes international marketing is an offensive move to prevent competitor inroads or a semioffensive move in response to a competitive threat. Sometimes the move is defensive and in retaliation for actual competitor moves. In the early 1990s U.S. automobile companies were slowly building sales programs in Japan, partly in response to Japanese inroads in the U.S. automobile market.

Yet another reason for international marketing is to establish a niche market position. Some firms have become global marketers by doing so, notably Rolls Royce and Rolex.[31]

International Finance

The international financial picture has received almost as much attention as the areas of international operations and international marketing. Since it became the largest stock market in the world in the 1980s, thereby influencing all other stock exchanges, the Tokyo stock market is now of great interest to many U.S. managers and managers in other countries.[32]

D I V E R S I T Y   E X H I B I T

A Religious Holiday

Roy Christoph was an oil company chemical engineer. His career had taken him to refinery operations in various parts of North and South America. By the time he was 45 he had developed a reputation as a hard-driving, able executive.

After many years of plant work, he was transferred to the head office of International Oil, an American company with operations in many parts of the world. In response to a request from the government of Pakistan, International was building a refinery in East Pakistan, and Christoph's job was to work on the planning of this refinery.

Shortly before the refinery was to start operations, one of the Americans who had been sent out to manage it took ill, and Christoph was asked to go to East Pakistan to take the man's place. He arrived there at about the time operations were to begin and found himself up against a very tight schedule.

Christoph's assistant, a Pakistani engineer named Avil, had received training in chemical engineering in the United States. Roy Christoph had not had time to form much of an opinion otherwise, but the man appeared technically capable.

Late one afternoon, a rush order came through for Christoph's action, and Avil was involved. Christoph told Avil that he would have to be in the office early the next morning. Avil quickly responded "I am sorry, Mr. Christoph, but tomorrow is Eid. It will not be possible for me to be here until late tomorrow. I thought you knew about the

day." (Eid-el-Fiter is celebrated after Ramadan as a thanksgiving after the fasting of one month. It is considered the most important of all the Muslim festivals. Such religious holidays are government-approved paid holidays, and every employer is expected to exempt workers for prayers.)

To this Christoph reacted forcefully: "I don't care if it's Christmas tomorrow! You better be here early and that's that." He stepped into his office and slammed the door shut, leaving Avil confused, in the outer office. Other Pakistanis in the office had heard the exchange, and rumors about it circulated quickly.

One hour later Christoph's telephone rang. It was the general manager of the refinery. In a very stern voice, he said, "Christoph, the plant's shutting down on a sudden walk-out. The Pakistanis say that you insulted their religion. They claim they won't go back to work until we fire you. What did you do? What can we do now?"

Discussion Questions

1. What action should the general manager take?
2. What action should Roy Christoph take?
3. What action should Avil take?
4. How might this incident have been avoided?

Source: Adapted from J. S. Ewing and F. Meissner, *International Business Management: Readings and Cases*, Belmont, CA: Wadsworth (1964): 455.

Many analysts have presented the idea that exchange-rate volatility is a major issue in itself.[33] This volatility may continue partly because of the increased use of debt financing by multinationals on a worldwide basis.[34]

As more and more foreign financial markets become linked electronically to each other on a real-time basis, the exchange-rate volatility can increase. The speed with which the world's stock markets crashed in unison in October 1987 demonstrated how foreign financial markets affect the volatility of international finance. The floating currency exchange rates in operation since the late 1970s have increased volatility. In the earlier fixed exchange-rate era, government regulations

FIGURE 3.9   *National Differences in Managerial Assumptions*

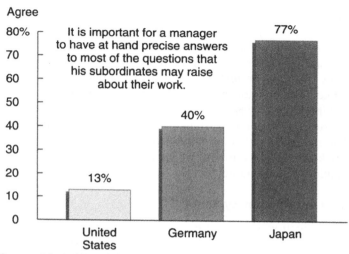

Source: Adapted from A. Laurant, "The Cross-Cultural Puzzle of International Human Resource Management," *Human Resource Management*, 25, no. 1 (Spring 1986): 93.

may have dampened volatility. With today's floating exchange rates, volatility is increased as investment funds seek the best market returns at electronic speeds. The Federal Reserve Board has seen some of its power to control U.S. interest rates diminished due to the size of the Japanese and German financial markets.[35] International mergers and acquisitions add to the diversity and complexity that characterize international finance.

International Human Resource Management

As many firms have decided to pursue opportunities in international operations, marketing, and finance, international human resource management (HRM) activities take on a new urgency. Extensive research in recent years has been devoted to the cultural differences that must be addressed in international HRM activities.[36]

An example of a cultural difference affecting management is presented in Figure 3.9, which illustrates the national differences in managerial assumptions about supervision. Such dramatic differences in the perceived role of management might explain different international HRM practices relating to participation in corporate governance.

International Research and Development

Research and development (R&D) has become a potent international weapon.[37] U.S. nondefense R&D spending as a percentage of gross domestic product increased by 20 percent in the decade of the 1980s relative to the decade of the 1970s.[38] It is forecast that spending in nondefense R&D in the United States will increase even further in the 1990s as many managers realize that spending on new-product development is necessary to provide value to customers.[39]

For sustainable performance, a firm must also be able to produce what it invents.[40] Thus the strength of R&D and operations programs becomes important in assessing a firm's international competitive strength.

Not only are U.S. firms spending more on R&D as part of an international strategy, but they are also protecting those investments in R&D more aggressively. Patent-infringement litigation has become an increasingly visible aspect of a firm's international interests. In 1988, for example, Texas Instruments earned nearly half its profit from successful patent-infringement litigation against nine competitors in Japan and South Korea. Other semiconductor companies, biotechnology companies, computer makers, and software firms have also been protecting their patents as part of an international R&D strategy.[41]

International Information Systems

Like R&D, information systems are increasingly becoming an international competitive weapon. One example is the airline computerized worldwide reservation systems (covered in detail in Chapter 16).[42] The extensive use of computers in manufacturing, often labeled computer-integrated manufacturing, allows firms to standardize operations throughout the world and reduce the time to manufacture items. Computerized inventory systems allow firms to accurately track inventory and to ship more quickly to other countries. As will be fully discussed in Chapter 16, extensive investments in computerized systems enable United Parcel Service to ship to many places in the world in minimum time. The strength of a firm's information systems is assuming importance in assessing the firm's international competitive strength.

CRITICAL THINKING QUESTIONS

1. Discuss the impact on other activities in the firm when a firm shifts its manufacturing operations to other countries (that is, becomes a hollow corporation).
2. Discuss the offensive and defensive characteristics of an international marketing program.

CHALLENGES TO MANAGEMENT IN THE UNITED STATES

In this chapter we have shown how the economic world has moved from an unchallenged market for U.S. firms to a competitive international marketplace in which Japanese and European firms offer customers both multiple alternatives and affordable quality. This situation presents new challenges to the management of U.S. firms. In the quality exhibit, Alcoa seems to understand the challenges as it considers delivering quality to customers throughout the world.

Total Quality and Demanding Worldwide Customers

Many customers throughout the world have become increasingly demanding; they expect flawless products and services. Appeals to nationalism and patriotism may

Q U A L I T Y   E X H I B I T

Excellence through Quality at Alcoa

Alcoa reflects its worldwide focus through their corporate statements of vision and values.

Alcoa's Vision

Alcoa is a growing worldwide company dedicated to excellence through quality—creating value for customers, employees, and shareholders through innovation, technology, and operational expertise. Alcoa will be the best aluminum company in the world, and a leader in other businesses in which we choose to compete.

Alcoa's Values for Quality and Excellence

We will provide products and services that meet or exceed the needs of our customers. We will relentlessly pursue continuous improvement and innovation in everything we do to create significant competitive advantage compared to world standards.

Source: Alcoa Corporation, Pittsburgh, PA.

work for a short time, but these sentiments can be short lived in the face of superior customer value from international competitors. "To survive in such an environment, managers must meet customers' needs by offering quality products and services that outperform the products and services of worldwide competitors. This is the driving force behind Total Quality Management."[43]

Total Quality and Global Competition

The growth of Japanese industry after World War II and the loosening of international trade barriers have opened up a new form of competition. Previously many U.S. firms concentrated on domestic competitors and paid little attention to quality. Some large Japanese firms found that they could compete with U.S. firms on the basis of quality. Those Japanese firms virtually rewrote the rules of international competition and forced U.S. firms to focus on quality.[44]

Firms consistently producing affordable high-quality products and services will be the international business survivors and growth engines of the 1990s. In competitive, worldwide, open markets where customers have alternatives to shoddy products and services, the low-quality producers will go bankrupt.

Even those firms that today operate without international competitors in their market risk international competitors entering in the future. Since the best defense is a good offense, maintaining customer loyalty through high-quality products is a way to prevent international competitive inroads.

CRITICAL THINKING QUESTIONS

1. Describe the role of quality in global competition in the 1990s.

2. Discuss the pros and cons of international competition for U.S. firms and their managers.

QUALITY CASE

Conclusion to the General Motors Case

Cadillac won a Baldrige Quality Award in 1992 by investing in manufacturing systems and focusing on customers' requirements. (Photo credit: Cadillac/Luxury Car Engineering and Manufacturing.)

There were rays of hope for GM as it began to produce high-quality cars in some of its divisions. Saturn had been started partly to learn how to build small cars that would be responsive to customers' demands for affordable quality. Saturn accomplished that goal and could not build cars fast enough to satisfy demand in 1993.

Cadillac won a Baldrige Quality Award in 1992. Its Seville Touring Sedan won a design award in 1993 for a high-quality engine design.

The Buick Park Avenue was in the top ten of the J. D. Powers Customer Satisfaction Survey for quality in 1993. The Buick LeSabre was named as a great family value in full-sized automobile transportation in 1992.

But the successes were not consistent throughout GM. In the early 1990s Oldsmobile's sales had fallen by 80 percent from their early 1980s levels. Rumors were rampant that GM would sell the Oldsmobile division. In 1993 GM slowed the gargantuan losses from 1992, but part of that was due to devaluation of the U.S. dollar, which made foreign cars more expensive relative to GM cars. As a company, GM still had high costs, inconsistent quality, shrunken market share, and a combative union. Ford and Chrysler took automobile market share from the Japanese in 1993.

Many called for the breakup of GM into separate companies. It was maintained that the separate companies would have a better chance of getting close to their customers, providing affordable quality, and winning the war with international competitors.

In the early 1990s GM seemed to be caught in a downward spiral. It was not clear that its short-term focus on stockholders' demand for profitability would pull it out of the biggest crisis it had encountered since the Great Depression. By not consistently concentrating on its customers and thereby defeating its worldwide competitors, GM was risking its future.

DISCUSSION QUESTIONS

1. In an era of intense international competition, how important is it for a company to provide affordable quality to customers?

2. What are the roles of management and unions in delivering affordable quality?

3. Discuss the managerial actions that need to be taken at GM for it to regain its former health.

4. Should GM try to sell its cars based on a patriotic appeal of "American cars"?

continued

Sources: "The World's Top Automakers Change Lanes," Fortune (October 4, 1993): 73–75; "Caddy's 295-HP Smoothie," Business Week (June 7, 1993): 69; "Dinosaurs?" Fortune (May 3, 1993): 41; "The UAW Fires a Shot Across GM's Bow," Business Week (September 14, 1992): 28; "Swollen GM Finds a Crash Diet Means Uncomfortable Labor," The Wall Street Journal (September 9, 1992): A1; "Saturn: GM Finally Has a Real Winner," Business Week (August 17, 1992): 87; "Top-Selling Cars for First Half," USA Today (July 14, 1992): B1; "GM's Leaders Go on the Record," Fortune (March 9, 1992): 51–52; "GM Posts Record '91 Loss of $4.45 Billion: Sends Tough Message to UAW on Closings," The Wall Street Journal (February 25, 1992): A3; "A Sad Day for GM Proves That the Market Rules," The Wall Street Journal (February 25, 1992): A18; "Can GM Remodel Itself?" Fortune (January 13, 1992): 28; "Detroit Paradox," The Wall Street Journal (February 15, 1989): 1.

SUMMARY

Global economic competition has exploded in the past two decades. U.S. competitiveness has declined as international competition has become stronger. U.S. business has lost market share in several industries to Japanese firms producing higher-quality goods at lower prices. International competition is likely to further intensify in the twilight of the twentieth century and in the beginning of the twenty-first century.

After being leveled in World War II, Japanese and European industries rebuilt with new technologies and new capital. The Japanese also devised new management systems based on ideas of Total Quality that increased the quality and lowered the costs of products and services. As international trade barriers declined, worldwide customers were able to choose among several companies for their purchases. Thus the customers started to demand high quality and low prices.

Occasionally, patriotism and protectionist fever run high. Such sentiments may give domestic firms a temporary respite from international competition as customers buy for reasons other than quality and price. However, domestic firms that rely on such sentiments in the long term and that fail to offer their customers affordable quality do so at their peril. In the long term most customers will demand affordable quality.

There is a growing possibility that the world economy will define itself into three international trading blocs, with totally open trade within the blocs and restricted trade across the blocs. These blocs would be the North American Free Trade Agreement (NAFTA) partners, member countries of the European Economic Area (EEA), and the Pacific Rim countries.

When evaluating international strategies, firms must weigh the advantages of global business systems relative to the advantages of local adaptation. Global businesses, multinational/multimarket businesses, "blocked" global businesses, or local/national businesses may result from that tradeoff.

When a firm decides to manufacture in another country or to launch an international marketing program, the firm must realize that such decisions impact most areas in the company, including R&D, finance, information systems, and human resource management. Each of these functional areas can contribute to the decision to compete internationally.

The rebuilding of Japanese and European industry after World War II, the spread of Total Quality as a system of management, the lowering of trade barriers, and the increasing demands of worldwide customers have introduced a globally competitive era. Firms producing consistently high-quality products and services at low prices have a strong advantage and should prosper in this new, internationally competitive marketplace.

EXPERIENTIAL EXERCISE

The Buy-American Quiz

I.   Only one of these automobiles is made in the United States. Which one is it? Match all the automobiles to their countries of origin. You may use the entries in the right column more than once.

_____	1. Pontiac LeMans	A. Canada
_____	2. Chevrolet Lumina	B. Korea
_____	3. Mercury Capri	C. Mexico
_____	4. Honda Accord	D. United States
_____	5. Dodge Stealth	E. Japan
_____	6. Mercury Tracer	F. Australia
_____	7. Plymouth Voyager	

Answers to this section are on page 89.

Source: *The Wall Street Journal* (January 24, 1992): A1.

II. After the quiz has been completed, the class should be divided into groups of six to eight persons. In each group there should be someone who owns, or whose family owns, a Honda Accord or any other Japanese nameplate automobile. There should also be someone who owns, or whose family owns, a General Motors product, someone with a Ford product, and someone with a Chrysler product. Each group should respond to the following questions:

1. Which car in the quiz is really American?

2. Can a car designed in Japan but manufactured in the United States really be an American car? Explain.

3. Will a car with a Japanese-sounding name like Honda or Toyota be viewed as American just because it is assembled in the United States?

4. Is it unpatriotic to buy a foreign car? Why or why not?

CHAPTER CASE

Sing's Chinese Restaurant

The Bali Hai Corporation started as a small Chinese restaurant in Boston, Massachusetts, in 1959. The restaurant was an exact replica of a Chinese pagoda. Over the years the restaurant, owned and managed by Arnold Sing, became known for its food and atmosphere. Customers were made to feel as if they were actually in China. In the last few years Sing decided to incorporate and open other similar restaurants throughout the country. Sing, who had come to the United States from China in the early 1940s, was very strict in keeping up his reputation for good food and atmosphere, and he had a policy of hiring only waiters of Oriental descent. He felt this added to his customers' dining pleasure and made for a more authentic environment. For kitchen positions, though, Sing hired any applicants who were qualified.

About a year ago in Sing's Bali Hai of Washington, DC, there was a shortage of waiters. An advertisement was placed in the paper for waiters, and the manager of the store was instructed by Sing to hire only Orientals. The manager was also reminded of Bali Hai's commitment to a reputation for good food and atmosphere. Two young men, one black and one white, both with considerable restaurant experience, applied for the waiter jobs. The manager explained the policy of hiring only Orientals to the young men, and he also told them he could get them work in his kitchen. The two men declined the positions and instead went directly to the area Equal Employment Office and filed a complaint. Sing's defense was that the policy was only to preserve the atmosphere of the restaurant. He said the Oriental waiters were needed to make it more authentic. Sing also added that he hired blacks, whites, and other races for his kitchen help.

Discussion Questions

1. Is Sing's defense a good one under the law? Why or why not?
2. Is this a case of preferential hiring?
3. Is this a case of reverse discrimination?

Source: Kenneth A. Kovach, "Sing's Chinese Restaurant," from T. L. Beauchamp and N. E. Bowie, *Ethical Theory and Business*, Englewood Cliffs, NJ: Prentice-Hall (1988): 393.

KEY TERMS

blocked global businesses Businesses forced into local adaptation despite the advantages of global business systems.

competitive benchmarking Analyzing what the best competitor or leading companies in the industry are doing to discover the products, processes, and practices that satisfy customer needs.

European Community (EC) Group of Western European countries that have agreed to eliminate trade barriers among themselves in order to encourage trade and improve economic development in Europe.

European Economic Area (EEA) All of the countries in the European Community and the European Free Trade Association.

European Free Trade Association (EFTA) Group of European countries that have agreed to cooperate among themselves to encourage trade.

experience curves Graph curves that cause the unit cost of production to decline at a constant rate as the cumulative production volume doubles.

global businesses Businesses that use the same processes throughout the world and market a nearly identical line of products throughout the world.

global business systems Systems that use the same business processes and operations throughout the world.

gross domestic product Value of all goods and services produced domestically.

hollow corporation   Firm that contracts out most of its manufacturing.

ISO 9000   Comprehensive standard specifying the management systems and processes a firm must possess in order to market certain products in the European Community.

local adaptation   Modification of a multinational organization's business operations to fit the requirements of specific countries.

local/national businesses   Businesses that adapt their operations and products to specific countries.

maquiladoras   Manufacturing plants in Mexico that perform low-wage operations, usually assembly of parts made in the United States.

multinational/multimarket businesses Businesses that require some degree of local adaptation in situations where there is limited economic advantage in global business systems.

process simplification   Simplification of systems and work flow to reduce both defects and time.

time-based competition   Competition based on doing the job faster than others so that the customer receives the product or service faster.

trade barrier   Impediment, usually quotas on quantity or tariffs on price or technical specifications on trade items, to prevent free trade among countries.

trade deficit   Condition existing when a country imports more than it exports.

trade surplus   Condition existing when a country exports more than it imports.

ENDNOTES

1. "Goodyear Squares Off to Protect Its Turf from Foreign Rivals," *The Wall Street Journal* (December 29, 1989): A1.
2. "Boeing's Dominance of Aircraft Industry Runs into Bumpiness," *The Wall Street Journal* (July 10, 1992): A1.
3. M. Prowse, "Is America in Decline?" *Harvard Business Review* (July-August 1992): 162.
4. "How American Industry Stacks Up," *Fortune* (March 9, 1992): 30.
5. I. Mitroff and S. Mohrman, "The Slack Is Gone: How the United States Lost Its Competitive Edge in the World Economy," *Academy of Management Executive* (February 1987): 66.
6. M. E. Porter, "Capital Disadvantage: America's Failing Capital Investment System," *Harvard Business Review* (September-October 1992): 65–82.
7. "Getting High Tech Back on Track," *Fortune* (January 1, 1990): 74.
8. Porter.
9. Mitroff and Mohrman.
10. W. Cole, "Competitive Economies and the Economics of Competition," in M. J. Stahl and G. M. Bounds, *Competing Globally Through Customer Value*, Westport, CT: Quorum Books (1991): 14–31.
11. Ibid., 16.
12. W. E. Deming, *Out of the Crisis*, Cambridge, MA: MIT Center for Advanced Engineering Study (1986).
13. J. M. Juran, *Managerial Breakthrough*, New York: McGraw-Hill (1964); K. Ishikawa, *What Is Total Quality Control?* Englewood Cliffs, NJ: Prentice-Hall (1985).
14. Ibid.
15. American Quality Foundation and Ernst & Young, "International Quality Study: The Definitive Study of the Best International Quality Management Practices," Cleveland: Ernst & Young (1991): 1.
16. "What If Japan Triumphs?" *Fortune* (May 18, 1992): 61.
17. "The Dark Side of 1992," *Forbes* (January 22, 1990): 85.
18. "A New Era Is at Hand in Global Competition: U.S. vs. United Europe," *The Wall Street Journal* (July 15, 1991): A1.
19. M. E. Porter, ed., *Competition in Global Industries* Boston: Harvard Business School Press (1986): 2–3.
20. "Mega Market," *Time* (August 10, 1992): 43; "Debate Rages Over Trade Pact," *USA Today* (August 10, 1992): B1.
21. "Who Gains from the New Europe?" *Fortune* (December 18, 1989): 84.

22. "Why Japan Will Emerge Stronger," *Fortune* (May 18, 1992): 46–56.

23. "World Business," *The Wall Street Journal Reports* (September 24, 1992): R26–R27.

24. "The Case for Protection," *Forbes* (February 17, 1992): 44-45.

25. M. J. Stahl, "Protectionism or Total Quality Management?" *Quality Progress* (December 1992): 41–43.

26. "Fear and Loathing of Japan," *Fortune* (February 26, 1992): 50.

27. "The Backlash Isn't Just Against Japan," *Business Week* (February 10, 1992): 30; "Honda's Star Gets Another Sequel," *New York Times* (August 27, 1993): C1.

28. J. Sheth and G. Eshghi, *Global Marketing Perspectives*, Cincinnati: South-Western (1989): vi.

29. J. Sheth and G. Eshghi, *Global Operations Perspectives,* Cincinnati: South-Western (1989).

30. "Made in the U.S.A.: Manufacturers Start to Do It Right," *Fortune* (May 21, 1990): 54–64.

31. Sheth, and Eshghi.

32. "The Tokyo Stock Market: And How Its Swings Affect You," *Business Week* (February 12, 1990): 74–84.

33. D. Lessard, "Finance and Global Competition: Exploiting Financial Scope and Coping with Volatile Exchange Rates," in Porter, *Competition in Global Industries*, 147–148.

34. W. Folks and R. Aggarwal, *International Dimensions of Financial Management*, Boston: PWS-Kent (1988).

35. "Fed Has Lost Much of Its Power to Sway U.S. Interest Rates," *The Wall Street Journal* (March 12, 1990): 1.

36. P. J. Dowling and R. S. Schuler, *International Dimensions of Human Resource Management*, Boston: PWS-Kent (1990): 685–698; N. J. Adler, *International Dimensions of Organizational Behavior*, 2nd ed., Boston: PWS-Kent (1991).

37. S. Johnson, "Comparing R&D Strategies of Japanese and U.S. Firms," *Sloan Management Review*, 25 (Spring 1984): 25–34; "Innovation: The Global Race," *Business Week* (June 15, 1990).

38. "Missed Opportunities," *The Wall Street Journal* (November 14, 1988): R21.

39. R. Keller and R. Chinta, "International Technology Transfer: Strategies for Success," *Academy of Management Executive* (May 1990): 33–43.

40. "What U.S. Scientists Discover, the Japanese Convert into Profit," *The Wall Street Journal* (June 25, 1990): 1.

41. "Going on the Offense," ibid., R37.

42. "Smart Factories: America's Turn?" *Business Week* (May 8, 1989): 142; "Race for Computerized Booking Systems Is Heating Up Among European Airlines," *The Wall Street Journal* (December 1, 1988): B3.

43. American Quality Foundation and Ernst & Young, 3.

44. "The Quality Imperative: What It Takes to Win in the Global Economy," *Business Week* (October 25, 1991): 7.

Answers to Buy-American Quiz I are 1 (B), 2 (A), 3 (F), 4 (D), 5 (E), 6 (C), 7(A).

Managerial Ethics and Corporate Social Responsibility

LEARNING OBJECTIVES

After reading this chapter, you should be able to accomplish the following:

- Discuss the implications of the definition of ethics—doing the right thing right the first time—for managerial decisions and behavior.

- Compare and contrast the five different managerial ethics bases.

- Discuss the arguments for a liberal corporate social responsibility on the part of managers.

- Discuss the arguments for a conservative corporate social responsibility on the part of managers.

- Describe the various positions a firm's managers might take on corporate social responsibility issues.

- Compare and contrast the three different kinds of stakeholder interest in corporations.

- Describe the relative importance of the government, ethical, societal, and competitive influences operating to shape corporate social responsibility decisions.

CHAPTER OUTLINE

Ethics, the Organization, and Management
   Concept of Ethics
   Ethics and Organizational Processes
   Ethics Bases for Managers
   Which Ethics Base?
   International Ethics
The Corporate Social Responsibility Debate
   Arguments for Liberal Corporate Social Responsibility
   Arguments for Conservative Corporate Social Responsibility
   Corporate Social Responsibility Positions
Multiple Stakeholder View
   Equity Stake
   Economic Stake
   Influencer Stake
   A Stakeholder Grid
   Stakeholder Conflict and Total Quality
Influences on Corporate Social Responsibility
   Government and Regulatory Influences
   Ethical Influences
   Societal Influences
   Competitive Influences

Cases and Exhibits
   Johnson & Johnson
   McDonnell Douglas
   Westinghouse Electric
   The FCPA
   Sloane Products
   Bluebird Smelter

Johnson & Johnson Recalls Tylenol

Johnson & Johnson has evolutionized Tylenol by adding tamper-proof packaging to protect its consumers. (Photo credit: AP/Wide World Photos.)

On September 30, 1982, Johnson & Johnson (J&J) announced that three people had died as a result of consuming Tylenol capsules laced with cyanide. Within the next two days, four more deaths from the same cause were announced. J&J's handling of the situation is regarded as a must-read for anyone studying managerial ethics and product liability issues.

At the time of the poisonings, Tylenol was a major brand for J&J, produced in both capsule and tablet form. Through years of concentrated marketing and advertising, J&J had built Tylenol into the number one over-the-counter analgesic brand, with 35.3 percent of that market. Sales of Tylenol in 1982 were $350 million, accounting for 7 percent of all J&J sales and 17 percent of all profits.

What were J&J managers to do? Some of their customers were dying from consuming one of their flagship products? The CEO and chairman of J&J, James E. Burke, stressed that the following J&J Credo, originally written in 1947 and modified in 1979, played a critical role when the company fashioned its response to the crisis.

JOHNSON & JOHNSON'S CORPORATE CREDO

We believe our first responsibility is to the doctors, nurses and patients, to mothers and fathers and all others who use our products and services. In meeting their needs everything we do must be of high quality. We must constantly strive to reduce our costs in order to maintain reasonable prices. Customers' orders must be serviced promptly and accurately. Our suppliers and distributors must have an opportunity to make a fair profit.

We are responsible to our employees, the men and women who work with us throughout the world. Everyone must be considered as an individual. We must respect their dignity and recognize their merit. They must have a sense of security in their jobs. Compensation must be fair and adequate, and working conditions clean, orderly and safe. We must be mindful of ways to help our employees fulfill their family responsibilities. Employees must feel free to make suggestions and complaints. There must be equal opportunity for employment, development and advancement for those qualified. We must provide competent management, and their actions must be just and ethical.

We are responsible to the communities in which we live and work and to the world community as well. We must be good citizens—support good

continued

works and charities and bear our fair share of taxes. We must encourage civic improvements and better health and education. We must maintain in good order the property we are privileged to use, protecting the environment and natural resources.

Our final responsibility is to our stockholders. Business must make a sound profit. We must experiment with new ideas. Research must be carried on, innovative programs developed and mistakes paid for. New equipment must be purchased, new facilities provided and new products launched. Reserves must be created to provide for adverse times. When we operate according to these principles, the stockholders should realize a fair return.

The subjects of corporate ethics and managerial ethical decision making have received much attention in organizations lately. A recent survey of ethics practices in business revealed that 45 percent of firms have enacted ethics codes since 1987. More than 80 percent of U.S. firms had ethics codes in the early 1990s.[1]

ETHICS, THE ORGANIZATION, AND MANAGEMENT

There has been an increasing number of cases of managers and the organizations they represent acting in highly publicized, unethical, yet legal ways. There have also been other cases in which managers have acted in highly visible, ethical, and admirable ways, as did the managers at Johnson & Johnson in the Tylenol recall. In this chapter we explore the different managerial approaches to dealing with ethical decisions, and then we broaden the discussion to the larger issue of corporate social responsibility.

Concept of Ethics

Ethics might be defined as doing the right thing right the first time. This concise definition underscores the importance of describing what is the "right thing." If there were not disagreements on what is the "right thing," then the issue of ethical behavior by managers would be far less controversial.

It is difficult to describe what is the right thing because there are so many different bases of ethics. A different base of ethics may give a different answer in a given situation. Later in this chapter we review five primary ethics bases for managers.

A decision involving ethics usually is made in the context that someone will be hurt or harmed in some way by the decision. The ethics exhibit in Chapter 1 asks: Is it ethical to shut down a plant that is the lifeblood of a company town? The ethics exhibit in Chapter 2 asks: Is it ethical to fire someone who has worked for a company for many years and is near retirement? The ethics exhibit in Chapter 3 asks: Is it ethical to conduct business in a country that practices blatant racial segregation? These are but a few of the ethical questions asked in this book.

Those few situations in which all bases of ethics produce the same answer are usually the easy questions that all agree upon. Is it ethical to continue to market a product that is known only by its producers to kill or mutilate its users? Is it ethical to blatantly ignore signed contracts? Prior to reviewing the ethics bases, it is important to understand the rest of the definition of ethics concerning doing the right thing right the first time.

Ethics and Organizational Processes

There is a close link between Total Quality Management and managerial ethics. TQM is concerned with the continuous improvement of organizational processes and systems to prevent defects. Nearly all organizations claim that they wish their managers to act ethically in deciding business issues. Therefore unethical managerial behavior can be described as a result of a defect in an organizational system.

The defect may be inadequate training for the manager in which the organization glossed over the importance of ethical decisions. This lack of thoroughness indicates that the training system needs to be improved. Or there may be conflicting signals from the reward system whereby short-term profits are stressed over all else. If this is the case, then the reward system needs to be revised. Once the organizational processes are aligned, then managers may be predisposed to do the right thing right the first time.

The issue of managers assuming responsibility for the ethical conduct of their employees and their organization is receiving increased attention today due in part to some highly publicized ethics cases. To communicate the importance of ethical decisions to managers, many organizations have published codes of ethics similar to that in the following ethics exhibit.

Ethics Bases for Managers

Ethics questions would be easy to decide if all questions could be resolved with the same ethics base. But the five different bases reviewed below show how different answers are possible to an ethical dilemma depending on which ethics base the manager is using.[2]

Eternal Law (Rule-Based Ethics)

The **eternal law approach to ethics** holds that there is a common set of moral standards apparent in nature or revealed in Scripture. This set of moral standards should be obvious to anyone who takes the time to study either nature or Scripture. Everyone should act in accordance with the common set of standards (eternal law). Some refer to the eternal law as "rule-based ethics," because it holds that one should adopt a set of general rules, or principles, that guides one's actions.[3]

Thomas Jefferson seemed to have been influenced by the eternal law in the framing of the Declaration of Independence in the United States in 1776. He wrote that certain truths were "self-evident" and that certain rights were "inalienable," including the rights to "life, liberty, and the pursuit of happiness." Another good example of the eternal law is the Golden Rule: "Do unto others as you would have others do unto you."

Religion is associated with the eternal law. Frequently, religious leaders interpret the eternal truths in Scripture. However, not all subscribe to the same religious lead-

E T H I C S   E X H I B I T

McDonnell Douglas Code of Ethics and Ethical Decision-Making Checklist

Code of Ethics

Integrity and ethics exist in the individual or they do not exist at all. They must be upheld by individuals or they are not upheld at all. In order for integrity and ethics to be characteristics of McDonnell Douglas, we who make up the Corporation must strive to be:

— Honest and trustworthy in all our relationships;

— Reliable in carrying out assignments and responsibilities;

— Truthful and accurate in what we say and write;

— Cooperative and constructive in all work undertaken;

— Fair and considerate in our treatment of fellow employees, customers, and all other persons;

— Law abiding in all our activities;

— Committed to accomplishing all tasks in a superior way;

— Economical in utilizing company resources; and

— Dedicated in service to our company and to improvement of the quality of life in the world in which we live.

Integrity and high standards of ethics require hard work, courage, and difficult choices. Consultation among employees, top management, and the Board of Directors will sometimes be necessary to determine a proper course of action. Integrity and ethics may sometimes require us to forgo business opportunities. In the long run, however, we will be better served by doing what is right rather than what is expedient.

Source: McDonnell Douglas Corporation, *MDC Policy Manual, Policy 2,* "Five Keys to Self-Renewal", 1993.

Ethical Decision-Making Checklist

Analysis

— What are the facts?

— Who is responsible to act?

— What are the consequences of action? (Benefit-Harm Analysis)

— What and whose rights are involved? (Rights/Principles Analysis)

— What is fair treatment in this case? (Social Justice Analysis)

Solution Development

— What solutions are available to me?

— Have I considered all of the creative solutions which might permit me to reduce harm, maximize benefits, respect more rights, or be fair to more parties?

Select the Optimum Solution

— What are the potential consequences of my solutions?

— Which of the options I have considered does the most to maximize benefits, reduce harm, respect rights, and increase fairness?

— Are all parties treated fairly in my proposed decision?

Implementation

— Who should be consulted and informed?

— What actions will assure that my decision achieves its intended outcome?

— Implement.

Follow-up

— Was the decision implemented correctly?

— Did the decision maximize benefits, reduce harm, respect rights, and treat all parties fairly?

ers. A disadvantage of the eternal law is that few individuals or religious leaders interpret nature or Scripture in the same way. In today's diverse society many do not follow Scripture. Moreover, there is no commonly accepted way to choose among the different interpretations. Therefore an interpretation of the eternal law that guides one person's actions may be different from another interpretation of the eternal law that guides another person's actions.

Utilitarianism   **Utilitarianism,** or the **utilitarian principle,** is a doctrine that a manager should act in ways to create the greatest benefits for the largest number of people. Utilitarianism arises from **teleological theory,** which stresses the outcome, not the intent, of managerial actions. Teleology comes from the Greek word *telos,* which means outcome or result. Thus a managerial decision is "right" if it results in benefits for others, and it is "wrong" if it results in damage or harm to others.

In following the utilitarian principle, a manager should be aware of the benefits and damages of a managerial action, such as closing a plant. If followed literally, the utilitarian principle would suggest seizing the assets of the few wealthy people who own Rolls-Royces and distributing those assets to large numbers of impoverished individuals. Herein lies the biggest drawback to utilitarianism; that is, the possibility of exploitation. Justifying benefits for the great majority of the population by extracting sacrifices from a small minority is the ethical fallacy in the "soak the rich" tax schemes that sometimes spring up in the legislature.

Universalism   **Universalism** is a doctrine that the ethics of a decision depend on the motives or intentions of the decision maker. Universalism arises from deontological theory, which is the opposite of teleological theory. Deontology is derived from another Greek word, *deon,* which means the duties or obligations of the individual. Thus personal intentions or personal motives can be translated into personal duties or obligations, because all would behave in the same universal fashion given the same situation.

Managers who scrupulously adhere to the terms of a contract may do so because they believe in the sanctity of contracts. Such a belief is consistent with universalism.

A disadvantage of universalism is the problem of objective interpretation. Persons subject to self-deception, or beliefs of self-grandeur, can justify unethical decisions by referring to their "lofty" motives. In distributing defective products in the market, a manager might argue that the company is trying to keep the price of the products low. In truth, the manager may be covering up a shoddy management system.

Although utilitarianism and universalism are the two most popular ethical bases for managers, these theories cannot be used to judge all ethical issues in all circumstances. The two ethical bases that we discuss next have been developed more on the basis of values than on principles.

Distributive Justice   **Distributive justice** is equity based on the primacy of the single value of justice. According to the idea of distributive justice, managers should act to ensure a more equitable distribution of benefits. This practice is assumed to be essential for social cooperation. The manager who attempts to hire the largest number of people and thereby to distribute salaries widely would be acting in accord with the idea of distributive justice.

An obvious problem with distributive justice is the basis for the distribution of benefits. Should benefits be distributed in accordance with needs or in accordance with accomplishments? Since social cooperation, needs, and equity are highlighted, the concern is that individual effort, risk taking, incentive, and achievement are downplayed.

Personal Liberty   **Personal liberty** is based on the primacy of the single value of individual choice. A managerial decision that violates individual liberty, even if it results in greater benefits for others, is not consistent with the idea of personal liberty. Personal liberty is based on equal opportunities for individual choice and exchange, not upon equal distributions of benefits. A pay system, which pays individuals in accordance with their own choices of how hard to work, is consistent with the idea of personal liberty.

A problem with the idea of personal liberty is that it does not ensure some minimum level of existence if an individual is not capable of working. Personal liberty assumes that others will voluntarily provide for the incapacitated individual through charity.

Which Ethics Base?

There does not appear to be a single ethics base, with standards for managerial decisions and actions, that can guide managers in all situations. A proposed ethical decision must be analyzed using the multiple ethics bases to see how it holds up under the scrutiny of the multiple approaches. Only after informed thought and analyses relative to the different ethics bases can the manager make a rational and ethical decision.

The experiential exercise at the end of this chapter presents four situations for analysis relative to the five ethics bases. The following diversity exhibit raises some interesting age-discrimination issues that require ethics-related resolution.

International Ethics

The existence of five different ethics bases complicates decisions concerning ethics by managers within the United States. The existence of different ethics standards in different countries further complicates the international manager's decisions concerning ethics issues. Since ethics is defined as doing the right thing right the first time, it is hard for a U.S. manager operating in a different country to know what is the right thing, since different standards may apply. In some countries, for example, gifts or gratuities are expected for public officials. U.S. standards may prohibit such actions, as the following international exhibit demonstrates.

DIVERSITY EXHIBIT

Severance Pay at Westinghouse Electric

In the early 1980s the Westinghouse Electric Corporation adopted a cost-saving policy pertaining to employees of retirement age (those *eligible* for retirement pension benefits) who have been *laid off by management*. Here "laid off" means that the employees were fired (at least temporarily) and did not voluntarily leave their positions. Westinghouse's policy, as is customary, was to provide severance pay to employees in the event that management determines they must lose their positions. Employees of retirement age and eligible for the corporation pension plan could, of course, elect to retire at the time of the layoff if they no longer wished to work.

Westinghouse's policy was framed as follows: No employee could receive both severance pay and retirement benefits. That is, laid-off union and management employees could not collect both severance pay and payments from the pension plan. They had to choose one or the other: An employee who did not retire could receive severance pay, and an employee who chose to retire (having been forced involuntarily into a loss of job) could not receive severance pay. No employee could receive the severance pay, look for a job, not find one, and then announce his intention to go on the company's retirement plan.

Management at Westinghouse thought this policy was justified for two reasons: (1) for cost control and (2) because employees would be "double dipping" if they received both severance pay and payments from a pension plan. The company also held that both the severance plan and the pension plan are voluntary programs not mandated by law.

Thirty-five employees at Westinghouse's Lester, Pennsylvania, plant objected to this justification and filed a lawsuit. They saw the issue as one of age discrimination. They held that severance pay is justified by rules about being involuntarily laid off, whereas pension benefits are warranted by the rules of retirement plans.

U.S. District Judge Marvin Katz of Philadelphia found in March 1986 that Westinghouse's policy did indeed involve "blatant, willful age discrimination" against older employees. The judge held that the policy had the effect of giving "employees who are eligible for retirement no practical choice but to take retirement benefit and forgo severance pay." The judge saw the severance-pay provision as a short-term way for an employee to think through his or her situation and alternatives. Pension plans, by contrast, are provisions for long-term retirement. To penalize an older employee by forcing him or her to limit or give up one in order to claim the other is age-based discrimination.

Westinghouse said its policy was not based on age but rather on whether the employee was eligible for a pension, regardless of age. But Judge Katz held that "age and retirement are, in fact, so closely linked that a criterion based on one is a criterion based on the other." Westinghouse vigorously objected to this finding and appealed the judge's ruling.

Discussion Questions

1. Is Westinghouse discriminating on the basis of age? Is it immorally discriminating? Willfully discriminating?

2. If both the pension plan and the severance plan are voluntary, can Westinghouse be held either morally or legally at fault for violating someone's rights? Should the acceptability of the policy be left to the free market of competition for employees?

3. Is it unfair that an employee cannot choose to take severance pay first and then later, having received the severance pay while looking for a job, choose to go into retirement?

Source: T. L. Beauchamp and N. E. Bowie, *Ethical Theory and Business*, 3rd ed., Englewood Cliffs, NJ: Prentice-Hall (1988): 392.

INTERNATIONAL EXHIBIT

The Murky Land of the FCPA

The Foreign Corrupt Practices Act (FCPA) became law in 1977, in the wake of foreign bribery scandals involving U.S. companies that shook the governments of Belgium, the Netherlands, Honduras, Italy, and Japan. One of the most notorious incidents involved an estimated $25 million in concealed payments made overseas by Lockheed Corporation in connection with sales of its Tristar L-1011 aircraft in Japan. This culminated in the resignation and subsequent criminal conviction of Japanese Prime Minister Kankuie Tanaka.

The FCPA, which makes it a crime for a U. S. corporation to bribe officials of foreign governments to obtain or increase business, is controversial, in part, because it seeks to forge a distinction between "bribes" (which it deems illegal) and "gratuities" (which the FCPA permits). The difference is murky, according to the FCPA's critics.

"The law marked the difference between gratuities paid to low-level officials and payments made to authorities," writes Duane Windsor in his book *The Foreign Corrupt Practices Act: Anatomy of a Statute*. "In many countries a payment to a customs official is a matter of course and a matter of economic necessity. A customs official may backlog an order or hinder a shipment by elaborately checking each imported item. The detrimental effect to the shipment is obvious. In response, lawmakers sought to delineate gratuities and bribes very clearly. But in reality the definition of gratuities was so vague that some people felt it had a chilling effect [on business]."

Source: A. Singer, "Ethics: Are Standards Lower Overseas?" *Across the Board* (A Conference Board Publication) (September 1991): 33. Reprinted by permission of Ethikos, Inc., Mamaroneck, New York.

CRITICAL THINKING QUESTIONS

1. Compare and contrast each of the five managerial ethics bases with the requirements of the law in general. Compare and contrast each of the five bases with the requirements of the specific law concerning product liability.

2. What are the implications of the definition of ethics (doing the right thing right the first time) for managerial training?

3. Six months into a new job as a manager, your superior directs you to implement a decision contrary to your sense of ethics. Discuss your alternatives.

THE CORPORATE SOCIAL RESPONSIBILITY DEBATE

There are several ways for a manager to make a decision.[4] The manager may use economic analysis, legal analysis, or ethics analysis.[5] In the preceding section we discussed the different ethics bases for the manager to consider when trying to do the right thing right the first time. Now we need to address the question of how the manager combines the economic, legal, and ethics analyses to make decisions that benefit society.

Corporate social responsibility is the obligation of the firm to use its resources in ways to benefit society. This is sometimes referred to as having a social action program, as having a social policy, or as community responsiveness.

WHEN IT COMES TO TEACHING
YOUR CHILDREN ABOUT RESPONSIBLE DRINKING,
YOU ARE THE LEADING AUTHORITY.

Anheuser-Busch uses its financial resources and advertising prowess to prevent underage drinking. The above photo and headline are part of an ad in the company's campaign to stop underage drinking before it starts. (Photo credit: Anheuser-Busch, Inc.)

There is considerable debate about how managers and firms should fulfill this responsibility. In this section we review the various arguments in the debate.

Arguments for Liberal Corporate Social Responsibility

Many arguments in favor of a liberal corporate social responsibility start by reviewing the role of business in society. In a book devoted to exploring that role, the authors indicated that there are three primary reasons why business should voluntarily assume a liberal corporate social responsibility.[6]

First, society expects it. This argument holds that since firms are creatures of society, they have an obligation to give something back to their creators. If the firms do not fulfill those obligations to the society that created them, then that society will place restrictions on their power.

Second, businesses' long-term self-interests are best served when those obligations are fulfilled. This stance of enlightened self-interest takes a long-term view of profitability. This argument holds that individuals who have a healthy physical environment, a good education, reasonable income, and a secure job make better employees and customers than do those who are poor or ignorant.[7]

Third, by fulfilling their obligations to society, firms will avoid future government regulation. Much of the current regulation of business has arisen from complaints over past business practices. For example, complaints in the 1970s about pollution of the environment led to the establishment of the Environmental Protection Agency. This argument holds that a proactive stance by business will prevent the establishment of future burdensome government regulations and the formation of entire government regulatory agencies. Although there will be costs involved in firms' proactively pushing corporate social responsibility before it is demanded by the government, it is generally less expensive to implement programs unhampered by government regulations than to react to government restrictions.

Arguments for Conservative Corporate Social Responsibility

Many managers counter that the most socially responsible action a company can engage in is to maximize its profits. This more conservative view is founded on four ideas.

First, profit maximization is the only legitimate purpose of business in capitalism. In capitalism managers are hired by owners and stockholders solely to maximize profits. Milton Friedman, the Nobel-Prize-winning economist, forcefully expressed this view and tied it into the role of capitalism in a free society: "There is one and only one social responsibility of business—to use its resources and engage in activities designed to increase its profits so long as it stays within the rules of the game. Few trends could so thoroughly undermine the very foundations of our free society as the acceptance by corporate officials of a social responsibility other than to make as much money for their stockholders as possible."[8]

Second, social responsibility subverts the market system. When firms pursue social-action programs, they incur costs that must eventually be passed on to consumers in the form of price hikes. Friedman argues that the allocative mechanism of price in the marketplace will then be distorted because of the added social costs.[9] As a result some goods will be artificially priced out of the market.

Third, the roles of business and government become confused. Many argue that the role of government is to implement social programs through the electoral process. Voters elect individuals who will implement those desired social goals. When business implements social goals, however, voters do not have an opportunity to participate in the selection of the specific social goals. This thwarts the purpose of an elected legislative body in a free society.

Fourth, business can become too powerful. If corporations become a primary instrument for social change, then they will have an added dimension of power at their disposal. When this power is combined with their economic power, business firms could become too influential in a society that relies on checks and balances to preserve its freedom.

Corporate Social Responsibility Positions

Given the conflicting arguments relating to corporate social responsibility, there are at least three different positions that managers might employ. These stereotypical positions are described in terms of increasing social activism.

The first position is **minimum legal compliance,** which means compliance with the minimum social requirements of the law. Some firms adopt this position because their slender profit margins and concern for short-term survival do not provide the flexibility to do much else.

Enlightened self-interest, the second position, is the use of social programs to gain an advantage in the marketplace. A firm might use a social responsibility program as a strategic weapon to communicate to the market that it is better than its competi-

FIGURE 4.1 *Corporate Social Responsibility Matrix for a Bank in the Pacific Northwest*

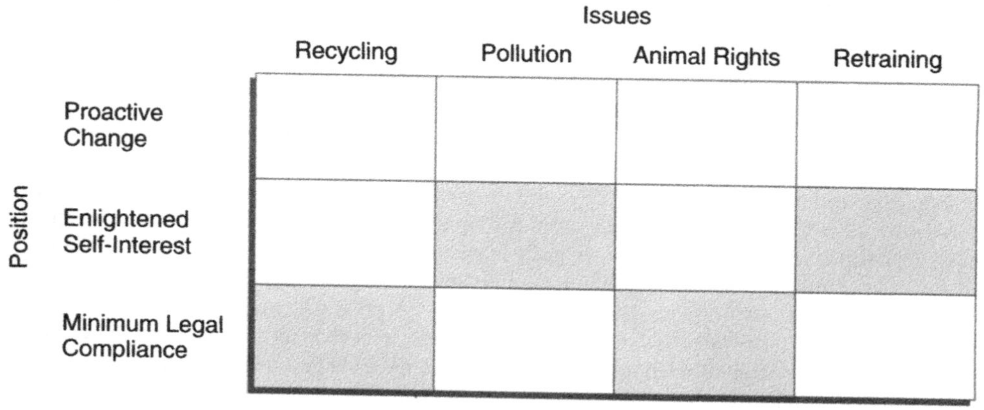

tors. This is consistent with the long-run, best-interest-of-the-firm stance that is expected to lead to long-term profitability. Some firms adopt this position or the minimum legal compliance position because they believe it to be the proper position.

The third position is **proactive change**, which is the active use of the firm's assets to improve society independent of a direct benefit to the firm. Managers taking such a position risk disapproval from owners and stockholders for going so far beyond the requirements of today's laws.

Managers and their firm might take different positions as a function of the nature of the specific decisions and the firm's customers. This would lead to a situation like that depicted in Figure 4.1. In a Total Quality sense, the position might be tied into the interests of the firm's customers. Certain decisions might be made in terms of "minimum legal compliance" if the firm's customers have little interest in those decisions beyond what is already in the law. Other decisions might be made in terms of "enlightened self-interest" if the firm's customers have a particular interest in those social issues.

For example, the customers of a bank with a regional check-processing facility in a lumbering area like the Pacific Northwest may have little interest in whether or not the checks are written on recycled paper. Thus "minimum legal compliance" may be the appropriate position on recycling. The same customers may not even want the bank to go beyond "minimum legal compliance" on animal rights issues because it might lead to unemployment, as happened with the Endangered Species Act. That act has been used to prohibit logging in vast areas in the Northwest, resulting in a dramatic increase in unemployment in the region. In other decisions the same bank's customers may want the bank to act in terms of "enlightened self-interest." Because of the unemployment just mentioned, the bank's customers may want the bank to actively implement worker-retraining programs. Also, the bank's customers may prize their clean air and thus expect the bank to take an "enlightened self-interest" position on pollution.

Q U A L I T Y   E X H I B I T

The Sloane Products Case

Sloane Products is a regional manufacturer of metal dispensers for paper products used in restaurants, hotels, and passenger terminals. The products bear the Sloane brand name and are advertised in trade journals. Sloane sells its products through wholesalers. There is no information on the amount of output eventually sold in minority-operated establishments. Sloane assumes the amount is relatively small. The manufacturing plant, however, is in an older metropolitan area with a large black population, though the plant itself is far from the center of the black neighborhoods and the firm has only a few black employees.

In response to pleas from the metropolitan chapter of the National Alliance of Business, Sloane's board adopted the following policy on minority purchasing:

Sloane managers are expected to make extra efforts to find minority suppliers and even to help minority enterprises adjust to Sloane's purchasing requirements. The board's instructions also made it clear that the effort was not expected to impose any serious disruption on Sloane's operations.

Right after the procurement directive was issued, Frank Gambetta, head of purchasing, had found a local firm, Diamond Carton Company, a black-owned and black-managed producer of corrugated boxes for shipping merchandise. For quotation purposes, Gambetta's office had given Diamond information on quantity, quality, sizes, and delivery requirements.

Diamond had admitted being new to the business but assured the people at Sloane that Diamond could meet the product and delivery specifications.

Diamond had sent quotations to Gambetta's office. After some negotiation, Diamond was awarded a contract by Sloane, which then reduced quantities purchased from other sources.

However, Diamond did not provide samples for preproduction approval at the time specified in the original agreement. When samples eventually appeared, they proved to be below standard. Gambetta and production chief Sam Fritzel then spent time helping the managers at Diamond work out the defects, and eventually Diamond did produce samples that could be approved.

First production deliveries were satisfactory, but since then every delivery has been either late or substandard. This has been going on for four months.

Fritzel is ready to end the agreement on the grounds that the relationship with Diamond is disrupting Sloane's operations.

Discussion Questions

1. Has Sloane done enough for Diamond to justify ending the agreement at the present time?

2. Is the fact that the relationship with Diamond is disrupting Sloane's operations good enough reason in itself for ending the agreement?

3. If Sloane does end the agreement with Diamond, does it have any obligation to find another minority supplier?

4. Given Sloane's geographical location, does it have any special moral obligation to the black community at all?

Source: T. L. Beauchamp and N. E. Bowie, *Ethical Theory and Business*, 3rd ed., Englewood Cliffs, NJ: Prentice-Hall (1988): 117–118.

C R I T I C A L   T H I N K I N G   Q U E S T I O N S

1. How are the arguments for a liberal corporate social responsibility and the arguments for a conservative corporate social responsibility aligned with political affiliation in the United States?

QUALITY CASE

Back to the Johnson & Johnson Case

The Tylenol poisonings became a publicity event without precedent in U.S. business. About 125,000 stories appeared in the print media, and it was estimated that the Tylenol brand received over $1 billion in adverse publicity. Immediately following the poisonings, the market share of the entire Tylenol line fell by 80 percent.

Johnson & Johnson (J&J) quickly issued the largest product recall in U.S. history—31 million bottles of capsules, with a retail value of over $100 million. Through ads and $2.50 coupons that offered an exchange of tablets for capsules, through 500,000 messages to the medical community and to distributors, and through public press releases, J&J forcefully communicated its actions.

These actions were taken by J&J even though it had been established that the poisonings were not due to a malfunction in the company's manufacturing process. It was determined that someone had purchased bottles of Tylenol capsules, injected cyanide into the capsules, and reintroduced the capsules into the distribution chain in the Chicago area. Only capsules were involved in the poisonings, since tablets were much harder to tamper with.

Within a few months J&J reintroduced the capsule form of Tylenol with a triple-sealed, tamper-resistant package. The flaps of the box were glued shut, the bottle's cap and neck were covered with a plastic seal, and the mouth of the bottle was covered with a foil seal. The box and the bottle were marked with the warning "Do Not Use If Safety Seals Are Broken."

It was estimated that out-of-pocket costs associated with J&J's decisive actions approached $200 million. It appeared, however, that J&J's forceful and quick actions had reestablished the public's trust in its products. In less than one year following the poisonings, Tylenol had regained nearly all of its former market share as its share approached 35 percent.

2. Describe five important social responsibility issues for a chemical manufacturer. For the firm complete a corporate social responsibility matrix on those issues.

Sometimes the best-intentioned corporate social responsibility policy does not meet expectations. Managers must then decide if it is in the enlightened self-interest of the organization to continue with the policy, as is illustrated in the quality exhibit.

MULTIPLE STAKEHOLDER VIEW

Stakeholders are the individuals and organizations that have an interest or stake in the activities of a firm. As industrial organizations have grown significantly larger since World War II, their power to affect the lives of many people has also grown. Thus there are an increasing number of stakeholders associated with the typical firm. These stakeholders have an equity, an economic, and/or an influencer stake in the firm.

Equity Stake

An **equity stake** in the company is associated with an ownership position. The equity stake varies as a function of the kind of power held by the stakeholder. The following examples refer to the primary orientation of the stakeholder.

The ownership position can range from formal ownership to a voting position of power, as with stockholders, directors, and other minority equity interests. The economic position of power is held by employee-owners. The political position of power is held by dissident stockholders.

There has been considerable criticism of many managers in the United States for overly focusing on the stakeholders with an equity stake and formal/voting power by stressing short-term profits. Such a focus has been associated with ignoring customers and losing customers to international competitors that provide more value to customers. An increasing number of U.S. managers are realizing that the best way to serve the interests of equity stockholders is by building a firm that provides more value to customers and increases market share in the long term.

Economic Stake

An **economic stake** is the result of direct market involvement with the company's marketplace activities. Formal or voting power is exercised by preferred debt holders. Economic power is exercised by a large group of stakeholders including suppliers, debt holders, customers, employees, and competitors. Political power is exercised by local and foreign governments, consumer lobbies, and unions that have an economic stake in the firm.

Influencer Stake

Groups with an influencer stake meet the expanded definition of stakeholders because they do not have much equity or economic interest. An **influencer stake** is interest associated with the firm's activities not due to marketplace or equity involvement.[10] Influencers may include those with formal or voting power such as outside directors and licensing bodies. Those with economic power include regulatory agencies that can affect prices. Those with political power include federal and state governments, trade associations, and environmental groups.

In recent years there has been an increasing number of laws that provide some of these groups with considerable legal power to back up their interest in the firm. In such situations managers must comply by force of law and government sanctions. Two examples are the Environmental Protection Agency and the Occupational Safety and Health Administration, which regulate issues concerning pollution and workplace safety, respectively.

A Stakeholder Grid

The various stakeholders described above are presented in Figure 4.2 as a function of the kind of stake and the kind of power they represent. The grid shows

FIGURE 4.2 *A Real-World Stakeholder Grid*

| | | Power | | |
		Formal or Voting	Economic	Political
Stake	Equity	Stockholders Directors Minority Interests	Employee/Owners	Dissident Stockholders
	Economic	Preferred Debt Holders	Suppliers Debt Holders Customers Employees Competitors	Local Governments Foreign Governments Consumer Lobbies Unions
	Influencers	Outside Directors Licensing Bodies	Regulatory Agencies	Federal and State Government Trade Associations Environmental Groups

Note: Grid location denotes the primary but not necessarily the sole orientation of each stakeholder.

Source: Adapted from *Strategic Management: A Stakeholder Approach,* by R.E. Freeman. Copyright © 1984 by Pitman Publishing Co.: 63.

the primary orientation of each stakeholder group, although some groups could be placed in more than one cell. Two conclusions can be drawn from Figure 4.2: (1) there are a large number of individuals and groups that have a stake in the typical firm, and (2) the nature of the stakeholders' interests vary as a function of the kind of power they possess.

Stakeholder Conflict and Total Quality

Given the large number of stakeholders with different interests and different power bases, there will naturally be situations of conflict among them. Managers can deal with the conflict partly by prioritizing the various groups. Historically, stakeholder conflict was thought to be a zero sum game in which one group gained advantage only at the expense of another group. Total Quality Management stresses the primacy of the customer and the importance of employees and suppliers in the management system of the firm. TQM strives to increase the health of the firm by strengthening the priority of the customer, supplier, and employee groups. A healthier firm should be better able to serve the equity and economic interests of the other stakeholder groups, as all ships rise with a rising tide.

FIGURE 4.3   *Constraining Influences on the Corporate Social Responsibility Decision*

CRITICAL THINKING QUESTIONS

1. Managers have traditionally paid considerable attention to the stakeholders in the four upper left quadrants of Figure 4.2, that is, the stakeholders with an equity or economic stake who have a formal/voting or an economic power with the firm. Those stakeholders with an influencer stake or political power have received relatively less attention from management. Forecast the trend of importance for those two groups.

2. Total Quality Management stresses the primacy of the customer and the importance of employees and suppliers in the management system of the firm. How do these TQM themes relate to the interests of the other stakeholders?

INFLUENCES ON CORPORATE SOCIAL RESPONSIBILITY

In addition to the previously mentioned arguments in favor of a liberal corporate social responsibility, there are a number of influences on any corporate social responsibility decision. These influences can be divided into four categories: government and regulatory influences, ethical influences, societal influences, and competitive influences (see Figure 4.3).

Government and Regulatory Influences

The powers of the government to regulate business in the United States are broad and deep. The U.S. Congress controls much business activity through its constitutional authority to regulate interstate commerce.

To implement its regulatory function, the federal government has established a number of regulatory agencies. A few of the more important ones are:

1. the Environmental Protection Agency (EPA), which develops and enforces standards for pollution;

An Occupational Safety and Health Administration inspector can have a significant impact on the health and safety conditions in the workplace. (Photo credit: OSHA/Department of Labor.)

2. the Equal Employment Opportunity Commission (EEOC), which prosecutes employment discrimination complaints based on race, gender, religion, creed, or national origin;

3. the Food and Drug Administration (FDA), which enforces standards for the purity and labeling of foods, drugs, cosmetics, and hazardous consumer products; and

4. the Occupational Safety and Health Administration (OSHA), which regulates safety and health conditions in the workplace.

These and other federal and state regulatory agencies are significant forces affecting liberal corporate social responsibility decisions.

Ethical Influences

As indicated earlier, there are at least five different managerial ethics bases. These bases act as internal self-regulating forces for corporate social responsibility decisions. Interest in managerial ethics is at a high point today, as managers' ethical standards are increasingly being evaluated as part of their performance.[11]

For managers to apply their own personal ethical standards to corporate decisions can be a complicated process. Even if the individual manager has been able to analyze a particular situation in terms of several of the five ethics bases and feels reasonably comfortable with the decision, then there are various stakeholder interests to satisfy. To deal with such situations, more than 80 percent of U.S. firms in the early 1990s had ethics codes to serve as guides.[12]

QUALITY CASE

Conclusion to the Johnson & Johnson Case

Calamity struck Tylenol capsules again in February 1986 when a Westchester, New York, woman died from cyanide-laced Tylenol capsules. Since Johnson & Johnson felt that it could no longer guarantee the safety of the product, J&J decided to discontinue the manufacture of capsules. Instead, it would market only tablets and a new product called a "caplet," which is an elongated, coated, easy-to-swallow tablet. That decision cost the firm about $150 million. Apparently it was a wise decision, as Tylenol's market share stood at 32 percent by July 1986. In describing the company's actions, J&J's president commented: "People think of this company as extraordinarily trustworthy and responsible, and we do not want to do anything to damage that."

That trustworthiness continues to be a major asset for the firm. Today J&J is one of the world's leading manufacturers and marketers of health care products. It offers a broad line of consumer products, prescription and over-the-counter pharmaceuticals, and various other medical and dental items. Sales in 1994 were forecast at about $17 billion, with about 50 percent of those sales outside the United States. Its reputation remains intact: J&J was one of only two firms ranked among America's ten "most admired" corporations in both 1992 and 1983.

Sources: Johnson & Johnson; "Johnson & Johnson," *Value Line Investment Survey* (June 18, 1993): 219; "Johnson & Johnson," *Standard & Poors Reports*, Standard & Poors Corporation (May 28, 1993): 1268; "America's Most Admired Corporations," *Fortune* (February 10, 1992): 41; R. Hartley, *Management Mistakes and Successes*, 3rd ed., New York: Wiley (1991): 365; M. L. Mitchell, "The Impact of External Parties on Brand-Name Capital: The 1982 Tylenol Poisonings and Subsequent Cases," *Economic Inquiry* (October 1989): 601–618; R. Jacobs, "Products Liability: A Technical and Ethical Challenge," *Quality Progress* (December 1988): 28;"Johnson & Johnson's Recovery," *New York Times* (July 5, 1986): 33; "Ranking Corporate Reputations," *Fortune* (January 10, 1983): 35; and "A Death Blow for Tylenol?" *Business Week* (October 18, 1982): 151.

Societal Influences

There are at least three different ways that society exercises its influence on a firm's corporate responsibility stance. The first and most powerful way is through market forces. The cumulative buying decisions of individual customers in the marketplace communicate society's preferences. If society prefers to buy "safe" cars and not buy "unsafe" cars, then society has voted its preferences on this corporate social responsibility issue.

The second way is through the electoral process. By voting for candidates with certain views on social responsibility issues, society expresses its preferences.

The third way that societal preferences are indicated is through the activities of influence groups. Influence groups use a variety of tactics including lobbying public officials, informing the public on certain issues, and organizing boycotts. Some examples of influence groups are Ralph Nader's Public Citizen (a consumer organization), the Sierra Club (an environmental organization), and Action for Children's Television (a special-interest organization).

Competitive Influences

Competitors directly affect the social responsibility decisions of corporations in the areas of product quality, safety, and economy. The Total Quality movement exists today largely because Japanese and German competitors gave U.S. customers high-quality, reasonable priced products from which to choose. In the mid-1990s it was very difficult to sell an automobile without antilock brakes and air bags because most of the competitors offered them and customers demanded them.

Competitors help to establish the norms for employment practices in an industry. Those firms that violate the norms on the downside usually incur the loss of skilled personnel.

CRITICAL THINKING QUESTIONS

1. In the 1970s and 1980s there were significant reductions in federal regulation in a variety of industries, among them the airlines, railroads, trucking, natural gas distributors, financial institutions, oil pipeline companies, and segments of the telecommunications industry. Forecast the trend of federal regulation of business over the next ten years.

2. How are competitors an influence on liberal corporate social responsibility decisions? How are competitors an influence on conservative corporate social responsibility decisions?

SUMMARY

Ethics is defined as doing the right thing right the first time. Unethical managerial behavior can be described as a result of a defect in an organizational system.

It is difficult to determine what is the right thing because there are so many different bases of ethics. There does not appear to be a single ethics base, with standards for managerial decisions and actions, that can guide managers in all situations. A proposed ethical decision must be analyzed using the multiple ethics bases to see how it holds up under the multiple approaches. Five different ethics bases are reviewed.

The eternal law approach to ethics holds that there is a common set of moral standards apparent in nature or revealed in the Scripture. Some refer to the eternal law as "rule-based ethics" because it holds that one should adopt a set of general rules, or principles, to guide one's actions.

Utilitarianism, or the utilitarian principle, maintains that a manager should act in ways to create the greatest benefits for the largest number of people. A managerial decision is "right" if it results in benefits for others, and it is "wrong" if it results in damage or harm to others.

Universalism holds that the ethics of a decision depends on the motives or intentions of the decision maker. Personal intentions or personal motives can be translated into personal duties or obligations, because all would behave in the same universal fashion given the same situation.

Distributive justice is based on the primacy of the single value of equity. According to the idea of distributive justice, managers should act to ensure a more equitable distribution of benefits.

Personal liberty is based on the primacy of the single value of individual choice. A managerial decision that violates individual liberty, even if it results in greater benefits for others, is not consistent with the idea of personal liberty.

Corporate social responsibility refers to the obligation of the firm to use its resources in ways to benefit society. Many arguments in favor of a liberal corporate social responsibility start by reviewing the role of business in society. First, society expects a liberal corporate social responsibility. Second, businesses' long-term self-interests are best served when these responsibilities are fulfilled. Third, the firm will avoid future government regulation.

Many managers counter that the most socially responsible action a company can engage in is to maximize its profits. This conservative view is founded on four ideas. First, in a capitalist economy, profit maximization is the only legitimate purpose of business. Second, corporate social responsibility subverts the market system. Third, the roles of business and government become confused. Fourth, business can become too powerful.

Given the conflicting arguments, there are at least three different positions that managers might employ. One position is minimum legal compliance, which means that the managers comply with the minimum social requirements of the law. Another position, enlightened self-interest, involves the use of social programs to gain an advantage in the marketplace. Proactive change, a third position, is the active use of the firm's assets to improve society independent of a direct benefit to the firm.

Stakeholders are the individuals and organizations that have an interest or stake in the activities of a firm. These stakeholders have an equity, an economic, and/or an influencer stake in the firm. An equity stake in the company is associated with an ownership position. An economic stake is the result of a direct market involvement with the company's marketplace activities. An influencer stake is interest associated with the firm's activities not due to marketplace or equity involvement.

In addition to the arguments in favor of a liberal corporate social responsibility, there are other influences on corporate social responsibility decisions. These are regulatory, ethical, societal, and competitive influences.

EXPERIENTIAL EXERCISE

Four Moral Problems for Resolution

Decide in your own mind what is "right" and what is "wrong" in these four short moral problems that need resolution. They are not simple problems. It is suggested that you make use of the five ethics bases discussed in the chapter.

Once you have analyzed the problems by yourself, join with four or five other students in your class to discuss the analyses of the problems relative to the five ethics bases.

Changing Corporate Pensions

In the spring of 1990 General Motors announced that it was planning to change the pension policies affecting its senior executives. In the past each pension had been calculated as a percentage of the last three years' average salary payments. In the future the pension would be a percentage of the last three years' average salary *plus* bonus payments. The bonus payments for senior executives at GM tend to equal or exceed their salaries; consequently the effect of this policy change would be to double or more than double the pension benefits for a limited number of persons. As an example, the pension for Roger Smith, chairman of GM, was expected to increase from $550,000 per year to $1,150,000.

The decision to increase the pension benefits for senior executives was made at a time when the company was also planning to reduce the pension benefits paid to mid-level retirees. Alarmed by the rapid increase in health care costs, GM had notified 84,000 former salaried employees that their health care coverage was being substantially lowered. The company was legally able to change provisions of the retirement coverage, as those provisions had never been part of a written contract.

Discussion Question

Is it "right" for the company to increase substantially the future pension payments of current senior executives and to decrease substantially the health care coverage of retired mid-level managers? Why or why not?

Making Political Contributions

In 1989 it was revealed that five U.S. senators had received approximately $1.8 million in campaign contributions from Charles Keating, chairman of Lincoln Savings and Loan Inc., of Orange County, California, during 1988, an election year. The donations were not technically campaign contributions. It is illegal for a single person or single company to donate more than $10,000 to the political campaign of a single candidate in a single year. Instead, the money had been given to the political causes that were expected to help the senators in their home states. For example, $900,000 had gone to a campaign to register voters in California. All the funds were then spent to register voters in heavily Democratic districts, which, of course, was beneficial to Senator Cranston, Democrat of California, one of the five who received the money.

In 1988 Lincoln Savings and Loan was undergoing a lengthy investigation by the federal government, which alleged improper loans and impending bankruptcy. The five senators met as a group with the regulators involved in the investigation on two separate occasions during the year and urged caution and delay. In defense of the senators, it should be explained that the national accounting firm retained by Lincoln and numerous economic consultants employed by Lincoln claimed that the savings and loan was not bankrupt and that the ongoing investigation appeared to be simply a personal vendetta against Keating by government officials.

Lincoln Savings and Loan did become insolvent in early 1989, and the company was then taken over by the government. At that time it was announced that the repayment of the federally insured depositors would cost the government (and consequently the taxpayers) $2 billion. The five senators have continually claimed that they did nothing wrong.

Discussion Questions

1. Was it "right" for Lincoln Savings and Loan to make large but legal campaign contributions to members of the U.S. Senate?
2. Was it "right" for members of the Senate to accept the contributions from Lincoln Savings and Loan and then intercede with the regulators on behalf of the donor?

Cutting Old-Growth Timber

In 1985 the Pacific Lumber Company of Scotia, California, was the largest private owner of redwood timberland in the United States and a firm that was widely respected by most environmentalists. The company had followed conservative logging practices since its founding in the late 1890s, never clear-cutting the land but always leaving some of the older trees to provide shade and protection for the new seedlings. The result was that the company was on a "sustained yield" basis, cutting slightly less than the annual growth each year, and the timberland was considered to be in excellent condition.

In 1982 the grandson of the founder of the Pacific Lumber Company died suddenly, leaving children too young to take over the management of the firm. A new group of managers was brought in, and they continued the traditional logging practices even though earnings remained lower than at most other timber companies on the West Coast—due, it was said, to the high cost of selective cutting. Some of the family's stock in the company was sold to pay estate taxes, and the new management group sold additional shares to raise money for debt repayment.

The family holdings of company stock were then less than 30 percent, and in 1985 Charles Hurwitz, who had made both a reputation and a fortune as a corporate raider, offered to buy the majority of the shares on the open market. The new management group fought Hurwitz's early efforts, but when he raised his bid to $700 million, financed by high-return, high-risk junk bonds, they were unable to compete and surrendered control.

To pay off the debt, the new owner quadrupled the rate of harvesting on company lands, clear-cutting the timber and ending the traditional practice of sustained yield logging. A forest survey just before the sale of the company showed a total value of $1.8 billion in redwood timber; at the new rate of harvesting, all of that would be gone in 18 years.

Discussion Question

Is it "right" for a new owner to clear-cut timber that has been preserved by the prior owners for nearly 100 years?

Pricing Essential Drugs

In 1987 azidothymidine (AZT) was the only drug that seemed to be effective against the acquired immunodeficiency syndrome (AIDS). AZT blocks the reproduction of the AIDS virus within the bloodstream of victims, thereby stabilizing their condition. AZT does not cure AIDS. It does, however, enable the patient in nonadvanced cases to continue living in the hope that a cure will be found.

AZT was developed by the Burroughs Wellcome Company, in cooperation with the federal government. Burroughs Wellcome is a midsize pharmaceutical company based in North Carolina. It is completely owned by Wellcome Ltd., which is a charitable trust located in Great Britain.

AZT was first synthesized in very minute amounts by a government-funded scientist at the National Cancer Institute in 1964. At the time it was believed that cancer might be a viral disease, and the drug was developed as a defense against viral infections. AZT was found to be ineffective in blocking the spread of cancer cells, and consequently it was neglected for the next 20 years. In 1984 a scientist at Burroughs Wellcome heard of the earlier effort, tried the drug against AIDS in laboratory animals, and found that it worked. The next five years were spent developing the production process (which is exceedingly complex in order to ensure the purity that is needed), conducting human trials, gaining regulatory approval, and starting the marketing process.

The drug is now being offered for sale at a retail price of $1.80 per tablet. The problem is that the typical patient requires 12 tablets per day, which amounts to $7,800 per year. An unfortunate paradox is that many of the 78,000 people diagnosed with the AIDS virus have no health insurance. Consequently, many are unable to pay for the drug that will prolong their lives.

Burroughs Wellcome has consistently refused to divulge precise cost data on the drug, but it does say that it is following pricing policies that are traditional in the pharmaceutical industry. Under those traditional policies, the manufactured cost (material, labor, and factory overhead) would be about 50 cents per tablet and the wholesale price $1.50. Administrative expenses, liability insurance, and future research and development would not be included in the manufactured cost estimate.

Discussion Question

Should a drug company follow traditional pricing policies, given that the resulting prices will make a given drug unaffordable to some dying patients?

Source: LaRue Tone Hosmer, *The Ethics of Management*, 2nd ed., Irwin, 1991, pp. 121–125. © 1991 Richard D. Irwin, Inc., Burr Ridge, IL.

CHAPTER CASE

Cost-Benefit Decision at Bluebird Smelter

Bluebird Smelter is owned by a larger, national mining company and located in Bluebird, a town of 12,000 in western Montana. The smelter, which has been operating profitably for 35 years with 125 employees, processes copper ore arriving by railroad.

Bluebird Smelter is the only major industrial pollution source in the valley. On sunny days when the air is still and during periods of temperature inversion over the valley, the action of the sun on smelter emissions contributes to photochemical smog similar to that in urban areas. Automobile emissions and agricultural activities are also sources of photochemical oxidants, but smelter emissions are far more important.

A group of economists from a prestigious research institute in another city picked the Bluebird Smelter as a test case for a research project on the health effects of pollution. The figures they produced led to debate among the various local groups involved in the controversy. The researchers looked at the operation of Bluebird Smelter in terms of costs and benefits to the community and to society. The accompanying table shows their basic calculations.

The Earth Riders (a small local environmental group) seized upon the study, arguing that if total costs of smelter operation exceeded benefits, then a clear-cut case had been made for closing the plant. It was already operating at a loss, in this case a net social loss of $730,000. Thus, in the eyes of the environmentalists, Bluebird Smelter was in social bankruptcy.

The smelter's managers and members of the Bluebird City Council, on the other hand, ridiculed the study for making unrealistic and overly simplistic assumptions. They questioned whether the costs were meaningful, citing other economists' estimates of the value of a human life that were much lower than $1 million. They argued that health risks posed by the smelter were less than those of smoking cigarettes,

Annual Benefits and Costs of Bluebird Smelter	
Benefits:	
Payroll for 125 employees at an average of $15,000 each	$1,875,000
Benefits paid to workers and families at an average of $1,000 each	125,000
Income, other than wages and salaries, generated in valley by the company	4,600,000
Local taxes and fees paid by the company	100,000
Social services to community and charitable contributions	20,000
Total	$6,720,000
Costs:	
Excess deaths of 5 persons at $1 million each[a]	$5,000,000
Other health and illness costs to exposed population	450,000
Crop and property damage from pollutants	1,000,000
Reduction of aesthetic value and quality of life	500,000
Lost revenues and taxes from tourism	500,000
Total	$7,450,000

[a] Calculated on the basis of recent court decisions compensating victims of wrongful death in product liability cases in Western states. The figure reflects average compensation.

drinking alcohol, or riding motorcycles and that benefits to the community were great. They even suggested that important costs had been left out of the calculations, such as sociological and psychological costs to workers who would be laid off if the plant closed.

Discussion Questions

1. Analyze the costs and benefits enumerated in the table. Are there items that belong in the table but are not included? Are there items in the table that should be deleted?

2. When making public-policy decisions, do you think a dollar value should be placed on human life? If your answer is no, how do you decide whether to spend an extra $100 million on highway safety? If your answer is yes, how do you decide how much a human life is worth?

3. Suppose it is true that the health risks posed by the smelter are less than those of smoking cigarettes. Does that mean that the smelter should not be closed down? That cigarettes should be banned?

4. Is the decision whether or not to close Bluebird Smelter the kind of decision that should be made by cost-benefit analysis?

Source: G. Steiner and J. Steiner, *Business, Government, and Society: A Managerial Perspective,* 7/e, 1994. Copyright © 1994 by McGraw-Hill. Reproduced with the permission of McGraw-Hill, Inc.

KEY TERMS

corporate social responsibility Obligation of the firm to use its resources in ways to benefit society.

distributive justice Equity based on the primacy of the single value of justice.

economic stake Stake in a company due to direct market involvement with the company's marketplace activities.

enlightened self-interest Use of social programs to gain an advantage in the marketplace.

equity stake Stake in a company associated with an ownership position.

eternal law approach to ethics Belief that there is a common set of moral standards apparent in nature or revealed in Scripture.

ethics Doing the right thing right the first time.

influencer stake Stake in a company based on an interest associated with the firm's activities not due to marketplace or equity involvement.

minimum legal compliance Compliance with the minimum social requirements of the law.

personal liberty Individual choice based on the primacy of the single value of liberty.

proactive change Active use of the firm's assets to improve society independent of a direct benefit to the firm.

stakeholders Individuals and organizations that have an interest or stake in the activities of a firm.

teleological theory Theory that stresses the outcome, not the intent, of managerial actions.

universalism Doctrine that the ethics of a decision depend on the motives or intentions of the decision maker.

utilitarianism (utilitarian principle) Doctrine that a manager should act in ways to create the greatest benefits for the largest number of people.

ENDNOTES

1. R. E. Berenbeim, "The Corporate Ethics Test," *Business and Society Review* (Spring 1992): 77–80.

2. These five rules are described in greater detail in L. T. Hosmer, *The Ethics of Management*, 2nd ed., Homewood, IL: Irwin: 1991: 108–120.

3. M. J. Stahl and D. G. Grigsby, *Strategic Management for Decision Making*, Boston: PWS-Kent (1992): 185.

4. This section draws heavily on Stahl and Grigsby, 189–193.

5. L. T. Hosmer, *The Ethics of Management*, 2nd ed., Homewood, IL: Irwin (1991): 102.

6. G. A. Steiner and J. F. Steiner, *Business, Government, and Society*, New York: Random House (1988): 182.

7. Committee for Economic Development, *Social Responsibilities of Business Corporations*, New York: CED (1981): 25–26.

8. M. Friedman, *Capitalism and Freedom*, Chicago: University of Chicago Press (1962): 24.

9. M. Friedman, "The Social Responsibility of Business Is to Increase Its Profits," *New York Times Magazine* (September 13, 1970).

10. R. Freeman, *Strategic Management: A Stakeholder Approach*, Boston: Pitman (1984): 58.

11. A. Bennett, "Ethics Codes Spread Despite Skepticism," *The Wall Street Journal* (July 15, 1988): 17.

12. R. E. Berenbeim, "The Corporate Ethics Test," *Business and Society Review* (Spring 1992): 77–80.

Planning and Strategic Management for Customer Value

5
CHAPTER

Decision Making, Problem Solving, and Continuous Improvement

LEARNING OBJECTIVES

After reading this chapter, you should be able to accomplish the following:

- Discuss the concepts of problems, decisions, and decision making.
- Explain the difference between programmed and nonprogrammed decisions.
- Describe the effect of bounded rationality on decision-making behavior.
- Discuss the relationships between managerial level, decision scope, and risk.
- Describe the use of standard operating procedures, decision rules, and expert systems in decision-making situations.
- Explain the seven-step nonprogrammed decision-making process.
- Outline the unresolved problems with rational decision making.
- Discuss the relationship between group decision making and cross-functional teams.

CHAPTER OUTLINE

Managerial Decision Making
  Decisions and Problems
  Structure
  Total Quality and Decisions
  Problem Finding
  Opportunity Finding
  Deciding Not to Decide
  Optimal Decisions versus Satisficing
Context of Managerial Decision Making
  Complex Streams of Decisions
  Uncertainty and Risk
  Decision Scope

Making Routine Decisions
  Decision Rules and Standard Operating Procedures
  Expert Systems
Making Nonroutine Decisions
  Define the Problem and Recognize the Need
  Diagnose and Analyze Causes
  Develop Alternatives
  Evaluate Alternatives
  Select the Best Alternative
  Implement the Best Alternative
  Monitor and Evaluate the Results
Problems with Rational Decision Making and Problem Solving
  Causes of Variation
  Continuous Improvement
  Recycling
  Psychological Biases
  Bounded Rationality
  Organizational Politics
  Escalation of Commitment
  Advantages and Disadvantages
  Implications
  The Customer Referent
Improved Decision Making
  Heuristics
  Understanding Variation
  Involvement of Customers
Cases and Exhibits
  Coca-Cola
  Procter & Gamble
  Levi Strauss
  T. H. Sandy Sportswear
  Time Value in Cultures
  Acme Supply Company

QUALITY CASE

Coca-Cola's Classic Planning Blunder

Coca-Cola's reintroduction of Coke Classic demonstrated the power consumers have to shape the behavior of a company. (Photo credit: UPI/Bettmann.)

During World War II Coca-Cola went with the GIs. The company saw to it that every man in uniform could get a bottle of Coca-Cola for five cents whenever he wanted, no matter what the cost to the company. Throughout the 1950s, 1960s, and early 1970s, Coca-Cola ruled the soft-drink market, despite strong challenges by Pepsi. It outsold Pepsi by two to one. But this was to change.

By the mid-1970s the Coca-Cola Company was a lumbering giant. Performance reflected this. Between 1976 and 1979 the growth rate of Coca-Cola soft drinks dropped from 13 percent annually to a meager 2 percent. As the giant stumbled, Pepsi-Cola found heady triumphs. First came the "Pepsi Generation," an advertising campaign that captured the imagination of the baby boomers with its idealism and youth. This association with youth and vitality greatly enhanced the image of Pepsi and firmly associated it with the largest consumer market for soft drinks.

Then came another management coup, the "Pepsi Challenge," in which comparative taste tests with consumers showed a clear preference for Pepsi. This campaign led to a rapid increase in Pepsi's market share from 6 percent to 14 percent of total U.S. soft-drink sales.

Coca-Cola, in reaction, conducted its own taste tests. Alas, these tests had the same result—people liked the taste of Pepsi better, and market share changes reflected this. By 1979 Pepsi had closed the gap on Coca-Cola, having 17.9 percent of the soft-drink market to Coke's 23.9 percent. By the end of 1984 Coke had only a 2.9 percent lead, while in the grocery store market it was now trailing 1.7 percent. Further indication of the diminishing position of Coke relative to Pepsi was a study done by Coca-Cola's own marketing research department. This showed that, in 1972, 18 percent of soft-drink users drank Coke exclusively, while only 4 percent drank only Pepsi. In ten years the picture had changed greatly; only 12 percent now claimed loyalty to Coke, while the number of exclusive Pepsi drinkers almost matched, with 11 percent.

What made the deteriorating competitive performance of Coke all the more worrisome and frustrating to Coca-Cola was that it was outspending Pepsi in advertising by $100 million annually. It had twice as many vending machines, dominated fountains, had more shelf space, and was competitively priced. Why was it still losing market share?

With the market share erosion of the late 1970s and early 1980s, despite strong advertising and superior distribution, the company began to look at the product itself.

continued

Evidence was increasingly suggesting that taste was the single most important cause of Coke's decline. Perhaps the original secret formula needed to be scrapped. And so Project Kansas began.

Under Project Kansas in 1982 some 2,000 interviews in 10 major markets were conducted to investigate customers' willingness to accept a different Coke. People were shown storyboards and comic-strip-style mock commercials and were asked series of questions. One storyboard, for example, said that Coke had added a new ingredient and it tasted smoother, while another said the same about Pepsi. Then consumers were asked about their reactions to the "change concept" (for example, "Would you be upset?" and "Would you try the new drink?"). Researchers estimated from the responses that 10 percent to 12 percent of Coke drinkers would be upset, and that half of these would get over it but half would not.

While interviews showed a willingness to try a new Coke, other tests disclosed the opposite. Small consumer panels or focus groups revealed strong favorable and unfavorable sentiments. But the technical division persisted in trying to develop a new, more pleasing flavor. By September 1984 it thought it had done so. It had developed a sweeter, less fizzy cola with a soft, sticky taste due to a higher sugar content from the exclusive use of corn syrup sweeteners, which is sweeter than sucrose. The new formula was introduced in blind taste tests, where consumers were not told what brand they were drinking. These tests were highly encouraging, with the new flavor substantially beating Pepsi, whereas in previous blind taste tests Pepsi had always beaten Coke.

Before adopting the new flavor, Coca-Cola invested $4 million in the biggest taste test ever. Some 191,000 people in more than 13 cities were asked to participate in a comparison of various unmarked Coke formulations. The use of unmarked colas was intended to eliminate any bias toward brand names. Fifty-five percent of the participants favored New Coke over the original formula, and New Coke also beat out Pepsi. The research results seemed to be conclusive in favor of the new formula.

Although the decision was made to introduce the new flavor, a number of ancillary decisions had to be reconciled. For example, should the new flavor be added to the product line, or should it replace the old Coke? It was believed that bottlers generally would be opposed to adding another cola. After considerable soul searching, top executives unanimously decided to change the taste of Coke and take the old Coke off the market.

Many managers relish the role of making decisions. Some feel that with decision-making authority comes a certain amount of power and influence. In this chapter we assert that power arises from quality products and services and from continuously improving consistent operations. Thus managers need to continuously improve their operations with a well-trained, problem-solving labor force so that the number of unique decisions becomes smaller.

MANAGERIAL DECISION MAKING

Throughout their careers, managers will make thousands of decisions. The art and science of decision making are frequently associated with managerial expertise. Indeed, a measure of managerial power and influence is the latitude managers have to make decisions without approval from other levels of management.

Decisions and Problems

A **decision** is a choice made from at least two alternatives. Making the choice is only part of the decision-making process. **Decision making** is the process of identifying alternatives and choosing one of the alternatives to solve a problem or address an opportunity. Which applicant to hire, which personal computer to buy, how to meet additional demand from department store customers near Christmastime, and how to increase service levels in a restaurant are all examples of opportunities requiring the decision-making process.

A **problem** is a situation that could prevent the organization from reaching its goals. How can we counter declining sales? Should we introduce a new product? What should we do with the old product if we introduce a new product? These are all problems requiring decisions.

Structure: Programmed versus Nonprogrammed Decisions

One way to classify decisions is by determining whether they are programmed decisions or nonprogrammed decisions.[1] **Programmed decisions** are decisions that are routine and repetitive and that are associated with standardized decision rules. Ordering replacement inventory on Monday morning is an example of a programmed decision. Deciding on the amounts of products to be reordered is done on the basis of decision rules resulting from prior outages of inventory.

Nonprogrammed decisions are decisions that occur so infrequently that standardized decision rules are not available to solve them. Restructuring a company by eliminating an entire layer of managers is an example of a nonprogrammed decision. Since such an issue is typically addressed only once or twice in the history of a company, standardized decision rules usually do not exist. Instead, what can be used is the seven-step decision-making process for nonprogrammed decisions that is outlined later in this chapter.

The terms *programmed decisions* and *nonprogrammed decisions* are two ends of a spectrum representing the degrees of standardization in the decision process (see Figure 5.1).

Total Quality and Decisions

Firms and managers that have implemented Total Quality Management have more stable processes and systems than do firms that have not implemented TQM. Stable processes and systems have less randomness and unpredictable variation associated with them. Therefore there should be fewer nonprogrammed decisions in TQM firms.

Conversely, firms that are constantly making nonprogrammed decisions need to ask if there is too much unexplained variation in their processes and systems. Should such firms apply quality tools like statistical process control to reduce the variation? The less unexplained variation there is, the fewer will be the nonprogrammed decisions. In Chapter 15 we discuss a number of tools that can be used to analyze the variation in processes.

FIGURE 5.1   *Structure in Decision Making*

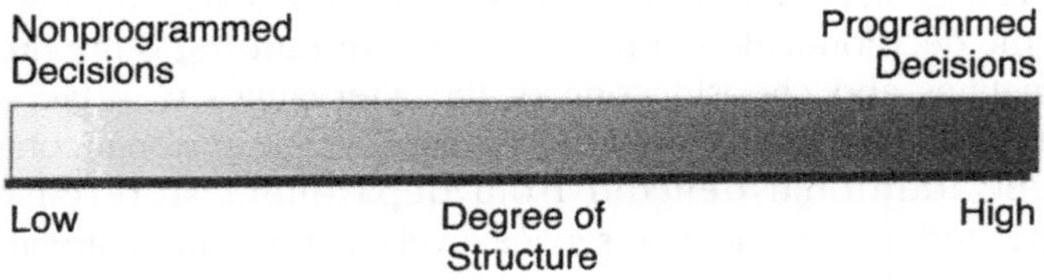

Nonprogrammed   Programmed
Decisions   Decisions

Low   Degree of   High
                              Structure

For example, a capsule-manufacturing firm found that there were too many defects in the hard gelatin capsules it was producing. Because of the number of defects, the firm had been making a number of decisions concerning accepting, inspecting, or rejecting batches of capsules. By implementing a quality improvement program that included statistical quality control and cross-functional teams, the company traced the source of many of the defects to variation in quality among its suppliers. After changing its purchasing procedures and thereby reducing the number of defects in supplied materials, the firm had fewer decisions to make about accepting, inspecting, or rejecting lots due to poor quality.

Problem Finding

Successful managers often go to great lengths to find and classify problems. Successful managers have a sense about which problems to delegate to others for solution, which problems to spend little effort on while solving them quickly, and which problems to concentrate on through all phases of their solution.

There are at least four situations that alert managers to problems: (1) a deviation from past experience, (2) a deviation from the plan, (3) others presenting problems to the manager, and (4) competitors outperforming the manager's organization.[2]

A deviation from past experience is one of the easiest for the seasoned manager to spot. An increase in customer complaints or a decrease in sales from repeat customers, for example, are easy to spot.

A deviation from the plan is also easily identified if the manager sets up a tracking system to measure actual performance relative to the plan. Failure to develop new products on time or failure to reduce the frequency of lost luggage by customers are two examples.

It is difficult for managers to ignore problems that are brought to their attention by others. When customers complain about unfilled orders or when subordinates complain about another employee who is sexually harassing them, it is dangerous to ignore the problems.

The superior performance of competitors may be more difficult to pinpoint, as they may mask their performance until it becomes public. Competitors may have a number of new products under development, for example, but not until those products are released into the marketplace do managers become aware that their own organization has fallen behind.

Opportunity Finding

An **opportunity** is a situation in the environment that may help the organization to reach or exceed its goals. Sensing those opportunities is an art form developed by experienced managers. The growth of two-wage-earner families has a major impact on the fast-food restaurant business. Understanding that growth and its impact as it develops is a significant opportunity. The following quality exhibit shows how Procter & Gamble seeks opportunity by trying to serve its consumers.

Deciding Not to Decide

Sometimes a manager decides not to decide. There are two recurring situations where such a nondecision may be appropriate.

First, is the decision the manager's to make? There are times when the decision is better handled by a subordinate. Such delegation is a good way to help develop the confidence and skill of subordinates. There are times when the decision is better handled by a superior. If the decision involves areas beyond the responsibility of the immediate manager, then it is better to let a superior field the decision. For example, a decision posed to a hotel sales manager affecting the food service may be better handled by the general manager.

Second, might the situation resolve itself? Some managers use delay as a tactic to see if the crisis atmosphere requiring a decision evaporates. New information might make the decision unnecessary.

Optimal Decisions versus Satisficing

Frequently, managers do not have the time or other resources to seek the best possible or optimal decision to a problem. An **optimal decision** is the one that is the best possible alternative of all alternatives. For example, a decision on an investment that yields the highest return of all alternatives is an optimal decision.

Instead, the manager may be more interested in a satisficing decision. **Satisficing** is choosing the first decision alternative that satisfies minimal decision criteria. In the investment example the manager may choose a safe investment alternative that satisfies minimum return criteria, such as investing in U.S. Treasury bills.

CRITICAL THINKING QUESTIONS

1. Define the concepts of problems, decisions, and decision making and programmed and nonprogrammed decisions.

2. Would you expect cross-functional teams to use optimizing or satisficing more often? Why?

CONTEXT OF MANAGERIAL DECISION MAKING

To appreciate the complexity of managerial decision making, it is necessary to understand the situation of the decision. This includes the pattern in prior deci-

Q U A L I T Y   E X H I B I T

Procter & Gamble: A Statement of Purpose

We will provide products of superior quality and value that best fill the needs of the world's consumers.

We will achieve that purpose through an organization and a working environment which attracts the finest people; fully develops and challenges our individual talents; encourages our free and spirited collaboration to drive the business ahead; and maintains the Company's historic principles of integrity and doing the right thing.

Through the successful pursuit of our commitment, we expect our brands to achieve leadership share and profit positions and that, as a result, our business, our people, our shareholders, and the communities in which we live and work, will prosper.

These are the principles that guide our actions as a Company and our attitudes about our employees:

— We will employ, throughout the Company, the best people we can find without regard to race or gender or any other differences unrelated to performance. We will promote on the same basis.

— We recognize the vital importance of continuing employment because of its ultimate tie with the strength and success of our business.

— We will build our organization from within. Those persons with ability and performance records will be given the opportunity to move ahead in the Company.

— We will pay our employees fairly, with careful attention to the compensation of each individual. Our benefit programs will be designed to provide our employees with adequate protection in time of need.

— We will encourage and reward individual innovation, personal initiative and leadership, and willingness to manage risk.

— We will encourage teamwork across disciplines, divisions and geography to get the most effective integration of the ideas and efforts of our people.

— We will maximize the development of individuals through training and coaching on what they are doing well and how they can do better. We will evaluate Procter & Gamble managers on their record in developing their subordinates.

— We will maintain and build our corporate tradition which is rooted in the principles of personal integrity; doing what's right for the long term; respect for the individual; and being the best in what we do.

These are the things that will enable us to achieve the category leadership that is our goal in every business in which we compete:

— We will develop a superior understanding of consumers and their needs. This is the foundation and impetus for generating the superior benefits and value consumers seek in other brands.

— We will develop strategies and plans capable of giving us the competitive advantage needed to meet our business objectives.

— We will create and deliver product and packaging on all our brands which provide a compelling advantage versus competition in bringing consumers superior benefits that best satisfy their needs. To do this we will be the world leader in the relevant science and technology.

— We will seek significant and sustainable competitive advantages in quality, cost and service in our total supply and delivery systems so as to meet our business objectives.

— We will have superior, creative marketing on all our brands. We will have enduring superior copy, and promotion programs distinguished by their creativity, effectiveness, and efficiency.

— We will develop close, mutually productive relationships with our trade customers and our suppliers. We will work with these partners in ways that are good for both of our businesses.

— We will promote a sense of urgency and a willingness to try new things. This will enable us to get better ideas working in the market ahead of competition.

— We will follow the principles of Total Quality to achieve continual improvement in everything we do. Whatever level of performance we have achieved today, we know that we can and must improve upon it tomorrow.

Source: Procter & Gamble, Cincinnati (1993).

FIGURE 5.2   *Decision-Making Conditions and Risk*

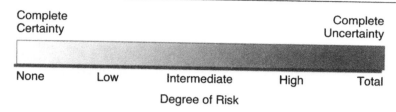

sion making, the riskiness of the decision, and the potential impact of the decision on the organization.

Complex Streams of Decisions

Henry Mintzberg, a noted scholar of managerial behavior, prefers to analyze patterns in streams of decisions.[3] He refers to these patterns as managerial strategy, arguing that to understand a manager, one must analyze a series of decisions by that manager and determine the pattern in the decisions. By analyzing a pattern of decisions from General Motors in the 1980s for example, many have concluded that GM's strategy was to yield lofty profits, not to maintain market share.

Uncertainty and Risk

Many managerial decisions are made under conditions of uncertainty and risk, with many pieces of information not being known at the time the decision needs to be made. Unfortunately, many decision makers do not react well to risky decision-making conditions. Many are not able to perceive correctly the amount of risk involved.[4] It is not unusual, therefore, for many managers to delay making decisions under conditions of risk or to seek out more information in order to reduce the amount of uncertainty. Figure 5.2 describes the various degrees of risk and of certainty or uncertainty associated with many managerial decisions.

In managerial decision making, **complete certainty** is the condition in which the manager knows all the information relevant to a decision and the outcome of the decision is exactly predictable. Conditions of complete certainty are usually associated with highly structured programmed decisions. **Complete uncertainty** is the condition in which the manager has little information relevant to a decision and there is no way to predict the outcome of the decision. Because of the riskiness associated with situations of complete uncertainty, most managers will avoid making decisions in such conditions. They will either seek more information or delay the decision until more information is available.

Decision Scope

The **scope of the decision** is the proportion of the organization affected by the decision. Corporate strategic decisions, like mergers, have a broad decision scope

FIGURE 5.3   *Types of Decisions and Managerial Levels*

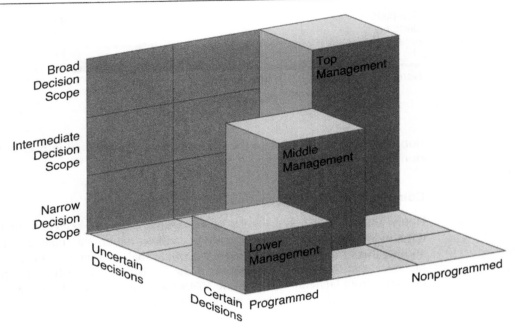

because they usually impact the entire organization. In general, the broader the scope of a decision, the higher the level of management involved in the decision. Figure 5.3 summarizes this relationship and the concepts of decision risk, certainty, and programmed versus unprogrammed decisions.

In situations with broad decision scope, people often seek information to reduce the risk in decision making. However, paying for that information from insiders raises an ethical issue, as the following ethics exhibit illustrates.

CRITICAL THINKING QUESTIONS

1. Why do some managers purposely procrastinate when faced with complete uncertainty?

2. How are managerial level, decision scope, and risk related?

MAKING ROUTINE DECISIONS: PROGRAMMED DECISIONS

As we have indicated, programmed decisions are routine, repetitive decisions associated with standardized decision rules. How they are made can be precisely described.

Decision Rules and Standard Operating Procedures

Standard operating procedures (SOPs) and decision rules are established ways of making routine decisions. SOPs and rules are usually expressed in the form of

E T H I C S   E X H I B I T

Levi Strauss Polices Working Conditions in International Apparel Manufacturers

In the last two decades, apparel manufacturers and retailers have been under intense international competition from low-priced garments assembled in countries where workers are paid very low-wages. The flood of imports was so strong in the 1980s that domestic textile manufacturers started a patriotic-themed "Made in the U.S.A." campaign using celebrities such as Bob Hope. The ads argued that "It does matter" where a garment was made.

To help understand the structure of the industry, you must know that the textile manufacturer is the firm that makes the cloth, an operation that is very capital intensive. Once the cloth is made, it is usually sold to an apparel manufacturer, who does the cutting and sewing of the fabric pieces into a garment. The labor-intensive sewing is sometimes referred to as assembly. In spite of some high-tech attempts to automate the sewing process with robots, most attempts have failed because of the flexibility of the fabric. The apparel operation is based on an individual worker, usually a relatively unskilled, patient, dexterous woman at a sewing machine.

The U.S. government hastened the movement of apparel manufacturers offshore when it provided special tariff relief for garments assembled in the Caribbean. Under Section 807 of the tariff code, the U.S. government ruled that no tariffs would be collected on the increased value associated with the labor added to a garment assembled in the Caribbean. This was part of an attempt to promote jobs, economic growth, and political stability in the Caribbean region. Partly because of this initiative and the competition from low-wage countries, tens of thousands of apparel manufacturing jobs were lost in the United States. Even though such jobs historically had been low paying with compensation not much more than $7 to 8 an hour plus fringe benefits, it is hard to keep costs down when wages in many developing countries are considerably less than $1 per hour with few or no fringe benefits. In the late 1980s, some textile plants in

the People's Republic of China paid a wage rate of $0.22 an hour, and some apparel plants in the Caribbean paid a wage rate of $0.80 an hour.

The domestic textile industry's "Made in the U.S.A." campaign had limited success. Many customers were interested primarily in the cost and quality of a garment and paid little attention to country of origin. So many large apparel firms had to decide between low-priced garments from low-wage countries, or lost sales due to the higher prices of garments sewn in the United States.

Liz Claiborne, a major women's apparel firm, contracted nearly all of its apparel manufacturing throughout the world. Wal-Mart advertised that most of its stores' goods were domestically manufactured, but there were several cases of internationally sourced goods. Lands' End, the mail order retailer, indicated if its garments were manufactured domestically or internationally. Levi Strauss, the world's largest supplier of brand-name apparel, contracted much of its apparel manufacturing throughout the world.

An issue with contracting such manufacturing to low-wage countries is that labor practices are deplorable in some countries due to non-existent or considerably less stringent labor laws than in the United States. Few low-wage countries have the multitude of laws covering equal employment opportunity, compensation and benefits, child labor, labor relations, and occupational safety and health that exist in the United States. (See Chapter 9 for a more in-depth coverage of labor laws.)

When such deplorable conditions become known, U.S. public pressure against such practices can be quite heated. As seen in the Dresser Industries case in Chapter 3, U.S. public pressure against apartheid in South Africa forced the withdrawal of most U.S. firms from that country. Such public pressure can result in boycotts against the other country or against the U.S. company doing business with firms in the other country.

continued

Deplorable working conditions in some low-wage countries raise an ethical dilemma for U.S. firms that purchase garments from manufacturers in such countries. Are the U.S. firms subsidizing such behavior?

Some U.S. firms have tried to enforce certain labor standards on international suppliers from a stance of enlightened self-interest (see Chapter 4) because domestic customers wanted it. This raises a whole series of questions. Some have charged that the U.S. firm's behavior is no less than meddling in the internal affairs of another country. Some have pointed out that by raising the cost of doing business in another company, the U.S. firm is in effect pricing that company and its workers out of future work because some international competitor will undercut prices with less costly labor practices.

Amid these charges, Levi Strauss has tried to ensure that its international garment contractors treat workers well in their plants. In 1992, Levi became the first in its industry to promote a broad set of guidelines for its contract plants that covered labor and the environment. Levi said it would inspect plants and cancel contracts for violators. Im Choong Hoe is an inspector for Levi who checks for health and safety hazards and abuses of workers' rights in contract plants in Southeast Asia from Bangladesh to Indonesia. His primary concern is worker safety and he frequently checks the number of fire extinguishers and exits in plants in case of fire. He says that a fire would be disastrous in some crowded plants killing many workers.

But if a contract is canceled, how does that help the welfare of displaced workers? To solve such a dilemma, Levi has designed some innovative approaches to protect workers. When a Levi inspector discovered that one of its contractors employed children, Levi continued to pay the children while they attended school at the factory rather than force the company to fire them and cause their families to lose needed wages.

As international joint ventures grow in importance and frequency, this ethical dilemma will be confronted by more U.S. managers. As more U.S. firms respond to public pressure, attention will be paid to working conditions in low-wage countries.

Discussion Questions

1. Does a U.S. firm have the right to meddle in the labor practices of another sovereign country?

2. Describe minimum compliance and enlightened self-interest approaches to this dilemma.

Sources: "Managing by Values: Is Levi Strauss' Approach Visionary—or Flaky?" *Business Week,* (August 1, 1994): 46–52."Levi Tries to Make Sure Contract Plants in Asia Treat Workers Well," *Wall Street Journal* (July 28, 1994): A1; D. Vogel, "Is U.S. Business Obsessed with Ethics?" *Across the Board* (December 1993): 31–33; D. Grigsby, "Liz Claiborne, Inc." in D. Grigsby and M. Stahl (Eds.) *Strategic Management Cases,* Belmont, CA, Wadsworth (1993): 54–73; A. Singer, "Ethics: Are Standards Lower Overseas?" *Across the Board* (September 1991): 31–34

if–then statements. The relationship involves one piece of information as an input and a simple response as a result. At Lands' End, for example, a simple rule may be if the customer returns an item, then honor the customer's request for another item or a refund with no hassle. In contrast, a discount retailer may have a standard operating procedure that if a customer returns an item, then the customer is asked to choose another item, but a refund is not issued. In both cases the SOP is meant to serve as a guide for making routine, programmed decisions. In both cases the SOP is consistent with the customer-value strategy of the organization.

Decision rules and standard operating procedures are appropriate when little risk is involved. As illustrated in the following diversity exhibit, they can be misleading when used in situations with risk.

D I V E R S I T Y   E X H I B I T

T. H. Sandy Sportswear

The Millers, Brad and Mary, moved to Tallahassee, Florida, in order for Mary to attend Law School at Florida State University. Brad graduated from Georgetown University with a degree in business administration and worked in retail management for five years. Brad graduated with top honors from Georgetown and had excellent recommendations from his former employers.

Tallahassee, Florida, is basically a college town, centering around two universities and the Florida State Legislature. The two universities are Florida State University and Florida A&M University. There is only one large shopping mall and a few department stores in Tallahassee, and jobs in retail management are quite scarce.

Upon arriving in Tallahassee, Mary started classes at the Law School and Brad began looking for a job. There were absolutely no openings anywhere in town for retail managers, and Brad eventually had to settle for a teller position at a local bank. Brad kept abreast of the retail job market in Tallahassee, and finally an opportunity came open.

T. H. Sandy, a women's discount sportswear retailer, advertised in the local newspaper for a store manager. Brad immediately made an appointment for an interview and sent in a resume, as requested in the ad. Brad arrived early for his interview and was given an application form to complete. The application form was a long one and included a question concerning sex of applicant. While completing the application form, Brad noticed that all the employees of T. H. Sandy were female and all of the other applicants waiting to be interviewed

were also female. Brad was finally called in for his interview, which he thought went very well. The interviewer told Brad that they had two more days of interviewing before a decision would be made and that he would be hearing from them in about a week. The next week Brad received a letter from T. H. Sandy informing him that he had not been chosen for the position and thanking him for his interest in the company. The letter gave no reason for their decision. Since this job was so important to Brad, he decided to visit the store and talk with the lady who had interviewed him.

In his meeting with the interviewer, Brad found out that the company had been very impressed with his experience and credentials, but had decided against hiring him because he was a male. The interviewer showed Brad a job description for the manager's position and pointed out that one of the duties of the manager was to supervise all areas of the store, including the dressing rooms. Because of this particular duty, the company felt that the position should be filled with a female. Brad left the store upset and discouraged.

After discussing the situation with his wife, who is now studying fair employment legislation, Brad considered filing a suit against T. H. Sandy for discrimination based on sex under Title VII of the Civil Rights Act of 1964.

Source: Kenneth A. Kovach, "T. H. Sandy Sportswear," from T. L. Beauchamp and N. E. Bowie, *Ethical Theory and Business*, Englewood Cliffs, NJ: Prentice-Hall (1988): 393–394.

Expert Systems

An **expert system** is a computerized decision-making aid to help decision makers decide with multiple pieces of information. The term *expert* (from *expertise*) refers to capturing the experience of some decision makers who have been successful in making similar decisions over many years.[5] The expertise is usually captured on a computer in a series of if–then decision rules. Unlike SOPs and rules involving a single piece of information, an expert system involves several seemingly unrelated pieces of information that collectively help form the decision. For example, in helping an insurance agent decide

FIGURE 5.4   *Seven Steps in Nonprogrammed Decision-Making Process*

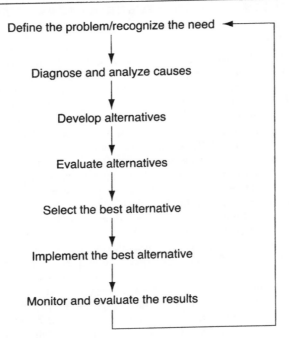

how much to charge an applicant for automobile insurance, the expert system may inquire about the age, accident record, traffic violations, kind of car, horsepower of car, and marital status of the applicant. The experience of successful claims adjusters has shown that young, single men with several accidents and traffic violations, and driving overpowered sports cars tend to have an abnormally high rate of accidents. Therefore the computerized expert system would advise the insurance agent to charge a high premium rate on an insurance policy for a person with these characteristics.

CRITICAL THINKING QUESTIONS

1. What are the uses of standard operating procedures, decision rules, and expert systems in decision-making situations?
2. How could an expert system be used in the registration process at your school?

MAKING NONROUTINE DECISIONS: NONPROGRAMMED DECISIONS

In making nonroutine decisions, typically there are several stages in a rational decision-making/problem-solving process. Although a particular situation is not routine, there are seven common steps that the decision maker can follow (see Figure 5.4). In the following discussion of these steps, a decline in sales is used as an example of a problem to be solved.

Define the Problem and Recognize the Need

The first step in making a nonroutine decision is to recognize that a decision must be made. There must be a general perception that something is wrong or that there is a specific perceived gap between the actual performance and the targeted objectives. Specific problem statements make the seven-step decision-making process easier.

This recognition that something is amiss may lead to a statement of the problem, such as "Sales are not so good." A more specific statement, such as "Sales are 12 percent below expectations," will facilitate the decision-making process.

Diagnose and Analyze Causes

In the second step the decision makers must try to understand why the problem exists. This diagnosis and analysis step draws on the experience of the decision makers. This is why many nonprogrammed decisions are made by middle and upper levels of management. In Chapter 15 we present a number of tools to analyze causes of problems.

Why are sales off? Is it because of the state of the economy? Is it because of the entrance of a new competitor in the industry? Is it because there are quality defects in the products offered for sale?

Develop Alternatives

Once the causes have been analyzed, the decision makers are in a position to develop alternatives. This third step is nonevaluative, with alternatives simply being listed in the hope of stimulating free thinking.

If the sales decline is due to the defect rate in the firm's products, should the firm lower prices in an attempt to compensate for the defects? Should an advertising campaign be started to stress the other positive features of the product? Should the firm initiate a substantial quality improvement program? Should the firm advertise its quality improvement efforts? Should the firm hire someone to investigate the quality problems in competitors' products?

Evaluate Alternatives

Once the alternatives have been developed, the next step is to evaluate them. This evaluation should include questions of soundness, probability of success, cost, and consistency with the firm's strategies.

Will lowering the price backfire by communicating an image of inferior goods? Might an advertising campaign backfire without substantial improvement in the quality of the products? Would investigating the quality problems of competitors be viewed as "dirty tricks"?

Select the Best Alternative

After evaluation of the alternatives, it is time to choose the best alternative. This step may be subjective, since it involves judgments about the probability of success and of fit with the firm's strategies.

QUALITY CASE

Back to the Coca-Cola Case

In January 1985 the task of introducing the new Coke was given to the McCann-Erickson advertising agency. Bill Cosby was to be the spokesman for the nationwide introduction of the new Coke scheduled for April. All departments of the company were gearing their efforts toward a coordinated introduction.

On April 23, 1985, Mr. Goizueta, chairman of Coca-Cola, held a press conference in Lincoln Center in New York City in order to introduce the new Coke. Invitations had been sent to the media from all over the United States, and some 200 newspaper, magazine, and TV reporters attended the press conference. However, many of them came away unconvinced of the merits of the new Coke, and their stories were generally negative. In the days ahead the news media's skepticism was to exacerbate the public nonacceptance of the new Coke.

The word spread quickly. Within 24 hours 81 percent of the U.S. population knew of the change, and this was more people than were aware in July 1969 that Neil Armstrong had walked on the moon. Early results looked good; 150 million people tried the new Coke, and this was more people than had ever before tried a new product. Most comments were favorable. Shipments to bottlers rose to the highest volume in five years. The decision looked unassailable. But not for long.

The situation changed rapidly. Although some protests had been expected, these quickly mushroomed. By mid-May calls were coming in at a rate of 5,000 a day, in addition to a barrage of angry letters. The company added 83 WATS lines, and hired new staff to handle the responses. People were speaking of Coke as an American symbol and as a longtime friend that had suddenly betrayed them. Some threatened to switch to tea or water. Here is a sampling of the responses: "The sorrow I feel knowing not only won't I ever enjoy real Coke, but my children and grandchildren won't either....I guess my children will have to take my word for it." "It is absolutely terrible! You should be ashamed to put the Coke label on it....This new stuff tastes worse than Pepsi." "It was nice knowing you. You were a friend for most of my 35 years. Yesterday I had my first taste of new Coke, and to tell the truth, if I would have wanted Pepsi, I would have ordered a Pepsi not a Coke."

In all, more than 40,000 such letters were received that spring and summer. In Seattle strident loyalists calling themselves Old Coke Drinkers of America laid plans to file a class action suit against Coca-Cola. People began stockpiling the old Coke. Some sold it at scalper's prices. When sales in June did not pick up as the company had expected, bottlers demanded the return of old Coke.

The company's research also confirmed an increasing negative sentiment. Before May 30, 53 percent of consumers said they liked the new Coke. In June the vote began to change, with more than half of all people surveyed saying they did not like the new Coke. By July only 30 percent of the people surveyed each week said that they liked the new Coke.

Anger spread across the country, fueled by media publicity. Fiddling with the formula for the 99-year-old beverage became an affront to patriotic pride. Robert Antonio, a University of Kansas sociologist, stated, "Some felt that a sacred symbol had been tampered with." Even Goizueta's father spoke out against the switch when it was announced. He told his son the move was a bad one and jokingly threatened to disown him. By then company executives began to worry about a consumer boycott against the product.

Selection of a quality improvement program may be viewed as the alternative with the highest probability of long-term success. This alternative may also have the best fit with the strategies of the firm.

Implement the Best Alternative

Once chosen, the alternative must be implemented. The implementation step often includes the allocation of funds and other resources.

The quality program must be funded and it must be communicated to the firm's employees, suppliers, and customers. The program may involve substantial training, modification of corporate policies, interaction with suppliers, and time.

Monitor and Evaluate the Results

Once the alternative has been implemented, results must be monitored and evaluated. Have we solved the problem that we started out to solve? This final step involves feedback to the first step as the conclusion of the decision-making process.

Is the quality of the products improving? Is it improving fast enough? Do customers perceive that the quality is improving? Is the quality of competitors' products improving faster? Are sales improving?

CRITICAL THINKING QUESTIONS

1. Describe the seven steps in the nonprogrammed decision-making process.

2. How were those steps applied in the case of Coca-Cola?

PROBLEMS WITH RATIONAL DECISION MAKING AND PROBLEM SOLVING

The rational decision-making model assumes that human decision makers are rational, that is, that they follow the prescribed seven-step process for making nonprogrammed decisions. Instead, much research has shown that human decision makers are prone to a number of biases and limitations that hamper their effectiveness as processors of information.

Causes of Variation

If rigorously followed, the seven-step model can be a time- and energy-consuming process. As a result, managerial decision makers may wish to move onto other issues that they have had to put on hold while making the decision at hand. Thus they probably will avoid doing the research into the system to investigate the cause of variation responsible for the problem in the first place. In many organizations managers are rewarded for solving problems and making decisions. They are not rewarded for determining the cause of variation.

In the example given above in our discussion of the seven-step process, investigation of the cause of variation in product quality might reveal that the variation was caused by defective raw materials from suppliers. The suppliers may have been responding to purchasing policies that awarded supply contracts on the basis of low bid and not necessarily high quality.

Continuous Improvement

The seven-step rational decision-making process is a discrete model. Thus there is a tendency to consider decisions and problems as discrete entities, to be considered one at a time. This works counter to the notion of continuously improving a system or process. Indeed, this discrete process focuses on exceptions to the system—called problems—not on improving the consistency of the process. For example, looking for ways to continuously improve the quality of products in the absence of customer complaints and problems may preclude a future problem.

Recycling

The seven-step model suggests that there is a definite beginning and a definite end to the decision-making process. The model does not recognize that sometimes in organizations lower-level managers go through the seven steps only to have the next higher level of management recycle them through the model with different information or assumptions. As other managers get involved in the decision, the process is recycled. All too often managers are recycled several times through the model. A problem may arise in that an earlier stated analysis or evaluation may be accepted as fact simply because it has been listed several times.

Psychological Biases

Managers are subjected to a number of biases in decision making. Even with training, it is difficult for many to overcome the effects of the biases.[6] Some of the more common biases that affect managerial decision making are described below.[7]

Problems Calibrating Probabilities   Many decision makers do not fully understand the nature of probability. Many overestimate the odds of an infrequently occurring event and underestimate the odds of a frequently occurring event.

Ignorance of Sample Size   Many decision makers do not pay attention to the sample size. A sample with three out of four indicating one preference does not necessarily mean that chances are 75 percent in the total population. Extrapolating to a large segment of the population on the basis of a small, nonrandom sample is one of the most commonly occurring problems for decision makers.

Bounded Rationality

Bounded rationality is the ability of decision makers to process only a limited amount of information. The rational decision-making model assumes that decision makers can consider all relevant information and evaluate all relevant alternatives. Partly because of bounded rationality, managers often satisfice rather than optimize. Very large numbers of managerial decisions are made under conditions of bounded rationality.[8] In an aptly titled article, "The Magic Number Seven, Plus or Minus Two," the authors showed that many human decision makers can consistently deal with only five to nine pieces of information in a decision-making task.[9]

INTERNATIONAL EXHIBIT

Understanding Time Values in Other Cultures

American business managers have encountered problems trying to understand time values in other cultures. One U.S. company lost a major contract opportunity in Greece because its managers tried to impose American customs on the Greek negotiators. Besides being too forthright and outspoken in the eyes of the Greeks, the Americans tried to set time limits for the meetings. The Greeks, however, considered time limits insulting and thus felt that the Americans showed a lack of finesse. The Americans also wanted the Greeks to first agree to principles, and then allow their subordinates to work out all the necessary details. The Greeks viewed this as a deceptive strategy; they preferred to handle all arrangements regardless of the time involved. **us**

Consider an unfortunate American manager who worked in the South Pacific. He foolishly hired local natives without considering the island's traditional status system. By hiring too many of one group, he threatened to alter the balance of power of the people. The islanders discussed this unacceptable situation and independently developed an alternative plan. It had taken them until 3:00 a.m. to do so, however. But since time was not important in their culture, they saw no reason to wait until morning to present their suggestions to the American. They casually went to his place of residence, but their arrival at such a late hour caused him to panic. Since he could not understand their language and could not imagine that they would want to discuss business at 3:00 a.m., he assumed that they were coming to riot and called in the Marines. It was some time before the company was able to get back to business as usual. **us**

Arabs typically dislike deadlines. An Arab faced with a deadline tends to feel threatened and backed into a corner. Many Americans, on the other hand, try to expedite matters by setting deadlines. As a result, hundreds of American-owned radio sets are sitting untouched in Middle Eastern repair shops because some Americans made the cultural mistake of requesting that the work be completed by a certain time. **us**

Source: David A. Ricks, *Blunders in International Business*, Cambridge, MA: Blackwell (1993): 3–5.

Organizational Politics

Organizational politics in decision making are activities that attempt to influence the outcomes of a decision. When political correctness guides managerial deliberations, then steps in the decision-making process, such as listing and evaluating alternatives, yield decisions that are not the best among all alternatives.

Escalation of Commitment

Escalation of commitment is an increase in commitment to a chosen course of action even though the ineffectiveness of that course of action has become obvious. Rational decision makers would not "double their bet," but pride, organizational politics, or inexperience sometimes cause managers to escalate their commitment to a defective decision. Throughout the 1960s many questioned the involvement of the United States in Vietnam, yet the U.S. government escalated its commitment over more than a ten-year period.

There are many advantages to group decision making, including support once a decision has been reached. (Photo credit: Joseph Pobereskin/Tony Stone Worldwide.)

In doing business in other cultures, it is important to understand their decision biases and organizational politics. As the following international exhibit shows, this includes ideas as simple as the meaning of time in different cultures.

CRITICAL THINKING QUESTIONS

1. How should bounded rationality impact the design of financial statements?

2. Will organizational politics impact decisions in a TQ organization less than in other organizations? Why or why not?

GROUP DECISION MAKING

Group decision making has its own advantages and disadvantages. These are particularly relevant in situations that involve cross-functional teams.

Advantages and Disadvantages

Group decision making is a decision-making process performed by more than one individual. This type of decision making is being used more frequently in organizations today than individual decision making. Prior to its wholesale adoption, however, it is prudent to be aware of several advantages and disadvantages associated with group decision making. These pros and cons are presented in Table 5.1. **Groupthink** is a process in which the group members are so concerned with group consensus that they are unwilling to evaluate options realistically and objectively.[10]

TABLE 5.1   *Advantages and Disadvantages of Group Decision Making*

Advantages	Disadvantages
1. More knowledge, experience, and broader perspectives are available.	1. Group deliberations are time consuming.
2. More alternatives can be evaluated.	2. Group compromise decisions may not produce the strong actions required.
3. Group discussion rigorously evaluates alternatives.	3. Groupthink allows consensus to become more important than the quality of the decision.
4. Group participation broadens support for the decision throughout the organization.	4. Accountability and individual ownership of the decision are lacking.

Implications for Cross-Functional Teams and Cultural Change

As more organizations implement cross-functional teams in a switch to Total Quality, group decision making will be used more often. In accord with the advantages noted in Table 5.1, cross-functional teams and group decision making are consistent. Using group decision making can help the organization switch its corporate culture from one dominated by individuals to one that operates through cross-functional teams. In a comprehensive study of the elements of success associated with TQM, one researcher included: "A decentralization of decision-making responsibility to a well-trained problem-solving labor force (i.e., employee participation in decision making)."[11]

The Customer Referent

Total Quality firms have a special commitment to provide value to their customers. Sometimes, for the sake of organizational politics, individuals ignore the customer. Group decision-making processes, especially if they are composed of cross-functional teams, increase the odds that the customer is the primary focus of the decision.

CRITICAL THINKING QUESTIONS

1. How are group decision making and cross-functional teams related?

2. How does the customer referent help the decision-making task?

IMPROVED INDIVIDUAL AND GROUP DECISION MAKING

To lessen the problems associated with decision making, there are a number of ways to improve the decision-making processes.

QUALITY CASE

Conclusion to the Coca-Cola Case

Company executives now began seriously thinking about how to recoup the fading prospects of Coke. In an executive meeting the decision was made to take no action until after the Fourth of July weekend, when the sales results for that holiday weekend would be in. The results were unimpressive. The decision was then made to reintroduce Coca-Cola under the trademark of Coca-Cola Classic. The company would keep the new flavor and call it New Coke. The decision was announced to the public on July 11, when top executives walked onto the stage in front of the Coca-Cola logo to make an apology to the public, without admitting that New Coke had been a total mistake.

Two messages were delivered to the American consumer. First, to those who were drinking the new Coke and enjoying it, the company conveyed its thanks. The message to those who wanted the original Coke was that "we heard you" and the original taste of Coke is back.

The news spread fast. ABC interrupted its afternoon soap opera to break the news. In the kind of saturation coverage normally reserved for disasters or diplomatic crises, the decision to bring back old Coke was prominently reported on every evening network-news broadcast. The general feeling of soft-drink fans was joy. Democratic Senator David Pryor of Arkansas expressed his jubilation on the Senate floor: "A very meaningful moment in the history of America, this shows that some national institutions cannot be changed." Even Wall Street was happy. Old Coke's comeback drove Coca-Cola stock to its highest level in 12 years.

On the other hand, Roger Enrico, president of Pepsi-Cola USA, said: "Clearly this is the Edsel of the '80s. This was a terrible mistake. Coke's got a lemon on its hands and now they're trying to make lemonade." Other critics labeled this the "blunder of the decade."

The most convenient scapegoat, according to consensus opinion, was the marketing research that preceded the decision. Yet Coca-Cola had spent about $4 million and devoted two years to the marketing research. About 200,000 consumers were contacted during this time. The error in judgment was surely not from want of trying. But when we dig deeper into the research efforts, some flaws become apparent.

The major design of the marketing research involved taste tests by representative consumers. After all, the decision point involved a different-flavored Coke, so what could be more logical than to conduct blind taste tests to determine the acceptability of the new flavor, not only versus the old Coke but also versus Pepsi? And these results were significantly positive for the new formula, even among Pepsi drinkers. A clear "go" signal seemed indicated.

But with the benefit of hindsight, some deficiencies in the research design were more apparent—and should have caused concern at the time. The research participants were not told that by picking one cola, they would lose the other. This turned out to be a significant distortion. Any addition to the product line would naturally be far more acceptable to a loyal Coke user than would be a complete substitution, which meant the elimination of the traditional product.

The symbolic value of Coke was the sleeper. Perhaps this should have been foreseen. Perhaps the marketing research should have considered this possibility and designed the research to map it and determine the strength and durability of this value. Would it have a major effect on any substitution of a new flavor?

continued

A natural human phenomenon asserted itself in this case—the herd instinct, the tendency of people to follow an idea, a slogan, a concept, to "jump on the bandwagon." At first, acceptance of the new Coke appeared to be reasonably satisfactory. But as more and more outcries were raised—fanned by the press—about the betrayal of the old tradition (somehow this became identified with motherhood, apple pie, and the flag), public attitudes shifted vigorously against this perceived unworthy substitute. And the bandwagon syndrome was fully activated. It is doubtful that by July 1985 Coca-Cola could have done anything to reverse the unfavorable tide. To wait for it to die down was fraught with danger, for who would be brave enough to predict the durability and possible heights of such a protest movement?

Could, or should, such a tide have been predicted? Perhaps not, at least as to the full strength of the movement. Coca-Cola expected some resentment. But perhaps it should have been more cautious and have considered a "worst-case" scenario in addition to what seemed the more probable, and been prepared to react to such a contingency.

DISCUSSION QUESTIONS

1. When a firm is facing a negative press, as Coca-Cola was with the new Coke, what recourse does the firm have? Support your conclusions.

2. Do you think Coca-Cola would have been more successful if it had introduced the new Coke as an addition to the line and not as a substitute for the old Coke? Why or why not?

3. For Coke customers, what other dimensions are there to customer value besides taste?

Source: Adapted from R. F. Hartley, *Management Mistakes and Successes*, New York: Wiley (1991): 67–84.

Heuristics

Heuristics are rules of thumb, or general cognitive strategies, used to simplify the decision-making process.[12] Heuristics are not as specific as the decision rules and standard operating procedures discussed earlier. The three most frequently used heuristics are availability, representativeness, and anchoring and adjustment.

Availability   Often people judge the chance of an event by comparing it with the available information in their memories. Availability is governed by recency and frequency of occurrence. Thus an insurance adjuster's estimates will be influenced by recent accidents and the most commonly occurring reasons for them.

Representativeness   Human decision makers judge the odds of an event by matching it with a preexisting category. An employee team may prejudge the work behavior of a new colleague, for example, by comparing him or her with similar other employees.

Anchoring and Adjustment   People tend to start a decision-making process by using a value from a similar process and then adjusting from that value.

Understanding Variation

Both individual and group decision-making processes can be improved if the decision makers increase their understanding of variation. If variation in the system is small, then a limited number of problems requiring decisions will be apparent. If variation is large, then many problems will surface. Some of these will be beyond the control of the decision maker.

Involvement of Customers

One promising way to improve the quality of decisions is to involve customers. Their presence reinforces the priority of customers as a prime strategy of the firm.

CRITICAL THINKING QUESTIONS

1. How do heuristics impact the group problem-solving task?

2. How can the involvement of customers help the decision-making task?

SUMMARY

Decisions are pervasive in organizational life. A decision is a choice made from at least two alternatives. Decision making is the process of identifying alternatives and choosing an alternative to solve a problem or address an opportunity. A problem is a situation lacking certainty.

The most common way to classify decisions is according to whether they are programmed decisions or nonprogrammed decisions. Programmed decisions are decisions that are routine and repetitive and that are associated with standardized decision rules. Nonprogrammed decisions are decisions that occur so infrequently that standardized decision rules are not available to solve them.

Bounded rationality is a recognition that the human mind can comprehend only a limited amount of information. Thus decision makers often satisfice: They choose the first decision alternative that meets minimal decision criteria. Such a satisficing decision is different from the optimal decision, in which the best possible alternative of all alternatives is chosen.

Most decisions are made under conditions of risk and uncertainty in which the outcome of the decision is not exactly predictable. Decision scope refers to the proportion of the organization affected by the decision. The scope of the decision and the riskiness of the decision vary as functions of organizational level. Top management is usually involved with nonprogrammed and uncertain decisions with broad decision scope. Middle management is usually involved with nonprogrammed and programmed decisions, risky and certain decisions, with intermediate decision scope. Lower management is usually involved with programmed and certain decisions with narrow decision scope.

Standard operating procedures and decision rules are established ways of making routine decisions. An expert system is a computerized decision-making aid to help decision makers decide with multiple pieces of information.

Nonroutine decisions are solved with a seven-step nonprogrammed decision-making process. The steps are: (1) define the problem and recognize the need, (2) diagnose and analyze causes, (3) develop alternatives, (4) evaluate alternatives, (5) select the best alternative, (6) implement the best alternative, and (7) monitor and evaluate the results.

There are some unresolved problems with rational decision making. It tends to ignore the concepts of causes of variation, continuous improvement, recycling, psychological biases, bounded rationality, organizational politics, and escalation of commitment.

Increasingly being used in organizations is group decision making, which allows cross-functional teams to flourish. Heuristics are rules of thumb that help individuals make decisions.

EXPERIENTIAL EXERCISES

Are Petty Thefts Permissible?

Assume that you have been the manager of a production plant for a few years. During that time employees have been involved in a number of petty thefts and minor shoplifting situations. You have allowed employees to take home small amounts of company products for their personal use. These products consist of batch overruns and leftovers with no commercial value. Recently the petty theft problem has mushroomed. Last night there was a major theft, with one or more persons stealing an expensive table saw.

Discussion Questions

1. What are you going to do about this theft of an expensive table saw?
2. How could this occurrence of a theft have been avoided?
3. What, if anything, will you do about the increasing number of petty thefts?

Source: Adapted from R. Fulmer, *Supervision: Principles of Professional Management,* Encino, CA: Glencoe (1976): 191.

Should We Keep Out Foreign Cars?

Opinion among both management and union leadership was sharply divided, but they all agreed on one point. They deplored the crippling impact that imported steel and steel products had on domestic production. Thousands of steelworkers had lost their jobs, and profit margins were sagging. Something had to be done. And whatever it was, it had to be aimed at the major cause of the problem—the imported automobile.

What should be done about it? It had been proposed at a major steel-producing plant that no imported cars be allowed inside the gates. Anyone arriving in a foreign car would be provided with transportation inside the plant. And that meant *anyone*: workers, executives, visitors, and delivery people.

Those sponsoring the motion claimed it was necessary because steelworkers and the steel industry had a significant interest in the success of American automobile companies. Those opposed contended that such an action was merely symbolic, and such symbolism was too expensive a price to pay for the curtailment of a personal freedom. Opponents also argued that it would lead to ill will at the plant between owners of domestic and imported cars. The issue went to a vote.

Discussion Questions

1. If you had a vote on this issue, how would you vote? Why?
2. It was assumed in the discussion that the major cause of the problem was the imported automobile. Is it possible that there were other causes? If so, what might they be?

Source: Adapted from V. Barry, *Moral Issues in Business,* 2nd ed., Belmont, CA: Wadsworth (1983): 218.

CHAPTER CASE

Acme Supply Company

Paul Conway was becoming somewhat of a legend at the Acme Supply Company. For the past two years he had attained the highest monthly sales volume of the 30-man salesforce. He consistently sold from 10 to 15 percent above the next highest salesman. As well as being the leading salesman, he was also looked upon by the rest of the salesforce as their "leader." He was known throughout the company as a "go-getter," "fast thinker," and, in the words of one of the other salesmen "could sell anything to anyone." In short, he was a born salesman.

Each salesman's job consisted of contacting customers in the field, selling them on the products, and maintaining and servicing the contract over a number of years. At the end of each day, the salesmen would phone in their orders to the order compiler. Each order, depending upon the number of products involved, had a normal "filling time" that was based on past experience and was well known by each salesman. The majority of the filling time was attributed to searching out the products in the stockroom, compiling each order, and moving it to a central disbursal point for distribution.

Other than "special rush orders," which usually involved large accounts that had to be delivered for special promotions, each order was filled and delivered within seven to ten days. The "special rush orders" required the individual attention of one of the stockroom men and could be filled and delivered within four to seven days. This special attention disrupted the overall coordination of search and compiling involved in filling the many daily orders, but it was acceptable for these special orders.

Paul was friendly with everyone in the company but was especially good friends with Mike Miller,

the order compiler who received the nightly phone orders. Paul had helped Mike obtain his job at Acme, and they lived in the same neighborhood. Paul also played golf each Saturday with Pete Talbot, the head of the warehouse stock department, and their wives were in the same bridge club.

Ron Taylor, one of the executive vice presidents of Acme, was visiting with Mike one evening at his office when Paul phoned in his orders. Three of the five orders were labeled "special rush." In talking with Mike, it became apparent that about half of Paul's orders were marked "rush." Later in the week, Ron was talking with Grant Pierson, one of Acme's better accounts. In the course of the conversation, Grant said, "I certainly like dealing with your man, Paul Conway. He always fills my orders in a minimum of time. That man knows how to deal with customers."

This situation bothered Ron, and he was wondering whether he should pursue the matter further.

Discussion Questions

1. Should Ron pursue the matter further? If so, to what extent? If not, why not?

2. What are Ron's responsibilities to reduce processing time? How well understood are customer requirements? What does continuous improvement mean in this organization?

3. Who needs training? What should be the nature of that training?

Source: A. F. Knapper, *Cases in Personnel Management,* Westerville, OH: Robin Enterprises (1977): 21–22.

KEY TERMS

bounded rationality Ability of decision makers to process only a limited amount of information.

complete certainty Condition in which the manager knows all the information relevant to a decision and the outcome of the decision is exactly predictable.

complete uncertainty Condition in which the manager has little information relevant to a decision and there is no way to predict the outcome of the decision.

decision Choice made from at least two alternatives.

decision making Process of identifying alternatives and choosing one of the alternatives to solve a problem or address an opportunity.

escalation of commitment Increase in commitment to a chosen course of action even though the ineffectiveness of that course of action has become obvious.

expert system Computerized decision-making aid to help decision makers decide with multiple pieces of information.

group decision making Decision-making process performed by more than one individual.

groupthink Process in which the group members are so concerned with group consensus that they are unwilling to evaluate options realistically and objectively.

heuristics Rules of thumb, or general cognitive strategies, used to simplify the decision-making process.

nonprogrammed decisions Decisions that occur so infrequently that standardized decision rules are not available to solve them.

opportunity Situation in the environment that may help the organization to reach or exceed its goals.

optimal decision Decision that is the best possible alternative of all alternatives.

organizational politics in decision making Activities that attempt to influence the outcomes of a decision.

problem Situation that could prevent the organization from reaching its goals.

programmed decisions Decisions that are routine and repetitive and are associated with standardized decision rules.

satisficing Choosing the first decision alternative that satisfies minimal decision criteria.

scope of the decision Proportion of the organization affected by the decision.

standard operating procedures (SOPs) and decision rules Established ways of making routine decisions.

ENDNOTES

1. G. Huber, *Managerial Decision Making,* Glenview, IL: Scott Foresman (1980).
2. W. E. Pounds, "The Process of Problem Finding," *Industrial Management Review* (Fall 1969): 1–19.
3. H. Mintzberg, "Patterns in Strategy Formation," *Management Science,* 24 (1978): 934–948.
4. M. J. Stahl, *Strategic Executive Decisions: An Analysis of the Difference Between Theory and Practice,* Westport, CT: Quorum Books (1989).
5. C. W. Holsapple, K. Tam, and A. B. Whinston, "Adapting Expert System Technology to Financial Management," *Financial Management* (Autumn 1988): 1–19.
6. A. Tversky and D. Kahneman, "The Belief in the 'Law of Numbers,'" *Psychological Bulletin* (1971): 105–110.
7. M. Bazerman, *Judgment in Managerial Decision Making,* New York: Wiley (1988).
8. H. Simon, "Making Management Decisions: The Role of Intuition and Emotion," *Academy of Management Executive* (February 1987): 57–63.
9. G. Miller, "The Magical Number Seven, Plus or Minus Two: Some Limits on Our Capacity for Processing Information," *Psychological Review* (1956): 81–97.
10. G. Whyte, "Groupthink Reconsidered," *Academy of Management Review* (1989): 40–56.
11. R. Cole, "Introduction, Special Issue on Total Quality Management," *California Management Review* (Spring 1993): 8.
12. A. Tversky and D. Kahneman, "Judgment Under Uncertainty: Heuristics and Biases," *Science* (1974): 1124–1131.

6
CHAPTER

Corporate and Competitive Strategy

LEARNING OBJECTIVES

After reading this chapter, you should be able to accomplish the following:

- Describe the importance of strategy to the manager.

- Elaborate on the idea that strategy is a pattern in a series of decisions.

- Discuss the concepts of strengths, weaknesses, opportunities, and threats in a SWOT analysis.

- Explain how mission, objectives, and strategies relate to each other in a strategic plan.

- Compare and contrast the impact of Total Quality on concentration and diversification strategies.

- Describe the difference and the similarity between corporate and business levels of strategy.

- Analyze an industry with Porter's Five Forces Model of Industry Competition.

- Discuss the importance of the six market-entry barriers.

- Compare and contrast the three generic competitive strategies.

- Explain the relationship of Total Quality to competitive strategy.

CHAPTER OUTLINE

The Nature of Strategic Management
  Strategy as a Series of Decisions
  Deliberate and Emergent Strategy
  Why the Need to Understand Strategy?
The Strategic Management Process
  Strategy Formulation
  Internal Strengths and Weaknesses
  External Opportunities and Threats
The Strategic Plan
  Mission-Objectives-Strategies
Total Quality and Corporate Strategies
  The Customer and Corporate Strategy
  *The Strength of Concentration and
    the Weakness of Diversification*
Business-Level Strategy
  Competing within the Chosen Industry
  Relationship to Corporate Strategies
Porter's Generic Competitive Strategies
  *Cost Leadership-Differentiation-
    Focus-"Stuck in the Middle"*
Porter's Five Forces Model
  Buyers and Bargaining Power
  Potential Entrants and Entry Barriers
  Suppliers and Bargaining Power
  Substitute Products and Services
  Competitors and Rivalry
  Plotting Competitive Groups
  Market Entry and Product Positioning
Total Quality and Competitive Strategy
  Competitors or Customers?
  Buyers or Customers?
  Suppliers or Partners?
  Cost Leadership
Cases and Exhibits
  Caterpillar and Komatsu
  Gender Differences
  Fast-Moving Bank
  Procter & Gamble
  Xerox
  Falls Church General Hospital

Caterpillar and Komatsu Compete Globally through Quality: Cat Concentrates and Komatsu Diversifies

By continuing to focus on meeting the requirements of its worldwide customers in heavy machinery, Caterpillar is beating its nearest competitor, Komatsu, which has decided to diversify. (Photo credit: Caterpillar, Inc.)

Caterpillar Inc. is the world's largest producer of earth-moving machinery. Its products include tractors, scrapers, graders, compactors, loaders, off-highway trucks, and pipe layers. Cat also makes diesel and turbine engines and lift trucks. Sales in 1994 were forecast to be $13.5 billion, 55 percent of them international sales. Cat's big yellow equipment is a symbol of U.S. industrial might and is found throughout the world.

Cat's fiercest global rival throughout the 1980s and 1990s has been Komatsu Ltd., of Tokyo. Komatsu's 1994 global construction equipment sales were forecast at $7.5 billion. Komatsu's rallying cry had been "Catch up to Caterpillar and surpass it."

It appeared for a while that Cat might lose. Komatsu had lower-cost labor in the 1980s. Cat's workforce was relatively more expensive in the 1980s.

In the mid-1980s Komatsu's U.S. market share was close to 15 percent. In 1988 Komatsu started a joint venture in the United States with Dresser Industries for manufacturing and distribution in Cat's backyard. The combined Komatsu-Dresser U.S. market share leaped to 20 percent. With Cat's U.S. market share in 1988 around 35 percent and holding, it appeared that Komatsu-Dresser might overtake Cat. In the face of such growing international competition, what was Cat to do?

A firm usually decides at the corporate level in which businesses it wishes to operate. Then it decides how to enter the chosen business. These decisions are in the realm of corporate-level strategy. The firm's executives must then decide how to compete in the chosen business. Decisions in this area form what is known as competitive-level strategy. These two levels of strategy and the impact of Total Quality Management on strategy are the subjects of this chapter.[1]

THE NATURE OF STRATEGIC MANAGEMENT

Strategic management consists of managerial decisions that relate the organization to its environment, guide internal activities, and determine long-term organizational performance. Such decisions are important because they are the precursors of many other managerial activities.

Strategy as a Series of Decisions

Henry Mintzberg, a noted management theorist, described strategy as a pattern in a stream of decisions.[2] He portrayed this idea by describing the patterns in the many decisions made at Volkswagenwerk over a 54-year period. From those decisions and the patterns they formed, the company's strategy of low-priced transportation may be spotted throughout the years that the Volkswagen was marketed throughout the world.

Mintzberg's idea that strategy is a pattern in a stream of decisions has two important implications. First, strategy is not necessarily apparent from the analysis of a single decision. To understand strategy fully, it must be viewed in the context of several decisions and the consistency among those decisions.[3] Second, the organization must be aware of decision alternatives in all of its decisions. Strategy may be viewed as the logic that governs the firm's choices from among all its decision options.

For example, a tobacco company, faced with long-term declining sales of tobacco products, might diversify into the consumer foods industry. In its diversification decisions it may opt for branded consumer foods wherein the tobacco company can continue to use its advertising and marketing expertise. This is the example of R. J. Reynolds Industries' acquisition of Nabisco in 1987 to become the giant consumer goods company RJR-Nabisco.[4] A product differentiation strategy of branded consumer products emerges as a pattern from these decisions. **Product differentiation** refers to a product that will be perceived by the customer as different or somehow unique. Thus strategy defines the firm's business as a response to its environment.

This chapter was influenced by F. Karakaya and M. J. Stahl, *Market Entry and Exit Barriers*, Westport, CT: Quorum Books (1991); M. E. Porter, *Competitive Strategy and Competitive Advantage*, New York: Free Press (1980 and 1985); M. J. Stahl and G. M. Bounds, *Competing Globally Through Customer Value: The Management of Strategic Suprasystems*, Westport, CT: Quorum Books (1991); and M. J. Stahl and D. W. Grigsby, *Strategic Management for Decision Making*, Boston: PWS-Kent (1991).

D I V E R S I T Y   E X H I B I T

Gender Differences in a Multinational Organization

You are a group of consultants and have been invited to advise an employee of an organization (multinational) on a problem that she has. Here is what she says to you:

"I feel myself to be more competent and more dynamic than my boss, who is quiet, reserved, and a rather political manager. My own style of open confrontation on issues works well for me but it has led my supervisor to downgrade me on appraisals of my work relationships. I have let him know that I disagree with his evaluation in this area, and that I feel that the style which he views as a handicap is actually one of my best assets. I am now getting the feeling that I'm hurting my career by being faced with this confrontation. What can I do?"

Discussion Questions

1. Prepare a set of concrete recommendations for the manager, and another set for the employee.

2. Present at least one other illustration of the kinds of confrontations people experience because of their different value orientations.

Source: P. Casse, *Training for the Multicultural Manager*, Washington, DC: Society for Intercultural Education, Training and Research (1982): 159.

Deliberate and Emergent Strategy

Is strategy always a purposeful process? Is strategy always the outcome of a planned effort toward goals that results in a pattern in a series of decisions? Might strategy also be the result of managers simply "muddling through" without an explicit plan? The cumulative effect of making small decisions regularly can result in a pattern in the stream of decisions.

Mintzberg contrasted *deliberate strategy* with *emergent strategy*.[5] Deliberate strategy had been viewed as a result of the strategic-planning process. **Deliberate strategy** is a strategy in which a firm decides on its goals and implements intended strategy to realize the goals. This view of strategy as a deliberate process ignores several possibilities.[6] Sometimes a firm may not intentionally set strategy. Its strategy may emerge from the lower levels of the organization as a result of its daily activities. Such emergent strategies might also be the result of the implementation process. Alterations in goals based on feedback during implementation may produce strategies that vary from their original design. **Emergent strategies** are those strategies actually in place in the organization. Strategies become apparent from a number of decisions, as noted in the performance appraisal decisions in the diversity exhibit.

Why the Need to Understand Strategy?

Why do managers throughout the organization need to understand strategy? Is not strategy the province of the most senior executives in the firm?

In an earlier, more stable era with very few international competitors, executives were soley responsible for strategy. Today managers throughout the organization should be involved in strategy formulation and implementation for several reasons.[7]

Most importantly, due to the rebuilding of other nations' industries after World War II and the elimination of many trade barriers, international competition has become feverish, as we saw in Chapter 3. Before the 1970s the United States had few significant international industrial competitors. In that period American firms could stay in markets for a long time with benign domestic competition. Today rapid change is the name of the game. Such change mandates that managers understand the forces requiring strategic change. With that understanding they can help formulate new strategic plans and implement the new strategies.

As ever-increasing numbers of U.S. firms become serious about Total Quality, managers at all levels need to understand the strategic and operational changes associated with TQ. Lower-level managers will become heavily involved with training and implementation of quality issues. In some firms these managers will be empowered to deal with customers and with managers in other areas. Managers must understand the corporation's strategy so that they can explain the strategy to others and elicit their support.

As the pace of technological change accelerates, the strategy, products, customers, and markets of many firms change at a quickening rate. To help shape and implement the new strategies and managerial processes, managers need to understand the technological and economic forces at work.

CRITICAL THINKING QUESTIONS

1. Why is strategy important for the manager? Should managers leave strategy to top-level executives? How have changes in quality and technology impacted the importance of strategy for managers?

2. Compare and contrast the view that strategy is a pattern in a series of decisions with the view that strategy can be found in the firm's latest annual report.

THE STRATEGIC MANAGEMENT PROCESS

Three major steps in the strategic management process are (1) strategy formulation, (2) implementation, and (3) evaluation and control. In working through these steps, firms analyze internal strengths and weaknesses as well as external opportunities and threats.

Strategy Formulation, Implementation, and Evaluation and Control

As depicted in Figure 6.1, the strategic management process involves decisions ranging from planning the strategy through control of operations. There are at least three steps in the process. **Strategy formulation** is decision making that determines the organization's mission and establishes its objectives and strategies. Some refer to strategy formulation as planning. **Strategy implementation** consists of the

FIGURE 6.1   *The Strategic Management Process*

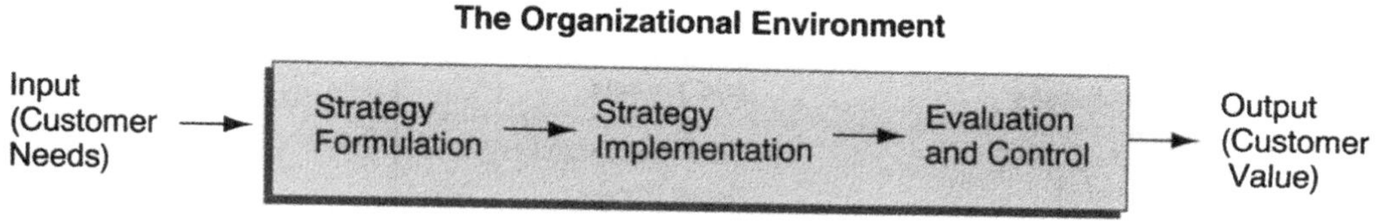

The Organizational Environment

Input
(Customer → | Strategy → Strategy → Evaluation | → Output
Needs) | Formulation Implementation and Control | (Customer
                                                            Value)

activities and decisions that are intended to carry out new strategies or support existing strategies. Some refer to strategy implementation as operational management.
Evaluation and control involve the activities and decisions that keep the process
on track. Evaluation and control include following up on goal accomplishment and
feeding back the results to decision makers.

When planning strategy, managers must analyze conditions in the internal environment of the organization *and* conditions in the external environment. This
analysis of internal *strengths* and *weaknesses* and external *opportunities* and *threats*
is so pervasive in strategic planning that it has its own acronym: **SWOT analysis**.

Internal Strengths and Weaknesses

Conditions internal to the organization are called internal strengths and weaknesses.
A **strength** is a condition or issue internal to the organization that may lead to a
customer benefit or a competitive advantage. Alternatively, a **weakness** is a condition or issue internal to the organization that may lead to negative customer value or
a competitive disadvantage. Most of these internal strengths and weaknesses are the
result of prior management decisions.[8] Table 6.1 shows the primary internal and
external conditions or issues examined in a SWOT analysis.

Horizontal systems and processes, a flat organizational structure, and a cus-
tomer-oriented corporate culture are obvious internal strengths. These strengths
are common to many firms that are serious about Total Quality Management and
about providing superior value to customers as a way to compete globally. These
strengths can be contrasted to bureaucratically oriented organizations with tall,
narrow organizational structures, many levels of non-value-added management,
and rigid job descriptions. These features discourage people from solving problems
or improving systems outside their immediate jobs. How often is the cry of "That's
not my job" an excuse for not satisfying the customer?

Competent, experienced, flexible managers are a definite asset. Managers who
understand customers and competitors and who are dedicated to continuous
improvement, information sharing, and involvement in planning and implementing
change are an indispensable asset.[9]

Strong finances can facilitate most decisions that management wishes to implement. Alternatively, a weak financial position with questionable debt levels weak-
ens and constrains any organization. A weak financial position can prohibit a firm
from responding to external opportunities and makes the firm more susceptible to
external threats.

TABLE 6.1   *Primary SWOT Analysis Issues*

Internal Strengths and Weaknesses	External Opportunities and Threats
Horizontal systems and processes	Customer value trends
	Social trends
Organizational structure	Demographic trends
Corporate culture	Economic trends
Management	Technological trends
Financial position	Regulatory trends
Operations	Physical trends
Marketing	Competitive trends
Human resources	
Research and development	

Source: Adapted from M. J. Stahl and D. W. Grigsby, *Strategic Management for Decision Making*, Boston: PWS-Kent (1991): 29.

In the early 1990s Trans World Airlines (TWA) was struggling for its very survival with high debt levels and mounting losses. Because of its weak financial position, it had sold some of its more lucrative international routes to raise cash. Selling the crown jewels left TWA in a weakened position to compete in the future.[10] In contrast, financially stronger Delta Airlines, American Airlines, and United Airlines were buying aircraft and lucrative, growing international routes from ailing airlines. Such purchases made those three airlines even stronger and more capable of serving customers and competing in the future.

Strengths in production/operations and in marketing are usually the internal strengths that brought an organization to its current strong position. Some examples of strengths in production/operations are systems capable of producing quality products and services, modern plant and equipment, flexible manufacturing systems, and state-of-the-art technology. Examples of strengths in marketing are a strong distribution system, products or services in demand by customers, competitive prices, and effective advertising. Some of Caterpillar's strengths in production and marketing are described in this chapter's quality case.

Some examples of strengths in human resources are the energy and training of the firm's human resources. The potential of trained human resources is not realized if work rules are restrictive, as General Motors learned in the 1970s. GM expended much effort in the 1980s and 1990s pursuing looser work rules to improve the productivity and the quality of its operations. In deciding on which plants to close as part of a restructuring in 1992, one GM plant was kept open and another GM plant was closed in part because of the looser work rules and higher quality at the plant kept open.[11] Many Total Quality firms today are investing 5 percent to 8 percent of their payroll in employee training. These are numbers unheard of a few years ago.

Q U A L I T Y   E X H I B I T

The Fast-Moving Bank

The marketing strategy of a certain bank was to develop and promote quick-response capabilities. This was done by flattening the structure required to make decisions.

The bank learned that its 24-hour time to process car loans was twice as quick as the competition. Instead of resting on its laurels, the bank changed its procedures to speed up on all kinds of banking; for example, it pushed loan approvals down to a low organizational level.

The natural next step was to market itself as "the fast-moving bank." One ad said: "Time is money. People shouldn't hold up banks, and banks shouldn't hold up people either."

By being first with the strategy, the "fast-moving bank" prevented other banks from copying its advertising strategy. However, the competitors were not too late to gain the other advantages of a flatter structure and quick response—lower costs, simpler systems, and better quality.

Source: R. J. Schonberger, *Building a Chain of Customers: Linking Business Functions to Create the World Class Company*, New York: Free Press (1990): 20; A. Ries and J. Trout, *Bottom-Up Marketing*, New York: McGraw-Hill (1989): 128–129.

Training in horizontal systems and processes is usually part of the training to increase quality and productivity, as the Capsugel division of the pharmaceutical firm Warner-Lambert discovered.[12] **Horizontal systems and processes** are flows of work and activities that span such vertical functions as purchasing, design, production, and marketing. Capsugel used such training so that its personnel would think horizontally in accord with the way value was created for its customers.

Computerized information systems can be a strength in providing products and services to the firm's customers. For some firms strong information systems can provide value directly to customers. American Airlines' Sabre reservation system allows travel agents to book reservations quickly for their customers.[13]

A research and development program that continually turns out new and valuable products is an internal strength that can pay dividends for years into the future. As new-product development cycle times shorten and as customers demand new technologies and new products *now*, R&D will receive increasing attention.[14] Merck has a very productive R&D program with many new pharmaceutical products in the R&D pipeline. This R&D strength helped Merck top the list of *Fortune*'s most admired companies for every year from 1987 through 1993.[15]

Internal strengths and weaknesses are inside the organization and under the influence of managers. Therefore it is assumed that the weaknesses can be changed. External threats can be more trying than the internal conditions, since external threats are not under the control of the firm's managers.

External Opportunities and Threats

An **opportunity** is an issue or condition in the environment external to the firm that may help it reach its goals. A **threat** is an issue or condition in the external

As Eastern Airlines discovered, any organization can go bankrupt if its costs are too high and its employees and management are adversaries. (Photo credit: A/P Wide World Photos.)

environment that may prevent the firm from reaching its goals. Very strong external opportunities or threats may even cause the firm to modify its goals and strategies.

Although opportunities and threats in the external environment are not under the direct control of the firm's managers, they must be responded to if the firm wishes to remain healthy and grow. Analyzing the external environment is labeled as **environmental scanning**.[16] High organizational performance is associated with the frequency and breadth of environmental scanning.[17]

The trends listed in Table 6.1 as external opportunities and threats may be opportunities or they may be threats, depending on the nature of the trend. Unlike the issues listed as internal strengths and weaknesses, external trends are not under the control of management. With adequate strategic planning, however, management can anticipate and respond to these external trends.

Managers must understand and even anticipate customer-value trends, since these trends can affect the products or services demanded and the way the firm operates. A good example of customer-value trends affecting the way a firm operates is the switch to "no-dicker sticker" pricing in the automobile industry in the early 1990s. Sales usually double about the first month or so, then stabilize into a pace 20 percent to 50 percent ahead of sales before the switch. No-dicker dealers slash expenses, mainly by cutting employees. Advertising expenses can also be cut because satisfied customers advertise widely by word of mouth.[18] Understanding value and delivering it to customers is so central to the essence of management that we shall devote all of Chapter 7 to the subject.

Social and demographic trends usually bring slowly developing, yet long-lasting change to organizations. For example, the shift to dual-career couples in the United States took many years to develop. Now that the trend is in place, it will be a long time (if ever) before this country returns to only one family member working. The dual-career couple has been associated with the popularity of disposable diapers and other labor-saving products and services. Now that the demand is established, the call for such products and services should stay strong for some time.

To recognize the changes in the economic environment, organizations spend considerable time and money on economic forecasts. Forecasts concerning recessions, expansions, inflation, international exchange rates, and other economic phenomena aid managers as they plan strategic moves.[19]

Firms also spend considerable amounts of time, money, and personnel on technological forecasting. The effects of technology and technological change on the firm, its customers, and its competitors are so important that they are analyzed in detail in a separate chapter (Chapter 17).

Changes in government regulation can have an extreme impact, because the rules of conducting business are sometimes changed abruptly through legislation. Managers usually pay close attention to potential regulatory changes. Managers frequently join industry associations to monitor potential changes and to influence the nature of the regulation.

Changes in the physical environment, such as acid rain and global warming, usually occur at a slow rate. Therefore the trends are easier to counter with a strategic plan.

Changes in competition, such as the entry of a new competitor, can be a dramatic threat. Extensive changes due to competitive threats underscore the importance of competitive strategy and competitor analysis. Being the first to market with a new product or service is a way to preempt competitors, as noted in the quality exhibit on page 151.

CRITICAL THINKING QUESTIONS

1. How are the three major steps in the strategic management process of strategy formulation, implementation, evaluation and control linked to each other?

2. As the pace of change in business quickens in the 1990s due to international competition, discuss the importance of a SWOT analysis. How frequently should a SWOT analysis be done in a changing environment?

THE STRATEGIC PLAN

After the SWOT analysis has been performed with the study of the firm's strengths, weaknesses, opportunities, and threats, then managers are able to formulate the strategic plan. The **strategic plan** is a plan which includes steps that the organization intends to take to achieve its mission, objectives, and strategies.

The strategic plan should be formulated to capitalize on external opportunities and internal strengths, and to work around external threats and internal weaknesses. Grow-and-invest situations are those in which firms can capitalize on external opportunities with internal strengths. Shrinkage or withdrawal situations are those in which firms have significant internal weaknesses or external threats that they cannot overcome.

Mission

A **mission statement** describes the business(es) the firm is in. The mission indicates why the organization exists.[20] Since it refers to the whole enterprise, there is only one mission statement per enterprise.

The mission should be written from the perspective of the customers rather than from that of the stockholders or any other group. The customer perspective, or attention to customer value, is a primary characteristic of Total Quality Management.[21]

Mission statements usually describe the firm's chief products or services, the customers or market served, the customer value provided, and the firm's activities. An example of a mission statement, printed in Eli Lilly's annual report, is as follows: "Eli Lilly and Company is a global research-based corporation that develops, manufactures, and markets pharmaceuticals, medical instruments and diagnostic products, and animal health products. The company markets its products in 110 countries around the world."[22] Understanding what the firm's customers require in 110 countries is a primary function of Lilly's management.

Objectives

After the *why* of the business has been defined, it is appropriate to describe the *what*. **Objectives** or **goals** are the kinds of results the firm seeks to achieve. Corporate objectives or goals refer to results targeted for the entire corporation. Goals can also exist at the business level, at a functional-area level like marketing, and at lower levels in the organization.

Objectives should be specific, measurable, time phased, and realistic. The realistic characteristic explains why objectives are considered *after* the mission statement has been prepared. The mission statement broadly determines what is achievable and desirable. For example, a 30 percent rate of growth in sales may be realistic in a rapidly growing biotechnology company. Such an objective is not realistic, however, in Caterpillar Inc. for sales of earth-moving equipment. Increasing attention is being paid to market share and sales growth objectives, as these goals show relative changes in value realized by customers. Many firms are concentrating on providing customer value in the 1990s as a competitive mandate and as an integral part of Total Quality.[23]

One year or less refers to a short-term objective, and five years or more refer to a long-term objective. The time between refers to a medium-term objective. Table 6.2 contains several examples of short- and long-term objectives.

There are three themes that may be found in objectives: (1) growth, (2) stability, and (3) restructuring. In a *growth* theme the firm attempts to grow and expand through significantly increased sales. Many firms in the biotechnology and computer software industry pursue growth, for example. Stability is pursued by firms in mature industries that do not expect significant growth, such as the aluminum industry. **Restructuring** consists of a series of actions aimed at downsizing or cutting back the scope of the firm. Firms in shrinking industries like the steel industry for example, have restructured in recent years.

TABLE 6.2   *Examples of Short- and Long-Term Objectives*

Objective	Measure	Short Term: 6 Months	Long Term: 5 Years
Customer satisfaction	Percent satisfied	60%	95%
Market share	Percentage	10%	15%
Growth	Dollar sales (millions)	$8	$12
Profitability	Return on assets	12%	16%
Stockholder value	Earnings per share	$1.40	$1.90

Strategies

After the objectives have been determined, the managers can decide how to achieve them. *Strategy* refers to *how* the organization will attain its objectives. The choice of strategy is so central to the understanding of strategic management that we devote the remainder of this chapter to corporate and competitive strategies and the entire next chapter to Total Quality and customer-value strategy.

CRITICAL THINKING QUESTIONS

1. How do mission, objectives, and strategies relate to each other in a strategic plan? Why is there a necessary order among the three?

2. Is the deliberate formulation of mission, objectives, and strategies more or less important in a rapidly changing, internationally competitive marketplace with demanding customers? Explain.

TOTAL QUALITY AND CORPORATE STRATEGIES

What is the implication of TQM for corporate strategy? Does the era of international competition in which customers have many choices of vendors have any implications for decisions concerning corporate strategy? The quality criteria for the Baldrige Award specifically rate strategic quality planning—including (1) strategic quality and company performance planning process and (2) quality and performance plans—in the award evaluation.

The Customer and Corporate Strategy

Before the advent of intense global competition, many managers chose corporate strategies with little regard for customer value. Many strategy models were based on complex financial calculations, with shareholder return a primary criterion.

QUALITY CASE

Back to the Cat–Komatsu Case

Instead of retreating in the face of fierce Japanese competition, Caterpillar has fought back hard on at least three fronts. First, Cat has made a dramatic investment in and commitment to quality. Its Plant-With-A-Future (PWAF) idea includes Total Quality Control (TQC), Computer-Integrated Manufacturing (CIM), and Just-In-Time (JIT) production. Conceptually, "PWAF is a purely customer-driven manufacturing philosophy." CIM uses computers throughout the manufacturing process for scheduling, machine control, and inventory tracking. JIT schedules the delivery of parts as they are needed rather than hold them in inventory, thereby helping to spot quality problems as they occur. Part of Cat's commitment to quality includes educating its suppliers in quality-improvement methods at the Caterpillar Quality Institute.

Second, Cat has kept a lid on its costs so that Komatsu does not achieve a substantial competitive cost advantage. This global competition has highlighted Cat's higher labor costs. To keep labor costs in line, Cat suffered a bitter, highly visible strike in 1992 by the United Auto Workers that was resolved only after Cat threatened to hire permanent replacements. Cat also kept its supplier costs low by educating its suppliers to use quality techniques as a way to reduce the cost of manufacturing.

Third, Cat has kept its dealer network strong to provide service to its customers. In 1992 Cat estimated that its 65 full-line U.S. dealers had a net worth of $1.72 billion, versus Komatsu-Dresser's net worth of $300 million for its 60 U.S. and Canadian dealers. Like many other firms serious about Total Quality, Cat recognized the importance of suppliers and dealers as part of Cat's system to provide value to the customer. Providing value to its customers was a large part of Cat's competitive strategy.

Today lower trade barriers and deregulated global commerce mark a new, internationally competitive era. Customers can now vote with their money, choosing from among competing international firms which provide the best value. This globally competitive environment forces managers to determine strategy with a customer focus. There are certain corporate strategies that will flourish in such a competitive, customer-focused environment.

The Strength of Concentration and the Weakness of Diversification

Understanding customers and their needs in narrowly defined markets is a formidable challenge. Market-share battles in such narrowly defined markets as airlines, automobiles, beer, motorcycles, and earth-moving equipment reveal how hard it is to provide superior value to customers in a single industry.

It is virtually impossible for managers in a widely diversified firm like LTV to provide superior value to customers in each of the different markets. Focused global competitors in one market will not stand still while diversified managers are tending to several other markets and other customers.

It is forecast, therefore, that concentration or related diversification will be the corporate strategies of choice in an era of global competition and TQM. **Concentration** focuses on a single product or market. **Related diversification** focuses on a few related products or markets. It is no accident that America's ten "most admired" corporations that have consistently shown up in *Fortune* magazine in the early mid-1990s are firms pursuing either concentration or related diversification. Firms like Merck, Rubbermaid, Wal-Mart, Liz Claiborne, Levi Strauss, Johnson & Johnson, Coca-Cola, 3M, Pepsico, and P&G repeatedly appear in the annual listing. These firms concentrate on certain products and markets.

In contrast, it is forecast that conglomerate diversification will decline in importance in an era of global competition and demanding customers. **Conglomerate diversification** is concerned with operations in unrelated markets or unrelated products.

CRITICAL THINKING QUESTIONS

1. How will international competition cause the customer to grow in importance in strategic planning in the 1990s?

2. Describe the impact of Total Quality on concentration and diversification strategies in the 1990s.

Over many years, Procter & Gamble has concentrated on consumer products. If it wishes to maintain its presence in that industry, it is important for P&G to maintain its consumers' confidence that it will do nothing to harm them. When faced with a controversial product, it is in P&G's enlightened self-interest to act vigorously, as the following ethics exhibit demonstrates.

BUSINESS-LEVEL STRATEGY

This section examines an important question relating to business-level strategy: How should the firm compete in its chosen business?

Competing within the Chosen Industry

Increasingly, strategy at the business level has been receiving attention in many U.S. companies because of the white-hot global competition described in Chapter 3. Prior to the onset of that global competition, many managers thought that it was not necessary to pay attention to competitive strategy. They thought that strategy was the province of the most senior executives in the firm. The speed of global competitors' moves has changed such thinking. Now managers throughout the firm must think in terms of the competition and competitors' moves relative to the firm's customers.

Although competitive strategy is not without its drawbacks, it does help the manager to think in terms external to the firm. Competitive strategy provides a framework for the manager to think about external issues, particularly competitive moves.

Even if the firm has operated in its industry for some time, its executives must address the question of how to compete. With the exception of monopolies, all

E T H I C S   E X H I B I T

Procter & Gamble Rely Case

Although doctors say they are now increasingly convinced that toxic shock syndrome (TSS) has been present for decades, P&G first became aware of it in June 1980, when the Center for Disease Control (CDC) in Atlanta contacted P&G and other major tampon manufacturers and requested data concerning tampon usage. At that time, there were no data to suggest a link between TSS and the usage of tampons.

Although the CDC's June study did not link any specific tampon to the occurrence of the disease, studies done by the state health departments of Wisconsin and Minnesota showed a statistical link to P&G's Rely brand tampons. In June, when P&G was notified of a possible problem with its product, it began to collect information about toxic shock and tampon usage, in general, and Rely, in particular. During July and August P&G's reaction was to begin laboratory testing with the suspected bacteria and to assemble a panel of scientific experts. P&G's microbiologists tested the suspected bacteria on Rely, and the results seemed to indicate that the material in Rely did not encourage the growth of the bacteria.

On September 15 the CDC announced the results of a study of cases of TSS sufferers in July and August. In the sample of 42 women, 71 percent had used the Rely tampon. The results of this study prompted the scheduling of a meeting between P&G, the Food and Drug Administration (FDA), and CDC officials.

The results of the CDC's second study put P&G on the defensive. In an attempt to retain a product for which it had spent more than 20 years' research and $74 million, P&G announced in a news release that the company had examined a summary of the CDC's data and believed the information too limited and fragmentary for any conclusions to be drawn. Edward G. Harness, chairman and chief executive of P&G, recalls he was "determined to fight for a brand, to keep an important brand from being hurt by insufficient data in the hands of a bureaucracy."

When the P&G representatives met face to face on September 16 with FDA and CDC officials, P&G arrived with a number of questions concerning the CDC study. But P&G also arrived

continued

companies compete by virtue of their daily operations. Therefore they have a de facto competitive strategy. If they do not understand the competitive forces shaping their industry and respond with an explicit competitive strategy, then they leave their success to chance.

Relationship to Corporate Strategies

As described earlier, corporate-level strategy is a choice of business in which to operate. Competitive business-level strategy is a choice of how the firm competes in the chosen business(es). Now we shall examine the relationship between these two choices.

The strategic-planning process and the SWOT analysis discussed earlier argue for consistency in the strategic plan if the plan is to be implementable and successful. A major difference between successful and failed acquisitions has been shown to be the consistency between the corporate and competitive levels of strategy.[24] If a company has developed expertise in one competitive strategy at the business level, then it should enter future businesses in which that same competitive strategy is important.

with a proposed warning label they were willing to put on its packages. The meeting ended with the FDA allowing P&G one week to study the CDC's findings and respond.

By September 18 P&G had halted production of the Rely tampon, perhaps because of the uncertainty about the necessity of a warning label, perhaps under the deluge of negative publicity. P&G's previously recruited group of experts was unable to positively refute the latest studies. "That was the turning point," Harness said. "I knew Sunday night what we had to do. We didn't know enough about toxic shock to act, and yet we knew too much not to act." Consequently, P&G announced on September 22 its voluntary suspension of sale of its product.

On September 23 the FDA and P&G began the drafting of a consent agreement. P&G had already started pulling back some 400,000 cases of Rely by this time. Under the agreement P&G denied any violation of federal law or any product defect, but agreed to buy back any unused product the customer still had, including P&G's $10 million introductory promotion free samples. It also pledged its research expertise to the CDC to investigate TSS, and agreed to finance and direct a large educational program about the disease, as well as issue a

warning to women not to use Rely. According to Chairman Harness, "This is being done despite the fact that we know of no defect in Rely tampons and despite evidence that the withdrawal of Rely won't eliminate the occurrence of TSS." As a result of the consent decree worked out between P&G and the FDA, P&G launched a broad educational campaign to inform women about TSS, the link between this disease and tampons, and the greater statistical link with the Rely brand. It also informed consumers about the voluntary withdrawal of Rely and the details of the refund offer.

Discussion Questions

1. As a result of its Rely experience, P&G withdrew from the tampon business. Compare and contrast P&G's actions with Ford's actions in the Pinto case in Chapter 17.
2. Relate P&G's decision to withdraw from the tampon business to its strategy of concentration in the consumer products industry.

Source: Archie B. Carroll and Elizabeth Gatewood, *Proceedings: Academy of Management 41st Conference*, 1981. Reprinted in M. W. Hoffman and J. M. Moore, *Business Ethics: Readings and Cases in Corporate Morality*, 2/e, McGraw-Hill, 1990, 394–396.

For example, if a firm in the consumer products industry is skilled at competing through advertising its branded products, that firm should stick to such a competitive strategy. The firm probably does not have the skill to compete in a business requiring the achievement of low cost through large capital-intensive plants for standardized products. Therefore the firm should enter and compete in only those businesses in which it can compete on the basis of the advertising of branded products.

Expertise in a particular competitive business-level strategy helps to determine the kinds of other businesses to enter. Thus competitive business-level strategy influences corporate-level strategy. This link stresses the corporate-level strategies of concentration or related diversification.

The sustainability of competence in a type of competition must be considered.[25] Sustained competitive advantage is likely if the company is committed to a particular kind of competitive strategy throughout its operations.[26]

An example of a firm having a sustained competitive advantage owing to a particular strategy is Compaq Computer. Compaq wrote the book on how to compete by offering low-priced personal computer clones to IBM computers. However, a year later, Compaq lost its competitive strategy and market share, and fired its president, Rod Canion. In 1991 Compaq was no longer the low-price leader and was no longer profitable. In the first half of 1992 it rediscovered its low-price strategy and set the computer industry ablaze with a PC price war that was to enable the company to regain market share. Its low-price strategy was so successful that Compaq had difficulty satisfying the demand for its low-priced computers.[27]

CRITICAL THINKING QUESTIONS

1. Compare and contrast corporate and competitive levels of strategy.

2. How does competitive strategy influence acquisitions?

PORTER'S GENERIC COMPETITIVE STRATEGIES

Michael Porter has been the most influential writer in the area of competitive strategy. He has described three separate generic strategies applicable in a variety of industries: cost leadership, differentiation, and focus.[28]

Cost Leadership

Cost leadership is having the lowest cost of operation in the industry. Cost leadership, not price leadership, is the generic strategy. A firm could be the lowest-cost producer yet not offer the lowest-priced products or services. That firm would enjoy profitability above the average in the industry. However, cost leaders often do compete on price, and with their low cost structures they are very effective at this form of competition.

Cost leadership is not easy to attain. There must be an organization-wide commitment to achieving a low-cost structure without ignoring quality and other demands of the customer. Cost leadership is pursued through low cost of quality, workforce productivity, economies of scale, experience, low wages, buyer bargaining power, and the like. **Economies of scale** refer to the use of large amounts of physical assets to lower the unit production cost.

A good example of cost leadership through economy of scale in the beer industry is Anheuser-Busch, which builds immense breweries with large productive capacity. This procedure spreads fixed costs over large quantities of production. Due to Anheuser-Busch's economies of scale in water processing, refrigeration, and packaging, its unit cost of production is lower than that of competitors with smaller plants.

Wal-Mart is the cost leader in the discount retail market. Like most cost leaders, it has achieved this cost leadership position through a variety of means. Wal-Mart uses buyer bargaining power from large-volume purchases. The firm has a very efficient, computer-intensive distribution system linked to some of its major suppliers. Wal-Mart makes use of economies of scale with extremely large, strategically located distribution centers, and its pays careful attention to store location. Wal-Mart is also the price leader in its industry. For all of these reasons, it was beating the competition in the 1990s.

By maintaining or reducing prices on a broad variety of goods, Wal-Mart provides greater value to its customers and strengthens its reputation for having everyday low prices. (Photo credit: Wal-Mart.)

There is a risk in seeking cost leadership through economies of scale and large capital investments. If demand for the product declines dramatically within a short time period, the large capital investment could be jeopardized. Dramatic declines in demand within a short time period are often due to a substitution effect. For example, in the 1980s, due to a fashion fad in which it was stylish to wear denim in several different ways, demand for denim skyrocketed. Whereas denim had been used primarily to make jeans for younger people and for work clothes, denim was suddenly popular for the additional uses of jeans for men and women of a variety of ages, and for skirts, jackets, and coats. An automobile manufacturer even upholstered in denim the interior of a special-edition automobile. Consequently, the textile industry expanded productive capacity to meet the demand created by the denim fashion fad. When the fad waned, demand for denim fell. Several large denim-producing plants with significant capital investment were obsolete.

Differentiation

As a competitive strategy, **differentiation** is supplying a product or service that will be perceived by the customer as different or somehow unique. A firm can achieve differentiation for its products or services in a number of different ways. It could build a brand image through extensive advertising. It might design extra features into the product or service to make it different from competing products or services. It could provide extra customer service with the product or service. It could operate an extensive dealer network for repair and distribution. It could attempt to ensure its marketplace perception as a distributor of only very high-quality items. It could offer a continuous stream of new products or services and be known as an innovator. Or, finally, it might be the first to market with new products or new services.

Differentiating firms assume that customers will pay extra for an item if they perceive that it is different. Such firms also assume that the nature of the difference is valued by the customer. However, there is a limit to how much of a premium customers will pay for a differentiated product or service.

Advertising frequently plays a large role in differentiation strategies, because customers must be convinced that there is something different about the product or service. For example, Merrill Lynch spends millions of dollars advertising on television. The ads try to convince us that Merrill Lynch has insight into financial investments that few others have.

Differentiating firms typically employ substantial consumer research efforts to identify changing consumer tastes. With such data the firms can be the first to market with a new and differentiated product. IBM and P&G are two examples of differentiators using large consumer research efforts. Additionally, both firms advertise heavily to persuade customers that their products or services meet the customers' tastes.

Federal Express is a good example of a firm employing a differentiation strategy. It boasts superior service, including guaranteed delivery next day, tracking of the package's location, and security of the package. Lands' End and L. L. Bean both provide superior service through quick delivery, a variety of sizes, stylish clothing, very high-quality merchandise, and no-hassle returns.

Caterpillar differentiates itself with a broad list of quality machines and an extensive dealer network for parts and repair. "Cats" usually do not break, but if they do, their owners know that they can get them fixed quickly. Throughout the world many construction firms willingly pay a price for such a supply and repair service. For them, the alternative is the high cost of a delayed construction project due to broken, idle construction equipment.

Focus

Focus is concentration on serving a particular target group, segment, or market niche. The focusing firm attends closely to the needs of the target segment, even more closely than does the cost leader or differentiator. Focus refers to the narrowness of the market served, or market niche, rather than the characteristics of the product or service.

When concentrating on the market niche, cost focus or differentiation focus are two alternatives. In **cost focus** the focusing firm offers a product or service to a market segment at a lower price than that of competitors. In **differentiation focus** the focusing firm offers to a market segment a product or service that is more differentiated than all competitors' comparable products or services.

A good example of differentiation focus is a Ferrari automobile. That sports car, with its meticulous attention to performance and image and with its extremely high price, is targeted at a very narrow market segment. Revco's senior citizen discounts on prescription drugs is an example of cost focus.

INTERNATIONAL EXHIBIT

Quality, International Competition, and the Customer at Xerox

In 1960 Xerox shipped its first copiers. Over the next 15 years it ruled an entire new industry that it had invented.

After 15 years of absolute industry dominance, Xerox became complacent and out of touch with its customers. In the late 1970s the company produced unacceptable-quality products and services at high prices. As a consequence Xerox lost dramatic market share to Japanese competitors like Canon, Minolta, and Sharp. Its market share tumbled from more than 90 percent in the early 1970s to less than 15 percent in the early 1980s. The butt of many office jokes became the phrase: "Copier temporarily *in order.*"

To regain customers and market share lost to the Japanese competitors, Xerox, under the leadership of David Kearns, launched its Leadership Through Quality strategy. "We redefined quality as meeting the requirements of our customers. It may have been the most significant strategy Xerox had ever embarked on. Quality actually decreases costs by reducing rejects, eliminating excessive inspections and field service, and most importantly, by diminishing the cost of business lost to competitors."

As a measure of the dramatic improvement, Xerox won the Baldrige Quality Award in 1989.

As of 1991 the firm reported the following results: "We have reduced our average manufacturing cost by over 20 percent despite inflation. We have reduced the time it takes to bring a new product to market by up to 60 percent. We have decreased our defective parts from 8 percent to less than three-hundredths of 1 percent. We are the first American company in an industry targeted by the Japanese to regain market share without the aid of tariffs or protection of any kind."

Quality, in terms of meeting customer requirements, had become an effective international competitive strategy for Xerox. The strategy yielded lower costs, faster production of new products, fewer defects, and regained customers.

Sources: D. Kearns and D. Nadler, *Prophets in the Dark: How Xerox Reinvented Itself and Beat Back the Japanese,* New York: Harper Business (1992): xiv; D. Kearns, "Foreword," in Stahl and Bounds, ix; R. Osterhoff, W. Locander, and G. Bounds, "Competitive Benchmarking at Xerox," in M. J. Stahl and G. M. Bounds, *Competing Globally Through Customer Value: The Management of Strategic Suprasystems,* Westport, CT: Quorum Books (1991): 788; D. Kearns, "Leadership Through Quality," *Academy of Management Executive* (May 1990): 86–89.

"Stuck in the Middle"

Porter maintains that there is a fourth, de facto strategy in business-level competitive strategy, which he has identified as "stuck in the middle."[29] It is not an a priori, purposeful strategy in itself. "Stuck in the middle" is the result of not successfully pursuing any of the three generic strategies.

Maybe the firm is not sure which of the three generic strategies is the best strategy for its industry. Sometimes the company is unwilling to commit the necessary financial resources to a market in order to achieve cost leadership through economies of scale. Perhaps the firm is not able to achieve differentiation with unequaled quality or with dealer networks. By not having the lowest costs, by not being differentiated in the minds of the consumer, or by not successfully targeting a market segment, the firm usually experiences weak profits and limited market share.

In the late 1980s, for example, Sears apparently recognized that it was stuck in the middle. It lowered prices across the board in a national campaign emphasizing its new lower prices. As the retailer had difficulty lowering its costs, it was still "stuck in the middle" in the early 1990s. It usually takes considerable work and time for large firms to change competitive strategies, as is evident in this chapters' international exhibit.

CRITICAL THINKING QUESTIONS

1. Give one example each of an automobile company or division of an automobile company that primarily follows one of the three generic competitive strategies.

2. How should Sears pull out of its "stuck in the middle" spot?

PORTER'S FIVE FORCES MODEL

As American industry became surrounded by intense foreign competition, Porter argued that strategy equates to how the firm competes against other firms in the marketplace. He stressed that strategy is not simply a collection of models and concepts at the corporate level of strategy. It also includes analyzing potential entrants, suppliers, buyers, substitutes, and competitors.[30]

Porter described the competitive forces shaping an industry in his Five Forces Model of Industrial Competition. The model, depicted in Figure 6.2, has been one of the most widely used models in strategic management. By analyzing the five forces, one can assess the forces driving competition in a specific industry and evaluate the odds of a firm's successfully entering and competing in that industry. Thus one can measure the industry's attractiveness for entry or exit, analyze competitive trends, and plot future strategy. The five forces are (1) potential entrants with their threat of entry, (2) buyers with their bargaining power, (3) suppliers with their bargaining power, (4) substitutes with their threat of substitute products or services, and (5) industry competitors with their rivalry among existing firms.

Buyers and Bargaining Power

Buyer power is the capability of buyers, purchasing agents, and customers of an industry to influence the price and the terms of a purchase. If buyer power is high, then the profit margins of incumbent firms tend to be low. If there are only a few buyers, or if the buyers are well organized, then buyer power may be high. If buyer power is high, the industry is unattractive to potential entrants who are considering entry. For instance, buyer power in the retail clothing industry is limited, as the buyers are so numerous. It is hard to exact price concessions from the retailer when there are numerous customers for the retailer.

Potential Entrants and Entry Barriers

The subject of creating and maintaining market entry barriers has received considerable attention from executives. If the incumbent firms in the industry can keep

FIGURE 6.2   *Forces Driving Industry Competition*

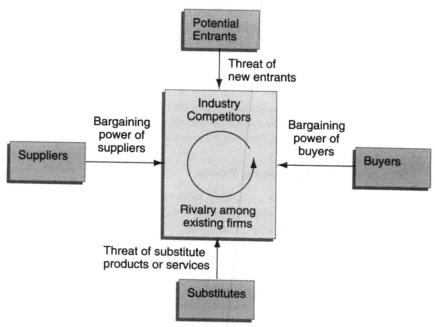

Source: Reprinted from *Competitive Strategy: Techniques for Analyzing Industries and Competitors* by Michael E. Porter. Copyright 1980 by The Free Press.

potential entrants at bay and dissuade them from ever entering the industry, the entire subject of competition and its impact on incumbent firms' profits becomes moot. The threat of new firms entering an industry is low if the incumbent firms have sufficient power to influence prices, control resources, and shape the nature of competition within that industry.

Harley-Davidson offers an example of the effect of potential entrants. In the 1970s many Harley executives thought that the barriers to entry into the upscale U.S. motorcycle industry were too high because of the capital requirements and customer loyalty. Consequently, they viewed the competition in terms of other U.S. firms and paid little attention to potential Japanese entrants. They did not regard the Japanese motorcycle companies as serious competitors, partly because the Japanese entered on the low-price end of the market. The U.S. firms took the Japanese firms seriously only after the Japanese firms, with their low prices and high quality, had made dramatic sales inroads into the higher-end U.S. motorcycle market.

Incumbent firms often spend substantial resources designing and building market-entry barriers. Substantial entry barriers limit the competition and can yield high profitability for the incumbents. The opposite is also true. In the retail clothing industry, entry barriers tend to be low, and consequently profit margins are limited. Entry barriers are low because there are few sustainable cost advantages to incumbents, only limited financing is required to lease retail store space, and it is difficult to differentiate the product. The potential for entrants to enter readily limits prices and profits.

Of all the entry barriers that have been studied, the three most important market-entry barriers are cost advantages of incumbents, product differentiation of incumbents, and capital requirements.[31] Cost advantages of incumbents accrue from a variety of sources, including economies of scale, experience effects, proprietary product or process technology, favorable access to raw materials, favorable location, and a TQM system that lowers the cost of quality. Product differentiation of incumbents refers to the brand identification and customer loyalties associated with the incumbent firms' existing products or services. Finally, the need to invest large amounts of financial resources creates the barrier to entry known as capital requirements.

Suppliers and Bargaining Power

Supplier power is the capability of vendors or suppliers to decide the price and the terms of supply. Suppliers include vendors of labor, raw materials, and capital goods such as machinery. If supplier power is high, then the profit margins of incumbent firms in the industry tend to be low. Low profit margins make an industry less attractive to potential entrants. A rough measure of supplier power is the number of suppliers in the industry. A large number of suppliers typically indicates low supplier power, and vice versa.

Supplier power in the domestic steel industry is formidable for the large, mature steel companies like Bethlehem Steel and Republic Steel. The United Steel Workers Union has near-monopoly supplier power on the supply of labor to the steel industry. The concentrated supplier power keeps the labor cost of large, mature domestic steel firms high. To get around such high supplier power, several small minimills, such as Nucor Steel, have been started in the recent past with nonunion, lower-cost labor. These minimills are able to keep their labor cost low and thus can compete with low-priced Japanese and Korean steel imports.

Substitute Products and Services

The availability of substitutes for an industry's products and services alters the power of incumbent firms. As the availability of substitutes rises and as the ease of substitution increases, the power of incumbent firms to control prices and the terms of the business declines. A good example of a competitive force arising from a substitute product is the substitution of aluminum for steel in many uses. "I'll grant that steel makes a good railroad rail," says David Reynolds, retired chairman and son of the founder of Reynolds Metals, "but anything else we've got a shot at."[32] Such substitution was partly responsible for the growth of the domestic aluminum industry and the shrinkage of the steel industry in the 1970s and the 1980s, when both industries were faced with global competition.

Competitors and Rivalry

Competitive rivalry among existing firms in an industry is the extent to which firms respond to competitive moves of other incumbent firms. In some industries an implicit "gentleman's agreement" seems to exist in which firms respect one another's market niches and follow a "live and let live" strategy. In other industries a "dog eat dog" idea prevails, cutthroat competition is the rule, and competitive moves are vigorously countered.

A good example of competitive forces shaped by the rivalry among incumbent firms is the domestic soft-drink industry. This industry is infamous for its "cola wars," in which millions of dollars in advertising are spent to protect a market share. So that one did not gain a competitive lead over the other, both Coke and Pepsi were experimenting with iced tea in the early 1990s.[33] In almost every situation the two firms aggressively matched each other's moves.

Porter's Five Forces Model offers a way to analyze the competitive dynamics in an industry. After such an initial analysis, competitive-group analysis can help with market-entry and product-positioning decisions.[34]

Plotting Competitive Groups

Several steps are involved in the graphic presentation of competitive groups. First, the important competitive dimensions in the industry are identified. **Competitive dimensions** are the specific factors used by firms to compete within the industry. Competitive dimensions are more specific, like quality, size of market served, number of products, dealer network, and the like, than the generic competitive strategies in the industry. For example, in the early 1990s one might argue that a primary competitive strategy in the airline industry was differentiation. However, to conduct a strategic group analysis, a specific description of differentiation based on number of markets served is required. After the competitive dimensions have been identified, the second step is the graphic mapping of the firm's dimensions together with the positions of its competitors. The third step is the analysis of the firm's position relative to its competitors.

Examples of competitive groups from the airline industry in 1981 and 1989 are presented in Figures 6.3 and 6.4. Those dates are chosen because they indicate the massive movement associated with deregulation in the 1980s. Cost and size of the airline are defined as the important competitive dimensions. Size is a proxy for how many different destinations are available to the traveler without switching airlines. Airline size is measured by available seat miles (ASM). Cost is measured by operating expense per ASM, which is a commonly used measure of airline cost structure.[35] In 1981 the major airlines operated with similar costs. This was associated with the government's regulation of prices, which provided little incentive for the airlines to reduce costs. As has been demonstrated in many industries, regulation of prices encouraged competition on bases other than price. Price competition among the airlines became relevant only after the industry had been deregulated. Then costs became very important. The 1989 plot of airline competitive groups in Figure 6.4 shows the different positioning of the airlines once cost assumed importance.

It is common to see a diagonal pattern in a strategic group map like the 1989 plot if one of the dimensions is cost/price and the other dimension is a specific form of differentiation. For many products and services, the customer demands more of the differentiated dimension or feature as the price increases. Many would argue:

FIGURE 6.3   *Competitive-Group Map of the Airline Industry: 1981*

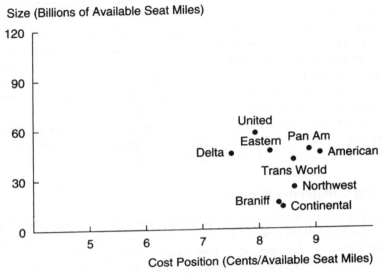

Source: *Moody's Transportation Manual,* (New York: Moody's Investor's Service, 1982) as adapted in M. J. Stahl and D. W. Grigsby, *Strategic Management for Decision Making,* PWS-Kent (1991): 92.

"You get what you pay for." It is the off-diagonal positions that may present unique opportunities for market entry or product positioning.

Market Entry and Product Positioning

Competitive-group analysis reveals the soundness of current competitive strategy, the need for repositioning in the industry, the wisdom of entering the industry, and how to position new products or services. A competitive-group plot can help a firm to decide where on the diagonal to position itself and anticipate industry-average profitability. If the firm can achieve an off-diagonal position, connoting greater differentiation at lower cost/price, it may realize above-average profitability. Off-diagonal, high-value positions can be achieved by different or proprietary technology, or by high-quality products or services that also lower the firm's costs, or by more differentiated products or services at the same cost.

CRITICAL THINKING QUESTIONS

1. Using Porter's Five Forces Model of Industry Competition, analyze the brewing industry.
2. Analyze entry into the domestic soft-drink industry in terms of the three market-entry barriers discussed in the text.

FIGURE 6.4   *Competitive-Group Map of the Airline Industry: 1989*

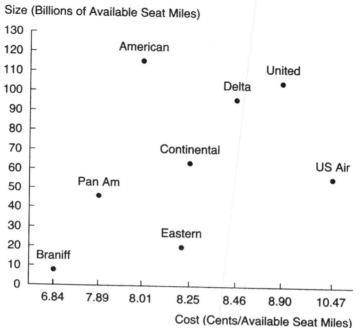

Source: 1989 annual reports of the eight airlines.

TOTAL QUALITY AND COMPETITIVE STRATEGY

In the introduction to this chapter, we highlighted the importance of competitive strategy. Prior to today's interest in competitive strategy, little attention was paid to the study of business-level strategy. Many firms, like GM, Harley-Davidson, and Xerox, rue the time when they ignored or underestimated their competitors, especially in the intense, internationally competitive arena in which many U.S. firms operate. But there are some risks associated with competitive strategy, and we shall consider these now.

Competitors or Customers?

By definition, competitive strategy involves concentrating on the firm's competitors. Competitors are at the heart of Porter's generic competitive strategies, competitors are at the center of Porter's Five Forces Model in Figure 6.2, and competitors are analyzed in competitive-group analyses. Such an emphasis on competitors frequently comes at the expense of concentrating on the customer. As we shall describe fully in Chapter 7, the customer and the satisfaction of customer needs are at the heart of Total Quality.

The best competitive strategy is a customer-value strategy. By concentrating on exceeding customer requirements, the firm will be in a better position than its competitors to retain current customers and win new customers.

Concentration on competitors usually results in the firm's pursuing a follower mentality. Such followership results in imitation rather than innovation. Clearly, a firm cannot be the early market entrant if it merely imitates the competition. In an era in which customers are constantly demanding new products with the latest technology, late market entrants pay a penalty in ignoring customers.[36]

Under a TQ banner, firms benchmark competitors primarily for the best processes and the best systems. Firms develop products and services through intense examination of customers' requirements. Customers *and* competitors are important—in that order.

Buyers or Customers?

The use of the term *buyer* instead of *customer* is unfortunate because it connotes a near-adversarial exchange. It certainly does not connote a partnering relationship. The background of the Five Forces Model of Industrial Competition connotes the near-adversarial exchange based on the bargaining-power idea. It suggests that if there is some way to weaken the bargaining power of the buyer, then all is well and the firm need not worry about satisfying customer requirements.

Suppliers or Partners?

In today's competitive world, which demands zero defect production and delivery, many Total Quality firms recognize their suppliers as partners in their system. The idea of supplier power based in industrial competition connotes the adversarial mentality described in the preceding section. GM's recent treatment of its suppliers that forced the suppliers to compete more vigorously on the basis of price caused many observers to wonder how much of an impact such a move would have on the quality of GM's products.[37] Some view a firm's willingness to treat suppliers as partners as the acid test in its commitment to Total Quality.[38]

Cost Leadership and Differentiation through Total Quality

A reading of Porter's generic competitive strategies suggests that most firms typically achieve only one of the generic competitive strategies. Some firms never achieve even one of the three strategies and remain "stuck in the middle."

Two separate analyses of Porter's generic competitive strategies argue that both cost leadership and differentiation are simultaneously achievable. Both may be required in order to achieve sustained competitive advantage in the industry. High quality, innovation, learning effects, and economies of scale are mentioned as conditions for achieving both generic competitive strategies.[39]

Several other researchers contend that flawless quality, and the systems that produce it, are the principal ways to simultaneously achieve both low cost and differentiation.[40] This is the chief concept of Total Quality Management that we stress throughout

QUALITY CASE

Conclusion to the Cat–Komatsu Case

Caterpillar's commitment to quality, its cost controls, and its networks of suppliers and dealers paid off in the early 1990s. Cat gained market share at Komatsu's expense in the United States "In four key products (crawler tractors, crawler loaders, hydraulic excavators, and wheel loaders), Komatsu-Dresser's unit market share dropped from 20.3 percent in 1988 to 18 percent in 1991. Cat's U.S. market share rose from 34.5 percent to 36.4 percent in the same period." Komatsu-Dresser's joint venture had problems in terms of realizing the goal of overtaking Cat. After suffering a loss associated with the strike in 1992, Cat's profits were growing strongly in 1993 and 1994.

Komatsu decided to diversify away from construction equipment, with only half of its sales in the mid-1990s in construction equipment. "Komatsu isn't only for a bulldozer anymore," says Satoru Anzaki, executive managing director of Komatsu's international operations.

Cat concentrated on its construction equipment business with quality, cost control, and networks of suppliers and dealers.

Its strategy of providing value to its customers became part of its competitive strategy. This helped Komatsu answer the corporate-strategy question of what business it was in by diversifying away from construction equipment.

DISCUSSION QUESTIONS

1. How important for its competitive strategy was Cat's strategy of providing value to its customers through quality, price, and dealer networks?

2. How did Komatsu's decision to diversify affect its competitive strength in construction equipment?

Sources: "Caterpillar," *Value Line Investment Survey* (May 14, 1993): 1344; "Caterpillar's Don Fites: Why He Didn't Blink," *Business Week* (August 10, 1992): 56–57; "Komatsu Throttles Back on Construction Equipment," *The Wall Street Journal* (May 13, 1992): A5; R. P. Vichas and T. Mroczkowski, "Caterpillar, Inc. in Latin America," in M. J. Stahl and D. W. Grigsby, *Strategic Management for Decision Making*, Boston: PWS-Kent (1991): 922–942; K. Kelly, "A Dream Marriage Turns Nightmarish," *Business Week* (April 29, 1991): 94–95; S. Cayer, "Welcome to Caterpillar's Quality Institute," *Purchasing* (August 16, 1990): 80–84.

this book. *Cost leadership is associated with low cost of quality, high workforce productivity, flat organizational structures, and short response times. Differentiation is associated with dedication to providing flawless quality and value to customers.*

This TQM strategy seems to have been employed successfully by many Japanese firms in several industries, including consumer electronics and automobiles.[41] Procter & Gamble, Xerox, and Warner-Lambert are three of the growing number of U.S. firms that have used quality to achieve both low cost and differentiation.[42] In the 1990s customers demand affordable quality. We discuss Total Quality and customer-value strategy at length in Chapter 7.

CRITICAL THINKING QUESTIONS

1. How does competitive strategy relate to Total Quality?

2. Discuss the utility of a single competitive strategy in an era in which customers demand affordable quality.

SUMMARY

Following Mintzberg, strategy is a pattern in a series of decisions. An analysis of internal strengths and weaknesses and of external opportunities and threats (SWOT analysis) is preparatory to deciding on the strategic plan.

All organizations interact with and are affected by the external environment in which they function. There are external opportunities to be capitalized on and external threats to be avoided. These external environmental issues include customer-value, social, demographic, economic, technological, regulatory, physical, and competitive trends.

Similarly, there are internal environmental issues that must be considered in formulating a strategic plan. These issues include horizontal systems and processes, organizational structure, corporate culture, management, financial position, operations, marketing, human resources, research and development, and information systems. When formulating and implementing the strategic plan, the internal strengths must be capitalized on and the internal weaknesses overcome.

The corporate strategic plan contains at least three elements: the mission (why), objectives (what), and strategy (how). The main element is the mission statement, which describes the business(es) the firm is in. Objectives are the specific kinds of results the organization hopes to achieve. They should be specific, measurable, time phased, and achievable.

Total Quality Management and current practice support the idea of concentration and relatedness in corporate strategy. Frequently, conglomerate diversification is an admission of a failure to compete.

The relationship between the corporate and business levels of strategy should be consistent. The firm should compete at the business level in ways in which the firm has competence. Doing so further supports concentration or related diversification as corporate strategies.

Porter modeled how firms compete in an industry with his Five Forces Model of Industrial Competition. One of the five forces measures entry barriers as a way to preclude competition in an industry. The three most important entry barriers are cost advantage of incumbents, product differentiation of incumbents, and capital requirements. Two of these entry barriers (cost leadership and differentiation) are especially important because they are two of Porter's three generic competitive strategies. As a generic business-level competitive strategy, cost leadership is production of the product or service at the lowest cost in the industry. Differentiation is the offering of a product or service that will be perceived by the customer as different or somehow unique. As a competitive strategy, the focusing firm serves a specific target group, segment, or market niche, and serves it well.

Competitive-group analysis is an important way to analyze the competitive structure of an industry. By plotting how the major firms in an industry compete along two dimensions, executives can decide how to position the firm.

A drawback of competitive strategy is the concentration on the firm's competitors and not on its customers. Total Quality is a primary way to achieve both low cost and differentiation and thereby to offer affordable quality to customers.

EXPERIENTIAL EXERCISE

The Costs of Keeping a Secret

With considerable anxiety Philip Cortez reread the engineering director's memo: "Call me at your earliest convenience about design specs for a new radial."

"New radial." That could mean only one thing—that his employer, National Rubber and Tire, wanted to beat its biggest competitor, Lifeworth, in getting an 80,000-mile, puncture-proof tire on the market.

Ordinarily such a memo would signal a challenge for an employee as conscientious and industrious as Phil Cortez. But until six months ago Cortez had been employed by Lifeworth. While there he had been instrumental in drawing up designs for a similar tire that Lifeworth was not only interested in producing but was also counting on to revitalize its sagging profit posture. In fact, so important did Lifeworth consider Cortez's work that when he announced his departure, Lifeworth's president reminded him of an agreement that Cortez had entered into when undertaking his work with Lifeworth. He had promised to refrain from disclosing any classified information directly or indirectly to competitors for a period of two years after his termination from Lifeworth. The president indicated in no uncertain terms that he considered Cortez's work on the new radial highly classified. Cortez assured the president that he anticipated no conflicts of interests, since National had given him every reason to believe that it wanted him primarily in a managerial capacity.

And now the memo was staring him in the face. Cortez responded to it that very afternoon and had his worst fears realized. As he'd suspected, the engineering director solicited Cortez's input on the matter of a new radial.

Cortez unhesitatingly explained his dilemma. While sympathetic to Cortez's predicament, the director broadly hinted that refusal to provide constructive input would result in a substantial disservice to National and was bound to affect Cortez's standing with the firm. "After all," the director said, "it's very difficult to justify paying a man a handsome salary and expediting his movement up the organizational ladder when his allegiances obviously lie elsewhere." The conversation ended icily with the director advising Cortez to "think about it."

Discussion Questions

1. Three volunteers are needed from the class to role-play Cortez, Lifeworth's president, and the engineering director. The students should role-play the first conversation between Cortez and Lifeworth's president, and then role-play the conversation between Cortez and the engineering director. They should emphasize Cortez's promise, his concern, and the engineering director's insistence.

2. After the role playing, the class should respond to the following questions:
   a. What are the ethics operating in this case?
   b. What are the likely effects of Cortez's alternatives?
   c. Is National Tire and Rubber merely following good business sense by trying to understand its chief competitor's moves? Explain.

Source: V. Barry, *Moral Issues in Business*, 2nd ed., Belmont, CA: Wadsworth (1983): 257.

CHAPTER CASE

The Falls Church General Hospital

Founded in 1968, the Falls Church General Hospital (FCGH) is a privately owned, 615-patient bed facility in Falls Church, Virginia. Falls Church is four miles from downtown Washington, DC, and is surrounded by affluent urban/suburban communities with a highly educated population composed largely of employees of the U.S. government and high-tech engineering firms.

FCGH, with 895 employees, provides a broad range of health care services, including drug/alcohol abuse wards, emergency rooms, X-ray and laboratory facilities, maternity wards, intensive- and cardiac-care units, and outpatient facilities. With strong competition from other comprehensive facilities such as George Washington University Hospital, Georgetown University Hospital, Fairfax General Hospital, and Arlington Hospital, FCGH has had to concentrate on offering high-quality treatment at reasonable prices. FCGH has not attempted to obtain all of the latest up-to-date diagnostic equipment (such as $350,000 CAT scanners), because its board felt it would not be cost effective to try to compete with the more research-oriented university hospitals such as Georgetown and George Washington. Even though FCGH is considered a "medium-to-large" hospital, it has attempted to stress personal attention to each patient. In January 1990 the hospital began a series of ads in the *Washington Post* highlighting its concerned doctors and nurses, its friendly support staff, and its overall philosophy that its employees care about their work and their patients.

Quality health care is a goal all hospitals profess, but few have developed comprehensive and scientific means of asking customers to judge the quality of care they receive. A tremendous amount of effort has been devoted to assessing the clinical quality of hospital care; books, journals, and papers on the topic abound. The problem, however, is that past efforts to measure hospital quality have largely ignored the perceptions of customers—the patients, physicians, and payers. Instead of formally considering customer judgments of quality, the health care industry has focused almost entirely on internal quality assessments made by the health professionals who operate the system. In effect, a system for improving health care has been created that all but ignores the voice of the customer.

The board of FCGH believes that all hospitals need to make the transformation from the current practice of attempting to ensure quality to measuring and improving the quality of care from both the external, customer perspective and the internal, provider perspective. Fueled by concerns in recent years about costs and medical practice variation and by the demand for greater social accountability, there is an emerging demand by patients and payers that quality health care be provided at best value.

As board president Dr. Irwin Greenberg recently stated at the annual FCGH meeting, "As the prices people pay in the future for given levels of service become more similar, hospitals will be distinguished largely on the basis of their quality and value as assessed by customers. We must have accurate information about how our customers, not just the health care professionals who work here, judge the quality of care in this institution. A recent survey of more than 200 hospitals showed that two-thirds routinely conduct patient satisfaction surveys."

In response to Dr. Greenberg's statement, and in light of the advertising campaign, hospital administrator Carla Kimball called a meeting of her department heads to discuss the issue of quality. "Can we deliver on our promises? Or are we in danger of failing to live up to the level of health care our patients expect, and do we risk losing them?" Ms. Kimball asked.

Annie Kerr, head of nursing, continued the debate. "I argue that surveys, such as the one Dr. Greenberg mentioned in his speech, are valuable. But how do we measure the quality of our health care? If we are serious about improving the quality of care, we need more *valid* and *reliable* data on which to act. We need answers to specific, quality-related questions about activities in areas that affect patients—admission, nursing, medical staff, daily care, and ancillary staff."

"I have an idea," said Merrill Warkentin, Kimball's staff director. "I just finished reading a book by John Groocock. He's the Vice President for Quality at TRW, a big manufacturer. He says there are 14 steps in TRW's internal quality audits. Why don't we consider his approach?" The steps start with quality to the customer as a way to beat the competition.

When the meeting ended, Ms. Kimball began to think about the whole issue of quality control in U.S. firms. It had worked in many manufacturing companies, but could the concepts of quality control really be used in a hospital?

Discussion Questions

1. Why is it important to get the patient's assessment of health care quality? Does a patient

have the expertise to judge the health care he or she receives?

2. How might a hospital measure quality?

3. How can a hospital compete with other health care providers through quality?

Source: Adapted from Robert Murdick, Barry Render, and Roberta Russell, *Service Operations Management*, Boston: Allyn & Bacon, 1990: 444–445.

KEY TERMS

buyer power   Capability of buyers, purchasing agents, and customers of an industry to influence the price and the terms of a purchase.

competitive dimensions   Specific factors used by firms to compete within the industry.

competitive rivalry   Extent to which firms respond to competitive moves of other incumbent firms.

concentration   Focus on a single product or market.

conglomerate diversification   Operations in unrelated markets or unrelated products.

cost leadership   Lowest cost of operation in the industry.

cost focus   Offer of a product or service to a market segment at a price lower than that of competitors.

deliberate strategy   Strategy in which a firm decides on its goals and implements intended strategy to realize the goals.

differentiation   Supplying a product or service that will be perceived by the customer as different or somehow unique.

differentiation focus   Offer, to a market segment, of a product or service that is more differentiated than all competitors' comparable products or services.

economies of scale   Use of huge physical assets to lower the unit production cost.

emergent strategies   Strategies actually in place in the organization.

environmental scanning   Analyzing the external environment.

evaluation and control   Activities and decisions that keep the process on track.

focus   Concentration on serving a particular target group, segment, or market niche.

horizontal systems and processes   Flows of work and activities that span such vertical functions as purchasing, design, production, and marketing.

mission statement   Statement that describes the business(es) the firm is in.

objectives or goals   Kinds of results the firm seeks to achieve.

opportunity   Issue or condition in the external environment that may help the firm reach its goals.

product differentiation   Process by which a product will be perceived by the customer as different or somehow unique.

related diversification   Focus on a few related products or markets.

restructuring   Series of actions aimed at downsizing or cutting back the scope of the firm.

strategy   Method of *how* the organization will attain its objectives.

strategic management   Managerial decisions that relate the organization to its environment, guide internal activities, and determine long-term organizational performance.

strategic plan   Steps which the organization intends to take to achieve its mission, objectives, and strategies.

strategy formulation   Decision making that determines the organization's mission and establishes its objectives and strategies.

strategy implementation　Activities and decisions that are intended to carry out new strategies or support existing strategies.

strength　Condition or issue internal to the organization that may lead to a customer benefit or a competitive advantage.

supplier power　Capability of vendors or suppliers to decide the price and the terms of supply.

SWOT analysis　Analysis of internal strengths and weaknesses and external opportunities and threats.

threat　Issue or condition in the external environment that may prevent the firm from reaching its goals.

weakness　Condition or issue internal to the organization that may lead to negative customer value or a competitive disadvantage.

ENDNOTES

1. R. J. Schonberger, "Is Strategy Strategic? Impact of Total Quality Management on Strategy," *Academy of Management Executive*, 6, no. 3 (August 1992): 80–87.
2. H. Mintzberg, "Patterns in Strategy Formation," *Management Science*, 24 (1978): 934–948.
3. H. Mintzberg and J. A. Waters, "Of Strategies, Deliberate and Emergent," *Strategic Management Journal*, 6 (1985): 257–271.
4. J. T. Wilson, "Strategic Planning at R. J. Reynolds Industries," *Journal of Business Strategy*, 6 (1985): 22–28.
5. H. Mintzberg and A. McHugh, "Strategy Formation in an Adhocracy," *Administrative Science Quarterly*, 30, no. 2 (June 1985): 160–197.
6. H. Mintzberg, "The Design School: Reconsidering the Basic Premises of Strategic Management," *Strategic Management Journal*, 11 (March–April 1990): 171–196.
7. R. D. Ireland et al., "Strategy Formulation Process," *Strategic Management Journal*, 8 (1987): 469–486.
8. Mintzberg, "The Design School."
9. Schonberger, "Is Strategy Strategic?"
10. "TWA May Go to Creditors, Employees: Rescue Plan Needs Union, Investor Approval," *USA Today* (August 4, 1992): B1.
11. "GM Posts Record Loss of $4.45 Billion, Sends Tough Message to UAW on Closings," *The Wall Street Journal* (February 25, 1992): A3.
12. W. Judge, M. Stahl, R. Scott, and R. Millender, "Long–Term Quality Improvement and Cost Reduction at Capsugel," in Stahl and Bounds, *Competing Globally Through Customer Value*, 703–709.
13. C. Harris, "Information Power," *Business Week* (October 14, 1985): 53–55.
14. C. Wilson and M. Kennedy, "Improving the Product Development Process," in Stahl and Bounds, *Competing Globally Through Customer Value*, 403–427.
15. "America's Most Admired Corporations," *Fortune* (February 8, 1993): 40–72.
16. D. C. Hambrick, "Environmental Scanning and Organizational Strategy," *Strategic Management Journal*, 3 (1982): 159–174.
17. R. L. Daft, J. Sormunen, and D. Parks, "Chief Executive Scanning, Environmental Characteristics, and Company Performance," *Strategic Management Journal*, 9 (March–April 1988): 123–139.
18. "'No–Dicker Sticker' Car Deals Ignite: Buyers Tired of Getting Beaten Up," *USA Today* (August 4, 1992): A1.
19. J. S. Armstrong, "The Value of Formal Planning for Strategic Decisions," *Strategic Management Journal* (1982): 197–211.
20. D. S. Cochran, F. R. David, and C. K. Gibson, "A Framework for Developing an Effective Mission Statement," *Journal of Business Strategies*, 2 (1985): 4–17.

21. H. C. Carothers, G. M. Bounds, and M. J. Stahl, "Managerial Leadership," in Stahl and Bounds, *Competing Globally Through Customer Value*.

22. *Eli Lilly and Company: Report to Shareholders*, 1991: 1.

23. "King Customer," *Business Week* (March 12, 1990): 88–94; D. A. Kearns, "Leadership Through Quality," *Academy of Management Executive* (May 1990): 86–89.

24. M. E. Porter, "From Competitive Advantage to Corporate Strategy," *Harvard Business Review* (May–June 1987): 43–59.

25. K. P. Coyne, "Sustainable Competitive Advantage—What It Is, What It Isn't," *Business Horizons* (January–February 1986): 54–61.

26. P. Ghemawat, "Sustainable Advantage," *Harvard Business Review*, 64, no. 5 (1986): 53–58.

27. "Compaq Can't Cope with Demand for Pro Linea PCs," *The Wall Street Journal* (July 10, 1992): B1.

28. Porter, *Competitive Strategy* and *Competitive Advantage*.

29. Ibid.

30. Ibid.

31. Karakaya and Stahl, *Market Entry and Exit Barriers*.

32. "Aluminum Producers, Aggressive and Agile, Outfight Steelmakers," *The Wall Street Journal* (July 1, 1992): 1.

33. "The Cola Kings Are Feeling a Bit Jumpy," *Business Week* (July 13, 1992): 112.

34. Porter, *Competitive Strategy*; K. O. Cool and D. Schendel, "Strategic Group Formation and Performance: The Case of the U.S. Pharmaceutical Industry, 1963–1982," *Management Science*, 33, no. 9 (1987):

1102–1124; T. Oliva, D. Day, and W. DeSarbo, "Selecting Competitive Tactics: Try a Strategy Map," *Sloan Management Review* 28, no. 3 (1987): 5–15.

35. E. E. Bailey, D. R. Graham, and D. P. Kaplan, *Deregulating the Airlines*, Cambridge, MA: MIT Press (1986).

36. C. Wilson and M. Kennedy, "Improving the Product Development Process," in Stahl and Bounds, *Competing Globally Through Customer Value*, 428–477.

37. "GM Tightens the Screws," *Business Week* (June 22, 1992): 30.

38. "Shrinking Supplier Bases," *The Wall Street Journal* (August 16, 1991): B1.

39. C. W. Hill, "Differentiation Versus Low Cost or Differentiation and Low Cost: A Contingency Framework," *Academy of Management Review*, 13, no. 3 (1988): 401.

40. J. Bowles and J. Hammond, *Beyond Quality*, New York: Putnam (1991); W. E. Deming, *Out of the Crisis*, Cambridge, MA: MIT Press (1986); D. A. Garvin, *Managing Quality: The Strategic and Competitive Edge*, New York: Free Press (1988); D. Griffiths, *Implementing Quality with a Customer Focus*, Milwaukee: Quality Press (1990); Stahl and Bounds, *Competing Globally Through Customer Value*.

41. K. Ishikawa, *What Is Total Quality Control? The Japanese Way*, Englewood Cliffs, NJ: Prentice-Hall (1985).

42. Kearns, "Leadership Through Quality," 86–89; W. Locander and W. Saxton, "Application to P&G"; and W. Judge et al., "Application to Capsugel," both in Stahl and Bounds, *Competing Globally Through Customer Value*.

Total Quality and Customer-Value Strategy

LEARNING OBJECTIVES

After reading this chapter, you should be able to accomplish the following:

- Explain how high quality and low cost can go together.

- Discuss the importance of management systems, especially customer-value systems, in producing high quality.

- Discuss the importance of the customer and total customer satisfaction in business-level strategy.

- Describe the role of benchmarking in quality improvement.

- Relate the ideas of customer value and best net customer value to the idea of quality.

- Discuss the importance of customer-value determination systems in organizations.

- Discuss the importance of Quality Function Deployment and new-product development systems in organizations.

- Explain why quality is at the heart of the rebirth of U.S. industrial competitiveness.

- Discuss the payoff from Total Quality Management.

CHAPTER OUTLINE

With Great Quality, Prices, and Dealers, Saturn Regains Customers Lost to Japanese Automakers 🇺🇸 ⚫

Saturn has achieved great quality through increased employee input into managerial decisions, as well as higher levels of employee training. (Photo credit: Saturn Corporation.)

Since the early 1970s U.S. automobile manufacturers, and General Motors in particular, watched as Japanese automakers gained the competitive edge for customers. GM's market share went into a tailspin, and its annual loss in 1992 was $23.5 billion, the largest ever recorded by a U.S. firm (see Chapter 3).

What would it take to regain customers from Honda, Nissan, and Toyota? How do you convince American customers, who have been burned repeatedly by poor quality, high prices, and high-pressure dealers from Detroit, that a new era has arrived in American automobiles?

The problems were so ingrained in its own systems of management and labor relations that GM decided to answer such a crisis with a completely new company, called Saturn. By starting Saturn, GM hoped to do what no U.S. automaker had accomplished in the two decades of the 1970s and 1980s. Saturn hoped to profitably build high-quality, low-priced small cars and thereby to regain customers and market share from Japanese models. Saturn's specific mission was to "market vehicles developed and manufactured in the United States that are world leaders in quality, cost and customer satisfaction through the integration of people, technology and business systems and to transfer knowledge, technology and experience throughout General Motors."

This was a costly, ambitious, and risky undertaking. GM's investment in creating Saturn was $5 billion. No one knew for sure if a U.S. firm, even a brand-new one, could wean U.S. consumers from the high-quality Japanese cars they had grown to love.

A SYSTEMS MODEL OF QUALITY

How can managers and their organizations yield superior quality at low cost? For many U.S. firms to embrace the idea of delivering superior quality to their customers as a business strategy, the firms first needed an answer to this question. For such a business strategy to be sustainable, it was important to link superior quality and low cost, as Saturn proved.

Quality and Low Cost

W. Edwards Deming is sometimes called the father of the Japanese and American quality movements. He made a seminal contribution to business strategy and practice when he showed how high quality *and* low cost can go hand in hand.[1] Joseph Juran, Kaoru Ishikawa, Philip Crosby, and others all taught the new logic of higher quality and lower costs.[2]

Before Deming's analysis, economists argued that quality, or any feature of a product, costs money. The more quality in a product, the higher the cost of the product, according to many economists.[3] Since many managers relied on inspection after production to achieve high quality, the economists were correct in observing that quality costs money. But it does not need to be that way.

Using the logic presented in Figure 7.1, Deming showed how high quality can lead to lower costs. For this logic to hold, quality cannot be inspected in at the end of the production process. Deming argued that quality is a strategy that must permeate an organization throughout its business activities. "Cease dependence on inspection to achieve quality. Eliminate the need for inspection on a mass basis by building quality into the product in the first place."[4]

The idea that high quality can be achieved at low cost was a watershed in business operations. Today firms pay attention to designing the product to eliminate recurring defects in production. Firms also design manufacturing processes so that operations are performed without errors, and firms manage systems to eliminate the cause of defects. Then they continuously improve the products or services and the processes to yield even greater value to customers. Organizations pay attention to the cost of quality—or to the cost of poor quality.

The Cost of Quality

The **cost of quality** is the cost incurred in producing poor-quality products and services. Included in the cost of quality are the costs of scrap, rework, warranty repair, inspection, and quality-related maintenance.[5] These costs are sometimes expressed as a percentage of cost of goods sold. In an earlier era many firms experienced a cost of quality of from 15 percent to 30 percent.[6] Firms that implement Total Quality usually experience dramatic declines in the cost of quality of 90 percent or more. Through continuous improvement of the products or services and the process, some firms relentlessly drive the cost of quality toward zero. Then affordable quality becomes a realizable goal. With lower costs and higher quality, the firms can provide more value to customers.

FIGURE 7.1   *The Pervasive Role of Quality*

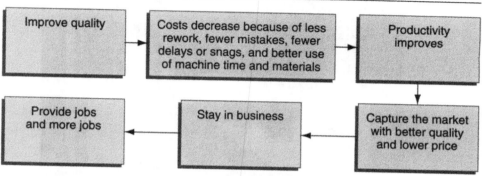

Source: Reprinted from *Out of the Crisis* (p. 3) by W. E. Deming, by permission of MIT and W. Edwards Deming Institute. Published by MIT, Center for Advanced Engineering Study, Cambridge, MA 02139. Copyright © 1986 by W. Edwards Deming.

Capsugel, a division of Warner-Lambert, makes hard gelatin capsules for the worldwide pharmaceutical industry. Capsugel has been lowering its cost of quality by one-half every five years. It does this primarily by eliminating inspection after production. In an earlier process the firm employed over 100 inspectors per plant to inspect the product *twice*. Redesign of the systems, including selecting a few suppliers based on quality, continuous process improvement, training of new behavior, and attention to customers, helped Capsugel accomplish the reductions in the cost of quality.[7]

Management Systems and Behavior

Total Quality is different from other strategies and systems in that TQ closely links strategies and systems. The management systems and behaviors necessary to yield the results called for by Deming and others are new.

In the balance of this book we describe these new systems and behaviors in greater detail. These systems and behaviors require firms to focus on external customers and on cross-functional horizontal systems and processes.[8]

Cross-functional systems are activities and resources that are linked to provide value to customers and that span at least two of the functions of design, production, marketing, and finance.[9] Cross-functional systems, which typically include personnel and resources from these functions, are associated with horizontal structures and flatter organizations, with fewer levels of management, less direct supervision, continuous process improvement, cross-functional teams, and more employee training.

We briefly describe two cross-functional systems in this chapter: the customer-value determination system and the new-product development system. We explore the managerial implications of horizontal processes and systems in greater detail in subsequent chapters. First, because of the intensity of international competition, it is necessary to understand the primacy of the customer.

Personal interviews are often used to determine needs of customers. (Photo credit: Michael Siluk/The Image Works.)

Global Competition

As we saw in Chapter 3, deregulated global competition has offered customers choices in many industries. Today, if a customer does not like a Lincoln, the customer can choose among Cadillac, Mercedes, BMW, Lexus, and Infiniti. But 30 years ago the only relevant choice may have been a Cadillac. Today if a customer does not like a Xerox copier, the customer can choose among Sharp, Minolta, and Canon. Twenty years ago the only choice may have been Xerox. Today if a customer does not like Caterpillar, the customer can choose Komatsu or Deere. The choices seemingly have no end. In such an environment, customers demand high quality and low price—and, as indicated later in this chapter, much more. Deming and international competition taught U.S. industry that it can, and it must, deliver superior value to customers.

Managers must heed the customer in this internationally competitive era or face bankruptcy. In the summary of a recent International Quality Study, the American Quality Foundation made the following bold statement concerning the importance of quality as a business strategy: "Quality improvement is the fundamental business strategy of the 1990s. No business without it will survive in the global marketplace."[10]

CRITICAL THINKING QUESTIONS

1. Explain how high quality and low cost can go together. Were the economists wrong who assumed that more quality means more costs?

2. Explain the importance of management systems, especially customer-value systems, in producing high quality.

TOTAL QUALITY AS A BUSINESS STRATEGY

Total Quality is a business strategy in that it shows managers how to operate within a business by focusing on customers. As we shall see later in this chapter, once managers focus on customers, then different managerial systems are needed to deliver value to customers.

Customers

As a business strategy, Total Quality focuses first and foremost on consistently satisfying customers and their needs.[11] The primary focus is the customer, not the competitor, as in competitive strategy (see Chapter 6). This is a major mind-set difference between customer-value strategy and competitive strategy. By delivering superior value to customers, the competitors are left in the dust.

A recent analysis of the impact of TQM on strategy listed 19 key ideas associated with TQM. The first and most important key idea listed is "Get to know the next and final customer."[12]

After watching Xerox nearly go bankrupt and then regain customers from the Japanese with its "Leadership Through Quality" strategy, David Kearns, former chairman of Xerox, offered an eloquent description of failure in a handbook for decline. The first chapter for decline reads as follows: "Assume you own the customer, that you know what he wants better than he does and that he will remain loyal to you no matter how much you abuse him." The chapter also advises you not to waste time measuring customer satisfaction and definitely not to pay attention to or respond to customer complaints.[13]

Robert Galvin was the chairman of Motorola when it won a Malcolm Baldrige National Quality Award. He seemed to understand the centrality of customers to the success of Motorola. In a description of Motorola's strategy, Galvin described Motorola's foremost goal of total customer satisfaction.[14]

In Chapter 1 we emphasized that the customer is at the core of Total Quality. How pervasive is this idea of the centrality of customers? In 1991 *Business Week* reported survey results indicating that about 90 percent of firms using quality strategies reported that they focused on customer satisfaction.[15]

Increasingly, U.S. customers are women, and women will demand companies that do not discriminate against them. Many international firms will be impacted by this trend, as is noted in the following international exhibit.

Total Customer Satisfaction

Meeting customer requirements is one level of customer commitment. That level may imply a reactive system to provide to customers what they request of the firm. Such a reactive mode is different from an expression of striving for "total customer satisfaction," "customer delight," or "exceeding customer expectations." The latter three expressions show that the firm may go beyond what the customer demands today to keep the customer as a customer tomorrow. For example, Eastman Chemicals expresses its vision thus: "To be the World's Preferred Chemical Company by focusing on exceeding customer expectations."[16]

INTERNATIONAL EXHIBIT

The Great Japanese Secret

There's little talk of Japanese management any more. That's partly because it is old news. It is also because those who wrote about it stressed the least important things—like quality circles and consensus management.

There is, however, one consistent strong belief among the early writers on Japanese management and those who wrote later about the real strengths, which were in quality, JIT, equipment policies,... and in development of the broad view.

Some of us Westerners, when we want to feel good about ourselves, point to Japan's gross underuse of half its human resources—the feminine half (who are generally excluded from influential occupations). Is the Western practice of pigeonholing people much worse?

Japan may resolve its cultural weakness. It is much easier for the West to resolve its failing, which is noncultural: It is just a matter of adopting continuing programs of cross-training and cross-functional shifts of people. Until then, the broad view remains as the great Japanese strength, and the Western weakness is the lack of it.

Source: Richard J. Schonberger, *Building a Chain of Customers: Linking Business Functions to Create the World Class Company*, New York: Free Press (1990): 130.

Ford estimates that it costs five times as much to attract a new customer as it does to retain an old one.[17] Such a commitment may mean providing better value than all other competitors, and it is associated with increasing the firm's market share through retaining old customers and winning new customers.

Lands' End, the high-performing, high-quality, mail-order clothing retailer, provides an example of the primacy of the customer. Lands' End's principles of doing business, stated in the following quality exhibit, reflect the companys's dedication to the customer.

Shareholder and Owners

What about the needs of the shareholders? Are not the purposes of management and companies to maximize the wealth of the owners? Does the primacy of the customer detract from owner needs?

A growing body of evidence shows that TQM, with its focus on the customer, is the way in a globally competitive marketplace to produce superior long-term financial value for owners.[18] Since 1988 winners of the Malcolm Baldrige National Quality Award have outperformed the stock market by nearly three to one, according to *Business Week*. Over that time the average Baldrige winner yielded a cumulative gain of 89 percent, whereas the Standard & Poor's 500 stock index delivered 33 percent.[19]

Two recent empirical studies have shown the superior business results associated with implementing quality as a business strategy. In 1991 the General Accounting Office reported to Congress on a study of 22 companies that were finalists for the Malcolm Baldrige National Quality Award in 1988 and 1989. According to the report: "Companies that adopted quality management practices experienced an overall

QUALITY EXHIBIT

Lands' End: Principles of Doing Business

Principle 1. We do everything we can to make our products better. We improve material and add back features and construction details that others have taken out over the years. We never reduce the quality of a product to make it cheaper.

Principle 2. We price our products fairly and honestly. We do not, have not, and will not participate in the common retailing practice of inflating mark-ups to set up a future phony "sale."

Principle 3. We accept any return, for any reason, at any time. Our products are guaranteed. No fine print. No arguments. We mean exactly what we say: GUARANTEED. PERIOD. ®

Principle 4. We ship faster than anyone we know of. We ship items in stock the day after we receive the order. At the height of the last Christmas season the longest time an order was in the house was 36 hours, excepting monograms which took another 12 hours.

Principle 5. We believe that what is best for our customers is best for all of us. Everyone here understands that concept. Our sales and service people are trained to know our products, and to be friendly and helpful. They are urged to take all the time necessary to take care of you. We even pay for your call, for whatever reason you call.

Principle 6. We are able to sell at lower prices because we have eliminated middlemen; because we don't buy branded merchandise with high protected mark-ups; and because we have placed our contracts with manufacturers who have proved that they are cost conscious and efficient.

Lands' End mail order retailing has been very successful due to its affordable quality, customer service, and guaranteed customer satisfaction. (Photo credit: Lands' End.)

Principle 7. We are able to sell at lower prices because we operate efficiently. Our people are hard working, intelligent and share in the success of the company.

Principle 8. We are able to sell at lower prices because we support no fancy emporiums with their high overhead. Our main location is in the middle of a 40-acre cornfield in rural Wisconsin. We still operate our first location in Chicago's Near North tannery district.

Source: Lands' End Inc. Annual Report (1992).

improvement in corporate performance. In nearly all cases, companies that used Total Quality Management practices achieved better employee relations, higher productivity, greater customer satisfaction, increased market share, and improved profitability."[20]

A large-scale data analysis of the relationship between quality and profit revealed that the higher the quality, the higher the profitability.[21] This positive relationship between quality and profitability held for both measures of profitability

FIGURE 7.2   *The Relationship between Quality and Profit*

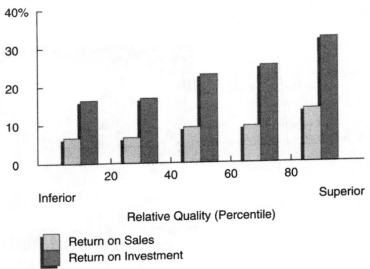

Source: Robert D. Buzzell and Bradley T. Gale, *The PIMS Principles*, New York: Free Press (1987), 107.

tested—return on sales and return on investment. **Return on sales** is a measure of profitability in which profits are expressed as a percentage of sales. **Return on investment** is a measure of profitability in which profits are expressed as a percentage of investment. Figure 7.2 shows graphically the positive relationship between quality and profitability.

Competitors

In our Chapter 6 discussion of the importance of competitors in the formulation and implementation of business strategy, we noted certain disadvantages of focusing on competitors. Principally, by concentrating on competitors, it is easy to lose sight of customers. This conflicts with the purpose of business strategy, which is to serve customers' needs.[22]

By following its competitors, the firm is destined to pursue a follower strategy. By never being first to market with a new product, it is destined to realize below-average financial returns. In one aspect, however, focusing on the competition is relevant in that it can help the firm find ways to improve processes and systems through the activity of benchmarking.

Benchmarking

Functional benchmarking is studying and possibly even emulating the best processes and systems in the world, whether in the firm's own industry or in another industry. Xerox developed benchmarking to a fine business practice, and these

FIGURE 7.3 *Managerial Focus on Competitors and Customers*

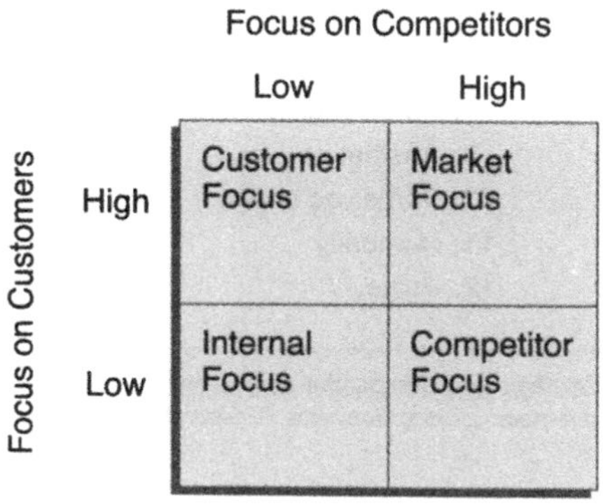

Focus on Competitors

		Low	High
Focus on Customers	High	Customer Focus	Market Focus
	Low	Internal Focus	Competitor Focus

practices have been thoroughly documented.[23] If Xerox benchmarked L.L. Bean's order entry and billing system, for example, such a practice would be called functional benchmarking.[24]

Competitive benchmarking is analyzing what the best competitor or leading companies in the industry are doing in order to discover the products, processes, and practices that satisfy customer needs. For example, if IBM studied and emulated how Microsoft designs new software for PCs, such a practice would be known as competitive benchmarking.

Competitive benchmarking of processes is the prime area for focusing on competitors. As we have so frequently emphasized, managers should focus on customers and their value requirements as the first step in designing, improving, and distributing products or services. Figure 7.3 presents in matrix format the managerial focus on customers and competitors. The dangers of an internal focus are described in Chapter 2 and throughout this book. Market focus combines high competitor focus for competitive benchmarking of processes with high customer focus for customer-value determination. Thus in Figure 7.3 market focus is the preferred quadrant.

CRITICAL THINKING QUESTIONS

1. What is the importance of the customer and total customer satisfaction in business-level strategy?
2. How are benchmarking and quality improvement related?

CUSTOMER VALUE

Providing value to customers is much more than simply eliminating defects. Customer value has many dimensions and must be systematically determined in the firm's products and services.

TABLE 7.1   *Multiple Dimensions of Quality*

1. Conformance to specifications	7. Durability
2. Performance	8. Serviceability
3. Quick response	9. Aesthetics
4. Quick-change expertise	10. Perceived quality
5. Features	11. Humanity
6. Reliability	12. Value

Source: D. A. Garvin, *Managing Quality: The Strategic and Competitive Edge*, New York: Free Press (1988): 49; and R. J. Schonberger, *Building a Chain of Customers: Linking Business Functions to Create the World Class Company*, New York: Free Press (1990): 83.

Multiple Dimensions

Deming, Juran, Ishikawa, Crosby, and others taught the business world that it could deliver high quality and low price to the customer simultaneously. That finding introduced an era of paying attention to the multiple dimensions of customer value. Quality no longer means just numeration of defects or adherence to an internal engineering specification. Quality means delivering value to customers in accord with their expectations.

Two researchers have together formulated a total of 12 dimensions of customer value.[25] Presented in Table 7.1, these dimensions clearly indicate that quality is more than the presence or absence of defects.

Value Realized and Value Sacrificed

Value can be either positive or negative, because value can be realized or it can be sacrificed. **Realized value** is value that the customer receives. It can include comfort, image, ease of use, reliability, consistency, enjoyment, and a host of other characteristics. **Sacrificed value** is value that the customer gives up. It can include time, money, energy, frustration, worry, and a number of other components. Therefore a two-dimensional view of customer value has been proposed. Both dimensions have multiple components.

It has been estimated that a satisfied customer will tell three other potential customers of his or her satisfaction. However, a dissatisfied customer will tell seven other potential customers of his or her dissatisfaction. It is important, therefore, for managers to pay attention to the value sacrificed by customers that could lead to dissatisfaction.

Customers demand customer value in many dimensions. In the case of a product with harmful side effects, who should make the decision concerning whether the positive effects outweigh the negative effects? As described in the following ethics exhibit, should the customer make the decision, or the firm, or the government?

E T H I C S   E X H I B I T

Hair Dyes

In January 1978 the Food and Drug Administration (FDA) announced it was considering a regulation that would require hair dyes containing the chemical 4-MMPD (4-Methoxy-M-phenylenediamine sulfate) to carry the following label: "Warning: Contains an ingredient that can penetrate your skin and has been determined to cause cancer in laboratory animals." The warning promised to have a significant effect on the sales of the major manufacturers of permanent hair dyes, including Clairol, Cosmair, Revlon, Alberto-Culver, Breck, Helene Curtis, and Tussy. The permanent hair dye sales of these companies had topped $300 million in 1977.

4-MMPD had been suspected of being carcinogenic since March 1975. The National Cancer Institute (NCI) subsequently tested 4-MMPD and found that it did indeed cause cancer in laboratory animals. In spite of these findings, however, the FDA was unable to do more than propose a warning label, since the 1938 Food, Drug, and Cosmetic Act, which regulates cosmetics, prohibits the FDA from banning the sale of hair dyes no matter how hazardous their contents. After a prolonged legal battle with the cosmetics industry, the FDA succeeded in imposing the proposed warning label.

When it was clear that the FDA would succeed in imposing the warning label, the major hair dye manufacturers implemented essentially similar strategies to avoid the label: They reformulated their hair dyes so that the new dyes contained no 4-MMPD. However, the companies refused to recall the old hair dyes that they had already distrib-uted to retailers and that would continue to be sold over counters for several years. They would affix no warnings to these dyes.

The response of Revlon differed somewhat from that of the other manufacturers. Revlon removed the offending 4-MMPD from its dyes and replaced it with a 4-EMPD (4-ethoxy-M-phenylenediamine sulfate), a substance with a chemical structure almost identical to 4-MMPD, but one that did not yet require a warning label. Several chemical experts later claimed that Revlon's 4-EMPD had a potential for causing cancer similar to that of 4-MMPD.

Until animal tests on 4-EMPD are completed, the FDA cannot move to require a warning label against the Revlon substance. Such tests take three to four years to complete, and processing a warning proposal takes another one or two years.

Discussion Questions

1. In your judgment, was the Food and Drug Administration right in ordering the warning label in January 1978? Why or why not?

2. In your judgment, was it enough, from an ethics point of view, for the cosmetics companies to fix the warning on their labels or did their duties extend beyond this? Explain.

3. What should management at Revlon do about 4-EMPD?

Best Net Value

The difference between value realized and value sacrificed is called **net customer value** or simply **net value**. A comparison of the net value for all competitive firms in the industry determines the **best net value**,[26] thereby giving the firm a target. The business objective is to move the firm's customers to a position of higher value realized and lower value sacrificed so that the best net value in the industry is offered.

Many view Federal Express as providing the best net value in domestic, rapid, small-package delivery. Federal Express charges a moderate price for consistent, next-day, secure delivery, by courteous employees, and package pickup at the sender's place of work. Sacrifice to the customer is minimized and value realized is substantial. The U.S. Postal Service does not yield such net value to customers.

Frequently, managers make organizational decisions based on saving money. However, customers have needs other than price reduction. As the diversity exhibit demonstrates, making decisions solely on the basis of saving money for the organization can be fraught with difficulty.

Customer-Value Determination Systems

Providing best net value implies that particular attention is paid to deciding what the customer requires. Such an important task requires the efforts of managers in several functions to fully understand value realized and value sacrificed. To pay it proper attention, such a cross-functional system needs to be formalized.

A good example is the worldwide customer satisfaction measurement system that Capsugel has in place. The system collects data from customers on a worldwide basis to determine what their requirements are and if they are being met by Capsugel. Managers are then held accountable to the customer satisfaction data. Sometimes, customers are impressed just because the firm cares enough to ask if they are satisfied.

At its Wixom, Michigan, Lincoln plant, Ford workers and managers review customer satisfaction/dissatisfaction data twice a month. "We are very customer-driven," says a company spokesperson, noting that meetings are held twice a month in the plant's large conference room to go over the results of Ford's competitive new-vehicle-quality studies, which provide detailed reports on what customers liked or didn't like about the Wixom-made cars.[27] These data help them to continuously improve the product and the manufacturing process to yield even greater value to customers.

New-Product Development Systems and Quality Function Deployment

New-product development systems in TQM firms are good examples of the use of cross-functional systems to create and deliver value to customers. The new-product development systems frequently utilize personnel from most of the functional areas in the company to work together on the design of the new product.

At Corning Laboratories teams consisting of representatives from research and development, manufacturing, and marketing guide prototypes from the labs to market.[28] Sometimes customers are on the teams.

It appears that many Japanese and German firms understand the importance of including customer expectations in the design of new products and services. However, the data in Figure 7.4 show that many U.S. firms had not yet adopted this business practice when the survey was done in the early 1990s.

A technique being used more often today to ensure that the design of new products and services is based on customer criteria is Quality Function Deployment

D I V E R S I T Y   E X H I B I T

The University Maids

Old State University had little experience with personnel administration. The faculty took care of itself, student wives held most of the secretarial posts, and there were few full-time employees in the traditional sense of the term. Therefore the president was very distressed when federal funds for research were withheld because a group of dormitory maids claimed they had been discriminated against by being laid off.

To reduce the cost of dormitory operation, the university was cutting the staff of maids from 60 to 45 (with the understanding that students would do more of their own housework). The 15 maids charged that they should have been eligible (on the basis of performance and seniority) to do other jobs in the university. More specifically, they asked to be assigned to positions of guard and watchman. To date, these jobs had always been filled by men, and there had been no transfers between these positions.

The president was loathe to approve this on several counts. He felt that it was dangerous for women to be guards, and he knew that guards had to be able to work night as well as day shifts. Intruders or prowlers would be less likely to be intimidated by a woman, particularly since some of the women were very slight of build. Also, he felt that these were not jobs suitable for the older women (although some of those dropped were quite young).

The male guards also objected to this request, on the grounds that it was unfair to have employees from another work group interfering with their seniority lines. In truth, the more recently hired guards were somewhat concerned that they might be displaced by women having longer service with the university.

Discussion Questions

1. The decision to drop the maids was made to reduce the cost of operating the university. What about the needs of the students for cleanliness? Should the university's managers explore the balance of these two needs among the students?

2. In making decisions based on cost containment, how should managers balance those decisions with customers' other needs?

Source: George Strauss and Leonard R. Sayles, *Personnel: The Human Problems of Management*, 4e, © 1980, p. 469. Reprinted by permission of Prentice-Hall, Englewood Cliffs, NJ.

(QFD). This technique starts with customer criteria, translates them into product or service requirements, and then translates them into product or service requirement measures. **Quality Function Deployment** is a customer-driven design system that attempts to achieve early coupling between the requirements of the customer, marketing, and design engineering.[29]

For example, in the design of a personal computer, customer requirements might be expressed as ease of use, portability, quality of graphics, affordability, and speed. The product requirements might then be expressed as menu-driven commands, open architecture, lightweight unit, compact size, high-resolution screen, medium price, and fast microchip. The product requirement measures might then be expressed as lightweight unit (less than 10 pounds), compact size (20" × 16" maximum outside dimensions), and medium price (greater than $2,000 but less than $3,000 per unit).[30]

Sea Ray Boats Division of Brunswick Corporation is a manufacturer and marketer of high-quality boats. The following quality exhibit illustrates the importance of customer requirements in a firm's TQ efforts.

FIGURE 7.4   *The Customer and New-Product Design across Countries*

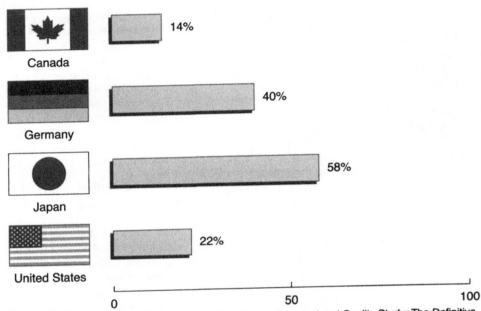

Percentage of Businesses Whose Departments Always or Almost Always
Translate Customer Expectations into the Design of New Products and Services

Canada — 14%

Germany — 40%

Japan — 58%

United States — 22%

0   50   100

Source: American Quality Foundation and Ernst & Young, "International Quality Study: The Definitive
Study of the Best International Quality Management Practices," Cleveland: Ernst & Young (1991): 21.

CRITICAL THINKING QUESTIONS

1. How are the ideas of customer value and best net customer value related to the idea of quality?

2. Describe the importance of a customer-value determination system in a technological firm with rapidly changing technology.

THE PAYOFF FROM TOTAL QUALITY

As documented in Chapter 3, U.S. industry has been under attack from intense global competition. Some industries were decimated in the 1980s. Some companies lost thousands of customers and retrenched into smaller-size organizations. However, there has been a rebirth of U.S. competitiveness in some industries and companies under the banner of Total Quality Management. Associated with this industrial renaissance are high quality, low costs, short cycle times, regained market share, and increased long-term profitability.

QUALITY EXHIBIT

Quality at Sea Ray Boats

To help us meet the challenge of continual quality improvement, Sea Ray has put together a program called P.A.C.E.—People Achieving Customer Expectations.

In a very real sense, quality is a closed loop, beginning and ending with the customer. The quality process starts when we seek to understand what it takes to satisfy customers in our marketplace.

Quality then goes full circle: We define specifications to meet the customer's requirements. We manufacture products and develop the services necessary to satisfy those requirements. Then we go back to the customer and get feedback: "How are we doing? Did we meet your expectations? How can we serve you better? What improvements and innovations would you like to see from us?"

So you see, in a pace-setting company, quality must mean more than just a product characteristic. Rather, it's an attitude that "the customer is king." That belief must permeate the entire company, driving every decision and involving every employee. When quality improvement becomes truly ingrained in the corporate culture, error rates and defects plummet. Productivity and customer satisfaction mushroom.

Through quality improvement efforts, Sea Ray has further enhanced the quality of its boats, as well as enhanced profitability. (Photo credit: Sea Ray Boat Division/ Brunswick Corporation.)

The goal of the P.A.C.E. program is to continuously improve the quality of our products and services and to enhance our ability to satisfy the customer.

Source: Brunswick Corporation, Sea Ray Boats Division (July 1991).

Improved Operating Performance

The most comprehensive study to date concerning the results of TQM firms is the 1991 GAO study of 22 companies that were finalists for the Malcolm Baldrige National Quality Award in 1988 and 1989. These firms' increased operating performance is illustrated in Figure 7.5. The firms reported average annual improvements of from 5 percent to 12 percent in reliability, on-time delivery, order-processing time, errors or defects, product lead time, inventory turnover, and costs of quality.[31]

High Quality

The quality gap is the gap relative to many international competitors that has been most noticeably closed by U.S. firms that have embraced TQM. As noted in Figure 7.5, the average decline in defects was about 10 percent per year for the Baldrige finalists.

FIGURE 7.5   *Improved Operating Performance of 22 TQM Firms*

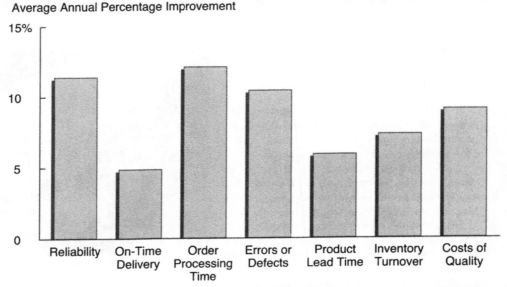

Source: U.S. General Accounting Office, "Management Practices: U.S. Companies Improve Performance Through Quality Efforts" (May 1991), GAO/NSIAD-91-190): 22.

One of the most obvious industries reporting improved quality is the automobile industry. A 1990 survey of over 1,000 consumers shows that most thought the quality of U.S. cars was almost as good as the quality of Japanese models (see Table 7.2). Although there are substantial differences among some auto makes in terms of quality, it is noteworthy that Saturn was ranked third in the J.D. Power Customer Satisfaction Survey within two years of its start-up.

Xerox, a 1989 Baldrige Quality Award winner, credits its "leadership through quality" efforts with its dramatic improvement in quality. The firm has improved designs and upgraded the quality of both its internal and external suppliers. Partly as a result, the number of defective parts at the Webster, New York, Xerox plant plunged from 10,000 parts per million in 1980 to just 360 ppm in 1989.[32]

The Corning, New York, plant of Corning Inc. produces ceramic filters to purify molten metals such as iron and steel. As part of its quality strategy, the plant has implemented several changes in organization, management, and personnel policies. These changes include the abandonment of shift supervisors and of inspection after production. There is also greater reliance on cross-functional teams, including the use of production teams with engineering and maintenance personnel, the location of sales and marketing in the plant to improve responsiveness to customers, and cross-training so that workers can rotate among jobs. The plant has achieved dramatically improved quality levels as measured in terms of customer rejects. Defect rates have dropped from 1,800 parts per million to just 9 ppm over a three-year period.[33]

TABLE 7.2   *American Quality Is Catching Up*

Percentage of respondents who agreed, disagreed, or were unsure that the quality of U.S. cars is almost as good as the quality of Japanese models:	
Agreed	71%
Disagreed	25%
Not sure	4%

Source: "Auto Quality," *Business Week* (October 22, 1990): 91.

Low Cost

As Deming predicted, when quality goes up due to systemic and process changes, then costs come down. Many firms have reported lower costs associated with such quality efforts. Affordable quality has thus become the reality in many markets.

Primarily due to high costs, Texas Instruments shifted production of its low-priced calculators to the Far East in 1982. With some determined people who wanted to prove that they could manufacture low-priced, high-quality calculators in this country, and with the encouragement of a major customer (Wal-Mart), the Lubbock, Texas, plant of TI regained the manufacturing. Its engineers and manu-facturing personnel designed the product and the manufacturing process concur-rently by designing the product for ease of assembly with only seven components. Thus the TI-25 calculator had the fewest parts of any scientific calculator in the world in 1990. TI selected top-quality suppliers, eliminated wasteful steps in the manufacturing process, and used a continuous-flow manufacturing process. Although TI did not publish the exact cost of manufacture, it apparently achieved its low-cost goal, since it priced the line of TI-25 calculators from $5 to $10 and sched-uled production of 2 million units in 1990.[34]

The Dana Corporation plant in Minneapolis makes hydraulic control valves used in heavy construction equipment. The TQ manager, Hank Rogers, described several low-tech changes the plant made without investing funds in new technology. Two themes were important: a just-in-time manufacturing system built around man-ufacturing cells, and extensive use of teams. "The teams are 'primarily self-directed,'" Rogers points out. "They elect their own team captains and tackle various continu-ous improvement projects—including setup reduction and preventative mainte-nance."[35] As a result, Dana has increased productivity by 32 percent, pared quality costs by 47 percent, reduced total inventory by 50 percent, improved return on investment by 470 percent, and increased return on sales by 320 percent.[36]

Short Cycle Times

One advantage of simplifying processes and working in cross-functional teams is reduced cycle time. **Cycle time** is the length of time required to complete an oper-ation. For a new product or service, this includes the time to design and deliver it to the customer. For an existing product or service, cycle time refers to the time it takes to fill a customer's order.

QUALITY CASE

Back to the Saturn Case

Saturn's business strategy for acceptance by customers in the fiercely competitive automobile marketplace was based on a simple idea—customers would perceive more value in a low-priced, high-quality Saturn than in competing models. Saturn's quality was world class, its prices were low, and its dealers treated customers well with no-haggle pricing.

The commitment to delivering such value to customers was extraordinary at General Motors, as its plummeting market share showed. GM had been accused by many of short-term-profit thinking for the sake of maximizing current earnings (see Chapter 3). However, the $5 billion investment in Saturn was made with the expectation that profits would not be made until the mid-1990s. In this case the customer was first, and short-term profits were second.

Saturn's quality was not an accident. Saturn's workers were members of teams with previously unheard of levels of input into decisions and very high levels of worker training by industry standards. All workers were on salary, and part of their pay was tied into reaching quality goals. As part of a horizontal system of management, suppliers and dealers were integral members of the Saturn team. Saturn had one of the tightest just-in-time (JIT) inventory systems in North America, in which parts were delivered from suppliers just as they were needed for use in the assembly process. This JIT system revealed the source of quality problems so they could be solved immediately. The team that designed the car included manufacturing personnel with experience in assembly and in manufacturing processes. Their input helped design a car that was easier to assemble and that allowed fewer chances for manufacturing errors.

Saturn's sales approach to no-haggle pricing, or no-dicker stickers, started a marketing revolution among car dealers. Because of its success in this area, Ford, Chrysler, and other divisions of GM also experimented with no-haggle pricing.

A good example of reduced cycle time in automobile design can be found at Chrysler. The automaker reorganized its staff into platform teams—groups representing all departments that work on one car or truck from start to finish. The team is able to resolve conflicts early and prevent a hard-to-build car or unreliable design from ever reaching production. Chrysler has also developed a Japanese-style cooperative relationship with its suppliers, recognizing that suppliers are part of its cross-functional team.[37] With its cross-functional teams and supplier partnering, Chrysler has cut $3 billion from its yearly costs, and it can bring a car to market as fast as the best worldwide competitors. Chrysler has shortened its new-car development cycle in the last five years from 54 months to 39 months and has done it with a smaller staff.

A good example of reduced cycle time in manufacturing can be found at Motorola's Boynton Beach, Florida, plant that produces customized pagers. The plant uses a simultaneous engineering effort in which the pager was redesigned for robotic assembly. It shrank its supplier base to 22 "best-in-class," sole-source suppliers, chosen for their extremely high quality levels. It also uses computer-controlled, "real-time," statistical process control that attempts preemptively to avoid quality problems rather than just count mistakes. The plant can begin producing customized pagers in lot sizes of

FIGURE 7.6   *Improved Market and Financial Performance of TQM Firms*

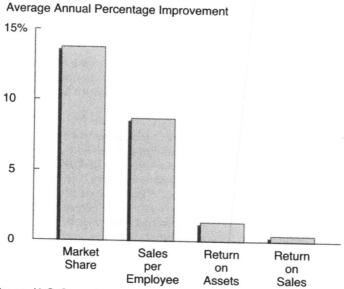

Source: U. S. General Accounting Office, "Management Practices: U. S. Companies Improve Performance Through Quality Efforts" (May 1991), GAO/NSIAD-91-190): 27.

one within 20 minutes after a salesperson enters an order via computer at Motorola's headquarters in Schaumburg, Illinois. The actual production of each pager, customized to the proper radio frequency, takes less than two hours. This includes manufacture of printed circuit boards, final assembly, testing, and packaging for shipment.[38]

In the Corning, New York, plant of Corning Inc., customer lead times have dropped from five weeks to a few days. Sometimes the plant can respond within 30 hours.

Regained Market Share and Improved Financial Performance

In addition to the preceding examples of improved operating performance, the longer-term issues of increased sales, market share, and financial performance must be considered. Two separate studies have shown that companies that furnish quality products can charge more for their products, with resulting higher profit margins.[39] A look back at Figure 7.2 emphasizes the dramatically higher profitability associated with higher quality.

Besides operating performance, the 1991 GAO study of 22 companies that were finalists for the Baldrige Quality Award in 1988 and 1989 collected data on market share increases, sales per employee, return on assets, and return on sales. The results are presented in Figure 7.6. Because it connotes increased value to customers and competitive strength, the most noteworthy increase is the 13.7 percent average annual increase in market share.[40]

Business Week recently published a special issue on quality, titled "The Quality Imperative: What It Takes to Win in the Global Economy." In the introduction the editors wrote: "Quality may be *the biggest competitive issue* of the late 20th and early 21st

QUALITY CASE

Conclusion to the Saturn Case

Within two years of its late-1990 start-up, Saturn had become an obvious success. Its cars were ranked third in a 1992 J.D. Power Customer Satisfaction Survey, based largely on the firm's nearly impeccable quality, low prices, and no-haggle pricing by dealers. The prices of some of the other cars in the top five were three or four times higher than Saturn's prices. The customer satisfaction ratings from the 1992 J.D. Power Customer Satisfaction Survey for the top five autos are listed in the following table:

J.D. Power Customer Satisfaction Ratings for Top Five Automobiles: 1992

Auto Make	Customer Satisfaction Rating
Lexus	179
Infiniti	167
Saturn	160
Acura	148
Mercedes-Benz	145
Industry Average	129

Source: "Saturn: GM Finally Has a Real Winner," *Business Week* (August 17, 1992): 87.

Saturn's dealers were selling an average of 100 cars each month, more than any other brand sold in the United States. Saturn dealerships were ranked by automobile dealers as the most valuable dealership to own in 1993. Six weeks before the 1992 model year was officially over, the Saturn dealers sold out of cars. In the spring of 1992 Saturn started to ship cars to Taiwan. In 1993 Saturn was operating near capacity with three shifts and was planning to export right-hand drive cars to Japan. In early 1994 Saturn reported its first-ever profit and lobbied General Motors for funds to start another plant.

Saturn showed that GM could produce cars to global standards of quality, price, and customer satisfaction, and thereby regain customers who had been lost to Japanese competitors. Also, Saturn showed that to be world class, it takes both long-term, executive-level commitment to superior customer value and systemwide team approaches with suppliers, dealers, and workers.

DISCUSSION QUESTIONS

1. How was Saturn's business strategy of very high quality and low prices different from other divisions of GM?

2. Why was it important for Saturn to implement team concepts in the design and production of its cars?

3. Why was it important for GM to establish a new company rather than simply produce a new model in an existing GM plant?

Sources: "GM Saturn Unit Trumpets Profit Turned in 1993," *The Wall Street Journal* (January 6, 1994): A4; *Saturn Mission*, Spring Hill, TN: Saturn Corporation, 1993; "Honda: The Dangers of Running Too Lean," *Fortune* (June 14, 1993): 113–114; "Labor's Days at GM," *The Wall Street Journal* (September 4, 1992): A1; "Fulfilling Buyers' Wishes, Saturn's Well Runs Dry," *USA Today* (August 18, 1992): B1; "Saturn: GM Finally Has a Real Winner," *Business Week* (August 17, 1992): 86–91; "Saturn's Success Breeds Low-Pressure Copycats," *The Wall Street Journal* (July 31, 1992): B1; "At Saturn, What Workers Want Is...Fewer Defects," *Business Week* (December 2, 1991): 117–118; "Saturn Does Right by Customers; When Will It Make Money?" *Automotive News* (June 3, 1991): 12; C. M. Solomon, "Behind the Wheel at Saturn," *Personnel Journal* (June 1991): 72–74.

By focusing on providing value to customers throughout the world, Procter & Gamble offers a variety of products in a global market. (Photo credit: Procter & Gamble.)

centuries."[41] Echoing that sentiment, Joseph Juran, one of the founders of the quality movement, recently remarked: "The twenty-first century will be the Century of Quality."[42] It appears that a number of U.S. firms are realizing the quality imperative.

CRITICAL THINKING QUESTIONS

1. Relate the demands of customers to the demands of shareholders/owners in a TQ firm.

2. Is TQ a matter of national competitiveness? Explain.

SUMMARY

Deming and others showed industry that high quality and low cost can go together. More inspection after the fact of production and more cost are not the way to achieve higher quality in a competitive era. For higher quality to happen, there must be improvement in horizontal systems and processes.

Quality is much more than defect elimination. As a business strategy, Total Quality Management focuses primarily on the customer and on the idea of providing customer value. Customer value is multidimensional and consists of value received and value sacrificed. Customer-value determination systems attempt to discover what the customer values and does not value. Best net customer value refers to the greatest difference between value received and value sacrificed among all competitors.

Customer-value systems that determine what the customer values and the design of new products to fulfill those customer values are crucial in quality improvement. Quality Function Deployment is a new-product development system that explicitly incorporates customer value in the design and in the design process.

Functional benchmarking refers to analyzing the processes and systems of the "best-in-class" firms to improve processes and systems.

Although severely battered by international competition in the late 1970s and throughout the 1980s, some U.S. firms have been experiencing a rebirth with Total Quality. Those that have implemented many TQM ideas are realizing higher quality, lower costs, shorter cycle times, increased market share, and greater profitability. Some U.S. firms are successfully competing globally on the basis of TQM.

EXPERIENTIAL EXERCISE

The Hidden Triangles

Objective: To discourage people from jumping to early conclusions before carefully analyzing the total picture from many angles.

Procedure: After studying Figure 7.7 for five minutes, determine the total number of triangles in the diagram. Compare your total with the totals found by your classmates.

Key: There are a total of 35 triangles in the diagram:

1. Ten small single triangles (without any intersecting lines in them)— for example, AFG.
2. Five tall triangles (each with an external side as a base, and containing five pieces)— for example, ABD.
3. Five long-base triangles (each with three pieces)—for example, ACJ.
4. Five triangles with two exterior sides (each with three pieces)—for example, EAB.
5. Ten triangles with two small triangles inside—for example, ABF.

Discussion Questions

1. Why didn't each of you discover all 35 triangles on your own?
2. Sometimes customers see things in a firm's products that managers do not. Describe the importance of managers' assessing customer value.

Source: Adapted from J. W. Newstrom and E. E. Scannell, *More Games Trainers Play*, New York: McGraw-Hill (1983): 121–123.

FIGURE 7.7 *The Hidden Triangles*

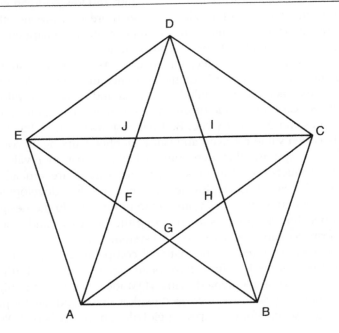

CHAPTER CASE

Champion International Paper Company

As the Pigeon River winds through the mountains of North Carolina, its waters are filled with bass and trout. About 25 miles before crossing into Tennessee, the river turns the color of coffee, and the only fish found in it are bottom-dwelling carp. In 1988 the Environmental Protection Agency determined that a process used to bleach wood pulp at the Canton, North Carolina, plant of the Champion International Paper Company was responsible for the pollution.

Environmental groups and the state of Tennessee appealed to the EPA to force Champion to treat the 45 million gallons of water per day it cycled out of and back into the river. The state of North Carolina, which had earlier approved the company's operating permit, entered the dispute on the side of Champion, claiming that the discharges affected only the color and not the quality of the water. The company claimed that the technology necessary to meet the EPA's standards did not exist and that enforcement would result in closure of the plant.

The controversy surrounding the Champion issue has far-reaching effects. On one side, if the plant closed down, not only would 1,650 plant workers be out of jobs, which paid an average annual salary of $40,000, but businesses in the community also would suffer and, in all probability, not survive. On the other side, Cocke County residents in Tennessee, whose per capita income is $8,600, compared to Haywood County (North Carolina) residents' per capita income of $12,097, attribute the area's high unemployment rate to the state of the Pigeon River. In 1989 Cocke County's unemployment rate was 10 percent, a low figure for that area where unemployment has been as high as 29 percent. This reveals a stark contrast to Haywood County's 1989 unemployment rate of 4.3 percent. Cocke County residents cite examples of investors who lost interest in the area after surveying the river's condition.

Environmental groups appealed to citizens of both states to support the EPA standard, emphasizing the benefits of scenic beauty and the economic impact of recreation and tourism in the entire area. An opposing grass-roots organization called "Save Champion" was formed in the Canton area, and it enlisted thousands of volunteers in its fight against the EPA. Newspaper and television ads were used to notify the organization's supporters of the times and locations of public hearings on the EPA permit, thereby ensuring packed houses of pro-Champion supporters. Letter-writing campaigns and door-to-door solicitation brought further pressure on the EPA and environmental groups. Emotions ran high as reports came in of leaders of the Dead Pigeon River Council in Tennessee receiving threatening phone calls and cars with Tennessee license plates being vandalized or stolen while in Haywood County.

The outcome of the Champion/Pigeon River controversy was a compromise agreement in which Champion agreed to work within existing technology to improve the water quality under strict monitoring by the EPA. In 1991 Champion began construction on an oxygen delignification process that would result in the reduction of chlorine use, eliminating dioxins that have been found to cause cancer in laboratory animals. Champion also has been cutting back on its freshwater consumption and is installing a new system to eliminate offensive odors from the air and water. Additionally, what was originally predicted to be a 1,000-employee reduction at the Champion plant has been reduced to a 300–400 cut, which the company hopes to achieve through retirement and attrition. Ross Kilpatrick, plant manager and vice president of operations at Champion, states that "there is no payout whatsoever on this [environmental improvements]." The residents of Cocke County might disagree.

Discussion Questions

1. Managers are asked to provide value to customers. What are the managers' other responsibilities to people impacted by a plant's operations?

2. How should managers balance the two responsibilities?

Sources: M. J. Stahl and D. W. Grigsby, *Strategic Management for Decision Making*, Boston: PWS-Kent (1991): 180; Luann Nelson, "The Waters of Strife: Paper Profits Have Polluted the Pigeon River and Sparked a War Between the States," *Business North Carolina* (April 1991): 36.

KEY TERMS

best net value   Strongest net value among all competitive firms in the industry.

competitive benchmarking   Analyzing what the best competitor or leading companies in the industry are doing in order to discover the products, processes, and practices that satisfy customer needs.

cost of quality   Costs incurred in producing poor-quality products and services.

cross-functional systems   Activities and resources that are linked to provide value to customers and that span at least two of the functions of design, production, marketing, and finance.

cycle time   Length of time required to complete an operation.

functional benchmarking   Studying and possibly even emulating the best processes and systems in the world, whether in the firm's own industry or in another industry.

net customer value (net value)   Difference between value realized and value sacrificed.

quality function deployment   Customer-driven design system that attempts to achieve early coupling between the requirements of the customer, marketing, and design engineering.

realized value   Value that the customer receives.

return on investment   Measure of profitability in which profits are expressed as a percentage of investment.

return on sales   Measure of profitability in which profits are expressed as a percentage of sales.

sacrificed value   Value that the customer gives up.

ENDNOTES

1. W. E. Deming, *Out of the Crisis*, Cambridge, MA: MIT Center for Advanced Engineering Study (1986).
2. J. M. Juran, *Managerial Breakthrough*, New York: McGraw-Hill (1964); K. Ishikawa, *What Is Total Quality Control?* Englewood Cliffs, NJ: Prentice-Hall (1985); P. Crosby, *Quality Is Free*, New York: New American Library (1979).
3. W. E. Cole, "Competitive Economies and the Economics of Competition," in M. J. Stahl and G. M. Bounds, eds., *Competing Globally Through Customer Value: The Management of Strategic Suprasystems*, Westport, CT: Quorum Books (1991): 14–31.
4. Deming, *Out of the Crisis*, 23.
5. Cole, "Competitive Economies and the Economics of Competition," 19.
6. R. J. Schonberger, *Building a Chain of Customers: Linking Business Functions to Create the World Class Company*, New York: Free Press (1990): 77.
7. W. Judge, M. Stahl, R. Scott, and R. Millender, "Long-Term Quality Improvement and Cost Reduction at Capsugel/Warner-Lambert," in Stahl and Bounds, *Competing Globally Through Customer Value*, 703–709.
8. D. A. Garvin, Managing Quality: The Strategic and Competitive Edge, New York: Free Press (1988): 49.
9. Stahl and Bounds, *Competing Globally Through Customer Value*, 2.
10. American Quality Foundation and Ernst & Young, "International Quality Study: The Definitive Study of the Best International Quality Management Practices," Cleveland: Ernst & Young (1991): 1.
11. J. Bowles and J. Hammond, *Beyond Quality: How 50 Winning Companies Use Continuous Improvement*, New York: Putnam (1991): 193.
12. R. J. Schonberger, "Is Strategy Strategic? Impact of Total Quality Management on Strategy," *Academy of Management Executive*, 6 (August 1992): 80–87.
13. D. A Kearns and D. A. Nadler, *Prophets in the Dark: How Xerox Reinvented Itself and Beat Back the Japanese*, New York: Harper Business (1992): 270.

14. R. W. Galvin, *The Idea of Ideas*, Schaumburg, IL: Motorola University Press (1991): 68.
15. "The Quality Imperative: What It Takes to Win in the Global Economy," *Business Week* (October 25, 1991): 38.
16. Eastman Chemical, *Strategic Intent*, Kingsport, TN (1993).
17. "Now Quality Means Service Too," *Fortune* (April 22, 1991): 100.
18. W. Copulsky, "Balancing the Needs of Customers and Shareholders," *Journal of Business Strategy* (November-December 1991): 44–47.
19. "Betting to Win on the Baldie Winners," *Business Week* (October 18, 1993): 8.
20. U.S. General Accounting Office, "Management Practices: U.S. Companies Improve Performance Through Quality Efforts" (May 1991), GAO/NSIAD-91-190: 1.
21. R. D. Buzzell and T. G. Bradley, *The PIMS Principles*, New York: Free Press (1987): 107.
22. K. Ohmae, "Getting Back to Strategy," Harvard Business Review (November-December 1988): 149–156.
23. R. C. Camp, *Benchmarking: The Search for Industry Best Practices That Lead to Superior Performance*, Milwaukee, WI: ASQC Quality Press (1989).
24. R. Osterhoff, W. Locander, and G. Bounds, "Competitive Benchmarking at Xerox," in Stahl and Bounds, *Competing Globally Through Customer Value*, 792.
25. Schonberger, *Building a Chain of Customers*, 83; Garvin, *Managing Quality: The Strategic and Competitive Edge*, 49.
26. G. H. Carothers, G. M. Bounds, and M. J. Stahl, "Managerial Leadership," in Stahl and Bounds, *Competing Globally Through Customer Value*, 78.
27. "America's Best Plants: Ford Motor," *Industry Week* (October 15, 1990): 52.
28. "Corning Laboratories," *Business Week* (October 25, 1991): 158.
29. W. A. Band, *Creating Value for Customers*, New York: Wiley (1991): 168–169; Y. Akao, *Quality Function Deployment: Integrating Customer Requirements into Product Design*, Cambridge, MA: Productivity Press (1990).
30. Band, *Creating Value for Customers*, 168–169.
31. U.S. General Accounting Office, 22–23.
32. "America's Best Plants: Xerox," 28.
33. "America's Best Plants: Corning," 40.
34. "America's Best Plants: Texas Instruments," 30.
35. "America's Best Plants: Dana," 47.
36. Ibid.
37. "Chrysler on the Road to Recovery," *USA Today* (March 6, 1992): B1.
38. "America's Best Plants: Motorola," 62.
39. V. K. Shetty, "Product Quality and Competitive Strategy," *Business Horizons* (May-June, 1987): 46–52; B. Stratton, "The Value of Implementing Quality," *Quality Progress* (July 1991): 70–71.
40. U.S. General Accounting Office, 27.
41. "The Quality Imperative," 4.
42. Joseph Juran, "Made in the U.S.A.: A Renaissance in Quality," *Harvard Business Review* (July-August 1993): 47.

Organizing for Total Quality

8

CHAPTER

Organizational Structure and Design

LEARNING OBJECTIVES

After reading this chapter, you should be able to accomplish the following:

- Explain the difference between formal and informal organizational structures.

- Discuss the ideas of authority, division of labor, specialization, delegation, and decentralization in organizations.

- Compare and contrast the various structural forms and their advantages and disadvantages.

- Analyze the different approaches to designing organizations.

- Describe the major differences between an organizational focus and a process focus.

- Discuss the importance of cross-functional integration, and describe two important cross-functional systems.

- Outline the trends in organizational structure.

CHAPTER OUTLINE

Q UALITY CASE

Ohio Printing Company

Employees, trained in quality improvement techniques at OPC, help solve problems with customers, and change the role of managers to facilitators. (Photo credit: David R. Frazier.)

If you work in a competitive industry, you know that every little edge you can gain on others in your field translates into more dollars for your company. Of course, one of the best ways to gain an edge is by providing customers with better-quality products or services than they can find elsewhere. And one of the best ways to do that is through the use of statistical process control (SPC) and cross-functional teams. SPC is the application of statistical thinking and statistical analysis of data to control and improve processes.

Members of the commercial printing industry face a number of problems peculiar to their operations, says Jerry Cozart, technical director for the Ohio Printing Company (OPC), Dayton, Ohio:

1. The printing industry is very competitive, and profits traditionally are not as high as they are in other industries.
2. Printing is a risky business. "The work may have to run through ten different stages, and if any one of those stages has a problem, then the whole job may have to be scrapped," Cozart says.
3. Traditionally, it has been very difficult to standardize anything in the industry. Unlike specialty printers, who can become very efficient and cost effective by handling only one line of work (such as newspapers or business forms), commercial printers must handle a variety of different projects (posters, labels, advertising brochures, annual reports, and so on), and thus must deal with a great deal of variability.
4. In recent years the trend has been toward more and more full-color printing, so in order to remain competitive, commercial printers must provide this service. However, full-color printing involves even greater degrees of variability and difficulty.

As a result of these challenges, OPC found itself practicing "crisis management" most of the time. Every color job, for example, was "like walking through a minefield," according to the company president, Bill Franklin. "Everyone knew something would go wrong; the only question was when."

Even the experienced press operators weren't comfortable with the new equipment. Also, salespeople remained constantly nervous, wondering when the problems would occur and how they would explain them to their waiting customers. Because of the lack of control, spoilage and rerun costs soared while profits suffered. "Even when we invested in a lot of new equipment designed to help us begin to standardize, we still found a lot of the same spoilage and rerun problems existing," adds Franklin.

continued

OPC realized that some changes needed to be made. So the company addressed three goals:

Goal 1: Implement adequate controls to stabilize operations. This would help to reduce spoilage and reruns (internal "failures") and eliminate poor-quality final work that ultimately is rejected by the customer (external "failures").

Goal 2: Blend the newest available technology with the skilled judgment and experience of the company's craftspeople to ensure consistent, problem-free work.

Goal 3: Place the focus for quality on the individual employees performing the jobs, not on inspectors.

The experienced quality professional will quickly realize that one possible solution for achieving these three goals is SPC. "One of quality expert W. Edwards Deming's points is that if you give employees responsibility for making a quality product, they will come up with a way to do it," says Franklin. "Then it's management's responsibility to change the process to make it possible for workers to put their ideas into motion."

Having recognized that, the company began to implement SPC. In this case the implementation was a matter of encouraging employee input. A short time before implementing these changes, the company had built on an addition to its facility and had sought the input of both suppliers and employees for workstation configuration and layout design.

"The company had previously operated in a rather traditional top-down manner," says technical director Cozart. "However, when people realized how effective employee participation was, they realized that it would be beneficial to obtain it for this process, too. SPC and employee involvement, in other words, came along together at the right time." So management called together the company's 80 employees, gave them an introduction to SPC and what was being planned, and asked for their assistance. "We knew that they would be uncomfortable doing things in a new way, but we also told them that we would listen to them, because they held the key to the success of SPC," says Franklin. But how do people do things in a new way with an old organizational structure?

WHAT IS AN ORGANIZATION?

Ever since people have joined together to accomplish goals, they have wondered about the best way to organize themselves.

Purpose: Goal Accomplishment

Alfred D. Chandler, one of the foremost writers in the area of organizational structure, offered the following definition of structure. "**Structure** can be defined as the design of the organization. The design has two aspects. It includes, first, the lines of authority and communication between the different offices and officers, and, second, the information and data that flow through these lines of communication and authority."[1]

Few would argue with Chandler's definition of structure. However, there is some disagreement about whether goals cause structure or structure causes goals.[2] Our purpose in this chapter is not to resolve the disagreement concerning the direction of causality. Rather it is to show that strategy and structure must be consistent if successful implementation of strategy is to occur.

Structure can also prevent goal accomplishment. *Fortune* magazine analyzed problems for the automobile industry and its future in a story, "U.S. Cars Come Back." The article was particularly interested in the disastrous effect of the 1984 reorganization at General Motors. When Jack Smith moved in as president in April 1992, he set about undoing the reorganization that GM had undertaken eight years before, stating "It's tough to operate when the structure isn't right. It just stops you cold."[3] Many people inside and outside the company blame the reorganization for many of the problems that afflict GM today. Instead of flattening the organization and getting closer to the customer, the reorganization did just the reverse.

Sometimes an organizational structure is so out of touch with the needs of the customer that the firm may start a new organization quite separate from the old organization. Witness the Saturn Corporation. GM wanted to prove to itself and to the world that it could design, manufacture, and market high-quality, reasonably priced small cars that would be preferred over imports. Rather than trying to achieve such a formidable goal in an existing division of GM, a whole new company, entirely removed from the corporate level of GM in Detroit, was started in Tennessee.

Diversity of Organizational Types

Figure 8.1 describes alternative structural forms in terms of complexity. The more divisionalized the organization becomes, the more complex is the structure. We define the various forms later in this chapter.

One way to understand the consistency between strategy and structure is to observe evolutions in structure as organizations grow more complex. As the strategy becomes more complex, the structure becomes more complex.[4]

Formal and Informal Structure

There are at least two types of structure in organizations that reflect the grouping of resources and the flow of work and of information: (1) the formal or explicit organization and (2) the informal or implicit organization.

Formal Structure   The **formal organization** is the structure specified in the organization chart. The **organization chart** diagrams the functions, departments, or positions in the organization and shows how they are related in patterns of formal authority. Generally, formal authority starts at the top of the organization and can be traced throughout the organization. Later in this chapter we show several examples of the formal organization and of organization charts.

The vertical dimension of an organization chart shows the number of reporting or hierarchical levels. Each vertical level describes another level of management. For example, a tall organization chart might have eight layers of management.

The horizontal dimension refers to the breadth of supervision and is measured by the number of employees supervised. This is sometimes called the **span of control.** Small spans of control denote extensive control and supervision. The Roman military was based upon the number 10 as the basis for spans of control. In the 1990s spans of control are growing larger as employees become more highly trained.

FIGURE 8.1   *Alternative Structural Forms*

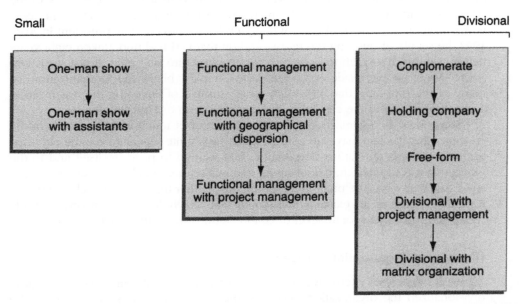

Source: R. C. Shirley, M. H. Peters, and A.I. El-Ansary, *Strategy and Policy Formation: A Multifunctional Orientation* (New York: John Wiley & Sons (1981), 239. Copyright © 1981 by John Wiley & Sons. Reprinted by permission of John Wiley & Sons, Inc.

Informal Structure   The informal organization is not explicitly drawn or formally communicated. The **informal organization** is reflected in the patterns of communication and influence associated with flows of information, work, and social activities of organizational members. Wise managers learn to use both the informal and the formal organization to get work done.

CRITICAL THINKING QUESTIONS

1. Elaborate on the principal purpose of organizations.
2. Discuss the relative importance of the formal and informal organizational structures in the 1990s.

AUTHORITY

Authority might be viewed as the glue that holds organizations together. Thus the source and flow of authority are important to the consideration of organizational structure.

Sources of Authority

Authority is "the right to give orders and the power to exact obedience."[5] Authority in organizations flows from the owners through the structure to managers.

Another view of authority holds that authority flows from those who are managed. This **acceptance view of authority** was promoted by Chester Barnard, who held that whether authority is present or not in any particular situation is determined by the receiver, not by the giver of the order. "A person can and will accept a communication as authoritative only when four conditions simultaneously obtain: (a) he can and does understand the communication; (b) *at the time of his decision* he believes that it is not inconsistent with the purpose of the organization; (c) *at the time of his decision* he believes it to be compatible with his personal interest as a whole; and (d) he is able mentally and physically to comply with it."[6]

For example, a manager may have the legitimate right to direct a subordinate at work and may direct that subordinate to ship some defective products. The subordinate might not comply because the subordinate either feels it to be an unethical act or does not feel that the act is consistent with the firm's quality strategy.

Owners

In U.S. capitalism the legitimate right to direct others starts with the owners of the organization. Ownership may be direct ownership in a small proprietorship or it may be diffuse ownership through thousands of stockholders. Legitimately, those who own the capital have the ultimate right to direct others to employ the owners' capital to earn a profit.

In a corporation the owners are referred to as stockholders. They hire managers as their agents to run the organization on behalf of the owners to produce a return on the owners' invested capital. **Agency theory** explains the relationship between owners and managers.[7] The costs that the owners incur in employing the managers to represent the interests of the owners are called agency costs. The first agency cost that the owners incur is the establishment of the first group of executives charged with running the organization. This group is known as the board of directors.

Board of Directors

The board of directors is the highest decision-making and authoritative body in organizations. The board, which usually consists of inside senior executives and outsiders, represents the interests of the stockholders in the running of the organization. Recently, the power and the percentage of outside directors have been increasing. The forced resignation of Robert Stempel as chief executive officer of General Motors in late 1992 is an example of the power of outside directors on the board.

The articles of incorporation or the legal charter of most corporations place a legal responsibility on the board of directors to represent the stockholders. The courts have enforced this legal responsibility, on the basis that it is the stockholders' capital that enables the organization to exist. The legal and financial systems are the bases of formal power and authority in most organizations.

Chief Executive Officers and Other Managers

The term *executive* is usually used to refer to senior-level managers in an organization who serve as officers of that organization. The highest-ranking executive, often called the chief executive officer (CEO), has ultimate responsibility for the management and performance of the firm.

The jobs of president and chairman of the board are also very senior positions. In some organizations all three titles are vested in one individual. In other organizations three different individuals have the titles and share the ultimate responsibility for the firm.

The next level is usually headed by a chief operating officer (COO). This executive has full responsibility for the daily operations of the entire organization.

The exact titles and duties of other executives (usually vice presidents), mid-level managers (usually general managers), and lower-level managers (usually department and group managers) vary from organization to organization. The titles are frequently a function of the specific organization.

Line and Staff Authority

In fulfilling their legal and financial responsibility, managers must cause others to act. **Line authority** is the direct chain of command from the board through the CEO and other managers in a direct chain to the nonmanagerial employee. Line managers are concerned with the design, production, sale, and distribution of the firm's products or services.

Specialists, called staff, are usually hired in large organizations to advise the line managers and administer functional policies. **Staff authority** is advisory; it is not direct command line authority.

The relationship between authority and responsibility can be indicated by observing that responsibility involves being accountable.[8] Responsibility always goes with authority in organizations. Managers are given authority so that they can direct others toward the goal accomplishment for which the managers are held accountable.

CRITICAL THINKING QUESTIONS

1. Describe the concept and flow of authority in organizations.

2. Discuss the relative importance of line and staff authority in the 1990s.

DELEGATION AND SPECIALIZATION

Once tasks have been divided and employees have specialized, managers must be held responsible for task accomplishment. Recognizing that they cannot perform all the tasks in the organization, managers delegate some tasks to others.

Delegation

Delegation is the assignment of authority and responsibility for the completion of specific tasks to subordinates. The delegation of a specific task means that the manager is still responsible for the accomplishment of the overall task.

FIGURE 8.2   *The Delegation Process*

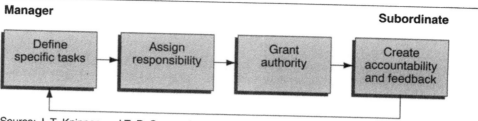

Source: J. T. Knippen and T. B. Green, "Delegation," *Supervision,* 51 (March 1990): 7–9.

For example, a manager who is responsible for the design of a new automobile may delegate authority and responsibility for the design of the engine to a subordinate manager. Although the higher-level manager is still ultimately responsible for the design of the overall automobile, that manager holds the subordinate manager responsible and accountable for the design of the engine.

How to Delegate

There are at least four steps in the delegation process (see Figure 8.2). Delegation may take on several forms, including: "Take action. I do not need to hear from you again." This form does not have the feedback loop shown in Figure 8.2 and is therefore not desirable. At the other end of the spectrum lies the following comment: "Look into the problem and let me know what you find out. I will decide the right course of action." This form has the obvious drawback that there is no delegation of authority. Assuming the skill and maturity of the subordinate, the preferred form of delegation is: "Look into this problem. You have authority to correct the problem. Let me know how you fixed it."[9]

Some managers have trouble delegating tasks because they have a need to closely "supervise" workers. This behavior can yield problems, especially if the amount or kind of supervision differs between genders, as is apparent in the diversity exhibit.

Decentralization

Delegation exists in most organizations to varying degrees as a function of the specific situation. In general, the amount of delegation in the organization refers to the degree of decentralization or centralization in the organization. **Decentralization** is the delegation of many tasks and of the associated authority to subordinates throughout the organization. Power and control are delegated to lower organizational levels in decentralized organizations. **Centralization** is the delegation of few tasks and of little authority throughout the organization. Power and control are kept at the upper levels in centralized organizations.

There is a fair amount of decentralization, for example, if sales personnel in an office equipment sales organization can negotiate terms of the sale when selling fax machines. Alternatively, the organization is quite centralized if the sales personnel must have approval from higher organizational levels for price, delivery date, quantity, and financing terms.

D I V E R S I T Y   E X H I B I T

Morale or Money

Bob Carson was supervisor of a highly technical department. The machinery in the department was competently operated by persons all younger than Carson. All but two of the operators were men. Clara, one of the women, was five months pregnant. She had been there when Carson was hired and had maintained an excellent work record.

Carson had instructed the operators that when on duty they had complete responsibility for and control of what happened on the machines. The work was of a highly technical nature and required great concentration to keep the input and output to and from the machine at a pace that would utilize it to its fullest capacity.

To emphasize the responsibility and control of the operators, Carson had stated that if he were in the machine room and got in the way, they were to "throw him out." Carson seemed incapable of keeping his fingers out of the pie, however, as he continually interrupted or corrected the operators.

The operator's job called for very little physical exertion, most of the time requiring only the pushing of buttons. Occasionally, though, it was necessary to lift objects associated with the work. Clara's fellow workers had been doing this for her during her pregnancy, but in one instance had forgotten, thereby creating a bottleneck. Clara was later reminded by Carson about keeping the work flowing steadily. In response, she did some lifting.

A few days after the incident, Clara had a miscarriage. Clara blamed Carson and accused him of discriminating against her because she was a woman.

At about this time, the whole department was due to come under annual review for budget changes. Since the department was relatively new and in need of additional funds for the expansion necessary to its survival, the manager wanted no one to "rock the boat." Clara intended to "sink the boat," the manager felt. The manager was faced with a dilemma. On the one hand, Carson might be a poor supervisor and the cause of Clara's miscarriage. On the other hand, whether it was Carson's fault or not, recognition of Clara's claim by high-level management could be a severe blow to the department's prestige and to its expectations of an increase in its budget. Furthermore, the other workers were threatening to back Clara in response to Carson's treatment.

Discussion Questions

1. How should the manager deal with Clara? Should he encourage her to delay, drop, or pursue her charges of discrimination?

2. Should Carson have permitted Clara's fellow workers to help her perform her job?

Source: A. F. Knapper, *Cases in Personnel Management*, Westerville, OH: Robin Enterprises (1977): 41–42.

Division of Labor and Specialization

As we indicated earlier in this chapter, the purpose of an organization is to facilitate goal accomplishment. An organization does that by dividing labor and tasks through specialization and then integrating the parts into a system. **Division of labor and specialization** mean that individuals perform narrowly specified tasks.

Early management and organization theorists were strongly in favor of division of labor and specialization. Max Weber described this concept as one of the prime characteristics of an ideal bureaucracy: "Labor is divided with clear lines of authority and responsibility. These divisions are legitimized as official duties."[10] One of the central ideas of Frederick Taylor's philosophy was "job specialization."[11] Henri Fayol argued that the more people specialize, the more efficiently they can perform their work. He further argued that division of labor increased total production by simplifying the tasks required of each worker.[12]

In earlier times, before the growth of large organizations with thousands of employees, the owner accomplished all the tasks. The owner as master craftsman— say a carpenter or tailor—worked with little help from others. The owner was knowledgeable of production, merchandising, and accounting. As organizations grew during the Industrial Revolution, it was no longer efficient for all employees to perform all the tasks of the organization. Dividing the tasks and encouraging employees to specialize ensured gains in productivity and efficiency.

An example of division of labor and specialization is found in a large automobile company like General Motors. Not only do people specialize in terms of engineering or production or marketing or accounting, but the assembly line takes the specialization concept further. On the assembly line, a worker is responsible for a narrow task like installing a side-view mirror.

Integration

One of the disadvantages of specialization is that the tasks become so minute and so specialized that it takes major managerial effort to integrate all the tasks. This may be why Fayol listed coordinating as one of the five managerial functions.[13] Many scholars view the integration of the activities of individuals and units as the very essence of management.[14]

The task of managing becomes more difficult as individual departments and their responsibilities become specialized. In an automobile-manufacturing plant, there may be specialization on the assembly line as well as in the engineering design function. Someone in manufacturing may assemble only the reverse gear in the transmission. One engineer in development may design only reverse gears in transmissions. Coordinating the activities of all other assemblers to yield a perfectly assembled car is a formidable task. The designers of the various parts must also be coordinated. Integrating across the two major areas so that the design ensures ease of manufacture and error-free manufacturing is a managerial challenge of the 1990s.

CRITICAL THINKING QUESTIONS

1. Is specialization or integration more important? Why?

2. Discuss the concepts of delegation and decentralization.

STRUCTURAL FORMS

Before discussing specific structural forms, we shall explore the two broad descriptions of organizational types—mechanistic and organic structures.

Mechanistic and Organic Structures

Mechanistic organizations occur in environments with stable technology and stable demands from customers.[15] In **mechanistic designs** tasks are fractionated and

FIGURE 8.3   *A Functional Organization*

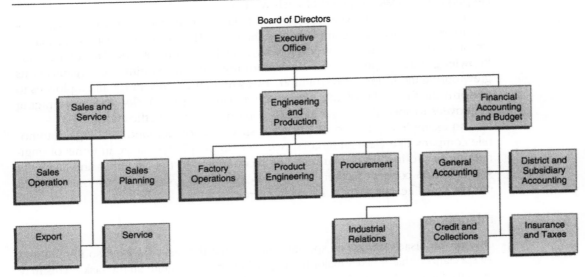

specialized. There is little emphasis on clarifying the relationship between tasks and organizational objectives. The structure of control, authority, and communication is primarily vertical between superior and subordinate.

Organic organizations are suitable in changing technological environments requiring innovation with trained workers. In **organic designs** tasks are more interdependent. There is more emphasis on relevance of tasks and organizational objectives. Control, authority, and communication are varied. Communication is vertical and horizontal, depending on where needed information resides.

Understanding the two broad classes of organizations known as mechanistic and organic sets the stage for discussion of the specific kinds of organization structures.[16]

Functional Structure

One of the most common organizational forms is the functional form. It is frequently found in firms pursuing a strategy of concentration or high relatedness. Like activities or like functions are grouped together in a **functional structure**. An example of a functional structure is given in Figure 8.3. If the organization becomes significantly larger, an extensive corporate staff may emerge that reports directly to the executive office in an advisory capacity.[17]

Advantages   The functional form is appropriate if the firm is pursuing a concentration or relatedness strategy (Chapter 6), or if the firm produces a single product or only a few closely related products. The functional structure allows for maximum specialization of effort and economy of scale. For example, if a firm is in the business of designing, manufacturing, and marketing only mainframe computers, then a functional structure may be appropriate.

FIGURE 8.4   *A Geographic Organization*

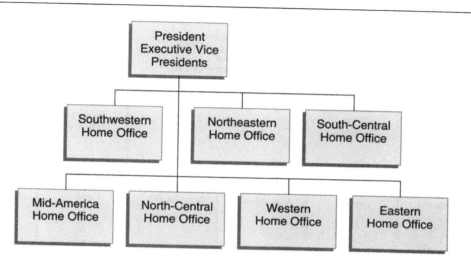

Disadvantages   In the functional organization coordination across the functions becomes increasingly difficult as the number of products, number of markets, or kinds of customers grow. In such situations a more complex structure becomes appropriate. In the mainframe computer example above, if the firm starts designing, manufacturing, and selling personal computers in addition to its mainframe business, then a more complex structure may be needed.

Geographic Structure

As the firm grows in geographic coverage, the simple functional form often evolves into a **geographic structure**. Like functions are grouped together within each geographic area but not across geographic areas. Figure 8.4 presents an example.

Advantages   In a geographic structure the organization can focus on the needs of the customers in each geographic segment. In the insurance industry, for example, customers in different parts of the country may have different needs due to different lifestyles and different risks.

Disadvantages   Duplication and coordination of activities across geographic areas can be expensive and may lead to an added layer of management.[18] For example, design and production of insurance policies can occur and be duplicated in more than one geographic area. If such design, production, and marketing activities become too customized to the customers in a specific area, then the image of the firm in the minds of customers may become blurred. It may be hard, for instance, to conduct a national advertising campaign if the products and services are customized by region.

FIGURE 8.5   *A Product (Division) Organization*

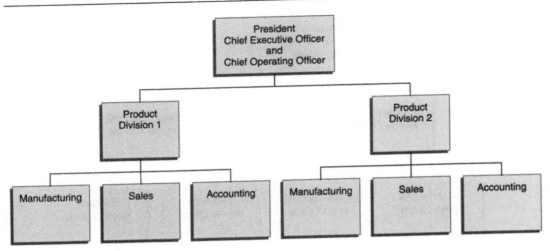

Product or Division Structure

The **product or division structure** is a logical evolution of the functional form. It is as if another functional organization were added in duplicate to the existing functional organization for the second product. Separate manufacturing, sales, and accounting activities are grouped together around products in a **product structure**. Figure 8.5 gives an example.

Returning to our computer example, a product structure is like having a separate company (division) for mainframe computers and a separate company (division) for personal computers. Even though common activities like manufacturing are found in both divisions, these activities are segregated by product as the basis for the divisional grouping.

Advantages   As with the functional form, in a product structure there is a high degree of specialization of effort. There may also be substantial economies of scale if the volume in each of the divisions is large enough to justify the separate facilities and workforces.

Disadvantages   Coordination across divisions can become exceedingly difficult. The degree of specialization causes personnel in one division to lose sight of customers and problems in another division. If customer needs evolve, the degree of specialization makes it difficult for employees to adapt to the new needs. For example, the mainframe people may not be able to think of the needs of customers in small organizations who need an intermediate-size minicomputer.

Customer-Focused Structure

In a **customer-focused organization** activities, personnel, and resources are grouped by common types of customers. For example, in our computer example, all

FIGURE 8.6 *A Customer-Focused Organization*

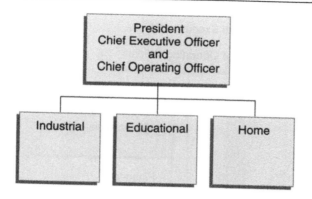

activities associated with industrial customers are grouped together, as are all activities associated with educational customers and all activities associated with home-use customers (see Figure 8.6).

Advantages In a customer-focused organization, the needs of the customer can be well served. By grouping activities associated with a customer segment, all functional activities (for example, production, marketing, finance) are targeted at specific kinds of customers.

Disadvantages If the customer group has varied needs, then the activities in a division can be varied. For example, in the industrial division of the computer company, activities associated with the design, manufacture, and sales of mainframe computers, minicomputers, and personal computers are all grouped together. There is also duplication of activities and personnel across divisions, as design, manufacture, and sales of personal computers are also conducted in the educational and home divisions.

Holding-Company Structure

Holding companies are conglomerations or collections of separate, seemingly unrelated groupings of businesses or divisions called strategic business units, or SBUs. Within each SBU or division there is some common important strategic dimension. Across SBUs there may be little commonality. Thus a holding company is like a multidivisional organization with an added layer of management. The function of management at the holding-company or corporate level is to loosely oversee a number of nearly autonomous companies. There are few functional specialists centralized at the corporate level. Figure 8.7 presents an example of an SBU structure.

Advantages The greatest advantage of a holding-company structure is diversification of risk.[19] It is assumed that the unrelated SBUs operate on different cycles and have different cash flows. Therefore in a year when one SBU is

FIGURE 8.7   *A Generic Strategic Business Unit Structure*

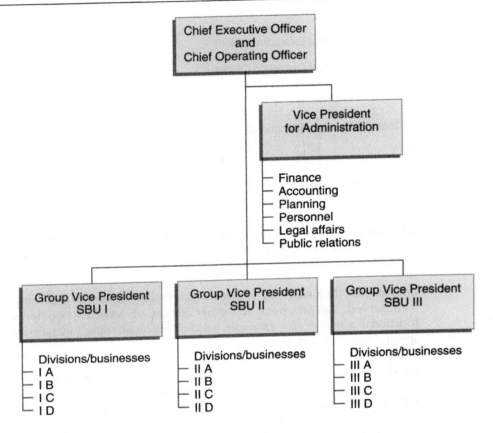

experiencing weak profits, the other SBUs may be having offsetting positive cash flows. In this way the risk to the investor is limited.

Disadvantages   There are several disadvantages associated with a holding-company structure. Coordinating the independent SBUs is difficult. By the very fact that the SBUs are unrelated in their core businesses, there is no expectation of positive fit among them. Budgeting and allocation of resources among such unrelated businesses can be difficult, since the corporate executives must compare apples and oranges. Financial control and operational control can be difficult, since the SBUs function on different cycles. Duplication of staffs and functions at the various levels is also a problem.[20]

Matrix Structure

The **matrix structure** is an overlay of businesses or projects on functional groupings. This structure coordinates activities and resources across functions associated

FIGURE 8.8 *A Matrix or Grid Organization: Dow Corning (1973)*

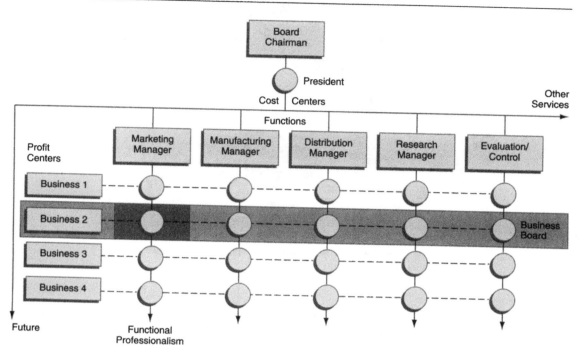

with a specific business while retaining functional specialization. Figure 8.8 shows the matrix organization at Dow Corning. The various businesses do not completely "own" the functional resources, as in a divisional or SBU structure. In a matrix structure, the businesses or product lines "borrow" the functional resources from the functions.[21] Matrix forms evolved in the aerospace and construction industries with the development of separate projects in those industries.[22]

Advantages The matrix structure helps managers to deal with a number of new products or businesses. Since the functions remain with their human and other resources, managers can dedicate resources to new products or businesses quickly. The matrix may be less expensive than duplicating the functional resources for each new product. Thus a matrix structure may be appropriate in high-technology industries or industries with frequently changing new products. Aerospace, computers, and electronics industries with streams of new products are examples where matrix organizations are used. Boeing uses a matrix organization when it starts a new aircraft.

Disadvantages Matrix forms have coordination problems even though increased coordination is the desired goal.[23] There may be recurring battles between the

Boeing often uses matrix structures to coordinate resources on new products like the 777 aircraft. (Photo credit: Boeing.)

business or product managers and the functional managers. Matrices may be expensive to operate because of the extra layer of management, and they may even be counterproductive in stable organizations with few products. Communications arising from two directions may be confusing, and some people are uncomfortable with reporting to more than one boss.

The use of cross-functional teams as a way to reap the benefits of a functional organization without the disadvantages is illustrated in the following quality exhibit.

CRITICAL THINKING QUESTIONS

1. Discuss the pros and cons of the various structural forms of organizations.

2. Forecast the future of matrix structure organizations.

CONTRASTING APPROACHES TO ORGANIZATIONAL DESIGN

Having outlined the specific structural forms of organizations, we now describe four different approaches to designing organizations.

Classical Approach

The classical approach focuses organization design efforts on patterns of authority, division of labor, and specialization to produce efficiency. This is an approach that leaves to chance the integration of activities to deliver value to the customer. This approach is represented by the internal-focus cell of Figure 7.3 and pays little attention to customers or competitors.

QUALITY EXHIBIT

Cross-Functional Teams at Potlatch

The Potlatch Corporation of Idaho manufactures and sells wood products, coated papers, pulp and paperboard, and packaging. It is in the forest products business. In the wood products industry, there are major functional differences between the foresters who raise the trees, the lumberjacks who cut them down, the sawmill operators who cut the logs into boards or process the logs into pulp, and those who process the pulp into paper. Because of these functional differences, the need for cross-functional integration is critical in this industry.

How much authority should managers retain and how much should employee teams have? Many companies have trouble answering this question, because they have always answered it one way in the past by placing considerable authority in the hands of managers. It is not always easy to make the transition in management style required for the delegation of authority to employee groups. Changing from a hierarchical structure to shared power for old established companies is a major change. Potlatch was able to make these changes in a number of its plants under the label of "Team Concept" and focus on the manufacturing processes.

"The first task was to divide lumber and plywood production line employees into teams," explained Gordon Haines, employee involvement coordinator at St. Maries, Idaho. Each team is a logical unit whose members can manage their work. "Each team controls one manufacturing process; each shift has its own set of teams. Supervisors are team members." The processes were designed by volunteers from both hourly and salaried employees over six months of twice-weekly meetings.

Both internal and external customers were identified by the teams. Four cross-functional teams wrote in-plant specifications. Each team was responsible for setting standards for its area. In doing so, it asked the following question: What does the downstream work team expect from the upstream teams? In trying to answer that question, the teams identified production problems and product defects. Then they traced the problems and defects through the mill to see how they affected other operations.

This problem and defect identification process led to the idea that a customer can be internal to the plant. The quality control manager, Mike Telford, commented on the growing influence of internal customers: "We came to realize that we have customers inside the plant too. If a log wasn't manufactured right, for example, it causes problems at the Chip-N-Saw or plywood lathe. These operators are customers of the guys running the debarker and cutoff saws. We plan to get to the point where a 'customer' can refuse an inferior product from a 'supplier' even if it means we have to shut down the line."

Sources: J. Ross, *Total Quality Management*, Delray Beach, FL (1993): 151; Potlatch Corporation, *Value Line Investment Survey* (October 23, 1992): 934; "'Team Concept' Involves Crews in All Aspects of Mills," *Forest Industries* (November 1991): 14.

Environmental Approach

As we saw in Chapter 6, the environmental approach argues that an organization should stay in touch with opportunities and threats in the external environment. A classic research study reported on the relationship of the kind of environment and the required organizational structure.[24] It found that a loose, flexible structure is best suited to a changing environment. Tight, stable structures are more appropriate in stable environments. Due to fierce international competition and rapidly changing technology, most environments today are uncertain and changing.

Although hierarchical organizations with close supervision and tight control may be appropriate for the military, they are no longer suitable in many organizations with demanding customers, international competitors, and rapidly changing technology. (Photo credit: Lockheed.)

Task Technology

A study linking type of manufacturing technology and required organizational structure indicated that there are three kinds of manufacturing technology. **Small-batch production** is production in batches of one or a few items designed to customer orders. **Mass production** is production of many items with the same specification. **Continuous process production** is nonstop production of the flow of work. "Different technologies impose different kinds of demands on individuals and organizations, and these demands have to be met through an appropriate structure." [25] The findings on the links between technology and structure are presented in Table 8.1. As mass production gives way to smaller-batch production in the 1990s, fewer firms will follow the formalized, centralized, vertical, mechanistic organization described in the table's mass production column.

Systems and Process Focus

Many of the problems associated with traditional, hierarchical organizations underlie the suggestion that a systems and process viewpoint is needed. In this book we consider the linkage between customer-value provision and managerial systems improvement to be the essence of management.

Organizations need to be viewed in terms of their business processes. [26] A **process** is a group of activities that takes an input, adds value to it, and provides an output to an internal or external customer. Key in this definition is the link with providing value to the customer.

TABLE 8.1 *Manufacturing Technology and Organizational Structure*

Structural Feature	Small Batch	Mass Production	Continuous
Formalization	Low	High	Low
Centralization	Low	High	Low
Written vertical communication	Low	High	Low
Verbal lateral communication	High	Low	High
Overall structure	Organic	Mechanistic	Organic

Source: Joan Woodward, *Industrial Organizations: Theory and Practice*, London: Oxford University Press (1965). Reprinted by permission of Oxford University Press.

In most organizational problems the process is the problem, not the employees. The process focus has the twin themes of improvement and teaming to provide value to the customer. Unfortunately, the organizational focus has the theme of assigning fault to individual employees in the pursuit of the bottom line. For example, the *Harvard Business Review* reported on a paper company that shifted emphasis from problem assignment to fixing the process that caused the problem. Positive results were forthcoming: "Six months out, customers were beginning to notice a marked difference in quality."[27]

The systems and process focus is key to continuous improvement. As such, it will be increasingly used by organizations as the basis of structure in the future.

The concept of viewing businesses from a process viewpoint has spread to include even the legal profession. A law firm in Tennessee describes its mission and strategy in a one-page document. In that document is a one-paragraph description of organizational design: "Structure. The business process is managed through empowered individuals and teams to provide service and value to our clients. Each individual takes ownership of responsibilities, with the support and encouragement of the rest of the team."[28]

CRITICAL THINKING QUESTIONS

1. Discuss the different approaches to designing organizations.

2. Forecast the future of the process focus.

KEY CONTINGENCIES FOR STRUCTURAL DESIGN

A number of criteria must be considered in designing organizational structure.

Customer Requirements

The single most important requirement for organizational design is responsiveness to customer requirements. If the current organizational structure precludes organizational members from focusing on customers, then that structure needs to be changed. Unfortunately, many pyramidal, functional structures that focus on their internal system of authority and division of labor are hampered in their attempt to focus on the customer.

In the following ethics exhibit, it appears that Dow Corning was insulated from its customers. When a manufacturing organization falsifies manufacturing records and produces products that harm customers, that organization is less than responsive to customers.

Technological Change

Another key contingency for organizational design is technological change. Studies have suggested that as the pace of technological change quickens, organizations need to be more flexible and more adaptive. As the pace of technological change is expected to intensify, the future may see more organic organizations with predominantly horizontal flows of work and communication.

International Competition

International competition increases the demands on organizational structure. Because of international competition, customers are more demanding that they receive the latest technological products and features. This increases the need for organizations to operate with reduced cycle times to deliver value to customers. Horizontal and matrix organizational structures are best suited for such a task. *Business Week* noted that in a global economy rigid structures will be swept away and corporations that can adapt will thrive.[29]

Size

The design of the organization is associated with its size. Small organizations are easier to integrate because of the proximity of the people and the general nature of their tasks. Conversely, large firms have special integration problems. A trend in organizational design in the 1990s is **downsizing,** which is the purposeful shrinking of organizations. General Motors and IBM are two examples of large organizations that have shrunk by tens of thousands of employees in the recent past.

Strategy

As mentioned earlier, strategy and structure should be related. After World War II the primary U.S. manufacturing strategy was long production runs of standardized products, which suggested a functional grouping. Today the model is shorter production runs of specialized products with changing technology, which suggests a systems and process framework.

Diversification of Products and Services

A holding-company structure is an appropriate organizational design for a firm that produces a series of diversified products. Such products may be unrelated and/or

E T H I C S   E X H I B I T

Dow Corning and Breast Implants

Breast implants had been on the market for over three decades and had been sold to approximately two million women. In 1991 questions concerning the safety of breast implants were raised. Claims were made that linked breast implants to cancer, problems with the immune system, and other illnesses.

Dow Corning and Bristol-Myers Squibb (BMS) Company, both manufacturers of implants, have come under intense public scrutiny. BMS manufactures implants covered in polyurethane foam. This foam covering has been shown in laboratory conditions to break down and release TDA, a chemical substance known to cause cancer in laboratory rats. Although BMS claims there are no reported cases of human cancer associated with polyurethane foam, the company has voluntarily stopped shipments of the implants and has notified doctors to delay using the product until a Food and Drug Administration (FDA) study is completed.

Dow Corning manufactures silicone implants, which have been known to leak. Although claims have been filed linking the silicone leaks to problems with the immune system, Dow Corning has maintained that there is no medical proof to support these assertions.

Consumers asked why more testing was not done before the implants were put on the market, why doctors did not inform them of the risks associated with the implants, and why the FDA moved so slowly in regulating this product. *Business Week* found evidence that the industry had been aware of studies linking implants to cancer and other complications long before women were informed of the risks. Thomas Talcott, a materials engineer at Dow Corning who quit his job in 1976 due to a dispute over the safety of implants, asserts: "Manufacturers and surgeons have been performing experimental surgery on humans." There were also allegations that manufacturing employees falsified records on the manufacturing of the implants.

In March 1992 Dow Corning announced that it was pulling out of the implant business, it offered to pay up to $1,200 per woman to have implants removed, and it set aside $10 million to fund implant studies. Even with these actions, however, Dow Corning is still faced with potential legal liabilities that could run as high as $1 billion. In early 1994 several manufacturers of silicone implants were negotiating a settlement with the courts in the amount of $4 billion.

Dow Corning received considerable badgering in the press over its handling of the situation. In an open letter to Dow Corning, *Business Week* published the Five Cardinal Rules for Crisis Management, which includes: "Rein in your lawyers, and face the public and the facts."

Discussion Questions

1. What is the responsibility of all managers, whether in engineering, manufacturing, sales, or legal departments, to deliver safe products to customers?

2. How do functional organizations make it easier to ignore customers?

Sources: "Dow Corning Employees Falsified Data on Breast Implants, Counsel Concludes," *The Wall Street Journal* (November 3, 1992): A3; S. McMurray and T. M. Burton, "Dow Corning Plans to Quit Implant Lines," *The Wall Street Journal* (March 19, 1992): A3, A6; "Here's What to Do Next, Dow Corning," *Business Week* (February 24, 1992): 33; Tim Smart, "Breast Implants: What Did the Industry Know, and When?" *Business Week* (June 10, 1991): 94–98; J. Seligmann, E. Yoffe, and M. Hager, "The Hazards of Silicone," *Newsweek* (April 29, 1991): 56; "New Worries About Breast Implants," *U.S. News & World Report* (April 29, 1991): 16.

they may be in unrelated markets. Today the trend is to concentrate on product lines and on providing the best value to customers. Thus the holding-company form should become increasingly rare in the future.

INTERNATIONAL EXHIBIT

Manufacturing Globally for Domestic Sales

An increasing number of U.S. firms have been manufacturing in other countries for sales in the United States. Manufacturing in a country different from the country where the design and marketing are performed only increases the need for the integration of design, manufacturing, and marketing.

The automobile industry has been pursuing global manufacturing in a substantial way, as reported by *Industry Week*: "Ford Motor, for example, is planning to import minicars built in South Korea, will produce cars for the Canadian market in a 70%-owned affiliate plant in Taiwan, and is building a plant in Mexico to export cars to the U.S. Chrysler Corp. is selling autos built by Mitsubishi Motors Corp. in Japan. General Motors Co. takes cars from Suzuki Motor Co., its Japanese

affiliate. A study by Arthur Andersen & Co. predicts that by the year 1995, some 25% of the auto parts that go into American-built cars will be produced in U.S.-owned plants abroad, up from the current level of 15%."

Industry Week also reported the same pattern in the consumer electronics industry, noting that Motorola was buying or building semiconductor and communications equipment plants in Taiwan, Japan, Hong Kong, Singapore, and Mexico.

Sources: M. J. Stahl and D. W. Grigsby, *Strategic Management for Decision Making*, Boston: PWS-Kent (1991): 198; "Exodus: Where Is U.S. Industry Going? It's Heading Where Many American Manufacturers Have Already Gone—Offshore," *Industry Week* (January 6, 1986): 29.

Technological Interdependence (Pooled, Sequential, or Reciprocal)

Technological interdependence can also influence structure. **Interdependence** is the degree to which organizational units depend on each other for resources to perform their tasks. There are three types of interdependence that influence structure.[30] Figure 8.9 shows these three kinds of interdependencies and the kind of coordination needed.

Pooled interdependence is the degree to which each unit is relatively independent because work does not flow among units. Fast-food restaurants are good examples. **Sequential interdependence** is the degree to which the output of one unit becomes the input of another unit. There is much more interdependence and sharing of resources in this form. A good example is a computer assembly line. **Reciprocal interdependence** is the degree to which the output of Unit 1 becomes the input for Unit 2, which transforms the input and sends it back to Unit 1 as its input. Colleges in a university are a good example: Students take courses in one college and then return to another college for higher-level courses.

Information-Processing Requirements

An organization's needs relating to the amount and the frequency of information processing influence its organizational design. Limited sampling of external information can be associated with an inwardly focused organization. A prison may have limited information needs and thus be an inwardly focused organization. Today the number of organizations that do not need frequent external information is limited

FIGURE 8.9   *Types of Interdependence*

1. Pooled

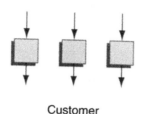

Customer

2. Sequential

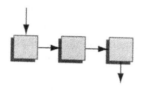

Customer

3. Reciprocal

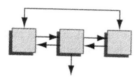

Customer

Note: Arrows indicate flow of work.

Source: Adapted from James Thompson, *Organizations in Action,* New York: McGraw-Hill (1967).

and growing smaller. Frequent sampling of information should be associated with many ties and mechanisms that are in touch with the external world. For example, an airline needs a great amount of information from the outside world in order to meet customers' needs.

CRITICAL THINKING QUESTIONS

1. How will customer requirements and international competition impact structural design in the 1990s?

2. Forecast the future for large organizations in the 1990s.

CROSS-FUNCTIONAL INTEGRATION

A prime purpose of management is the creation and improvement of systems. We shall now describe some of those systems-related tasks, emphasizing cross-functional tasks.

Cross-Functional Systems

A good way to view an organization is as a system rather than as a chain of command. The latter view has several of the inherent organizational problems described earlier. The systems view focuses on the processes needed to deliver value to the customer.

Figure 8.10 shows a systems view of an organization. It focuses on delivering value to consumers, in contrast to the chain of command view, which focuses on vertical authority. Note the cross-functional systems associated with design and redesign, production and distribution (including suppliers and customers), and consumer research. One researcher has noted that a typical organization's business processes might include new-product development, materials management, and customer needs analysis.[31] Although the process titles differ slightly from those in Figure 8.10, the processes are the same.

Because of their centrality to most businesses, there are at least four cross-functional systems that should exist in nearly all business organizations: the customer-value determination system, the new-product design and development system, the logistics and materials system, and the information flow system.

The Customer-Value Determination System   This system is the one that is arguably the most important cross-functional system, yet it is the most frequently ignored in many organizations. In large organizations there is a tendency to take customer requirements for granted. Comments like the following are often the prelude to organizational decline: "We understand the customer. Otherwise we would not have grown to our current large size." Elements of this cross-functional system were discussed in Chapter 7.

The New-Product Design and Development System   In this internationally competitive era with its rapidly advancing technology, customers are demanding the latest in new products and services. Firms need systems to take customer requirements and rapidly mix them with the latest technology to deliver new value. We shall describe this system in detail in Chapter 17.

The Logistics and Materials System   Organizations need to cross-functionally manage the acquisition, transformation, and distribution of materials. This system includes supplier/purchasing functions, materials transformation/manufacturing functions, and distribution functions. Suppliers are part of this system. We shall cover in detail the supplier and operations management aspects of this system in Chapter 18.

An example of the cross-functional nature of the logistics and materials system may be found at the Watervliet, New York, Army Arsenal. The system spans the four vertical functions of quality control, operations, engineering, and resource

FIGURE 8.10   *The New Way to View an Organization: The System*

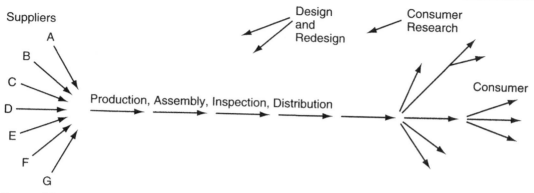

Source: Adapted from W. E. Deming, *Out of the Crisis*, Cambridge, MA: MIT Press (1986): 4.

management. Prior to viewing its work in terms of cross-functional systems, the arsenal had been having quality problems with the cannons it designed and manufactured. "It just fell through the crack" was a familiar expression. The cross-functional system required ownership from one manager across the other three functions. **System ownership** can be defined as one manager having authority and responsibility for activities in the system. Some of the experienced managers found that system ownership was discomforting, because they had been accustomed throughout their careers to thinking in vertical organizational terms. "In cross-functional systems the reporting/tasking lines begin to resemble a network (spider web) structure as opposed to an hierarchical (tree branch) structure."[32]

Information Flow   The march of information technology is having a dramatic impact on the design of organizations. Earlier structures were characterized by division of labor and specialization, as we have already noted. Today's principles are integration and cross-functional unification. Owing to networks of computers, company departments are fusing, and organizations are growing so closely allied with customers and suppliers that organizational boundaries between them are dissolving.[33] In Chapter 16 we shall discuss information flow in much greater detail.

System Ownership and Boundary Positions

Flows of work and communication in cross-functional systems do not follow the neat lines found in vertical organizations. Overlaps, as opposed to clean lines of definition, are the more common occurrences.

There are also questions of system ownership. In the logistics and materials flow system described in the Watervliet case, there are activities from the four functional areas of quality control, operations, engineering, and resource management. Frequently the manager who is willing to operate in the cross-functional mode becomes the system owner.

Individual Cross-Functional Integrators

In traditional, functionally organized firms, there are often integration and coordination problems. Rather than redesign the organization around processes and cross-functional systems, some organizations add individuals whose job it is to integrate across the functions. The existence of these individuals, although well intentioned, is a Band-Aid approach to a structural design issue. Rather than acknowledging that the work flows horizontally and setting up horizontal structures, individual cross-functional integrators exist in a vertical world. These individual cross-functional integrators go by various titles, the more popular being special assistant, coordinator, facilitator, and integrator. As the titles suggest, the individuals usually have little influence in the organization.

Cross-Functional Groups

As one of his 14 points, Deming noted the importance of cross-functional groups: "Break down barriers between departments. People in research, design, sales, and production must work as a team, to foresee problems of production and in use that may be encountered with the product or service."[34]

Some cross-functional groups have the same problems as individual integrators. Because certain groups such as councils, committees, task forces, and problem-solving teams are temporary, their ability to influence real work is limited.

Alternatively, some cross-functional groups are long lived and are serious attempts to integrate activities in recognition of the horizontal work flow.[35] Titles like project team and cross-functional team suggest long-lived attempts to perform the integration role of cross-functional systems.

CRITICAL THINKING QUESTIONS

1. Discuss the importance of cross-functional integration.
2. List the four main cross-functional systems common to many organizations. Describe their purposes.

TRENDS IN STRUCTURAL FORMS

From our discussion thus far of the many issues associated with organizational structure and design, we note certain definite trends.

Customer-Driven Structure

The decade of the 1990s may be remembered in business as the decade of the customer. As we saw in Chapter 3, customers on a global basis are being offered many alternatives from which to choose. Due to advances in quality and technology, many of the choices are affordable. The customer can be demanding in this globally competitive environment.

QUALITY CASE

Back to the Obio Printing Company Case

The company contracted with two local professors with SPC training experience to develop a training program specifically for the Ohio Printing Company (OPC). The first training group consisted of 23 employees. They were taught to place emphasis on prevention rather than on inspection, to share data with coworkers who handled jobs before and after their operation, and to apply various SPC techniques to printing applications.

During training, the 23 employees broke up into four project teams, with employees from different departments on the same team. One team, for instance, was composed of four pressmen, a prepress technician, and an estimator.

Management selected four problems and allowed each team to choose the one on which it wanted to work. The teams began working on the problems while they were still receiving training, then continued with them after the training was complete. The problem-solving process that the teams used involved defining the causes of the problem, collecting data on a limited test basis, beginning to analyze results, and continuing to monitor the process as new procedures were implemented.

One team tackled the problem of uneven ink-drying times. While some jobs dried within the time expected, others took much longer. Still others never dried and had to be scrapped. At first, some of the employees suggested that changes in humidity and temperature in the pressroom were causing the problem. To test out this hypothesis, they plotted temperatures, humidity levels, and drying times, but they found no correlation.

Next they noticed that the batches of slow-drying jobs all came from one stock. After standardizing the stock and still not completely solving the problem, they began to monitor ink and fountain solution characteristics, and found that this was the real cause. That is, most of the variations in drying time were caused by fluctuations in these properties. The team then developed a procedure to monitor these properties on a regular basis and to keep them within specified limits.

In such an era organizations must be responsive. If they are not, they might lose their customers, as some firms like General Motors, Harley-Davidson, and Xerox found out in earlier years. Cross-functional customer-value determination systems are becoming increasingly important for the survival of organizations.

Even in its organization chart (Figure 8.11), KLM Airlines in Europe stresses the importance of being customer-driven. The chart shows customers at the top, being served by nonmanagerial employees, who are supported by mid-level managers, with top-level management at the bottom.[36] KLM has inverted the traditional command-and-control pyramid that had top management ruling the organization. Federal Express uses a similar inverted pyramid with the external customer at the top, served by front-line employees, with support from mid-level managers, and top-level management at the bottom.[37]

In both organizations there is a realization that the structure exists to deliver value to the customer. Both structures also recognize that customer-value informa-

FIGURE 8.11   *KLM Organization Chart*

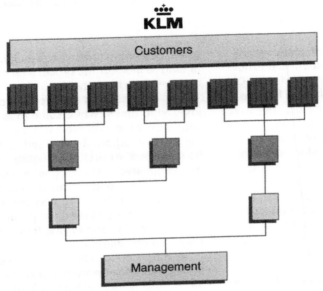

Source: W. J. Vrakking, "Customer Orientation Within the Organization," in W. Mastenbroek, *Managing for Quality in the Service Sector,* Oxford, England: Basil Blackwell (1991): 68.

tion and customer-value delivery flow from the customer and from those employees closest to the customer.

Since both firms are in service industries, this may be an area where service firms are able to implement a TQ concept more readily than manufacturing firms. By definition, service firms are in direct, perpetual contact with external customers. Manufacturing firms might not be. It may be easier, therefore, for some service firms to emphasize the customer-driven feature of their structures than for some manufacturing firms.

Flattened Structure

The trend to downsize may be strengthened by the increased focus on managing processes rather than managing people. Cross-functional systems and processes link cross-functional work teams. Organizing around systems and processes, as opposed to functions, permits self-managed work teams and allows companies to dismantle unneeded supervisory structures.[38]

The unneeded supervisors can be reassigned as process and cross-functional system improvement specialists, as was done at Milliken and Company. Milliken's structure has become so flat that some shifts in textile plants have no "supervisors" on them. But the shifts have well-trained cross-functional teams that can get the work done and solve problems.[39]

Such actions will cause organizations to become increasingly flat. The future organization may look more like a rectangle than a pyramid. If communication patterns were drawn inside the rectangle, then the organization would resemble a spider web.

Flexibility and Adaptability

As rapidly changing technology brings more new products to the marketplace, organizations will need to adapt to the new products and the associated customers. Since new products are being introduced more quickly, organizations must become more flexible. The structure of today may not be the structure of tomorrow. In the internationally competitive environment of the 1990s with its rapidly changing technology, it is crucial for organizations to adapt rapidly, shorten cycle times, and quickly introduce new products to market. Many of the mechanistic, pyramidal, functional, overly specialized organizations described earlier in this chapter are not suited to such an environment.

As defined in Chapter 6, **restructuring** involves a series of actions aimed at downsizing or cutting back the scope of the firm. Today restructuring is a term that has become part of our everyday vocabulary, seen often in newspaper reports of developments in the business world.

Cross-Functional Systems and Processes

Tomorrow's customer-driven organization may be a collection of a few cross-functional systems and processes. At the minimum, these would include the customer-value determination, new-product design and development, information flow, and logistics/material flow cross-functional systems. In 1993 *Business Week* reviewed structural trends in a feature story entitled "The Horizontal Corporation." That article advised managers to destroy the hierarchy. "Instead of creating structure around functions or departments, build the company around its three to five 'core processes.'"[40]

When Chrysler introduced its new line of LH cars in late 1992, it proudly described how it had designed and developed the cars in less time than its competitors. Chrysler stated that a primary reason for the shorter cycle time for design and development was its implementation of flatter horizontal organizational structures using cross-functional teams.[41]

Many firms may not be ready to switch from a pyramid to a series of cross-functional systems. Before making that dramatic switch, an organization might use a matrix structure. The matrix retains the old functions but has cross-functional mechanisms overlaying those functions.

Cross-functional, self-managed work teams operate many of the cross-functional processes in organizations. Teams are such an important topic that we shall devote Chapter 14 solely to a discussion of them.

CRITICAL THINKING QUESTIONS

1. Discuss the trends in organizational structure.

2. Discuss the impact of downsizing and flattening of organizational structures on career prospects for students.

Conclusion to the Ohio Printing Company Case

The measures taken by the team to eliminate the problem of uneven ink-drying times was immediately successful. Spoilage rates dropped from 20 percent to 1 percent. As a result, inventory was reduced, jobs could be performed faster, and the Ohio Printing Company (OPC) was able to reduce its price for such jobs while at the same time increasing its market share and improving its profits. In fact, the savings on this project alone over the course of one year paid for the cost of the SPC training program.

"This project also clearly illustrated that employees are willing, and in some cases eager, to follow new procedures when those procedures have been designed—not by managers—but by respected colleagues," says technical director Cozart.

In addition to the dollar savings, there have been other benefits that OPC can point to as a result of its SPC team approach:

1. Gaps between departments have begun to close. Employees now communicate with one another and help co-workers solve problems. Employees have also begun to realize that management is listening to their ideas, and mutual trust has begun to flourish.

2. Supervisors have become better communicators and better listeners. Instead of functioning as department problem solvers and overseers, supervisors work with employees to solve problems. They now function more as facilitators, tapping the skill and knowledge of the craftspeople. "Supervisors today are concerned about building a climate that allows employee input, reduces employee fear, and encourages quality," says Franklin, the company's president.

3. Individually, employees have become analytical about their jobs and the work they do. "They feel very involved in the management of their jobs," adds Cozart.

4. The company's salesforce has much more confidence in the quality and timeliness of the jobs they bring in from customers. Now there isn't nearly as much chance of jobs "blowing up in their faces."

5. OPC is now considered one of the best printers in the region. "We have regained some customers that were lost in the past, and we now enjoy an excellent reputation," Cozart asserts.

OPC has also started to research and compile the quality requirements of individual customers. "Quality for one is not necessarily quality for another," Cozart explains.

Finally, the company has plans to begin working with its suppliers of paper, ink, and photographic materials to improve their quality. Eventually, OPC plans to limit its business to the ones that show the most improvement. "We used to shop around for the best price," Cozart concludes, "but now we look for the best quality and service."

DISCUSSION QUESTIONS

1. How does the SPC process with cross-functional teams complement the organizational structure?

2. How does the SPC process with cross-functional teams change the role of management?

Source: Copyrighted material reprinted with permission of *Quality Excellence Achieved: Quality Assurance Blueprints for Action from 50 Leading Companies* and the Bureau of Business Practice, 24 Rope Ferry Road, Waterford, CT, 06386.

SUMMARY

The primary purpose of an organization is to accomplish goals, preferably customer-relevant goals. There are at least two kinds of organization that the manager can use to achieve these goals. One is the formal organization that is depicted in organization charts. The other is the informal organization that consists of the patterns of communication and influence among employees.

Authority is the right of managers to direct subordinates. This right flows from the owners through the top-level managers and then through the organization. However, this authority must be viewed in the context of what the subordinates will accept. The organization chart is the picture of the organizational structure. The chart has both vertical (number of layers) and horizontal (span of control) dimensions.

Managers cannot possibly accomplish all the required tasks in an organization. Therefore they delegate to subordinates the authority and responsibility for task accomplishment. Decentralization refers to the pattern of delegation throughout the organization. A basic concept of organization is division of labor and specialization in which tasks are divided so that individuals can become specialists at certain tasks. The attendant challenge for managers is to integrate the specialized tasks into meaningful output that will provide value to customers.

There are several organizational forms. Functional organizations group similar tasks. Geographic organizations repeat the structure in each major location. Product or division organizations group activities associated with common products. Customer organizations group activities associated with types of customers. Holding companies have strategic business units that are collections of divisions with commonality within the SBU and little commonality across the SBUs. Matrix organizations overlay product or business organizations on a functional structure.

The different approaches to designing organizations are the classical, environmental, task-technology, and systems and process approaches. A systems and process approach groups activities associated with the provision of customer value. Alternatively, an organizational approach is concerned with authority, reporting relationships, and control independent of the customers.

The need to integrate across functions has become increasingly important in recent years due to several changes in the business world. Increased international competition has been associated with customers' increased demands for quality. Rapidly changing technology has been associated with shortened cycle times.

There are at least four cross-functional systems common to many organizations. The customer-value determination, new-product design and development, logistics and materials, and information flow systems are common to many organizations attempting to provide greater value to customers. These systems are usually implemented by cross-functional teams.

Organizations are becoming increasingly customer-focused and increasingly reliant on customer-value determination systems. Firms are also becoming smaller by downsizing themselves, as it is easier to stay in touch with customers when smaller. Organizational structures are becoming flatter as cross-functional teams are assuming many of the functions previously performed by managers. Organizations are also becoming more flexible and more adaptable as customer needs continue to change rapidly. This adaptation may take the form of matrix and cross-functional systems organizations with decreased emphasis on vertical, hierarchical forms.

EXPERIENTIAL EXERCISE

Choosing a Global Structure

To illustrate the relationship of certain strategic choices to appropriate structural choices, let's play a game. With your class divided into groups of five individuals, each group will play the game. Each individual in the group represents one of the companies (A, B, C, D, or E) described below:

> *Company A*: Pharmaceutical company with manufacturing operations in 23 countries and sales in 48 countries. The company manufactures and sells a major line of painkillers as well as a small number of specialty drugs.
>
> *Company B*: Oil company conducting research and development, exploration, extraction, refining, wholesaling, and retailing operations worldwide.
>
> *Company C*: Accounting firm with 20 percent of its business outside of the United States through associates in five countries. Clients are mainly North American multinational corporations with overseas operations.
>
> *Company D*: Manufacturing company with sales and manufacturing facilities in 15 countries. The company manufactures a wide range of products, from electronic parts to sports equipment.
>
> *Company E*: Retail company with stores specializing in fashion, sports equipment, hardware, and office furniture, located in the United States; exports to Canada.

The individuals each have ten units that may be used to pay for the acquisition of the structure (L, M, N, O, or P in the accompanying figure) they feel is best for their particular company. Note that *product* refers to any product, service, or group of products or services.

> *Step 1*: The individuals in the group write on a piece of paper a choice of structure and how much (of the ten units) their company is willing to pay for this structure.
>
> *Step 2*: Within each group, structures are assigned on the basis of these choices as follows: If only one player has chosen a particular structure, he or she is awarded that structure and pays the stated number of units for it. If two or more players have chosen the same structure, the one paying the most gets the chosen structure and the other(s) bid on the remaining structures. In the case of a tie, the parties get to bid again until the tie is resolved. If the tie cannot be resolved (that is, if the players bid all of their units), then the instructor acts as mediator and assigns the available structures at random.
>
> *Step 3*: If an individual has a change of mind, he or she may negotiate with one or more players in the group to trade structures.
>
> *Step 4*: The instructor announces the "winning solutions," and the individual and group scores are calculated. Scores are based on "correct choices" as well as on unused points as follows: Individuals score +15 for having a company/structure match and add to this any unused units. Each group adds together all individual scores for an overall group score.

Source: Reproduced from Betty Jane Punnett, *Experiencing International Management*, 1989: pp. 34–35, with the permission of South-Western College Publishing. Copyright 1992 by South-Western College Publishing. All rights reserved.

Structure L

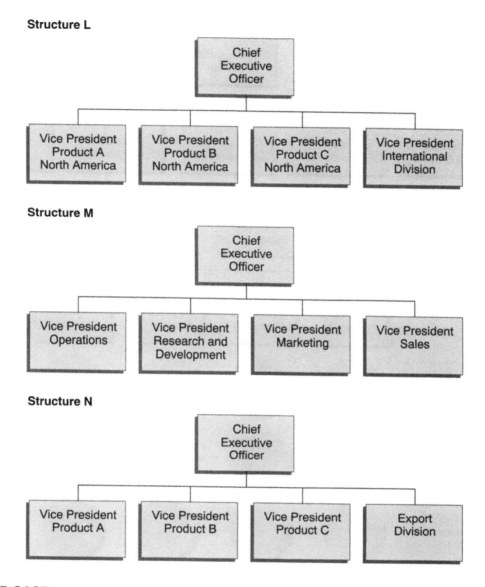

Structure M

Structure N

CHAPTER CASE

TQM in a Small Company: Marlow Industries

Ray Marlow, founder and president of Marlow Industries, manufacturer of thermoelectric cooling devices, was commenting on how the company had won the 1991 Malcolm Baldrige Quality Award in the small-business category. "We have a bad habit of calling it our quality program when it really is a quality system," he explained. "A system is something that has a beginning and no ending. We have programs within our system, but it's an ongoing, continuous thing and the people in our company know this."

Marlow was most proud of the company's enormous, colorful map of a fantasy sea voyage

Structure O

Structure P

covering one wall of the company lunchroom. Designed and painted by a company employee, the scene charts the voyage of the company to "World Class Quality . . . and Beyond," complete with the company's beginnings in the Sea of Darkness and its movement through the Tropic of Excellence and on toward Malcolmland and the Baldrige Straits. Another example of employee commitment is the *Quality Policy* accompanied by a *Quality Pledge*, which Marlow's people know by heart. It reads: "I pledge to make a constant, conscious effort to do my job right today, better tomorrow, recognizing that my individual contribution is critical to the success of Marlow Industries."

Tracing his actions that ultimately led to the Baldrige Award, Marlow commented, "Despite the fact that ever since the company's founding in 1973 we promoted ourselves as a 'quality' company, the only problem was we didn't know what it meant."

The company was typical of the many smaller firms that were suppliers to the electronics industry. In the mid-1980s prime manufacturers, the purchasers of Marlow's product, were beginning to move from in-house production of components to single-source suppliers. Moreover, the suppliers had to be ranked as first-tier or "blue ribbon." The prime manufacturers were moving to quality production and demanded the same of their suppliers. As Marlow's customers became more exacting, he knew

that action had to be taken. A well-meaning attempt to instill quality by meeting each week with the company's hourly personnel simply wore Marlow ragged while leaving top and middle management out of the process.

Discussion Questions

1. What is the difference between a quality program and a quality system? Why would a system be more appropriate?

2. Should the implementation of TQM be from the top down or the bottom up?

3. Why did Ray Marlow's attempt to instill quality management by talking to hourly personnel fail?

Source: Joel E. Ross, *Total Quality Management: Text, Cases, and Readings*, Delray Beach, FL: St. Lucie Press (1993): 62.

KEY TERMS

acceptance view of authority   Presence of authority in a particular situation is determined by the receiver, not by the giver of the order.

agency theory   Theory explaining the relationship between owners and managers.

authority   Right to give orders and the power to exact obedience.

centralization   Delegation of few tasks and of little authority throughout the organization.

continuous process production   Nonstop production of the flow of work.

customer-focused organization   Grouping of activities, personnel, and resources by common types of customers.

decentralization   Delegation of many tasks and of the associated authority to subordinates throughout the organization.

delegation   Assignment of authority and responsibility for the completion of specific tasks to subordinates.

division of labor and specialization   Performance by individuals of narrowly specified tasks.

downsizing   Purposeful shrinking of organizations.

formal organization   Structure specified in the organization chart.

functional structure   Grouping together of like activities or like functions.

geographic structure   Grouping together of like functions within each geographic area but not across geographic areas.

holding companies   Conglomerations or collections of separate, seemingly unrelated groupings of businesses or divisions called strategic business units, or SBUs.

informal organization   Organization reflected in the patterns of communication and influence associated with flows of information, work, and social activities of organizational members.

interdependence   Degree to which organizational units depend on each other for resources to perform their tasks.

line authority   Direct chain of command from the board through the CEO and other managers in a direct chain to the nonmanagerial employee.

mass production   Production of many items with the same specification.

matrix structure   Overlay of businesses or projects on functional groupings.

mechanistic designs   Structures in which tasks are fractionated and specialized.

organic designs   Structures in which tasks are interdependent.

organization chart   Chart that diagrams the functions, departments, or positions in the organization and shows how they are related in patterns of formal authority.

pooled interdependence   Degree to which each unit is relatively independent when work does not flow among units.

process   Group of activities that takes an input, adds value to it, and provides an output to an internal or external customer.

product or division structure   Grouping together of separate manufacturing, sales, and accounting activities around products.

reciprocal interdependence   Degree to which the output of Unit 1 becomes the input for Unit 2, which transforms the input and sends it back to Unit 1 as its input.

restructuring   Series of actions aimed at downsizing or cutting back the scope of the firm.

sequential interdependence   Degree to which the output of one unit becomes the input of another unit.

small-batch production   Production in batches of one or a few items designed to customer orders.

span of control   Number of employees supervised.

staff authority   Advisory, not direct command line, authority.

structure   Design of the organization.

system ownership   One manager has authority and responsibility for activities in the system.

ENDNOTES

1. A. D. Chandler, Jr., *Strategy and Structure*, Cambridge, MA: MIT Press (1962): 16.
2. D. J. Hall and M. A. Saias, "Strategy Follows Structure," *Strategic Management Journal* (1980): 156.
3. "U.S. Cars Come Back," *Fortune* (November 16, 1992): 58.
4. J. R. Galbraith and D. A. Nathanson, *Strategy Implementation*, St. Paul: West Publishing (1978): Chapter 8.
5. Fayol, *General and Industrial Management*, London: Pitman (1949): 20.
6. C. Barnard, *The Functions of the Executive*, 30th anniv. ed., Cambridge, MA: Harvard University Press (1968): 165.
7. M. C. Jensen and W. H. Meckling, "Theory of the Firm," *Journal of Financial Economics*, 3 (1976): 305–360.
8. Fayol, *General and Industrial Management*, 20.
9. H. Sherman, *It All Depends*, University, AL: University of Alabama Press (1966): 83–84.
10. M. Weber, *The Theory of Social and Economic Organization*, New York: Oxford University Press (1947): 328.
11. F. W. Taylor, *Scientific Management*, New York: Harper (1911).
12. Fayol, *General and Industrial Management*, 19.
13. Ibid.
14. B. Victor, "Coordinating Work in Complex Organizations," *Journal of Organizational Behavior* (1990): 187–199.
15. T. Burns and G. Stalker, *The Management of Innovation*, London: Tavistock (1961).
16. M. J. Stahl and D. W. Grigsby, *Strategic Management for Decision Making*, Boston: PWS-Kent (1991): Chapter 6.
17. Galbraith and Nathanson, Chapter 8.
18. R. C. Shirley, M. H. Peters, and A. I. El-Ansary, *Strategy and Policy Formation*, New York: Wiley (1981): 238–250.
19. A. C. Hax and N. C. Majluf, *Strategic Management*, Englewood Cliffs, NJ: Prentice-Hall (1984): 383–399.
20. Ibid.
21. Galbraith and Nathanson, 7–10.
22. D. I. Cleland and W. R. King, *Systems Analysis and Project Management*, 3rd ed., New York: McGraw-Hill (1983).
23. D. I. Cleland and W. R. King, eds., *Project Management Handbook*, 2nd ed., New York: Van-Nostrand Reinhold (1988).
24. Burns and Stalker, *The Management of Innovation*.

25. Joan Woodward, *Industrial Organizations: Theory and Practice*, London: Oxford University Press (1965).

26. H. J. Harrington, *Business Process Improvement: The Breakthrough Strategy for Total Quality, Productivity, and Competitiveness*, New York: McGraw-Hill (1991): 9.

27. H. Sirkin and G. Stalk, "Fix the Process, Not the Problem," *Harvard Business Review* (July-August 1990): 30.

28. Andersen, McClintock, and Range, "Statement of Mission and Vision" (1992): 1.

29. "Reinventing America," *Business Week* (1992): 60.

30. J. Thompson, *Organizations in Action*, New York: McGraw-Hill (1967).

31. Harrington, 35.

32. G. Conway and H. Carothers, "Application to Government: U.S. Army, Watervliet Arsenal," in M. Stahl and G. Bounds, *Competing Globally Through Customer Value*, Westport, CT: Quorum Books (1991): 748–787.

33. J. Bowles and J. Hammond, *Beyond Quality*, New York: Putnam (1991): 159.

34. W. E. Deming, *Out of the Crisis*, Cambridge, MA: MIT Press (1986): 24.

35. "Staying Power: Motorola Illustrates How an Aged Giant Can Remain Vibrant," *The Wall Street Journal* (December 11, 1992): A1.

36. W. J. Vrakking, "Customer Orientation Within the Organization," in W. Mastenbroek, *Managing for Quality in the Service Sector*, Oxford, England: Basil Blackwell (1991): 68.

37. *Blueprints for Service Quality: The Federal Express Approach*, New York: American Management Association Membership Publications Division (1991): 17.

38. "The Search for the Organization of Tomorrow," *Fortune* (May 18, 1992): 95.

39. Bowles and Hammond, 159.

40. "The Horizontal Corporation," *Business Week* (December 20, 1993): 76.

41. "Unfortunately, Most Cars Are Ruined When They Run into Barriers Like These," *Business Week* (October 26, 1992): 1.

9
CHAPTER

Managing Human Resource Systems

LEARNING OBJECTIVES

After reading this chapter, you should be able to accomplish the following:

- Discuss the idea that human resource problems are defects in the human resource system.

- Describe ways to improve the HR system to eliminate the frequency and severity of discrimination defects.

- Compare and contrast the legal environment of HR issues today with the legal environment in 1960.

- Discuss the role of human resource planning in growing and in shrinking organizations.

- Explain the major steps in the HR process.

- Describe the use of application forms, interviews, tests, assessment centers, reference checks, and physical examinations as selection devices.

- Explain the importance of training and development of employees, and the importance of reward systems in TQ organizations.

- Compare and contrast the benefits of cooperative and adversarial labor–management relations in a TQ environment.

CHAPTER OUTLINE

Human Resource Systems
>   *Human Resource Processes and Systems*
>   *Problems as System Defects*
>   *Human Resource Systems and Total Quality*

The Legal Environment of Human Resources
>   *Discrimination and Diversity*
>   *Federal Laws*

Human Resource Processes
>   *HR Planning*
>   *Recruitment*
>   *Selection and Hiring*
>   *Training and Development*
>   *Performance Appraisal*
>   *Rewards*
>   *Longevity or Exit*

Labor Relations
>   *Why Unions?*
>   *Collective Bargaining*
>   *Grievance Process*
>   *Labor–Management Actions*

Cases and Exhibits
>   *NationsBank*
>   *Stopping Sexual Harassment*
>   *Michel Pierre*
>   *Promus*
>   *Student Code of Ethics*
>   *Vacation*
>   *To Be Sick*

NationsBank Trains and Rewards Quality

Ed Dolby, consumer banking executive, and the keys to NationsBank customer satisfaction. (Photo credit: NationsBank Corporation.)

NationsBank Corporation is the third-largest bank holding company in the United States, with assets of $156 billion in 1993. It has over 60,000 employees in over 2,000 offices in 9 states and the District of Columbia.

NationsBank Corporation was formed in late 1991 from the merger of NCNB Corporation and C&S/Sovran Corporation. Three years earlier NCNB Corporation had been formed as the result of an acquisition of First Republic Bank of Texas by NCNB of North Carolina. Through a series of acquisitions in the 1970s and 1980s, NCNB had grown from a small North Carolina bank into a powerhouse in U.S. banking.

A bank that had grown that big that fast was very interested in the quality of its diverse operations. In pursuing the quality issue, NationsBank asked: How good is good enough?

Is 99% Good Enough? What is an acceptable level of Quality at NationsBank? If 99% is good enough, then . . .

— 58,585 checks will be deducted from the wrong checking accounts each day.

— $450,000,000 in domestic funds transfers will be deposited into the wrong account daily.

— 1,241 customers each month will not be able to complete a transaction at an ATM because the system will be down.

— $12,000,000 in dividends or interest payments for securities invested would be misdirected daily.

— 24,808 Bankcard payments will not show up on the customers' accounts next month.

— 47,147 personal statements will be distributed in the next month with errors in them.

Recognizing that 99 percent is not good enough, NationsBank launched a massive quality improvement process. Central to that process is its Quality Definition and Quality Fundamentals. The Quality Definition is: "Delivering the value our customers expect." The Quality Fundamentals are as follows:

Focus on the Customer: Understanding and responding to customer expectations is in the best interest of the company.

continued

Customer satisfaction leads to growth and profitability.

Involve Everyone: Quality is the responsibility of every associate. Our success as a service organization depends on the contributions of all associates.

Practice Prevention: Attack the root cause of problems, not just the symptoms. Quality can be best achieved by preventing problems rather than by detecting and correcting them after they occur.

Improve Continuously: Getting a little better every day is important to staying ahead of ever-changing customer needs. Improvement is the cornerstone of achieving and maintaining customer satisfaction.

Value Teamwork: Effective teams provide the collective intelligence to generate the best actions for Quality improvement. Teamwork promotes cooperation, communication, and mutual support, causing the total organization to exceed the sum of its parts.

Be Innovative: Quality requires applying creative solutions to problems.

DISCUSSION QUESTIONS

1. With 60,000 employees from a number of other prior corporations, how could NationsBank ensure consistency in the application of its Quality Fundamentals?

2. What was the role of its human resources in such a task?

Human resources play a huge role in the success of any organization. Managers increasingly recognize that systems must be designed to maximize the potential of the organization's current and future human resources.

HUMAN RESOURCE SYSTEMS

Human resources are not just the skills and the number and kinds of people in an organization. The organization's human resource systems are a very important part of the organization's assets.

Human Resource Processes and Systems

We recall from Chapter 8 that *processes* are groups of activities that take an input, add value to it, and provide an output to an internal or external customer. *Systems* are collections of processes and resources. Many organizations view process improvement to yield improvements in customer value as the key to organizational success. This idea strikes to the heart of *Total Quality Management* which is a systems approach to management that aims to continuously improve value to customers by designing and continuously improving organizational processes and systems.

In this chapter we treat the human resource (HR) system from the process perspective, examining the HR subprocesses and the flow of human resources in the organization through the various subprocesses. This survey includes HR planning, recruitment, selection and hiring, training and development, performance appraisal, and rewards. The goal of these subprocesses is longevity of high-performing individuals. Figure 9.1 presents this view of the HR process.

FIGURE 9.1   *The Human Resource Process*

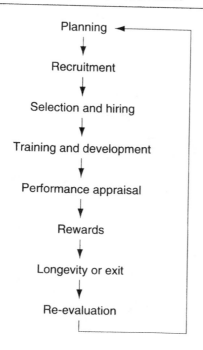

Viewing human resources from the process perspective helps managers in at least two ways. First, it helps managers understand the integrated-systems nature of many HR activities. Some organizations have viewed HR activities as isolated functions, with certain functions not being integrated with other functions. Sometimes managers who are conducting the recruiting and hiring do not integrate their activities with those managers who are designing the reward system. The result may be that one kind of talent is hired, while another kind of behavior is rewarded.

Problems as System Defects

The systems view also helps the manager to see HR problems as defects in the system, not necessarily the fault of any one manager. Partly for this reason, the Saturn Corporation refers to its HR processes as "people systems." This view also recognizes that a person's problematic behavior may be salvageable through training and appropriate rewards.

For example, failure to properly serve the customer may be the result of inadequate training. An incident of alleged sexual harassment may be due to a failure in the selection process or in the training process. This view is apparent in the following diversity exhibit, which demonstrates the preventive aspect of dealing with sexual harassment.

D I V E R S I T Y   E X H I B I T

Stopping Sexual Harassment Before It Begins

Sexual harassment lawsuits have catapulted management's handling of harassment complaints into a position of considerable importance.

Today more than ever before, male and female employees work, travel, eat, and socialize together. Thus the pin-up pictures and obscene language that thrived in previously all-male domains must give way to the sensitivities of female coworkers. Managers must ask themselves this: Are sexual jokes, invitations for drinks after work, or casual touching unwelcome or unlawful? And when an unwelcome incident occurs, managers and supervisors must know what to do to try to avoid legal consequences.

The Equal Employment Opportunity Commission (EEOC) released its Policy Guidance on Current Issues of Sexual Harassment in March 1990, advising managers how to avoid lawsuits:

Antiharassment Policies

The most important thing is to adopt a policy against sexual harassment. Include procedures for employees who feel they have been harassed to come forward and develop a procedure for resolving their complaints.

Design the complaints procedure to encourage victims to come forward. Do not require a victim to complain first to the offending supervisor. It is critical to ensure confidentiality as much as possible and provide effective remedies, including protection of victims and witnesses from retaliation for speaking out.

Other steps include affirmatively raising the subject of harassment, expressing strong disapproval, developing appropriate sanctions, inform-

Sexual harassment is a defect in the human resource system either because the person has not been adequately trained or does not believe that the penalties are high enough. (Photo credit: Frank Herboldt/Tony Stone Images.)

ing employees of their legal right to raise the issue of harassment under Title VII of the Civil Rights Act of 1964, and developing methods to sensitize all concerned. The following is a suggested policy:

Sexual harassment of employees or applicants for employment will not be tolerated.

Any employee who feels that he or she is a victim of sexual harassment by a supervisor,

continued

Human Resource Systems and Total Quality

Many managers in TQ organizations recognize that human resources are the only appreciating asset. Other assets, such as buildings and equipment, depreciate over time no matter how well they are maintained. With education, training, and experi-

coworker, or customer should bring the matter to the immediate attention of (the person's supervisor or a designated person in the personnel department). An employee who is uncomfortable for any reason about bringing the matter to the attention of his or her supervisor should report the matter to (the designated person in the personnel department).

Complaints of sexual harassment will receive prompt attention and be handled in a confidential manner to the extent possible. Prompt disciplinary action will be taken against persons who engage in sexual harassment.

Of course, you need to tailor the policy of your company. But, at a minimum, it should set out in strong terms that the company prohibits sexual harassment and must describe what procedures the employee should follow to complain about harassment to company officials other than his or her immediate supervisor.

Next, communicate the policy to all supervisors and employees. Include the policy in the employee handbook, explain the policy at employee meetings and post it on bulletin boards. Videotapes are available to help educate employees and supervisors.

Handling Complaints

In handling sexual harassment complaints, you must guard against subsequent litigation by the complaining employee and by the subject of the complaint. First, the EEOC guidelines state you must investigate the complaint immediately and thoroughly.

Include in the investigation an interview of the complaining party by someone experienced in employee investigations. Ask the employee to sign a written statement of the facts. Since credibility is often an issue in these cases, it is advisable for two company representatives to attend all interviews.

Consider interviewing any witnesses to the alleged harassment. A word of caution here: Be very careful about what you reveal to coworkers about the investigation. For example, if you tell someone an explicit detail of the complaining party's charges, you may expose yourself to a subsequent claim by the accused on the grounds of libel or intentional infliction of emotional distress. This need for confidentiality applies throughout the investigation.

Second, the EEOC guidelines say to take immediate corrective action, "by doing whatever is necessary to end the harassment, make the victim whole by restoring lost employment benefits or opportunities, and prevent the misconduct from recurring. Disciplinary action against the offending supervisor or employee, ranging from reprimand to discharge, may be necessary . . . The employer should make follow-up inquiries to ensure that harassment has not resumed and the victim has not suffered retaliation."

If the investigation is inconclusive, you may nevertheless want to remind the supervisor of the company's policy on sexual harassment, and offer the complaining employee a transfer to another area or supervisor. But remember, a knee-jerk decision to discharge an alleged harasser before the facts are clear can lead to a claim of wrongful termination or defamation.

In an era in which men and women work closely together, claims of sexual harassment are more prevalent. A strong antiharassment policy, supported by effective and well-planned preventive and/or corrective action, will go a long way to insulate your company from liability.

Source: Reprinted by permission of American Management Association from Robert K. McCalla, "Stopping Sexual Harassment Before It Begins," *Management Review* (April 1991): 44–46. American Management Association, New York. All rights reserved.

ence, human resources can increase in value over time. As resources, people are to be valued, not viewed as dispensable.

Consistent with this view of people as resources is the trend to empower employees, especially teams. **Empowerment** is sharing with nonmanagerial employees the power and authority to make and implement decisions. Empowerment is a theme in most HR issues today.

There are two HR areas receiving much attention under the TQ banner. One is training and the other is reward systems. In a TQ organization, training of new individual and team-based skills is critical to initiating and sustaining quality improvement. The kinds of team-based skills and behaviors needed, as well as empowerment issues, are covered in greater detail in Chapter 14.

Robert Galvin, chairman of Motorola, which won a Baldrige Award in the late 1980s, described the importance of training. He included in a list of the "Welcome Heresies of Quality" an Old Truth: "Training is overhead and costly." That view, Galvin stated, has been replaced by a New Truth: "Training does not cost."[1] Obviously, there is an out-of-pocket cost for training. However, many managers recognize training as a way to gain future customer satisfaction and reduce future costs by training employees how to do it right the first time. Backing up Galvin's New Truth, Motorola estimated that it has earned $30 for every $1 it has invested in quality training.[2]

Deming recognized the importance of training in his 14 Points of Management. One of those points is: "Institute a vigorous program of education and self-improvement."[3] It is noteworthy that many organizations have taken Deming's point to heart, as many are spending 5 percent to 7 percent of payroll on training today. That figure compares with the era of Galvin's Old Truth, when organizations spent less than 1 percent of payroll on training.

The other HR process that has received much attention in Total Quality organizations is the reward process. A recent review of the common elements of success in many Total Quality Management efforts noted the importance of realigning the reward and measurement systems, both formal and informal, to support the new TQM directions.[4] This may be easier said than done, as old reward systems that reinforce old forms of individual behavior may be hard to change. Even as IBM was losing billions of dollars in the early 1990s, it still lavished millions of dollars on annual "Golden Circle" celebrations for its top salespeople.[5] What was the message about the importance of team behavior?

To be sure, there are other HR processes requiring improvement in TQ organizations. Training and rewards have been only the most visible processes in established organizations. For the TQ efforts to be sustainable, there is also a need for further improvement of the HR processes of selection, promotion, performance appraisal, and the development of future leaders.[6]

CRITICAL THINKING QUESTIONS

1. What are the advantages and disadvantages of cutting training budgets in a recession?

2. Describe the conditions that make human resources (a) an appreciating asset, and (b) a depreciating asset.

THE LEGAL ENVIRONMENT OF HUMAN RESOURCES

Human resource systems and processes are conducted in the midst of a variety of laws governing their behavior. These laws are so pervasive that they impact nearly every aspect of the HR system. Since nearly all organizations publicly profess that they wish to conform with the law, HR decisions and practices that are illegal are viewed as a defect in the HR system. In the Total Quality tradition of designing the system correctly, rather than correcting a problem after it occurs, we shall discuss the legal issues before reviewing the entire HR process.

Discrimination and Diversity

Common to much of the legislation, especially in the area of equal employment opportunity, are the concepts of discrimination and affirmative action. **Discrimination** is the practice of taking HR actions based on criteria that are not job relevant. As such, discrimination is a defect in the HR system. Not hiring women for jobs they could perform as well as men, for example, constitutes discrimination. Not paying those of Asian descent the same as others constitutes discrimination. **Affirmative action** is taking positive steps to promote employment opportunities for qualified people in protected groups that are currently underrepresented in the organization. Purposely seeking and hiring qualified blacks when they are underrepresented in the organization is an example of affirmative action.

As exemplified in the diversity exhibits throughout this book, there are two reasons why an organization benefits from a diverse workforce. First, discrimination is illegal. Second, the U.S. culture is becoming increasingly diverse. If a firm hires and promotes only one class or group of individuals and discriminates against others, that firm is losing the potential contributions of the other classes. Those other classes can help the firm interact with, and understand, an increasingly diverse customer base.

Federal Laws

There are a number of federal laws governing various HR issues. There are also state laws, but because these vary from state to state, they are not reviewed here. The most noteworthy of the federal laws are in the areas of equal employment opportunity, compensation and benefits, labor relations, and occupational safety and health (see Table 9.1). Rather than being an exhaustive listing of the legal issues concerning HR, the table is meant only to reinforce the idea that there are a number of laws concerning employment practices. Some examples relating to those issues are presented in the exhibits and cases in this book, especially in the diversity exhibits. The following international exhibit presents a dilemma involving discrimination.

TABLE 9.1   *Noteworthy Federal Laws Impacting Human Resources*

Law	Area of Impact
1. *Equal Employment Opportunity:*	
Civil Rights Act, Title VII (1964), amended by the Equal Employment Opportunity Act (1972)	Prohibits discrimination in the employment relationship on the basis of race, religion, color, gender, or national origin.
Executive Orders 11246 (1965) and 11375 (1967)	Require organizations with federal contracts to eliminate discrimination through affirmative action.
Age Discrimination in Employment Act (1967), amended in 1978 and 1986	Prohibits discrimination against those aged 40 through 65 and restricts mandatory retirement.
Vocational Rehabilitation Act (1973)	Forbids discrimination based on physical or mental handicap.
Vietnam Era Veterans Readjustment Act (1974)	Prohibits discrimination against Vietnam era veterans and extends affirmative action to Vietnam era veterans.
Pregnancy Discrimination Act (1978)	Prohibits employment discrimination on the basis of pregnancy or childbirth.
Americans with Disabilities Act (1992)	Prohibits discrimination against disabled individuals.
2. *Compensation and Benefits:*	
Fair Labor Standards Act (1938)	Sets minimum wage and requires overtime pay for work in excess of 40 hours per week.
Equal Pay Act (1963)	Prohibits differences in pay between men and women for substantially equal work.
3. *Labor Relations:*	
National Labor Relations Act (Wagner Act) (1935)	Mandates procedures for employees to form a labor union, and requires management to bargain collectively with a legally formed union of employees.
Labor–Management Relations Act (Taft-Hartley Act) (1947)	Limits the power of unions, allows the president of the United States to prevent or end a strike hazardous to national security, and increases management's rights in a union-organizing campaign.
4. *Occupational Safety and Health:*	
Occupational Safety and Health Act (OSHA) (1970)	Mandates safety and health standards in work organizations.

CRITICAL THINKING QUESTIONS

1. Since discrimination is viewed as a defect in the HR system, describe ways to improve the HR system to eliminate the frequency and severity of such defects.

2. Some countries have stronger legislation than the United States in the HR arena, and some countries have weaker legislation. Describe the impact on managers and employees as they work for global organizations and shift from country to country.

I N T E R N A T I O N A L   E X H I B I T

Michel Pierre

Harry Austin was a chief project engineer in the Research and Development Center of a large aerospace and electronics manufacturer. A corporate vice-president directed the center. Each assistant director coordinated several related projects. Each chief project engineer supervised a dozen or more teams working on parts of the project. The teams were reassigned periodically as jobs were completed and new ones begun. The Center permitted its engineers to request work assignments, believing that this improved morale and professional development. A staff assistant to the vice-president kept records of each engineer's education, experience, and current assignment in the Center. The staff assistant occasionally assigned new men and others who did not express a preference.

One team under Harry Austin included Michel Pierre, a young African who had attended a British missionary school in his country and graduated from a U.S. engineering institute on a scholarship. He was spending a two-year internship with the company before returning to a job with the government in his native country. He was one of fifty foreign interns in the Center. Austin found Pierre to be shy around Americans but above average in his job. He worked well with little supervision; consequently, Austin, who had many pressing problems, did not know him well personally. One of the other members of the team was John Eaton, also a new employee. Austin found that Eaton knew his job but required attention and sympathy at times. Eaton constantly bragged to his fellow workers about his fame as a college basketball player. As Austin praised and encouraged Eaton in his work, the younger man began to seek Austin's advice and shifted his conversations from stories of basketball prowess to subjects of mutual interest.

One day several weeks after Michel Pierre joined the company, Austin entered his office and found a scribbled note from Thomas Ballentine, director of the Center: "See me immediately—T.B." Wondering what he wanted, Austin went to Ballentine's office at once.

Ballentine began the conversation, "Michel Pierre and John Eaton are on your project, aren't they?"

"That's right, they're on the same design team."

"Well, I want Michel moved."

"What on earth for?" Austin asked.

"I have heard that Eaton is prejudiced."

"Prejudiced? You mean because Mike's black?"

"That's right. I don't want the African boy annoyed any while he's here working for us."

"Well, good grief, I've worked with them more closely than you, and I certainly haven't noticed it. I'll admit Eaton has had some problems adjusting, but I don't think prejudice is one of them. In fact, he seems to be fascinated with some of Mike's stories about life in Africa."

"Please don't argue with me," Ballentine replied as though he had not heard. "Just move Michel to some other team."

"Mr. Ballentine, that team is due to be broken up in a few weeks anyway; we can separate them then. Besides, if I lose Mike, I'll either have to bring in someone else and train him for the job or else overload the other two men until they finish their design."

"I don't care what you do about that, just move the African boy as soon as you can—preferably by tomorrow."

Ballentine would not say where he had "heard" his information.

Since Austin was used to impulsive, soon-forgotten decisions of the director and had no openings anywhere on his thirteen other teams, he did nothing immediately. Two days later, Ballentine approached him in the employee dining room and asked whether he had transferred Michel Pierre.

Discussion Questions

1. Should Michel Pierre be transferred to minimize confrontations resulting from racial prejudice? Why or why not?

2. Would a transfer be a favor to Michel Pierre? Why or why not?

3. What alternatives are open to Austin in response to Ballentine's order?

4. What alternatives do you recommend that Austin pursue?

Source: A. F. Knapper, *Cases in Personnel Management*, Westerville, OH: Robin Enterprises (1977): 43–44.

Q U A L I T Y   E X H I B I T

Better People at Promus

The vision of Promus Companies is based on the concept that customer retention is directly linked to employee retention:

— We will hire, *train, train* and *retrain* the best people who are selected for their service orientation.
— We will deliver the best service primarily with front-line people and their immediate supervisors, all of whom are empowered to guarantee satisfaction to our customers.
— We will have reward, recognition and retention programs so we will be the em-

ployer of choice with the highest level of employee retention.
— We will have a diverse workforce in a climate of open communications, mutual trust and individual dignity where every employee can achieve his or her own potential.
— We will create structures, systems, human resource policies, training and development, and hiring standards that will permit operating with five or less layers in each business unit.

Source: M. D. Rose, "Promus 2000: A Company That Fulfills Our Vision," *Vision* (Spring 1993): 3.

HUMAN RESOURCE PROCESSES

Now that we have established the importance of the legal environment, we can describe HR processes. As noted in Figure 9.1, the processes consist of HR planning, recruitment, selection and hiring, training and development, performance appraisal, and rewards. The hoped-for result of the processes are high-performing individuals who stay with the organization.

This HR process emphasis is apparent in the Promus Companies. Promus is a major hospitality company that includes Harrah's casinos and three lodging chains—Embassy Suites, Hampton Inn, and Homewood Suites. The company is pursuing a strong growth strategy that includes specific people-related elements, as the quality exhibit reveals.

Human Resource Planning

Human resource planning, the first step in the HR process, involves forecasting staffing needs and determining the steps needed to fulfill those needs.

Forecasting Staffing Needs   The most important step in forecasting staffing needs is a review of the organization's objectives and strategies (see Chapters 6 and 7). This includes reviews at both the corporate/enterprise level and the business unit level. If the organization is pursuing growth objectives, then there may be a need to expand the size of the firm's human resources.

For example, the Promus Companies anticipate doubling in size in the mid-1990s through the construction of new casinos and new inns. That strategy requires a doubling of the number of employees in a relatively short time period. Recruiting, selecting, hiring, training, and developing are critical processes in such an environment. Alternatively, in the early and mid-1990s IBM has been cutting the size of its workforce at both the managerial and nonmanagerial levels. Given its much-advertised corporate policy of no layoffs throughout its history, IBM tried to shrink its labor force through voluntary turnover before it realized it could not meet its employment goals without layoffs. In 1993 it resorted to layoffs. Termination and outplacement processes are critical in such an environment.

Forecasting Internal Supply   Once staffing needs have been forecast, managers are in a position to forecast the internal supply of human resources. A forecast of internal supply is derived from examining the kinds of human resources internal to the organization, the demographics of those resources (especially years until retirement), and the stability of the people presently employed.

This process may include a **job analysis,** which is a systematic study of what is done, when, where, how, why, and by whom in current and predicted jobs.[7] The job analysis can be used to write job descriptions and job specifications. A **job description** is a written statement of job duties and responsibilities. A job description frequently includes working conditions, and the tools, materials, and equipment used to perform the job. A **job specification** is a list of the skills, abilities, education, experience, and other qualifications needed for the job. Whereas job descriptions and job specifications in the past had been written narrowly and had focused on the individual, today many TQ organizations are concerned with broader descriptions and specifications that are relevant to teams.[8] The horizontal flows of work and horizontal structures described in Chapter 8 support this trend toward broader job descriptions and team-relevant specifications.

The job analysis may include a human resource audit. A **human resource audit** is a cataloguing of the strengths and weaknesses of current personnel. For example, the HR audit may uncover weaknesses in the information technology skills of current employees at a time when the organization is entering an information-system-intense business.

Forecasting External Supply   Once managers have forecast internal supply, they are in a position to forecast external supply. As with forecasting internal supply, this includes a review of skills, abilities, education, experience, and other qualifications needed for the job. Especially if the organization has always hired locally, this forecast may have implications for training to fill gaps.

Correcting Shortage or Surplus   From the forecasts and the comparisons of supplies and needs, the organization is in a position to correct the imbalances. If there is a surplus in the organization, management needs to decide the value of the human resources to the enterprise and if it will carry a surplus until normal turnover and retirements correct the situation. If there is a dramatic imbalance, and if management cannot tolerate the costs of carrying the surplus personnel, then it might resort to involuntary pay cuts, part-time work, early retirements, and terminations.

Alternatively, if there is a shortage of human resources in certain areas, cross training and hiring are alternatives. A dramatic shortage may require hiring patterns broader than those the firm has used in the past. These are all possible elements in the planning process that can be summarized as follows:

1. Forecast staffing needs.
2. Forecast internal supply.
3. Forecast external supply.
4. Compare needs with supplies.
5. Correct shortage or surplus.

Recruitment

Once the organization has decided to hire employees to fill certain positions, managers need to attract applicants to those positions. **Recruiting** is the process of attracting individuals to apply for jobs. Recruiting is usually done for specific open positions in the short term. Sometimes managers will recruit very talented individuals in the long term for positions that may come open later. The persons who are recruited by managers may come from inside or outside the organization.

Internal recruiting is the process of attracting current employees to apply for higher-level jobs in the organization. Many firms have "promote from within" policies, and union contracts may require it.[9] Internal recruiting has the advantages of being less costly than external searches. Also, internal recruiting can help retain high-performing individuals who might otherwise leave if there were no advancement opportunities.

External recruiting is the process of attracting individuals from outside the organization to apply for jobs. Applicants may be attracted through a variety of sources, including newspaper advertisements, state employment agencies, private employment agencies, and current employee referrals.[10] External recruiting covers a larger pool of candidates than does internal recruiting.

The recruiting and hiring process has two separate dimensions: The organization wants to attract candidates while the individual is trying to select a job. The economic costs of attracting the wrong person for the job can be substantial for the organization. The psychological costs can also be substantial for the individual. Hiring the wrong manager—one who either quits or must be fired—can cost the organization up to $75,000.[11]

One way to deal with this problem is through realistic job previews. A **realistic job preview (RJP)** is a job outline that gives applicants a real picture (both positive and negative information) about the job and the organization.[12] RJPs help individuals self-select into the job on the basis of realistic information. Since the individual's expectations for the job are based on reality, the individual's subsequent satisfaction is enhanced and the odds of turnover are less. Without RJPs the individual's expectations may be unrealistic, and subsequently unmet, resulting in dissatisfaction and turnover.

There are a number of ethics issues that arise in the recruiting process impacting both the recruiter and the applicant. The Student Code of Ethics shown in the following exhibit is an ethics code for students involved in the recruiting process at Carnegie Mellon University.

ETHICS EXHIBIT

A Student Code of Ethics

Release of Information Authorization

I authorize the Career Opportunities Center at GSIA to release pertinent information about me to prospective employers. This authorization includes full participation in campus interviews, placing a resume in the GSIA Resume Book and mailing or faxing resumes to employers who request them. It also allows the professional staff of the COC to discuss my qualifications with employers when requested, with the exception of grade and transcript information. This authorization applies to both permanent and summer intern recruiting.

Name: *Please Print* _____

Signature: _____

Date: _____

———————— OR ————————

I do not wish to utilize the Career Opportunities Center's services at this time. If I should want to avail myself of the services offered in the future, I will inform you.

Name: *Please Print* _____

Signature: _____

Date: _____

Personal Information

For our computer bid system information, we ask for you to complete the information below.

Citizenship Status, check one

☐ US Citizen   ☐ Permanent Resident
☐ FI Student Visa   ☐ Other _____

Expected Graduation date: _____
Years of fulltime work experience _____
Undergrad degree in _____

The Career Opportunities Center

✦✦✦✦✦✦✦✦✦✦✦✦✦✦✦✦✦✦✦✦✦✦✦

Registration Form
Code of Ethics
Personal Information

Confidential

continued

Code of Ethics

The code of ethics that follows applies to the job search as conducted under the guidance of the Career Opportunities Center. It is the belief of the COC and its Student Support Committee that deviation from this code may project a negative image of the students and subsequently of the class and school. Once a reputation is tarnished through questionable conduct the damage may be irreparable. If you plan to utilize the COC or any of its resources, we ask that you read this code, and then sign it, indicating your understanding and willingness to abide by its tenets. Students who violate this code will be subject to penalties that have been set up by the GSIA Honor Code Committee.

○ Candidates must present their qualifications and interests accurately. Falsifying data, such as GPA, date of graduation, institutions attended, prior work experience, and eligibility to work in the United States is not only unethical but with most firms is grounds for immediate dismissal.

○ It is expected that candidates will make an earnest effort to learn about the company with whom they are interviewing. Failure to do so tells the company that the candidate has little interest and reflects poorly on the school and Career Center.

○ Candidates are expected to interview only when genuinely interested in the positions for which the organization is interviewing. For example, it is not acceptable to take an interview on a marketing schedule when the candidate's interest is in finance, without having received direct approval from the company. Interviewing for practice takes advantage of recruiters and limits interviewing opportunities for other students who may be sincerely interested in the positions being offered.

○ Candidates are expected to adhere to common rules of courtesy when attending company sponsored events. If a student signs up to attend an event it is expected that the student will attend and will stay until the event is over.

○ Candidates must notify organizations of their acceptance or rejection of offers as soon as that decision is made but certainly no later than the deadline prescribed by the company. Candidates should expect offers to be confirmed in writing, and likewise, should notify the company by telephone first and follow up with a courteous letter. Requests for extensions of decision deadlines should be made as early as possible—not at the last minute.

○ Candidates should honor an accepted offer as a contractual agreement. Upon accepting a position, candidates should withdraw from interviewing and notify the COC of their decision. Continuing to interview after accepting an offer, or reneging on an accepted offer is unethical.

○ Students should understand that abuse of COC resources including, but not limited to, the PROfit bidding system, the calling cards and GSIA phones, unauthorized removal of library resources and abuse of fax privileges constitutes a violation of this code of ethics and the GSIA Honor Code.

I have read and understand the above Code of Ethics and agree to abide within them for the duration of my stay at GSIA.

_____

Signature   Date

The Career Opportunities Center discourages employers from requesting grade information during the initial on-campus interview. This type of questioning during second interviews and plant trips is left to the discretion of company. Additionally, companies that you contact through your own efforts are not required to adhere to this policy. Please report to a COC staff member any company behaviors that you feel may be a violation of state, civil, or federal laws.

Source: Edward R. Mosier, Carnegie Mellon University, Graduate School of Industrial Administration.

Selection and Hiring

Selection is the process of determining the applicants' qualifications and of choosing the best applicant for the job. The selection process includes at least three steps:

1. Application
2. Determination of qualifications
3. Choice of best applicant

The process starts once the applicant indicates that he or she is interested in the job, extends through the phase of determining qualifications, and is completed when the choice is made of whom to hire. If the applicant rejects the employment offer, then the manager usually offers the job to the next best qualified applicant if there is more than one applicant. If there is only one, then the manager can repeat the entire process. In an increasing number of TQ organizations, the selection process is conducted by peers on the work team.[13]

In determining qualifications, the selection devices used include application forms, interviews, tests, assessment centers, reference checks, and physical examinations. When using any of these devices, the manager should examine its validity. **Validity** is the relationship between applicants' scores on the device and applicants' future job performance. Devices with low validity do not help the manager select the best person for the job and may be discriminatory.

Application Forms   An **application form** is a written document to collect information on the applicant's educational background, previous work experience, and other job-related demographic data. The form should not contain questions that are irrelevant to the job, as such questions may be discriminatory.[14] The applicant's job resume or vita may also be attached to the application form. The application form is often used by the interviewer as a basis for discussion and further exploration.

Interviews   Interviews are widely used to select applicants in nearly all organizations and for most jobs. Yet interviews are poor predictors of subsequent job performance. Nonetheless, they will probably continue to be used so that both the organization and the individual can collect face-to-face information.[15]

The interviewer must be careful not to ask questions in the interview that may be viewed as discriminatory. Partly for this reason and partly because there are ways to make the interview more productive, many organizations offer training for their managers on how to interview. Because of the importance of interviews to managers and applicants, the Experiential Exercise in this chapter simulates interviews.

Tests   A **job test** is a written or computer-generated test that measures a specific attribute, skill, or personality dimension relevant to the job. Because some tests are good predictors of subsequent job performance and some are not, validity is an especially important issue here. To help ensure validity, managers should make certain that testing conditions relating to amount of time and environment are consistent across applicants.[16]

Assessment Centers   An **assessment center** is a simulation of many of the important tasks in the job, conducted with a number of relevant exercises and situations. The experiential activities may cover a two- or three-day time period. Although assessment centers are relatively expensive to administer, they are a popular selection device because they can be a valid predictor of the candidate's future success.[17] Although assessment centers are used primarily for managerial jobs, their use is spreading to other jobs.

Reference Checks   **Reference checks** are questions addressed to former employers, former co-workers, and other acquaintances concerning the experience and behavior of the job applicant. Most of the persons listed by the job applicant as references will probably be positively biased in favor of the applicant. However, useful information can often be obtained from a reference check that could not be obtained from other sources. If the manager can find some sources in addition to the references provided by the applicant, a wealth of unbiased information may become available.

     To produce the most open form of communication, reference checks are usu- ally done verbally rather than by letter. Letters of reference have the greatest chance of being positively biased in favor of the applicant.

Physical Examinations   If the job requires substantial manual effort, the employer may require a physical examination to determine physical capability to perform the job. Or if the job requires some particular physical characteristic, like keen eyesight in a pilot, the organization may test for that characteristic with a physical examination. Additionally, a number of employers require a physical examination prior to extending health or life insurance.

Training and Development

Training and development (T&D) is the process of developing knowledge, skills, and behaviors in people that will enable them to better perform their current and future jobs. As indicated earlier in this chapter, training is an area receiving much attention in TQ organizations today. There is an increased understanding that orga- nizations must spend massive amounts of time and money on T&D to increase their competitiveness. This view is growing as more organizations come to see that human resources are their only appreciating asset. Many organizations today are spending 5 percent to 7 percent of their payroll on T&D.

     In the past T&D had stressed functional, technical, and specific job-related skills. Today many TQ organizations stress a broad range of teaming skills, cross- functional issues, quality issues, and diagnostic and problem-solving skills.[18]

     Decades ago a common view was that T&D was for the enrichment of the individ- ual and independent of a payoff for the organization. Today many see T&D as a way to ensure the consistent delivery of value to customers through highly capable employees.

Today, since human resources are the only appreciating asset of an organization, many organizations stress team training. (Photo credit: Frank Herholdt/Tony Stone Worldwide.)

Since many of these employees operate in cross-functional teams, much of the T&D in TQ organizations includes training for team building and for teamwork. This is such an important topic that we shall devote all of Chapter 14 to a discussion of teams.

The Training and Development Process   The T&D process consists of several steps (see Figure 9.2). The evaluation step signifies that organizations expect a payoff from their T&D processes.

Continuous improvement is the constant refinement and improvement of products, services, and organizational systems to yield improved value to customers. The feedback loop in Figure 9.2 indicates that, in the spirit of continuous improvement, T&D is not a one-time event but a lifelong process. The earlier view of training was that people receive an inoculation of education in high school or college that lasts throughout their careers. Many organizations today recognize that due to the massive changes occurring in the business world, booster shots of T&D are needed throughout employees' careers.

Training and Development Methods   A variety of methods is used to accomplish the objectives of the T&D program. A popular T&D method is **on-the-job training (OJT),** which is learning how to perform the job on the work site under the guidance of an experienced employee. Other T&D methods are classroom training, computer-assisted instruction, conferences, and visits to other organizations to study their processes (benchmarking).

Performance Appraisal

Performance appraisal is an important process in organizations because it signals to members the kinds of behaviors that subsequently might be rewarded.

QUALITY CASE

Back to the NationsBank Case

Hugh McColl, Jr., the CEO of NationsBank, commented on the importance of people in the NationsBank organization: "Our company prides itself on the people it employs. They are smart, creative, aggressive and very hard workers. They have lots of good ideas that, when implemented, help this company grow, save money or be a better citizen. They are what makes NationsBank such a great company."

Recognizing the importance of people to its future, and the importance of quality, the firm addressed the role that training plays in the customer satisfaction cycle. The accompanying chart presents the quality process, the customer satisfaction cycle, and associated processes. Note the number of processes in which training is necessary.

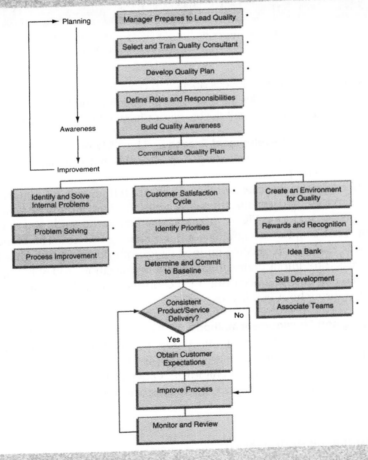

*Training necessary

Source: NationsBank, Charlotte, NC (1993).

FIGURE 9.2   *The Training and Development Process*

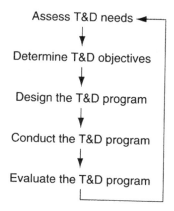

Assess T&D needs

Determine T&D objectives

Design the T&D program

Conduct the T&D program

Evaluate the T&D program

Performance appraisal is the process of evaluating how well individuals and teams are performing their jobs.

In many traditional organizations, performance appraisal was based on supervisory review of individual goal accomplishment tied into financial performance. In many TQ organizations today, performance appraisal is based on customer, peer, and supervisory review of team goal accomplishment tied into improvements in quality and customer-value delivery.[19] Figure 9.3 is an example of managerial performance appraisal done by direct and indirect reports (subordinates), supervisors, self, and others at the Union Pacific Railroad. Note the dimensions of the appraisal, particularly the inclusion of Customer Focus and Teamwork.

Recall from Chapter 1, *management* is defined as the creation and continuous improvement of organizational systems that when used by organizational members lead to increased value for the customers of its products or services. A theme of this book is the primary responsibility of managers to improve systems and processes. This theme suggests that performance appraisal for managers should be tied primarily to progress in systems improvement, rather than to improvement in output measures. If the system is improved, then improvement in output measures will follow.

How important is this task of systems and process improvement for managers? Deming commented on the potential for payoff from managerial improvement activities when he estimated the percentage of problems associated with the system. "I should estimate that in my experience most troubles and most possibilities for improvement add up to proportions something like this: 94 percent belong to the system [*responsibility of management*], 6 percent special"[20] (emphasis added). If 94 percent of the problems are the responsibility of management, then managers should not hold employees responsible for those problems in performance appraisal.[21]

There are a number of potential problems with the performance appraisal process. Many of the traditional methods of supervisory evaluation of individual goal accomplishment are inherently subjective. As such, they set up a potential conflict situation with the evaluator or supervisor expressing judgment. Many indi-

FIGURE 9.3 *Managerial Performance Appraisal: Union Pacific Railroad*

UNION PACIFIC RAILROAD
MANAGEMENT BEHAVIOR QUESTIONNAIRE

Person Rated: _____

NO. RESPONSES

Rated by
Direct Report
Indirect Report
Supervisor
Self
Other

SOCIAL SECURITY #

How frequently does the person being rated exhibit the following leadership behaviors?

Rating scale columns: No Opportunity To Observe | Almost Never | 2 | 3 | 4 | Almost Always

Communication

1. Explains own needs and expectations, including both the *what* and the *why*
2. Listens for understanding by asking relevant questions and summarizing
3. Provides me with balanced, timely feedback
4. Coaches me in using and improving my skills
5. Manages conflict constructively by looking for win/win solutions
6. Demonstrates sensitivity to the needs and diversity of the audience

Customer Focus

7. Ensures complete understanding of both internal and external customer needs
8. Demonstrates commitment to customer needs in prioritizing responsibilities and deliverables
9. Allocates resources and provides assistance to ensure customer commitments are met
10. Seeks feedback on meeting the needs of both internal and external customers

Empowerment

11. Builds trust by showing respect and appreciation, by listening and being fair
12. Assigns responsibilities which challenge me and build confidence in my abilities
13. Encourages me to pursue training and development opportunities
14. Provides me with sufficient information, authority, and resources to accomplish objectives
15. Supports employee involvement and coaches me in the practice of the Principles of Quality Management
16. Gives me credit that is specific and meaningful

Teamwork

17. Provides teams with clear directions
18. Shares appropriate information with all team members
19. Uses interpersonal skills effectively to build consensus
21. Focuses on group results and offers assistance to ensure customer needs are met

Innovation/Change

21. Sees situations from others' points of view
22. Looks beyond existing ways of doing things for innovative solutions
23. Encourages me to take risks in search of continuous improvement
24. Anticipates and plans for change, explaining why changes need to be made

Judgment/Decisiveness

25. Makes timely decisions, seeking diverse points of view and using all available data
26. Develops contingency plans based on known risk factors
27. Sets a good example of business ethics
28. Acknowledges own mistakes

Goals/Results

29. Inspires and motivates the work group toward world class standards
30. Communicates expectations related to the Business Objectives, including responsibilities, measures, and targets
31. Achieves established targets through effective root cause analysis, corrective action, implementation, and evaluation/recognition of progress
32. Personally uses the Principles of Quality Management and the problem-solving process to make decisions
33. Identifies and removes barriers to continuous improvement

Source: Union Pacific Railroad, Omaha, NE (1993).

viduals associate this with subsequent punishment or lack of reward. To deal with the problem, many organizations have made the process appear more objective through extensive paperwork and documentation, which further complicates the process.[22] For these reasons, and a recognition that customer value is often provided by teams, many organizations have moved to team output measures with customer and team evaluation. Today many measures are more directly tied to customer-relevant outcomes.

Rewards

As noted earlier in this chapter, reward processes have undergone change in TQ organizations. A recent review of traditional reward systems characterized them as based on competition for individual merit increases. In contrast, TQ-based reward systems consisted of team- or group-based rewards, including financial rewards and nonfinancial recognition.[23] Several organizational TQ journeys have failed because of the inability to redesign the reward system to support the values of TQ, including teaming.[24]

Compensation   **Compensation** is the monetary payments (wages, salaries, bonuses—current and deferred) used to reward employees. The last part of the definition—"used to reward employees"—is important. The manager needs to ask what kind of behavior is being rewarded. Is the pay system rewarding team or group behavior, individual performance, or longevity independent of performance?

Compensation in some TQ organizations is tied to achieving quality-relevant goals. At Eastman Chemical Company, a 1993 Baldrige Award winner, all employees are involved in an employee stock ownership plan (ESOP). About 3 percent of employee wages is committed to the ESOP. By involving all employees, as opposed to involving only executives as at some companies, Eastman reinforces the spirit of teamwork in its workforce.[25] At the Saturn Corporation 5 percent of employees' compensation is dependent on achieving quality-relevant goals.

Benefits   **Benefits** are tangible items of value in addition to compensation that an organization provides to its employees. Since benefits are usually tied to employment, not performance, about the only form of behavior that is rewarded is joining the organization and staying with the organization. When managers tie benefits to behavior, they need to be mindful of the kind of behavior they are rewarding, as noted in the Chapter Cases at the end of this chapter.

Benefits had at one time been referred to as "fringe benefits." Now that benefits typically add about one-third of payroll to an organization's costs, benefits are not fringe.

Traditional benefit schedules offer few choices for employees. Today cafeteria benefit schedules in which employees can choose among several benefit options are popular. The choice is consistent with the trend of giving more power to employees, as we shall see in Chapter 14 in our discussion of teams.

Recognition   A number of organizations use recognition to reward individual and team performance. Awards, prizes, public acclaim in meetings, and company

QUALITY CASE

Conclusion to the NationsBank Case

In addition to training, NationsBank noted the importance of rewards and recognition in its quality improvement process. Presented in the following table are categories and examples of the kinds of behavior that the organization rewarded and recognized. The table recognizes that rewards and recognition are meant to reinforce certain kinds of behavior.

What kinds of rewards and recognition should be used? The figure on page 267 provides a variety of examples. Most of the examples are not expensive monetarily.

However, they provide recognition that can be a powerful reinforcer of behavior.

Several business writers and security analysts were suggesting in the mid-1990s that NationsBank was not finished growing. Some speculated that it would become a nationwide, broad-spectrum, financial services firm. Based on the information in this case, it appears that NationsBank understands the importance of training, rewards, and recognition as it implements quality processes in the

Behaviors That Managers Reward and Recognize

Category	Example
Improving customer satisfaction	Continuous improvement of processes involved in customer research Quicker response on inquiry information Increase in positive feedback from customers and clients
Increasing revenue and reducing costs	New sources of income identified Supplies, paper reduced Cost-effective methods identified Unnecessary processes eliminated Improving communication methods with units working different shifts
Improving accuracy	Creative research to determine root cause of problem Personal computer program replaces manual process
Improving work environment	New cross-training program Associate accountability for crisis management during manager's absence
Improving methods and procedures	Establishing customer checkpoints on a project that saves systems expense Developing an on-the-job training program for new hires

Source: NationsBank, Charlotte, NC (1993).

continued

customer satisfaction cycle. The firm should be well positioned for growth.

DISCUSSION QUESTIONS

1. Do the concepts of Total Quality apply equally to service and manufacturing organizations? Explain.

2. For training, reward, and recognition processes, how important is it to reinforce a quality emphasis?

Sources: F. Barnes, "NCNB, Inc.," in D. Grigsby and M. Stahl, *Strategic Management Cases*, Belmont, CA: Wadsworth (1993): 156–180; "Is 99% Good Enough?" Charlotte, NC: NationsBank (1993); "Quality Definition," Charlotte, NC: NationsBank (1993); "NationsBank," *Value Line Investment Survey*, New York: Value Line Inc. (September 10, 1993): 2030; "NationsBank Corp.," *Standard NYSE Stock Reports*, New York: Standard & Poor's Corp. (August 16, 1993): 1626M; *Quality Through Rewards & Recognition Process Guide*, Charlotte, NC: NationsBank Services Inc. (January 1993): 3.

Getting Creative: What Kinds of Rewards and Recognition Work?

Level 1	Level 2	Level 3
Certificates of Achievement	Gift certificate	National Conference/ seminar attendance
Balloons	Desk/office accessories	Travel/vacation package
Recognition in staff meeting	Cross pen with NationsBank logo	Gift certificate
Flowers	Portfolio/Pad Holder	Major event tickets
Special parking space (designated Associate of the Month parking in a lot that is free for NationsBank)	Recognition plaque/trophy	Annual "GEM" Award
	NationsBank marketing items	Donation to charity in associate's name
Telephone call from management	Parking space (where there is a charge for parking)	QuickCash
Letter from management		Associate Incentive Plan
Mention in the "Times"	External seminar (local)	
Mention in newsletter	Departmental meal with management	
Meal with management		
Appreciation social	Staff outing	
NationsBank marketing items	Associate of the year	
Casual day	Weekend travel (local)	
Associate of the month	Entertainment/event tickets	
Movie tickets	Paid day(s) off	
Movie rentals	Quarterly "GEM" Award	
Ribbons	Dinner for two	
Banners	Donation to charity in associate's name	
T-shirt	QuickCash	
Departmental trophy on loan to winner		
Special department or team performance may receive any of the above in addition to food brought in by associates or an Associate Appreciation Day.	Special department or team performance may receive any of the above in addition to a staff meal that is catered or a staff outing that is a meal or an event.	

The above examples are provided to spark your imagination. Add other items as appropriate for your situation.

Source: NationsBank, Charlotte, NC (1993).

publications are ways to recognize performance. Mary Kay, the retail cosmetics company, is noted for using the power of recognition at annual meetings and through pink symbols to motivate a salesforce.[26]

Longevity or Exit

The hoped-for result of the entire HR process is the continuation of high-performing employees in the organization. If the organization retains these employees, then its HR processes are effective. Sometimes employees leave the organization either of their own volition or because management determines they are no longer making a contribution and should be terminated. If too many valued employees leave, or if too many low performers need to be terminated, managers need to ask how the HR system can be improved.

CRITICAL THINKING QUESTIONS

1. Why are job descriptions and specifications written more broadly in TQ organizations than in non-TQ organizations?
2. Describe the importance of flexible human resources in a growing or a shrinking organization.
3. How do the HR processes in TQ organizations compare with the HR processes in traditional organizations?

LABOR RELATIONS

Thus far in this chapter we have assumed that management is interacting directly with employees. However, it must be recognized that a significant number of employees interact with management through unions. Although the percentage of employees represented by unions has been in a long downward spiral, HR issues are more constrained in those organizations with unions.

Why Unions?

Many managers prefer not to deal with unions because union contracts restrict the freedom of managers to deal with employees over issues of wages, benefits, working conditions, and other HR issues. The whole process of negotiating a union contract, administering the contract through the grievance process, and working with a union on a daily basis can severely impact the operations of a firm.[27] **Labor–management relations** is the process of dealing with employees who are represented by a union.

Unions were very popular and powerful in the United States in the early and mid-1900s. They have been declining dramatically in the last few decades, with membership in several unions down by one-third in the last two decades.[28] Given the protection provided by federal law (see Table 9.1), many workers have decided that they do not need the representation provided by unions.

There are actions that management can take to preclude a union from being voted in by workers. If managers treat employees fairly, provide equitable wages, benefits, and working conditions, and if they give employees a way to have complaints resolved, then there is a low probability of a union. Employees join unions because they believe that union representation will provide advantages that they cannot gain by themselves.

Collective Bargaining

Collective bargaining is the process of negotiating a labor contract between management and labor. This process can be lengthy and adversarial, because it usually determines wages, benefits, working conditions, and other HR issues for the life of the contract. The contract is the basis of labor relations for the life of the contract, which is usually three years.

Grievance Process

The **grievance process** is the process for interpreting the contract and for settling disputes during the life of the labor contract. Grievances can be adversarial at the time that they are being resolved and they can be time consuming. However, they provide a mechanism to interpret and enforce the contract so that employees need not resort to strikes and other labor actions.[29]

Labor–Management Actions

Labor–management relations can be cooperative or they can be adversarial. Cooperative labor–management relations are a definite asset for a firm, especially for one in a competitive situation. By working together, management and labor can find ways to lower costs and provide superior value to customers. Many unions are working with managers in a TQ environment to provide such value to customers. These unions recognize that the enemy is *not* management; rather, it is international competitors.

Unfortunately, there were some managers and union members in General Motors and the United Auto Workers in the 1990s who acted as if the enemy were each other. In January 1994 the UAW struck a Louisiana GM plant because the plant tried to increase productivity as a way to lower its costs.[30] That was in a time period when Japanese auto firms were selling an increasing number of cars made in the United States at an increasing profit.

Adversarial labor–management relations make it nearly impossible to implement significant, lasting change that will benefit customers. Adversarial situations can be marked by a number of confrontations between management and labor. Labor can engage in a strike in which it refuses to come to work. Labor can promote a boycott in which it asks others not to buy the firm's products or services. Management can implement a lockout in which it refuses to let employees come to work, or management can hire strike breakers, who are nonunion workers, to do strikers' jobs. Such actions usually leave scars that last for years.

CRITICAL THINKING QUESTIONS

1. There have been a number of laws passed concerning employment issues that restrict the freedom of managers in organizations. Are managers better off working under the constraints of the law or working with unions? Explain.

2. Explain the importance of cooperative labor–management relations in implementing a continuous improvement culture.

SUMMARY

The human resource system is viewed from the process perspective. The HR subprocesses and the flow of human resources in the organization through the various subprocesses include HR planning, recruitment, selection and hiring, training and development, performance appraisal, and rewards. The hoped-for result of these subprocesses is longevity of high-performing people. Many managers recognize that human resources are the organization's only appreciating asset.

Viewing human resources from the process perspective helps managers in at least two ways: (1) it helps managers understand the integrated-systems nature of many HR processes, and (2) it helps managers see HR problems as defects in the system, not necessarily as the fault of any one manager.

Two HR areas receiving much attention under the TQ banner are training and reward systems.

HR systems and processes are conducted in the midst of a variety of laws governing their behavior. The most noteworthy of the federal laws are in the areas of equal employment opportunity, compensation and benefits, labor relations, and occupational safety and health. Since nearly all organizations publicly profess that they wish to conform with the law, HR decisions and practices that are illegal are viewed as defects in the HR system.

Discrimination refers to HR actions based on criteria that are not job relevant. Thus discrimination is a defect in the HR system. There are two reasons why an organization benefits from a diverse workforce: (1) discrimination is illegal, and (2) U.S. culture is becoming increasingly diverse.

HR planning involves forecasting staffing needs and the steps needed to fulfill those needs. These steps are forecasting the internal and external supply, comparing needs with supplies, and correcting the shortage or surplus.

Recruiting is the process of attracting individuals to apply for jobs. Internal recruiting refers to encouraging current employees to apply for higher-level jobs in the organization. External recruiting refers to attracting individuals from outside the organization to apply for jobs.

Selection is the process of determining the applicants' qualifications and choosing the best applicant for the job. The selection process consists of application, determination of qualifications, and choice.

There are a number of selection devices used to determine applicant qualifications, among them application forms, interviews, tests, assessment centers, reference checks, and physical examinations.

Training and development refers to the process of developing knowledge, skills, and behaviors in employees that will enable them to better perform their current and future jobs. The training and development process consists of assessing T&D needs, determining T&D objectives, and designing, conducting, and evaluating the T&D program.

Performance appraisal is the process of evaluating how well individuals and teams are performing their jobs. Traditional reward systems view appraisal as competition for individual merit increases. TQ-based reward systems are based on team- or group-based rewards, including financial rewards and nonfinancial recognition.

The anticipated result of the entire HR process is the continuation of high-performing employees in the organization. If too many valued employees leave or if too many low-performing employees need to be terminated, then managers need to ask how the HR system can be improved.

EXPERIENTIAL EXERCISE

The Awful Interview

Employment interviews are frequently traumatic experiences. Interviewers know what they are looking for, and the interviewees don't. Interviewers are prepared, and the interviewees are not. Interviewers are relaxed, and the interviewees are tense. The cards are stacked in the interviewers' favor, it seems.

Interviewers are also notorious for asking disconcerting questions: "Tell me about your goals in life. Why do you want to work for International Widgets?" If job hunters answer such questions candidly but impulsively, they may never be hired. ("My only goal in life is to get a job so I can begin to find out whether I really like it" or "I want to work for International Widgets because I don't have any other likely looking offers right now.") Anyone who has been confronted with questions such as these will understand why we have titled this exercise "The Awful Interview."

Job hunters should not let interviewers catch them by surprise. This exercise is based on the assumptions that (1) practice can help prepare for interview situations, and (2) honesty really is the best policy. Job hunters who concentrate on giving a prospective employer the impression that they are just the person wanted are employing a defensive strategy. They may become so preoccupied with projecting an "image" that they have little energy left for the real problem of showing the interviewer the careful thought they have given to planning their career.

In this exercise all members of the class will together develop a list of the ten most awful questions that they know, from their own or others' experience, have actually been asked in job interviews. An "awful" question is one that would be threatening or difficult to answer honestly in a job interview. When completed, the list should be written down for use in the remainder of the exercise.

The class will then divide into groups of three or four, each student choosing others who might be helpful in providing feedback on his or her interviewing style.

One member of each group volunteers to answer the first question, and another member is chosen to ask the question. Selecting a question from the list of the ten most awful, the interrogator asks the interviewee the first question. The interviewee must try to answer the question as truthfully and honestly as possible. After the answer is given, other members of the group provide feedback to the interviewee on how they experienced the answer.

Upon completion of the feedback, the interviewee becomes the interrogator, selects a question and a new interviewee, and another round begins. The rounds are continued until each person has answered at least three questions or until time is called.

Class members should summarize in writing (for their use only) how they felt they performed, answering these questions: What questions did I handle well? What were my strengths? What questions did I handle poorly? What questions asked of others would I have found difficult to answer? What can I do to deal more effectively with the questions that gave me problems?

The entire class should then reconvene for discussion.

Discussion Questions

1. What did you learn during the exercise about how to answer interviewers' questions more effectively?
2. Do you think employment interviewers obtain valid data in interviews? Why or why not?
3. If you were an interviewer, what kinds of questions would you ask?
4. Why is the interview so widely employed as a selection device?
5. What steps can the interviewee take to ensure a more effective interview?

Source: Adapted from R. J. Lewicki, D. D. Bowen, D. T. Hall, and F. S. Hall, *Experiences in Management and Organizational Behavior,* 3rd ed., New York: Wiley (1988): 268–270.

CHAPTER CASE

Vacation

Ronald worked for about six months out of a year for a company as an extra employee. The company and the union had detailed provisions for earning vacation. These, in part, stated that a person with Ronald's seniority had to work 110 days in the preceding year to earn a two-week vacation. In 1973 Ronald had worked 101 days and thereby earned no vacation for 1974. Near the end of December 1974, Ronald calculated that he was going to have only 108 days of work for 1974 and, consequently, not earn a vacation for 1975.

Ronald's supervisor heard through the grapevine that Ronald had offered $20 to anyone who would lay off sick on Ronald's days off so he would be called in for work. Thus Ronald was hoping to pick up two days of work and earn a vacation in 1975. This offer was most attractive, as the employee could lay off and draw sick pay plus the $20 offered by Ronald. The supervisor wondered whether it was his area of concern if Ronald were in fact trying to do this, and, if so, what he should do about it.

Discussion Questions

1. Should the supervisor be concerned with Ron's scheme to "earn" a vacation? If so, what should that concern be?
2. Is there a need to change the method of determining how vacations are earned? Or should there be a redefinition of eligibility? Explain.

Source: A. F. Knapper, *Cases in Personnel Management,* Westerville, OH: Robin Enterprises (1977): 80.

To Be Sick?

On May 1 the union had negotiated a new sick-pay agreement. The agreement stated, in part, that all employees with more than three years of service were entitled to ten days of sick leave a year and that at no time could more than twenty days be accumulated. Sick pay was full salary for the employee on his normal job. The rule further stated a doctor's certificate might be requested.

The new rule differed from the old one, which stated that sick-pay benefits would be paid only if no extra expenses were incurred by the company because of an employee's sickness.

In the past six years only two days of work had been missed because of sickness in John's group. The work was of such a nature that, when an employee was sick, someone else had to be found to perform his duties. Thus under the old rule no one drew sick pay in this work group because additional expenses were incurred in hiring replacements for sick employees.

The new agreement had been in effect two months and there were already five days of sick leave used. One employee had used three days and another two. Neither of these employees had missed any work in the preceding six years. One employee had brought the company doctor's certificate, which was not required, and the other had not. This much sickness worried the superintendent, because too much time off would create problems with relief help. These employees were already drawing twenty days a year vacation. The question mulled over by the superintendent was how to stem attempts to misuse sick leave.

Discussion Questions

1. Was the superintendent showing appropriate concern? Why or why not?

2. What suggestions do you have for the superintendent?

Source: A. F. Knapper, *Cases in Personnel Management*, Westerville, OH: Robin Enterprises (1977): 33.

KEY TERMS

affirmative action Taking positive steps to promote employment opportunities for qualified people in protected groups that are currently underrepresented in the organization.

application form Written document to collect information on the applicant's educational background, previous work experience, and other job-related demographic data.

assessment center Simulation of many of the important tasks in the job, conducted with a number of relevant exercises and situations.

benefits Tangible items of value in addition to compensation that an organization provides to its employees.

collective bargaining Process of negotiating a labor contract between management and labor.

compensation Monetary payments (wages, salaries, bonuses—current and deferred) used to reward employees.

discrimination Practice of taking HR actions based on criteria that are not job relevant.

empowerment Sharing with nonmanagerial employees the power and authority to make and implement decisions.

external recruiting Process of attracting individuals from outside the organization to apply for jobs.

grievance process Process for interpreting the contract and for settling disputes during the life of the labor contract.

human resource audit Cataloguing of the strengths and weaknesses of current personnel.

human resource planning Forecasting staffing needs and determining the steps needed to fulfill those needs.

internal recruiting Process of attracting current employees to apply for higher-level jobs in the organization.

job analysis   Systematic study of what is done, when, where, how, why, and by whom in current and predicted jobs.

job description   Written statement of job duties and responsibilities.

job specification   List of the skills, abilities, education, experience, and other qualifications needed for a job.

job test   Written or computer-generated test that measures a specific attribute, skill, or personality dimension relevant to the job.

labor–management relations   Process of dealing with employees who are represented by a union.

on-the-job training (OJT)   Learning how to perform the job on the work site under the guidance of an experienced employee.

performance appraisal   Process of evaluating how well individuals and teams are performing their jobs.

realistic job preview (RJP)   Job outline that gives applicants a real picture (both positive and negative information) about the job and the organization.

recruiting   Process of attracting individuals to apply for jobs.

reference checks   Questions addressed to former employers, former co-workers, and other acquaintances concerning the experience and behavior of the job applicant.

selection   Process of determining applicants' qualifications and of choosing the best applicant for the job.

training and development (T&D)   Process of developing knowledge, skills, and behaviors in people that will enable them to better perform their current and future jobs.

validity   Relationship between applicants' scores on the device and applicants' future job performance.

ENDNOTES

1. R. Galvin, *The Idea of Ideas*, Schaumburg, IL: Motorola University Press (1991): 100.
2. R. Blackburn and B. Rosen, "Total Quality and Human Resource Management: Lessons Learned from Baldrige Award-Winning Companies," *Academy of Management Executive*, 7, no. 3 (August 1993): 56.
3. W. E. Deming, *Out of the Crisis*, Cambridge, MA: MIT Center for Advanced Engineering Study (1986): 24.
4. R. Cole, "Introduction—Special Issue on Total Quality Management," *California Management Review*, 35, no. 3 (Spring 1993): 8.
5. "As IBM Losses Mount, So Do the Complaints About Company Perks," *The Wall Street Journal* (October 27, 1993): A1.
6. Blackburn and Rosen, "Total Quality and Human Resource Management," 49.
7. E. McCormick, "Job and Task Analysis," in M. Dunnette, Ed., *Handbook of Industrial and Organizational Psychology*, Chicago: Rand McNally (1976): 651–696.
8. Blackburn and Rosen, "Total Quality and Human Resource Management," 51.
9. B. Dumaine, "The New Art of Hiring Smart," *Fortune* (August 17, 1987): 78–81.
10. P. Farish, "HRM Update: Referral Results," *Personnel Administrator* (1986): 22.
11. Dumaine, "The New Art of Hiring Smart."
12. M. Suszko and J. Breaugh, "The Effects of Realistic Job Previews on Applicant Self-Selection and Employee Turnover, Satisfaction, and Coping Ability," *Journal of Management* (Fall 1986): 513–523.
13. Blackburn and Rosen, "Total Quality and Human Resource Management," 51.
14. J. Ledvinka, *Federal Regulation of Personnel and Human Resource Management*, Boston: PWS-Kent (1982).
15. R. Arvey and J. Campion, "The Employment Interview: A Summary and Review of Recent Research," *Personnel Psychology*, 35 (1982): 281–322.
16. F. Schmidt and J. Hunter, "Employment Testing," *American Psychologist* (October 1981): 1128–1137.
17. T. Hanson and S. Balestreri, "An Alternative to Interviews: Pre-Employment Assessment Process," *Personnel Journal* (June 1985): 114.
18. "Back to School for Honda Workers," *New York Times* (March 29, 1993): D1–D3; Blackburn and

Rosen, "Total Quality and Human Resource Management," 51.

19. Ibid.

20. Deming, *Out of the Crisis,* 315.

21. K. Carson, R. Cardy, and G. Dobbins, "Upgrade the Employee Evaluation Process," *Survey of Business,* College of Business, University of Tennessee (Summer-Fall 1993): 29–32.

22. D. McGregor, "An Uneasy Look at Performance Appraisal," *Harvard Business Review* (September-October 1972): 133–134; G. Rider, "Performance Review: A Mixed Bag," *Harvard Business Review* (July-August 1973): 61–67.

23. Blackburn and Rosen, "Total Quality and Human Resource Management," 51.

24. Cole, "Introduction—Special Issue on Total Quality Management," 8.

25. "Eastman Chemical to Start New Era," *Knoxville News-Sentinel* (December 5, 1993): D1.

26. "Mary Kay's Lessons in Leadership," *Fortune* (September 20, 1993): 63–77.

27. C. Heckscher, *The New Unionism,* New York: Basic Books (1988).

28. "What Us Worry? Big Unions' Leaders Overlook Bad News, Opt for Status Quo," *The Wall Street Journal* (October 5, 1993): B1.

29. J. Magenau, J. Martin and M. Peterson, "Dual and Unilateral Commitment Among Stewards and Rank-and-File Union Members," *Academy of Management Journal* (June 1988): 359–376; J. Cain and M. Stahl, "Modeling the Policies of Several Labor Arbitrators," *Academy of Management Journal,* 26 (1983): 140–147.

30. "GM Settles Strike at Louisiana Plant Sparked by Effort to Boost Productivity," *The Wall Street Journal* (January 17, 1994): A2.

10

Organizational Culture and Change

LEARNING OBJECTIVES

After reading this chapter, you should be able to accomplish the following:

- Relate Schein's three levels of organizational culture to each other.

- Discuss the importance of symbols, stories, heroes, slogans, and ceremonies in communicating and reinforcing organizational culture.

- Describe the kinds of organizations that would favor Adapters, Rebels, Good Soldiers, and Mavericks.

- Relate organizational socialization to indoctrination.

- Describe each of the four corporate cultures—Tough-Guy, Macho Culture, Work-Hard/Play-Hard Culture, Bet-Your-Company Culture, and Process Culture—as a function of their environments.

- Discuss the five factors associated with changing an organizational culture.

- State why it takes so long to change organizational cultures.

CHAPTER OUTLINE

Organizational Culture
  Observable and Not Observable Culture
  Managerial Reinforcement Actions
Purposes of Culture
  Socialization
  Behavioral Conformity
Environment and Culture
  Tough-Guy, Macho Culture
  Work-Hard/Play-Hard Culture
  Bet-Your-Company Culture
  Process Culture
  Changing Environments and Changing Cultures
Cultural Change
  The Need for Cultural Change
  Crisis and Cultural Change
  Culture and the Status Quo
  Organizational Culture and Total Quality
Cases and Exhibits
  Promus
  AT&T
  Disney
  Union Carbide
  Velsicol Chemical
  American Overseas, Inc.

Corporate Culture and Promises at Promus

To help fulfill its Promise to customers at the Promus Corporation, managers' desks are in the lobby in Embassy Suites to ensure customers easy access to management. (Photo credit: Embassy Suites/Promus Companies.)

The Promus Companies Inc. was formed in 1990 in connection with a restructuring of Holiday Corporation. At that time Holiday Inns was separated from the other lines of business. Today Promus is a major hospitality company with an extensive casino gaming business and three different-branded lodging chains.

The casinos are operated under the Harrah's name. In 1993 Promus was the only company that operated a casino in each of the five largest land-based gaming markets in the continental United States. This includes Harrah's casinos in Atlantic City, Las Vegas, Reno, Lake Tahoe, and Laughlin, Nevada. With over 300,000 square feet of casino space, Harrah's was positioned as a major player in the gaming industry.

The lodging chains include Embassy Suites, Hampton Inn, and Homewood Suites. Embassy Suites offers two-room suites consisting of a separate living room and dining/ work area, plus a wet bar, and a traditional bedroom. Hampton Inn hotels are limited-service facilities aimed at the value-minded customer. Homewood Suites offers two-room suites aimed at the extended-stay customer.

When Promus was formed in 1990, the challenge for its managers was to design processes to deliver more value to customers in highly competitive markets. How could Promus define itself and differentiate itself in the minds of customers and other stakeholders?

Michael D. Rose, chairman and CEO of Promus, understood the need to differentiate Promus and to communicate that differentiation to all stakeholders. "We strongly believe in the relationship of a well-defined vision, values, and practices (creating a culture) to the long-term success of our business. We communicate with employees and stakeholders to create common culture, values, and practices in a highly decentralized operating environment. Even the name Promus was chosen for its internal communication value— as a word in Latin that means 'to serve,' and in its anglicized pronunciation connotes our 'promise' of *guaranteed* satisfaction."

This question of defining itself and communicating values needed to be answered at a time when gaming and casinos were being redefined in the minds of customers. Whereas in the past it had a negative connotation, gaming was being redefined as an acceptable form of adult entertainment in the 1990s. In 1992, 90 percent of surveyed adults indicated that casino gaming was an acceptable form of adult entertainment. With average losses per customer of around $55 per visit, the cost of casino entertainment was comparable to the cost of other forms of entertainment.

ORGANIZATIONAL CULTURE

Organizational culture is a key means to communicate the goals of the organization and the appropriate behavior in attaining those goals. In this section we consider the nature of organizational culture and how managers can reinforce culture.

Observable and Not Observable Culture

Organizational culture consists of the key values and beliefs that are shared by organizational members. As such, culture may not be readily observable. There are, however, signs and symbols of culture that can be observed.

The most noted writer in the area of organizational culture is Edgar Schein, who argues that there are both observable and not observable levels of culture. Schein speaks of values and beliefs and of the underlying assumptions in the not observable part of culture.[1]

The values and beliefs are core to the definition of culture and are at the center of organizational culture. Values and beliefs are not necessarily observable. However, in some organizations they may be written and widely communicated, as in the case of the Promus "Promises" (see page 281) and "The Penney Idea" described in Chapter 1. If the values and beliefs are not directly observable, they can be inferred from the explanations given by organizational members for their behavior.

Another aspect of culture that is not observable are the assumptions underlying the values and beliefs. These assumptions are the very foundation of the organization's culture. Indeed, the assumptions may be so widely shared by organizational members that they are unaware of them.

The observable part of culture in all organizations consists of the artifacts and the behavior of its members.[2] **Artifacts** are the signs and products of culture. Although this part of organizational culture is readily observable, it may be hard to interpret without knowledge of the underlying values and beliefs. For example, some may consider it inefficient for the general manager in Embassy Suites to have a desk located in the lobby. All the interruptions from people when the desk is in the open may prevent the general manager from completing his or her "work." However, the Promus value concerning the primacy of customers described in the organization's "Promises to Our Customers" (page 281) explains the nature of that behavior.

The observable part of organizational culture builds on the not observable parts. Those three parts and the building block idea are depicted in Figure 10.1.

The artifacts and behavior may take several noteworthy forms: symbols, awards, stories, heroes, slogans, and ceremonies that signify organizational values. Generally speaking, **symbols** are objects that convey meaning to others. Organizational awards are usually symbols of the behavior that the organization is trying to reinforce.

Stories are descriptions of actual organizational events that characterize the values of the organization. To symbolize the cooperation between management and the union at the Saturn Corporation, for example, employees tell stories of how a team of managers and union members studied and traveled together for nearly a year to design the new corporation.

Heroes are individuals who personify the culture of the organization. Bill Gates, founder and CEO of Microsoft, with his hard-working, risk-taking, innovative

FIGURE 10.1   *Three Dimensions of Organizational Culture*

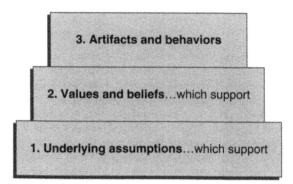

Source: Based on E. Schein, *Organizational Culture and Leadership,* San Francisco: Jossey-Bass (1985): 14.

ways, is a god-like hero at Microsoft. That firm has grown to be the world's largest software firm in large part because of his vision and actions.

Slogans are short sayings that capture key organizational values. As we saw in Chapter 7, Lands' End captures much of its organizational culture with its slogan: "GUARANTEED. PERIOD.®" The corporation feels so strongly about the saying that it repeats it in most of its advertising. Lands' End has even registered the saying in its unique form of all capital letters and a period after each word with the government to protect this unique form. Caterpillar has a slogan of "24-hour parts service anywhere in the world." This communicates its corporate value of meeting the customer's needs.

Ceremonies are special activities that communicate organizational values. Graduation ceremonies at universities are meant to communicate the importance of learning on a campus.

Sometimes values, beliefs, and underlying assumptions become so accepted that managers are not even aware they are there. Did the managers in the following diversity exhibit assume that women "belonged" in certain jobs and that men "belonged" in certain other jobs?

Managerial Reinforcement Actions

To reinforce the desired organizational culture, managers need to know the key levers and mechanisms to use. Schein offered the following bases for managerial actions to reinforce organizational culture:

1. The behaviors managers measure and control.
2. Managers' reactions to crises.
3. Modeling and coaching of expected behaviors.
4. Criteria for allocation of rewards.
5. Criteria for selection, promotion, and termination of employees.[3]

DIVERSITY EXHIBIT

The AT&T Settlement Case

In January 1971 the Equal Employment Opportunity Commission (EEOC) brought charges of discrimination [to the Federal Communications Commission] against American Telephone and Telegraph Company (AT&T) on grounds of discrimination in hiring and promotion. AT&T denied the charges and presented statistics showing (1) that 12.4 percent of its workforce was from minority groups, (2) that while only 2.9 percent of its management positions were held by minorities, 9.3 percent of those recently promoted were from minority groups, (3) that women constituted 55.5 percent of all employees and 33.5 percent of the management and professional staff, etc. Meanwhile, women workers became upset over a contract negotiated by their own union that apparently offered better pay for craft jobs that were held mostly by men. Women's salaries would have been set at roughly 65 percent of those for men (by the women's calculations). While union and management began negotiations, the EEOC pressed charges.

AT&T produced 100,000 pages of documents and statistical arguments intended to prove its innocence, and the EEOC filed 30,000 pages of counter argument. The EEOC not only supported the women's charges of economic discrimination, but argued that sex stereotyping was prevalent in hiring and promotion. They argued that the company was set up to funnel women into operators' jobs and men into management positions. AT&T argued that what it did was no different than airlines' practices of training stewardesses and pilots and adduced statistics to prove its point. The EEOC in turn used statistics to show that 99.9 percent of all operators were female, only 1.1 percent of (more highly paid) craft workers were female, etc. Meanwhile, at least one other government office (the GSA) expressed disagreement with the EEOC position, finding an equal employment plan submitted by AT&T highly favorable.

Eventually AT&T settled with the EEOC out of court. Though complicated, the main provision was that AT&T would pay lump sums of money totaling $15 million to 13,000 of its female and 2,000 of its male employees who had suffered discrimination, and would grant $23 million in pay increases to 36,000 workers who had suffered from job discrimination (plus a commitment of $25 million to $35 million over another five-year period). AT&T further agreed to alter its patterns of hiring and to set goals and timetables to upgrade female and minority employees. However, Bell never formally admitted that it was guilty of any charges brought by the EEOC.

Source: T. L. Beauchamp and Norman E. Bowie, *Ethical Theory and Business*, Englewood Cliffs, NJ: Prentice-Hall (1979): 582–583. Reprinted by permission of Prentice-Hall.

These actions send powerful signals concerning what is valued by the organization. The levers relating to the reward system and to the hiring and termination system send powerful and durable signals about the organization's culture. As we shall see later in this chapter, changing the culture can be difficult simply because these levers are so long lasting.

CRITICAL THINKING QUESTIONS

1. Why should managers focus on the values and beliefs aspect of organizational culture? Why not simply focus on the behavior of organizational members?
2. How do reward systems and hiring and termination systems reinforce corporate culture?

Q UALITY CASE

Back to the Promus Case

One of Promus's first steps was to create and communicate a vision of itself. "OUR VISION is to provide the BEST EXPERIENCE to our gaming and hotel customers by having the BEST PEOPLE trained, empowered and pledged to excellence, delivering the BEST SERVICE, QUALITY & VALUE to every customer, every time . . . GUARANTEED." The vision was further detailed in a set of values labeled "The Promus Companies Promises":

"Promus is a company founded on the idea of a promise and a commitment to excellence to our customers, our employees, our franchisees, our shareholders, and our communities. Fulfilling our promises will make us the premier hospitality company in the world. Our promises are as follows:

Promises to Our CUSTOMERS

Excellent service, high-quality products, and outstanding value to every customer, every time . . . backed by our 100% satisfaction guarantee. Continual improvement in the quality and value of our products and services by listening to our customers.

Promises to Our EMPLOYEES

The opportunity to develop to their full potential in a climate of dynamic growth, teamwork, and open communication. Recognition and reward for superior performance against measurable goals. A company that encourages risk-taking and adapts its organization to the needs of our customers and our employees. Leadership that values a diverse work force, with the highest standards of integrity, ethics, mutual trust, and individual dignity.

Promises to Our SHAREHOLDERS

To be industry leaders in financial performance, producing extraordinary results, not just extraordinary efforts. To create opportunities for our people to be significant shareholders who manage the corporation's assets as their own and create value for all shareholders.

Promises to Our FRANCHISEES and BUSINESS PARTNERS

To create growing brands with clear competitive advantage delivering superior financial returns. To choose franchisees and business partners who share our vision and intense commitment to customers and employees.

Promises to Our COMMUNITIES

We will add value to our communities by our products, services, and sharing our financial resources to achieve a positive impact on our employees, their families, and our fellow citizens. The people of the Promus Companies will be volunteers and leaders because people make the difference in every community."

As a symbol of the Promise to customers, every general manager's desk at Embassy Suites hotels is located in the lobby so that guests have easy access to management. As a way to implement the Promise to employees, Promus established the Harrah Institute of Casino Entertainment to train Harrah's employees on the Promus way of conducting business.

What was the link between the Promises and the future of the company?

PURPOSES OF CULTURE

Organizational culture serves several important purposes in the life of the organization and its members. Culture is a way for new members to learn what is important in the organization and to guide their behavior. Culture also communicates values to customers and other external stakeholders.

Socialization

New members in an organization undergo an intense learning process relating to organizational life called socialization. **"Organizational socialization** is a process by which new members learn and adapt to the new organization that they have joined."[4] In socializing new members, organizations create a series of events designed to replace the nonconforming old values the individuals may hold with the new organizational values. Training, communication, and reward systems play a significant part in organizational socialization activities.

In addition to the formal organizational socialization process, there is also an **informal socialization,** which is the process by which a new member learns and adapts to the informal organization. The primary source of informal socialization is the work group or team, which can exert powerful standards for work behavior and output on its members. This is such an important topic that we treat it in much greater detail in Chapter 14.

The organizational and informal socialization processes may be complementary or they may conflict. Wise managers ensure that they are complementary.

Behavioral Conformity

A prime purpose of organizational culture, and of socialization in particular, is behavioral conformity. The organization is interested in its members behaving in ways that further organizational goals. Faced with such pressures for conformity in values and behavior, members have at least four choices: conform or not conform to the values and beliefs of the organization, or conform or not conform to the behavior prescribed by the culture.[5]

Figure 10.2 depicts the four different combinations of cultural and behavioral conformity. Rebels probably will not be in the organization for too long, as they reject both the organizational values and the appropriate behavior. The military and other rigid hierarchies like Good Soldiers, because they conform on both dimensions. Some organizations highly value Mavericks, because they preserve the culture and values while adding diversity to the behavioral menu of employees. Adapters are of less value, because in the long term they do not further the culture of the organization.

The following quality exhibit illustrates some of the socialization that Disney's employees experience. Socialization helps them to understand the corporate value relating to customer service.

CRITICAL THINKING QUESTIONS

1. Describe the kinds of organizations that would favor Mavericks over Good Soldiers.

2. Compare and contrast socialization with brainwashing.

FIGURE 10.2 *Culture Caricatures: Analytical Scheme for Studying Cultural Nonconformity*

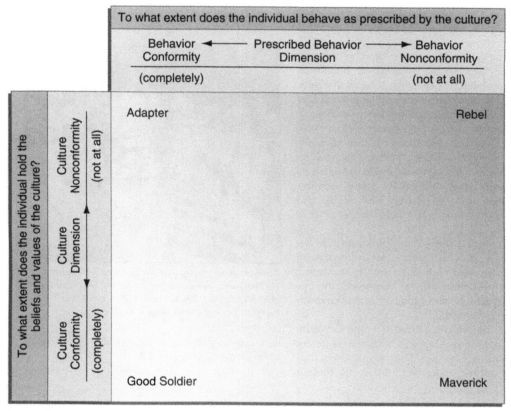

ENVIRONMENT AND CULTURE

The Promus corporate culture described in the Promus case was deliberately designed and communicated to stakeholders early in the life of the organization. The executives designed the culture to fit the organization's environment. Whether their organization's culture is newly designed or has evolved over time, managers must ask if it fits the environment.

There are at least two critical dimensions of the environment in determining its fit with the organization's culture.[6] These two dimensions are (1) the riskiness associated with the organization's activities, and (2) the speed with which managers get feedback on the success of decisions and strategies. The combinations of these two dimensions have been labeled as four separate corporate cultures by two prominent writers on the topic of corporate culture, Terrence Deal and Allan Kennedy.

Q   U   A   L   I   T   Y   E   X   H   I   B   I   T

Disney's Service Strategy: The Culture Is the Key

The answer to how Disney does it is the corporate culture, or "the way we do things around here." "Corporate culture" is certainly a buzzword these days, but it is nevertheless a useful term in explaining how the company's quality strategy works.

The organization defines quality service as a series of behaviors exhibited by cast members in the presence of guests. These behaviors include smiling, making eye contact, using pleasant phrases, performing their role functions, and implementing the many other details that add up to the "personal touch" in the eyes of the guests.

At the core of the Disney philosophy is the belief that people (both guests and cast members) are products of their environment. To the degree that an environment can be controlled, the appropriate reactions of people within that environment can be predicted.

Disney, therefore, strives to control, within good business sense, as much of the environment at the resort as possible. Both the experience of the guest and the experience of the cast, though

The culture at Disney, symbolized through costumes and uniforms, stresses to employees the importance of customer service. (Photo credit: AP/Wide World Photos. Copyright Walt Disney Productions.)

adhering to different standards, are orchestrated to be as positive as possible.

continued

These four cultural labels are obviously simplifications. Within organizations different divisions or functions may have somewhat different cultures. Many marketing departments, for instance, are characterized with cultures separate from manufacturing. Nevertheless, organizations have a predominant culture. Successful organizations seem to have a consistent culture that fits their environment, unlike unsuccessful organizations.

Tough-Guy, Macho Culture

The **Tough-Guy, Macho Culture** is characterized by organizations and managers who regularly take high risks and get quick feedback on whether their actions were right or wrong.[7] Because of the high risk and quick feedback, this may be the most trying of all corporate cultures. Construction, management consulting, advertising, television, the entertainment industry, and sales of big-ticket items are examples. The big sale, the big movie, the big project, the one big anything—all characterize this culture.

Because it is a stressful culture with the high risk and high speed, burnout can be a problem. Thus it is not unusual to see large rewards associated with successes.

The company's philosophy of guest service was established by Walt Disney with the opening of Disneyland on July 17, 1955. He was committed to providing a "good show" through themed entertainment.

In essence, Walt took his greatest film creations and translated them into a form of three-dimensional reality. He took a theater audience and lifted them onto the stage, surrounded them with sets and props, and had them interact with actors and actresses (the cast members). In a way, he put the guests in the middle of the action, engaging all five senses and enabling them to experience the show scene by scene in a preplanned sequence.

Disney views its show as a live performance and the physical setting as a movie set. Everything must be carefully designed and constructed to bring home the feeling of theme and service to the guest. . .in a word, quality. Each day, the set must be perfect, restored to its shiny luster so guests can "shoot the movie through their eyes."

The concept of show business is extended throughout the culture and helps in attaining the "buy in" of the cast. From the beginning, an employee is not hired for the job but, rather, cast for a role in the show. Cast members wear costumes, not uniforms. They play before an audience of guests, not a crowd of customers. When they are in a guest environment, they are "on-stage"; when they are in an employee environment, they are "backstage."

This vernacular communicates to cast members that they are in show business. They are not necessarily to be themselves when on stage, but rather to play a role. The role calls for an "aggressively friendly" approach, one that incorporates smiles, enthusiasm, sincerity, high energy, and concern for the happiness of the guest. In short, a cast member is a host or hostess.

The culture at the resort continues to evolve and change. Its purpose, however, remains the same: to support the cast in exceeding the needs and expectations of the guests.

Source: R. Johnson, *The Journal of Business Strategy*, 12 (September-October 1991): 39–40.

The "stars" who make the successful decisions, whether in the entertainment industry or in any other industry, are usually richly rewarded.

It is unfortunate that the label is male oriented, for of all the types of corporate culture, this one probably discriminates least against women. A star is a star, regardless of gender.

Work-Hard/Play-Hard Culture

The **Work-Hard/Play-Hard Culture** is characterized by action and fun, low risk, and quick feedback.[8] Sales organizations, computer hardware and software companies, consumer electronics, and chain restaurants are all examples. In this corporate culture the name of the game is a high number of small risks, as no one sale will make or break the salesperson. This is coupled with quick decisive feedback as the sale is either made or not made.

The Work-Hard/Play-Hard Culture is labeled to include the words *play hard* since visible celebrations of successful achievers are routine. Mary Kay, the national retail cosmetics firm, is noted for Mary Kay conventions that celebrate successful salespersons. IBM celebrates successful sales agents at yearly gatherings. Some computer software and biotechnology firms celebrate a week of hard work with Friday "beer busts."

A danger in this culture is that high levels of activity and sales volume can distract from attention to quality. Attention to detail and the needs of the individual customer can sometimes suffer in the push for the next sale or the next new product.

Bet-Your-Company Culture

The **Bet-Your-Company Culture** is noted for high-risk decisions and a slow-feedback environment.[9] It may be years before managers in this culture learn if some high-stakes decisions pay off for the organization. Organizations with large projects or programs that take years to develop and then years to pay off exemplify this corporate culture. If the decisions on the projects are correct, then the organization may benefit from years of success. The converse is also true. Aerospace companies like Boeing and Lockheed and capital goods companies like Caterpillar and Cincinnati Milacron are examples of this culture.

Sometimes organizations that are not normally characterized by this culture find themselves in a bet-your-company situation. The decision that must be made is all the more gut-wrenching since the managers are not accustomed to making such decisions. In the early 1980s Chrysler made a bet-your-company decision when it launched the K-Car series of cars. IBM bet the company when it launched the System 360 family of computers in 1964. That decision and that family of computers earned the firm billions of dollars and dominance of the computer industry for many years.[10]

Process Culture

The **Process Culture** is characterized by slow feedback and low-risk decisions.[11] Managers often find it difficult to measure the effectiveness of a decision because of the long time spans and the large number of low-risk decisions involved. Thus they sometimes concentrate on the process, or the way the activities are carried out. Government agencies, utilities, and financial-services firms are examples of process culture firms.

If the processes are tied to designing and delivering customer value, then the organization can be an effective Total Quality player. Competition in the marketplace can go a long way toward helping the organization focus on its customers and tying processes to customer value. If the processes are not tied to customer value, then the firm can drift and be known as an ineffective bureaucracy. The absence of competition is associated with processes that are not linked to customer value.

Now that the four cultures have been defined and described, they can be depicted as a function of the two key environmental dimensions of risk and speed of feedback. Figure 10.3 shows the four cultural types as a function both of the risk associated with the organization's activities and the speed with which managers get feedback on the success of decisions and strategies.

Changing Environments and Changing Cultures

The corporate cultures and environmental descriptions outlined above are pure types in that corporate culture is depicted as a function of certain types of environ-

FIGURE 10.3   *Corporate Culture as a Function of the Environment*

Speed of Environmental Feedback

	Fast	Slow
High	Tough-Guy, Macho Culture	Bet-Your-Company Culture
Low	Work-Hard/Play-Hard Culture	Process Culture

(Risk)

Source: Based on T. Deal and A. Kennedy, *Corporate Cultures: The Rites and Rituals of Corporate Life,* Reading, MA: Addison-Wesley (1982): 107–108.

ments. In today's intense internationally competitive business environment, the speed of environmental feedback is quickening. Also, because of the concern for quality, much attention is being paid to process issues in organizations. Thus in the future some of the characteristics of the Process Culture may merge with the cultures defined by greater rapidity of environmental feedback.

Different environments give birth to different cultures. Note the different values between the two countries in the following international exhibit.

CRITICAL THINKING QUESTIONS

1. Describe the impact of increasing speed due to international competition on the Bet-Your-Company Culture and the Process Culture.

2. How will the attention to processes needed to yield the consistent quality demanded by customers affect the four types of culture?

CULTURAL CHANGE

As the speed of environmental change increases, organizational cultures must also change. Yet many of the cultural changes are painfully slow.

The Need for Cultural Change

As environments change, the organizational cultures must adapt. Yet many corporate cultures require several years to change and then do so only with much effort.[12] Throughout all of the recent turmoil signaling that IBM needed to change dramatically, the company continued to be known for its rigid bureaucracy and concern for rules.[13]

Many firms have recognized the importance of changing corporate culture as they launch new strategies. New strategies based on quality may conflict with old strategies that may have emphasized schedules and productivity. Xerox and Harley-Davidson are two examples of firms that took years to change corporate cultures in

INTERNATIONAL EXHIBIT

Union Carbide's MIC Plants in the United States and France

One of the most famous industrial accidents in the twentieth century happened on December 3, 1984, when a tragic toxic gas leak of methyl isocyanate (MIC) occurred at a Union Carbide plant in Bhopal, India, killing at least 1,750 people and leaving thousands of others sick and incapacitated. That plant was closed and never reopened. In subsequent litigation, U.S. District Judge John F. Keenan called the case "the most significant, urgent, and extensive litigation ever to arise from a single event."

Although its own internal inspections and reports had warned of potential problems in controlling reactions and of failures both in India and at a similar plant at Institute, West Virginia, Union Carbide took the position that potential problems had been handled and that both plants were operated in accordance with proper safety standards. It suggested sabotage as a likely but not conclusive explanation of the "accident" in India and sharply criticized the way Indian supervisors had loosely implemented the company's safety standards.

Subsequent investigation indicated that there had been more than 70 generally small MIC leaks at the Institute plant from 1980 to 1984. That plant was closed for a five-month period after the Bhopal disaster, but it was reopened after presumably thorough inspections by Union Carbide, the state of West Virginia, EPA, and OSHA. Before reopening the plant, Union Carbide put in place $5 million in new safety equipment, introducing new safety monitors and a new cooling system that was thought to "solve" the problems that had arisen in India.

A year later, on April 1, 1986, Union Carbide was fined $1.3 million by the U.S. Labor Department for 221 safety violations at the Institute plant. This was the largest such fine in history. OSHA inspectors charged that Union Carbide had intentionally underreported the number of injuries at the plant and had maintained defective safety equipment. Secretary of Labor Brock said the findings showed a "laissez-faire attitude" toward worker safety. However, none of these violations involved the MIC unit, and no one had died. No units were closed.

Less widely discussed and investigated is a relatively obscure Union Carbide facility in Beziers, France, that uses large quantities of MIC in order to produce an insecticide. Beziers is also in a region of France that has one of the highest unemployment rates in that country. The French are well aware of the safety concerns that have arisen about Union Carbide facilities. However, workers have made it clear that they are much more concerned about losing their jobs than they are about injury from toxic gases. Shortly after Bhopal, Environment Minister Huguette Bouchardeau had the plant inspected and declared it safe. Local officials have made it clear that jobs at this facility are critical to the area's economic viability. Bouchardeau further noted that "in France, there are at least 300 companies that present comparable risks. If we reacted emotionally to the catastrophe [in India], there would be an industrial disaster in France."

Source: T. Beauchamp and N. Bowie, *Ethical Theory and Business*, 3rd ed., Englewood Cliffs, NJ: Prentice-Hall (1988): 253–254. © Tom L. Beauchamp.

the direction of greater emphasis on quality. Even after years of change, including winning a Baldrige National Quality Award and regaining market share from Japanese competitors, Xerox's culture is still changing. David Kearns, former chairman of Xerox, describes the change process as "a Race with No Finish Line."[14]

E   T   H   I   C   S   E   X   H   I   B   I   T

Velsicol Chemical Corporation

On December 24, 1975, the administrator of the Environmental Protection Agency of the U.S. government, Russell E. Train, issued an order suspending certain uses of the pesticides heptachlor and chlordane. A federal act seemed to give him authority to do so, but both the secretary of agriculture and the manufacturer of the pesticides, Velsicol Chemical Corporation, joined in asking for a public hearing on the decision. Train and the EPA adduced considerable evidence to indicate that these pesticides, which were widely used in the environment to control pests, produced cancer in laboratory animals. Testing on laboratory animals was the sole basis for the inference that the pesticides posed a cancer threat to humans, although it also was conclusively demonstrated that residues of the chemical were widely present in the human diet and in the tissues of those persons exposed.

Velsicol stood to lose a substantial amount of money unless existing stocks of the pesticides could be sold, and the EPA administrator did allow the company to sell limited stock for use on corn pests (for a short period of time). The Environmental Defense Fund believed strongly that no sale should be permitted, and it sought an injunction against continued sale. During the course of the public hearing, Velsicol argued both that its product should not be suspended unless the governmental agency could demonstrate that it is unsafe, and that any other finding would be a drastic departure from past federal policy. However, both the agency and the judge argued that *the burden of proof is on the company* (that is, the company must be able to prove that its product is safe). Since most issues about environmental and human safety turn on a demonstration of either safety or hazardousness, this burden-of-proof argument was strongly contested in the hearing. The judge found in favor of the agency largely because he believed the animal tests demonstrated a "substantial likelihood" of serious harm to humans. EPA officials subsequently considered backing down on this suspension ruling.

Discussion Questions

1. Should Velsicol have been allowed to sell its existing stock? Why or why not?

2. Should the "burden of proof" be placed on the company rather than on the government? Why or why not?

3. In what respects, if any, was Velsicol treated unfairly by the government?

Source: Adapted from T. Beauchamp and N. Bowie, *Ethical Theory and Business*, 3rd ed., Englewood Cliffs, NJ: Prentice-Hall (1988): 254–255.

Crisis and Cultural Change

Frequently it takes a survival crisis, or a near-death experience, to energize an organization to change its culture from one set of values to another set of values. As noted in the Harley-Davidson case in Chapter 1, Harley had lost over two-thirds of its market share and millions of dollars before it changed its culture to value quality. Xerox saw its market share go from nearly 100 percent to less than 15 percent before it changed its values.[15] Why must organizations nearly go bankrupt before they change?

Different organizations have different ethical values. In the ethics exhibit note some of the differences between Johnson & Johnson (Chapter 4) and Velsicol on the issue of product safety.

FIGURE 10.4 *How Culture Perpetuates Itself*

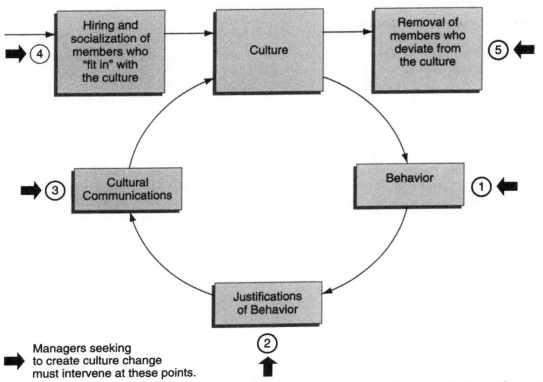

Culture and the Status Quo

There are several processes at work to keep corporate cultures stable and resistant to change. Figure 10.4 presents a model of some of the stabilizing and reinforcing factors that act to keep culture in a staus quo situation.

It has been argued that managers attempting to change culture are most successful if they attempt to change it in the sequence shown in the figure.[16] The first thing to change is people's behavior. Through direction, reward, training, or other means, managers must change the behavior of the organization's members. Training takes time, and it takes years to change reward systems, because there are too many stories in the organization of the old behaviors that had been rewarded.

Then there must be cultural justifications for the behavior. New rituals, new stories, and new heroes are needed to justify the new behaviors.

These new cultural artifacts, stories, symbols, and rituals need to be widely and consistently communicated. P&G managers, for example, often repeat the story of a P&G production line worker who, in order to solve a quality issue, called a customer and investigated the amount of time and the temperature at which the cus-

Q UALITY CASE

Conclusion to the Promus Case

Chairman and CEO Michael Rose commented on the link between the "Promises" and the future of Promus through the medium of corporate reputation: "By adhering to the Promises we intend to build a reputation unlike any other company. Our emphasis on values, integrity and Promises has become the foundation of our successful growth strategy, particularly in casino entertainment, where reputation means so much to each new community and its citizens."

It appears that Promus's reputation paid off, as a number of new casino projects were approved by various government agencies in 1993. Harrah's was selected to be a joint-venture partner in the first casino in New Orleans. Harrah's was also a joint-venture partner for a casino on an Indian reservation in Alabama. Two riverboat casinos were approved for Joliet, Illinois, two in Mississippi, two in Missouri, and one in Louisiana. Promus also continued to expand the lodging chains by opening a number of new Hampton Inns.

Promus's profitability and stock price delivered on the Promus Promises to shareholders in the first four years of operation. In that time profitability tripled, and the stock price quadrupled from 1990.

DISCUSSION QUESTIONS

1. Discuss the importance of corporate culture in a hospitality company.

2. How have the Promus Promises paid off for the company's stakeholders?

Sources: Personal communication, Michael D. Rose (September 17, 1993); "Promus Companies," *Value Line Investment Survey*, New York: Value Line (September 3, 1993): 1787; "Promus Companies," *Standard & Poor's*, New York: Standard & Poor's Corporation (August 23, 1993): 1870F; M. D. Rose, "Promises: What They Mean to Us," *Vision* (Mid-Summer 1993): 1–2; "1992 Annual Report," The Promus Companies, Memphis, TN: 5; The Promus Companies Promises, The Promus Companies, Memphis, TN.

tomer had baked a Duncan Hines angel food cake.[17] This story emphasizes how production line workers, not just corporate executives, get involved in quality improvement.

The fourth step that managers must take to impact culture involves the hiring and socialization of members who match the culture. If new managers and employees are hired who already have the desired values, there are few time lags for training and socialization before the new employees can act on those values.

Lastly, a way to reinforce a culture is to remove those organizational members whose behavior deviates from the cultural values. Their removal reduces the variance in behavior and sends to those in the organization powerful signals relating to appropriate behavior. Today termination is viewed as a last resort, because it is increasingly difficult to terminate employees and because organizations have substantial investments in human resources. Many firms would prefer to pursue the other four steps first.

Organizational Culture and Total Quality

A Total Quality culture has distinct organizational values and beliefs. Transforming an organizational culture that is not based on customer value, continuous improvement, and cross-functional processes into one based on these TQ values is a large-scale, multiyear task. As we have already noted, the new culture needs to take on some of the Process Culture characteristics relating to concern for processes and systems.

An inwardly focused company needs to become primarily customer focused. Shortly after Lou Gerstner took over as CEO at IBM in 1993, he remarked: "I have never seen a company that is so introspective, caught up in its own underwear, so preoccupied with internal processes. Some dealings required 18 signatures. It was bureaucracy run amok."[18] From 1986 to 1993 IBM had taken $28 billion in write-offs, and in 1993 its stock was off 75 percent from its peak in 1987.[19]

The philosophy of continuous improvement needs to be part of the new TQ culture. In many organizations the idea of a continuous stream of small improvements is alien to the idea of "If it's not broke, don't fix it."

The themes of customer focus, horizontal process management, and continuous improvement need to become central to the values and culture of the organization. As Figure 10.4 suggests, that transformation may take years, particularly if the organization had been successful with its old culture. The historical successes of IBM and GM in different environments made it hard for them to change their cultures in a new, internationally competitive environment in which customers demand affordable quality and other dimensions of value.

The experiential exercise on page 293 deals with organizational culture in terms of the way members of an organization interact with its customers. The exercise focuses on the importance of customer groups in an academic setting.

CRITICAL THINKING QUESTIONS

1. Compare and contrast the time it would take to change the organizational culture in a university versus in an industrial organization owned by stockholders.

2. Explain why cultural change takes so much time.

SUMMARY

Organizational culture consists of the key values and beliefs that are shared by organizational members. As such, culture may not be readily observable. In addition to values and beliefs, another aspect of culture that is not observable are the assumptions underlying the values and beliefs. These assumptions, which are the very foundation of the organization's culture, may be so widely shared by organizational members that they are unaware of them.

The observable part of culture in organizations consists of the artifacts and the behavior of its members. The artifacts and behavior may take several noteworthy forms including symbols, stories, heroes, slogans, and ceremonies that signify the organizational values.

Managers need to know the key levers and mechanisms to use to develop and reinforce the desired culture. These actions include the behaviors managers measure and control, their reactions to crises, modeling and coaching of expected behaviors, criteria for allocation of rewards, and criteria for selection, promotion, and termination of employees.

New members in an organization undergo an intense learning process relating to organizational life called socialization. Organizational socialization is a process by which a new member learns and adapts to the new organization that he or she has joined.

A prime purpose of organizational culture, and of socialization in particular, is behavioral conformity. The organization is interested in its members' behaving in ways that further organizational goals. Faced with such pressures for conformity in values and behavior, members have at least four choices: conform or not conform to the values and beliefs of the organization, or conform or not conform to the behavior prescribed by the culture.

Two critical dimensions in determining the fit between the environment and the organization's culture are (1) the riskiness associated with the organization's activities, and (2) the speed with which managers get feedback on the success of decisions and strategies. The combinations of these two dimensions have been labeled as four separate corporate cultures. The Tough-Guy, Macho Culture is characterized by organizations and managers who regularly take high risks and get quick feedback on whether their actions were right or wrong. The Work-Hard/Play-Hard Culture is characterized by action and fun, low risk, and quick feedback. The Bet-Your-Company Culture is noted for high-risk decisions and a slow feedback environment. The Process Culture is characterized by slow feedback and low-risk decisions.

As environments change, the organizational cultures must change. Yet many corporate cultures require several years to change and then do so only with much effort. Frequently it takes a survival crisis to energize an organization to change its culture from one set of values to another set of values.

There are several processes at work to keep corporate cultures stable and resistant to change. In the sequence of organizational change, the first thing managers must change is people's behavior. Then there must be cultural justifications for the behavior. New rituals, new stories, and new heroes are needed to justify the new behaviors. These new cultural artifacts, stories, symbols, and rituals need to be widely and consistently communicated. The fourth step that managers must take to impact culture involves the hiring and socialization of members who match the culture. Lastly, a way to reinforce a culture is to remove those persons whose behavior deviates from the cultural values.

EXPERIENTIAL EXERCISE

Who Are the Customers?

Organizational culture consists of the key values and beliefs shared by organizational members. An all-encompassing value of the organization is the way its members interact with its customers. First, there must be identification of those customer groups. Second, there must be agreement on the relative priority of various customer groups. Third, there must be shared understanding of the value components that the various customer groups require.

This experiential exercise addresses those three issues in the context of the university, college, or school of which you are a member. As a student at your university, college, or school, you have firsthand knowledge of the customers of the institution.

This exercise has two parts. First, you should complete both parts A and B as an individual. Then, the instructor should divide the class into groups ranging in size from four to six people. Your group should then complete the exercise. After the group scores have been agreed upon, your group should rejoin the rest of the class. Each group should report its group's findings to the class for comparison and discussion. If you are at a large university with multiple campuses, colleges, and schools, your instructor needs to decide the organizational level that is to be analyzed.

Part A

List the ten most important customer groups of your institution. Distribute 100 points indicating the importance of those customers. The most important receives the most points. If you do not believe there are ten important customer groups of your institution, then list the most important ones. Be sure that they add to 100 points.

	Individual Scores		Group Scores	
	Identity	Points	Identity	Points
Customer # 1				
Customer # 2				
Customer # 3				
Customer # 4				
Customer # 5				
Customer # 6				
Customer # 7				
Customer # 8				
Customer # 9				
Customer # 10				
	Total	100	Total	100

Part B

For the five most important customers in Part A, indicate the two most important components of customer value (Chapter 7) they require. First complete Part B as an individual, then complete it as a group.

1. Two most important value components (a and b) for the most important customer group from Part A.

Individual List   *Group List*

a. _____   a. _____
b. _____   b. _____

2. Two most important value components (a and b) for the second most important customer group from Part A.

Individual List	*Group List*
a. _____	a. _____
b. _____	b. _____

3. Two most important value components (a and b) for the third most important customer group from Part A.

Individual List	*Group List*
a. _____	a. _____
b. _____	b. _____

4. Two most important value components (a and b) for the fourth most important customer group from Part A.

Individual List	*Group List*
a. _____	a. _____
b. _____	b. _____

5. Two most important value components (a and b) for the fifth most important customer group from Part A.

Individual List	*Group List*
a. _____	a. _____
b. _____	b. _____

CHAPTER CASE

American Overseas, Inc.: Which Culture is Important?

After the division of India into two countries, India and Pakistan, American Overseas Corporation began operating in Karachi. Business increased at a satisfactory rate. The company's U.S. staff rose in ten years to eight. More local staff was also employed over time to handle the increased business. However, the salary paid to the local personnel never exceeded the salary paid to the U.S. managerial group.

Richard Lowry, the general manager, had joined the company ten years before as a junior executive. He had gone to American Overseas immediately after graduating in business from a small California college. His rise had been consistent in the company. He believed that he had a fine career with several promotions ahead. Karachi was his first overseas assignment.

Theodore Sanderson, manager of freight and transportation, was about 55 years of age. Unlike the other Americans, he had long service with American Overseas, including several international assignments, before being sent to Pakistan four years before. Joe Fowler, was a 28-year-old engineer, and a bachelor, with just a year in Karachi.

While members of the Pakistani community might feel that American's personnel had no interest in them, Richard Lowry would not have understood their viewpoint. When he took over as general manager, he felt the need for informal gatherings of local managers to create a more friendly atmosphere in and outside the office. In addition, he wanted to invite high government officials and managers from other firms to these parties. Thus, he hoped to foster better relations with the local community, generate business, and create high-level contact with the government.

Therefore, Lowry began asking local managers, their wives, and local dignitaries to cocktail parties. The occasions for these parties were usually American holidays such as New Year's Eve, Christmas Eve, and the like. Lowry gave such parties whenever a senior executive from American's headquarters or from one of its overseas divisions, visited Karachi.

One of the local employees, a Pakistani named Mahmoud Bekery, had joined American soon after graduation from the University of Karachi. Richard Lowry, who had hired him, had indicated that

American's policy was to advance a man on the basis of merit and regardless of racial background, religion, or anything other than merit. Since Bekery was well-educated, Lowery assured him that his future with the company should be a bright one. Pakistan was growing and progressing, and it was American Overseas' policy to grow along with it.

Bekery, a bachelor, was a devout Muslim. He neither drank alcoholic beverages nor smoked tobacco. A short while after joining American Overseas, Bekery was invited to one of Lowry's parties. This one was in honor of the vice president in charge of Eastern and Far Eastern operations. The party was attended by several other American Overseas people from various branches. The party was held in one of Karachi's best hotels. The entire management group was invited, along with their wives.

At the party, the company doctor, Dr. Yasin, and his wife were sitting with Joe Fowler, who had come alone. By 10 p.m. Fowler had clearly drunk too much. He said to Mrs. Yasin, apparently under the influence of the drinks, "What a great night! I suggest you don't go home with your husband tonight. I'll take you home with me. You know the doctor is getting old. I can't see you spoiling such a great night with him. I am not too drunk to drive you to my house."

Bekery noticed that Dr. Yasin himself was drinking heavily and did not appear to be disturbed by the conversation. Nor was he disturbed when Fowler received an emergency call from the company offices but refused to leave unless Mrs. Yasin went with him. With some difficulty, others persuaded him to go without her. Mrs Yasin, clearly embarrassed by the situation, convinced her husband to take her home.

Elsewhere in the party, Lowry was paying court to the wife of another manager. Meanwhile, the vice president was dancing consistently with one of the company secretaries. Neither paid any attention to what was going on elsewhere. They both urged the Pakistani employees and the Americans to drink and eat heartily.

The episodes at the party disturbed Bekery. On the following day, he sought out one of the senior Pakistani employees and explained that he was upset by the party. He wondered what it meant in terms of American Overseas and its attitudes. The other man replied:

"These parties are given by the management to encourage the local managers to bring their wives and become culturally modernized in the Western sense. Mr. Lowry probably feels that the old local traditional way of living so that sexes do not mix together should be a thing of the past.

"To promote this modernization, management has adopted a few methods. If other things are equal, such as experience, qualifications, and so forth, those who are sociable and bring their wives to such parties stand a better chance for promotion over those who are equally competent but are still traditionalist.

"For example, I am a university graduate and have been with the company for the last 15 years. I have earned my promotions the slow, hard way. But I know a local manager who joined the company only five years ago as a senior clerk. He is now a department manager. He is below average in productivity, and managerial skill, and he is only a high-school graduate. His subordinates know his job better than he does. Yet he is one of Mr. Lowry's favorites. The reason—because he is successful at supplying call girls to Mr. Lowry."

"As for me, although I have generated more business than anybody else in the office, I know I am not in Mr. Lowry's good books. Mr. Sanderson has been fighting my case for promotion for the last three years, but it seems that Mr. Lowry does not agree. I think I am not sociable according to his definition, for I do not bring my wife to these parties. I am afraid that my present position is the end of the line for me in this company. I should be seeking a position elsewhere where I stand a better chance for career progress. I can compete successfully with others in all respects; but I refuse to compete in dishonorable practices."

"This type of behavior, favoritism, and behind-the-scenes activities is not only destroying my morale and impairing my efficiency, but it is having the same effect on others who hold our old cultural traditions dear. After seeing those in the company who are after the so-called Western type of modernization, and who prosper by doing so, we who still believe in the old ways of living are placed on the horns of a dilemma. You had better be thinking about how you will decide."

Discussion Questions

1. How would you decide?
2. What are the responsibilities of U.S. managers doing business in a foreign culture regarding those culture's values?

3. What should the U.S. managers do to prevent Pakistani managers from quitting?
4. Whose culture, the American or local Pakistani, is more important? Why?

5. What should be done about the parties?

Source: Adapted from J. S. Ewing and F. Meissner, *International Business Management*, Belmont, CA: Wadsworth (1964): 425–428.

KEY TERMS

artifacts   Signs and products of culture.

Bet-Your-Company Culture   Culture noted for high-risk decisions and a slow-feedback environment.

ceremonies   Special activities that communicate organizational values.

heroes   People who personify the culture of the organization.

informal socialization   Process by which a new member learns and adapts to the informal organization.

organizational culture   Culture consisting of the key values and beliefs that are shared by organizational members.

organizational socialization   Process by which new members learn and adapt to the new organization that they have joined.

Process Culture   Culture characterized by slow feedback and low-risk decisions.

slogan   Short sayings that capture key organizational values.

stories   Descriptions of actual organizational events that characterize the values of the organization.

symbols   Objects that convey meaning to others.

Tough-Guy, Macho Culture   Culture characterized by organizations and managers who regularly take high risks and get quick feedback on whether their actions were right or wrong.

Work-Hard/Play-Hard Culture   Culture characterized by action and fun, low risk, and quick feedback.

ENDNOTES

1. E. Schein, *Organizational Culture and Leadership*, San Francisco: Jossey-Bass (1985): 14.
2. Ibid.
3. Ibid., 223–243.
4. E. Schein, "Organizational Socialization and the Profession of Management," in L. Boone and D. Bowen, *The Great Writings in Management and Organizational Behavior*, Tulsa, OK: Penn Well Books (1980): 392.
5. V. Sathe, "Implications of Corporate Culture: A Manager's Guide to Action," *Organizational Dynamics* (Autumn 1983): 15.
6. This section was influenced by T. Deal and A. Kennedy, *Corporate Cultures: The Rites and Rituals of Corporate Life*, Reading, MA: Addison-Wesley (1982): Chap. 6.
7. Ibid., *Corporate Cultures*, 107.
8. Ibid., 108.
9. Ibid., 108.
10. "IBM: A Special Company," *Think* (September 1989): 51.

11. Deal and Kennedy, *Corporate Cultures*, 108.
12. J. Lorsch, "Managing Culture: The Invisible Barrier to Strategic Change," *California Management Review* (1986): 95–109; "The Difficult Task of Changing Corporate Culture: The Case of Corning Glass," *The Wall Street Journal* (April 22, 1983): 1.
13. "The Corporate Culture at IBM: How It Reinforces Strategy," *The Wall Street Journal* (April 8, 1982): 1.
14. D. Kearns and D. Nadler, *Prophets in the Dark: How Xerox Reinvented Itself and Beat Back the Japanese*, New York: Harper Collins (1992): 257.
15. Ibid., xiv.
16. Sathe, "Implications of Corporate Culture: A Manager's Guide to Action," 5–23.
17. "Procter & Gamble Rewrites the Marketing Rules," *Fortune* (November 6, 1989): 91.
18. "Rethinking IBM," *Business Week* (October 4, 1993): 88–89.
19. Ibid., 87.

Behavioral Processes

PART

4

11
CHAPTER

Leadership

LEARNING OBJECTIVES

After reading this chapter, you should be able to accomplish the following:

- Describe the differences between management and leadership.
- Explain the differences between formal and informal leaders.
- Relate the concept of power to the concept of leadership.
- Define the five bases of power; compare and contrast them.
- Discuss the traits approach to leadership.
- Explain the behavioral styles approach to leadership.
- Compare and contrast the Leadership Continuum, the Consideration and Initiating Structure Approach, and the Managerial Grid.
- Describe the Situational/Contingency Approach to Leadership.
- Compare and contrast Hersey and Blanchard's Situational Leadership Theory, Fiedler's Leadership Contingency Model, the Vroom-Yetton-Jago Decision Involvement Model, and the Path-Goal Theory.
- Describe the role of a transformational leader in a Total Quality organization.
- Relate the concept of leaders as empowerers and the concept of self-managed work teams to the traditional concepts of leadership.

CHAPTER OUTLINE

Defining Leadership
- *Importance of Leadership*
- *Managers: Leaders or Administrators?*
- *Formal versus Informal Leadership*
- *Organizational Leadership versus Interpersonal Leadership*

Power
- *What Is Power?*
- *Five Bases of Power*
- *Power and Networking*
- *Using Power Responsibly*

Responsibility and Accountability
- *Relationship of Responsibility and Accountability*
- *Levels*
- *Scope*

The Traits Approach
- *List of Leadership Traits*
- *Limits of the Traits Approach*

Behavioral Styles Approaches
- *Leadership Continuum*
- *Consideration and Initiating Structure*
- *Leadership Grid*

Situational/Contingency Approaches
- *Hersey and Blanchard's Situational Leadership Theory*
- *Fiedler's Leadership Contingency Model*
- *Vroom-Yetton-Jago Decision Involvement Model*
- *Path-Goal Theory*
- *Comparing the Situational/Contingency Approaches*

Contemporary Issues in Leadership
- *Transformational/Charismatic Leadership and Total Quality*
- *Leadership and Empowerment in Total Quality*
- *Self-Managed Work Teams*

Cases and Exhibits

- *Government Agencies*
- *Bendix*
- *Western Food Products*
- *Investment-U.S.*
- *Evaluating Quality/Service*
- *Sales Quotas*

TQM and Leadership in Government Agencies

David Kearns, a transformational leader and past CEO of Xerox, understood the importance of TQ when he became Undersecretary of Education. (Photo credit: Xerox Corporation.)

Is Total Quality Management appropriate for federal, state, county, and municipal governments? Many government agencies would answer yes and look to the private sector for guidance. In New York State Governor Mario Cuomo introduced the Excelsior Award, similar to the Baldrige Award, to recognize quality in business, education, and government. President Clinton ordered the development of a TQM effort for state agencies in Arkansas when he was governor.

Eastman Kodak and Minnesota Mining and Manufacturing (3M) are among the compa-

nies that have turned their TQM successes into profit centers that market consulting services to government agencies. Kodak is headquartered in Rochester, New York, which is in Monroe County. A Kodak spokesman commented: "We've been going through a quality management program for several years and we began to think that this could be applied to government as well. We've seen improvement in the business environment and assume that the same kinds of improvement can be made in government."

Monroe County officials were searching for a model that could be applied to the management of the county government. The county director of operations said, "We've been involved for three years in something called 'organization development.' We brought experts to talk to our people about productivity and budgets but it wasn't what we were looking for. The Kodak program met our criteria. The model we were looking for would have to focus on quality and productivity, which TQM does. It focuses on customer satisfaction, and for our purposes taxpayers are our customers."

The Kodak effort resulted in a partnership with the Greater Rochester Metro Chamber of Commerce and the Center for Governmental Research. The partnership's goal was to bring TQM to all county departments. Such partnerships require leadership of public sector officials, because applying TQM to the public sector is not government business as usual.

Dr. Martin Luther King, Jr. was one of the most power-ful, yet referent leaders of the twentieth century as he espoused values that many respected. (Photo credit: Wide World.)

DEFINING LEADERSHIP

What do Lee Iacocca, David Koresh, Ronald Reagan, Adolf Hitler, Winston Churchill, and Martin Luther King all have in common? Although some had base motives, all were great leaders. All had strong influence on their followers. In this chapter we examine leaders and the process of leadership, because leadership is very important in organizational life.

Importance of Leadership

Just how important is leadership? Leadership is especially important in Total Quality organizations, because TQ involves dramatic change to a new and improved way of doing business and managing operations. It takes influencial leaders to cause followers to change.

There is no known case of a firm sustaining strong TQ strategies and practices throughout the organization without the vocal and personal leadership of the firm's executives. A recent review of the elements of success in transforming organizations along TQ lines stressed the primary role of leadership in helping organizations and their employees make that transformation.[1] In fact, leadership is so important in a TQ organization that it is a crucial factor in the Baldrige National Quality Award and the European Quality Award. 🔵🔵

Managers: Leaders or Administrators?

We recall from Chapter 1 that *management* is the creation and continuous improvement of organizational systems that when used by organizational members lead to increased value for the customers of its products or services. Thus management is tied to the customer. Management is not strictly internally focused administration.[2]

Administration is the operation of internal systems. In bureaucratically administered organizations, therefore, administration can be completely divorced from the customer. Thus an administrator in a government agency that has not yet implemented Total Quality may be a bureaucratic administrator who consistently follows the rules while ignoring the customer.

Leadership is the ability to influence people toward the accomplishment of goals. Leadership is associated with the determination of the goals, a vision for the future, and the process of change to reach the goals and the future. Leadership is about helping people do things they would not normally do.

Formal versus Informal Leadership

Formal leadership is associated with the individual who has the explicit designation from the organization as the leader. Whether elected or appointed, the formal leader has the position of leader of the group.

Within a group, **informal leadership** is associated with the individual who influences group members even without the organization's formal designation. The formally designated leader is wise to partner with the informal leader to help influence organizational members. This is particularly true in Total Quality organizations that have empowered individuals to work on systems improvement to deliver greater value to customers. Entire levels of formally designated managers may be eliminated and replaced by trained leaderless groups. Teams without a formally designated leader may operate to serve the customers' needs. As earlier indicated, some of Milliken and Company's textile plants operate without formally designated leaders, as does much of the Saturn Corporation.

Organizational Leadership versus Interpersonal Leadership

Leaders are found both in organizations and in interpersonal situations. The biggest difference is the establishment and communication of goals. An organizational leader will spend considerable effort to formulate and articulate the goals to be implemented, thereby establishing the direction for change. Articulation of the goals enables the organizational members either to buy into the goals or reject them. For example, executives at Saturn ask the workers to buy into the notion of producing high-quality cars in self-managed groups.

An interpersonal leader may try to influence others for the sake of his or her individual needs and personal goals. Gang leaders are examples of interpersonal leaders who influence others to do things that are out of the mainstream of acceptable behavior.

CRITICAL THINKING QUESTIONS

1. Relate the differences between management and leadership to the concept of strategy.

2. Discuss the importance of informal leaders in TQ organizations.

POWER

Central to any consideration of leadership is a discussion of power. It is important to understand how power operates and to be aware of the different bases or sources of power.

What Is Power?

Power is the potential ability to influence others' attitudes or behavior. Whereas power refers to potential, leadership refers to the actual use of that power to influence others. In most organizational settings we are interested in the ability to influence behavior.

Five Bases of Power

The ability to influence others arises from at least five different bases or sources of power: coercive, expert, legitimate, referent, and reward.[3] All five power bases are predicated on the followers' perception that the power holders can influence or mediate some outcome. The perception may be different from the reality, but what is important is that the power holders maintain the perception or image that they can influence the desired outcomes.

Effective managers maintain as many of the power bases as possible. Then they can match the use of those bases to the specific person or situation.

Coercive Power   **Coercive power** arises from the perception in the followers that the power holder has the ability to mediate punishment. Sometimes the power holder may not actually be able to administer the punishment, but fosters the impression that he or she does control the punishment. In many organizations the formal leaders can only recommend punishment to be administered by the personnel office. Punishment in organizational settings may be both intrinsic and extrinsic. It may take the form of criticism, a letter of reprimand, a demotion, a pay cut, suspension, or termination from employment. Unintended consequences of punishment are resentment, hostility, and sabotage. Leaders who administer punishment are advised, therefore, to punish in private, fit the punishment to the infraction, and be consistent.

Expert Power   **Expert power** derives from the perception by the followers that the power holder has needed information or special knowledge for the followers. Information can be a source of power in many organizations. Such expert power may be held, for example, by professional employees and secretaries who are not in formal leadership positions. Corporate accountants working on the details of the latest employee stock ownership plan may have expert power. This power base may be completely independent of formal power. It is important for expert power holders to promote an image of expertise, maintain credibility, and avoid threatening the self-esteem of others.

Legitimate Power   **Legitimate power** arises from the followers' perception that the power holder has the proper right to direct activities because of the position occupied. Legitimate power is usually associated with formal authority in organizations and has a base in a position description or a charter. In organizations it is not unusual to see legitimate power reflected in symbols like size and location of offices, amount and quality of office furniture, perks, signature authority, and spending authority. To maintain legitimate power, power holders are advised to follow proper channels to communicate the legitimacy of their requests, to exercise power regularly to let others know that the power is real, and to verify that the requests are appropriate. Department heads who remind people that they are the "boss" are relying on legitimate power.

Referent Power   **Referent power** arises from the followers' identification and respect for the power holder and from their desire to be like the power holder. Referent power, which can be the most powerful of all the power bases, is associated with charisma, trust, respect, emotional involvement, imitation, and a willingness to follow. Political leaders, like President John Kennedy, and religious leaders, like Pope John Paul II, usually score high on referent power. Referent power can be especially powerful if the power holders select subordinates like themselves—individuals who cherish similar values, traits, experiences, and behaviors. A leader who reminds followers of some individual or organizational value such as integrity or teamwork is relying on referent power.

Reward Power   **Reward power** stems from the followers' perception that the power holder can mediate valued rewards. The rewards may be both intrinsic, like praise and recognition, and extrinsic, like a promotion, pay raise, or favorable performance appraisal. To maintain reward power, leaders should control as many rewards as possible. To influence behavior with rewards, leaders need to offer coveted rewards, offer credible rewards, and link the rewards to desired behavior. For example, offering a trip to Hawaii to the top sales performer may have no reward power for a person who hates to travel.

Power and Networking

Power flows in many directions in organizations that use cross-functional teams and leaderless groups. It is common, therefore, for leaders to maintain contacts or networks of individuals and groups in organizations. Such networks can be sources of information for expert power and channels to distribute power.

Using Power Responsibly

Organizational leaders who have several power bases at their disposal must be careful to use the power responsibly. Several power bases in one leader can result in very powerful, all-encompassing control over others. For example, Adolf Hitler had at his disposal several power bases that he used to destroy millions of people. Some in the Nixon White House used power for illegal personal gain. In most busi-

DIVERSITY EXHIBIT

Bendix Politics

In June 1979 William Agee, chairman of Bendix Corporation, hired Mary Cunningham to serve as his executive assistant. Mary Cunningham was described as an "unusually brilliant," "uncommonly ambitious," "politically astute," "beautiful," "sophisticated," "poised" woman with "high ideals."

Almost immediately after arriving from the Harvard Business School, she was assigned to put her extensive financial analytical skills to work on some major Bendix investment projects. One of her largest projects was an analysis of the possible acquisition of the Warner and Swasey Company, a machine-tool business. The investment looked good. Bendix already had a machine-tool business that, together with the acquisition of Warner and Swasey, would make Bendix the second largest U.S. machine-tool builder. Relying on the analysis, Agee purchased Warner and Swasey in April 1980 for $300 million. The buy paid off: Warner and Swasey was holding $65 million in liquid assets and $40 million in stock, which, when disposed of, made the real purchase price $195 million.

In June 1980 Bill Agee promoted Mary Cunningham, then only 29, to vice president for corporate and public affairs. Both handsome people, the two necessarily worked and traveled together, and gossip started when first Cunningham and then Agee separated from their spouses. By now, the two were working closely together. A company staff person described Cunningham with the words: "She's his key advisor; she counsels him on the most important things in the company." But some insiders sensed trouble. Later a Bendix executive commented, "She is very smart and she knows how corporations work—that's

how she's done so well—but when it came to her relationship with Bill Agee, she didn't act smart, she didn't use her political sense."

Several Bendix managers now began to complain that Cunningham had too much access to Agee and that he was becoming increasingly inaccessible to others. The feelings of the managers were further ruffled when Agee had Cunningham carry out an in-depth analysis of Bendix's automotive business in June 1980. Cunningham angered several managers when she inspected the floors of the automotive plants without first telling the plant managers that she was going to do so. Bendix managers (including William Panny, the president of Bendix) afterward harshly criticized the three-volume analysis that Cunningham and her seven-person staff (derisively referred to as "Snow White and the Seven Dwarfs") had produced. The Cunningham report, according to the managers, was unenlightening and did not contain anything they did not already know.

In September 1980 Agee fired William Panny. According to *Fortune* magazine, it was rumored in Detroit that several Bendix executives had earlier gone to Panny to "complain" about Cunningham's relationship to Agee. Panny, according to the *Fortune* rumor, was "planning" to bring the matter to the Bendix board of directors, but Agee fired him before he had the chance. A few hours later Jerome Jacobson, a Bendix executive, resigned from his position as vice president for strategic planning.

Matters then became more heated. According to author Gail Sheehy, who interviewed both Cunningham and Agee, "anonymous letters" were

continued

ness organizations there are checks and balances on the application of power through formal organizational controls like spending limits and the need for another person to countersign.

Because top-level executives have access to several power bases, they need to use the power responsibly, as noted in the diversity exhibit.

being sent to Bendix board members, making "malicious references" to the conduct of the pair. The letters, according to Sheehy, urged board members to "investigate their relationship" at once.

Agee acted quickly. First he arranged meetings with Bendix's top managers and with the board's executive committee. To each group he said the same thing: The rumors going around were utterly false; he and Cunningham had "no romantic involvement." Then he moved to promote Cunningham to the vacated position of vice president for strategic planning. At the fateful company meeting of September 24, he announced her promotion and simultaneously attempted to lay "the female issue" to rest. The next day, however, the story was reported in the nation's newspapers along with the rumors suggesting that Cunningham's rapid promotions were due to her "romantic involvement" with Bill Agee.

The day the news broke in the papers, Cunningham decided she had to move quickly if she was to outmaneuver "them." (She did not know who had sent the anonymous letters.) Her first instinct was to resign, since this would prevent the board from firing her first and would ensure that Agee would not be compromised by her continuing presence in the company. But by the next day she had instead decided to request a temporary leave of absence from the company. This tactic would leave her with a palatable option should the board want her to leave, but at the same time it would pressure the board to take the option of retaining her. Since the board had publicly approved her promotion only a few days earlier, it would probably not be willing to reverse itself publicly so soon afterward. Consequently, on September 28 she submitted to the board a letter requesting an "immediate but

temporary" leave that "should not be construed in any sense as tantamount to resignation." The letter continued by explaining that a resignation would set "a dangerous precedent" in that it would enable "female executives to be forced out of a company through malicious gossip" and would also "tend to confirm the most base and erroneous assumptions suggested by the media."

The next afternoon a committee comprised of a few members of the Bendix board of directors met and decided to announce in the name of the board that they had "complete confidence" in Cunningham and that "it would be unjust for a corporation to respond to speculation in the media by accepting her request." After the meeting one of the board members gave her a bit of advice: She should be careful because she was being used by others to get at Agee and if the thing went on for much longer, Agee's position would be in danger.

The drama was not yet over. Cunningham was still unsure whether it might be better for her to resign. When the full board met a few days later and the members discussed the issue among themselves, a large number felt that she should not continue on at Bendix. Too many difficulties would confront her if she continued in her present role, they felt. This was made known to Cunningham. Subsequently, on October 9, she resigned.

Discussion Questions

1. Was Cunningham treated fairly?
2. Did Agee act smartly? Why is it important for a leader to be above reproach and suspicion?

Source: Adapted from M. G. Velasquez, *Business Ethics: Concepts and Cases*, 2nd ed., Englewood Cliffs, NJ: Prentice-Hall (1988): 403–407.

CRITICAL THINKING QUESTIONS

1. How does the concept of power compare to the concept of leadership?
2. Describe the bases-of-power approach to leadership. Compare and contrast the five bases of power.

RESPONSIBILITY AND ACCOUNTABILITY

Two concepts aligned with any discussion of authority and power are those of accountability and responsibility. These subjects deserve special attention today in Total Quality organizations as cross-functional teams and self-managed groups create special power issues.

Relationship of Responsibility and Accountability

Responsibility is the duty to perform assigned activities. In accepting a particular job, the individual accepts the responsibility to perform the activities and tasks associated with that job. Since the tasks are often assigned by the formally designated leader, the new employee implicitly accepts the authority of the leader by accepting the job. In some leaderless groups the tasks are assigned by agreement of the group and the informal leader.

Accountability is the obligation to report on and justify the accomplishment of assigned tasks. Leaders are held accountable, just as are others, to justify the accomplishment of assigned tasks. Accountability and responsibility can extend in two directions.

Although managers can lay responsibility and accountability on subordinates for work, it does not mean that the energies of the subordinates are necessarily fully utilized. The ethics exhibit shows that managers risk losing subordinates if they ask them to do things that are less than ethical.

Levels

Formal leaders high up in their organization are frequently responsible and accountable for the activities of all those reporting to them through the organizational structure. A plant manager is responsible and accountable for the activities of the nonsupervisory employees, the first-level supervisory or shift managers, as well as the second-level manufacturing, engineering, accounting, and maintenance departments. Indeed, the plant manager is responsible and accountable for all assigned tasks and goals for the entire plant. The plant manager cannot delegate responsibility but holds subordinate levels accountable to accomplish their assigned tasks.

Scope

Sometimes responsibility and accountability extend laterally due to the scope of the job's activities. For example, the accountability of a staff position like plant safety manager extends throughout the plant. However, the safety manager may have no formal power over the line employees. In such a situation the safety manager needs to rely on informal power and several power bases to influence the line employees.

CRITICAL THINKING QUESTIONS

1. Relate the ideas of responsibility and accountability.
2. Relate the responsibility of managers to act ethically with their responsibility to perform their assigned job duties.

E T H I C S   E X H I B I T

The Manager as an Activist

Jay Schlister drove slowly in the late evening traffic. He turned the dial on the FM radio hoping to pick up some soothing music as he had not yet adjusted to the hassle of big city traffic. Today he was more impatient than usual because he knew that arriving home late would eliminate the possibility of a bite to eat before he left again for his meeting with the Association of American Scientists (AAS).

Jay looked forward to the meeting as he did all of the Association's meetings. He found that his membership yielded many benefits. The lectures given at the beginning of each meeting were informative and interesting. The social afterward gave him a chance to discuss and debate scientific topics of current controversy and mutual interest with other scientists, some of whom were quite well known in their fields. The meetings were truly stimulating, often educational, and sometimes provided him with ideas that were useful in his job.

Jay worked for Western Food Products Inc. At Western he was a member of a research team that worked in the area of product development. Because Western's products were chemical in nature, the job was perfect for Jay, who had only two years before earned his degree in chemistry at State Tech. Though Jay was considered a member of the research and product development team, he found that "team" was somewhat of a misnomer, since he and the other members usually worked on different projects. The research team had a number of junior scientists, and generally one or two of these were assigned to each team member as assistants. Each team member with his assistant(s) worked on assignments developed by management in conjunction with marketing research and sometimes at the suggestion of individual R&D members.

Although Jay found the AAS meetings to be very stimulating, he found that sometimes they were a source of conflict. An example of this had occurred recently. In one particular meeting, the speaker, a nutrition specialist, had delivered a powerful presentation deploring the use of additives and preservatives in food products. The scientist provided evidence that such products might cause possible genetic mutation. The expert predicted impending health and genetic doom if use was continued at its present increasing rate.

Jay had listened with special interest and some guilt because he knew that most of Western's currently marketed products contained additives and/or preservatives. The argument was not a new one to Jay, but the speech did give him a sense of personal responsibility. Afterward, in discussing the matter with others, a research scientist from a company making only health foods had told Jay about research his company had done to eliminate additives and preservatives from their products. Though he could not reveal company secrets, he did alert Jay to the existence of extensive public research in the area.

Jay had gone to work the next day with enthusiasm. He could not wait to tell his fellow

continued

Influencing others is a major issue in the study of leadership. There are three major approaches to the study of leadership. The Traits Approach examines the characteristics or traits that leaders have in common. The Behavioral Styles Approach examines the behaviors of leaders. The Situational/Contingency Approaches look at a complex interaction of the leader, the followers, and the situation to explain leadership.

team members of the meeting and its topic. The team's reaction surprised Jay. Several members seemed disinterested, one scoffed at the idea, and others, while seemingly interested, had little comment. All wandered off to begin their day's work except for Alex Geopola, a seasoned veteran in R&D, having been at Western 23 years. Geopola said, "Jay, don't worry yourself with the thoughts you're having now. We went through all of this six years ago when the scientific reports on sugar began to surface. Management didn't buy it then and they won't buy this now."

Although Jay respected Geopola, he was not about to quit. Over several weekends, he researched the area from the sources given him at the meeting and began to develop some ideas to modify several of Western's products. When he felt he had put together a strong argument, he met with Roy Martin, director of market development, who headed both marketing research and product development. Roy Martin listened carefully to Jay's presentation and when he had finished, Roy said, "Jay, I can see you have done a lot of work on this and we really appreciate it. Now, I've listened to your view, so you listen to the way that management sees it. It's basically a matter of costs. We face tremendous competition out there, Jay, and we cannot waste time and money on unnecessary projects. Now I know you don't see this as an unnecessary project, but we do. The law does not prohibit the use of additives and preservatives in our products. Scientists warn against their use but consumers are still willing to buy our products and ultimately they are the ones who matter. Other companies have made the switch under pressure from various groups, so

the danger has been reduced. The volume of our products cannot significantly affect the public and maybe by the time our volume is high enough to make a difference we can afford to make modifications. Right now we have to think about developing products that sell or else we will not be able to stay in the marketplace."

Jay was upset by what Martin had said, and he left the office feeling frustrated and helpless. He could not understand how Martin and management could knowingly risk the public's health to meet company goals. He began to wonder if he was in the right job and considered a move, but Lynn and the children had just gotten settled and he hated to move them again. For weeks he could muster little interest in his current research assignment because of his overriding interest in the nutrition problem. Lately he had considered using his assistant and company time to work on his problem, but he feared that doing so might cost him his job if Martin heard about it. As the weeks passed, Jay became more resigned to the fact that he might have to subordinate his own values to company goals.

Discussion Questions

1. Do you agree or disagree that Jay should subordinate his own values to company goals? What are your reasons?

2. Do you agree with Roy Martin and, assuming he is a reliable spokesperson, therefore agree with management's position? Why or why not?

Source: J. R. Glenn, Jr., *Ethics in Decision Making*, (New York: John Wiley & Sons, 1986), 219–221. Copyright © 1986 John Wiley & Sons, Inc. Reprinted with permission of John Wiley & Sons, Inc.

THE TRAITS APPROACH

The **Traits Approach to leadership** studies the characteristics or traits that leaders have in common.

List of Leadership Traits

Many studies of leadership traits have been made and a variety of traits have been discussed. One of the more popular lists includes the following leadership traits:

1. Intelligence at least equal to the average of the group
2. Verbal ability
3. Past achievement in scholarship and athletics
4. Emotional maturity and stability
5. Persistence and a drive for continuing achievement
6. A need for status and economic success [4]

Limits of the Traits Approach

On the surface, the traits approach makes sense. However, many follow-up studies reveal disagreement about which traits predict effective leader behavior.[5] The traits may indicate only the minimally required levels necessary for effective leadership. The traits may not explain the sufficient conditions. Many of the traits are also found in nonleaders. A new, diverse workforce may place new demands on leaders and negate some of the old traits. For all of these reasons, the Traits Approach has been discredited and is not widely used in organizations today.

CRITICAL THINKING QUESTIONS

1. Relate the list of leadership traits to today's diverse workforce.

2. Relate the list of leadership traits to the needs of cross-functional, self-managed work teams in TQ organizations.

BEHAVIORAL STYLES APPROACHES

There have been several useful attempts to explain leadership by examining the behavioral styles of leaders. By examining the behavior of leaders, maybe we can infer what is needed for effective leadership. One of the frequently cited models of leader behavior is the leadership continuum.

Leadership Continuum

One study found that in their leadership styles some leaders were boss-centered and some were subordinate-centered.[6] A **boss-centered** or **autocratic leader** is a leader who tends to centralize authority. A **subordinate-centered** or **democratic leader** is a leader who delegates authority to others. The study also found that these two styles were actually two ends of a continuum, as depicted in Figure 11.1.

The figure indicates that there is a whole range of behaviors from which a leader may choose. Some leaders choose a style to fit a situation or to fit the specific subordinates. However, most leaders have a preferred pattern or style of leadership behavior that they rely on most of the time. Since many leaders have a preferred style of leadership behavior, they are attracted to certain organizational cultures where there is a fit between their preferred leadership style and the culture. For example, the military is noted for a command-and-control culture that would seem to foster a boss-centered leadership style. Alternatively, universities and research

FIGURE 11.1 *Leadership Continuum*

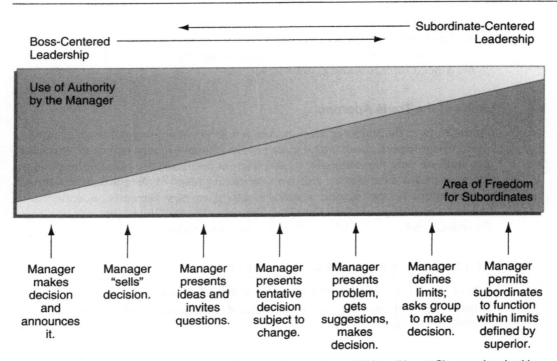

Source: Reprinted by permission of the *Harvard Business Review*. An exhibit from "How to Choose a Leadership Pattern" by Robert Tannenbaum and Warren Schmidt (May–June 1973): 164. Copyright 1973 by the President and Fellows of Harvard College; all rights reserved.

organizations are noted for participative cultures where subordinate-centered leadership styles are appropriate.

Although the study noted that managers have a preferred style or pattern of leadership, there is some adaptability in the model. There may be forces at work in the manager, in the subordinates, or in the situation that could cause the leader to vary a leadership style.

Consideration and Initiating Structure

A number of research studies on leadership were conducted at the Ohio State University and are called the OSU studies.[7] These studies found that there are two broad dimensions of leader behavior. One is called consideration and the other is called initiating structure. **Consideration** is the extent to which the leader is aware of subordinates, respects their ideas, and establishes mutual trust, warmth, and friendship. **Initiating structure** is the extent to which the leader is task oriented and directs subordinates' work activities toward goal accomplishment.

The strict authoritarian leadership style of the military may not be appropriate in many other rapidly changing organizations today. (Photo credit: Comstock.)

The researchers at OSU found that a leader could be engaged in both behaviors to varying degrees. Position on one of the behaviors did not necessarily imply position on another one of the behaviors. A leader could score any one of four combinations of low or high on the two dimensions. Figure 11.2 contains the OSU model.

Originally, it was assumed that effective leaders scored high-high on the two dimensions. However, a number of recent studies show that the specific situation must be taken into account before a forecast about leader effectiveness can be made. In many Total Quality organizations today employing well-trained cross-functional teams, high initiating structure on the part of a formal leader can be counterproductive.[8]

FIGURE 11.2 *Consideration and Initiating Structure as Leadership Styles*

Consideration		Low Structure and High Consideration	High Structure and High Consideration
	High	Low Structure and High Consideration	High Structure and High Consideration
	Low	Low Structure and Low Consideration	High Structure and Low Consideration
		Low	**High**

Initiating Structure

FIGURE 11.3   *The Leadership Grid* ®

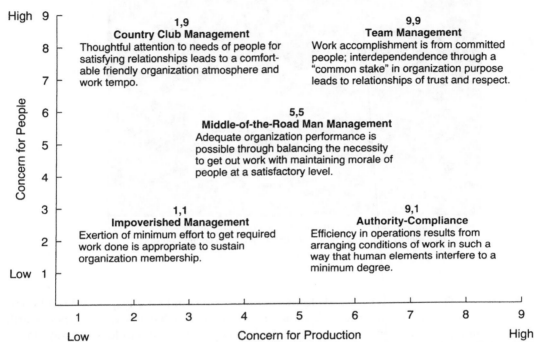

Source: The Leadership Grid® figure from *Leadership Dilemmas–Grid Solutions,* by Robert R. Blake and Anne Adams McCanse (formerly the Managerial Grid Figure by Robert R. Blake and Jane S. Mouton) Houston: Gulf Publishing Company, p. 29. Copyright © 1991, by Scientific Methods, Inc. Reproduced by permission of the owners.

Leadership Grid

The idea of two dimensions of leader behavior has been further developed in another study.[9] Rather than just high-low levels as in the Consideration/Initiating-Structure model, the study described nine different levels on each dimension. Thus leader behavior could be described as any one of 81 different combinations. The study's description of concern for people is analogous to the OSU description of consideration. Similarly, the later study's concern for production parallels the OSU description of initiating structure. The 81 combinations, with descriptions of the five most popular combinations, are shown in Figure 11.3. The study strongly suggests that the 9,9 leadership style is the most effective.

CRITICAL THINKING QUESTIONS

1. Compare and contrast the Traits Approach and the Behavioral Styles Approach to leadership.

2. Describe the Leadership Continuum, the Consideration and Initiating-Structure Approach, and the Leadership Grid. Compare and contrast the three approaches to leadership.

FIGURE 11.4 *The Situational Theory of Leadership*

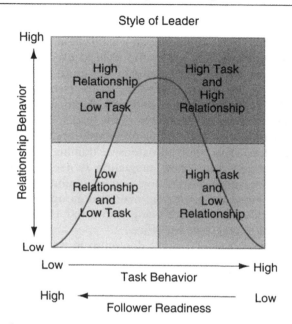

Source: Adapted from Paul Hersey and Kenneth H. Blanchard, *Management of Organizational Behavior: Utilizing Human Resources,* 6th ed., p. 306. Copyright 1993. Reprinted by permission of the Center for Leadership Studies, Inc.; Escondido, CA.

SITUATIONAL/CONTINGENCY APPROACHES

Some of the models of leadership discussed above are too simplistic. Some offer prescriptions that are universal, like high consideration and high initiating structure, are uniformly desirable. A shortcoming of several of the models is that they do not consider the specific situation. Recent evidence strongly suggests that effective leadership styles are contingent on the situation.

Hersey and Blanchard's Situational Leadership Theory

A major situational approach to leadership is Paul Hersey and Kenneth Blanchard's Situational Leadership Theory. The theory starts with two dimensions, comparable to the models in Figures 11.2 and 11.3, and adds the readiness of followers as the major situation to be reconciled.[10] Figure 11.4 illustrates the theory.

The **Situational Leadership Theory** is a contingency approach to leadership that links the leader's relationship behavior and task behavior to the readiness of followers. **Readiness of followers** is their ability to perform their job independently, their ability to assume additional responsibility, and their desire to achieve success. Follower readiness has little to do with chronological age.

The bell-shaped curve in Figure 11.4 prescribes when a specific leadership style should be used as a function of the readiness of followers. The theory holds that leader behavior should shift from (1) high task and low relationship to (2) high task and high relationship to (3) high relationship and low task to (4) low task and low relationship as followers move from low readiness to high readiness. A follower is at low readiness at the point of joining an organization and prior to training. High task behavior is an appropriate leadership style to use with a follower who needs direction at that time. As the individual receives more training and accumulates more job experiences, the leader may evolve to less task behavior.

As the individual becomes fully trained and well experienced, low task behavior and low relationship behavior are needed from the leader. This is the situation in many Total Quality organizations that spend previously unthinkable amounts on training. Once the individual has received extensive training and is working in a cross-functional self-managed team, little interaction is needed with the formal leader. Indeed, many TQ organizations are investing in continual, extensive employee training and are evolving to leaderless, self-managed groups. In terms of organizational structure, layers of leadership are being eliminated as the training is being done by the group and/or a large training office.

In 1993 Honda of America used a slight downturn in production as a way to intensify its commitment to worker training. In its Ohio plant Honda doubled the amount of technical training for workers from 5,000 hours to 10,000 hours in the first quarter of 1993.[11] The technical training included study of the jobs of co-workers. In this way Honda increased the ability of the workers to function without direction from a formal leader. This practice of using slowdowns in production to increase training contrasts with the United Auto Workers and the Big Three from Detroit, all of which use slowdowns to give workers time off with pay.

Fiedler's Leadership Contingency Model

One of the most comprehensive and complex contingency models of leadership is Fiedler's model. A central feature of Fiedler's theory is the extent to which the leader's style is relationship oriented and task oriented. Relationship orientation is conceptually related to the consideration and the concern for people expressed in the earlier theories, and task orientation is comparable to the initiating structure and the concern for production. The leader's style is measured by the **Least-Preferred Co-worker (LPC) scale,** which is a questionnaire that measures relationship orientation versus task orientation according to the leader's description of his or her least-preferred co-worker.

Fiedler's Contingency Theory of Leadership states that leadership success is determined by the degree of task structure, the degree of leader-position power, and the relationship between the leader and the followers.[12] **Leader–member relationship** is the extent to which the leader feels accepted by the followers. **Task structure** is the degree to which the task and the goals are clearly outlined. **Leader-position power** is the extent to which the leader has formal authority over subordinates.

Since there are three variables at each of two levels, there are eight possible combinations (2×2×2) of situational characteristics. Those eight combinations are depicted as conditions 1–8 in Figure 11.5. Situation 1 is most favorable to the leader since leader–member relations are good, the task is structured, and there is strong leader-position power. Situation 8 is most unfavorable to the leader because each of

FIGURE 11.5   *Fiedler's Leadership Contingency Model*

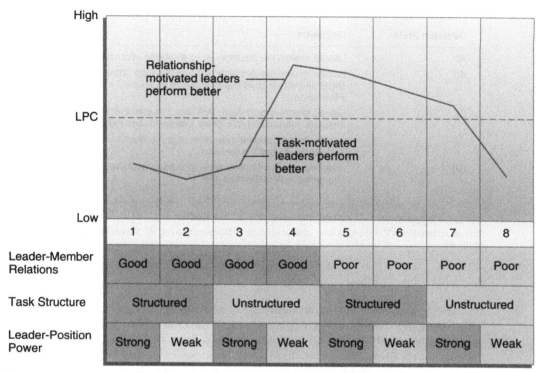

Source: Fred E. Fiedler and Martin M. Chemers, *Leadership and Effective Management* (Glenview, IL: Scott, Foresman, 1974), p. 80. Reprinted by permission of Fred E. Fiedler.

the three variables is rated low. Situations 2–7 are all intermediate degrees of favorableness for the leader. The model hypothesizes the degree of relationship orientation and the degree of task orientation appropriate in each of the eight situations.

Fiedler's model shows how to modify the situational variables to fit the leader's style, rather than how to modify the style to fit the situation.[13] The model argues that there is not one best leadership style. It also suggests that leaders are made, not born. Unfortunately, Fiedler's model is rather complex and therefore seldom used.

Vroom-Yetton-Jago Decision Involvement Model

Named for its three contributors, the **Vroom-Yetton-Jago (VYJ) Decision Involvement Model** is a decision-based theory of leadership.[14] The model holds that organizational decisions should be of high quality (positively related to organizational performance) and should be accepted by subordinates.

The VYJ model says that there are five different ways that the leader can make decisions. These five decision styles range from autocratic, through consultative, to group focused and are described in Table 11.1.

TABLE 11.1   *Decision Styles in the Vroom-Yetton-Jago Model*

Decision Style	Definition
AI	Leader makes the decision using available information.
AII	Leader makes the decision using information obtained from subordinates. Subordinates' only role in decision making is to provide information.
CI	Leader shares the problem with subordinates individually and requests information and ideas. Leader makes the decision alone.
CII	Leader and subordinates work as a group discussing the problem. The leader makes the decision.
GII	Leader and subordinates work as a group discussing the problem. The group makes the decision.

Note: "A" means autocratic, "C" means consultative, and "G" means group.

Source: Adapted from V. Vroom, "A New Look at Managerial Decision Making," *Organizational Dynamics* (Summer 1973): 67.

The VYJ model, shown in Figure 11.6, is a model to help leaders determine which decision style to use in a given situation. In some of the decision paths, there is more than one feasible, or suitable, decision style. In this case the leader may choose a style from among the alternatives. The choice should be a function of the amount of time available and the need to develop subordinates' decision-making skills. When there is little time, the leader should choose the more authoritative style. When there is a need to develop subordinates' decision-making skills, the leader should choose the more participative style.

Many Total Quality organizations are trying to develop the decision-making and problem-solving styles of subordinates so that cross-functional teams of subordinates can solve problems. Thus more organizations are recognizing the need for the more participative decision-making styles. The VYJ model has some promise in that it can describe that trend. Unfortunately, the model is complex and somewhat difficult for the practicing manager to apply.

Path-Goal Theory

The Path-Goal Theory of Leadership is another contingency model of leadership that tries to explain leadership effectiveness as a function of the situation.[15] The **Path-Goal Theory** stresses the leader's role in clarifying for subordinates how they can achieve desired rewards through job performance. Thus the leader's role is to increase the subordinate's motivation to attain personal and organizational goals. As shown in Figure 11.7, the leader increases the subordinate's motivation by clarifying the subordinate's path to the available rewards, or by increasing the desired rewards linked to job performance, or by both means.

FIGURE 11.6 *Leadership Decision Model*

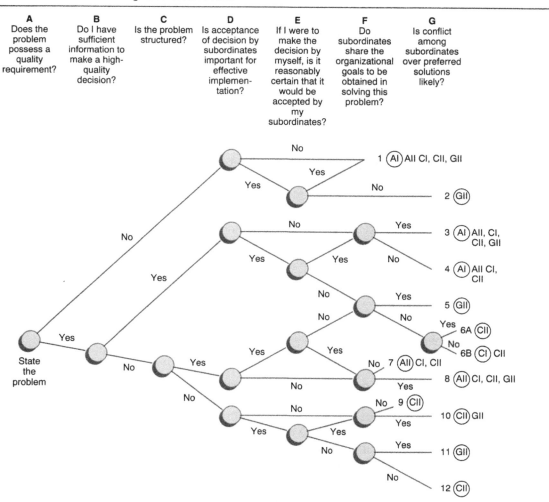

A	B	C	D	E	F	G
Does the problem possess a quality requirement?	Do I have sufficient information to make a high-quality decision?	Is the problem structured?	Is acceptance of decision by subordinates important for effective implementation?	If I were to make the decision by myself, is it reasonably certain that it would be accepted by my subordinates?	Do subordinates share the organizational goals to be obtained in solving this problem?	Is conflict among subordinates over preferred solutions likely?

Source: Adapted and reprinted from *Leadership and Decision-Making*, by Victor H. Vroom and Phillip W. Yetton, by permission of the University of Pittsburgh Press. © 1973 by University of Pittsburgh Press.

Comparing the Situational/Contingency Approaches

Situational/contingency approaches to leadership are more powerful than simple two-dimensional models that do not consider the situation. Some of the situational/contingency approaches to leadership are also so complex that they are difficult to remember and apply. Fiedler's model and the Vroom-Yetton-Jago model are quite complex, with 8 and 13 different combinations, respectively. The Path-Goal model is appealing because it links the subordinate's desired rewards to job accomplishment. Hersey and Blanchard's Situational Theory of Leadership explains the diminished role for leaders after the followers' readiness has been increased through

FIGURE 11.7   *Leader Roles in the Path-Goal Model*

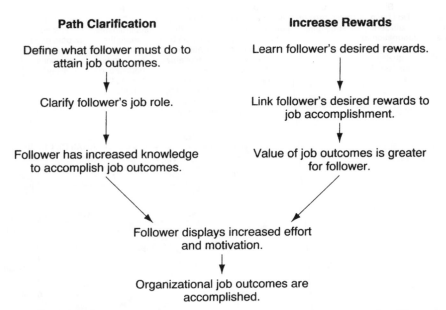

Source: Adapted from B. M. Bass, "Leadership: Good, Better, Best," *Organizational Dynamics,* 13 (Winter 1985): 26–40.

training and experience. Thus the Situational Theory of Leadership is consistent with much of the current practice in TQ organizations.

Situational Theories of Leadership tell us that the actions a leader takes in one situation may differ from those taken in another situation. The international exhibit asks whether it is appropriate to offer a payment in a foreign culture in which such payments are not the exception.

CRITICAL THINKING QUESTIONS

1. Describe the situational/contingency approach to leadership. Compare and contrast this approach to leadership with the traits approach to leadership and the behavioral styles approach to leadership.

2. Compare and contrast Hersey and Blanchard's Situational Leadership Theory, Fiedler's Leadership Contingency Model, the Vroom-Yetton-Jago Leadership Decision Involvement model, and the Path-Goal Theory. Which model or theory seems to best represent the leadership practices in many TQ organizations?

CONTEMPORARY ISSUES IN LEADERSHIP

In addition to the traditional leadership models and theories already reviewed in this chapter, there are some current trends in leadership that are worthy of review.

INTERNATIONAL EXHIBIT

Would You Give a Bribe?

Investment-U.S., a company headquartered in the United States, recently entered into a trading agreement with an Indian company. The Indian company agreed to act as representative for the U.S. company on the basis both of product information provided by Investment-U.S. and government incentives provided by the Indian government. Mr. Smith, marketing vice president of Investment-U.S., is in India to ensure the success of the project. He is surprised to find that the initial shipment has been held up in customs because government import restrictions have not been complied with due to insufficient data, even though this information had been supplied previously by the U.S. head office. The information is vital to the implementation of the agreement.

Mr. Smith is approached by a junior clerk in the Indian company who explains that his predecessor was very disorganized and that the material has probably been misfiled. The clerk suggests that if he were to work overtime he could probably find the material, but the Indian company does not pay for overtime and the clerk wants to be appropriately recompensed.

Discussion Question

Assume you are Mr. Smith and you believe that you are being asked for an illegal payment. Would you agree to the payment? Why or why not?

Source: Adapted from Betty J. Punnett, *Experiencing International Management*, Boston: PWS-Kent (1989): 38.

Transformational/Charismatic Leadership and Total Quality

Individuals who have exceptional impact on their organizations and its people are referred to as charismatic or transformational leaders.[16] **Transformational** or **charismatic leaders** are leaders who through their personal vision, energy, and values inspire followers and thus have a major impact on organizational success. Charismatic leaders articulate a vision or higher-level goal that captures followers' commitment and energies. They lead by example and are careful to behave in accord with the values they espouse for the followers. Charismatic leaders rely on referent power as a primary power base.

Mother Teresa, Martin Luther King, Winston Churchill, and Mahatma Gandhi are examples of transformational or charismatic leaders. Unfortunately, Adolf Hitler and Jim Jones of Jonestown, Guyana, were also charismatic leaders. The power of the charismatic or transformational leader is independent of the "goodness" of the vision articulated by the leader.

When he took over as CEO at Xerox in 1982, it would have been easy for David Kearns to maintain the status quo. However, as an act of transformational leadership, he helped the organization and its members to recognize that they must change dramatically and quickly to deliver quality to the customer in order to survive and grow.[17] He helped them see that they were in a new era of fierce international competition from several Japanese copier firms like Canon, Minolta, and Sharp, all of which had targeted Xerox. Since Xerox could no longer take its customers for granted, it had to reinvent itself and find new ways to deliver value to customers.

QUALITY CASE

Back to the Government Agencies Case

Total Quality Management is spreading to public agencies throughout the country with the help of companies with TQM experience. One of the best known is the Philadelphia Area Council of Excellence (PACE). PACE has spread TQM concepts to government, schools, and small businesses in the greater Philadelphia area. Many hoped that by improving efficiency and quality, PACE would attract new industry to the area.

Other cities have also started Area Councils of Excellence patterned after PACE. A Knoxville, Tennessee, Area Council of Excellence (KACE) was formed in 1992 with an objective similar to that of PACE. Patterned after PACE, other Area Councils of Excellence have started in Austin, Texas, Charlotte, North Carolina,

Cincinnati, Ohio, Columbia and Spartanburg, South Carolina, Indianapolis, Indiana, Kansas City, Missouri, Kingsport and Memphis, Tennessee, Pittsburgh and Erie, Pennsylvania.

The Watervliet Army Arsenal in Troy, New York, has been implementing many of these TQM concepts, including customer-value determination and cross-functional systems management. Its successes have been all the more remarkable because that arsenal is nearly 200 years old.

The city of Madison, Wisconsin, has implemented continuous quality improvement in many of its city departments. The implementation is noteworthy because of the various constituencies involved, including voters, city council, and 14 unions.

Kearns also influenced universities to change in a Total Quality direction when he initiated the Total Quality Fora series of meetings between industry and academia in 1989. His ideas had something to do with the theme of this book and the very idea of writing this book. Kearns left the well-paying and highly respected job as CEO of Xerox to become Undersecretary of Education so that he could help improve the quality of the nation's educational system.

The quality exhibit, which is taken from the book, *21st Century Leadership*, reveals some of the issues a visionary leader must deal with in helping an organization transform itself in terms of quality leadership.

Leadership and Empowerment in Total Quality

The role of managers as leaders as defined in this chapter is increasingly being questioned in Total Quality organizations. An increasing number of organizations recognize that the role of the manager is to establish, stabilize, and continuously improve the system and processes of work for employees.

Such a concept of management suggests that managers work on the systems and processes. Once the systems and processes have been established, managers concentrate on training employees to enable them to operate those systems and processes. Managers should also empower employees to solve problems in real time rather than refer all problems to managers. **Empowerment** is sharing with non-

Q U A L I T Y   E X H I B I T

Evaluating Your Quality/Service Initiative

We urge you to review the following list of key ingredients in an effective Quality/Service Initiative to see if you are covering all the bases. You may find that some elements need to be strengthened or added.

1. Are you leading a quality/service revolution that becomes part of the vision, values, and culture of your organization?

2. Are you continuously empowering and involving every single person in the organization?

3. Are you "married" to your customer? Have you made your customer a co-creative, co-active partner in the design and implementation of your quality/service process?

4. Are you making quality and service contagious?

5. Are you always telling the truth? First, to your employees. Second, to customers, suppliers, and distributors.

6. Are you passionate and enthusiastic about the Quality/Service Initiative?

7. Are you establishing a new language around quality and service, and then constantly communicating in this language?

8. Are you creating a learning organization? Educate, educate, educate.

9. Are you identifying the specific market niches where you can be most competitive?

10. Are you benchmarking, visiting others, and focusing on "best practices"?

Continuous renewal of superior service and total quality is the key to thriving inside our enterprises as well as out into our communities and nation in the 21st century.

Source: Lynne Joy McFarland, Larry E. Senn, and John R. Childress, *21st Century Leadership: Dialogues with 100 Top Leaders*, New York: The Leadership Press (1993): 177–180.

managerial employees the power and authority to make and implement decisions. Such an empowerment role is less directive than several of the traditional leadership models we discussed earlier in this chapter.

Such a role is also consistent with high readiness employees in the Hersey and Blanchard quadrant who require little direct interaction of the leader with the followers (see Figure 11.4). Flatter organizational structures with broader spans of control further limit the interaction and direction of the leader with the subordinates.

Self-Managed Work Teams

Some organizations are training subordinates so thoroughly in cross-functional teams that the traditional role of managers as leaders has changed. **Self-managed work teams** have the power to make the operating decisions and operate the systems designed by managers. Milliken and Company reported that some of its plants operate second and third shifts without managers in the plant. The Saturn Corporation is structured such that self-managed groups of employees perform most of the traditional managerial/supervisory functions. Besides limiting the role of traditional formal leadership in organizations, these trends also underline the impor-

In its quality processes, Heinz understands that quality begins with leadership and ends with customer satisfaction. (Photo credit: Heinz U.S.A.)

tance of continual employee training. Teams and empowerment are so important that we shall devote Chapter 14 to these topics.

The importance of leadership, education, and teamwork in a quality policy is emphasized in the Heinz Quality Policy illustrated in Figure 11.8. It all starts with leadership and ends with customer satisfaction.

CRITICAL THINKING QUESTIONS

1. Discuss the concepts of (a) leaders as empowerers and (b) self-managed work teams.

2. Relate to the traditional concepts of leadership the concepts of (a) leaders as empowerers and (b) self-managed work teams.

FIGURE 11.8 *Star-Kist Foods Inc. Quality Pyramid*

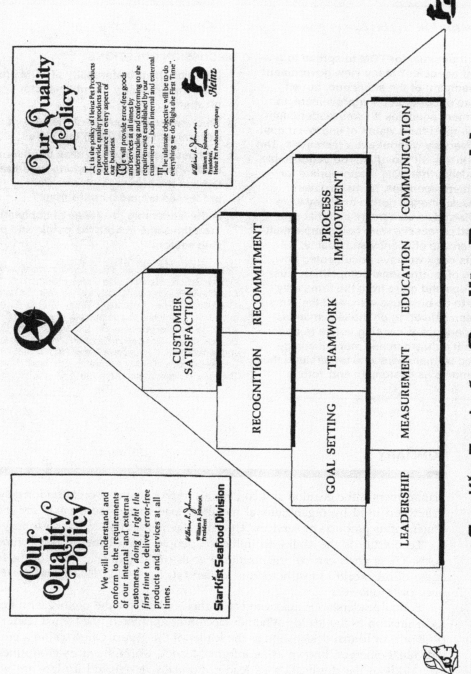

Our Quality Policy

It is the policy of Heinz Pet Products to provide quality products and performance in every aspect of our business

We will provide error-free goods and services at all times by understanding and conforming to the requirements established by our customers — both internal and external

The ultimate objective will be to do everything we do "Right the First Time".

William R. Johnson,
President,
Heinz Pet Products Company

Heinz

Our Quality Policy

We will understand and conform to the requirements of our internal and external customers, *doing it right the first time* to deliver error-free products and services at all times.

William R. Johnson,
President

Star-Kist Seafood Division

CUSTOMER SATISFACTION

RECOGNITION | RECOMMITMENT

GOAL SETTING | TEAMWORK | PROCESS IMPROVEMENT

LEADERSHIP | MEASUREMENT | EDUCATION | COMMUNICATION

Star-Kist Foods, *Inc.* **Quality Pyramid**

Source: H.J. Heinz Company.

Sources: Joel E. Ross, *Total Quality Management*, Delray Beach, FL: St. Lucie Press (1993): 126; "The Chamber's Role in Total Quality Management," *Chamber Executive*, 19, no. 1 (January 1992): 2–8; G. Conway and G. H. Carothers, "Application to Government: U.S. Army, Watervliet Arsenal," in M. J. Stahl and G. M. Bounds (eds.), *Competing Globally Through Customer Value*, Westport, CT: Quorum Books (1991): 748–787; J. Sensenbrenner, "Quality Comes to City Hall," *Harvard Business Review* (March-April 1991): 64–75.

QUALITY CASE

Conclusion to the Government Agencies Case

Why is it unusual for TQM to spread to government agencies? Many view government as a champion of the staus quo, not an advocate of continuous improvement. In government agencies it takes leadership to enlist support for a vision of improved quality and service without extra resources. The status quo is, all too often, too comfortable.

It appears that TQM is appropriate for government agencies. Many taxpayers would welcome the notion that they were being viewed as customers and that systems and processes were being implemented to increase efficiency and quality.

In this book we have documented how, because of international competition, customers demand more from the firms they choose to do business with. And the firms have been delivering on those demands. This experience is causing voters to understand that if they demand more, it can be delivered by managers who understand their requirements as customers and voters.

DISCUSSION QUESTIONS

1. Describe the transferability of TQM practices from industry to public-sector organizations.
2. Who are the customers of the various government agencies in this case?
3. Discuss the appropriateness of government agencies benchmarking organizations in the business sector. What processes are most appropriate?
4. Is the leadership challenge of applying TQM the same in both the public and private sectors?

SUMMARY

Management is the creation and continuous improvement of organizational systems that when used by organizational members lead to increased value for the customers of its products or services. Thus management is tied to the customer.

Leadership is the ability to influence people toward the accomplishment of goals. These goals can be organizational goals or the personal goals of the leader. Some of the world's most notorious leaders, such as Adolf Hitler, had great influence over followers.

Formal leadership is associated with those who have the organization's explicit designation as the leader. Whether elected or appointed, the formal leader has a positional or formal designation as the leader of the group. Often within a group an individual emerges, known as an informal leader, who influences group members even without the designation as leader. Formally designated leaders are wise to partner with the informal leader to help influence organizational members.

Power is the potential ability to influence followers' attitudes or behavior. The ability to influence arises from at least five different bases or sources of power: coercive, expert, legitimate, referent, and reward. Coercive power arises from the perception in the followers that the power holder has the ability to mediate punishment. Expert power refers to the perception by the followers that the power holder has needed information or special knowledge for the followers. Legitimate power refers to the followers' perception that the power holder has the proper right to direct activities because of the position occupied. Referent power arises from the followers identifying with the power holder and wanting to be like the power holder. Reward power stems from the followers' perception that the power holder can mediate valued rewards.

The traits approach to leadership studies the traits or characteristics that leaders have in common. Few of the same traits have been found to exist in all effective leaders.

The behavioral styles approach to leadership examines the behavior of leaders. Two broad dimensions have been observed that relate to the behavior of the leader and that focus on the task or on the subordinates. The Leadership Continuum, the Consideration and Initiating Structure Approach, and the Leadership Grid$_®$ are three models in the behavioral styles approach to leadership.

The situational/contingency approach to leadership examines the situation and argues that effective leadership is a function of the situation as well as of the leader and the followers. Hersey and Blanchard's Situational Leadership Theory, Fiedler's Leadership Contingency Model, the Vroom-Yetton-Jago Decision Involvement model, and the Path-Goal Theory are four popular situational approaches. Hersey and Blanchard's Situational Leadership Theory seems to be consistent with much of the current leadership practices in TQ organizations.

Transformational or charismatic leaders are leaders who through their personal vision, energy, and values inspire followers and thus have a major impact on organizational success. Many TQ journeys start and are sustained by transformational leaders who have an unyielding vision of the importance of serving the customer. The concepts of leaders as empowerers and of self-managed work teams observed in many TQ organizations challenge the traditional concepts of leadership.

EXPERIENTIAL EXERCISE

Supervising a Supervisor

Your class should be divided into discussion groups of from three to five students, with each group as demographically diverse as the class roster will permit. Each group should answer the questions for each of the eight scenarios presented below. The questions for each scenario should be answered in sequence before proceeding to the next scenario.

Tom is a long-time company employee who supervises the shipping department. Assume that you are the general manager to whom he reports. Recently you have received a large number of complaints about Tom's department. Customers have been receiving incorrect or incomplete shipments. Promised deadlines are not being met. Employee turnover is unusually high. The situation has deteriorated to the point where you now feel compelled to act. Until now you have been reluctant to act because Tom has been with the company for 36 years, and at age 58 he is nearing retirement.

1. What would you do in this situation? Why?

Consider each of the following scenarios of additional information to see how they might affect your final decision.

Scenario 1

Tom was your first supervisor when you joined the company. He was most helpful to you, and in fact you felt that to a certain extent he is responsible for your career success so far. Even though you passed him on the corporate ladder, he was never resentful, and the two of you have remained close friends.

2. Is it ethically responsible to let personal feelings of loyalty or friendship enter into a business decision? If you answer yes, please explain under what circumstances you might consider this to be appropriate behavior. If you answer no, please specify the costs of your decision.

Scenario 2

At home last night you read a magazine about the high percentage of men who die within two years of retirement. The article concludes that those people who have little or no outside activities are the most likely candidates. You know that Tom is just such an individual.

3. As a superior, do you have any moral stake in the likely fatality of one of your subordinates? Why or why not?

Scenario 3

Tom asks for an appointment with you. When you meet, he tells you that although he has no concrete proof, he is certain that some employees in his department are purposely making mistakes in order to make him and the company look bad.

4. What implications does this scenario have for responsible decision making? What would you do next? If Tom is lying, how should this figure into your decision?

Scenario 4

Paul, a promising young employee in your department whom you have been thinking of selecting as Tom's replacement, comes to tell you that he has been offered a job by another company. In previous conversations with him, you have indicated that when a higher position became available in the company, he would be given serious consideration. Now he tells you that unless he can be assured of a higher position soon, he feels he must pursue the opportunity that has been offered to him.

5. What would you say to Paul in this situation? What factors would you consider, and how should they relate to each other? Is there an ethical dilemma here? Why or why not?

Scenario 5

Your boss calls you in for an annual performance evaluation. In the course of the interview, problems in the shipping department are cited as one of your major shortcomings. You sense that this situation might affect your annual salary increase.

6. What would you say to your boss? How would you define the moral problems present in this situation?

Scenario 6

John, your best salesperson, angrily calls you to let you know that he has just lost a major account. The customer received three incorrect shipments in two weeks.

7. What would you say to John? To what extent are you obligated to these additional parties, and how does this obligation relate to the others already acknowledged?

Scenario 7

Tom asks you for an appointment and confides that he has had a drinking problem. He says that he knows that this is what has caused his poor performance at work, but he shows you his card confirming that he has joined AA and assures you that in the future there will be great improvement.

8. What would you say to him? What actions would you take?

Scenario 8

Your boss calls you and offers you a promotion to general manager of a much larger plant. You know you will accept the promotion and will therefore be leaving the company shortly.

9. How will this opportunity affect your decision about Tom?

Source: Adapted from J. R. Glenn, Jr., *Ethics in Decision Making*, New York: Wiley (1986): 68–78.

CHAPTER CASE

Sales Quotas

Loco Department Stores operated a retail outlet in a medium-sized Midwestern city. Harry, 25 years old, was the head of the men's clothing department in the store and supervised four other employees. With the exception of one saleswoman, all of the workers, including Harry, were male college students.

The employees were paid an hourly wage with no commission. Each worker had a separate money drawer to work out of and recorded his sales at the end of a day's work. Two employees, Kurt and Fred, had been working in the department for only a few months, but the other workers had held their jobs for at least a year.

Until a change in policy, the employees operated under a mutual agreement of sharing the easy and hard duties. Each employee took his turn waiting on the "tougher" and "undesirable" customers. The company, Harry, and the employees had always emphasized the cooperative effort of selling, without any special notice of dollar sales for each individual.

Then Harry convinced the management that department sales would increase if he could develop a friendly competitive atmosphere in the department. He thus set up a chart that stated monthly sales quotas for each worker. Management agreed to give a monthly bonus to the worker who sold the greatest dollar amount over his quota.

The previous cooperative atmosphere soon degenerated into something quite different from "friendly competition." In order to secure greater sales, employees raced to wait on the easier and more desirable customers while ignoring, as long as possible, the more troublesome buyers. Most of the time Kurt and Fred were forced to wait on the latter group, letting the senior employees have the big sales from established customers. Being junior employees, Kurt and Fred were scheduled to work hours when store traffic was light, yet their quotas were based on the same rate as the senior employees' quotas. Besides the growing friction among the workers that resulted from the new policy, customer complaints about service were increasing in number, and the total dollar sales for the department had not increased as anticipated.

Hoping to return to the old system, Kurt approached Harry about the problem. Harry refused to acknowledge any problem and stated that the new system separated "the men from the boys." Harry felt that if Kurt and Fred tried harder, they could receive the monthly bonus that had gone to the senior employees the first four months; he failed to see why they could not raise their dollar sales as he and the other employees had done. Kurt needed the job to meet college expenses but believed that something must be done about the new system if he and Fred were to remain on the job.

Discussion Questions

1. What conditions must necessarily exist for incentives (commissions in this case) to be successful?

2. What arguments might Kurt find effective in discussing the problem with Harry?

3. If Harry rejects Kurt's arguments, what should Kurt do?

Source: Adapted from A. F. Knapper, *Cases in Personnel Management*, Westerville, OH: Robin Enterprises (1977): 28–29.

KEY TERMS

accountability   Obligation to report on and justify the accomplishment of assigned tasks.

administration   Operation of internal systems.

boss-centered (autocratic) leader   Leader who tends to centralize authority.

coercive power   Power arising from the perception in the followers that the power holder has the ability to mediate punishment.

consideration   Extent to which the leader is aware of subordinates, respects their ideas, and establishes mutual trust, warmth, and friendship.

empowerment   Sharing with nonmanagerial employees the power and authority to make and implement decisions.

expert power   Power derived from the perception by the followers that the power holder has needed information or special knowledge for the followers.

Fiedler's Contingency Theory of Leadership   Theory that leadership success is determined by the degree of task structure, the degree of leader-position power, and the relationship between the leader and the followers.

formal leadership   Leadership associated with the individual who has the explicit designation from the organization as the leader.

informal leadership   Leadership associated with the individual who influences group members even without the organization's formal designation.

initiating structure   Extent to which the leader is task oriented and directs subordinates' work activities toward goal accomplishment.

leader–member relationship   Extent to which the leader feels accepted by the followers.

leader-position power   Extent to which the leader has formal authority over subordinates.

leadership   Ability to influence people toward the accomplishment of goals.

least-preferred co-worker (LPC) scale   Questionnaire that measures relationship orientation versus task orientation according to the leader's description of his/her "least preferred co-worker."

legitimate power   Power arising from the followers' perception that the power holder has the proper right to direct activities because of the position occupied.

Path-Goal Theory   Contingency leadership theory that stresses the leader's role in clarifying for subordinates how they can achieve desired rewards through job performance.

power   Potential ability to influence others' attitudes or behavior.

referent power   Power arising from the followers' identification and respect for the power holder and from their desire to be like the power holder.

responsibility   Duty to perform assigned activities.

reward power   Power stemming from the followers' perception that the power holder can mediate valued rewards.

self-managed work teams   Teams of workers who have the power to make the operating decisions and operate the systems designed by managers.

Situational Leadership Theory   Contingency approach to leadership that links the leader's relationship behavior and task behavior to the task readiness of followers.

subordinate-centered (democratic) leader Leader who delegates authority to others.

task readiness of followers Subordinates' ability to perform their job independently, their ability to assume additional responsibility, and their desire to achieve success.

task structure Degree to which the task and the goals are clearly outlined.

Traits Approach to leadership Approach that studies the characteristics or traits that leaders have in common.

transformational (charismatic) leaders Leaders who through their personal vision, energy, and values inspire followers and thus have a major impact on organizational success.

Vroom-Yetton-Jago (VYJ) Decision Involvement model Decision-based theory of leadership.

ENDNOTES

1. R. Cole, "Introduction," Special Issue on Total Quality Management, *California Management Review* (Spring 1993): 8.
2. G. H. Carothers, G. M. Bounds, and M. J. Stahl, "Managerial Leadership," in M. J. Stahl and G. M. Bounds (eds.), *Competing Globally Through Customer Value*, Westport, CT: Quorum Books (1991): 80.
3. J. R. French and B. Raven, "The Bases of Social Power," in D. Cartwright and A. Zander (eds.), *Group Dynamics*, Evanston, IL: Row, Peterson (1960): 607–623.
4. R. M. Stogdill, "Personal Factors Associated with Leadership: A Survey of the Literature," *Journal of Psychology* (January 1948): 35–64.
5. E. Jennings, "The Anatomy of Leadership," *Management of Personnel Quarterly* (Autumn 1961).
6. R. Tannenbaum and W. Schmidt, "How to Choose a Leadership Pattern," *Harvard Business Review* (March-April 1957): 95–101.
7. R. M. Stogdill and A. E. Coons (eds.), *Leader Behavior*, Research Monograph 88, Columbus: Ohio State University Bureau of Business Research (1957).
8. P. C. Nystrom, "Managers and the High-High Leader Myth," *Academy of Management Journal* (1978): 325–331.
9. R. S. Blake and J. S. Mouton, *The Managerial Grid III*, Houston: Gulf Publishing (1985).
10. P. Hersey and K. Blanchard, *Management of Organizational Behavior*, 6th ed., Englewood Cliffs, NJ: Prentice-Hall (1993).
11. "Back to School for Honda Workers," *New York Times* (March 29, 1993): D1.
12. F. A. Fiedler, *A Theory of Leadership Effectiveness*, New York: McGraw-Hill (1967).
13. F. A. Fiedler and L. Mahar, "A Field Experiment Validating Contingency Model Leadership Training," *Journal of Applied Psychology*, 64 (June 1979): 247–254.
14. V. Vroom and P. H. Yetton, *Leadership and Decision-Making*, Pittsburgh: University of Pittsburgh Press (1973); V. Vroom and A. G. Jago, *The New Leadership*, Englewood Cliffs, NJ: Prentice-Hall (1988).
15. M. G. Evans, "Leadership and Motivation: A Core Concept," *Academy of Management Journal*, 13 (March 1970): 91–102; R. J. House, "A Path-Goal Theory of Leader Effectiveness," *Administrative Science Quarterly*, 16 (September 1971): 321–328; R. J. House and T. R. Mitchell, "Path-Goal Theory of Leadership," *Journal of Contemporary Business*, 3 (Autumn 1979): 81–97.
16. R. J. House, "A 1976 Theory of Transformational Leadership," in J. G. Hunt and L. L. Larson (eds.), *Leadership: The Cutting Edge*, Carbondale: Southern Illinois University Press (1976): 189–207; B. M. Bass, "Leadership: Good, Better, Best," *Organizational Dynamics*, 13 (Winter 1985): 26–40; N. M. Tichy and D. O. Ulrich, "The Leadership Challenge—A Call for the Transformational Leader," *Sloan Management Review*, 26 (Fall 1984): 59–68.
17. D. T. Kearns and D. A. Nadler, *Prophets in the Dark: How Xerox Reinvented Itself and Beat Back the Japanese,* New York: Harper Business (1992).

12

Motivation for Total Quality

LEARNING OBJECTIVES

After reading this chapter, you should be able to accomplish the following:

- Compare and contrast motivation and leadership.
- Relate Maslow's Hierarchy of Needs Theory to Herzberg's Two-Factor Theory of Motivation.
- Describe McClelland's Socially Acquired Needs Theory.
- Relate Expectancy Theory to the Path-Goal Theory of Leadership.
- Explain Equity Theory.
- Discuss the ethics of Organizational Behavior Modification.
- Compare and contrast reinforcement theory and the process theories of motivation.
- Explain the Job Characteristics Model.
- Describe job simplification, job rotation, job enlargement, and job enrichment.

CHAPTER OUTLINE

The Nature of Motivation
  Motivation Defined
  Importance of Motivation
  Individual Motivation and System Performance
Content Theories of Motivation
  Maslow's Hierarchy of Needs Theory
  Alderfer's ERG Theory
  Herzberg's Two-Factor Theory
  McClelland's Socially Acquired Needs Theory
Process Theories of Motivation
  Equity Theory
  Expectancy Theory
  Path-Goal Theory
Reinforcement Theory
  Operant Conditioning
  Kinds of Reinforcement
  Organizational Behavior Modification and Total Quality
Job Design for Total Quality
  Job Simplification
  Job Rotation
  Job Enlargement
  Job Enrichment
  Job Characteristics Model
Cases and Exhibits
  IBM Rochester
  Federal Express
  Insider Trading
  Georgia and Mary
  Coconut International Ltd.
  Sam

IBM Rochester Motivates Employees for Total Quality and Wins a Baldrige

With the challenging goal of organizational survival as a great motivator, IBM/Rochester produced a computer in record time, increased market share every year of its first four years, and won a Baldrige Award for its actions. (Photo credit: IBM/Rochester.)

A principal product of the IBM Rochester, Minnesota, site in the 1980s was mid-range computers. At one point in the early 1980s, it had about 40 percent of the commercial mid-range market. Its primary products in this area were System 36 and System 38 computers.

Questions about shrinking market share were raised in 1985. Answers indicated that Rochester was going below 10 percent market share. Competitors like Digital Equipment Company (DEC) and Hewlett-Packard (HP) were gaining customers at IBM's expense. Although the business for mid-range computers was growing, IBM Rochester was rapidly losing market share. And it had some aged products. The System 36 came out in 1983 and the System 38 had been out since 1981.

A replacement product in the development stage, code-named Fort Knox, was killed in 1985. It had become too expensive for the low-end customer and did not have enough functions for the high-end customer. IBM seemed to be losing the mid-range market.

In 1985 Steve Schwartz became the head of Advanced Business Systems, the business unit that "owned" the Rochester site. Schwartz had spent considerable time at IBM Japan and was familiar with Japanese business processes and high quality standards. Schwartz offered the following observations of the challenges ahead for IBM Rochester at the time he took over:

> When I arrived, Rochester had a rather old product line which didn't compare at all favorably with the offerings of DEC and some others. Worse yet, they didn't even have a plan on the boards to replace that obsolete product. Market share was dropping and we needed a new product fast. This wasn't a case of a good business trying to get even better at that point. It was nothing less than a survival situation. And, believe me, survival does tend to motivate people to change.

THE NATURE OF MOTIVATION

One of the most frequently used terms among managers is *motivation*. It is a mis-understood term that has been used to praise some managers ("Coach Holtz is a great motivator") and to explain poor performance ("I was just not motivated"). Recognizing the importance of motivation for the individual and for managers, we review in this chapter several models of motivation, their implications for managers' jobs, and their relationships with Total Quality.

Motivation Defined

There are several definitions of motivation. Some relate to the sources of motivation. Is motivation an internal state, or is motivation externally reinforced and controlled by others? Can managers provide incentives to others by linking rewards to desired work outcomes in a process of motivation?

To begin to answer these questions, we offer our definition of motivation. Since managers cannot observe an internal state in an individual, we define motivation such that it is observable. **Motivation** is the amount of energy and the direction of energy displayed by an individual.[1] An individual can be greatly motivated in one setting but poorly motivated in another. Thus it makes no sense to make a general statement about the person's motivation without knowing the amount and the direction of energy expended.

For example, a college student can display high motivation to perform on a football team. He may practice football vigorously, and after practice he may consistently lift weights to increase his strength. Yet the same student may display poor motivation to perform in the classroom. Without being pressured to participate in classes and to attend study hall, the student may display no effort to do well academically. To fully describe the motivation, therefore, it is necessary to describe the direction of the effort and energies.

Importance of Motivation

Motivation is critical to understanding job performance. When motivation is mixed with the individual's ability, then the manager can forecast the individual's performance. Many organizations invest heavily in training to increase the ability of employees to perform their jobs. If the person's ability is nonexistent, then the resulting performance can be disastrous no matter how high the motivation is. For example, a person may be highly motivated to fly a jet aircraft. But a crash may result if that person does not have the flying ability derived from training.

Motivation and ability interact to yield high individual performance. The interaction is described as a multiplicative effect, that is:

$$\text{Performance} = \text{Motivation} \times \text{Ability}.$$

If either motivation or ability is zero, then the resulting performance is zero.

FIGURE 12.1 *Motivation and System Effects on Performance*

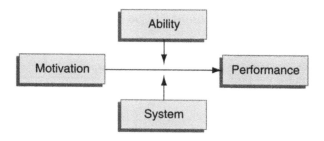

Individual Motivation and System Performance

What is the role of the system in determining performance? Let us recall from earlier chapters the definitions of processes and systems. *Processes* are grouped activities that take an input, add value to it, and provide an output to an internal or external customer. *Systems* are collections of processes and resources. Noting that systems are the responsibility of management, Deming estimated that 94 percent of problems are caused by the system.[2] To achieve the best performance from motivated employees, management must provide a consistent system that allows them to perform at a high level.[3]

One of the prime functions of management is to design and improve the system that employees operate as noted in our definition of management given in Chapter 1: *Management* is the creation and continuous improvement of organizational systems that when used by organizational members lead to increased value for the customers of its products or services. For employees to perform well, managers need to design stable processes with the right activities and the right resources at the right time. Part of the systems management work is the design and consistent operation of rewards and incentives systems tied to desired behavior. These systems reinforce motivation and channel motivated behavior in the desired directions.

The combination of motivation, ability, and the system yield job performance, as depicted in Figure 12.1.

The role of motivated employees in delivering value to customers is discussed in the following quality exhibit. Federal Express won a Baldrige Award partly because it understands the role of motivated people in a service business.

CRITICAL THINKING QUESTIONS

1. What is the manager's role in the motivation of employees?

2. How do motivation, ability, and the system interact to yield performance?

CONTENT THEORIES OF MOTIVATION

A group of theories of motivation, referred to as **Content Theories of Motivation**, focus on the internal needs that motivate people. Some of the Content Theories are

Q U A L I T Y   E X H I B I T

Federal Express's People-First Environment Helps Win a Baldrige

Frederick W. Smith, founder, chairman, and chief executive officer of Federal Express, emphasized the role of people in the company for the firm's success. "Customer satisfaction begins with employee satisfaction. When people are placed first, they will provide the highest possible service, and profits will follow." That emphasis helped the firm to be the first in the service category to win a Baldrige Award in 1990. FedEx was started in 1973 as a provider of overnight air express service. The firm's emphasis on people and customer satisfaction is described in Federal Express's Quality Proclamation:

> Federal Express's service policy is to create a satisfied customer at the end of each transaction. We will achieve 100 percent customer satisfaction by performing 100 percent to our standards, as perceived by the customer. To realize this goal, we will strive relentlessly to enhance quality in order to improve productivity. This proclamation is signified by the following symbol used to represent our commitment to achieve 100 percent customer satisfaction (quality) and 100 percent service levels (productivity), while remaining dedicated to the principles of our People-Service-Profit philosophy.

The Federal Express Philosophy and Service Commitment

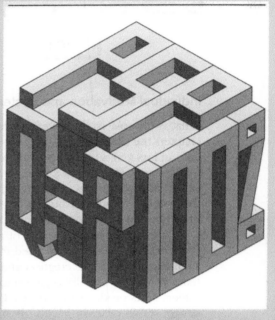

Source: Reprinted by permission of American Management Association from "Blueprints for Service Quality: The Federal Express Approach" by Briefing Staff, 1991, from *AMA Management Briefing:* 15; © 1991. American Management Association, New York. All rights reserved.

popular simply because they have been around for a long time. However, they are not uniformly relevant in today's workforce, as can be seen in the descriptions below. The most popular of the Content Theories of Motivation for the workplace are Maslow's Hierarchy of Needs Theory, Herzberg's Two-Factor Theory, Alderfer's ERG Theory, and McClelland's Socially Acquired Needs Theory.

Maslow's Hierarchy of Needs Theory

Abraham Maslow developed a popular content theory of motivation.[4] **Maslow's Hierarchy of Needs Theory** states that people are motivated by five groups of needs and that these needs exist in a hierarchical order. The theory argues that

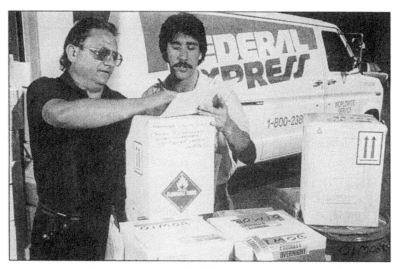

It is the motivated, nonmanagerial Federal Express employees who deliver value directly to their customers. (Photo credit: Federal Express Corporation.)

lower-order needs must be satisfied before higher-order needs are activated. The five groups of needs, their hierarchical order, and their definitions are as follows:

1. **Physiological needs** are basic human physical needs. These include food, water, sex, air, and survival.
2. **Security needs** are the needs for safety and security in both physical and economic terms. These include freedom from physical danger and a need for economic security through job security.
3. **Belongingness needs** are the needs to be accepted, included, and loved by others.
4. **Esteem needs** are the needs for attention, respect, recognition, and status.
5. **Self-actualization needs** are the needs for self-fulfillment and maximization of potential.

Physiological needs and security needs are considered lower-order needs, whereas the other three needs are considered higher-order needs. Figure 12.2 presents the need hierarchy and examples of how the various needs are fulfilled on the job.

There has been substantial criticism of Maslow's Hierarchy of Needs. The most important criticism is that there is little evidence that all people follow the need hierarchy that the theory indicates.[5] In today's diverse workforce with many individuals having different backgrounds and needs, there are numerous examples of individuals who do not follow the theory's order of needs.

Individuals of different ethnic backgrounds, for instance, may have different needs. Those from different countries may have different needs. Many people in developing countries may be primarily interested in physiological and security needs, whereas many in developed countries may be interested in higher-order

FIGURE 12.2 *Maslow's Hierarchy of Needs and Job Examples*

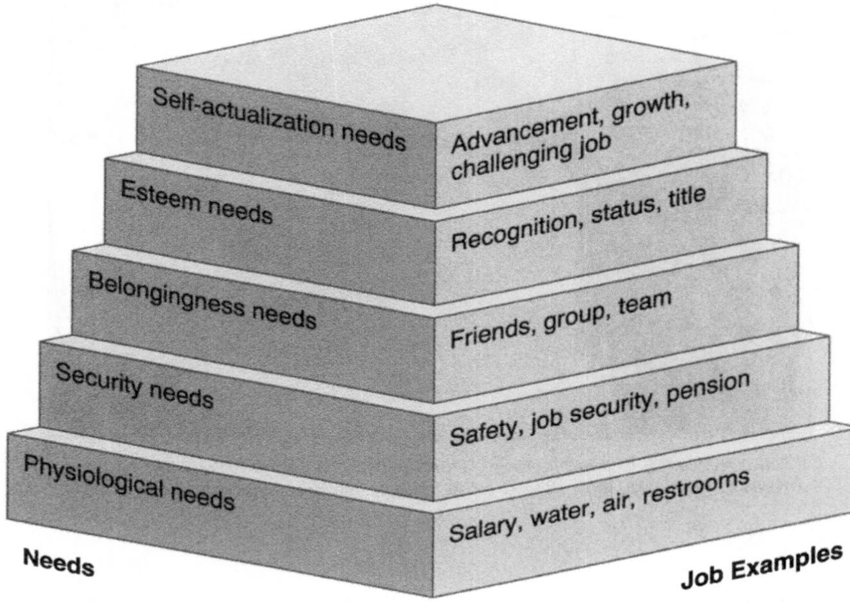

needs. Thus managers need to be aware of the differing needs of their workers and not assume that they will all respond uniformly.

Alderfer's ERG Theory

Partly in response to criticism of Maslow's theory, Clayton Alderfer presented a modified theory. His **ERG Theory** states that people are motivated by the three needs of existence, relatedness, and growth in a flexible hierarchical order.[6] (ERG = existence, relatedness, growth.) Existence needs address Maslow's first two needs of physiological needs and security needs. Relatedness needs encompass belongingness needs and social esteem needs. Growth needs include self-esteem and self-actualization needs.

Alderfer proposed that the three needs are in a flexible hierarchical order, unlike Maslow's strict hierarchical order. ERG theory also argued that more than one need could simultaneously motivate behavior.

The ethics exhibit on page 341 presents a situation in which it appears the lower-order needs had been satisfied. Nevertheless, the individuals engaged in illegal activity for the sake of millions of dollars of illegal gains. This seems to support Alderfer's flexible ERG Theory.

Herzberg's Two-Factor Theory

Herzberg's Two-Factor Theory states that the variables that determine motivation and satisfaction on the job are different from the variables that cause dissatisfaction

The international manager must not assume that what motivates the Western manager will necessarily motivate those of a different culture. (Photo credit: Charles Gupton/Tony Stone Images.)

and a lack of motivation.[7] Herzberg labeled the first set of variables as motivators or satisfiers. The second set consists of hygienes or dissatisfiers. The motivators are directly related to the work itself and arise from the content of the job. The hygienes relate to the environment or context of the job. Figure 12.3 presents Herzberg's Two-Factor model.

There has been some controversy about the way that Herzberg derived his theory. However, the theory is worth studying today because some job design techniques, cross-functional teams, and flatter organizational structures draw from both of Herzberg's factors. Later in this chapter we review some of the popular job design techniques that consider Herzberg's motivators.

McClelland's Socially Acquired Needs Theory

David McClelland formulated the **Socially Acquired Needs Theory**, which relates to the three needs of need for achievement, need for affiliation, and need for power.[8] McClelland argued that individuals acquire these three needs in differing degrees as a result of various childhood and life experiences—hence the term *socially acquired.* Unlike some of the other content theories, McClelland's theory assumes that different people have the three needs in differing amounts.

Need for Achievement (n Ach) is reflected in striving to accomplish difficult but feasible goals and later receiving feedback about personal performance. People high in n Ach do well in challenging jobs, with moderate risks and personal feedback on their individual performance. Jobs in sales, engineering, accounting, and management are examples of jobs well suited to those with high n Ach.

FIGURE 12.3 *Herzberg's Two-Factor Model: Motivation and Hygiene Factors*

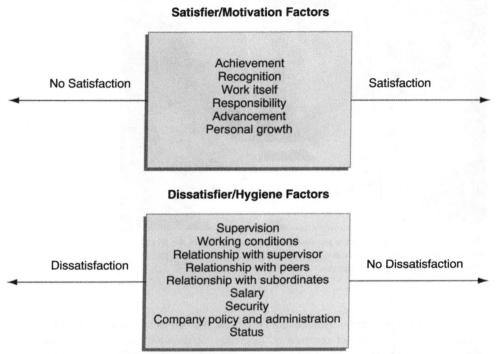

Source: Adapted from Frederick Herzberg, "One More Time: How Do You Motivate Employees?" *Harvard Business Review* (September–October 1987): 109–120.

Need for Affiliation (n Aff) refers to behavior aimed at establishing and maintaining friendly relationships with others. Those high in n Aff are attracted to jobs having much interaction with others and opportunities to establish friendships and be part of a tightly knit group. Nurses, social workers, and clergy are examples where high n Aff is an attribute.

Need for Power (n Pow) refers to influencing the activities or thoughts of a number of others.[9] High n Pow is manifested in jobs with opportunities to influence others. Managers, executives, leaders, and military officers are examples of positions where high n Pow is usually an asset.[10]

Barring significant life events like promotion, demotion, or the death of a loved one, these three needs change very slowly among adults. The principal implication for managers, therefore, is in terms of selecting, recruiting, and matching people and jobs. Selecting a high-need achiever for a sales job with challenge and feedback on personal performance may be a good match. Selecting the same high-need achiever for a dull, repetitive job with no accountability for personal performance could cause the individual to quit after a time in the job. Assigning a person with very low need for power into a team leader job could be very frustrating for the individual and those on the team. Cross-functional teams and groups (see Chapter 14) require careful matching of people to the various jobs and teams.

E T H I C S   E X H I B I T

Ethics and Insider Trading

In the 1980s insider trading—investing in publicly traded stocks on the basis of "inside" information that is not yet available to other investors—greatly undermined public confidence in the U.S. financial community. The news media have reported incident after incident of insider trading, which often yielded huge profits to those with inside information. As a result, the reputations of many respected organizations and individuals have been tarnished as the Securities and Exchange Commission (SEC) continues to investigate questionable securities transactions.

The most dramatic of the recent insider trading scandals began in 1986 when Dennis B. Levine, a merger specialist at the investment banking firm Drexel Burnham Lambert Incorporated admitted that he gave confidential inside information to arbitrageur Ivan F. Boesky. Levine and Boesky struck a deal: Levine provided valuable inside information to Boesky (as well as several others) in exchange for as much as 5 percent of the profits Boesky earned from that information. Levine

notified Boesky in advance of merger and takeover announcements—based on information he obtained from Drexel Burnham Lambert clients. Boesky then purchased stock in those companies on the assumption that the stock would increase in value when the public learned about the merger or takeover. For example, when Boesky learned that Nestlé S.A. was going to purchase Carnation Company, a leading pet food and consumer products manufacturer, he bought Carnation shares. When the news became public, Carnation's share price increased, and Boesky made a profit of more than $28 million.

In many cases Levine and Boesky's insider trading activities were not only unethical but also illegal. Boesky paid a $100 million Securities and Exchange Commission penalty, the largest ever for insider trading. In 1987 he was sentenced to three years in prison, despite his cooperation with authorities in their investigation of other insider traders.

continued

CRITICAL THINKING QUESTIONS

1. How does McClelland's Socially Acquired Needs Theory differ from the other content theories of motivation?

2. Of the four major theories discussed in this section, which has the strongest message concerning the importance of careful matching of people with specific jobs? Which has the weakest message? Elaborate on your answers.

PROCESS THEORIES OF MOTIVATION

Process Theories of Motivation focus on how people choose certain behaviors to satisfy their needs and how they judge their satisfaction. Three popular work-relevant process theories are Equity Theory, Expectancy Theory, and the Path-Goal Theory.

Equity Theory

Equity Theory states that individuals base their behavior on perceptions of their rewards and inputs relative to the rewards and inputs of relevant others.[11] The

Congress and the public wondered why Boesky had not been caught earlier, for the investigation revealed that New York Stock Exchange computers flagged 47 suspicious trades by Boesky between 1983 and 1986, many of them executed before merger announcements. Ironically, Boesky was fairly well respected as an arbitrageur; he had been invited to speak at leading business schools and had published a book arguing that his takeover attempts were a public service. Apparently, there is plenty of opportunity for insider trading in the financial community. It has been suggested that the SEC contributed to insider trading when it allowed Boesky to sell stocks and other securities before public disclosure of his crimes. (This concession was made because Boesky promised to cooperate with the SEC and testify against others involved in the scandal.) This special treatment—perhaps the ultimate use of inside information—saved Boesky an additional $100 million because the news of the scandal reduced the value of the securities.

As the Boesky-Levine insider trading scandal unfolded, the press hinted that many more insider traders might have been involved with their illegal activities. By early 1990, nine people had either been convicted and paid fines, served time in prison, or both, for their roles in the affair.

Nonetheless, many insider traders in the scandal will probably never be caught, although the SEC is still investigating.

The Boesky-Levine scandal and others involving investment bankers and securities traders have strained relationships between investment bankers and their clients. There is a new atmosphere of caution and mistrust on Wall Street. In the past many merger and takeover deals were sealed with a handshake, or even concluded over the phone. Now companies worry that their investment bankers will sell information about their business to the highest bidder. The doubt and suspicion have led some clients to demand written promises of confidentiality.

Discussion Questions

1. Legal issues aside, why do many people consider insider trading to be unethical?

2. What justification might Boesky and Levine have used to defend their actions?

3. Discuss the forces that may have driven Boesky and Levine to such behavior.

Source: O. C. Ferrell and John Fraedrich, *Business Ethics: Ethical Decision Making and Cases*, 1991, 202–206. Copyright © 1991 by Houghton Mifflin Company. Reprinted with permission.

inputs include job effort and performance, but they also include education, experience, and other qualifications. Individuals form a ratio as a basis of comparison:

$$\frac{\text{Outcomes}_{\text{self}}}{\text{Inputs}_{\text{self}}} \quad ? \quad \frac{\text{Outcomes}_{\text{relevant other}}}{\text{Inputs}_{\text{relevant other}}}$$

A feeling of equity or fairness exists if the ratios are equal. The ratios can be unequal if the individual receives too many outcomes/rewards for his or her level of inputs relative to the comparison other. If the ratios are perceived as being unequal, then the individual will take one of four actions:

1. *Change inputs.* The individual may increase or decrease his or her inputs. Since education, experience, and other inputs are fixed in the short term, job effort and attendance are usually changed if inequity is perceived.

2. *Change outcomes.* The individual may request a raise or a promotion, may engage in illegal actions like theft, or may take legal action to correct the inequities. The latter is particularly relevant if the individual is in a class protected by the law, as we saw in Chapter 9.

3. *Distort perceptions.* The individual may change the perception of his or her inputs relative to the relevant other, if it is not possible to change the outputs or the individual's inputs. The individual may focus on a different relevant other.

4. *Leave the job.* The individual, if he or she believes the inequitable situation cannot be resolved, may exit the scene rather than continue to endure the inequity.

It is difficult to predict, before the behavior occurs, which of the four alternatives an individual will choose. However, recognizing the severity of some of the alternatives, managers are advised to prevent the perceived inequity by ensuring equitable outcomes for given inputs for all workers.

As the diversity exhibit indicates, outcomes can include a number of seemingly minor issues, such as the use of a copier machine. Inequitable situations concerning outcomes can be filled with dangers in the workplace.

Expectancy Theory

Expectancy Theory is a powerful theory of motivation because it can explain a broad series of motivated behaviors and because it ties to the behaviors of the leader. **Expectancy Theory** states that people make decisions about behavior based on the value of the rewards, the linkage of the rewards to the behavior, and the odds that they can accomplish the behavior.[12] These three variables have specific meaning. **Valence** is the value or attractiveness of a specific reward. **Instrumentality** is the perceived linkage between the reward and the work behavior. **Expectancy** is the perceived probability that if individuals put forth the effort, they will perform successfully. Figure 12.4 shows how the three variables combine to predict performance.

In equation form, the three terms are multiplicative:

$$\text{Motivation} = \text{Valence} \times \text{Instrumentality} \times \text{Expectancy}.$$

The multiplicative relationship means that all three terms must be high for motivation to be high.[13] Conversely, if one of the terms is low, then motivation is low, no matter how high the other terms may be. For individuals to seriously seek a job with a specific company, they must first value the outcomes associated with the job (pay, location, benefits, the work itself), that is, they must have a high valence for the outcomes. Second, the individuals must perceive that those outcomes are associated with the job, that is, that they have a high instrumentality. Third, the individuals must perceive that if they try to get the job, the job will be forthcoming.

As indicated in the following international exhibit, individuals respond to the incentives and instrumentalities established by managers in accord with fulfilling the valences of the individuals. These may be different from the manager's goals.

DIVERSITY EXHIBIT

Georgia and Mary

It had been a practice in the accounting department for supervisors as well as rank-and-file employees to use the Xerox copier machine for personal use. Although not responsible for the departmental budget, Mary was in charge of the use of the machine. Supposedly, she was to see that the copier was used only for company business. However, the nature of the work done in the department made it difficult for Mary, or anyone else, to determine when the copier was being used for company business and when it was being used for personal business.

Everyone in the department realized the freedom with which employees utilized the machine. In fact, even department heads and supervisors had been known to "run off a few" copies of letters, articles, and various other literature for personal use. Everyone seemed content with the procedure until Georgia approached Mary about using the copier for some one-page fliers.

Georgia, a black supervisor in the department, had been more militant in her backing of the "black power" philosophy in recent months. She wished to use the machine to run off 1,000 copies of an announcement directed to blacks informing them of a private mass meeting the next week. Georgia first asked Mary whether she could use

the machine; Mary refused, stating that the material was "for personal use and was too controversial." After the incident, Mary reported the situation to her boss, who backed her actions. He clearly told her not to let Georgia use the machine for any material of that nature.

The next day Georgia again approached Mary. This time she *told* Mary that she was going to use the machine and proceeded to make copies of the bulletin. Although she knew it would likely cause trouble, Mary did not attempt to stop Georgia. Mary pondered about what to do, since she knew other employees had used the machine for personal items and had not even shown the courtesy Georgia had shown by asking to use the machine for personal matters.

Discussion Questions

1. Define the basic problem. Does Mary have a problem with Georgia?

2. Of what importance to the case are Georgia's race and organizational affiliation?

3. What action should be taken by whom? Why?

Source: A. F. Knapper, *Cases in Personnel Management,* Westerville, OH: Robin Enterprises (1977): 39.

Path-Goal Theory

The Path-Goal Theory of Leadership covered in Chapter 11 is similar to the Expectancy Theory of Motivation. The *Path-Goal Theory of Leadership* stresses the leader's role in clarifying for subordinates how they can achieve desired rewards through job performance.[14] In the Path-Goal Theory the leader determines individ-

FIGURE 12.4 *Expectancy Model of Motivation*

INTERNATIONAL EXHIBIT

Coconut International Ltd.: Reverse Motivation in a Developing Country

The management group of Coconut International of Ceylon was concerned with increasing the company's production of combed coconut fiber for export. Specifically, management was searching for ways to increase productivity from individual workers. However, the attitudes of Ceylonese employees raised unique problems. Thus, conventional methods of stimulating productivity had not proved successful.

Coconuts are stripped of their husks, split, and dried into copra. The copra is shipped abroad to be processed into oil. This export is one of Ceylon's major foreign-exchange sources. Recently other coconut products such as fibers have found expanding markets. Increased demand for fibers had led to Coconut International's concern with worker productivity.

Coconut International was one of Ceylon's major exporters of fiber. The firm had a processing plant in Colombo, the country's capital. Recovery of fiber from the husks of coconuts was done at various mills. The mills were located to the north and northeast of Colombo in the coconut-producing areas. The fiber was delivered to Coconut International, which stored, sorted, graded, baled, and exported the commodity. The company received two kinds of fibers: mattress and bristle. Distinguished by its longer staple, the latter type could be further processed by combing. It was then tied into bundles. The product was used in the production of fiber brushes.

For the purpose of combing brush fiber, it had been customary in Ceylon to use women. Coconut International employed more than 300 women for this purpose. The women were paid on a piece rate, on the basis of a hundredweight (112 pounds) of fiber combed. Rates varied according to the quality of combing, but had risen in recent years from $1.20 to $1.80 per hundredweight for the upper quality limit.

Since payment was on a piece-rate basis and because of local customs, Coconut International had never kept a strict check on attendance or on the number of hours worked each day by employees. Many women came to work in their spare time. They worked as long as they felt like it. They returned home to prepare meals and attend to their children, or when they were bored with the tiring combing process.

In the past, the company had been content to accept these conditions of work for its women operatives. While production was not effectively organized, this had not been particularly significant. Combing was a hand operation not involving machinery. Normal daylight was adequate for the combers. Weather conditions in Colombo required little more than a roof on the combing building. The irregular output of the women actually made checking their production fairly simple, since it combined to produce a fairly steady, if limited, yield. No timekeeping records were necessary. Most importantly, everybody seemed satisfied.

continued

uals' desired rewards (valences). For example, some like to travel and consider travel a reward. Others may be afraid of flying and view travel as a punishment.

The leader's role also includes clarifying the instrumentalities so that individuals understand the linkage between desired rewards and relevant job behavior. Managers must be careful that they link rewards to the desired job behaviors. Too often, incentive systems reward inappropriate forms of behavior. This may be true in Total Quality organizations that are trying to reward customer-relevant and team-relevant behavior amid older cultures that rewarded financial criteria and individual performance. Expectancy Theory and Path-Goal Theory offer some guidance in such situations by guiding the manager to think through the design of the appropriate instrumentalities.

However, two things occurred together which made increased production important. The first of these was an increase in foreign demand for combed fibers, which Coconut International was anxious to meet since management was profit-oriented. The second was a continuing decline in Ceylon's foreign-exchange position. This situation concerned the government and led it to encourage those companies in the export trade to do what they could to expand sales abroad. Therefore, Coconut International had both economic and political reasons for producing more combed fiber.

One way to increase output was to hire more employees. Since Ceylon had a chronic unemployment problem, it was not difficult to find women willing to work. However, space limitations prevented any significant expansion in the company's labor force. Moreover, the country's labor laws prohibited the use of female workers in a night shift. Thus, a two- or three-shift operation was impossible. Displacement of less productive workers in favor of new ones who might be more productive, would likely cause difficulties with the government department of labor or with labor organizers. Since the company had never developed production norms, dismissal of an employee for what Coconut International might consider low production would not necessarily be accepted as adequate cause.

Management recognized that one solution might be to work toward the development of production standards. Management also believed that this should be prefaced by enforcement of attendance and of working hours. However, an attempt to do this merely led to strong resentment by the workers. Any effort to attract women outside normal working hours seemed also destined to fail, since nearly all of the female workers were married and occupied with home duties at those times.

The next step taken was to increase payment for fiber combed. Management hoped that this would lead to greater output. However, to the surprise of the Coconut International management, the result was not increased production, but poor attendance. Apparently, the workers had developed earnings objectives of their own. When this individual earnings objective was reached, the employee merely failed to report for work. An increase in the piece rate made it possible to secure this objective in less time. Thus, the employee saw little reason to put in more time to earn more than she wanted.

Coconut International's management was considering what it might do. Better enforcement of hours and attendance records was a long-run objective. However, it could not be implemented at once. One manager suggested using appeals to produce more goods because of the country's need for export sales. However, management doubted that the typical worker would be moved by patriotic appeals. Ceylon had been independent only since 1948. National fervor was strongest among intellectuals and government employees. Coconut International employees were concerned with little more than food, shelter, clothing, and some relatively simple pleasures.

Source: Adapted from J. S. Ewing and F. Meissner, *International Business Management: Readings and Cases*, Belmont, CA: Wadsworth (1964): 456–458.

Whether they are called instrumentalities (in Expectancy Theory) or paths and goals (in Leadership Theory), the importance of goals in motivation needs to be emphasized. The second part of the IBM Rochester case stresses the importance of goals.

CRITICAL THINKING QUESTIONS

1. Is Equity Theory more relevant in an organization that is growing or in one that is downsizing? Elaborate on your answer.

2. How can Expectancy Theory be used to help managers change the culture of an organization?

Back to the IBM Rochester Case

In early 1986 Steve Schwartz installed Tom Furey as head of the Rochester lab, which was responsible for the design and development of the hardware and software of the new product line. Started in late 1985, the new line was code-named Silverlake and resulted in the AS/400 system.

The Silverlake project was both a key to survival and a key to redefining the mid-range market. New standards would have to be set in development, production, organization, coordination, and cooperation—both in the Rochester plant and with their customers and suppliers. Furey articulated some shorter-range objectives in pursuit of the longer-term vision:

— We must cut the product development cycle time in half on the new product—from 60 months to 30. We must be ready to roll out the product by mid-1988.

— Software must be ready when hardware is. We cannot afford the luxury of fully designing the hardware and then turn it over to the software developers. Software and hardware must be developed side by side and concurrently.

— We are a business—not a function. We need all functions—Manufacturing, Marketing, Product Service—to be involved upstream in the design phase, not just Engineering.

— This business is global in scope, not just domestic. [By 1986, 60 percent of all Rochester systems were sold outside the United States.] Therefore, we will be ready to ship to foreign customers at the same date as domestic [rather than the traditional several months lag].

— The new product will receive the most favorable market reception in our history. This will partially be due to its high quality and utility and partially due to the fact that we will secure customer inputs and reactions far upstream of the announcement date and fold these into the finalized product offering.

Furey's next step was to put in place several cross-functional teams representing hardware design, software design, and manufacturing concerns. Thus hardware, software, manufacturing processes, and customer service feedback systems could be designed concurrently rather than in the previous linear fashion.

continued

REINFORCEMENT THEORY

To varying degrees, the theories of motivation that we have discussed focus on the internal needs of the individual. **Reinforcement Theory** focuses on the relationship between behavior and its consequences. The interest here is in changing the individual's job behavior through the selected use of rewards and punishments.

Operant Conditioning

Operant conditioning and learning are central to Reinforcement Theory. **Operant conditioning** is the concept that individuals learn through past positive or negative consequences how to gain rewards or avoid punishments in the future. B. F. Skinner, the father of operant conditioning, has argued that reinforcement theory

A sign in one office at IBM Rochester states: "Once you have a clear vision, decisions become easier, commitment becomes clearer, purpose becomes constant." The broad range of commitment needed to implement Market-Driven Quality (MDQ), IBM's version of Total Quality Management, was indicated by the following:

— A key to effective linkage for quality management was the sharing of systems—manufacturing and logistics, marketing and service.

— Twelve customer and business partner councils are held each year, all over the world. Approximately ten customers attend each session. Business partner councils represent thousands of customers.

— Rochester made use of best-of-breed benchmarking for cost, reliability, and customer satisfaction. In this process the firm takes the best of the best competition and builds a mythical competitor. This provides a target to set a direction of competition for each element of the product or service.

— Education expenditures were five times the industry average. This level of education investment was considered necessary

for the organization to work toward a market-driven culture.

— The customer partnership call process contacts customers 90 days after a system is shipped. Employees at the Rochester site make these calls. The process is informative both for the customer, who gets to talk directly to the source of product design, and for the employee, who learns from direct user feedback.

— Morale surveys were conducted annually, with 95 percent participation. Rochester also conducted biannual surveys to test awareness, understanding, and attitude on market-driven quality.

The customer satisfaction and customer involvement served as an envelope around the entire product planning, design, introduction, and support process that emerged in the development of the AS/400. These initiatives were all a part of a mosaic that transformed the organization as the AS/400 was developed. The goal had been to balance the historic IBM culture of respect for the individual and support of innovation with the benefits of team participation and group accomplishment. Cross-functional teams played a significant role in the redesign of business processes.

can explain human behavior by knowing the consequences and the timing of the consequences.[15] Operant conditioning is based on a simple **law of effect**, which states that people tend to repeat behavior that is rewarded and not repeat behavior that is not rewarded.[16]

The concept is powerful in its simplicity and everyday examples. As children, we learn not to touch a hot stove. As students, we learn to study for tests if grades are important. As adults, we learn not to insult police when stopped for speeding. We learn these behaviors because of their consequences.

Kinds of Reinforcement

There are four kinds of reinforcement available to systematically reinforce desirable behavior and discourage undesirable behavior: positive reinforcement, negative reinforcement, punishment, and extinction.[17]

Positive Reinforcement **Positive reinforcement** is the application of positive consequences (rewards) following a desired behavior. Its purpose is to stimulate the desired behavior and increase the odds that it will be repeated. By definition, the consequence must be perceived as positive and valued by the individual. For example, some people do not like to fly. Therefore "rewarding" them with a trip after achieving a challenging goal may be viewed as punishment. This highlights the importance of the manager's first determining what is valued by employees before trying to reinforce their behavior.

Negative Reinforcement **Negative reinforcement** is the removal of an unpleasant consequence following a desired behavior.[18] This is also known as avoidance learning, since the individual learns how to avoid the unpleasant consequence. Like positive reinforcement, the purpose is to increase the odds that the desired behavior will be repeated. For example, a parent who stops harassing a child about playing a loud sound system when the child turns down the volume is using negative reinforcement.

Punishment **Punishment** is the application of negative or unpleasant consequences following an undesirable behavior. The purpose is to decrease the odds of the undesirable behavior being repeated. Verbal reprimands, written reprimands, and suspensions without pay associated with absenteeism are examples of punishments. Punishment as a reinforcement strategy has limitations, since it does not show the individual what the correct behavior is.

Extinction **Extinction** is the removal of all reinforcements following an undesirable behavior. As with punishment, the purpose is to decrease the odds of the undesirable behavior being repeated. Ignoring or isolating a poorly performing individual may show the person that the poor performance will not yield desirable results.

Positive reinforcement is the most powerful of the four kinds of reinforcement in work settings in the long term. Such reinforcement shows the individual the correct behavior, and it provides the rewards the individual seeks. Monetary awards and recognition for top sales performance are two examples of positive reinforcement.

Organizational Behavior Modification and Total Quality

Organizational Behavior Modification (OB Mod) is the deliberate attempt to change human behavior in work organizations through the application of operant conditioning. For the reasons mentioned above, most organizations implementing OB Mod use positive reinforcement as the mainstay.

Since organizations that try to remake themselves along the lines of Total Quality must change individuals' behavior, OB Mod has some applications. In trying to change peoples' behavior toward a greater TQ emphasis, Eastman Chemical uses a variety of reinforcers, among them social reinforcements like a record-breaking ceremony, letters sent home, and newspaper and newsletter articles. Social reinforcements can be especially potent because they involve the support and approval of others. Tangible reinforcements include a miniature wrench for a fix of a quality problem, potted plants for helping to "grow sales," a surveyor's transit for "surveying our customers," and thousands of ham biscuits for thousands of team meetings to improve quality issues.[19] The ham biscuits became symbolic as a social reinforcer that the group was solving a quality issue.

CRITICAL THINKING QUESTIONS

1. How does Reinforcement Theory differ from content theories of motivation?

2. Give an example of each of the four kinds of reinforcement a professor could use in a class.

JOB DESIGN FOR TOTAL QUALITY

Some of the job design techniques that are based on combinations of the motivational theories we have outlined above are job simplification, job rotation, job enlargement, job enrichment, and the Job Characteristics model.

Job Simplification

Job simplification attempts to reduce the number of different tasks an individual performs in the job. As described in Chapter 2, Frederick Taylor believed his scientific system of management would increase worker productivity through the application of scientific principles. Taylor also wanted to increase worker welfare through higher wages.

Unfortunately, two of Taylor's principles were associated with fragmentation of the work and divisions between workers and managers. Those two principles were job simplification and division of responsibility between workers and management.[20] Job simplification fosters an isolationist attitude in which the individual workers are encouraged to think in terms of their immediate tasks and immediate job. This is done sometimes at the expense of seeing how the whole enterprise delivers value to the customer. Division of responsibility between workers and management can yield the same behaviors as job simplification. Additionally, such division can suggest that the function of managers is to control the behavior of others, not to improve systems to yield greater value to customers. Job simplification also assumes that individuals are motivated primarily by financial compensation and that they do not require any social reinforcement. For these reasons job simplification is not widely used today.

Job Rotation

Job rotation refers to moving employees from one job to another. Its purpose is to prevent boredom and to cross-train. For example, a sales clerk may be rotated into the customer service department in order to understand how customers respond after the sale. Job rotation is being used with more frequency today, because it helps workers understand the cross-functional systems that yield value to customers.

Job Enlargement

Job enlargement refers to broadening the scope of the job by adding more tasks to it. For example, a sales clerk's job may be enlarged by adding inventory checking and store cleaning at the end of a shift. Job enlargement by itself does not restructure the way the work is done, nor does it add any managerial tasks into the job.

Job Enrichment

Job enrichment refers to adding some managerial decision-making authority and Herzberg's motivators to the job. For example, the sales clerk may be given some authority in the decision of what cash registers to buy and how to lay out the merchandise to appeal to the customers.

It is not unusual to see more than one of these job design strategies employed simultaneously. A good example of enlargement can be found at Ford's Walton Hills stamping plant outside Cleveland. Historically narrow job descriptions have been broadened. Some job descriptions have been merged with other job descriptions to create fewer job classes. For example, many of the production workers now perform their own maintenance. In the past, maintenance was done by a separate group of workers.

Examples of enrichment can also be found at the Ford plant. "Plant management also gave more autonomy to workers. For instance, Bob Kubec and his partner, Mark Asta, now run a transfer press—a highly technical press that stamps sheets of metal—with very little supervision. Both men were involved in buying and setting up the press."[21]

Job Characteristics Model

The Job Characteristics model proposed by J. Richard Hackman and Greg R. Oldham is a recent job design technique developed from the psychological aspect of the individual worker level.[22] The **Job Characteristics model** is a job design theory based on core job dimensions, employees' critical psychological states, and their work behavior. The model is illustrated in Figure 12.5.

Core Job Dimensions Hackman and Oldham listed five factors associated with the motivational potential of a job. They assert that the more these five core job dimensions can be designed into the job, the higher will be the workers' motivation and job performance.

1. **Skill variety** is the number of activities in a job and the number of skills used in the performance of the job. For example, a simplified manufacturing job based on division of labor, such as installing the left side mirror, is low in skill variety.

2. **Task identity** is the extent to which the worker performs the total job with a definable beginning and a definable end. The worker who installs the left side mirror has less task identity than the workers in a team that assembles the entire car body.

3. **Task significance** is the extent to which the worker perceives that the job has importance and impact on the company or its customers. Installing the

FIGURE 12.5 *The Job Characteristics Theory*

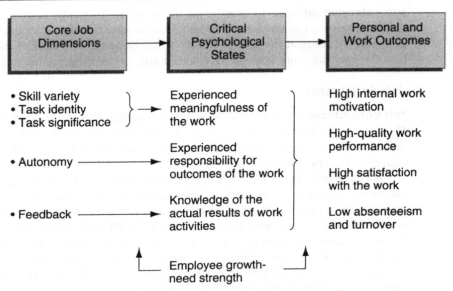

Source: From J. R. Hackman and G. R. Oldham, "Motivation Through the Design of Work: Test of a Theory," *Organizational Behavior and Human Performance*, vol. 16. Copyright © 1976 by Academic Press, Inc.

side mirror may have low task significance unless the worker understands the importance of proper installation to customer satisfaction and to sales for the firm.

4. **Autonomy** is the extent to which the worker has discretion in the performance of the job. An individual worker on an assembly line may have little autonomy, but the team that plans the work and decides how to assemble the car has considerable autonomy.

5. **Feedback** is the extent to which the worker learns about the outcomes of his or her performance. Providing automobile assemblers with customer satisfaction data is an example of feedback.

Critical Psychological States   The Job Characteristics model states that the five dimensions combine to yield three critical psychological states. Furthermore, the model reveals that the three states are intermediate positions leading to enhanced work performance. **Experienced meaningfulness of the work** refers to how satisfying the work itself is. **Experienced responsibility for outcomes of the work** is associated with the amount of autonomy. **Knowledge of the actual results of work activities** is knowledge acquired through feedback.

IBM Rochester made extensive use of feedback directly from customers to the AS/400 design and manufacturing team. We discuss this Total Quality practice of feedback from customers directly to employees in the conclusion to the IBM Rochester case.

QUALITY CASE

Conclusion to the IBM Rochester Case

Benefits of early supplier involvement at IBM Rochester were manyfold. Since 1990 lead times had been reduced by 80 percent, and supplier defect rates had improved almost 60 percent. More and more long-term relationships were evolving with key suppliers. In fact, 69 percent of production dollars were being spent with alliance suppliers. Concurrently, from 1985 there had been a 54 percent reduction in the number of production suppliers. The net result was that the bulk of production dollars were being spent with approximately 50 suppliers.

With the advent of the AS/400 development program, the development process was restructured so that it integrated customers and suppliers into the process. Development cycle times had been reduced by 50 percent since 1987. The AS/400 was developed in under 28 months.

The initial shipment of products occurred in August 1988. The product took off from that point as a hot seller. Later IBM called it the most successful product launch in IBM history. In the first four years of its life, the AS/400 gained market share every year. Editors and readers of *Information Week* cited the AS/400 as one of the ten best products and services of 1992. *Corporate Computing* named the AS/400 one of 1993's "best buys."

In October 1990 IBM Rochester was notified that it had won a Malcolm Baldrige National Quality Award. People at the Rochester plant like to say that it took over 10 years and over 8,000 people to win the Baldrige Award. With that long-term perspective and over 8,000 motivated people, the quality journey continues at IBM Rochester.

DISCUSSION QUESTIONS

1. Relate the content, process, and reinforcement theories of motivation to Steve Schwartz's comment: "It was nothing less than a survival situation. And, believe me, survival does tend to motivate people to change."

2. IBM Rochester made extensive use of feedback directly from customers to the AS/400 design and manufacturing team. Relate this Total Quality practice to McClelland's Need for Achievement, Herzberg's Motivators, and Hackman and Oldham's Job Characteristics model.

3. Discuss the motivational impact of ambitious goals in the AS/400 project and in many Total Quality systems.

Source: Reprinted by permission from *IBM Rochester: The Quality Journey Continues* by B. Konsynski. Copyright 1992 by International Business Machines Corporation.

Employee Growth-Need Strength One variable moderating all the relationships described above is **employee growth-need strength**, which means that different workers have different needs to grow and develop. Those with low needs do not respond very well to applications of the Job Characteristics model, whereas workers with a high growth-need strength do respond well to such applications. As workers today are receiving more and more training related to the importance of providing value to customers and the importance of working on horizontal processes in cross-functional teams, employee growth-need strength seems to be increasing.

Personal and Work Outcomes   The Personal and Work Outcomes associated with the Job Characteristics model include a customer-relevant outcome of high-quality work performance. The other outcomes of high internal work motivation, high satisfaction with the work, and low absenteeism and turnover may be viewed as intermediate outcomes to provide the customer-relevant work outcome. These intermediate outcomes facilitate the high-quality work performance, lower the costs of operations, and provide value to external customers.

A popular job design technique that builds on several of the motivational and job design techniques in this chapter uses autonomous groups and self-managed work teams. These require structural changes and changes in the focus on processes in the organization. In Chapter 14 we shall fully explore this topic.

CRITICAL THINKING QUESTIONS

1. Using the Job Characteristics model, analyze the job of a professor.
2. Describe the challenges of implementing job rotation, job enlargement, and job enrichment with a unionized workforce.

SUMMARY

Motivation is the amount of energy and the direction of energy displayed by an individual. Motivation is critical to understanding job performance. When motivation is combined with the individual's ability, then the manager can forecast the individual's performance.

Content Theories of Motivation focus on the internal needs that motivate people. The most relevant of the Content Theories of Motivation for the workplace are Maslow's Hierarchy of Needs, Herzberg's Two-Factor Theory, Alderfer's ERG Theory, and McClelland's Socially Acquired Needs Theory.

Maslow's Hierarchy of Needs Theory states that people are motivated by five groups of needs and that these needs exist in a hierarchical order. ERG Theory states that people are motivated by the three needs of existence, relatedness, and growth in a flexible hierarchical order. Herzberg's Two-Factor Theory states that the variables that determine motivation and satisfaction on the job are different from the variables that cause a lack of motivation and dissatisfaction. McClelland's Socially Acquired Needs Theory refers to the three needs of need for achievement, need for affiliation, and need for power.

Process Theories of Motivation focus on how people choose certain behaviors to satisfy their needs and how they judge their satisfaction. Three popular work-relevant process theories are Equity Theory, Expectancy Theory, and the Path-Goal Theory.

Equity Theory states that individuals base their behavior on perceptions of their rewards and inputs relative to the rewards and inputs of relevant others. Expectancy Theory states that people make decisions about behavior based on the value of the rewards, the linkage of the rewards to the behavior, and the odds that they can accomplish the behavior. The Path-Goal Theory of Leadership stresses the leader's role in clarifying how subordinates can achieve desired rewards through job performance.

Reinforcement Theory focuses on the relationship between behavior and its consequences. Operant conditioning and learning are central to Reinforcement Theory. Operant conditioning is the concept that individuals learn through past positive or negative consequences how to gain rewards or avoid punishments in the future. Operant conditioning is based on a simple law of effect which states that people tend to repeat behavior that is rewarded and not repeat behavior that is not rewarded. There are four kinds of reinforcement available to systematically reinforce desirable behavior and discourage undesirable behavior: positive reinforcement, negative reinforcement, punishment, and extinction. Organizational Behavior Modification (OB Mod) is the deliberate attempt to change human behavior in work organizations through the application of operant conditioning.

Some job design techniques are based on combinations of the preceding motivational theories, among them job simplification, job rotation, job enlargement, job enrichment, and the job characteristics model.

Job simplification attempts to reduce the number of different tasks an individual performs in the job. Job rotation refers to moving employees from one job to another for the purpose of preventing boredom and of cross-training. Job enlargement refers to broadening the scope of the job by adding more tasks to it. Job enrichment refers to adding some managerial decision-making authority and Herzberg's Motivators to the job. The Job Characteristics model is based on core job dimensions, employees' critical psychological states, and their work behavior.

EXPERIENTIAL EXERCISE

What Do People Want from Their Jobs?

The objective of this exercise is to give participants an opportunity to discuss what factors motivate employees. The class should be divided into groups of 3 to 5 persons each. On the form below, "What Do People Want from Their Jobs?" each person should indicate which of the 10 items listed he or she believes to be *most* important in contributing to employee morale. The items should be weighted from 1 to 10, with 10 assigned to the most important item, 9 to the second most important, and so on, in a reverse weighting order.

Then each group should total the individual weights within the group, ranking the 10 items in the "Group" column. Your instructor will provide you with data on how supervisors and employees have ranked the items.

Discussion Questions

1. In comparing your group's ratings with those in the "Employees" column, what factors might account for the differences of opinion?
2. What might be a reason for the evaluations in the "Supervisors" column being so different from those in the "Employees" column?
3. If this form were to be used in your department (office, etc.), how similar do you think the results would be?

Individual	Group	Factors	Supervisors	Employees
		High wages		
		Job security		
		Promotion in the company		
		Good working conditions		
		Interesting work		
		Personal loyalty of supervisor		
		Tactful discipline		
		Full appreciation of work done		
		Help on personal problems		
		Feeling of being in on things		

Source: J. W. Newsdron and E. E. Scannell, *Games Trainers Play*, New York: McGraw-Hill (1980): 121–123. Copyright 1980 McGraw Hill. Reprinted with permission.

CHAPTER CASE

SAM

Sam Ford was rapidly becoming the main topic of discussion for the workers on the E-shift. For the past year he had been working in the jeep-transportation department at a large manufacturing plant. His attendance record was good, and his work was considered far above average by his immediate supervisor. This supervisor, a generally disagreeable person, also considered Sam the informal leader of the transportation department. This feeling was shared by the foremen and the other workers.

Lately, though, several supervisors had seen Sam breaking different safety regulations. Most of the violations would have called for no more than a verbal reprimand, so the supervisors let them slide. Finally, Sam was caught by the plant safety supervisor without his safety glasses on. This resulted in his being laid off without pay for five working days.

It was the plant's policy that safety glasses must be worn to gain admittance to the plant and must be worn at all times in the plant. This policy was established to ensure that there would be no loss of sight from an accident or from a resulting fire. This written policy stated that employees caught not wearing their safety glasses would for the first offense get a five-day layoff and then for a second offense get another five-day suspension.

Within a few days of his return to work, Sam was again caught by the same safety supervisor without his safety glasses. The supervisor informed Sam in an angry voice, "I am getting tired of writing you up for stupid mistakes." Sam replied, "Why don't you go home and soak your head." The supervisor then struck Sam, at which point Sam proceeded to beat the supervisor unconscious.

Sam was laid off work until the company could decide what action to take regarding the fight. After a brief meeting the next day, Mr. Green, the transportation supervisor, informed Sam that he was terminated. A union steward then asked Mr. Green about the fate of the safety supervisor. Mr. Green replied, "He will remain at work, as far as I know." The union steward immediately stepped to the telephone and called the union president. From the ensuing conversation Mr. Green learned that a wildcat strike might be ordered over the firing of Sam and the retention of the supervisor.

Mr. Green knew that it was the company's stated policy that whoever started or was involved in a fight would be terminated immediately. Mr. Green was beginning to wonder whether the company had made a mistake in its decision and what the company should do now.

Discussion Questions

1. What can Mr. Green do to prevent the wildcat strike?

2. What do you think of the company's policy that "whoever started or was involved in a fight" would be terminated?

3. What possible explanations might be given for Sam's apparent change in behavior?

4. Could Sam's immediate supervisor or the foremen have prevented Sam's case from progressing as far as it did?

Source: Adapted from A. F. Knapper, *Cases in Personnel Management*, Westerville, OH: Robin Enterprises (1977): 86–87.

KEY TERMS

autonomy Extent to which the worker has discretion in the performance of the job.

belongingness needs Needs to be accepted, included, and loved by others.

Content Theories of Motivation Theories relating to the internal needs that motivate people.

employee growth-need strength Concept that different workers have different needs to grow and develop.

Equity Theory Theory that individuals base their behavior on perceptions of their rewards and inputs relative to the rewards and inputs of relevant others.

ERG Theory Theory that people are motivated by the three needs of existence, relatedness, and growth in a flexible hierarchical order.

esteem needs Needs for attention, respect, recognition, and status.

expectancy Perceived probability that if individuals put forth the effort, they will perform successfully.

Expectancy Theory Theory that people make decisions about behavior based on the value of the rewards, the linkage of the rewards to the behavior, and the odds that they can accomplish the behavior.

experienced meaningfulness of the work Degree of satisfaction in the work itself.

experienced responsibility for outcomes of the work Responsibility associated with the amount of autonomy.

extinction Removal of all reinforcements following an undesirable behavior.

feedback Extent to which the worker learns about the outcomes of his or her performance.

Herzberg's Two-Factor Theory Theory that the variables determining motivation and satisfaction on the job are different from the variables causing dissatisfaction and a lack of motivation.

instrumentality Perceived linkage between the reward and the work behavior.

Job Characteristics model Job design theory based on core job dimensions, employees' critical psychological states, and their work behavior.

job enlargement Broadening of a job's scope by adding more tasks to it.

job enrichment Adding some managerial decision-making authority and Herzberg's motivators to the job.

job rotation Moving employees from one job to another.

job simplification   Attempt to reduce the number of different tasks an individual performs in the job.

knowledge of the actual results of work activities   Knowledge acquired through feedback.

law of effect   Concept that people tend to repeat behavior that is rewarded and not repeat behavior that is not rewarded.

Maslow's Hierarchy of Needs Theory   Theory that people are motivated by five groups of needs and that these needs exist in a hierarchical order.

motivation   Amount of energy and the direction of energy displayed by an individual.

need for Achievement (n Ach)   Striving to accomplish difficult but feasible goals and later receiving feedback about personal performance.

need for affiliation (n Aff)   Behavior aimed at establishing and maintaining friendly relationships with others.

need for power (n Pow)   Influencing the activities or thoughts of a number of others.

negative reinforcement   Removal of an unpleasant consequence following a desired behavior.

operant conditioning   Concept that individuals learn through past positive or negative consequences how to gain rewards or avoid punishments in the future.

Organizational Behavior Modification (OB Mod)   Deliberate attempt to change human behavior in work organizations through the application of operant conditioning.

Path-Goal Theory of Leadership   Theory that stresses the leader's role in clarifying for subordinates how they can achieve desired rewards through job performance.

physiological needs   Basic human physical needs.

positive reinforcement   Application of positive consequences (rewards) following a desired behavior.

Process Theories of Motivation   Theories that focus on how people choose certain behaviors to satisfy their needs and how they judge their satisfaction.

punishment   Application of negative or unpleasant consequences following an undesirable behavior.

Reinforcement Theory   Theory that focuses on the relationship between behavior and its consequences.

security needs   Needs for safety and security in both physical and economic terms.

self-actualization needs   Needs for self-fulfillment and maximization of potential.

skill variety   Number of activities in a job and the number of skills used in the performance of the job.

Socially Acquired Needs Theory   Theory relating to the three needs of need for achievement, need for affiliation, and need for power.

task identity   Extent to which the worker performs the total job with a definable beginning and a definable end.

task significance   Extent to which the worker perceives that the job has importance and impact on the company or its customers.

valence   Value or attractiveness of a specific reward.

ENDNOTES

1. R. Steers and L. Porter, *Motivation and Work Behavior*, 5th ed., New York: McGraw-Hill (1991).
2. W. E. Deming, *Out of the Crisis*, Cambridge, MA: MIT Institute for Advanced Engineering Study (1986): 315.
3. G. Dobbins, R. Cardy, and K. Carson, "Examining Fundamental Assumptions: A Contrast of Person and System Approaches to Human Resource Management," *Research in Personnel and Human Resources Management* (1991): 1–38.
4. A. Maslow, *Motivation and Personality*, New York: Harper & Row (1954).
5. D. Hall and K. Nougaim, "An Examination of Maslow's Need Hierarchy in an Organizational Setting," *Organizational Behavior and Human Performance*, 3, no. 1 (1968): 12–35.
6. C. Alderfer, *Existence, Relatedness, Growth: Human Needs in Organizational Settings*, New York: Free Press (1972).
7. F. Herzberg, "One More Time: How Do You Motivate Employees?" *Harvard Business Review* (January-February 1987): 109–120.

8. D. McClelland, *The Achieving Society*, New York: Van Nostrand (1961); D. McClelland, *Power: The Inner Experience*, New York: Irvington (1975); D. McClelland and R. E. Boyatzis, "Leadership Motive Pattern and Long-Term Success in Management," *Journal of Applied Psychology*, 67 (1982): 737–743.

9. M. Stahl, *Managerial and Technical Motivation: Assessing Needs for Achievement, Power and Affiliation*, New York: Praeger (1986): 131.

10. Ibid., 121–124.

11. J. Adams, "Toward an Understanding of Inequity," *Journal of Abnormal and Social Psychology*, 67, no. 5 (1963): 422–436.

12. V. Vroom, *Work and Motivation*, New York: Wiley (1964): 17.

13. M. Stahl and A. Harrell, "Modeling Effort Decisions with Behavioral Decision Theory: Toward an Individual Differences Version of Expectancy Theory," *Organizational Behavior and Human Performance,* 27 (1981): 303–325.

14. R. J. House, "A Path-Goal Theory of Leader Effectiveness," *Administrative Science Quarterly* (September 1971): 321–328.

15. B. F. Skinner, *Beyond Freedom and Dignity*, New York: Knopf (1971).

16 E. Thorndike, *Animal Intelligence*, New York: Macmillan (1911).

17. B. F. Skinner, *Science and Human Behavior*, New York: Macmillan (1953); B. F. Skinner, *About Behaviorism*, New York: Vintage Books (1974).

18. L. Miller, *Behavior Management: The New Science of Managing People at Work*, New York: Wiley (1978).

19. V. Dingus, "The Strategy for Achieving Quality of Management," presentation at Eastman Chemical/University of Tennessee Continuous Improvement Workshop, August 10, 1993.

20. F. W. Taylor, *Scientific Management*, New York: Harper (1911).

21. "Team Spirit: A Decisive Response to Crisis Brought Ford Enhanced Productivity," *The Wall Street Journal* (December, 15, 1992): A1.

22. J. Hackman and G. Oldham, *Work Redesign*, Reading, MA: Addison-Wesley (1980).

13

CHAPTER

Communication

NUMMI

As a joint venture between Toyota Motor Corporation and General Motors Corporation, NUMMI showed that people from two different international cultures can communicate and work together based upon mutual trust. (Photo credit: New United Motor Manufacturing.)

NUMMI stands for New United Motor Manufacturing Inc., a 50-50 joint venture between Toyota Motor Corporation and General Motors Corporation, which are, respectively, the third largest and the largest companies in the world. NUMMI, which began production in late 1984, assembles smaller-size cars designed by Toyota. It is located in Fremont, California, and employs about 2,500 people. The plant receives components and parts from Toyota plants and suppliers in Japan and from suppliers in the United States. The cars it assembles are sold to marketing organizations belonging to both parent companies.

NUMMI was conceived during the early 1980s, an admittedly tumultuous time for the automobile industry in America. High energy prices and changing consumer preferences had resulted in an expanding demand for smaller, high-quality, more fuel-efficient cars. Japanese automobile producers, Toyota among them, were operating under a program of Japanese export quotas on cars shipped to the United States, a program intended (1) to give U.S.-based producers "breathing time" to adjust their production to meet market needs and federal standards on increased fuel efficiency, and (2) to encourage Japanese automakers to establish production plants in the United States.

One could speculate at length about the factors that motivated Toyota and GM to join together to form NUMMI. At the time, however, articles in the press focused on two important considerations.

Toyota found the idea of producing in the United States attractive for short-term reasons, such as the quota, and for long-term reasons, such as its own business philosophy and the global competitive environment facing the auto industry. At the same time, it was interested in lowering the risks associated with beginning U.S. production by bringing in a partner knowledgeable about U.S. marketing and labor–management practices and by learning how to manage successfully in the United States. GM, on the other hand, was comparatively inexperienced in small-car production and in the shop-floor, worker–management, and vendor–supplier relationships that were needed to make such production cost competitive. It saw the joint venture with Toyota as an opportunity to participate, in a substantial way, with one of the world's foremost cost-competitive producers of

continued

high-quality small cars—and to learn from the experience and transfer what it learned to other GM operations. From this perspective, GM's participation in NUMMI would serve to enhance GM's potential for future success in small-car production.

Thus there were sound business reasons for creating NUMMI. Lowering the risks associated with possible future financial and operating commitments of impressive magnitudes motivated both Toyota and GM to come together in NUMMI.

But NUMMI involved other risks—risks that were intrinsic to its very nature. Could Toyota's Japan-based management system be implemented successfully in the United States? NUMMI would be breaking new ground and creating a distinctive, hybrid corporate culture reflecting both Japanese and American culturally based traits and culturally influenced institutions. At the beginning, neither GM nor Toyota was really sure that an experiment like NUMMI could succeed.

Communication processes are spread throughout organizational life. People are constantly transmitting information, and hopefully meaning, to others. The importance of good communication increases as organizations become more diverse. As organizations become international in their scope of operations and in their personnel, clear communications become critical. The NUMMI case indicates the importance of good communication across people of different nationalities and different experiences. The case also shows the importance of lateral communication processes in an organization using cross-functional teams.

THE COMMUNICATION PROCESS

Communication is the process by which information is shared and understood by two or more persons. To appreciate this definition, we must understand that **data** are symbols or characters without meaning or value and **information** consists of data with meaning or value. A string of numbers represents data, but if the data are arranged to represent sales by month, for each type of automobile, by dealer, then the numbers are information. Communication is concerned with the process of sharing and understanding the information.

A Model of One-Way Interpersonal Communication

There are numerous ways to share information. One way is simply to transmit it. However, the mere act of transmission does little to ensure that the information has been understood. Without the understanding there is, by definition, no communication.

Figure 13.1 is a representation of one-way interpersonal communication. The prime characteristic of one-way communication is that there is no feedback from the receiver to the sender. Without the feedback the sender is not sure that the information has even been received. Nor is the sender sure that the information has been understood with the intended meaning.

FIGURE 13.1 *One-Way Communication Model*

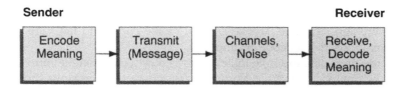

A tragic example of what can happen when the sender is not sure that the information has been received and understood is contained in the *Exxon Valdez* oil spill disaster in Alaska. Some have argued that the entire disaster could have been avoided if Mr. Cousins, the acting captain of the ship, had verified that the order he issued to turn the *Exxon Valdez* right had been received and understood.

A Model of Two-Way Interpersonal Communication

Figure 13.2 is a model of the two-way communication process. The most important difference between Figures 13.1 and 13.2 is the feedback loop in Figure 13.2. Feedback is meant to verify the receipt and understanding of the information by the receiver of the meaning sent by the sender. Let us examine each step in the two-way communication process.

The Sender   The **sender** (or **source**) is the person or group who wishes to transmit meaning to another person or another group. The sender is not interested in the words, data, or symbols themselves, but uses them only as conveyers of meaning when arranged and transmitted in certain ways. For example, if a firm decides to initiate a major Total Quality strategy, the executives will attempt to communicate that fact to all managers and employees. The executives must decide how to communicate the meaning of the TQ strategy to the firm, its employees, and customers.

FIGURE 13.2 *Two-Way Communication Model*

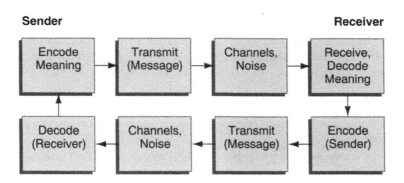

Encoding Once the sender has decided on the meaning to be communicated, the message must be encoded. **Encoding** is putting the meaning of the message into appropriate symbols for transmission. Words are the most frequently used symbols. However, sign language, smoke signals, Morse code, and flags are other symbols that may be used to encode meaning.

In the preceding example the executives must decide on the form of the message about the firm and TQ. What words or even physical expressions should be used to communicate the importance of the firm's decision to launch the TQ strategy?

Selecting a Medium After encoding the message, the executives must decide what channel of communication should be used to transmit the message. **Channels** are mediums of communication. Should the executives send a memo, use electronic mail, design a videotape, arrange for "town hall" meetings with employees, or hold training sessions?

Channels contain **noise**, which is any disturbance or interference that reduces the clarity of the communication. To overcome noise in the channel, most good communicators will use several channels, including written, electronic, and physical channels. Few things speak as loudly as the leader's physical actions relating to the importance of a message.

Transmitting To **transmit** means to send across. Literally, the sender is sending a message across the channel to the receiver.

The Receiver The **receiver** is the person or group who perceives the sender's message. By definition, if there is no receiver, there is no communication.

Decoding Decoding is the complement of encoding. **Decoding** is the process of the receiver's translating the symbols in the message into the meaning of the message. Managers sometimes send confusing messages. If, for example, a major new quality initiative is explained with constant reference to increased productivity and cost reduction, then many may perceive that increased customer satisfaction and customer retention are of lesser importance.

Feedback **Feedback** is the reversal of the communication process in which the receiver expresses a reaction to the sender's message. The existence of feedback differentiates between one-way and two-way communication processes.

For information to be understood by both parties in any communication process, there must be honesty in the exchange. This is especially true in sales, as is shown in the following ethics exhibit.

CRITICAL THINKING QUESTIONS

1. What is the most important difference between one-way and two-way communication processes?
2. Why are communication processes especially important in a firm making a transition to Total Quality?

E T H I C S   E X H I B I T

Bait and Switch

A computer store was having a sale on a limited number of computer systems. A person who bought one of the systems was so pleased with the purchase that he convinced a friend to buy one too. The friend called the store, described the system in detail to a salesman, and asked whether she could obtain a system identical to her friend's system. The salesman said yes, so the woman agreed to come to the store.

When the woman arrived at the store, she found that the salesman had configured a system with a different monitor. When she asked about this difference, the salesman told her it was "functionally equivalent" to her friend's monitor. The only difference was that her friend's monitor had some switches that allowed the monitor characteristics to be changed, whereas the monitor in her system relied on software signals to switch characteristics. Otherwise, the monitors were equivalent and had the same cost.

Discussion Questions

1. Was the salesman's response during the telephone conversation ethical? Why or why not?
2. "Bait and switch" is a sales practice in which the customer is attracted to a specific promised item and later switched to another, less attractive item for sale. Discuss the ethics of such a sales practice. Analyze the "bait and switch" practice using the two-way communication model.

Source: R. Dejoie, G. Fowler, D. Paradice, *Ethical Issues in Information Systems*, Boston: Boyd & Fraser (1991): 223.

PROBLEMS AND BARRIERS

Some issues often present barriers to communication. The manager needs to be aware of these barriers in order to overcome them.

Perception

Perception is the interpretation of a message by a receiver. Different receivers can perceive or interpret the same message in different ways. Two of the biggest sources of perceptual differences are differences in education and experience between the sender and the receiver.

Managers typically have higher levels of formal education and broader experience levels than nonmanagers. These differences can be the source of perceptual differences and communication problems between managers and nonmanagers. Therefore it is the manager's responsibility to ensure that the attempted communication fits the educational and experience levels of the receivers. One of the most important steps that senders could take to ensure effective communication is to use symbols that they know will be perceived by the receivers in the intended way.

Noise

As we discussed, noise is any disturbance or interference that reduces the clarity of the communication. An example of noise is a manager trying to talk to a subordi-

Back to the NUMMI Case

The joint-venture agreement between GM and Toyota gave Toyota the responsibility for operating the Fremont, California, plant and established an eight-person board of directors consisting of four Toyota representatives and four GM representatives. Although the board is the ultimate decision-making body, it cannot by itself change the joint-venture contract. Toyota runs the plant, and this situation can be changed only if both Toyota and GM agree.

In implementing its responsibility for running the plant, Toyota has drawn on its experience with its production system in its Japanese plants, an experience that reflects substantial and compelling Toyota-specific and "Japanese" influences and characteristics. Those influences and characteristics determine the entire NUMMI system, a system that differs noticeably from that found in "traditional" U.S. automobile plants.

As the automobile assembly line at NUMMI moves along, teams of employees work together on the car, installing, for example, the battery and battery cables or certain dashboard components. Each team is responsible for its increment of work on each car. Quite importantly, each team is also responsible for assigning specific tasks among its members, and these assignments may rotate hourly, daily, weekly, or whatever—as the team may wish. Each team sets its own tasks sequence and is responsible for the quality of its work.

If a team is having difficulty with the number of tasks it has to complete during the time it has the car, the allocation of tasks within the team or among teams may be changed. The key is to have each team working productively on each car during the time allotted.

The members of each NUMMI team generally get together about 10 to 15 minutes before starting time to exercise as a group and to socialize. These activities take place at a "team room," which is right on the shop floor. The team room also serves as a meeting place when work-related issues need attention. Each team uses a structured, systematic technique for identifying and resolving any scheduling and quality problems that it may face.

As expected, training is important and varied at NUMMI. Workers must be able to do all the jobs within their team's jurisdiction. They are also encouraged to work occasionally on other teams and to learn the jobs of those teams too. There is only one pay grade, or job classification, for production workers at NUMMI. All production workers are paid the same wage after 18 months of service. There are also three higher pay classifications—one for maintenance technicians, the others for tool and die, and tool and die tryout personnel.

NUMMI utilizes the "just-in-time" inventory system that Toyota developed in Japan. All components, parts, and subassemblies flow together in a continuous process paced by the main assembly line. Suppliers deliver their products to the NUMMI plant on a nearly continuous basis—in some cases every few hours or so. There is minimal receiving inventory and little receiving testing or inspection of supplier-provided parts.

NUMMI works with qualified suppliers on a long-term basis. The team approach is again key here. Suppliers work on the design and quality of their products, with substantial assistance from NUMMI when required. Purchase relationships are of indefinite duration. Suppliers know what is expected of them in terms of product schedule and quality. They also know that NUMMI will help them solve problems.

nate while the subordinate is trying to save a computer file. Similarly, a manager talking on the phone in a busy office may not hear the secretary's message. To overcome noise in the channel, most good communicators will use several channels, including written, electronic, and physical channels.

Language

A difference in language is an obvious barrier to communication. Even if there is a competent translation of the words from one language to another, the meaning frequently does not come through as intended. Most people who have ever spoken through a translator understand the frustration of sensing that the meaning has not been transmitted. To lessen or preclude such problems, many firms are requiring competency in a foreign language as a prerequisite for employment. Even if they have no overseas operations, many firms in California, Florida, Texas, and other southwestern states require competency in Spanish among their employees.

As more firms extend operations to foreign countries, the language issue is becoming widespread. Capsugel, a division of the pharmaceutical firm Warner-Lambert, has learned to use the language of quality to transcend the international language barrier. The language of statistical process control (see Chapter 15) provides a means of communication among individuals who speak different languages. This improved communication has increased the amount of information transferred among individuals from different parts of the world who speak different languages. Capsugel has plants in the United States, Belgium, France, Great Britain, Italy, Japan, and the People's Republic of China.[1]

By having different meanings attached to the same word, a language itself can be confusing. The 500 most common English words have an average of 28 definitions each.[2] Some of the different definitions of the word *run* are apparent in the following sentences. Mickey Mantle scored a *run*. She has a *run* in her hose. He was hired to *run* the marketing division. A *run* on some banks was associated with the start of the Great Depression. Since her father owns the business, she has complete *run* of the place. Did Mr. Cousins *run* the *Exxon Valdez* aground? Will Ross Perot *run* for president again? What story do you want to *run* in the company newsletter? Please have the clerk *run* those papers over in time for the afternoon mail *run*. Given the multiple definitions, the sender must use the word in the context that will be understood by the receivers for the intended meaning.

Information Overload

Information overload means that the processing information ability of senders and receivers has been exceeded. Some refer to information overload as bounded rationality. There is a limit to the amount of information that the sender can encode and the amount that the receiver can decode. In an article aptly titled "The Magical Number Seven, Plus or Minus Two," the author showed that many people can consistently deal with only five to nine pieces of information.[3] The number decreases if the sender or the receiver is under stress or is distracted by noise.

Information overload can be an issue when a firm launches a Total Quality strategy. For the TQ initiative to be successful, nearly all employees and managers need to be trained. The language of TQM relating to new tools, skills, concepts, organizations, and the like can be confusing. Management needs to keep the training program understandable. Employees and managers must be able to speak the new language so they can effectively communicate on new ways of doing business and delivering value to customers.

In the following diversity exhibit, communication on the core issue of comparable pay across genders declined dramatically when an illegal strike was called. The stress of dealing with the strike, and its question of illegality, prevented some of the managers from communicating on the basic issue of comparable pay. The communication process broke down because of the stress, the noise, and the information overload.

CRITICAL THINKING QUESTIONS

1. How are the sender, encoding, noise, perception, and feedback related in a communication process?

2. How can information overload occur when a firm initiates a TQ strategy?

IMPROVING INTERPERSONAL COMMUNICATION

Interpersonal communication is a critically important and all-pervasive process in organizations. Such an important process needs to be worked at continually for clarity and improvement. Areas for improvement include recognizing noise in face-to-face communication, active listening, choice of communication channels, and nonverbal communication.

Overcoming Noise in Face-to-Face Communication

One of the greatest barriers in face-to-face communication is noise in the channel. The sender should attempt to minimize the noise or the interference with the message.

A manager who tries to communicate with a secretary while the secretary is on hold on the telephone is competing for only part of the secretary's attention. Similarly, a manager who tries to communicate with a secretary while the secretary is working on a word processor can hold only part of the secretary's attention due to the interference of the word processor. In general, managers (senders) should attempt to communicate only when they have the undivided attention of the receivers. Otherwise, they are competing with noise, and the outcome of the communication attempt is unpredictable.

Active Listening

In the outdated command-and-control organizational model, it was assumed that expertise resided in the vertical hierarchy. Thus managers issued directives and employees implemented those directives. In today's Total Quality organizations, with their flatter organizational structures and cross-functional teams, expertise is found throughout the organization. Communication can occur in a number of directions,

D I V E R S I T Y   E X H I B I T

Comparable Pay in San Jose

On Sunday, July 5, 1981, the city employees of San Jose, California, went on strike. The strike was unusual: For the first time in U.S. labor history, workers were striking over the issue of equal pay for "comparable" work. Striking city employees agreed that men and women always received equal pay when they held the same job. But, they said, jobs that women traditionally filled paid less than those that men traditionally filled. These "disparities," city workers held, were discriminatory and had to end. The strike was unusual for a second reason: It was illegal. Civil Service regulations stipulate that city workers do not have the right to strike.

The strike arose out of a study commissioned by the San Jose city council in 1979, which was designed to find whether women were paid less than men for nonmanagement city jobs. The city council, which had been pressured to do the study by the City Worker's Union (the American Federation of State, County and Municipal Employees—AFSCME), asked Hay Associates, a consulting firm, to prepare the study.

Hay Associates began its study by sending a questionnaire to all city employees. The questionnaire asked each one to describe the tasks, problems, requirements, responsibilities, and working conditions involved in his or her job. The Hay consultants then had the city's personnel department review these questionnaires and conduct on-the-job interviews with about 20 percent of the employees. On the basis of these questionnaires and interviews, the personnel department wrote new job descriptions for each city job, indicating its duties, requirements, responsibilities, and working conditions.

Hay Associates then convened a committee of ten city employees and asked them to rate the new job descriptions of 225 nonmanagement city government jobs, using Hay's widely respected rating system and guided by Hay consultants. The committee was comprised of workers familiar with many job classifications and included four union members and one management representative. The committee met with the Hay consultants two or three times a week for five months to review the new job descriptions and assign points

to each job in each of four categories: know-how, problem solving, accountability, and working conditions. The discussions of the committee were often heated, since a final judgment could not be made until seven of the ten members reached agreement. Using tables provided by Hay Associates, the committee had to assign points to each job in each of the four categories.

The assignment of points used complicated criteria that took into account every aspect of the four categories. The Hay criteria, for example, took into account both the scope and depth of knowledge required by each job, including knowledge of practical procedures and techniques and skills gained through formal training and education or experience. Other categories measured human relations requirements for each job. Using these guides, the committee gave each job a numerical rating that constituted the "value" of the job and was intended to be a measure of the utility of the job relative to the needs of the organization and to other jobs in the organization.

Once the committee had assigned numerical ratings to each job, jobs with comparable values were grouped together into the same "job grade." Jobs dominated by women were paid less than jobs dominated by men, even when, as the numerical ratings assigned by the Hay committee suggested, those jobs involved equal or "comparable" requirements.

In order to develop a method of comparing salaries, the Hay consultant group used a complicated statistical formula to compute the average or "trend" salaries of jobs with the same numerical ranking. The formula took into account the relative value of each job to the city organization based on comparisons with other jobs and salaries of comparable numerical ranking. These averages were depicted as a "trend line" on a graph with average salaries on one axis and numerical rankings on the other axis. The "trend line" thus was supposed to indicate what a job would pay if salary were based solely on the value of the job as computed by the Hay study. The Hay study found that the salaries of most jobs dominated by women fell 2 percent to

continued

10 percent below this trend line (that is, below the computed average salary of jobs with the same numerical value), while jobs dominated by men were 8 percent to 15 percent above the trend line (above the computed average salary of jobs with the same numerical value).

Nine months and $100,000 later the committee finished its work and Hay Associates submitted a report of its results. A few months after that the city workers went on strike demanding that the salaries of all jobs filled predominantly by women should be raised to the levels of the Hay study trend line.

By Tuesday, July 7, 1981, striking city workers had shut down virtually all city construction projects and closed 13 of the city's 16 libraries. The hardest-hit city services were libraries, city garages, the city clerk's office, the auditors' office, and the finance office.

Earlier on the afternoon of July 8, the city council had instructed City Manager Francis Fox to send a letter to all striking workers warning them that the work stoppage was "an illegal strike" according to civil service ordinances, which stated that "failure to report for duty. . .within 48 hours. . .may be deemed to constitute resignation from the Service and the position may be declared vacant. If you fail to return, you will be considered as having resigned."

City Manager Fox and union negotiator Frank LeSueur met over the next few days to consider a compromise. By the weekend they had reached a tentative agreement, subject to the approval of the city council, that would provide $3.2 million over four years to bring all jobs up to the Hay trend line. On Sunday, July 12, the city council met to consider the tentative settlement worked out by Fox and LeSueur. The council unanimously voted to reject it. When its vote was announced outside the council chambers, a bitter crowd of union members and union officials broke open the closed doors of the chambers and charged into the meeting room, loudly denouncing the council's vote as "unbelievable arrogance and carelessness." Angered, Fox promised that he would push forward with his plan to fire all striking workers on Monday.

After the disturbance council members went back to work and developed two broad counterproposals. The first proposal, called "Plan A," promised general wage increases of 8.5 percent each year for the next two years but provided nothing for comparable pay adjustments; instead, under this plan, the council would promise to put the issue of comparable pay before city voters on the following November ballot. The second proposal, called "Plan B," offered general wage increases of 7.5 percent in 1981-1982 and 8 percent in 1982-1983 for the 2,000 workers represented by the union; also, this plan would set aside $1.4 million for comparable-pay adjustments for female-dominated jobs. Discussion of the proposals during the meeting was heated. Plan A was unanimously approved early in the discussions. But Plan B was strongly opposed by some. Both Francis Fox and Mayor Janet Hayes had earlier vowed not to go above a 6 percent wage increase, although both were strongly in favor of some comparable-pay adjustments. Other council members were unequivocally opposed to any comparable-pay adjustment. Eventually, however, Plan B also received the required six votes.

On Monday morning at 11 a.m., both general proposals were presented to the union at a secret meeting at a hotel near the airport. Under Plan B female-dominated jobs would increase at a faster rate than male-dominated jobs: female-dominated jobs would receive the general 7.5 percent wage increase plus an additional percentage increase designed to bring these jobs closer to the Hay trend line, while male-dominated jobs would receive only the general 7.5 percent wage increase. Librarians (a female-dominated category), for example, would receive a 7.5 wage increase plus another 7.5 percent comparable-pay adjustment increase. Typist clerks (the largest female-dominated category) would receive a 3.5 percent comparable-pay adjustment in addition to the 7.5 percent general wage increase.

On Monday night the city council met once again to make a final decision on Plan B. Several council members still objected to the plan and insisted that the city manager should follow through with his promise to fire striking workers. The majority of the council, however, were in favor of the plan and voted to adopt it as their official offer by a vote of 8 to 3. The next day union members met and voted 295 to 27 to accept the city council's offer of Plan B.

Source: "Comparable Pay in San Jose" in *Business Ethics: Concepts and Cases,* 2/e, M. G. Velasquez ed., © 1968, pp. 344–352. Reprinted by permission of Prentice-Hall, Inc., Englewood Cliffs, NJ.

including from the bottom up. Therefore listening by managers is critically important in today's organizations.[4] **Listening** means receiving messages in a thoughtful manner that leads to an understanding of the meaning in the messages. Listening is a recognition that the receiver has responsibility in the communication process.

Many people do not listen well. They prejudge the message or the sender and formulate their response to the sender while the sender is still transmitting. Effective listening requires at least two behaviors on the part of the listener. First, the listener must engage in active listening, not passive tolerance of the sender. Active listening means becoming involved in the communication process by asking questions and paraphrasing what the sender has said. Second, the listener must not prejudge the sender or the message. Receivers who start to formulate a response, even while the sender is speaking, are poor listeners. As communication processes become more dispersed in organizations, the importance of managerial listening will grow and become a critical managerial skill.

Choice of Communication Channels

The choice of communication channel has much to do with the effectiveness of the communication attempt. Placing a complex, nonroutine message in the company newsletter is not a good choice of communication channel for such a message. To ensure effective interpersonal communication, there should be a match between the richness of the communication channel and the complexity or routineness of the message. **Channel richness**, or **channel information capacity**, is the amount of information that can be transmitted and understood in a communication attempt. Face-to-face meetings are channel-rich encounters in which much original and complex information can be communicated and in which active listening and feedback ensure the transmission of meaning. In contrast, routine bulletins posted on bulletin boards or sent through electronic bulletin boards are lean communication channels appropriate for simple, routine messages.

Figure 13.3 illustrates the interrelationship of channel richness, message complexity, and choice of communication medium. The figure indicates that the more complex messages require more channel-rich mediums like face-to-face meetings, whereas simple messages can be transmitted with channel-lean media like routine bulletins or newsletters. Although video or teleconferencing approaches the richness of face-to-face meetings, these methods make it difficult to assess the nonverbal aspect of communication.

The potential for communication problems is compounded across different cultures. As shown in the following international exhibit, in its foreign locations McDonald's lessens this potential by hiring local talent.

Nonverbal Communication

Nonverbal communication is the process by which information is shared and understood by two or more persons using actions and behaviors rather than words.[5] Body language, seating arrangements, and attire can all be powerful behavioral cues in the communication process.

FIGURE 13.3 *Message Complexity and Channel Richness*

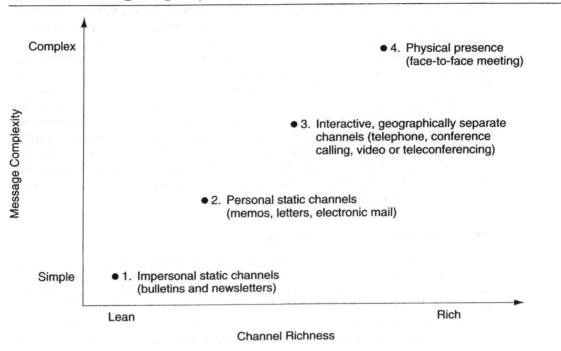

If the receiver has his or her arms folded and a stern facial expression, then the sender may correctly perceive resistance to the message on the part of the receiver. If the sender stays seated behind a formidable desk, thereby separated from the receiver as opposed to walking around the desk to be with the receiver, then the receiver may perceive a formal, commanding tone in the message. If the sender is attired casually, then the receiver may perceive a certain degree of informality in the communication, as opposed to the formality of a message emanating from a sender in a business suit and tie.

Nonverbal communication, if properly used, can powerfully reinforce the message intended in the verbal communication. Paying attention to nonverbal communication can be an important part of active listening.

CRITICAL THINKING QUESTIONS

1. How is nonverbal communication related to active listening?

2. What is the role of ethics in the communication process?

ORGANIZATIONAL COMMUNICATION

In today's Total Quality organizations, communication processes extend throughout the organization in a number of different ways. The formal and the informal, the

I·N·T·E·R·N·A·T·I·O·N·A·L   E·X·H·I·B·I·T

McDonald's: Adaptation through Local Ownership

Because of foreign ownership which hires local talent to help avoid cultural communication problems, McDonald's is one of few U.S. restaurant chains to operate successfully overseas. (Photo credit: Reuters/Bettman.)

McDonald's, by virtue of its U.S.-based franchising style of operation, was especially well suited for foreign adaptation when it expanded internationally. Its mode of operation in the United States had been to expand through selling franchises. There were two primary advantages to this: rigorous proven operating standards and controls, combined with the enthusiastic entrepreneurial leadership of its franchisees. When this method of expansion was exported overseas, it was found that a hidden benefit was the ability to adapt to local conditions. This has been referred to by

some management consultants as "tight-loose" management. Operating procedures are tight while allowing for individual creativity to adapt to unique circumstances. This has resulted in different marketing methods for different market conditions and, in some cases, menu modifications. For example, a berry-based soft drink is offered in Brazil, while a local fruit-based shake is offered in Malaysia, Singapore, and Thailand. Also, in Japan suburban locations, similar to those found in the United States, are shunned in favor of urban sites that consumers can reach without a car.

While McDonald's does have a limited number of wholly owned subsidiaries overseas, it has realized that staffing with locals and high levels of autonomy are necessary.

The results of this strategy of adaptation are impressive. Industry analysts have said that only McDonald's and Kentucky Fried Chicken are making acceptable profits on their foreign restaurants. Kentucky Fried Chicken, it should be noted, has a style of operation and cultural adaptation similar to that of McDonald's. While this means of foreign-market entry is certainly not suitable for many firms, it does emphasize the necessity of focusing specific attention on the issue of foreign cultural adaptation.

Source: R. C. Maddox, *Cross-Cultural Problems in International Business,* Quorum Books (1993): 43–44. Reprinted with permission of Greenwood Publishing Group, Inc., Westport, CT. Copyright © 1993 Greenwood Publishing Group.

vertical and the horizontal must all be used in concert by the effective communicator in a multipronged communication network throughout the organization.

Formal Communication

Formal communication is communication that flows along the lines of the organization prescribed by management. Years ago in a hierarchical organization, this had meant top-down communication. In many TQ organizations today, this means top-down, and bottom-up, and horizontal communication, all in accord with designated cross-functional systems and processes.

Formal communication flows horizontally in a hospital, for example, following a patient as the patient moves across departments from chemotherapy, to diet and nutrition, to physical therapy. Such horizontal communication is as legitimate as communication within the physical therapy department. Similarly, formal communication flows laterally in the Chrysler Design Center, which includes design, manufacturing, and marketing in the development of a new car. Such horizontal communication is as valid as communication within the design department.

For formal communication to be effective in an organization, managers and employees must believe the messages. As demonstrated in the following quality exhibit, honesty in communications figures prominently in the principles at Chick-fil-A, a large Atlanta-based restaurant chain.

Informal Communication

Informal communication is communication that flows in the organization independent of the structure prescribed by management. Nearly every organization has an informal communication network, sometimes known as a grapevine, independent of the formal structure and formal communication channels. Cafeterias, mail rooms, break rooms, wellness clubs, and other places where employees gather are places where informal communication networks are found. Wise managers not only are aware of such communication networks, but they also use them as part of the communication process.

Vertical Communication

Vertical communication is communication that flows upward or downward in the organization. Many managers are good at issuing communications to lower levels in the organization and thus have come to regard vertical communication primarily as top-down communication. However, effective managers also recognize the importance of upward communication and will reinforce bottom-up communication. Such upward communication is a recognition of feedback and the value of a two-way communication process. Sometimes upward communication is not pleasant for managers because it may reveal that all is not well in the organization. Nonetheless, the manager committed to continuous improvement recognizes that feedback from lower organizational levels is needed to recognize problems as a prelude to system improvement. Managers who do not encourage upward communication are akin to the ostrich with its head stuck in the sand.

Lateral Communication

Lateral communication flows horizontally within the organization. As Total Quality has spread throughout organizations, the use of cross-functional teams to design and improve systemwide horizontal processes has exploded. Because much work is done horizontally, much communication flows horizontally. For example, new-product design and development teams at Xerox that include members from most functional areas are rich in horizontal communication processes. Not only is there lateral com-

Q U A L I T Y   E X H I B I T

Principles at Chick-fil-A

We are people who have strong beliefs about how business should be conducted. We gladly state these beliefs. . .not with any claim of perfection. . .but as principles toward which we continually strive.

Customers First:

Our customers are the focus of everything we do. We do whatever it takes to satisfy their needs. When it comes to serving customers, we are flexible. . .both as individuals and as an organization.

Working Together:

Teamwork is essential to meeting the needs of our customers. Our operators, team members and staff work together as an independent team to achieve success.

Continuous Improvement:

Continuous improvement and innovation lead to success. Whether the innovation is in products—

the original boneless breast of chicken sandwich— or in services—our original mall restaurants—we are dedicated to continuous improvement.

Personal Excellence:

We strive for excellence in all that we do. Our behavior must be honest, upright and sincere. Personal excellence means doing what you say you will do, when you say you will do it, as you say it will be done. . .doing things right the first time every time.

Stewardship:

We strive to be good stewards of all that is entrusted to us. . .our time, talents, treasures, and natural resources. We believe the best decisions are made with a long-term perspective.

Source: Chick-fil-A, Atlanta, GA (1993).

munication within the teams, but there is also lateral communication with the functional home offices in production, marketing, finance, and the like. In such a fashion, a large part of the organization is kept abreast of the development of the new products.

Communication Networks

The effective communicator combines formal and informal communication processes together with vertical and horizontal communication processes. All the communication processes are used in concert in a multipronged communication network throughout the organization. By crisscrossing the entire organization in a number of ways, effective communication is reinforced. As shown in the following conclusion to the NUMMI case, by using both vertical communication processes and horizontal processes through teams, managers span the organization with a communication network.

CRITICAL THINKING QUESTIONS

1. What are the roles of formal and informal communication in a communication network?

2. How can a manager strengthen informal communication flows?

QUALITY CASE

Conclusion to the NUMMI Case

Ringi is the Japanese participatory approach to decision making. Communication with the objective of understanding is a hallmark of *Ringi*. This approach underlies NUMMI's team system. A corollary of the Japanese participatory approach is that problems are identified and solved at the bottom levels in the hierarchy—which possesses a detailed knowledge of whatever the situation demands. Management does not impose solutions; workers don't pass problems up.

Kaizen is the Japanese concept of continuous improvement. The plant is a "living" institution. It is constantly learning and changing. Work teams focus on how to improve what they are doing. Job rotation and cross-training, which give workers a more complete perspective on the production process, are relevant.

The concept of "purity of intent" is rooted in Japanese culture. Individuals are seen as being meant to think for themselves and to take action—sometimes significant action, if that is felt to be needed. For example, any NUMMI worker can stop the assembly line if he or she believes this is necessary for safety, quality, or other important purposes. And management would recognize the action as acceptable even if it turned out to be the wrong thing to do, since the worker's intent was correct. From the management perspective, however, the support of management and the other team members ensures that the action would never turn out to be the wrong thing to do.

Before assessing NUMMI's performance, it is important to note that there are really four partners in this joint venture—not just Toyota and GM. The United Auto Workers (UAW) and the employees themselves are also very important partners. The UAW has been especially accommodative in developing "new" ways of doing things. For example, it has accepted wage systems and pay classifications that depart significantly from the traditional ones. The work environment

continued

COMMUNICATION AND TOTAL QUALITY

In many organizations Total Quality is a change from traditional ways of doing business with an internal and profit focus. Focusing on the customer requires new ways of operating and behaving. The leadership pointing to a new vision of the future requires extensive and multidimensional communication of that vision to all concerned. Managers, employees, and suppliers must understand the importance of TQ to the organization before they can commit themselves to such a vision.

The Importance of Communication in Total Quality Management

TQM is an abbreviation for Total Quality Management. However, when executives and employees are out of sync, some refer to TQM as Total Quality Mayhem. This caused the authors of a book on quality to remark: "Until consensus is reached between executives and employees about how to go about achieving quality, there will be a great deal of wasted effort—or no effort at all."[6]

at NUMMI is much less adversarial than when the same plant was run by General Motors (and eventually shut down). The evidence is solid on this: At any given time five or six grievances (that is, workers' complaints against management that allege a violation of the labor agreement) are usually outstanding at NUMMI. Yet a few years back the outstanding grievances typically totaled at least 1,000. Absenteeism at NUMMI is about 5 percent to 6 percent, versus 20 percent or more in the earlier operation. Interestingly, about 80 percent of the workers now covered by the labor agreement at NUMMI also worked at the plant under the prior operator.

How has NUMMI been doing? Quite well, apparently, in terms of its union–management relations and in terms of its employee relations. Moreover, the Toyota production system and methods of workforce organization have been implemented at NUMMI and are operating well.

Compared to Toyota plants in Japan, NUMMI is also doing quite well. Product quality at NUMMI is as high as that at Toyota's plants in Japan. Worker efficiency is close to that of Toyota's plants in Japan and higher than was originally expected.

Because employee turnover rates are higher in California than in Japan and because NUMMI's workforce has less experience with the Toyota system than has Toyota's workforce in Japan, management feels that worker efficiency at NUMMI is about as high as possible.

DISCUSSION QUESTIONS

1. How are the number of filed grievances a reflection of the quality of communication between labor and management?

2. Describe the major cultural differences between the traditional U.S. managerial system that had been practiced in a unionized plant and Toyota's management approach practiced at NUMMI.

3. Compare and contrast the Japanese concept of "purity of intent" with the traditional adversarial relationship between labor and management in many U.S. plants. How do these two concepts affect communications?

Source: This was written by Professor Duane Kujawa. It appeared with permission from New United Motor Manufacturing, Inc. in R. Grosse and D. Kujawa, *International Business*, (2nd ed.) Richard D. Irwin, © 1992, and is herewith reprinted with permission.

Communications are important in all organizations, but they are especially important in TQ organizations because of the importance of horizontal processes involving people of varied organizational allegiances. For example, people in marketing may have the same allegiance and speak the same language and use similar assumptions. Personnel in production may have their own set of assumptions, allegiances, and technical jargon. In a TQ organization with cross-functional teams, communication is extremely important in helping personnel deal across these different sets of jargon, assumptions, and allegiances.

One TQ study has offered the Ten Commandments of Continuous Improvement, which includes a commandment on communication. It urges managers to discuss the undiscussibles.[7] In some corporate cultures that have had a history of success breeding arrogance, it is near-heresy to admit that quality needs to be improved. It would be unspeakable to admit that the firm needs an enterprise-wide, indefinite commitment to redesigning horizontal processes and refocusing on the customer.[8] That is why some TQ efforts take years in the birthing. Like an alcoholic who must admit that he or she has a problem before recovery can begin, an organization in need of a commitment to the customer and quality must first admit that the organization needs to improve the quality of its products and services.

There is an openness in many TQ organizations to examine the data. And there is an idea that managers should manage by fact, not by edict. As some have said, "In God we trust; all others bring data."

Total Quality Communication Guidelines

Communication is so important to a TQ process that recent lessons from Baldrige winners included "Steps for Developing a Communication Strategy." These include stating quality objectives in the business plan in the same way that costs and schedules are included. The steps also include requiring each unit to prepare an annual communication plan in support of the organization's implementation plan.[9]

Some advise selecting a name for the firm's Total Quality effort.[10] It is interesting to observe how many organizations have followed this communication advice and selected a custom name for their corporate Total Quality effort. To name a few, Alcoa refers to its "Excellence Through Quality"; Allied Signal refers to its "Total Quality Leadership"; IBM refers to its "Market-Driven Quality"; Procter & Gamble refers to its "Total Quality"; and Xerox refers to its "Leadership Through Quality." Each firm must brand a title to fit its own unique history and culture.

CRITICAL THINKING QUESTIONS

1. Why is it important for each organization to devise its own language for its TQ processes?
2. Discuss the relative importance of vertical and lateral communication processes in TQ organizations.

SUMMARY

Communication is the process by which information is shared and understood by two or more persons. Understanding, not simply the transmittal of data without meaning, is the critical element.

One-way communication and two-way communication differ primarily because of a feedback loop from the receiver to the sender in the two-way model. The feedback helps the sender verify that the receiver has understood the meaning.

In order to transmit meaning over a medium or communication channel, the sender encodes the meaning into appropriate symbols. These symbols are usually words, although sign language, smoke signals, flags, and Morse code have also been used as symbols in the communication process.

Perception is the interpretation of the message by the receiver. Feedback helps the sender to know if the perceived meaning is the intended meaning. The more noise or interference there is in the communication channel, the less likely it is that the receiver has perceived the meaning intended by the sender.

Information overload means that there is too much information in the chosen channel at the time, thereby preventing understanding. Thus the sender should carefully match the richness or information capacity of the channel to the complexity of the message. Channel-rich exchanges like face-to-face meetings may be needed for complex, nonroutine messages. Alternatively, channel-lean exchanges like organization bulletins may be appropriate for simple, routine messages.

Active listening is an increasingly important managerial skill. In active listening the receiver accepts some of the responsibility for understanding the meaning of a message. Paying attention to nonverbal communication is a tool of active listening and increases the odds of effective interpersonal communication.

Organizational communication today takes many paths and forms. The effective communicator recognizes that both formal and informal communication processes can be used to increase the odds of effective communication. As many TQ organizations become flatter with more cross-functional teams, lateral communication processes grow in importance along with upward communication processes. The effective manager recognizes that downward vertical communication is only one form of communication.

Communication is especially important in organizations making a shift to a TQ strategy because of the change involved. Organizational members must be informed of the change, lest chaos result. To communicate the importance of the TQ strategy, it is important for executives to show by their nonverbal communication—that is, by their behavior—that they are committed to TQ. To communicate the link between the firm's culture and TQ, it is not unusual for an organization to invent a unique label to identify its own TQ efforts.

EXPERIENTIAL EXERCISES

Distortions in Verbal Communication

The class should be separated into teams of six to eight members. The exercise is divided into two separate cycles.

Cycle 1

Only the initial sender in each team silently reads the following message:

> The final exam will be given on Monday, unless the preceding Friday is a holiday, in which case the exam will be on the succeeding Wednesday. The exam will be in Room 440 of Building 313 at 2 p.m. and will cover the last half of the text and all the cases.

The initial sender then whispers the message to his or her neighbor, who whispers it to the next person, and so on until every member of the team has received the message. The receiver is not to ask the sender any questions nor talk to the sender. The final member of the team to hear the message tells the rest of the team what he or she heard.

Cycle 1 Discussion Questions

    a. How badly was the final message distorted?
    b. How much important information was left out?
    c. What new information was added?
    d. How did the message get changed in the process of successive transmittals?

Cycle 2

This is a similar process, but this time feedback and two-way communication are used. Again, only the initial sender in each team silently reads the following message:

> The midterm test will be given on Friday, unless the preceding Wednesday is a holiday, in which case the test will be on the succeeding Monday. The test will be in Room 223 of Building 527 at 9 a.m. and will cover the first half of the text and the first seven cases.

The initial sender then whispers the message to his or her neighbor, who whispers it to the next person, and so on until every member of the team has received the message. This time, in order to confirm the message, each receiver is to repeat the message to the sender in a whisper as he or she thought it was heard. The sender and the receiver should verbally confirm the accuracy of the message in a whisper. The final member of the team to hear the message tells the rest of the team what he or she heard.

Cycle 2 Discussion Questions

> **a.** How badly was the final message distorted?
> **b.** How much important information was left out?
> **c.** What new information was added?
> **d.** How did the message get changed in the process of successive transmittals?

Headbands

Group size: Ten to fifteen members. In a large group a small group performs while the remaining members observe.

Time required: Approximately 45 minutes.

Materials: One headband for each participant. The headbands can be made of heavy paper or 5" × 7" cards with 10" strings attached to the ends of the cards (so that the cards can be tied around the heads of the participants). Each headband is lettered with a felt-tipped marker to show a particular role and an explanatory instruction as to how other members should respond to the role. Examples:

Comedian:	Laugh at me.	*Insignificant:*	Ignore me.
Expert:	Ask my advice.	*Loser:*	Pity me.
Important person:	Defer to me.	*Boss:*	Obey me!
Stupid:	Sneer at me.	*Helpless:*	Support me.

Physical setting: A circle of chairs—one for each participant—is placed in the center of the room.

Process:

> **I.** The facilitator selects 10 to 15 volunteers to demonstrate the effects of role pressure.
> **II.** He places a headband on each member in such a way that the member cannot read his own label, but the other members can see it easily.
> **III.** The facilitator provides a topic for discussion and instructs each member to interact with the others in a way that is natural for him. Each is cautioned not to role play but to be himself. The facilitator further instructs the group to react to each member who speaks by following the instructions on the speaker's headband. He emphasizes that they are not to tell each other what their headbands say, but simply react to them.

IV. After about 20 minutes, the facilitator halts the activity and directs each member to guess what his headband says and then take it off and read it.

V. The facilitator then initiates a discussion, including any members who observed the activity. Possible questions are:

1. What were some of the problems of trying to "be yourself" under conditions of group role pressure?
2. How did it feel to be consistently misinterpreted by the group, for example, to have them laugh when you were trying to be serious, or to have them ignore you when you were trying to make a point?
3. Did you find yourself changing your behavior in reaction to the group's treatment of you, for example, withdrawing when they ignored you, acting confident when they treated you with respect, giving orders when they deferred to you?

Source: Adapted from *Handbook of Structured Experiences for Human Relations Training* (1981), University Associates #203: 25–26.

CHAPTER CASE

Teamwork and the Art of Listening

The chief executive of an international organization and his top management group (about 15 people) asked a competent mid-level manager to temporarily leave his managerial position and advise the management group on how to improve the internal functioning of the firm. After four months the advisor sent a confidential report, recommending to the chief executive a six-month program of experimentation with a more participatory management style, that is, one calling for the managers concerned to change their behavior. A meeting was called, and the night before the meeting three members of the management group warned the advisor that they would say plainly that he had written nonsense.

The next day, understandably apprehensive, the advisor briefly presented his proposal. The chief executive looked smilingly around the table and the silence seemed eternal. He widened his smile and asked whether the silence meant that all agreed with the advisor. . .and the silence was more impressive than ever. With an even bigger smile, he said that he liked the advisor's proposals. Before he had finished his statement, eight hands were raised, including those of the three critics of the report. All had very positive comments and suggestions and constructive questions, and the advisor's recommendations were discussed and adopted without a single dissent. The advisor was asked to implement his proposals and to report to the same top group at the end of the six-month experimental program, with a recommendation for a further and presumably more extensive program.

Minutes of this meeting and recommendations were distributed to the whole staff. Subsequently, the advisor was prevented by middle-level managers from implementing *any* part of his program, and his short report at the end of the six months never reached the chief executive, who in turn never asked for another meeting on the subject.

Discussion Questions

1. In the top management meeting why wouldn't anyone say anything before the chief executive had spoken?
2. Why were the proposals approved by all members of the meeting, including the three persons who disagreed with the proposals?
3. Why didn't the chief executive ever ask for the report on the experimental program?
4. Did the chief executive really listen to the advisor when approving his proposals?

Source: Adapted from P. Casse, *Training for the Multicultural Manager,* Washington, DC: Society for Intercultural Education, Training and Research (1982): 140–141.

KEY TERMS

channel richness or **channel information capacity** Amount of information that can be transmitted and understood in a communication attempt.

channels Mediums of communication.

communication Process by which information is shared and understood by two or more persons.

communication networks Use of both vertical communication processes and horizontal communication processes throughout the organization.

data Symbols or characters without meaning or value.

decoding Process of the receiver's translating the symbols in the message into the meaning of the message.

encoding Putting the meaning of the message into appropriate symbols for transmission.

feedback Reversal of the communication process in which the receiver expresses a reaction to the sender's message.

formal communication Communication that flows along the lines of the organization prescribed by management.

informal communication Communication that flows in the organization independent of the structure prescribed by management.

information Data with meaning or value.

information overload Processing information ability of senders and receivers has been exceeded.

kaizen Japanese concept of continuous improvement.

lateral communication Communication that flows horizontally within the organization.

listening Receiving messages in a thoughtful manner that leads to an understanding of the meaning in the message.

noise Any disturbance or interference that reduces the clarity of the communication.

nonverbal communication Process by which information is shared and understood by two or more persons using actions and behaviors rather than words.

perception Interpretation of a message by a receiver.

purity of intent Japanese assumption that the worker's intent was correct even if the result of the worker's decision was not good.

receiver Person or group who perceives the sender's message.

ringi Japanese participatory approach to decision making.

sender (source) Person or group who wishes to transmit meaning to another person or another group.

transmitting Sending across.

vertical communication Communication that flows upward or downward in the organization.

ENDNOTES

1. W. Judge, M. Stahl, R. Scott, and R. Millender, "Long-Term Quality Improvement and Cost Reduction at Capsugel/Warner-Lambert," in M. Stahl and G. Bounds, *Competing Globally Through Customer Value*, Westport, CT: Quorum Books (1991): 708.

2. C. G. Pearce, R. Figgins, and S. Golen, *Principles of Business Communication*, New York: Wiley (1984): 516.

3. G. A. Miller, "The Magical Number Seven, Plus or Minus Two: Some Limits on Our Capacity for Processing Information," *Psychological Review*, 63 (1956): 81–97.

4. C. G. Pearce, "Doing Something About Your Listening Ability," *Supervisory Management* (March 1989): 29–34.

5. T. I. Sheppard, "Silent Signals," *Supervisory Management* (March 1986): 31–33.

6. P. Townsend and J. Gebhardt, *Quality in Action*, New York: Wiley (1992): 18, 96.

7. J. Bowles and J. Hammond, *Beyond Quality: How 50 Winning Companies Use Continuous Improvement*, New York: Putnam (1991): 194.

8. "Dinosaurs: IBM, Sears, GM," *Fortune* (May 3, 1993): 36–42.

9. W. Schmidt and J. Finnigan, *The Race Without a Finish Line: America's Quest for Total Quality*, San Francisco: Jossey-Bass (1992): 268–269.

10. Schmidt and Finnigan, *The Race Without a Finish Line*, 272–279

14

CHAPTER

Teams and Groups

LEARNING OBJECTIVES

After reading this chapter, you should be able to accomplish the following:

- Compare and contrast the role of managers in a flat organization and the role of teams in the same type of organization.

- Relate the concept of self-managed teams and the customer-value strategy.

- Describe the three team issues of involvement, empowerment, and self-management.

- Explain the stages of team development.

- Discuss the interaction of team cohesiveness and team performance norms on team performance.

- Describe the differences between formal and informal team leaders.

- Compare the advantages and disadvantages of team decision making.

CHAPTER OUTLINE

Motorola's Six Sigma Approach to Total Quality Renews the Firm

By winning a team competition held at corporate headquarters in Chicago, the "Road Runners" team from Motorola's Land Mobile Products sector in Malaysia reinforced the importance of teams in a global TQ process. (Photo credit: Motorola University.)

Motorola was founded in 1928 by Paul Galvin, who led the company until his death in 1959. His son, Robert Galvin, was chief executive officer from 1959 until 1986 and continued on the Motorola board until 1990. His son Christopher Galvin was assistant chief operating officer prior to being named president in 1993.

The company had over 120,000 employees and about $17 billion in sales in 1993. International business accounted for about 52 percent of sales. All of its products and services were in the area of electronics, including mobile radio and paging systems, semiconductors, integrated circuits, cellular phones and systems, space communications, and computers.

In such an industry new-product development and adaptability to rapidly changing technology are critical to survival. How is a company the size of Motorola continually renewed?

In the early 1980s Motorola stressed quality improvement with a goal of a tenfold improvement in quality levels in five years. In 1987 Motorola adopted a formal Total Quality initiative that it named "Six Sigma." Six Sigma refers to a defect rate of no more than 3.4 per million opportunities for error. In 1988 its Total Quality process won Motorola one of the first Malcolm Baldrige National Quality Awards. The six steps in Motorola's Six Sigma process are as follows:

— Identify the work you do (your "product").
— Identify who your work is for (your "customer").
— What do you need to do your work, and from whom (your "supplier")?
— Map the process.
— Mistake-proof the process and eliminate delays.
— Establish quality and cycle-time measurement and improvement goals.

continued

The Six Sigma process is implemented in the context of the Motorola culture. Motorola's fundamental objective, key beliefs, goals, and initiatives are printed on a small card for employees to carry and has been translated into 11 languages for Motorola's worldwide operations. The contents of the card are as follows:

Side 1:

OUR FUNDAMENTAL OBJECTIVE

(Everyone's Overriding Responsibility)

Total Customer Satisfaction

Side 2:

KEY BELIEFS—*how we will always act*

— Constant Respect for People
— Uncompromising Integrity

KEY GOALS—*what we must accomplish*

— Best in Class
  — *People*
  — *Marketing*

— *Technology*
— *Product: Software, Hardware and Systems*
— *Manufacturing*
— *Service*
— Increased Global Market Share
— Superior Financial Results

KEY INITIATIVES—*how we will do it*

— Six Sigma Quality
— Total Cycle Time Reduction
— Product, Manufacturing and Environmental Leadership
— Profit Improvement
— Empowerment for all, in a Participative, Cooperative and Creative Workplace

DISCUSSION QUESTIONS

1. What does "empowerment for all" mean in such a large organization with over 120,000 employees?
2. What is the role of teams in a process such as Six Sigma?

TEAMS AND PROCESSES IN ORGANIZATIONS

In this book we focus on the role of managers today. We have seen that due to intense international competition and demanding customers with alternatives, the managerial role has changed in recent years. The new role stresses providing value to customers by improving cross-functional systems.

But what is the role of employees in this era of less direct supervision? How do employees function in a cross-functional organization? In this chapter we address these questions by describing the role and functioning of teams in organizations.

Team Defined

A **team** is a collection of two or more persons who interact regularly to accomplish common goals.[1] Teams have been around as long as organizations have been around. Wherever people regularly interact to accomplish goals, whether in formal or informal settings, teams exist. For example, assembly teams in the Saturn Corporation work together to assemble cars. Surgical teams in a hospital work together to complete complicated surgeries.

The terms *team* and *group* may be used almost interchangeably. In many TQ organizations today the term *team* is more frequently used for at least two reasons.

First, because of the cross-functional nature of many teams, the term *cross-functional team* arose. Second, it is possible to discuss teamwork as a spirit and as a corporate cultural value.

The Role of Teams in Total Quality

Teams have been praised as the key to some Total Quality organizations. In many cases teams have helped to transform the organization and its managerial practices to focus on cross-functional issues. The Motorola quality case that opens this chapter presents an example where widespread adoption of cross-functional teams has enabled the organization to pursue its quest for quality.

In other organizations, however, the wholesale adoption of teams without managerial leadership to yield value to customers has been associated with the end of the quest for quality. Florida Power and Light, for example, implemented hundreds of teams in the name of quality improvement. The firm was even the first in this country to win the Deming Prize, which previously had been awarded in Japan only to Japanese firms for outstanding quality progress. However, FP&L's quality journey was halted when the cost of the program could no longer be justified relative to the value it provided to customers.[2]

Cross-functional teams are essential to implement the new managerial role to yield increased value to customers. However, the teams go hand in hand with management's assumptions of its new role and flattened organizational structure. Jack Welch, CEO of General Electric and leader of its rebirth in the 1980s and 1990s, has become a spokesperson for organizational change. He described the critical importance of cross-functional teams and project teams in the new flattened architecture of GE with fewer layers of management.[3]

The Role of Management in Total Quality

In Chapter 1 we defined *management* as the creation and continuous improvement of organizational systems that when used by organizational members lead to increased value for the customers of its products or services. *Systems* are collections of processes and resources, and *processes* are groups of activities that take an input, add value to it, and provide an output to an internal or external customer.

Managers' work on systems is crucial to the concept of management, and it is inherently cross-functional since the crucial systems are cross-functional. Managers create and improve systems that are operated by individuals and teams.

Many customer-relevant systems are cross-functional. For example, the new-product design and development system described in Chapter 8 is cross-functional. That system usually has representation from finance, engineering, production, marketing, and other organizational units. People working in teams populate such cross-functional systems.

The Thermos Corporation designs, manufactures, and markets leisure products. It recently replaced its bureaucratic culture with flexible interdisciplinary teams, which included customers and suppliers, to yield an award-winning design for a new electric grill. Without the interdisciplinary teams, Thermos guessed that it would have produced a modification of an existing gas grill, rather than the revolutionary electric design that won awards.[4] Managers designed the system for new-product design and development that was implemented by teams.

What is the role of management in such an organization? Managers design and improve systems operated by teams and individuals. Deming addressed this as one of his 14 points in describing the work of managers. "Break down barriers between departments. People in research, design, sales, and production must work as a team, to foresee problems of production and in use that may be encountered with the product or service."[5]

CRITICAL THINKING QUESTIONS

1. Describe the demands placed on individuals as team members in a Total Quality organization versus the demands placed on individuals in a vertical, hierarchical organization.

2. Discuss the educational and training needs of people who work in teams versus those who do not.

TYPES OF TEAMS

There are several different types of teams in organizations. Some customer-relevant teams are cross-functional, some are within a discipline. Some teams are permanent, some are temporary. Many teams today have the common characteristic that they contain members from a variety of areas in the firm.

Cross-Functional Teams

A **cross-functional team** is a team with members from at least two of the functions of design, production, marketing, and finance. Thus cross-functional teams are usually horizontal, with members from identical levels in different functions, or they may be diagonal teams, with members from slightly different levels in different functions. A cross-functional team may be depicted in a manner similar to the matrix or grid organization in Figure 8.8 (page 221).

Cross-functional teams implement and operate the cross-functional systems described in Chapter 8. These four critical cross-functional systems are the customer-value determination system, the new-product design and development system, the logistics and materials system, and the information flow system.

Cross-functional teams are sometimes referred to as interdisciplinary teams. In its "Statement of Purpose," Procter & Gamble listed the eight principles that guide its actions as a company, including its teamwork principle: "We will encourage teamwork across disciplines, divisions and geography to get the most effective integration of the ideas and efforts of our people."[6]

It would be difficult to imagine TQM as it is known today without cross-functional teams. Motivated, trained, and integrated cross-functional teams make it possible to deliver greater value to customers, at lower cost, with less supervision, and with flatter organizational structures.

Committees and task forces are two common types of cross-functional team. A **committee** is a long-lasting team, usually cross-functional, that is designed to deal with activities that recur. A college admission committee, for example, usually has members from several disciplines in the college to add breadth to the admission process. A **task-force/problem-solving team** is a temporary team, usually cross-functional, that is designed to deal with unique problems. For example, a task force is usually formed to investigate the cause of an aircraft accident and consists of members from several government agencies, the airline involved, the pilots association, and the manufacturer of the aircraft.

Formal and Informal Teams

A **formal team** is a team officially created by the organization as part of the formal organization structure. Formal teams, sometimes referred to as formal groups, may appear on organization charts. An X-ray department in a hospital and a loan department in a bank may be thought of as formal teams.

An **informal team** is a voluntary team not officially sanctioned by the organization. Informal teams sometimes form because they have common interests, such as recycling, or for social reasons, such as after-work sports teams. Experienced managers often work together with informal teams to form communication and influence networks. In doing so, managers must be careful not to cause the formation of informal teams that are in opposition to management, as happened in the following diversity exhibit.

Employee Involvement Teams

Employee involvement teams are teams formed to increase the participation and involvement of employees in their jobs in order to increase the value provided to customers. Suggestion groups and quality circles are good examples. Quality circles and many other employee involvement teams do not have the power to make changes in the work or the system. Rather, such teams are basically study groups that recommend changes to managers.[7] This suggests a traditional approach to organizations, with "managers" holding the power to make and implement decisions.

Employee involvement is considered an early step toward using the full capability of employees in organizations.[8] Thus employee involvement is scored as only 40 points out of a possible 1,000 points in the Baldrige National Quality Award criteria. To further tap the capabilities of teams for the continuous improvement and delivery of value to customers, teams must be empowered. The quality exhibit on page 392 shows how much teams can accomplish.

Empowered Teams

Empowerment is sharing with nonmanagerial employees the power and authority to make and implement decisions.[9] Empowered cross-functional teams share with managers the power to operate the cross-functional systems designed by managers.

DIVERSITY EXHIBIT

Mark Williams, Director of Dissident Employees

The Montgomery Construction Company is the prime subcontractor on the Clear Springs nuclear generating station. The generating station, being built by the Greater Eastern Gas and Electric Company, is considered of major importance in meeting the future electrical needs of a portion of the New England area. The project is also of great importance to Montgomery Construction because it ensures a minimum of two years' work at a time when area construction is generally in a depressed state.

In charge of the project for Montgomery is Mark Williams. Williams, who is now 30 years old, joined Montgomery 7 years ago on completion of his degree in electrical engineering at the University of Maryland. Although Williams supervised several minor jobs in the past, this is his first chance at a really important project. He believes that the confidence expressed in his ability by the allocation of this project may mean future advancement if he does his work well.

The company is now six months into the project, and Williams is encountering a morale problem. The problem is characterized by the division of workers into two seemingly hostile groups. The attitudes and positions of each group can be seen by considering the circumstances and feelings of two very different workers—Tom Beyer and Robert Tipton.

Tom Beyer is 50 years old. Following graduation from high school, Beyer joined the navy. It was in the navy, during the five years of World War II in which he served, that Beyer received his first electronics training. In 1946, following his discharge, he joined the New England Electrical Workers Union as an apprentice. Four years later,

in 1950, he was granted full status as an electrician. In the following years Beyer worked on almost all of the major projects in the New England area. He takes great pride in his work. Often he points to a construction project of years past and tells a story that occurred during its building.

Robert Tipton is a 24-year-old inner-city dweller from an impoverished background. At the end of the tenth grade, as the oldest of eight brothers and sisters, he was forced to drop out of school to help support the family. Because of his lack of education, Tipton quickly went through a succession of menial jobs and spent most of his time unemployed. Two years ago, as part of the JOBS program, Tipton was enrolled in a special trade program to learn electronics. Shortly thereafter he was admitted into the union's apprenticeship program. Last year, under a plan to bring more minorities into the construction trades, Tipton was admitted as a full journeyman. The Clear Springs job is Tipton's first as a journeyman.

During the first six months of work, Williams used two different forms of supervision on Beyer and Tipton, even though they frequently work side by side performing similar tasks. Williams has been very general in his direction of Beyer, believing that Beyer, with his vast storehouse of knowledge and his long experience, can be entrusted with a job and can be left to perform it in the best way possible. Williams has been heard to say that he is almost in awe of the skill with which Beyer performs his work.

On the other hand, Tipton has been given close supervision. As Williams explains it, several factors have caused him to watch Tipton more closely.

continued

By sharing power with employees to operate systems, managers are free to work on providing more value to customers and on improving systems. John Sculley, former chairman and CEO of Apple Computer, commented on the importance of empowering employees. "Our old, ineffective, hierarchical model will need to be replaced

First, because this is the first major job on which Tipton has worked, he can be expected to make mistakes through his lack of experience. Second, Williams feels that he needs to be nearby in order to give the encouragement and support needed by Tipton to build up his confidence in himself. Also, close supervision seems appropriate for Tipton because he is one of the first workers to achieve full status under the new training program, and management is very interested in his development as a means of evaluating the success of the program.

The other workers tend to identify with either Beyer or Tipton. The older, more established workers are treated by Williams in much the same way that he handles Beyer. The workers under the new program are all handled in a manner similar to the supervision given to Tipton.

Williams's differential treatment is being interpreted in very different ways by each group of workers. Beyer and his group feel that Williams's actions are just another example of management's practice of ignoring the problems of the good, steady worker while pampering some special-privilege group. They believe that Williams's close attention to the newer workers is also a result of Tipton's and his associates' inadequacies and incompetencies. Beyer and colleagues say that Tipton and associates are not fully prepared for the important responsibilities being given to them. Beyer's group believe that the assignment of important jobs to Tipton's group is "a real crime because in a tight labor market well-qualified men are being forced to live on unemployment while those incompetents are being nursed along. Those guys should still be apprentices."

Tipton and his co-workers see the controversy in quite another light. To them, the close supervision they are receiving while others work under freer supervision is another form of discrimination. It is apparent to Tipton and his group that Williams is watching them so that he can find an excuse to get them off the job at the first opportunity. It seems to them that Williams is always present when one of Tipton's group makes a mistake, but Williams never seems to notice errors made by the Beyer group. Also, just having Williams watching them so closely makes Tipton and his group overly nervous. "Who wouldn't make mistakes with someone watching over your shoulder and questioning every move you make?"

Under these conditions Williams is facing a serious morale problem. Productivity is down, costs are climbing, and the project is slipping behind schedule. To Williams a successful project and subsequent promotion appear to be in definite jeopardy unless something is done soon.

Discussion Questions

1. Mark Williams is applying a leadership approach to the old-line workers that is quite different from the approach he is using with the younger, inexperienced workers. Is this dual approach wise in this situation? Why or why not?

2. Is the fact that the young workers are from an underprivileged, economically depressed background a factor in the dissension that occurs? Why or why not?

3. To avoid these difficulties, what actions could have been taken by the Montgomery Construction Company and other companies in a similar position?

Source: Jeff O. Harris, Jr., *Managing People at Work*, (New York: John Wiley & Sons, 1976), 515–517. Copyright © 1976 John Wiley & Sons, Inc. Reprinted with permission of John Wiley & Sons, Inc.

by the new empowerment model of putting critical thinking and decision-making skills into the hands of a fully educated workforce."[10]

Empowerment is a partner of a flattened organization with few layers of managers. Thus there is little direct supervision of employees. The organization implementing empowerment also fosters a participative culture that values employees.

Q U A L I T Y   E X H I B I T

Quality Action Teams and Recycling at Federal Express

In 1989, when the Federal Express SuperHub sorting facility in Memphis began recycling aluminum cans to raise money for charity, a can recycler noted that the company might be missing other, potentially profitable recycling opportunities.

Employees formed a QAT, a Quality Action Team, including both management and hourly representatives. In its Focus phase the QAT identified a number of substances and products with recycle or reuse value—steel, batteries, paper, wood, plastic, oil, and tires—that the company was paying to have removed by refuse haulers.

In its Analyze phase the QAT identified the root causes of missed recycling opportunities as lack of awareness vis-à-vis the monetary value of such items and absence of a system for monitoring recyclable materials.

The QAT developed a quality action plan, which suggested performing a number of tasks:

— Draw up a comprehensive list of items with recycle or second-use value.
— Establish collection points for recyclable materials within the SuperHub.
— Create a manual system for tracking the monthly volume and monetary value of all recycled or reused materials.
— Identify vendors to either purchase the materials or provide disposal services free in return for the right to resell or reuse materials.
— Implement a recycling awareness communication program, which would, among other things, post notices on SuperHub bulletin boards, submit articles to the SuperHub newsletter, and produce segments on TV (via a regularly scheduled SuperHub news program on FXTV).

With approval from the vice president of operations, the QAT's plan was executed. For fiscal year 1990, the first year of the SuperHub recycling

Needing little supervision, Federal Express's empowered teams at the superhub sorting facility in Memphis unload and reload planes to deliver value to customers. (Photo credit: Chris Sorensen.)

effort, the program returned more than $196,000 to the company's bottom line.

The QAT has summarized its experience in a booklet that is now available to divisional quality facilitators and to the managing directors of other Federal Express facilities. Leaders of the QAT are advising others within the company who may be interested in pursuing similar recycling opportunities.

Source: Reprinted by permission of American Management Association from "Blueprints for Service Quality: The Federal Express Approach" by Briefing Staff, 1991, from *AMA Management Briefing*: 72–73, © 1991. American Management Association, New York. All rights reserved.

Figure 14.1 shows how empowerment, a flat organization, and a participative culture are complementary.

FIGURE 14.1 *Empowerment Leadership Model*

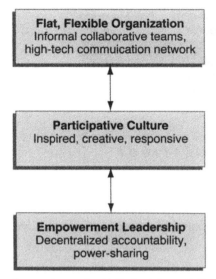

Source: Lynne Joy McFarland, Larry E. Senn, and John R. Childress, *21st Century Leadership: Dialogues with 100 Top Leaders,* New York: The Leadership Press (April 1993): 64.

Eastman Chemical Company summed up the ten principles that constitute its Quality Policy and that include an empowerment principle: "Create a culture where people have the knowledge, skills, authority, and desire to decide, act, and take responsibility for results of their actions and for their contribution to the success of the company."[11]

Self-Managed Work Teams

Self-managed work teams have the power to make the operating decisions and to operate the systems designed by managers. These teams plan, set priorities, organize, coordinate with others, measure, take corrective action, solve problems, and deal with team personnel issues.[12] As such, they act as traditional managers act in hierarchical organizations. Self-managed work teams require a high level of training and a high level of trust from management.[13] Although some refer to self-managed work teams as autonomous teams, they are not autonomous since they are tied to systems designed by managers.

A good example exists at the Saturn Corporation, where teams plan and control much of the work, including work methods, quality improvement, and personnel decisions. Some Milliken textile plants with no "supervisors" in the plant on the second and third shifts is another good example of a company with self-managed work teams.

Figure 14.2 presents a comparison of the relative amount of power that different kinds of teams possess.

FIGURE 14.2 *Teams and Power in Organizations*

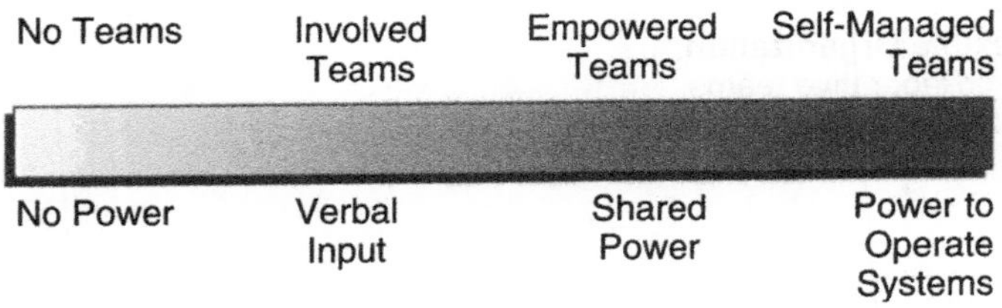

No Teams	Involved Teams	Empowered Teams	Self-Managed Teams
No Power	Verbal Input	Shared Power	Power to Operate Systems

CRITICAL THINKING QUESTIONS

1. What is the role of managers in organizations using self-managed work teams?
2. Discuss the circumstances under which self-managed teams would be expected to further the promotion of a diverse workforce. Under what circumstances would you expect self-managed teams to hinder the promotion of a diverse workforce?

TEAM AND GROUP PROCESSES

As is apparent from our discussion to this point, teams are an important feature of organizational life. It is essential, therefore, to understand how teams develop, how their standards are set, how they maintain cohesiveness, and how they are led.

Stages of Team Development

Teams go through a predictable development sequence of four stages: mutual acceptance, decision making, motivation, and control.[14]

Mutual Acceptance   In this initial phase members get to know each other. They test different behaviors to see which behaviors are acceptable and which are not. Barriers start to disappear.

Decision Making   In this second phase members learn how to function as a team. They develop team structure, patterns of communication, and methods of making decisions. There are advantages and disadvantages to team decision making, and we shall discuss these later. In the 1980s, due to a lack of empowerment, many quality circles never advanced beyond this point.

Motivation   In this phase members accept their roles as members of the team and develop cohesiveness as a group. They work together to accomplish the team's goals. Unfortunately, not all teams advance to this stage. Some get stuck in the decision-making phase due to differences among team members or failure to accept the team leader. Also, performance norms are formed. We shall describe their impact later.

Q UALITY CASE

Back to the Motorola Case

Quality has become a way of life at Motorola. It is a key driver—driven not only by management, but also by teams of employees at every level throughout the company, a team process begun in the 1960s.

In 1990 the team process was formalized as a total customer satisfaction, problem-solving team competition. During that year more than 2,000 teams were formed. Training was made available on analytic techniques, and judging criteria were announced. By 1992 the number of teams had increased to 3,700; 24 teams competed at the corporate finals for the gold. The panel of judges for the final selection was—and continues to be—the senior management of the company. The criteria for the competition are:

Teamwork	Results
Project selection	Institutionalization
Analysis techniques	Presentation
Remedies	

All of the teams must function within the context of a quality plan. If they do not, mayhem will result.

Control   In this most mature of all the phases, the members have fully accepted the team's leader and fully accept and support the team's goals. Team cohesiveness is so strong that members control nonconforming behavior. If the team's norms are supportive of the formal organization, the team could be a high-performing, self-managed team.

As we see in the following international exhibit, team work is a major aspect of the commitment to Total Quality. Statistical process control and other quality tools are also part of the TQ package.

Team Cohesiveness

Cohesiveness is the extent to which members are committed to the team and willing to remain a part of the team.[15] Cohesiveness is the glue that binds the team together. If the team is supportive of the organization's goals, then a cohesive team can be a definite asset. In this situation managers try to make the team even more cohesive via interteam competition and such rewards as praise. If a cohesive team does not support the organization's goals, it may be necessary to train the team extensively, to increase the size of the team to water it down, or even to disband the team.

Team Norms

A **team norm** is a standard of behavior that is accepted by team members and that guides their behavior. Norms are informal and unwritten, but they are nevertheless real guides to behavior. Frequently, teams develop performance norms relating to acceptable job performance, especially concerning productivity.

INTERNATIONAL EXHIBIT

Involvement through Team Work in the UK

A large American-owned multinational, code-named Qualchem, has outlets throughout the world. It sells high-quality specialty chemicals for use in both the domestic and the commercial markets. It is a leader in its market, and the major marketplace change over the last decade has been the continuing challenge of Japanese companies and products. Indeed, in recent years one of the major influences on corporate strategy, as well as on employment policy, has been the perceived threat of Japanese import penetration into the United States and the more competitive markets of the world.

Over 100,000 people are employed by Qualchem worldwide, of which nearly 8,000 work in the United Kingdom across a number of sites in different parts of the country. The bulk of these are employed at the head office and at the principal production site, which includes a sizable research division and a distribution department. Two other sites employ smaller numbers of staff, who are engaged in production of raw materials and products for use in the main factory. In all cases products are sold in both British and European markets. The smallest of the company's units in Britain has just over 200 staff, but the policies that it implements are broadly in line with those adopted at the other sites. If anything, however, this site is slightly further down the team-working road because of its size and the nature of the technology employed at the site.

The parent company, Qualchem—like many others in the chemical industry—publishes a set of corporate principles that is distributed to all employees. The preface to this is written by the United Kingdom chairman, and it states that the booklet "is an expression of the way in which we intend to manage the company, taking account of the external influences which are crucial to our business interests." He continues by asking employees to "help make these statements a living commitment, by developing the beliefs into plans for *continuous improvement.*"

Qualchem's mission comprises five goals, of which two are particularly relevant for this exhibit: (1) recognize that the firm's people are its most important asset, and (2) adopt quality as a way of life. The "people" policies and practices, which are fairly typical of this kind of progressive organization, include commitments to the best health and safety standards, equity of treatment, effective channels of communication, a superior employment package, stability of employment, and high performance standards from the staff.

The "quality" policies refer to visible and reinforced managerial commitment to quality, an emphasis on customers (both external and internal to the organization), quality as a measure of performance, and clarity of employee goals and objectives. The final point has a clear relevance for employee involvement; it states that "we will create an environment that encourages quality by ensuring that the contribution of all employees to the quality process is maximized by *training, team building, leadership, and ensuring individuals are responsible for their own processes.*"

continued

The interaction between team cohesiveness and team norms can be used to predict team work performance. Figure 14.3 describes the interaction. For a team with low performance norms, extensive training may be required to raise the norms. Sometimes, the only effective action that managers of teams with low performance norms can take is to disband them.

Team working is one part of Qualchem's World-Class Manufacturing Strategy, the other two parts being performance management and statistical process control (SPC). SPC is a key part of the quality improvement program, and this aims to provide the teams with a mechanism for assessing the quality of production as well as a methodology that will help them to overcome problems. Ultimately, all operators will be trained in the use and meaning of statistical techniques that are relevant to their part of the operation.

Performance management is a system designed to seek and achieve continuous improvement in the key aspects of each individual's or team's work, and it operates according to "reinforcements of good behavior." These reinforcements can be either tangible or social (for example, visits organized for the team, a contribution to a local charity, a beer bust, a badge, a word of thanks from the plant manager). The crucial point is that they are meant to reinforce actions that management defines as good for the business (section, department, plant). According to managers, this appears to have been well received in the U.S. plants, but they are less sure about its general application in Britain—despite some evidence that it has gone down well with certain shop-floor teams—because of differing cultures and traditions.

The third strand of World-Class Manufacturing is the team-working concept, and this is being extended across the whole company. This concept has developed well at the smallest site particularly with process operators in the chemical plants who are now covered by a single grade.

The move toward World-Class Manufacturing has been bolstered by two further employee relations practices. First, the company aims to devote 5 percent of each employee's time (on average each year) to training and development, and this includes not only technical-skills training but also team-building exercises as well. An example of the former would be the provision of specific packages, often delivered in conjunction with local technical colleges, for different grades of staff—say multiskill training for craftworkers or simple maintenance skills for process operators. Another would be training in how to interpret controls in the plant, their meaning and significance, and their relevance for quality. An example of the latter would be outward-bound courses designed to develop team spirit and decision making within groups and to reduce barriers between different grades of staff. While these sorts of exercises have become more common for managers over the last decade, at Qualchem they have been extended to manual workers as well.

The second element that underpins team working, and appears necessary for it to work effectively, is a revamped pay package that drastically reduces the number of grades on the shop floor. Under the new system there are four principal grades: ancillary work/laborer, process operator, craftworker, team leader. Each grade has a "start" and "established" rate, although variations are possible due to shift allowances and other fringe benefits. Pay levels for a process operator on shifts are high, not only for the industry but also compared with average wages for many white-collar and managerial staff in other sectors.

Source: Adapted from M. Marchington, *Managing the Team: A Guide to Successful Employee Involvement*, Cambridge, MA: Blackwell (1992): 123–126.

Team Leadership

A **formal team leader** is the person explicitly designated by the organization to lead the team. As illustrated in Figure 14.4, the supervisor model (A) was based on a formal supervisor–subordinate relationship. Even in the formal team leader model (B), many formal team leaders operate today in a more collaborative fashion on a peer level. In the coach model (C), some team leaders operate as a coach who lets the team call its own plays until asked for guidance by the team.

FIGURE 14.3 *Team Cohesiveness, Team Norms, and Work Performance*

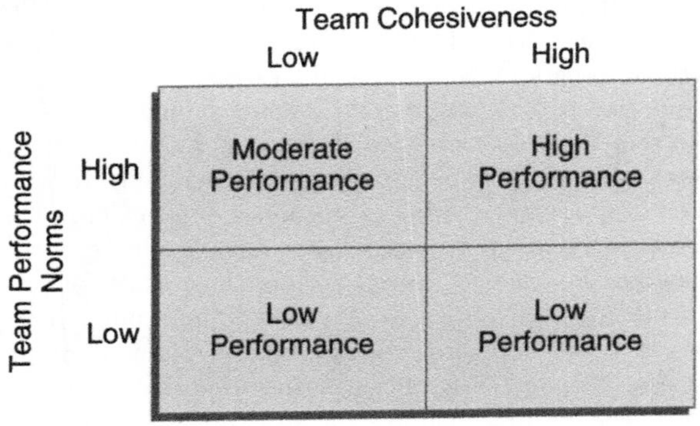

Team Cohesiveness

		Low	High
Team Performance Norms	High	Moderate Performance	High Performance
	Low	Low Performance	Low Performance

An **informal team leader** is a person who influences team members even without the explicit leadership designation by the organization. Such a leader usually draws on referent or expert power as described in Chapter 11. *Referent power* arises from the follower's identification and respect for the power holder and desire to be like the power holder. *Expert power* refers to the perception by the follower that the power holder has needed information or special knowledge for the follower. Informal team leaders have influence only as long as they represent the team's interests.[16]

FIGURE 14.4 *Team Leadership Models*

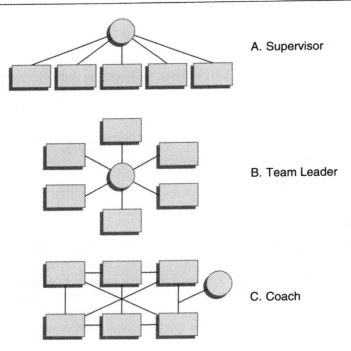

A. Supervisor

B. Team Leader

C. Coach

Frequently, the formal and informal team leaders are two different persons. The wise formal leader works with the informal leader and enlists his or her help to keep the team's performance norms high and team cohesiveness high (see Figure 14.3). If the two leaders are at odds, then the team's performance could be low.

As illustrated in Figure 14.5, cross-functional teams aligned with the organization are capable of innovative solutions. In the ad the firm credited the cross-functional team with the innovation.

CRITICAL THINKING QUESTIONS

1. Describe two situations that could prevent a team from completing the complete team development process.

2. How can a manager raise the performance norms of a group?

TEAM DECISION MAKING

With today's trend toward a team environment, there are several advantages of team decision making, among them broad-based participation and a number of original ideas. However, team decision making is not without its faults, which may include narrow-mindedness and deciding on risky options. By being aware of the team's behavior and by working directly with the team or through the informal leader, managers should capitalize on the advantages and minimize the disadvantages of team decision making.

Advantages of Team Decisions

Some of the noteworthy advantages of team decisions are diverse information, ease of communication, likelihood of acceptance, and economy of time.[17]

Diverse Information   Team members come from different backgrounds, bringing diverse views and information to the team. This breadth of information may help the team to examine issues from various perspectives and to formulate alternative solutions.

Communication   Because the team members have been involved in the formulation of the decision, they are already aware of the decision. Thus it is easier to communicate the decision to all concerned.

Acceptance   Because they were involved in formulating the decision, the team members are more likely to accept the decision and even to become avid proponents of implementing the decision.

Time   Team decisions take less time than a series of individual decisions from functional organizations if the team is a true cross-functional team. With the various functions already represented on the cross-functional team, time is not wasted

FIGURE 14.5   *Solution Credited to a Cross-Functional Team at American Express Benelux*

TRAVEL RELATED SERVICES

Simplifying expense vouchers

Business travelers from the Benelux countries of Belgium, the Netherlands and Luxembourg who charge their expenses on the American Express® Corporate Card now find submitting expense vouchers is easier and faster with a new automated system developed by an 11-person team. The cross-functional team from Travel Management Services (TMS) Benelux created a statement that details, by item and category, charges made on the Corporate Card during a business trip.

The resulting system summarizes charges by category, which can be organized according to the specific administrative needs of a company, and provides detailed information on each charge, including the cost in foreign and local currency and the rate of exchange. American Express' worldwide computer data network automatically tracks different categories of expenses, no matter where they are incurred. Original receipts are attached to the statement, and there is room for the employee to add additional explanations.

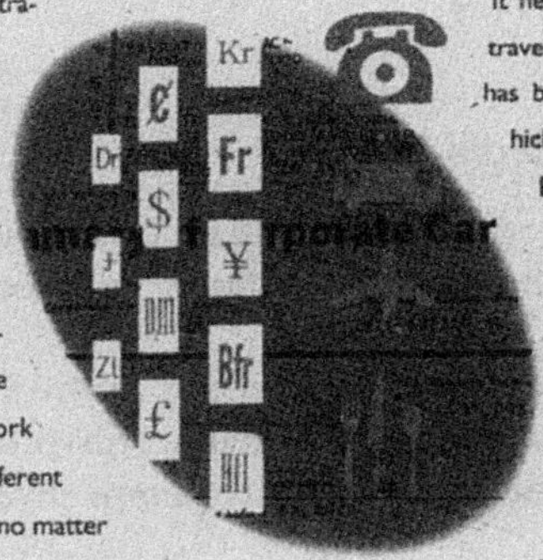

"The more a traveler uses the Corporate Card for business, the easier it is to submit expenses," explained team leader Cecile Quaedackers, manager of TMS Sales in Amsterdam, the Netherlands. "A process that used to take an exasperating hour of organizing, explaining and currency converting now only takes five minutes, even for the most complex trip."

The new expense voucher was developed over six months by representatives from Sales, Systems, Customer Service and Finance, who met with customers to learn what they needed.

It helped TMS sign a major travel and Card customer and has become an ongoing vehicle for getting American Express more timely payments from Corporate Cardmembers.

"The automated expense voucher is also expected to increase Cardmember loyalty significantly," Quaedackers said.

"Cardmembers, attracted by our simple way of reconciling expenses, will insist on using our Corporate Card."

TEAM MEMBERS

Kees Bakker, Jeanette Graveland, Cynthia v.d. Hulst, Philip Nauta, Wim Ockhuijsen, Guy Opdebeeck, Cecile Quaedackers, Annemieke Schmitz, Anne Tire, Lieve Waere and Willeke Wenno

Source: R. Heller, *TQM The Quality Makers: The Leaders and Shapers of Europe's Quality Revolution,* St. Gallen, Switzerland: Norden Publishing House Ltd. (1993): 197.

E T H I C S   E X H I B I T

The Chrysler Odometer-Tampering Affair

In 1987 the Chrysler Corporation faced criminal charges of tampering with the odometers on thousands of new cars. In a 16-count indictment, Chrysler and two of its executives were charged with systematically disconnecting or replacing odometers on at least 60,000 vehicles. According to the charges, company employees drove new cars and trucks with the odometers disconnected for as long as five weeks and up to 400 miles. The vehicles were then shipped to dealers, who were not notified of their previous use and who sold them to customers as new. Moreover, at least 40 vehicles shipped to dealers as new had actually been involved in accidents and repaired, sometimes inadequately. The government accused Chrysler of depriving its customers of knowledge about the prior mileage and accidents through "false and fraudulent pretenses." Charged with conspiracy to commit odometer fraud, wire fraud, and mail fraud, the company pleaded "no contest" in December 1987.

The evidence against Chrysler included memos from managers that urged employees to disconnect the odometers of vehicles driven more than 40 or 50 miles. Plant managers and quality control officers also were told to disconnect the odometers on new automobiles that would be used by company managers. Occasionally, however, employees forgot to disconnect the odometers. In these cases new odometers were installed to disguise the actual mileage before the cars were sent to dealers for sale.

Chrysler's practice of odometer tampering was discovered when a number of company managers who were stopped for speeding told Missouri Highway Patrol officers that the speedometers and odometers in the company-owned cars did not work. The Missouri Department of Revenue subsequently asked Chrysler to stop the practice of driving vehicles with disconnected odometers. Chrysler managers were then instructed not to tell police that their odometers did not work. These incidents prompted an eight-month investigation by the U.S. Attorney's Office, Missouri law enforcement officials, and the U.S. Postal Inspection Service.

When charges were brought against the company, Chrysler chairman Lee Iacocca at first accused the government of misinterpreting a legal

continued

coordinating across the various functions in the organization. Witness the cross-functional platform teams at Chrysler that have cut the company's new-product development time from five years to three years. As we saw in Chapter 5, if the team is not a true cross-functional team, decision making will take more time.

Disadvantages of Team Decisions

The chief disadvantages of team decisions are risky shift, time, and groupthink.[18] These disadvantages may preclude using team decision making in some situations.

Risky Shift   In many cases, cohesive teams recommend more risky decisions than individuals recommend. In this situation, the team members reinforce each other and a spirit of invincibility grows.

and routine test-drive program. Company executives claimed that the law on odometer fraud applied only to used cars, and that turning off new-car odometers was therefore legal. Chrysler acknowledged disconnecting odometers on test vehicles, but asserted the practice was favorable to buyers. Test drives are necessary to determine a car's quality, company officials said, but the mileage accumulated in testing should not reduce the buyer's warranty coverage; therefore the company disconnected the odometers.

Nevertheless, a week after the indictments Chrysler announced that it had stopped disconnecting odometers on test-driven automobiles. The company now places notices in cars sent to dealers explaining why mileage has accumulated on their odometers. This is the policy currently followed at Ford and General Motors. In addition, Chairman Iacocca issued a public apology, announcing that Chrysler had made a "mistake." Disconnecting odometers was a "lousy idea," he said, but emphasized the importance of test drives. Iacocca promised that the practice would not be repeated. The company also placed two-page advertisements in national newspapers declaring that Chrysler would extend the warranties on test cars and replace cars that had been damaged during test drives but were later sold as new.

Chrysler was the first automaker ever to be brought to court for odometer tampering, although used-car dealers have often been accused of rolling back the mileage on their vehicles. Since the passage of the federal odometer-tampering law of 1973, there have been many fewer incidents involving used-car rollbacks. Millions of new cars may have been sold with incorrect odometer readings, however. The Justice Department claims that Chrysler had been disconnecting odometers for more than 30 years. General Motors is also investigating reports that some employees may have violated company policy by disconnecting odometers as cars rolled off the assembly line.

Discussion Questions

1. Discuss the ethics issues involved in this case.

2. Do you think Chairman Iacocca's response to the situation was correct? If not, what actions should have been taken to resolve the situation?

Source: O. C. Ferrell and John Fraedrich, *Business Ethics: Ethical Decision Making and Cases*, 1991, 173–175. Copyright © 1991 by Houghton Mifflin Company. Reprinted with permission.

Groupthink   **Groupthink** is the reinforcement of team members by the team to the point that the members lose their ability to evaluate alternatives critically.[19] Everyone on the team then accepts a specific alternative without questioning its pros and cons.

Groupthink is apparent in the ethics exhibit about the Chrysler odometer-tampering affair. Indeed, it is not unusual to see groupthink operating in situations involving the unethical behavior of many people. The team culture can cause team members to rationalize their own unethical behavior.

CRITICAL THINKING QUESTIONS

1. Compare the advantages and disadvantages of team decision making in new-product development teams.

2. Compare the advantages and disadvantages of team decision making in military combat teams.

QUALITY CASE

Conclusion to the Motorola Case

The importance of quality will continue to intensify as Motorola approaches the twenty-first century. Customers are continually raising the bar of excellence. A simplified plan for quality improvement at Motorola is given below:

Top-Down Commitment and Involvement

Understand customer's needs
↓
Evaluate and improve processes to meet needs
↓
Develop measurement systems to track progress
↓
Educate, reward, communicate
↓
Set reach-out goals

Motorola continues to set reach-out goals. Its metrics have changed from parts per million to parts per billion, and the company is going forward with a goal of a tenfold reduction in defects every two years.

Now, as has been true throughout Motorola's history, there is a drive to do better, an aim for *renewal* strongly support-ed by senior management, but also pervasive throughout the entire organization. In a way, quality breeds quality. The Six Sigma initiative and Motorola's culture of renewal seem to be working as Motorola's earnings and sales were growing close to 20 percent per year in the mid-1990s. Motorola's stock value had more than quintupled in the five years following its receipt of the Baldrige National Quality Award in 1988.

DISCUSSION QUESTIONS

1. If Motorola is at Six Sigma, how can it achieve a goal of a tenfold reduction in defects every two years?

2. The majority of Motorola's sales are outside of the United States. Describe the problems and opportunities of reinforcing its Six Sigma quality initiative in the cultures of the United States, Europe, and China.

Sources: "Motorola," *Value Line Investment Survey*, New York: Value Line Publishing (October 29, 1993): 1069; R. W. Galvin, *The Idea of Ideas*, Schaumburg, IL: Motorola University Press (1991): 215; "Quality Renewal," Schaumburg, IL: Motorola Inc. (1989): 6; R. Buetow, "The Motorola Quality Process," Schaumburg, IL: Motorola Inc. (January 15, 1987).

SUMMARY

A team is a collection of two or more persons who interact regularly to accomplish common goals. The terms *team* and *group* may be used almost interchangeably, although *team* is more frequently used for at least two reasons: (1) because of the cross-functional nature of many teams, the term *cross-functional team* arose, and (2) it is possible to discuss teamwork as a spirit and as a corporate cultural value.

Cross-functional teams are essential to implement the new managerial role described throughout this book to yield increased value to customers. The teams go hand in hand with management's assumptions of its new role and with flattened organizational structures.

Managers' work on systems is crucial to the concept of management, and it is inherently cross-functional since the crucial systems are cross-functional. Managers create and improve systems that are operated by individuals and teams. People working in teams flesh out such cross-functional systems.

A cross-functional team is a team with members from at least two of the functions of design, production, marketing, and finance. Thus cross-functional teams are usually horizontal, with members from identical levels in different functions, or they may be diagonal, with members from slightly different levels in different functions.

Cross-functional teams implement and operate the cross-functional systems described in Chapter 8. These four critical cross-functional systems are the customer-value determination system, the new-product design and development system, the logistics and materials system, and the information flow system.

Committees and task forces are two common types of cross-functional teams. A committee is a long-lasting team, usually cross-functional, that is designed to deal with activities that recur. A task-force/problem-solving team is a temporary team, usually cross-functional, that is designed to deal with unique problems.

A formal team is a team officially created by the organization as part of the formal organization structure. An informal team is a voluntary team not officially sanctioned by the organization. Experienced managers often work with informal teams as communication and influence networks.

Employee involvement teams are teams formed to increase the participation and involvement of employees in their jobs in order to increase the value provided to customers. Quality circles were an early form of employee involvement team.

Empowerment is sharing with nonmanagerial employees the power and authority to make and implement decisions. Empowered cross-functional teams share with managers the power to operate the cross-functional systems designed by managers. Empowerment is paired with a flattened organization with few layers of managers. Thus there is little direct supervision of employees.

Self-managed work teams have the power to make the operating decisions and to operate the systems designed by managers. Such teams plan, set priorities, organize, coordinate with others, measure, take corrective action, solve problems, and deal with team personnel issues.

Teams follow the predictable development sequence of mutual acceptance, decision making, motivation, and control.

Cohesiveness is the extent to which members are committed to the team and willing to remain a part of the team. Cohesiveness is the glue that binds the team together. A team norm is a standard of behavior that is accepted by team members and guides their behavior. Though informal and unwritten, norms are real guides to behavior. The interaction between team cohesiveness and team norms can be used to predict team performance.

A formal team leader is a person explicitly designated by the organization to lead the team. An informal team leader is a person who influences team members even without the organization's explicit leadership designation. Frequently, the formal and informal team leaders are two different persons. The wise formal leader works with the informal leader and enlists his or her help to keep the team's performance norms high and team cohesiveness high. If the two leaders are at odds, then the team's performance could be low.

With today's trend toward a team environment, there are several advantages of team decision making, among them diverse information, communication, acceptance, and time. Disadvantages of team decision making are narrow-mindedness (groupthink) and deciding on risky options. Managers must try to capitalize on the advantages and minimize the disadvantages of team decision making.

EXPERIENTIAL EXERCISE

Brainstorming

Research indicates that creativity can be cultivated by the use of simple and practical exercise. All too often, however, the spark of innovative thinking is dampened by killer phrases like "We tried it last year," "We've always done it that way," and a host of similar comments.

To acclimate participants by flicking on their innate green light of creativity, a sample brainstorming session might be used. The basic ground rules of brainstorming are:

1. No critical judgment is permitted.
2. Free-wheeling is welcomed (that is, the wilder the idea, the better).
3. Quantity, not quality, is desired.
4. Combination and improvement of ideas are sought.

With these four basic rules in mind, the class should be divided into groups of four to six persons. Their task for 60 seconds will be to suggest all the ways they can think of for using a paper clip. Have someone in each group merely tally the number of ideas, not necessarily the ideas themselves. At the end of the one minute, ask the groups to report first the number of ideas they generated, and then get a sampling of some of the seemingly "crazy" or "far out" ideas. Suggest that sometimes these "silly" ideas may turn out to be very workable.

Alternatively, the group might think of ways to improve the standard (nonmechanical) lead pencil.

Discussion Questions

1. What reservations, if any, do you have about the suggested technique?
2. What kinds of problems is brainstorming best suited for?
3. What potential applications in the workplace can you see for brainstorming?

Source: Adapted from J. Newstrom and E. Scannel, *Games Trainers Play*, New York: McGraw-Hill (1980): 109.

CHAPTER CASE

Gapbuster Teams and Customers at Norwest Financial

Follow the process. Refer to the credit manual. Do it by the book. Yes, controls *are* important. Managing risk is essential. But wait a minute. What does the *customer* want? Are we exceeding customer expectations? How do we know? Good questions. But you need more than questions. You need a team problem-solving process to get at the heart of this stuff. At Norwest, it's called "Gapbusters," employees coming together as teams to identify and bridge "gaps" between customer expectations and service reality. Last year, more than 600 Norwest employees worked together in teams to change existing procedures in order to put customers first, save money, improve operating efficiency, and improve communications.

Examples? Streamlining the approval process so certificates of deposit can be reissued immediately. Developing a training course to help customer-contact employees remember customer names early in a relationship. Or giving every customer-contact employee on the bank floor a recipe box with index cards containing productivity tips suggested by employees of that bank location (Which employees in our bank are bilingual? When I've got an urgent customer need, whom do I call?).

"Gapbusters say a team can accomplish a lot more than one person," says Marketing Vice President Cynthia Gray. "The process smooths the way so customers can receive the very best service when they come to Norwest. We've made progress but we still have a long way to go, especially across business lines. Gapbusters never ends. There will always be room for improvement." The process is working. Annually, Norwest asks customers at each of its 410 banking locations how they think Norwest bankers are doing in service delivery, solving prob-

Empowered teams, particularly at service-oriented companies such as Norwest Financial, can best determine where improvement is most needed. (Photo credit: Marc Norberg Studio.)

lems, proactive service and communication. Bank presidents and their staff team review the results and suggest ways to close any service gaps which customers perceive.

Discussion Questions

1. Compare the advantages and disadvantages of proximity to customers in a service firm.

2. Describe the advantages and disadvantages of empowered teams in a service firm.

Source: Norwest Corporation Annual Report (1992): 12.

KEY TERMS

cohesiveness   Extent to which members are committed to the team and willing to remain a part of the team.

committee   Long-lasting team, usually cross-functional, that is designed to deal with activities that recur.

cross-functional team   Team with members from at least two of the functions of design, production, marketing, and finance.

employee involvement teams   Teams formed to increase the participation and involvement of employees in their jobs in order to increase the value provided to customers.

empowerment   Sharing with nonmanagerial employees the power and authority to make and implement decisions.

formal team   Team officially created by the organization as part of the formal organization structure.

formal team leader   Person explicitly designated by the organization to lead the team.

groupthink   Reinforcement of team members by the team to the point that the members lose their ability to evaluate alternatives critically.

informal team   Voluntary team not officially sanctioned by the organization.

informal team leader   Person who influences team members even without the explicit leadership designation by the organization.

self-managed work teams   Work teams that have the power to make the operating decisions and to operate the systems designed by managers.

task-force/problem-solving team   Temporary team, usually cross-functional, that is designed to deal with unique problems.

team   Collection of two or more persons who interact regularly to accomplish common goals.

team norm   Standard of behavior that is accepted by team members and that guides their behavior.

ENDNOTES

1. C. Larson and M. LaFasto, *Teamwork*, Newbury Park, CA: Sage (1989).
2. J. J. Evelyn and N. DeCarlo, "Customer Focus Helps Utility See the Light," *Journal of Business Strategy* (January-February 1992): 8–12; R. Wood, "A Hero Without a Company," *Forbes* (March 18, 1991): 112–114.
3. "Revolutionize Your Company," *Fortune* (December 13, 1993): 114–118.
4. "Payoff from the New Management," *Fortune* (December 13, 1993): 103–110.
5. W. E. Deming, *Out of the Crisis*, Cambridge, MA (1986): 24.
6. *A Statement of Purpose*, Cincinnati, OH: Procter & Gamble (1993): 2.
7. B. Dale and C. Cooper, *Total Quality and Human Resources*, Oxford, England: Blackwell (1992): 111–112.
8. M. Marchington, *Managing the Team: A Guide to Successful Employee Involvement*, Oxford, England: Blackwell (1992): 115–123.
9. L. McFarland, L. Senn, and J. Childress, *21st Century Leadership*, New York: Leadership Press (1993): 64.
10. Ibid., 63.
11. *Eastman Quality Policy*, Kingsport, TN: Eastman Chemicals Company (1993).
12. W. A. Band, *Creating Value for Customers*, New York: Wiley (1991): 189; A. B. Godfrey,

"Ten Areas for Future Research in Total Quality Management," *Quality Management Journal* (October 1993): 57.
13. J. Bowles and J. Hammond, *Beyond Quality: How 50 Winning Companies Use Continuous Improvement*, New York: Putnam (1991): 98.
14. J. Heiner and E. Jacobson, "A Model of Task Group Development in Complex Organizations and a Strategy of Implementation," *Academy of Management Review*, 1, no. 4 (1976): 98–111.
15. M. Shaw, *Group Dynamics*, 3rd ed., New York: McGraw-Hill (1981); G. Manners, "Another Look at Group Size, Group Problem Solving and Member Consensus," *Academy of Management Journal*, 18 (1975): 715–724.
16. H. Jessup, "New Roles in Team Leadership," *Training and Development* (November 1990): 79–83.
17. D. Cartwright, "Determinants of Scientific Progress: The Case of Research on the Risky Shift," *American Psychologist*, 28, no. 3 (March 1973): 222–231.
18. Ibid., 238.
19. I. Janis, "Groupthink," *Psychology Today* (November 1971): 43–46; *Victims of Groupthink*, 2nd ed., Boston: Houghton Mifflin (1982).

Control and Systems Improvement

15
CHAPTER

Statistical and Other Quality Tools for Systems Improvement

LEARNING OBJECTIVES

After reading this chapter, you should be able to accomplish the following:

- Describe the steps in the traditional management control cycle.
- Contrast corrective action and systems improvement.
- Relate common and special causes of variation.
- Describe the role that statistical thinking plays in systems improvement to yield better value for customers.
- Compare and contrast stable and unstable processes.
- Discuss the manager's role in systems improvement for stable and unstable processes.
- Describe control charts and the six other quality tools: Pareto charts, histograms, scatter plots, check sheets, cause-and-effect diagrams, and flowcharts.

CHAPTER OUTLINE

Traditional Management Control
- *Determine Objectives*
- *Establish Financial and Economic Measures*
- *Measure Performance*
- *Take Corrective Action*
- *Process and Systems Improvement versus Control*

Managing in the Presence of Variation
- *Statistical Thinking*
- *Common Causes of Variation*
- *Special Causes of Variation*
- *Customer-Relevant Measures*

Statistical Process Control
- *Control Charts and Run Charts*
- *Stable Processes*
- *Unstable Processes*
- *Process and Systems Improvement*
- *Capable Processes*

Six Other Quality Tools
- *Check Sheets*
- *Pareto Analysis and Charts*
- *Histograms*
- *Scatter Plots*
- *Cause-and-Effect Diagrams*
- *Flowcharts*

Cases and Exhibits
- *Eastman Chemical Company*
- *Alcoholic Employees*
- *Diversity through Values*
- *ICL*
- *Sea Ray Boats*
- *Bhopal*
- *Capsugel/Warner-Lambert*

Eastman Chemical Company

Eastman Chemical won a Baldrige Award in 1993 by concentrating on process improvement and SPC as key parts of their Total Quality efforts.
(Photo credit: Eastman Chemical Company.)

Eastman Chemical Company had been a major division of Eastman Kodak Company. It was started in 1920 to provide chemicals to the parent company in the photographic business. Over the years Eastman grew into a major chemical company, with 1993 world-wide sales of about $4 billion. On January 1, 1994, it was spun off from the parent firm and became an independent company.

Headquartered in Kingsport, Tennessee, Eastman has plants in several states in the United States and in several other countries. Eastman makes more than 400 products, including plastics for soft-drink bottles, acetate filters for cigarettes, polymer pellets for steering wheels, and other hard-molded plastic products.

The chemical industry is a highly competitive industry, with significant investments in the plant and equipment that produce the chemicals and chemical products in high volume. Anyone who has ever visited a chemical company knows that the investment in plant and equipment is substantial. Many chemical companies run their plant and equipment around the clock because shutting them down would cause problems in many of the processes and clog the equipment.

The complex plant and equipment yields many activities and processes to transform raw material or generic chemicals into finished chemicals, or products ready for shipment to customers. This makes the flow of material and the processes especially important in a chemical company.

Eastman also recognized that the chemical industry was a globally competitive business. Over the last two decades international competitors like Hoechst Celanese and BASF sold chemical products in the United States, as well as in many other countries. Many countries had their own chemical companies.

DISCUSSION QUESTIONS

1. Eastman described its "Strategic Intent (Vision) to be the world's preferred chemical company." How would Eastman grow and prosper in such an industry?

2. In a globally competitive business, how would Eastman realize its strategic intent?

Today managers are charged with improving the quality of the products and services offered to customers by their organizations. This requires improvement in the systems and processes that yield the products and services. Such steps require proactive managerial actions different from those found in traditional, reactive management control systems.

TRADITIONAL MANAGEMENT CONTROL

Controlling means ensuring that the organization is actually achieving its planned objectives. The traditional management control process, which unfortunately included the notion of corrective action after the product has been produced or the service has been rendered, consists of the several steps described below (see Figure 15.1).[1]

Determine Objectives

Planning and control are linked in the first step of determining objectives. *Planning* is deciding in advance what the organization's objectives ought to be and what its members ought to do to attain those objectives. Thus many managers speak of their planning and control system.

Objectives should be specific, measurable, time phased, and realistic. Specificity and realism are important in that these characteristics mean that the goals are achievable. There is little positive motivational impact on employees—and there may even be negative motivational impact—if they think they cannot achieve the goal.

The objectives, which express a hope for the future in terms of goals, may be short-, medium-, or long-term goals. Short-term goals may be accomplished within one year, medium-term goals within one to five years, and long-term goals within five years or more.

Establish Financial and Economic Measures

Goals should be measurable so that managers can determine if progress is being made toward accomplishing them. These goals usually are expressed as output goals in economic and financial terms, such as an increase in total dollar sales or an increase in profitability.

Measurement often implies priority. Many managers have found that you get what you measure. If managers measure financially relevant behaviors, then many organizational members rightly conclude that financial goals are most important for the organization. This may also suggest that owners and stockholders are the most important stakeholders for the organization.

Measure Performance

Once the goals have been set and the measures determined, then managers must measure the actual performance. Obviously, there is a time lag between setting a goal and measuring the actual performance. If the goal is a long-term goal of over five years, the time lags are often too long to allow for corrective action. A problem with most output-relevant goals is that there is a considerable time lag between when the activities are performed and when the output like profitability is measured.

FIGURE 15.1   *Traditional Management Control Cycle*

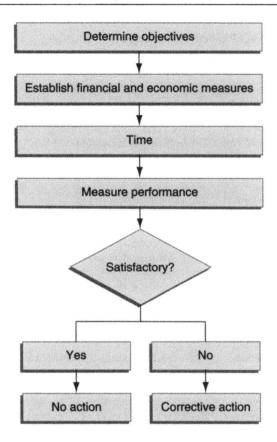

The following ethics exhibit demonstrates how in some ethical situations a time lag associated with certain output measures may not be tolerable. The manager may need to confront the situation and address the process before the situation has deteriorated. Waiting until the output has been measured may be too late.

Take Corrective Action

If the actual performance is not in line with the objective, then corrective action is taken. Because of the time lags and the output orientation of many measures, it is rare that such corrective action treats the cause or source of the problem. The feedback of information may simply determine how realistic the organization's goals may be in the future.

Having "fixed" the problem, the manager typically advances to the next problem to be "solved." Herein lies the weakness in traditional management control: Without treating the cause of the problem, without improving the process that caused the problem, the problem will likely recur. And another manager will be rewarded for "fixing" another problem.

E T H I C S   E X H I B I T

How to Confront—and Help—an Alcoholic Employee

Unless you work for a very small company, at least one of your colleagues probably has a drinking problem. And if you're a manager, the odds are that you haven't done anything about it.

Most managers dread the idea of confronting an alcohol abuser. They don't know what to say. In some fields, such as journalism and sales, drinking may seem such an integral part of the job that it seems unfair to single anyone out. And you can almost count on getting the runaround. "No one but alcoholics will talk so much about how little they drink," says Eugene McWilliams, chairman of the National Council on Alcoholism and Drug Dependence.

Delicate Art. Still, McWilliams and other experts say intervention is often the only way to get an alcoholic into treatment. Fortunately, such tactics are especially effective at work. "The reality that your job is on the line is usually quite an eye-opener," says Carol Cepress, who runs a program that helps businesses deal with alcoholics at the Hazelden treatment center in Center City, Minnesota.

But intervention doesn't work if it's not done right. Once you suspect a problem, begin documenting instances in which job performance has fallen short. Absenteeism is one problem characteristic of the alcoholic employee. The drinker may habitually leave the office early or arrive late and take more days off than others. Accidents, errors, and an overall decline in quantity or quality of work are increasingly evident. An alcoholic's mood swings may also lead to a rise in conflicts with other employees.

Once you have marshaled the facts, set up a meeting. But don't get right to the point. That's the last thing the experts recommend. Instead, they advise managers not even to mention drinking, let alone diagnose alcoholism.

Instead, says Susan Swan-Grainger, executive director of Employee Assistance of Central Virginia, which provides EAP services for some 20,000 employees from different companies, "keep the discussion focused on performance." Outline the shortcomings, insist on improvement, and then ask if there is anything you can do to help.

The alcoholic employee will probably promise to improve. But almost inevitably, performance problems will recur, often within just a few weeks. Now it's time for a tougher session. At this meeting, Swan-Grainger says, still avoid the issue of drinking, and say: "I don't know what's wrong with you, but I want you to see an employee assistance counselor." To give the worker an extra push, Swan-Grainger advises setting up the appointment yourself.

This approach leaves the diagnosis and treatment recommendations to trained counselors. But you can increase the odds of success by "telling them that if performance doesn't improve, they'll be disciplined," says Dr. Gary M. Kohn, the corporate medical director at United Air Lines Inc.

Consider how American Telephone & Telegraph Company handled Steven, 36, a middle manager in its international operations who was addicted to both alcohol and cocaine. Steven, who asked that his last name not be used, says he was coming into work late every day, often on little or no sleep. Early last year, while exploring a possible transfer within AT&T, he ran up a four-figure balance for personal expenses on his corporate credit card. With this, AT&T nixed the transfer, and his boss urged Steven to see a counselor—without accusing him of anything specific. Steven entered treatment in May and has been sober since. His performance has improved, and he recently got another transfer he wanted.

Many managers put off confronting employees like Steven, often in the belief they're being kind. To the contrary, confrontation may be the kindest course. Steven says that intervention "saved my life." And AT&T seems to have reclaimed a young worker whose gratitude and restored ability could result in years of productive service.

Source: William C. Symonds and Peter Coy, "Is Business Bungling Its Battle with Booze?" Reprinted from March 25, 1991 Issue of *Business Week* by special permission, copyright © 1991 by McGraw-Hill, Inc.

Process and Systems Improvement versus Control

Continuous improvement is the constant refinement and improvement of products, services, and organizational systems to yield improved value to customers. *Processes* are groups of activities that take an input, add value to it, and provide an output to an internal or external customer. *Systems* are collections of processes and resources. Systems and process improvement to yield improved products and services is the major difference between Total Quality Management and traditional management control that stresses corrective action after the fact.

This difference strikes to the very core of how management is defined. *Management* is the creation and continuous improvement of organizational systems that when used by organizational members lead to increased value for the customers of its products or services. A major theme of this book is the primary responsibility of managers to improve systems and processes. The tools for process and systems improvement covered herein, important as they are, are not the primary message.

How important is this task of process and systems improvement for managers? Deming commented on the potential for payoff from managerial improvement activities when he estimated the percentage of problems associated with the system: "I should estimate that in my experience most troubles and most possibilities for improvement add up to proportions something like this: 94 percent belong to the system [*responsibility of management*], 6 percent special" (emphasis added).[2]

The common elements of success in many TQM efforts were recently noted, and prominent among them was: "Systematically improving the quality of all business processes from an internal and (especially) external customer perspective."[3]

Process and systems improvement aims to continually improve processes and systems to yield continually improved value to customers before problems occur. In this way problems are prevented, rather than being corrected after they occur. Rather than inspection and repair after production and delivery, process and systems improvement activities decrease the chance that defects or problems will occur.

Many managers argue: "If it isn't broke, don't fix it." Managers in TQ firms counter: "If it isn't perfect, make it better." This improvement theme requires several tools and different ideas, including understanding the kinds of variation in a process, as we shall discuss in the next section.

The following diversity exhibit shows how Eastman Chemical Company promotes diversity through a set of values called "The Eastman Way." These values relating to people are meant to shape the system in regard to diversity rather than deal with diversity problems after they have occurred.

CRITICAL THINKING QUESTIONS

1. How does the short-term orientation of some managers reinforce the idea of corrective action?

2. Relate the idea of process and systems improvement to the concept of the customer as a stakeholder.

THE EASTMAN WAY

Eastman people are the key to success. We have recognized throughout our history the importance of treating each other fairly and with respect. We will enhance these beliefs by building upon the following values and principles:

Honesty and Integrity
We are honest with ourselves and others. Our integrity is exhibited through relationships with coworkers, customers, suppliers, and neighbors. Our goal is truth in all relationships.

Fairness
We treat each other as we expect to be treated.

Trust
We respect and rely on each other. Fair treatment, honesty in our relationships, and confidence in each other create trust.

Teamwork
We are empowered to manage our areas of responsibility. We work together to achieve common goals for business success. Full participation, cooperation, and open communication lead to superior results.

Diversity
We value different points of view. Men and women from different races, cultures, and backgrounds enrich the generation and usefulness of these different points of view. We create an environment that enables all employees to reach their full potential in pursuit of company objectives.

Employee Well-Being
We have a safe, healthy, and desirable workplace. Stability of employment is given high priority. Growth in employee skills is essential. Recognition for contributions and full utilization of employees' capabilities promote job satisfaction.

Citizenship
We are valued by our community for our contributions as individuals and as a company. We protect health and safety and the environment by being good stewards of our products and our processes.

Winning Attitude
Our can-do attitude and desire for excellence drive continual improvement, making us winners in everything we do.

E.W. Deavenport, Jr.
President

EASTMAN

Source: Eastman Chemical Company, Kingsport, TN (1993).

MANAGING IN THE PRESENCE OF VARIATION

Variation in outputs, systems, and processes has considerable significance for managerial practice. Different kinds of variability in output have different implications for managerial behavior and for the systems associated with yielding value for customers. Confusion concerning the causes of variation can lead to inappropriate managerial behavior.[4]

Statistical Thinking

Statistical thinking stresses that all work activities are part of larger processes with variation. Statistical thinking recognizes that all processes have variability and that variability can arise from two different causes—common cause and special cause. Deming commented on the importance of managers' recognizing variation and attempting to reduce it. "Understanding of variation, special causes and common causes, and the necessity to reduce constantly the variation from common causes, is vital."[5]

The major factors involved in many TQM failures have recently been noted: "The overreliance on statistical methods, and the underreliance on statistical methods."[6] The underreliance means that statistical methods are very important, but the overreliance means that they cannot be the sole feature of TQ.

Data are used to understand the variation and its causes in a process. Many TQ organizations are fond of the saying: "In God we trust. All others bring data."

Learning about variation in a process precedes improving the process. Reducing variation with data analysis is at the heart of systems and process improvement. Note that "statistical methods, process emphasis, and continual improvement" are some of the principles in Eastman's Quality Policy, which is reproduced in the following continuation of this chapter's quality case.

Common Causes of Variation

Common causes of variation are those system sources that affect each and every result in a series.[7] All the data are within the boundaries of variation in the historical data. Common-cause variation is always present in a system, although the assignable cause or causes may not be found. There may be many sources of variation or many causes of variation in the system. The result of these causes is predictable, as is a certain amount of noise or chance variation in the data.

Figure 15.2 is an example of common-cause variation. Given the current system and processes behind the data, a certain amount of fluctuation in units produced per labor hour is predictable. The variation is within a certain predictable range.

Special Causes of Variation

Special causes of variation are present at isolated times to yield variation in addition to that produced by common causes.[8] As such, special-cause variation is sporadic and is not predictable. Although the data are not predictable, they can be linked with an assignable event. Thus special-cause variation is also known as signal or assignable variation. The data associated with special-cause variation are few in number.

FIGURE 15.2 *Common-Cause Variation*

Source: R. S. Sanders, M. Leitnaker, and G. Ranney, "Managing in the Presence of Variation," in M. J. Stahl and G. M. Bounds, *Competing Globally Through Customer Value,* Quorum Books, 1991, 255. Reprinted with permission of Greenwood Publishing Group, Inc., Westport, CT. Copyright © 1991 Greenwood Publishing Group, Inc.

Figure 15.3 is an example of special-cause variation. The last data point in the series is not predictable from the range of the data before it. There is a special cause of variation in the last data point that requires further investigation to determine the assignable event.

This distinction between common and special causes of variation is crucial to system improvement activities. Frequently, confusion between these two sources of variation leads to mistakes in managerial attempts to improve the system. Deming reminded us of this confusion when he wrote about these two mistakes:

> *"Mistake 1.* To react to an outcome as if it came from a special cause, when actually it came from common causes of variation.
>
> *Mistake 2.* To treat an outcome as if it came from common causes of variation, when actually it came from a special cause."[9]

Most variation in a system arises from common causes of variation. Knowledge of the system based on data and experience, combined with some of the quality improvement tools, will help the manager discover the common causes of variation.

Customer-Relevant Measures

To improve the system, the manager should determine which measures to follow. What data should be collected?

Statistical thinking causes the manager to recognize that activities are parts of processes. Many processes do not suffer the time lag that many output-relevant measures suffer. For example, "the fraction of customer service requests taking more than five days to answer" is a real-time process measure. It does not have the time lag of measuring return on assets for the year.

FIGURE 15.3 *Special Cause Variation*

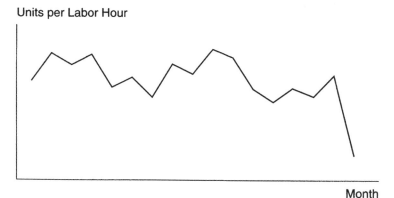

Source: R. S. Sanders, M. Leitnaker, and G. Ranney, "Managing in the Presence of Variation," in M. J. Stahl and G. M. Bounds, *Competing Globally Through Customer Value,* Quorum Books, 1991, 255. Reprinted with permission of Greenwood Publishing Group, Inc., Westport, CT. Copyright © 1991 Greenwood Publishing Group, Inc.

Total Quality Management is a systems approach to management that aims to continuously increase value to customers by designing and continuously improving organizational processes and systems. To continuously improve value to customers, managers improve systems. It is useful to ask: If the system is not customer relevant, then what is the purpose of the system?

Examples of customer-relevant measures for managers are sales, percentage growth in sales, time to introduce new products, and market share. Examples of customer-relevant service measures are service time and number of complaints. Examples of customer-relevant manufacturing measures are customer-relevant product characteristics (weight, dimensions, color, chemical composition), and percentage not meeting customer specifications. Customer-relevant administrative measures are number of errors and time to complete the activity.

The following international exhibit shows how ICL, a European computer firm, uses continuous improvement of processes to deliver more value to customers. The point values in the exhibit refer to a maximum of 1,000 points on The European Quality Award. In 1993 ICL won The European Quality Prize.

CRITICAL THINKING QUESTIONS

1. Give an example of a common cause of variation and a special cause of variation associated with the length of time to receive treatment in a hospital emergency room.

2. How could the use of statistical thinking help improve the registration system at your college or university?

STATISTICAL PROCESS CONTROL

Based on statistical thinking and a recognition of common and special causes of variation, statistical process control (SPC) is used in many organizations to improve

I N T E R N A T I O N A L   E X H I B I T

Quality the ICL Way: 1993–1997

Quality and Customer Care

Our goal is to exceed our customers' expectations and to delight them with personal service; we call it Customer Care. If Customer Care is one critical success factor, the other is continuous improvement, involving everyone in making small improvements in products, services and processes and in the way they work for customers. We have developed a new continuous improvement process called dELTA, the aim of which is to "improve a thousand things by 1 percent rather than one thing by 1,000 percent." However, Conformance Quality remains fundamental and in 1993 the Executive Management Committee assigns the highest priority to improving product delivery performance and reliability, and to making ICL easier to do business with in the specific area of invoicing.

The Four Phases of Quality Improvement

We will continue to structure our plans across four phases. The characteristics and TQ capability of a business division that has reached maturity in a phase are described below and in the accompanying illustration.

1. Conformance Quality
— Prevention operates throughout the division, which is registered to ISO9000. Products are validated against agreed customer requirements and processes are designed, not simply allowed to evolve.

— Independent market research proves that products and services consistently meet customers' requirements. *The Executive Management Committee assigns the highest priority in 1993 to improving product delivery performance and reliability and to make ICL easier to do business with in the specific area of invoicing.*

— TQ capability is at least 450 points on the Strategic Quality Model.

2. Customer-Driven Quality
— All staff are constantly involved in implementing measures to improve customer care, and managers talk more about customers than about business numbers.

— Independent surveys—which have been used for at least two years—confirm that customer satisfaction is higher than the division's two best direct competitors. *The target remains unchanged. Customer Satisfaction must be higher than the two best direct competitors in each of our chosen markets, worldwide, by the end of 1994.*

— TQ capability is at least 600 points.

3. Market-Driven Quality
— Continuous improvement is a way of life, and ideas for improvement are continuously sought from suppliers, partners and customers.

continued

processes. **Statistical process control (SPC)** is the application of statistical thinking and statistical analysis of data to control and improve processes. SPC uses control charts to understand stable and unstable processes, to reduce variation, and to improve the system.

Control Charts and Run Charts

Data collection of customer-relevant measures and plots of the time-ordered data are an essential part of SPC. A **run chart** is a time-ordered plot of data associated with a process. Figures 15.2 and 15.3 are examples of run charts.

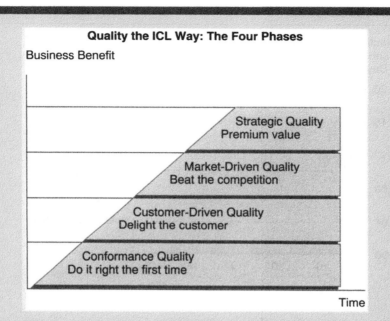

Quality the ICL Way: The Four Phases

Business Benefit

Strategic Quality
Premium value

Market-Driven Quality
Beat the competition

Customer-Driven Quality
Delight the customer

Conformance Quality
Do it right the first time

Time

The dELTA continuous improvement process will be introduced throughout the company, and the immediate target is 150,000 dELTA ideas in 1993 with the rates of adoption and involvement both at 50 percent.

— Best Practice Benchmarking is in use and TQ capability is at least 750 points.

4. Strategic Quality

— Best Practice Benchmarking is a way of life.

— Customers consistently receive premium value systems, products and services.

— The division has an international reputation for quality and customer care.

— TQ capability is at least 900 points. In 1993 the targets are 600 points on the Strategic Quality Model (SQM) in UK and Personal Systems and 450 points for Europe and International. We remain committed to having every business division's capability assessed at greater than 750 points by the end of 1994.

Source: Courtesy of ICL, London, England. (1993).

A **control chart** is a run chart with statistically determined upper (upper control limit—UCL) and lower (lower control limit—LCL) control limits drawn on either side of the process average. The control limits define the noise or random variation in the process. Data outside of the limits indicate a signal or assignable variation due to a special cause. SPC can be used to examine stable and unstable processes.

Stable Processes

A **stable process** is one in which the process measure shows no evidence of special-causes of variation. A control chart for a stable process contains the data within the upper and lower control limits, as in Figure 15.4. A stable process is sometimes referred to as a *consistent process* or an *in-control process*.

FIGURE 15.4 *Stable Process*

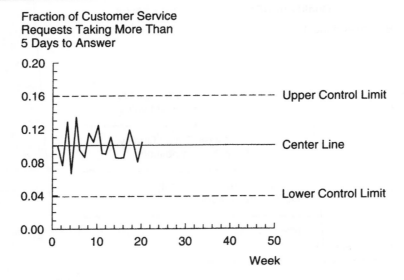

There are several advantages to stable processes. The greatest is process predictability: Process performance, costs, and quantities can be anticipated with stable processes. Another advantage is in terms of process improvement: Planned process improvements can be measured and evaluated with data.

A stable process does not necessarily mean that the product or service will meet the customer's needs. *In-control* or *stable* means only that the process is predictable and consistent. For example, the drive-in system at a bank may consistently yield waiting times ranging from zero to 12 minutes with an average of 6 minutes. However, customers may demand waiting times of less than 6 minutes.

Unstable Processes

An **unstable process** is one in which the process measure shows evidence of special causes of variation. A control chart for an unstable process contains some of the data outside of the upper and lower control limits. In Figure 15.5 the two data points occurring above 0.16 fraction of customer service requests are evidence of special causes and an unstable process. An unstable process is sometimes referred to as an *out-of-control process* or an *inconsistent process.*

Unstable processes are hard to predict because the manager never knows when there will be a special cause of variation that will produce data beyond the range of experience. Process improvement is difficult in unstable processes because special causes of variation may mask the effects of an improvement.

Eliminating special causes is an important managerial action in movement toward stable processes. Timely data are required so that special causes can be determined quickly. After the specific, temporary, or local problem has been cor-

FIGURE 15.5 *Unstable Process*

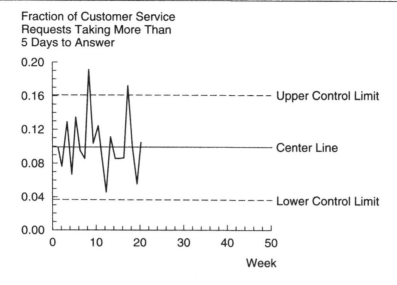

rected, the manager should prevent the special cause from recurring. Once the special causes have been eliminated and the process is stable, then the manager can move to improve that stable process.

In noting the importance of eliminating special causes of variation, Deming found himself in agreement with Juran: "Removal of a special cause of variation, to move toward statistical control, important though it be, is not improvement of the process. Removal of a special cause only brings the system back to where it should have been in the first place [quoting a lecture by Dr. Juran]. In repetition, as Dr. Juran also said, the important problems of improvement commence once you achieve statistical control."[10]

Process and Systems Improvement

Once the process is stable with no special causes of variation, process improvement means that features of the process that are always present need to be changed. This usually requires managerial action for improvement, because fundamental changes in the system are often required, and such changes usually necessitate expenditure of funds. Different equipment, different procedures, more operator training, more equipment maintenance, and different suppliers are all examples of changes to improve the system.

Improving a stable process may involve reducing the variation and/or changing the average of the process. Figure 15.6 shows both kinds of improvements to stable processes. Both forms of changes in the system should yield process improvements with greater value to customers.

FIGURE 15.6 *Improving a Stable Process*

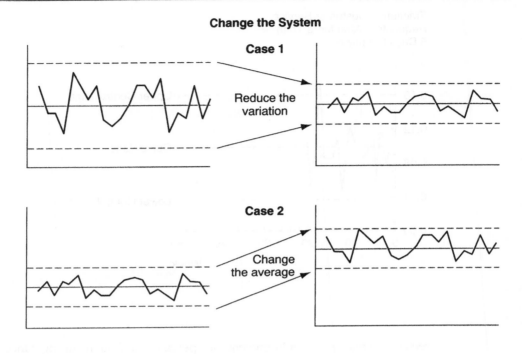

Capable Processes

The purpose of process improvement is to yield processes that meet customers' requirements. A **capable process** is one that meets customers' requirements. Process capability is a process requirement in addition to process stability.

The following quality exhibit shows how Brunswick Corporation's Sea Ray Boats Division uses process improvement to reduce the cost of quality.

CRITICAL THINKING QUESTIONS

1. How could a control chart help you to improve your body weight in a year?

2. Describe stable and unstable processes using basketball and football analogies.

SIX OTHER QUALITY TOOLS

Statistical process control is the tool most often used to improve systems. However, there are other tools that can be just as important, in certain applications, in identifying ways to change the process and improve the system.

QUALITY EXHIBIT

The Cost of Quality at Sea Ray Boats

The Cost of Quality

The cost of quality (COQ) is often described as revenues wasted on activities that do not add value to the product or service of a company. The COQ can be broadly defined as all the costs of doing things wrong or doing things over. These are real costs with real dollars attached to them. The COQ is an essential measurement of quality improvement because it is real and it is nonconfrontational. Since the COQ is the responsibility of everyone, no group or individual need be defensive about it. Everyone can freely discuss ways to increase operational efficiency without fear of finger pointing. Using the COQ, we can measure the time or materials spent to do things over. And we do this without having to find a scapegoat.

Ignoring the cost of quality can be very expensive for businesses today. Can you imagine any manager reporting that he's spending 20 percent of his earnings inspecting, testing, and fixing what he's just built? Yet this is typical of what is spent today by most businesses.

Lowering the Cost of Quality

As you focus on pleasing your customers, consider everything you do that does not add value to the process. Without complaining or placing blame, identify all the internal "hassles" that waste your time. Things like needless paperwork, waiting for approvals, and telephone tag are all time consuming and add very little to the process. Over the years a "layer of hassles" builds up to the point that people feel powerless to change it.

We know we must take control of the spiraling cost of quality. But first we must identify the

By involving employees such as Nancy Luster at all levels in quality improvement, Sea Ray has further enhanced the already high-quality boats. (Photo credit: Sea Ray Boat Division/Brunswick Corporation.)

offending time wasters and verify their cost in terms of wasted time and materials. Then we must reduce or eliminate those activities without sacrificing product quality. This is often done by refining or eliminating systems and controls that have outlived their intended use. If you have difficulty determining which systems have outlived their use, ask your employees, they'll know.

Source: *PACE Program Manual*, Sea Ray Boats Division of Brunswick Corporation, Knoxville, TN (1993): 4.

Check Sheets

A **check sheet** is a table, usually in matrix form, to record the frequency of problems. A check sheet records the frequency of problems by type of problem and is usually the first step in turning opinion into data. Figure 15.7 is an example of a check sheet.

QUALITY CASE

Back to the Eastman Chemical Case

Eastman Chemical Company decided to focus on quality by tying process improvement to customer requirements. In describing its quality journey, Eastman focused on the role of customer requirements, continual process improvement, and statistical process control. "In 1980, Eastman established a goal to be the First in Quality. While Eastman's Marketing organization worked to define customer needs, Manufacturing established statistical process control (SPC) systems to identify the capabilities within processes. This led to the implementation of improvement breakthroughs as processes were brought into line to meet customer fitness-for-use requirements."

To implement this quality emphasis, Eastman formulated and widely disseminated its Quality Policy, which is reproduced on page 427. Note the emphasis on processes throughout the Quality Policy. Processes are tied to continual improvement through statistical methods to satisfy customers.

The Eastman Way (page 416) deals with Eastman's approach to human resources. Its approach to diversity builds on a set of people values as part of a process, rather than trying to correct demographic data after the fact.

Top management leadership and training also figure importantly in Eastman's focus on quality. Earnie Deavenport, chairman and CEO of Eastman, remarked: "My senior management team has a quality meeting every week." Each employee spends a substantial amount of time each year learning about TQM methods.

continued

A check sheet is a quick and simple way to collect data about a homogeneous population. If the population is heterogeneous, however, it should be grouped first into separate, similar groups and sampled separately.

It is important for the manager to ensure that there is no fear of attribution, which might lead to recording false instead of actual data. It is also important for the manager to ensure that instructions are understood and consistently followed. Since the data are often used for a Pareto analysis (see next section), the data must be accurate and consistent.

FIGURE 15.7   *Check Sheet*

Problem	Day 1	Day 2	Day 3	Day 4	Total
A	///		//		5
B		/	/		2
C	//				2
D		///	/	//	6
Total	5	4	4	2	15

QUALITY POLICY

Quality Goal

To be the leader in quality and value of products and services

Quality Management Process

- Focus on customers.
- Establish mission, vision, and indicators of performance.
- Understand, standardize, stabilize, and maintain processes.
- Plan, do, check, act for continual improvement and innovation.

Operational Policy

- Achieve process stability and reliability.
- Control every process to the desired target.
- Improve process capability.

Principles

Customer Satisfaction	Anticipate, understand, and excel at meeting customer needs.
Continual Improvement	Improve the current level of performance of processes, products, and services.
Innovation	Search for and implement creative processes, products, and services.
Process Emphasis	Focus on processes as the means to improve results.
Management Leadership	Create and maintain a shared vision, constancy of purpose, and supportive environment that includes appropriate recognition and reinforcement.
Empowerment	Create a culture where people have the knowledge, skills, authority, and desire to decide, act, and take responsibility for results of their actions and for their contribution to the success of the company.
Statistical Methods	Understand the concept of variation and apply appropriate statistical methods for continual improvement and innovation.
Employee Development	Encourage and support lifelong learning and personal growth.
Partnerships	Build long-term relationships with customers and suppliers.
Assessment	Assess performance and benchmark against world's best.

E.W. Deavenport, Jr.
President

EASTMAN

FIGURE 15.8 *Pareto Chart Showing Final Inspection Rejects: Automotive Hose Division*

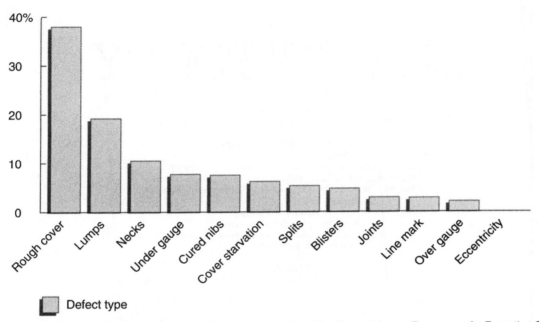

☐ Defect type

Source: Courtesy of BTR Hose. Barrie Dale and C. Cooper, *Total Quality and Human Resources: An Executive Guide*, Cambridge, MA: Blackwell (1992): 213.

Pareto Analysis and Charts

Pareto analysis is a technique that indicates which problems to solve and in what order.[11] It is based on the belief that most problems stem from only a few causes. This is often known as the 80/20 rule, since in many processes 80 percent of the problems are associated with only 20 percent of the causes.

Ranking data concerning problems with the most common problems at the top and the least common at the bottom allows the construction of a Pareto chart. A **Pareto chart** is a vertical bar graph that shows each problem area along the *x*-axis in descending order and percentages or frequency counts on the *y*-axis.

Figure 15.8 is an example of a Pareto chart. It shows data on rejects of automotive hoses from BTR Hose, a European firm. Note that about 60 percent of the rejects are associated with the first two causes.

Pareto analysis and charts are used in process improvement to indicate the relative importance of problems and to determine the order in which they should be solved. The process should be improved and the results remeasured. An improvement similar to that in Figure 15.6 should be observed. Then the problem with the next highest percentage of frequency should be selected and the process associated with it improved. This cycle of problem identification and process improvement should be repeated continuously.

Histograms

A **histogram** is a graphic representation of the frequency distribution of measured data. A histogram takes measured data and displays the distribution using the class intervals or values as a base. Thus a histogram resembles a bar chart in which the bars represent frequency of data.

Figure 15.9 is an example of a histogram. It shows the frequency distribution of the pH factor of effluent of a manufacturing process at Grace Dearborn Ltd., a European firm.

A histogram reveals the amount of variation in a process. Tall, narrow distributions reveal limited variability, whereas flat, wide distributions display more variability.

Histograms also show whether the data are symmetrical. Such observations can be compared with managers' understanding of what the shape of the data should be. Many processes show normal or bell-shaped distributions, as in Figure 15.9.

A shortcoming of histograms is that they show variability at only one point in time. A control chart is used to show variability over time.

Scatter Plots

A **scatter plot** displays graphically what happens to one variable when another variable changes, in order to test a theory that the two variables are related.[12] A scatter plot is designed so that the *x*-axis shows the measurement values of one variable and the *y*-axis shows the measurement values of the second variable.

Figure 15.10 is an example of a scatter plot with a positive relationship. A negative relationship would be denoted by the data sloping from the upper left to the lower right.

The direction and tightness of the data around a line indicate the strength of the relationship between the two variables. The more the data approach a straight line, the stronger the relationship between the two variables.

Scatter plots are useful in determining if process improvements can be made by changing one variable in order to improve another variable. A drawback to the use of scatter plots is that even if the data suggest that a relationship exists between the two variables, a cause-and-effect relationship has not been demonstrated. Further research on the process is needed.

Cause-and-Effect Diagrams

A **cause-and-effect diagram** is a simple graphic picture of the causes that go into the makeup of a common effect. The diagram is meant to represent the relationship between a certain effect and all the possible causes associated with that effect. Cause-and-effect diagrams are often referred to as fishbone diagrams because of their skeletal shape, with the effect (a specific problem) as the head and the possible causes as the bone structure of the fish. The diagrams are also referred to as Ishikawa diagrams because of Kaoru Ishikawa's early advocacy of their use.[13]

Figure 15.11 is an example of a cause-and-effect diagram. The diagram is used to help uncover the root causes of waste in a chemical process at Grace Dearborn

FIGURE 15.9 *Histogram: Effluent Analysis—pH*

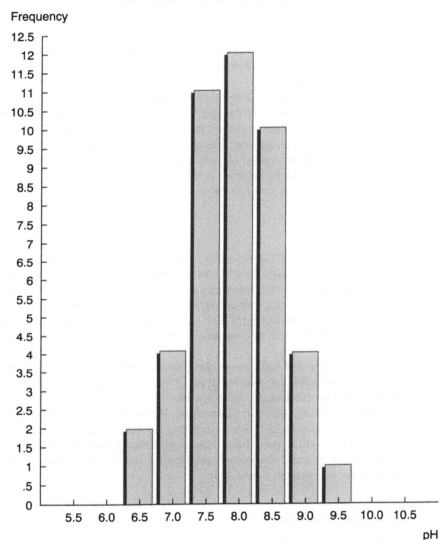

Histogram: Effluent Analysis—pH

Source: Courtesy of Grace Dearborn Ltd., Barrie Dale and C. Cooper, *Total Quality and Human Resources: An Executive Guide,* Cambridge, MA: Blackwell (1992): 206.

Ltd., a European firm. Figure 15.11 is referred to as a 6M cause-and-effect diagram because it deals with six Ms, where environment is the sixth M (Mother Nature). A simpler cause-and-effect diagram might contain 4Ms or 5Ms or other factors.

FIGURE 15.10   *Scatter Plot*

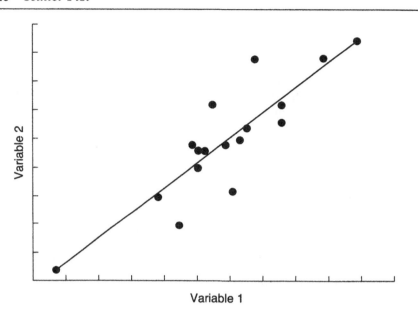

FIGURE 15.11   *Cause-and-Effect Diagram*

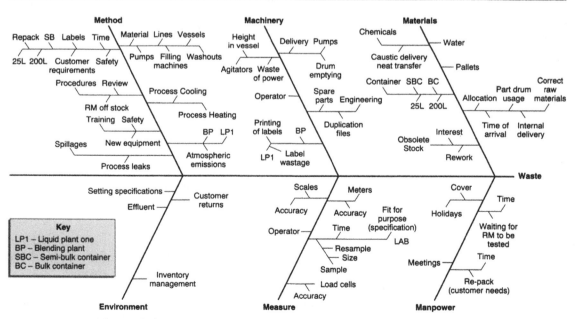

Source: Courtesy of Grace Dearborn Ltd., Barrie Dale and C. Cooper, *Total Quality and Human Resources: An Executive Guide,* Cambridge, MA: Blackwell (1992): 216.

Conclusion to the Eastman Chemical Case

Eastman Chemical Company's long quality journey has paid off handsomely for the firm. Its decade-old quality improvement journey helped to generate above-average sales from new products, high customer satisfaction, and a strong safety record.

In October 1993 Eastman was notified that it had won a Malcolm Baldrige National Quality Award. Its quality journey was not a short trip. Commenting on the award, Deavenport remarked: "This high honor is the culmination of over a decade of just plain hard work at finding out what our customers wanted and then putting the processes into place that satisfied their needs. Not a simple job for a company with over 7,000 customers worldwide, but we did it—year by year."

Its parent, Eastman Kodak Company, under pressure from the financial community to boost its stock price, had decided earlier to spin off Eastman Chemical Company on January 1, 1994. Reflecting Eastman's optimism over winning the Baldrige and its confidence as it prepared for the future as an independent company with $4 billion in sales worldwide, Deavenport commented: "We can't think of any better way to introduce ourselves to the world."

DISCUSSION QUESTIONS

1. On the basis of the Eastman case, discuss the importance of tying process improvement to customer requirements.

2. Why is a reputation for quality so important for a company just establishing itself as an independent organization?

Sources: "Kodak Unit, Ames Rubber Are Given Baldriges Amid Tougher Standards," *The Wall Street Journal* (October 19, 1993): A22; "Eastman Chemical Shows It's Ready to Leave the Nest," *USA Today* (October 19, 1993): 4B; "Strategic Intent," Kingsport, TN: Eastman Chemical Company (1993); "Eastman Chemical Company's Quality Journey," Kingsport, TN: Eastman Chemical Company (1993); "Eastman Wins '93 Nationwide Quality Award," *Knoxville News-Sentinel* (October 19, 1993): C1.

A flowchart can also be used to show the structure of an organization, especially if the organization is principally horizontal. Figure 15.12 is a cause-and-effect diagram for the Total Quality effort at the United Kingdom's post office—the Royal Mail.

The Royal Mail has been associated with impressive levels of customer service. Figure 15.13 benchmarks the reliability of the Royal Mail against other European Community post offices. The data indicate that TQ at the Royal Mail is paying off for customers.

Flowcharts

A **flowchart** is a pictorial representation showing all the steps of a process.[14] It is used to depict, with a set of symbols, all the steps in a particular process.

Flowcharts use conventional symbols to define activities.[15] One convention is that a rectangle represents a process, a triangle represents a decision, and a circle represents contribution or participation. Figure 15.14 is a flowchart for a family with two small children on a vacation involving driving to the destination.

FIGURE 15.12   *Total Quality Cause-and-Effect Diagram: The Royal Mail*

Source: R. Heller, *TQM The Quality Makers: The Leaders and Shapers of Europe's Quality Revolution,* St. Gallen, Switzerland: Norden Publishing House Ltd. (1993): 26.

FIGURE 15.13   *Benchmarking Royal Mail Reliability*

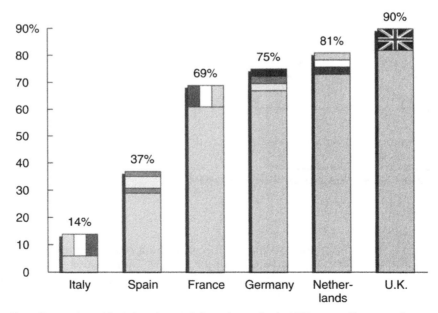

Note: Percentage of first-class letters delivered next day in 1992 across European Community.

Source: R. Heller, *TQM Quality Makers: The Leaders and Shapers of Europe's Quality Revolution,* St. Gallen, Switzerland: Norden Publishing House Ltd. (1993): 244.

FIGURE 15.14   *Flowchart for a Family Vacation*

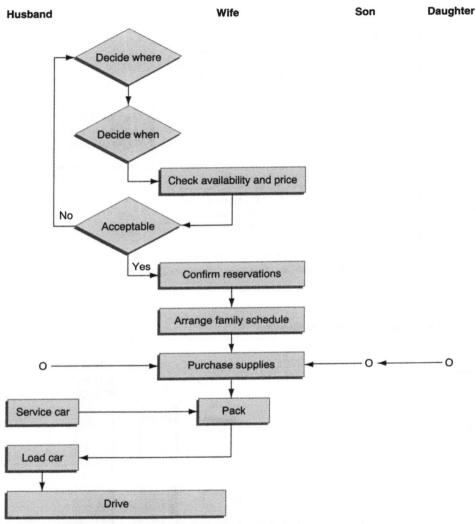

Note: O = input of information from husband, son, and daughter to wife (mother)

For process improvement to occur, it is important that each stage of the process be included so that attention can be focused on activities in which problems have occurred. One way to do this is to draw a flowchart of the steps that the process actually follows, and then draw a flowchart of the steps the process *should* follow. In the family vacation example of Figure 15.14, there are several changes that could be made to the flowchart to improve the process, depending on the workloads of the parents and the ages and maturity of the two children.

CRITICAL THINKING QUESTIONS

1. Construct a flowchart of a job search process that you will use in your last year in college.

2. Relate the use of the six quality tools discussed above to the use of control charts.

SUMMARY

Today's managers are charged with improving the quality of the products and services offered by their organizations. This requires improvements in the processes and systems that yield the products and services. Process improvement requires proactive managerial actions that differ from those in traditional reactive management control systems.

There is a problem with financial output goals of a considerable time lag between when the activities are performed and when the output, such as an increase in profitability, is measured. If the actual performance is not in line with the objective, then corrective action is taken. Because of the time lags and the output orientation of the financial measures, it is rare that such corrective action can treat the cause or source of the problem. This is the weakness of traditional management control: Without treating the cause of the problem, the problem will likely recur.

Continuous improvement refers to the constant refinement and improvement of products, services, and organizational systems to yield improved value to customers. Systems improvement aims to improve the processes and system to yield continuously improved customer value before problems occur. In this way problems are prevented, rather than being corrected after they occur. Instead of inspection and repair after production, systems improvement activities decrease the chance that defects or problems will occur.

Statistical thinking stresses that all work activities are part of larger processes with variation. Variability can arise from two different causes—common cause and special cause.

Common causes of variation are those system sources that affect each and every result in a series. Common-cause variation is always present in a system, although the assignable cause or causes may not be found. The result of these causes is a predictable amount of noise or chance variation in the data.

Special causes of variation are present at isolated times to yield variation in addition to that produced by common causes. Special-cause variation is sporadic and is not predictable. Although the data are not predictable, they can be linked with an assignable event. Thus special cause variation is also known as signal or assignable variation.

Total Quality Management is a systems approach to management that aims to continuously improve value to customers by designing and continuously improving organizational processes and systems. To continuously improve value to customers, managers should look for customer-relevant measures in deciding what to improve.

Statistical process control (SPC) is the application of statistical thinking and statistical analysis of data to control and improve processes. SPC uses control charts to understand stable and unstable processes, reduce variation, and improve the process.

A control chart is a run chart (a time-ordered plot of data associated with a process) with statistically determined upper and lower limits drawn on either side of the process average. The control limits define the noise or random variation in the process. Data outside the limits indicate a signal or assignable variation due to a special cause. Data within the limits are due to predictable, common-cause variation.

A stable process is one in which the process measure shows no evidence of special causes of variation. A control chart for a stable process contains the data within the upper and lower control limits. A stable process is sometimes referred to as an in-control process or a consistent process. Since stable processes are predictable, managers can proceed with process improvement.

An unstable process is one in which the process measure shows evidence of special causes of variation. A control chart for an unstable process contains some of the data outside the upper and lower control limits. An unstable process is sometimes referred to as an out-of-control process or an inconsistent process. Unstable processes are hard to predict. This makes process improvement difficult because the variation due to the special causes may mask the effects of the improvement.

Once the process is stable, process improvement means that features of the process that are always present need to be changed. This usually requires managerial action because fundamental changes in the system are often required. Improving a stable process may involve reducing the variation and/or changing the average of the process.

SPC is a tool often used to improve processes. There are other tools used to improve processes that are just as important in certain applications. In certain applications the other tools identify ways to change the process and improve the system.

A check sheet is a table, usually in a matrix form, to record the frequency of problems. A check sheet records the frequency of problems by type of problem and is usually the first step to turn opinion into data.

Pareto analysis is a technique that indicates which problems to solve and in what order. A Pareto chart is a vertical bar graph that shows each problem area along the *x*-axis in descending order and percentages or frequency counts on the *y*-axis. Pareto analysis and Pareto charts are used in process improvement to indicate the relative importance of problems and to determine the order in which they should be solved.

A histogram is a graphic representation of the frequency distribution of measured data. A histogram reveals the amount of variation in a process.

A scatter plot displays graphically what happens to one variable when another variable changes, in order to test a theory that the two variables are related. Scatter plots are useful in determining if process improvements can be made by changing one variable in order to improve another variable.

A cause-and-effect diagram is a simple graphic picture of the causes that go into the makeup of a common effect. The diagram represents the relationship between a certain effect and all the possible causes associated with that effect. Cause-and-effect diagrams are often referred to as fishbone diagrams.

A flowchart is a pictorial representation showing all the steps of a process. Flowcharts focus attention on activities in the overall process in which problems have occurred, thereby enabling process improvement to occur.

EXPERIENTIAL EXERCISE

Financial Compensation for the Victims of Bhopal

Seven engineers and scientists from the Union Carbide Corporation were sent to Bhopal to assist in the safe disposal of the remaining MIC at that site and to investigate the reasons for the accident. They were not permitted to interview operators of the Sevin process or to inspect the MIC storage tank and related piping. They were permitted to obtain samples of the residues from the nearly ruptured tank; through experimentation they were able to replicate reactions that led to residues with the same chemical properties in the same proportions. The account, therefore, is a hypothesis for the tragedy, not a proven series of events.

On December 3, 1984, some 2,000 people were killed and 200,000 were injured when a cloud of poisonous methyl isocyanate (MIC) gas was accidentally released from the Union Carbide Company plant in Bhopal, India. The MIC was used to manufacture Sevin, a plant pesticide that was distributed widely throughout India for use on that country's corn, rice, soybean, cotton, and alfalfa crops. It was said that the use of Sevin increased the harvest of the food crops by over 10 percent, enough to feed 70 million people.

The accident apparently occurred when between 120 and 240 gallons of water were introduced into a tank containing 90,000 pounds of MIC. The tank also contained approximately 3,000 pounds of chloroform, which is used as a solvent in the manufacture of MIC; the two chemicals should have been separated before storage, but that had not been done for some time in the operating process at Bhopal.

The water reacted exothermically (producing heat) with the chloroform, generating chlorine ions, which led to corrosion of the tank walls, and the iron oxide from the corrosion in turn reacted exothermically with the MIC. The increase in heat and pressure was rapid but unnoticed because the pressure gauge on the tank had been inoperable for four months and the operators in the control room, monitoring a remote temperature gauge, were accustomed to higher-than-specified heat levels (25°C rather than the 0°C in the operating instructions) due to the continual presence of the chloroform and some water vapor in the tank. The refrigeration unit built to cool the storage tank had been disconnected six months previously. The "scrubber," a safety device to neutralize the MIC with caustic soda, had been under repair since June. An operator, alarmed by the suddenly increasing temperature, attempted to cool the tank by spraying it with water, but by then the reaction was unstoppable, at a probable 200°C. The rupture disc (a steel plate in the line to prevent accidental operation of the safety valve) broke, the safety valve opened (just before, it is assumed, the tank would have burst), and over half the 45 tons of MIC in storage were discharged into the air.

Following the accident, Union Carbide officials in the United States denied strongly that their firm was responsible for the tragedy. They made the following three statements in support of that position:

1. The Bhopal plant was 50.9 percent owned by the American firm, but the parent corporation had been able to exercise very little control. All managerial and technical personnel were citizens of India at the insistence of the Indian government. No Americans were permanently employed at the plant. Safety warnings from visiting American inspectors about the Sevin manufacturing process had been ignored.

2. Five automatic safety devices that had originally been installed as part of the Sevin manufacturing process had, by the time of the accident, been either replaced by manual safety methods to increase employment, shut down for repairs, or disconnected as part of a cost-reduction program. The automatic temperature and pressure warning signals had been removed soon after construction. The repairs on the automatic scrubber unit

had extended over six months. The refrigeration unit had never been used to cool the tank and had been inoperable for over a year.

3. The Bhopal plant had been built in partnership with the Indian government to increase employment in that country. Union Carbide would have preferred to make Sevin in the United States and ship it to India for distribution and sale, because the insecticide could be made less expensively in the United States due to substantial economies of scale in the manufacturing process.

Warren Anderson, chairman of Union Carbide, stated that while he believed that the American company was not legally liable for the tragedy due to the three points above, it was still "morally" responsible, and he suggested that the firm should pay prompt financial compensation to those killed and injured in the accident.

Class Assignment

The class should be divided into groups of five to seven persons. Assume that the question of legal liability for the accident at Bhopal never will be settled, due to differences in the laws of the two countries and the difficulties of establishing jurisdiction. Assume, however, that the American company is morally responsible for the tragedy, as admitted by the chairman, because it was the majority owner and yet did not insist that the unsafe process be shut down. Each group should answer the following questions:

1. What factors would you consider in setting just financial compensation for each of the victims?

2. What is the responsibility of managers to ensure the safe operation of facilities before problems occur?

3. The Bhopal disaster occurred when all the safety devices were inoperative in the process. Relate the concept of special cause variation to this situation.

Source: LaRue Tone Hosmer, *The Ethics of Management*, 2nd ed., Irwin (1991): 58–60. © 1991 Richard D. Irwin, Burr Ridge, IL.

CHAPTER CASE

Long-Term Quality Improvement and Cost Reduction at Capsugel/Warner-Lambert

Capsugel, a division of Warner-Lambert, manufactures and distributes two-piece, hard-gelatin capsules to pharmaceutical companies worldwide. It has plants in the United States, Belgium, France, Japan, Mexico, Thailand, Brazil, and China.

Capsugel's customers often fill the capsules using high-speed filling machines that frequently operate at the rate of 150,000 capsules per hour, or 42 capsules per second. If just one capsule is defective (too thick, broken, or misaligned), the entire filling machine jams. This is expensive, as it means a loss of raw materials and production time. In addition, the product undergoes rigorous screenings owing to its obvious impacts on users' health. In sum, "functional" product quality is very important to Capsugel's customers.

In order to reduce the labor intensity of the filling process, Capsugel's pharmaceutical customers are demanding higher and higher levels of capsule quality so that their filling machines can be run with the least amount of labor. The president of Capsugel summarized this trend as follows: "Nearly fifteen years ago, most of our customers used semi-automatic filling machines. These were relatively labor intensive, so defects were caught fairly quickly. Today, most of those machines are fully automated with hardly any operator oversight. In the future, we expect our customers to move to operator-less machines. That represents a whole new ballgame for us—zero defects!"

Capsugel has always been committed to continuous cost reduction and quality improvement, but by the end of the 1970s most improvements were incremental. Frustrated with the status quo, the general manager at its largest plant, Charles Hoover, began searching for breakthrough ideas. Increasingly impressed with the power of improved quality, Hoover required that the rest of his management team become knowledgeable about various quality improvement techniques, including statistical process control.

From 1982 to 1989 the various Capsugel plants experimented with quality improvement projects, and dramatic improvements resulted. The accompanying figure shows the drop in defects. Because the management at the South Carolina plant was most committed and most knowledgeable about quality improvement and SPC techniques, it became the major innovator.

In mid-1989 Hoover was promoted to president of Capsugel. He immediately attempted to spread the SPC approach to the rest of the plants. First, he revised a program that had originated in 1980. This was a program aimed at encouraging cooperation between plants that were normally competitive. When one plant successfully implemented an innovation in the production process, it was rewarded in various ways and then required to share that innovation with the other plants. By applying SPC to this program, innovations spread more quickly.

Second, Hoover required that all of the plants lower their cost of quality by one-half every five years. The cost of quality was computed as the cost of scrap, inspection, customer complaints, lab testing, and quality appraisal as a percentage of cost of goods sold. The immediate result of this mandate was that each of the plants needed to reduce or eliminate all its inspection operations as quickly as possible. This had dramatic implications for the rest of the process because no longer could the machine operators assume that their defects would be identified and removed by the 100 percent to 200 percent manual inspections that occurred after the capsules were produced. In essence, this ambitious goal of reduction or elimination of defects required the machine operators to be responsible for both productivity and capsule quality. This requirement placed greater demands on the production floor to "get their process under control" and "do it right the first time."

Third, Hoover committed much time and capital to training the top 34 production managers in an intensive two-week course in SPC techniques and philosophy. Hoover recognized that rather than relying on staff personnel, the line managers must lead the change effort.

Through years of applying SPC and process improvement, Capsugel has dramatically increased the levels of quality, eliminated hundreds of inspectors, and reduced the cost of quality (Photo credit: Warner-Lambert Co.).

As one attendee stated, "We knew management was serious about this program when they flew so many folks from five different countries to Belgium and then South Carolina . . . It must have cost a bundle."

Finally, Hoover made perhaps the strongest institutional change of all: He required all future capital requests to be justified by SPC. Since capital expenditures are the lifeblood of organizations like Capsugel, this policy required that even the skeptics learn the SPC language in order to do their jobs.

These efforts resulted in dramatic benefits, and some short-term successes helped to guarantee future benefits. First, this quality improvement program served to reduce or eliminate the emotional appeals and unsystematic analysis behind capital budgeting that had existed in the past. As one plant manager stated, "In the past, folks came with subjective opinions. This led to battles and guys with the loudest voices won. Today, we make capital expenditure decisions with a lot more facts and less emotion. SPC has reduced the turf battles and politics."

Second, the program helped to transcend the language barrier. Being spread all over the world, SPC had the unintended benefit of providing a means of communication between parties who spoke different languages. This not only improved communication between the widely dispersed plants, but it also pro-

Trends in Major Defects at Capsugel

Percentage of 1981 Defects

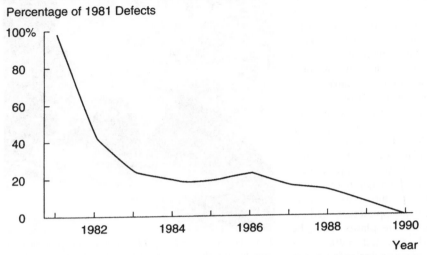

Source: W. Judge, M. J. Stahl, R. Scott, and R. Millender, "Long-Term Quality Improvement and Cost Reduction at Capsugel/Warner-Lambert," in M. J. Stahl and G. M. Bounds, *Competing Globally Through Customer Value*, Quorum Books (1991): 705. Reprinted with permission of Greenwood Publishing Group, Inc., Westport, CT. Copyright © Greenwood Publishing Group, Inc.

vided an important communication tool between the plants and their suppliers and buyers. This improved communication reduced friction and raised the amount of information transferred between parties.

Third, quality levels began to improve dramatically and productivity began to rise. The "quality gap" between Capsugel and its competitors has widened, and Capsugel is now proactively seeking out quality problems before the customers present them. In this way Capsugel expects to build cost effectively for the future and to strengthen its already solid competitive position.

Discussion Questions

1. Based on this case, what is the role of widespread use of SPC in changing corporate culture?

2. Based on this case, what is the role of widespread use of SPC in a multinational firm operating in different parts of the world?

Source: This case is a summary of a longer case by W. Judge, M. J. Stahl, R. Scott, and R. Millender, "Long-Term Quality Improvement and Cost Reduction at Capsugel/Warner-Lambert," in M. J. Stahl and G. M. Bounds, *Competing Globally Through Customer Value*, Westport, CT: Quorum Books (1991): 703–709.

KEY TERMS

capable process   Process that meets customers' requirements.

cause-and-effect diagram   Simple graphic picture of the causes that go into the makeup of a common effect.

check sheet   Table, usually in matrix form, to record the frequency of problems.

common causes of variation   System sources that affect each and every result in a series.

control chart   Run chart with statistically determined uper and lower control limits drawn on either side of the process average.

controlling   Ensuring that the organization is actually achieving its planned objectives.

flowchart   Pictorial representation showing all the steps of a process.

histogram   Graphic representation of the frequency distribution of measured data.

Pareto analysis   Technique that indicates which problems to solve and in what order.

Pareto chart   Vertical bar graph that shows each problem area along the *x*-axis in descending order and percentages or frequency counts on the *y*-axis.

run chart   Time-ordered plot of data associated with a process.

scatter plot   Graph showing what happens to one variable when another variable changes, in order to test a theory that the two variables are related.

special causes of variation   Causes present at isolated times to yield variation in addition to that produced by common causes.

stable process   Process in which the process measure shows no evidence of special causes of variation.

statistical process control (SPC)   Application of statistical thinking and statistical analysis of data to control and improve processes.

statistical thinking   Viewpoint that all work activities are part of larger processes with variation.

unstable process   Process in which the process measure shows evidence of special causes of variation.

ENDNOTES

1. This section was influenced by Chapter 6, "Evaluation and Control," in M. J. Stahl and D. W. Grigsby, *Strategic Management for Decision Making*, Boston: PWS-Kent (1992): 160–176.
2. W. E. Deming, *Out of the Crisis*, Cambridge, MA: MIT Center for Advanced Engineering Study (1986): 315.
3. R. Cole, "Introduction," Special Issue on Total Quality Management, *California Management Review*, 35, no. 3 (Spring 1993): 8.
4. R. S. Sanders, M. Leitnaker, and G. Ranney, "Managing in the Presence of Variation," in M. J. Stahl and G. M. Bounds, *Competing Globally Through Customer Value*, Westport, CT: Quorum Books (1991): 253–274.
5. Deming, *Out of the Crisis*, 136.
6. Cole, "Introduction," 7.
7. Sanders, Leitnaker, and Ranney, "Managing in the Presence of Variation," 255.
8. Ibid., 256.
9. W. E. Deming, *The New Economics for Industry, Government, Education*, Cambridge, MA: Massachusetts Institute of Technology for Advanced Engineering Study (1993): 102.
10. Deming, *Out of the Crisis*, 338.
11. B. Dale and B. Cooper, *Total Quality and Human Resources: An Executive Guide*, Oxford, England: Blackwell (1992): 212.
12. Goal/QPC, *The Memory Jogger: A Pocket Guide of Tools for Continuous Improvement*, Methuen, MA (1988): 44.
13. K. Ishikawa, *Guide to Quality Control*, Tokyo: Asian Productivity Organization (1976).
14. Goal/QPC, *The Memory Jogger*, 9.
15. R. M. Currie, *Work Study*, London: Pitman (1989).

16
CHAPTER

Management Information Systems

LEARNING OBJECTIVES

After reading this chapter, you should be able to accomplish the following:

- Describe the basic components of a management information system (MIS).
- Explain the different roles of management information systems.
- Discuss the information needs of external and internal customers.
- Describe the impact of computers in the workplace.
- Compare and contrast the information requirements of first-line management and top-level management.
- Explain the design and implementation criteria of an effective MIS.
- Describe the customer-value role of an MIS.

CHAPTER OUTLINE

The Evolution of Management Information Systems
Origins of Management Information Systems
The Need to Organize and Comprehend Information
Types of Information Processing
Basic Components of Management Information Systems
The Future of Management Information Systems
The Roles of Management Information Systems
Transaction/Bookkeeping Role
Strategic Planning Role
Competitive-Weapon Role
Customer-Value Role

The Information Needs of External and Internal Customers
Accessibility
Timeliness
User Friendliness
Security
Accuracy
The Impact of Computers in the Workplace
Effects of Computers on Performance
Effects of Computers on Global Competition
Effects of Computers on the Organization
Telecommuting
Designing and Implementing an Effective Management Information System
Determine Goals for External and Internal Customer Value
Tailor Information to Level of Management
Determine Nature of Information
Design Hardware and Software
Test the Management Information System
Implement the Management Information System
Deal with Resistance to Change
Monitor, Maintain, and Continuously Improve the Management Information System

Cases and Exhibits
Pitney Bowes
International Airlines
Ethics, Students, and Computers
Sunstrand
United Parcel Service
Fidelity Investments

Pitney Bowes Mailing Systems

Armed with information on customer expectations, Customer Satisfaction Teams at Pitney Bowes Mailing Systems implement Customer-Driven Quality improvements. (Photo credit: Hank Morgan/ Rainbow.)

Like many other firms driven by the spirit of Total Quality Management, Pitney Bowes Mailing Systems (Stamford, CT) strives to be the best in its industry. Its vision describes its reach and international presence. "Our vision . . . to be a dynamic, responsive, highly competitive business organization that gives the highest priority to capturing new and growing mailing preparation and processing markets worldwide. Concurrently, we shall enhance our dominant position in our postage meter and mailing machine business through vigorous promotion in North America and aggressive expansion in Europe and Asia Pacific."

In order to effectively implement their vision, Pitney Bowes Mailing Systems is guided by its innovative version of TQM, referred to as Customer-Driven Quality. Herb Schneider, Vice President of Total Quality at Pitney Bowes, described their TQ system. "It is truly a customer-driven quality process. The process starts with the customer, develops measures to address customer expectations, provides information to employees on customer-relevant criteria, and ties training and the reward system into performance on those customer-relevant criteria." Customer-Driven Quality (CDQ), is intended to remind all levels of management that the customer is the ultimate priority.

Recognizing that different customer groups have varying expectations, Herb Schneider stresses the importance of understanding customer expectations by business segment. "Each business segment is challenged to fully understand its customers' expectations. Qualitative and quantitative expectations and their relative priority are based on primary customer marketing research, not indirect information from field sales and service personnel. Performance standards are based on achieving a '100 percent very satisfied' rating from our customers. Customer expectations are assessed continuously to assure we adapt to changing requirements. Understanding customer expectations is a key factor in achieving Customer-Driven Quality throughout Mailing Systems."

DISCUSSION QUESTIONS

1. How are these customer expectations measured?
2. Likewise, once the information on the customers' expectations is measured, how is it then communicated to employees?

In this chapter we explore the managerial uses of computer-based management information systems for internal organizational purposes and for external customer value purposes. Simply defined, a **management information system (MIS)** is a set of computer hardware and software that gathers, organizes, summarizes, and reports information for use by managers, customers, and others.

This broad definition of MIS, which includes use of information systems to provide value to external customers, is consistent with the theme of this book concerning the essence of management. We recall the definition of Total Quality Management as a systems approach to management that aims to continuously increase value to customers by designing and continuously improving organizational processes and systems. Thus the design and operation of an MIS, as a key system that can provide value to customers, should be integral to TQM in the organization.

Management information systems consist of more than just the latest computer hardware and software specifications. Although computers are critical to MIS today, in this chapter we shall not attempt to educate readers to become experts in computer hardware and software jargon.

Historically, managerial uses of MIS were focused on making internal operations faster, more accurate, and more efficient. Today the more exciting uses of MIS are those that provide additional value for external customers. Those managers who find ways to bring additional value to their external customers with the firm's MIS will gain additional market share. The managers at Pitney Bowes seemed to understand the use of MIS to deliver such value to customers, as will become apparent in subsequent parts of the Pitney Bowes case.

THE EVOLUTION OF MANAGEMENT INFORMATION SYSTEMS

The use of computers and management information systems has grown explosively since the first large-scale electronic computer was used in the 1940s. Large mainframe computers, requiring well-trained technical staffs for their operation, became popular in the 1960s for accounting and inventory control. A **mainframe computer** is a large, powerful computer that serves as the core of many computer operations. Today nearly every company uses computers of various sizes throughout their operations. Most managers use computers for word processing, calculations (spreadsheets), and graphics. More and more managers are using electronic mail as a way to communicate both within and outside of the organization.

The computer industry has grown from nothing five decades ago to one of the fastest-growing industries in this country. Names like IBM, Digital, Microsoft, Intel, and Apple have become household words.

In the face of the pervasive growth of computers in business, managers should remember that computers and MIS are tools, not ends in themselves. Computerized systems have not yet yielded the hoped-for increases in white-collar productivity, even though computer budgets within companies rose throughout the 1980s.[1] An MIS should be viewed as a tool to provide value either to external customers or to internal customers. Computers can offer a dazzling array of high-tech features, but if value is not provided, the manager needs to ask why not and seek solutions.

An important message of this chapter is that those firms that find new ways to offer value to customers through their MIS will gain new customers. This message is consistent with the theme of this book: *The central purpose of management and organizations is to provide value to customers.* The information delivered from an MIS can be as valuable as the base product or service the firm provides to its customers. For example, Federal Express's package locator service provides additional value to customers. The service tracks the location of a package throughout its journey and delivery in case a customer needs to confirm delivery or verify that the package is on its way.

Origins of Management Information Systems

Managers have always had some kind of management information system. Prior to the advent of the computer and the formal study of management information systems, they always had systems, no matter how informal, to collect, analyze, summarize, and store information.[2]

The formalized study of MIS developed in the 1960s as computer power became widely available. Management information systems at that time performed mostly a "bookkeeping" function. Today the power and speed of computers have transformed the MIS into a tool for organizations to provide value to customers and to increase the organization's efficiency.

The Need to Organize and Comprehend Information

Managers need to organize and interpret large amounts of seemingly unrelated facts into meaningful themes for managerial action. Herein lies the difference between "data" and "information" and the justification for many a multimillion dollar MIS. As defined in Chapter 13, *data* are symbols or characters without meaning or value, and *information* consists of data with meaning or value. For example, there are millions of individual purchases at Wal-Mart each year. The records of those individual purchases are data. The summarization of those transactions and comparison with the prior year's sales translate the data into information that managers might use to make inventory decisions.

Types of Information Processing

There are three types of management information systems that need to be understood for managerial purposes: transaction-processing systems, decision support systems, and expert systems.

Transaction-Processing Systems

A **transaction-processing system (TPS)** is a management information system designed to record and summarize routine transactions for an organization. A transaction-processing system does not involve much analysis or summarization of the data for managerial decision making. However, a TPS can provide much value to the customer at the point of the transaction. National Car Rental uses customer-activated computer terminals at the point of rental to speed up rental and return of cars. The customer can rent the car without waiting in line to see an agent, as the computer already has stored information on the customer's credit card number, driver's license, and car preferences. At the point of return, the customer can use the computer terminal to calculate rental charges and can pay the bill with a credit card without waiting in line for a clerk. The computer challenge for organizations today is to find more ways to use the power of the computer to provide more value to the customer.

Decision Support Systems   A **decision support system (DSS)** searches for, analyzes, summarizes, and reports information needed for specific decisions. Whereas a transaction-processing system is used primarily at the point of the transaction, the DSS starts with information that is already in existence in the organization. Although the customer may come in contact with the transaction-processing system, the DSS is a decision-making aid for organizational members. For example, if a manager is planning to replace some machinery, a DSS collects the data on machine costs, useful life, maintenance, and other budgeting issues, summarizes the information, and reports it to the manager.

A special application of a DSS that permits interaction among members of a group is a **group decision support system (GDSS).** A GDSS searches for, analyzes, summarizes, reports, and interactively shares with group members the information needed for specific group decisions. A GDSS is used in a situation where it is appropriate to make a decision as a group. A GDSS may be used, for example, in a capital-budgeting situation where there is a multimillion-dollar proposal being developed to buy new equipment. The proposal would require the active involvement of several persons in a group.

Expert Systems   An **expert system** is a computerized decision-making aid that enables decision makers to use multiple pieces of information to make decisions in the manner of experts. To understand expert systems, it is useful to know what artificial intelligence is. **Artificial intelligence** is the use of information technology to make computers "think" like humans and mimic the human mind. Expert systems are an application of artificial intelligence in decision-making situations.[3] Through a series of "if-then" decision rules, expert systems duplicate the thinking processes that expert managers and expert professionals use to make decisions. Thus a less experienced person can draw upon expertise that has been quantified in a computer.

An early application of expert systems arose in the insurance industry. In dealing with a customer applying for insurance coverage on an automobile, an expert system leads the insurance agent through a series of questions to determine information that will allow an assessment of the risk of the applicant. Information on age, driving experience, gender, marital status, arrest record, DUI record, and accident record may be requested. The cumulative risk is used to determine rates. The questions asked by the expert system are most likely derived from the experiences of several senior agents who have observed risk patterns through many years of experience.

Basic Components of a Management Information System

The basic design of a management information system is simple. As Figure 16.1 indicates, an MIS consists of only five major elements:

1. The **input medium** is the computer hardware used to enter data into the computer. The input medium can be a keyboard, scanner, light pen, tape drive, disk drive, CD, or other computers.

2. The **storage device** is the computer hardware used to store the data after the data have been entered. The storage device can be a magnetic tape, floppy disk, or hard disk.

3. The **processor**, or **central processing unit (CPU)**, is the computer hardware that organizes, analyzes, and summarizes the data. The CPU is the "brains" of the MIS. In the language of personal computers, the "chip" is the processor. Ads for many personal computers may note "Intel inside," for example, referring to the maker of the processor for IBM and IBM-compatible personal computers.

4. The **output medium** is the computer hardware used to deliver the results of the computer operations to the user. The output medium can be a video screen or cathode-ray tube, printer, tape, floppy disk, hard disk, or other computers.

5. The **software** is the set of instructions that tells the computer hardware what to do. The software consists of the operating system and the applications program. The **operating system** is the set of computer instructions that performs the scheduling of jobs and housekeeping chores in the computer. In personal computers, for example, MS-DOS is a common operating system.
   Applications software is the set of instructions that tells the computer how to perform certain custom tasks like word processing, accounting, or graphics. WordPerfect (word processing), Lotus (spreadsheet), and Harvard Graphics (graphics) are some popular applications programs for personal computers.

As a measure of the evolution of management information systems, input and output mediums have changed considerably in the last two decades. Previously a mechanical form (punched cards) had been a primary form of input and output. Today the primary form of input and output is electronic, whether it be keyboard, disk, touch-sensitive video screen, or another computer. The electronic revolution and video screens have made it easier to provide value to the customer via the MIS. An automated teller machine (ATM) is a prime example of bringing value to the customer by utilizing such video input and output mediums.

The Future of Management Information Systems

No one has the power to accurately predict the future, especially in the rapidly changing, high-technology world of management information systems. However, advances in computer hardware and software already on the drawing board provide hints of the future for information systems. Dramatic advances are expected in the areas of portability and networking.

FIGURE 16.1   *Basic Components of a Management Information System*

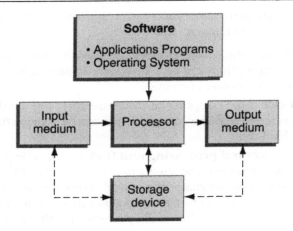

Portability   Computer technology is getting lighter, cheaper, faster, and more powerful. Thirty years ago the primary form of computing depended on large, mainframe computer installations. These required huge input and output devices, climate-controlled rooms, and staffs of computer experts conversant with computer science terminology. In the 1980s desktop personal computers transformed the computer world by bringing computer power to individuals at their desk at an affordable price.

The future will yield even smaller, more powerful, portable computers with more efficient software so that individuals can compute almost anywhere with the same power they might have in an office. In a special forecast of technology, *The Wall Street Journal* expressed the opinion that in the future we will give up little for portability.[4] *Business Week*, in discussing the future of the home computer, predicted that it will recognize voice and handwriting as input.[5] Such advances in information technology will continue to change the way work is done both in the office and in the home.

Networking   As more personal computers are used in the workplace, and as those computers become more powerful, there will be increasing needs to link these computers together to share common information. **Networking** is the linking together of individuals in an MIS to share information. Networking systems and software are rapidly spreading in offices. It is common to find those in a department linked together in a network, with several personal computers sharing some common data and the same printer.

CRITICAL THINKING QUESTIONS

1. Describe some ways that innovative uses of output mediums can deliver more value to customers in the banking industry.

2. What are some ethnic-diversity issues associated with the use of expert systems in the insurance industry?

An ATM is a prime example of providing value to the customers. (Photo credit: Mark Antman/The Image Works.)

THE ROLES OF MANAGEMENT INFORMATION SYSTEMS

Management information systems can serve at least four different roles in the organization. The first two roles (transaction/bookkeeping and strategic planning) have a traditional, internal focus. The second pair of roles (competitive weapon and customer value) have a more recent, external focus.

Transaction/Bookkeeping Role

Management information systems can be used to record, store, and report transactions. In doing so, the MIS performs a bookkeeping function.

This traditional role is the least exciting and least imaginative role for an MIS. In this application the awesome power of the MIS is used for the straightforward functions of recording, storing, summarizing, and reporting on transactions. The transactions are usually recorded and summarized in financial terms. In this role the MIS serves primarily as an internal tool, albeit a fast, accurate, and expensive one. When using an MIS only in this capacity, managers take a cost-centered view: Since the MIS is an expense with little direct bearing on providing value to customers, costs of the MIS are to be minimized.[6]

Many banks have used large computers to record, summarize, and report to customers on checking accounts at the end of the month. The banks have used the information internally as a way to track cash flow. This expenditure to clear and record millions of check transactions was large, because the MIS usually required mainframe computer power. Little value was provided to customers except for end-of-the-month statements. Not until customers could access their accounts through automatic teller machines, which are computer terminals, was much value provided

TABLE 16.1   *Components of an Industry Profile*

What industry is to be described?
— Name
— Geographic coverage
What is the industry's size, growth, structure?
— Number of firms
— Sales
— Market shares
— Industry structure
— Life cycle stage
What are the industry's marketing
strategy and tactics?
— Market targets
— Marketing objectives
— Marketing mix
What changes in the industry's size and marketing
strategy/tactics are anticipated?
— Size and strength
— Market targets
— Marketing objectives
— Marketing mix

Source: Robert B. Woodruff and Ernest R. Cadotte, "Analyzing Market Opportunities for New Ventures," *Survey of Business* (Summer 1987): 14. Reprinted with permission.

to customers. By tying into the bank's MIS, ATMs provide quick, 24-hour, 7-day, local banking service.

Strategic Planning Role

Management information systems are used as an integral part of the strategic planning process, as described in Chapter 6. They are used to collect, analyze, and report information on demographic, regulatory, economic, marketplace, and competitive trends that are useful in strategic planning. For example, computers may be tied to industry databases to track sales of competitors by kind of product, product features, and price. It is not unusual to find corporate computers tied to several large external databases relating to industry, marketplace, and demographic trends of all kinds. Computers are often used in strategic planning to perform computerized simulations of alternative strategies and their results. The MIS may be viewed as a strategic decision support system and as a strategic intelligence system.[7]

Reams of information are needed in this strategic planning role. Just to complete an industry profile requires considerable computer power. Table 16.1 lists the types of information needed for an industry profile. The last type of information—marketing mix—includes decisions on products, prices, promotion, distribution, and services.[8]

TABLE 16.2 *Components of a Key Competitor Profile*

Who are the key competitors?

— Companies serving the same markets

— Companies successful in meeting demand

What is the key competitor's financial size and strength?

— Sales

— Profit margins

— Total assets

— Debt

— Equity

— Various financial ratios

What are the key competitor's technical, marketing, and management capabilities?

— Mission and business objectives

— Market share position and trends

— Management capabilities and limitations

— Technical and operating capabilities

— Target market strategies

— Access to key resources

What changes are anticipated?

— Size and strength

— Market targets

— Marketing objectives

— Marketing mix

Source: Robert B. Woodruff and Ernest R. Cadotte, "Analyzing Market Opprotunities for New Ventures," *Survey of Business* (Summer 1987): 15. Reprinted with permission.

Competitive-Weapon Role

The view of a management information system as a competitive weapon for the firm is relatively new.[9] As we saw in Chapter 6, a danger for the firm in focusing on the competition is that managers sometimes lose sight of the customers.[10]

Table 16.2 gives an idea of the types and amount of information that must be generated to construct a key competitor profile. Such a volume of information requires a computer, especially when the managers test several different answers to the questions concerning a competitor's capabilities and changes.

By focusing on its competitors, the firm is almost always late to market with new products and services, as it will wait until the competitors have tested the market. By following the leader, the firm is giving up substantial market share. In following, the firm may have a viable position as number two or three, but it will operate in the shadow of the early market entrant.

By focusing on the current competition, the firm may also ignore new competitors. General Motors collected reams of information on Ford and Chrysler, but for a dangerously long time it assumed that the Japanese automakers were not worth worrying about.

Note that there is no mention of the customer in Table 16.2. A problem with viewing an MIS as a competitive weapon is that this view may ignore the changing needs of the customer. A firm may have a powerful, high-speed MIS capable of accurately tracking levels of internal inventories relative to competitors' sales. However, the MIS says nothing about the desirability of the products by the customer. Accurate tracking of buggy whips is of little value to customers with automobiles. Peter Drucker, the frequently cited management theorist, reminds us that firms must become information based and deliver more value to customers with information.[11]

Customer-Value Role

In situations where the management information system is viewed in the customer-value role, the value of the information merges with the value of the firm's product. The information itself becomes a service alongside the other products and services of the organization. Banks that electronically transfer funds provide value to customers in terms of speed and security in addition to the actual transmission of the funds. Some automobile service stations offer credit card payment at the pump by connecting to computers from the pump, thereby providing additional customer value of speed and convenience.

An organization might use its MIS to construct a customer profile by analyzing customer data relating to customers' buying behavior and their needs.[12] Table 16.3 lists the detailed reams of information needed to construct a customer profile. The amounts of information needed represent an efficient utilization of the power of an MIS to understand how to provide more value to customers.

Some airlines have found ways to provide value to customers through the MIS, as demonstrated in the international exhibit on page 456.

CRITICAL THINKING QUESTIONS

1. Compare and contrast the different roles of management information systems. Which role will assume even greater importance in the future?

2. Many organizations attempt to provide more value to their customers through an MIS by making information more accessible. Accessibility sometimes interferes with security. Which issue is more important to customers? Why?

THE INFORMATION NEEDS OF EXTERNAL AND INTERNAL CUSTOMERS

In this section we highlight the most obvious information needs of external customers in an era of information technology. We should remember, however, that these now-obvious needs were not apparent in the recent past when computers first became popular. Firms that discover still newer ways to provide value to customers through an MIS will increase their market share.

TABLE 16.3 *Components of a Customer Profile*

What are customers like as people?
— Needs and wants
— Important use situations
— Activities and interests
— Opinions and attitudes
— Demographic characteristics
— Values
How do people decide to buy?
— Problem recognition
— Search for and use of product information
— Evaluation of alternatives
— Purchase procedures
— Satisfaction with past purchases
What outside influences are affecting buying?
— Population and social forces
— Legal forces
— Technological forces
— Economic forces
— Natural forces

Source: Robert B. Woodruff and Ernest R. Cadotte, "Analyzing Market Opportunities for New Ventures," *Survey of Business* (Summer 1987): 14. Reprinted with permission.

Internal customers have information needs not unlike those of external customers. All organizational members who use an MIS are internal customers of the information systems department that designed and implemented the MIS.

Accessibility

To be of value to them, information must be accessible to customers. If they cannot readily access specific information when they need it, that information has little value.

A classic example of providing value to customers through accessibility of information is the American Airlines Sabre reservation system. American found a way to deliver a dimension of value to customers that its rival United Airlines did not have. United's reservation system listed United's flights exclusively. American's reservation system provided all airlines' schedules so that travel agents would use its system all the time. However, because American listed its own flights first, many agents never looked further. By making all the flight schedules accessible, American provided additional value to customers, and thereby gained additional customers.[13]

I N T E R N A T I O N A L   E X H I B I T

International Airlines, MIS, and Customer Value

Some international airlines are providing value to their customers by entering into joint ventures, linking their management information systems together, and advertising the combined benefits to the public. The linked systems provide more combined flights throughout the world, make reservations easier to complete, and offer transferable frequent-flyer points from one airline to another for future free travel.

Delta Airlines has joint ventures with KLM, Lufthansa, Swissair, Japan Airlines, and Air New Zealand. By including the schedules of those five international joint-venture partners in its computerized reservation system, Delta can span the world for its customers even though Delta aircraft do not fly to many of the international destinations that some of its partners do. The schedules offer many more flights and easier reservations.Transferable frequent-flyer points can also be earned from flying on one of the international partner airlines and transferred to the customer's Delta frequent-flyer account. If a customer takes a round-trip Air New Zealand flight from the United States to New Zealand and earns 16,000 frequent-flyer points on Air New Zealand, those points can be transferred to the customer's Delta frequent-flyer account for future free travel on Delta. The frequent-flyer points are credited in Delta's MIS automatically.

USAir has entered into a similar arrangement with British Air. Schedules, reservations, and frequent-flyer points have been merged. In that joint venture there was also a cash infusion by British Air into USAir to strengthen USAir. Such a financially cemented joint venture suggests that customers will see further services from the combination.

Some airlines have merged their informations systems so that customers can make seamless reservations and effortless transfers among partner airlines. (Photo credit: George Disario/The Stock Market.)

By entering into partnerships with other international airlines, Delta Airlines is able to offer its customers additional international routes. (Photo credit: Delta Airlines.)

Timeliness

Information is of little value to customers if it is not timely. They need current information to make timely decisions. Indeed, customers frequently need **real-time information**, which is information that immediately reflects the underlying reality. American Hospital Supply Company (AHSC) designed a computerized way to provide its customers with real-time information on purchasing inventory. AHSC's customers are purchasing agents for hospitals and clinics. By placing a computer terminal in each customer's office, AHSC's system provided order entry, invoicing and billing, inventory control, and shipping with a high degree of timeliness and accuracy. Since AHSC could then deliver computer-ordered hospital supply items within 24 hours, customers were able to reduce their inventory stock levels from 75 to 30 days. Thus the customers' purchasing and inventory financing costs decreased substantially.[14]

User Friendliness

For information from management information systems to be of value to customers, the information must be understandable. User friendliness means that the MIS is easy to use due to simple-to-follow instructions. Described earlier in this chapter, National Car Rental's system for renting and returning rental cars uses a touch-screen-operated system with just a few options per screen. The system is quick and easy for customers to operate.

Security

Customers have a need for secure information if the information concerns their own assets and their own behavior. For example, automatic teller machines need to display information in such a way that only the customer has access to the information. Security codes and personal identification numbers (PIN) need to be configured so that only the owner has access to his or her own funds. Recently Fidelity Investments, the nation's largest mutual fund company, tried to make access easier for its customers so that they could easily conduct business over the phone. However, Fidelity discovered that it had made access too easy, since anyone with a push-button telephone could gain access to the accounts of Fidelity customers. Fidelity fixed this security issue by requiring callers to key in their PIN and their Social Security number to gain access to their accounts.[15]

Accuracy

Information quality is the degree to which information accurately portrays reality. Just as external customers demand accurate information to make decisions, internal customers also need the same accuracy in information for decision-making purposes. USAA is one of the country's largest automobile insurers. When customers call in to check or change information in their insurance policies, the USAA agent must have an accurate information database.

E   T   H   I   C   S   E   X   H   I   B   I   T

Two Ethical Issues Involving Students and Computers

1. Jeff, a university student, obtained a part-time job as a data entry clerk. His job was to enter personal student data into the university's database. Some of this data was available in the student directory, but some of it was not. Jeff was attracted to a student in his algebra class and wanted to ask her out. Before asking her, though, he decided to access her records in the database to find out about her background. Were Jeff's actions in accessing a fellow student's personal information ethical?

2. Karen, a student at a university, learned to use an expensive spreadsheet program in her accounting class. Karen would go to the university microcomputer lab, check out the spreadsheet software, complete her assignment, and return the software. Signs were posted in the lab indicating that copying software was forbidden. One day, she decided to copy the software anyway so she could work on her assignments at her apartment. If Karen destroyed her copy of the software at the end of the semester, was her action ethical? If Karen never intended to destroy her copy of the software at the end of the semester, was her action ethical?

Source: R. Dejoie, G. Fowler, and D. Paradice, *Ethical Issues in Information Systems*, Boston: Boyd & Fraser (1991): 164, 224.

Customers need precise information relevant to their needs. The fact that the individual customer is one of a few million is no reason for the organization to be approximate. A bank with assets of $100 billion may not be particularly affected by whether the balance in Sam Smith's account is $1,111.11 or $11,111.11. However, the exact information is critical to Sam as an individual customer.

The ethics exhibit demonstrates some of these issues relating to security and accessibility.

CRITICAL THINKING QUESTIONS

1. Describe the areas in which the information needs of external customers might be different from the information needs of internal customers.

2. Many computer systems have become more user friendly in the last decade. Yet many people are afraid of using computers. What can an organization do to increase the user friendliness of its systems for external customers?

THE IMPACT OF COMPUTERS IN THE WORKPLACE

Forty years ago computers were in their infancy and were found in only a few military and research applications. Today computers are pervasive in the workplace, in schools, and in many homes. With so many activities computerized in the workplace, it is difficult to imagine an office, factory, or business activity without many computer applications.

Effects of Computers on Performance

In the last two decades over 40 percent of the spending by U.S. firms on plant and equipment has been on information systems technology, amounting to over $1 trillion.[16] There is substantial evidence that there have been major performance improvements in many parts of the economy as a result of this investment in information systems. In the past 20 years managers have witnessed quantum improvements in manufacturing, new-product development, provision of information to customers, and the globalization of business. Many manufacturing firms are producing more products with fewer people, partly because of the productivity enhancements associated with information systems that accurately track inventory, schedule production, automatically order materials, and route distribution with scanners and bar codes tied to the firm's MIS. Financial services firms, like Merrill Lynch, are delivering more financial products and information to customers by being tied to multiple electronic financial markets. Many financial services brokers and bankers can quote interest rates on many kinds of investment because they are linked to many financial markets. In both the manufacturing and service sectors, computers have been associated with numerous productivity and quality improvements.

At Boeing computers are used extensively to design the company's latest airplane—the 777. With its computer-aided design (CAD), Boeing hopes to lower the cost of design, lower the cost of maintenance, and lower the number of design defects to be corrected after initial production. Boeing is gambling billions on the 777 and using a radical CAD. The CAD enables the company to skip the usual paper drawings and full-scale mock-up and to go straight from computer images to fabrication and assembly. Over 200 "design/build" teams, with cross-functional membership from customers (the airlines), mechanics, salespeople, engineers, and assemblers, are integrated by the CAD.[17]

Effects of Computers on Global Competition

Management information systems that have no national boundaries are a means of enhancing international competition. In the airline industry, for example, firms with computerized worldwide airline reservation systems can offer value to customers that other firms cannot, as we saw in the international exhibit earlier in this chapter.[18] In the financial services industry, firms electronically linked to the world's major financial markets in New York, London, Frankfurt, Tokyo, and Hong Kong can provide real-time financial information to customers needing to deal in international currencies.

The MIS can tie together a firm's internationally dispersed resources as if they were in the next building.[19] At some international firms the power of management information systems is speeding new-product development by eliminating distances and borders. At Texas Instruments (TI) designers and engineers around the world now send detailed designs instantly over the computer network so that TI employees anywhere can work on them simultaneously. The time needed to develop a calculator shrank 20 percent as soon as TI began sending drawings electronically in 1989.[20]

Back to the Pitney Bowes Case

Particularly in a service business like mailing, Pitney Bowes recognized the importance of setting goals and communicating expectations. Current performance for each customer expectation is measured and serves as a baseline from which goals can be set for exceeding customers' expectations.

Many TQM processes stress the importance of employees having the right skills and tools in order to provide the customer with what they need. To help implement its vision statement, Pitney Bowes also recognized the importance of having customer-relevant information available to the employee. This empowers the employee to act appropriately at the point of a customer query. "We shall be driven by . . . our commitment to assuring that our employees have the tools,

skills, information, responsibility, and authority to satisfy customer expectations."

Herb Schneider discussed the critical role of information being in the hands of the employee at the point when they come in contact with the customer. "A critical performance standard is to resolve 100% of customers' queries in the first call. To accomplish that, we move data and decision support to the front line employee. The information is now available first hand and an empowered employee can make the necessary decisions to meet the customer's expectation. Our ability to meet the performance standard is dependent on the information system delivering information to employees, since the customer's first call is most important."

Effects of Computers on the Organization

As noted in Chapter 8, many organizations are becoming flatter as levels of management are being eliminated. Networks of computers are an important enabling force in this movement toward flatter organizations, since an MIS allows managers to stay in touch with a larger number of people. Rather than receiving reports from middle levels of managers, upper levels of management can link into the status of work at many organizational levels in the firm's MIS. The MIS can summarize both vertically and horizontally.

Information is one of the integrating processes between first-line and top-level management that is permitting the elimination of many mid-level managers. Whereas the job of many mid-level managers had been collecting, analyzing, and reporting information, those tasks are now being performed by a decision support system in numerous organizations. Whereas the role of some middle managers had been to make expert decisions, that role is being served by expert systems in some organizations. As the organizational flattening process progresses, the information needs of both first-line management and top-level management will become more alike in the future.

The spread of real-time management information systems has been having a dramatic effect on the organization horizontally. Well-integrated systems serve to tie together several diverse functions in the organization.[21] The flow of information is a

D I V E R S I T Y   E X H I B I T

Older Workers and Retirees at Sundstrand Data Control Inc.

This aerospace electronics firm makes avionic computer systems, airborne recorders and flight data systems for commercial and military aircraft, flight recorders, and a variety of measurement devices (acceleratometers, transducers, thermal switches) for use in aerospace, ground transportation, and the petrochemical industry. Located in the state of Washington, Sundstrand employs 1,600 people and is experiencing shortages of electronic and mechanical design engineers, drafters, circuit board designers and assemblers, skilled electronic technicians, and precision mechanical assemblers.

To combat this situation, Gary Hedges, Sundstrand's personnel manager, began recruiting older workers and retirees in three ways: among the company's own annuitants, through a contract engineering employment firm in Seattle, and via newspaper ads which read, "Retired? Sundstrand needs you."

The greatest number of recruits have come through the contract engineering firm. Over the past three years, Sundstrand has had between 30 and 40 employees on contract in the above-named categories. When the company finds someone it wants to hire as a permanent employee, it is free to do so after 90 days without further fees to the contracting company. Hedges has hired two 67-year-old engineers in this manner.

Because Sundstrand has a young workforce, it has only 35 annuitants. Six of these have come back to work, three engineers, one supervisor, one assembler, and one 69-year-old machinist. These workers have a choice regarding compensation. They can be considered temporary employees, receive an hourly wage and continue to draw their pensions. Or they can return as full-time workers, receive their salaries and fringe benefits, stop the pension while continuing to accrue credits toward a second retirement.

The newspaper ads have not been effective as yet, but Hedges is hoping to get some response. At the moment, he has between 20 and 40 jobs waiting to be filled.

Source: B. Jacobson, *Young Programs for Older Workers*, New York: Van Nostrand Reinhold (1980): 74–75.

critical cross-functional system that needs to be designed and managed, as we discussed in Chapter 8. In the previously cited Boeing example, the MIS allows over 200 "design/build" teams to be integrated horizontally through the utilization of computerized information.

The diversity exhibit shows how organizations needing highly educated workers for information systems technology work have found that age is no barrier to such work.

Telecommuting

By transmitting computer information over telephone lines, computers linked through modems have made a new kind of work arrangement possible. **Telecommuting** means that rather than physically commuting to the office on a daily basis, employees work on computers at home or other places and send the results of their computer work to the office. This pattern has made it possible for some employees to work at home who otherwise may have had to quit due to the constraint of commuting.

Advances in PCs have made it possible for managers to access organizational databases and communicate with customers while away from the office. (Photo credit: Ed Bock/The Stock Market.)

In 1993 National Cash Register (NCR) was experimenting with telecommuting in its salesforce. The experiment was motivated by at least two factors. One was an attempt to relieve the stress of commuting for its employees. The other was an attempt to save on office space. NCR recorded success with telecommuting, particularly in sales. Since experienced salespeople function with little management and respond to the motivation of sales commissions, the amount of contact needed with others in the organization is minimal.[22]

Telecommuting is not appropriate for some activities in an organization. Those employees needing considerable face-to-face interaction with others or specialized equipment will most likely continue to come to a central workplace.[23]

CRITICAL THINKING QUESTIONS

1. How will the flattening of organizations affect the information needs of lower-level managers?
2. How will the spread of computers in the home, interactive communication systems, and teleconferencing over video screen telephones affect the need for workers to come to a common workplace?

DESIGNING AND IMPLEMENTING AN EFFECTIVE MANAGEMENT INFORMATION SYSTEM

Some organizations have horror stories about expensive yet botched attempts to implement a new management information system. Others have success stories

Q U A L I T Y   E X H I B I T

United Parcel Service

Today UPS managers sing the praises of their five mainframe computers, their worldwide network, and their computer-controlled conveyor belts for routing packages. Chief Executive Officer Kent Nelson says there is a good reason to be bullish on all this technology: "We realized that the leader in information management will be the leader in international package distribution—period." However, this enthusiasm for the benefits of information systems was not always apparent.

In 1980 many UPS managers did not see the need for a change from a manual system. After all, they had improved manual package handling to the point that UPS had the industry's lowest costs. And UPS profits kept setting records.

But customers kept getting choosier, rival Federal Express was getting stronger, and computers were getting cheaper. By 1983 management realized that it could no longer keep ahead just by improving manual processes. Nelson, then senior vice president, created a task force to plot an information-technology strategy. He guessed that computer-based systems would someday identify, route, and track packages better than humans. UPS spent lavishly: $50 million for a global data net-

work; $100 million for a data center; $350 million for the Delivery Information Acquisition Device, a handheld computer for drivers; and $150 million on a cellular data network and a machine-readable label that holds more data than bar codes.

But there were mistakes. Nelson says that at first the company focused too much on hardware and too little on what customers wanted. Meanwhile, FedEx was designing systems to automate customers' mailrooms and delivering packages the next day.

The costs of automation constrained profits in the late 1980s, but UPS sales and earnings rebounded in the early 1990s. At FedEx Alan B. Graf, Jr., chief financial officer, says: "Long term, it's Federal Express vs. UPS. They're tough competitors." UPS may have made a wise investment in MIS, as FedEx withdrew from the intra European market in the early 1990s.

Sources: "After a U-Turn, UPS Really Delivers," *Business Week* (May 31, 1993): 92–93; "Federal Express," *Value Line Investment Survey*, New York: Value Line Publishing (March 26, 1993): 259; UPS: Up from the Stone Age," in "The New Realism in Office Systems," *Business Week* (June 15, 1992): 128.

about gaining new customers with increased value delivered with a new MIS. The success stories usually come only after several years of effort and many millions of dollars have been spent in implementing the MIS. As a prelude to discussing the steps in the design and implementation of a new MIS, the qualtiy exhibit describes one such success story.

Determine Goals for External and Internal Customer Value

The first and most crucial step in the design and implementation of a new MIS is determining what customer value the system will address. To proceed with the design of a new MIS without understanding customer-value goals is like starting on a journey without having a destination in mind. Implementing a new MIS just to have executive bragging rights on the use of the latest technology does not make sense. It does make sense to leave some room in the MIS for growth in case new forms of customer value need to be added in the future.

TABLE 16.4   *Information Requirements by Managerial Level*

Characteristics of Information	First-Line Management	Top-Level Management
Function	Operational control and systems improvement	Strategic planning, customer-value determination, and systems improvement
Type of decisions	Programmed and routine[a]	Nonprogrammed and nonroutine[a]
Source	Internal	Mostly external
Time horizon	Past and present	Future
Scope	Cross-functional at similar level	Entire organization
Level of summation	Detailed	Summary
Frequency of use	Very frequent	Frequent

[a]Programmed and nonprogrammed decisions are discussed in Chapter 5.

Citibank, the largest bank in the United States, has always been a heavy promoter of automated teller machines. It recognized early that its customers wanted access to their funds 24 hours a day, 7 days a week. At one point Citibank was the only bank in Japan to have ATMs open 24 hours a day. More recently, Citibank recognized that its customers in the United States were of different international backgrounds. Then it modified its ATMs to function in nine different languages. Recognizing that some of its customers were apprehensive of computer terminals, it made its ATMs user friendly with touch-sensitive screens. Citibank's ATMs also permit a customer to buy or sell mutual funds, to pay on a credit card balance, or to make a mortgage payment. This full picture of the value to be provided to customers from the ATMs drove a design of more than simply receiving or depositing funds.

Tailor Information to Level of Management

Different levels of management in the organization have different information needs. Therefore the MIS should serve different needs across different levels of management. The designer of the MIS needs to understand which level of management it will serve. Table 16.4 shows how information requirements differ by managerial level.

In many TQ organizations the information requirements of first-line management listed in Table 16.4 are becoming the information requirements of self-managed teams. Thus the MIS must be designed to deliver such information to these teams as well as to first-line management.

Information is a powerful commodity and it can serve many purposes. As we showed earlier in the chapter, computers are helping to merge the two different sets of needs listed in the table. If organizations continue to flatten, the needs of the two levels may more fully merge in the future. Today, however, the MIS designer needs to be mindful of the managerial level the MIS is meant to serve.

Determine Nature of Information

The exact kinds of information required must be determined, including the level of detail or summation, the time period covered, and the units of measurement. For example, at Sea Ray, a manufacturer and marketer of high-quality recreational boats, the manufacturing manager may want to know exactly how many boats are being worked on today. The CFO may not care about the number of boats in process but may want to know the dollar value of the inventory tied up in the partially completed boats. The sales manager may not be interested in work in process but may be interested in knowing how many completed boats are in inventory. All of these persons may be interested in comparing today's information with similar information from a year ago, whereas the first-level managers may be interested only in the information for today. The designer of the MIS at Sea Ray needs to take into account all of these kinds of required information.

Design Hardware and Software

Once the information requirements have been established, selection of the hardware and software can proceed. As indicated in Figure 16.1, this includes the input medium, the software (both the applications programs and the operating system), the processor, the storage device(s), and the output medium. Some suggest that the applications software is the most crucial decision in that this determines the operations the customers of the MIS can perform. Since information technology is changing so rapidly and yielding higher levels of performance at lower costs, it is advisable, for growth purposes, to buy more computer capability than is absolutely needed today.

Important decisions in this area include whether to use large mainframe computers, mid-sized minicomputers, or numerous personal computers. If personal computers are to be used, decisions need to be made on whether to use stand-alone systems or networked systems. In the area of software, there is a much higher chance users will be satisfied with the MIS if the software is user friendly.

Test the Management Information System

Once the MIS has been designed, it must be thoroughly tested before becoming operational. This step is critical for an MIS in financial services where customers can conduct their own transactions, for the wrong kinds of "bugs" in the MIS may enable thieves to conduct transactions involving customers' assets. This testing step is also important for large organization-wide systems in which thousands of customers and many departments could be impacted by bugs in the system. To help with any required debugging, some designers, hardware engineers, and software engineers should stay on the project as it is turned over to the users.

Implement the Management Information System

Implementation of an MIS involves documentation (detailed printed instructions), installation, and training. It does little good to spend millions of dollars on the latest hardware and software if personnel do not know how to use the system. Today many organizations view training in a new MIS as part of the investment in the new capability. The training needs to be done by individuals who speak everyday English, not just computerese. Otherwise some users will be intimidated by the technical nature of the training and will not fully learn how to use the MIS.

At this point individuals with backgrounds in technical writing should be added to the documentation effort. The documentation needs to be written so that a typical user can understand it, not just a user with a degree in computer science.

Deal with Resistance to Change

There are several reasons why individuals and organizations resist a new MIS:

1. Disruption of established departmental boundaries
2. Disruption of the informal system
3. Individuals with stake in old system
4. A staid organizational culture
5. Nonparticipatory implementation of change[24]

As we saw earlier in the chapter, information is cross-functional and cuts across organizational lines. Management must prepare employees for the new organizational patterns, both formal and informal. There will always be individuals with a stake in preserving the old system, as they may have built up expertise and power in that system. By rewarding continuous improvement, management can ensure a more flexible and accepting culture that encourages members and organizations to experiment with improvements. Most assuredly, management can use a participatory process in planning and implementing a new MIS or any other organizational change. In the UPS quality exhibit, management described a participatory implementation involving a task force as a crucial step in the success of switching to the company's MIS.

Monitor, Maintain, and Continuously Improve the Management Information System

The MIS needs to be monitored for problems and maintained. This requires that some trained personnel remain on staff after installation. These personnel will be needed to serve in a "help" role for the users of the MIS.

Once installed, an MIS, like all other systems, needs to be continuously improved. The driver for the continuous improvement is the evolving needs of customers or the inclusion of new customer groups with new needs. For example, as the time demands on business travelers grow, many hotels have added video checkout through the televisions in customers' rooms by linking the hotel's MIS into the televisions. Thus an existing MIS was improved to deliver more value to customers by adding a new input medium.

Software companies usually offer annual updates to software rather than a complete redesign. Some personal computers are designed today so that it is easy to replace the old processor chip with a new processor chip as an upgrade. To take advantage of the latest upgrades in both software and hardware without replacing

FIGURE 16.2 *Designing, Implementing, and Improving a Management Information System*

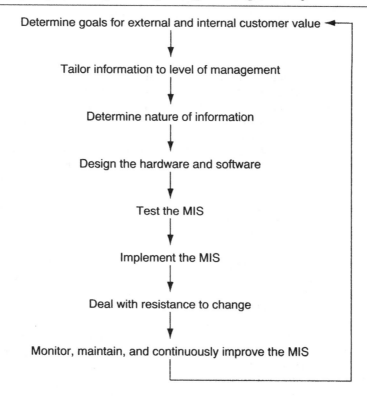

Determine goals for external and internal customer value

↓

Tailor information to level of management

↓

Determine nature of information

↓

Design the hardware and software

↓

Test the MIS

↓

Implement the MIS

↓

Deal with resistance to change

↓

Monitor, maintain, and continuously improve the MIS

the entire system, computer systems, both large and small, should be designed with improvements in mind.

This theme of continuous improvement completes the MIS design cycle. Figure 16.2 illustrates the entire design, implementation, and MIS improvement process.

CRITICAL THINKING QUESTIONS

1. Describe the most important design and implementation criterion of effective management information systems.

2. How will the flattening of organizations affect the design of management information systems?

Conclusion to the Pitney Bowes Case

How does an individual design an information system to meet the criteria of providing customer-relevant information to front line employees? One way is to start with customer requirements and implement those into the information systems design process.

At Pitney Bowes, Customer Satisfaction Teams control the improvement process. In order to articulate Customer-Driven Quality expectations and implement them in the information system design and operation, the firm has asked its Customer Satisfaction Teams to define the information systems support needed to implement the imporovements. Additionally, Pitney Bowes formed two specialized Customer Satisfaction Teams, the Data Requirements Customer Satisfaction Team and the Data Accuracy Customer Satisfaction Team, to deal with specific information issues. These teams specifically address ways that the information system can help employees to meet customer expectations. These two teams complement several other Customer

Satisfaction Teams and Cross-Functional Teams in the organization.

Herb Schneider summarized the key role of information and the information system in Pitney Bowes' Customer-Driven Quality system. "The information system contains key customer-relevant standards. It is our job to 'productionize' measurements. For example, the information system must deliver actionable, customer-relevant information to empowered employees."

DISCUSSION QUESTIONS

1. Describe the importance of actionable, customer-relevant performance measurements in an information system.

2. Compare and contrast the importance of customer-relevant performance measurements in an information system for manufacturing firms and service firms.

Sources: "Customer-Driven Quality Outline," Pitney Bowes Mailing Systems, Stamford, CT, August, 1992; Personal interview, Herb Schneider, July 8, 1994.

SUMMARY

Computerized management information systems are an extension of the manual information systems that were used by managers for centuries. Managers have always had a need to understand how their operations are performing, what their competitors are doing, and what their customers value. Computers, with their expensive, complicated, high-speed input and output devices, automate and speed up the processes. As computers become lighter, faster, cheaper, and more powerful, organizations will find an increasing number of ways to use information technology in a variety of roles throughout their operations.

In their brief history since World War II, management information systems have served several different roles. Many systems were introduced into organizations to serve a transaction or bookkeeping role. In this role the purpose of the MIS was to cut costs, improve speed, process greater volume, and increase accuracy. In a strategic planning role, the MIS is used to collect, analyze, summarize, and disseminate information dealing with external changes and forecasted changes that may affect the future of the firm. In a competitive-weapon role, the MIS is used to track competitors and their products and actions to help managers decide on competitive responses. In a customer-value role, the MIS is used to provide customers with timely, accurate, accessible information that has value for the customer.

The information needs of both external and internal customers include accessibility, timeliness, accuracy, understandability and user friendliness, and security. Those managers who find new ways to provide these values to customers will gain new customers for their organizations.

Management information systems have had far-reaching effects in the workplace. As a cross-functional system in many organizations, an MIS can enable an organization to evolve to a flatter organizational structure by providing decision support systems and expert systems support.

Information is a unique resource in an organization. The kind and quantity of information that is valuable to managers depend on their role and level in the organization. Information can tie together diverse parts of an organization, including multinational operations. The costs of poor information and of not providing customers with the information value that they demand are usually far greater than the investment cost in a state-of-the-art MIS.

There are several steps to be followed in the design and implementation of a new MIS. The first and most important is determining what value it provides to external customers and internal organizational members. Then the designers of the system must tailor the required information to the various levels of management, determine the nature of the information, design the hardware and software, test the MIS, implement it, deal with resistance to change, and monitor, maintain, and continuously improve the MIS.

EXPERIENTIAL EXERCISE

The Truth, Family Obligations, and a Costly New MIS

Recently, Tom was promoted to the position of Regional MIS Manager for a large company. Over several years he had worked hard to win the promotion.

Dick, the Director of Corporate MIS and Tom's supervisor, called Tom to his office. Dick had just been informed that the CEO had received an anonymous letter from an employee about the company's recently installed and very expensive MIS. This letter stated that the MIS was not achieving the expected results.

Tom was aware that the system's actual performance was poor and had previously reported this performance problem to Dick. Dick had politely listened to Tom while providing only positive feedback on the system's performance to the CEO. Dick had been the original supporter of the new MIS.

Dick told Tom that the CEO expected that a reply to the employee's letter would be sent, and he requested that Tom draft the reply. Dick instructed Tom that the reply should state that the MIS has been performing as forecasted and that all savings estimated in the original MIS implementation plan were being achieved.

Tom was very upset by Dick's order, believing that corporate executives were being misled to protect a questionable decision. Tom left Dick's office very disturbed.

Feeling very anxious, Tom later returned to Dick's office and stated his concern. Dick insisted on the content of the reply to the letter. Dick said that if Tom did not provide the requested reply, he would seriously question Tom's ability to perform as regional MIS manager.

Tom now is very worried about Dick's threat, for his family would suffer financial and emotional hardship if he were to be fired from his hard-won position. Tom's wife, Ellen, recently gave birth to their second child and quit her job in sales to spend more time with their newborn and their two-year-old. Tom tells Ellen of the quandary on the phone, and they both talk of the impact on their family if Tom were to lose his job.

Assignment

1. Three volunteers should be sought from the class to role-play Tom, Dick, and Ellen. The students role-playing the characters of Tom and Dick should role-play the first and then the second conversation between the two men. They should emphasize Tom's concern and Dick's insistence. Then the students role-playing Ellen and Tom should role-play the conversation between them. The student role-playing Ellen should review her decision to quit her job to raise their children and her concern about the impact on the family if Tom lost his job.
2. After the role playing, the class should discuss the following questions:
   a. Is Tom's duty to obey Dick?
   b. Is Tom's duty to tell the truth to the CEO?
   c. What are Tom's obligations to his family?
   d. What is Ellen's stake in this situation?
   e. Is Tom risking his own credibility and his career by falsifying statements to the CEO?

CHAPTER CASE

Making Service Personal at Fidelity Investments

In the competitive world of financial services, providing flawless, personalized service to every customer is both a challenge and a necessity. When you have over five million customers, and are adding more daily, the challenge is formidable indeed. Fidelity Investments, the giant mutual fund company, has managed to meet that challenge with a combination of management savvy, innovation, a keen focus on customer research, and technology. Lots and lots of technology.

"The financial services industry is very dependent on technology today," says Fidelity chairman and CEO Edward C. Johnson III. "For Fidelity, computers serve two purposes that are absolutely essential: They allow us to serve our customers better and they allow us to keep our expenses within reasonable limits."

The company has put millions of dollars behind its technology vision. State-of-the-art technology has helped catapult Fidelity to the top of the mutual fund industry. Fidelity now manages more than $220 billion in assets in approximately 200 mutual funds. Through its "invisible" technology, and such innovations as check writing, a customer magazine, and financial planning tools, Fidelity has made dealing with an investment company less intimidating for customers.

Fidelity's reliance on sophisticated technology starts at a basic level: When customers call, which they do at the rate of about 200,000 calls a day, operators attempt to answer 85 percent of the calls in less than 20 seconds. More than two-thirds of the calls are handled by a computer system, with no human intervention. A computer-switching system

Fidelity Investments, the largest mutual fund company in the United States, practices rapid response to customer inquiries in order to lower costs and provide value to customers. (Photo credit: Peter Vidor Photography.)

monitors the call loads at each of Fidelity's four telephone centers and distributes the remaining calls among its 2,000-plus representatives.

But getting the calls answered is only part of the plan. Fidelity has focused an enormous amount of attention on personalizing service. Fidelity representatives receive special training in problem solving and customer relations. And, of course, they are supported by technology. For example, the fastest growing area for new growth at Fidelity over the past year has been 401(k) accounts. Here, again, technology played a role. Fidelity's sophisticated computer system allows employees to tailor their 401(k) retirement plans to their own needs while still staying

within their employer's ground rules for "allowable" investments. Fidelity programmed the thousands of trading restrictions and rules required by employers into a computer server, which in turn is linked to Fidelity representatives' workstations. Now when a customer calls to make a trade, the server instantly tells the representative's computer if the employee's plan allows that transaction.

Coming soon from Fidelity is the "workstation of the future," an easy-to-use platform that will allow representatives to see an instant snapshot of all of a customer's accounts. Fields will be customized to allow a representative to offer a customer the kind of information he or she has requested in the past, increasing the level of personal service and—not coincidentally—sales.

"Successfully implemented, the workstation of the future can help us provide superior service to customers and improve our internal productivity," Johnson says. "Higher customer satisfaction and increased productivity are not competing goals; they are both desired end results of a well-integrated, well-thought-out quality strategy."

Discussion Questions

1. Describe the kinds of value that a financial services organization can provide to customers with an MIS.

2. Is it easier to provide value to customers with an MIS in service or manufacturing organizations? Why?

Source: "Quality '93: Empowering People with Technology," *Fortune* (September 20, 1993): 130.

KEY TERMS

applications software   Instructions that tell the computer how to perform certain custom tasks like word processing, accounting, or graphics.

artificial intelligence   Use of information technology to make computers "think" like humans and mimic the human mind.

decision support system   System that searches for, analyzes, summarizes, and reports information needed for specific decisions.

expert system   Computerized decision-making aid that enables decision makers to use multiple pieces of information to make decisions in the manner of experts.

group decision support system (GDSS)   System that searches for, analyzes, summarizes, reports, and interactively shares with group members the information needed for specific group decisions.

information quality   Degree to which information accurately portrays reality.

input medium   Computer hardware used to enter data into the computer.

mainframe computer   Large, powerful computer that serves as the core of many computer operations.

management information system (MIS)   Set of computer hardware and software that gathers, organizes, summarizes, and reports information for use by managers, customers, and others.

networking   Linking together of individuals in a management information system to share information.

operating system   Set of computer instructions that performs the scheduling of jobs and housekeeping chores in the computer.

output medium   Computer hardware used to deliver the results of the computer operations to the user.

processor, or **central processing unit (CPU)**   Computer hardware that organizes, analyzes, and summarizes data.

real-time information   Information that immediately reflects the underlying reality.

software   Set of instructions that tells the computer hardware what to do.

storage device   Computer hardware used to store data after the data have been entered.

telecommuting   Work process in which employees work on computers at home or other places and send the results of their computer work to the office, rather than physically commuting to the office on a daily basis.

transaction-processing system   Management information system designed to record and summarize routine transactions for an organization.

user friendliness   Concept that an MIS is easy to use due to simple-to-follow instructions.

ENDNOTES

1. "The New Realism in Office Systems," *Business Week* (June 15, 1992): 128–133.
2. M. Morton and J. Rockart, "Implications of Changes in Information Technology for Corporate Strategy," *Interfaces* (January-February 1984): 84–95.
3. G. Ashmore, "Applying Expert Systems to Business Strategy," *Journal of Business Strategy* (September-October 1989): 46–49.
4. "Technology: No Compromises," *The Wall Street Journal* (November 16, 1992): R8.
5. "Your Digital Future," *Business Week* (September 7, 1992): 56.
6. W. R. King, "Strategic Planning for Information Resources," *Information Resource Management Journal* (Fall 1988): 2–3.
7. J. C. Camillus and A. L. Lederer, "Corporate Strategy and the Design of Computerized Information Systems," *Sloan Management Review* (Spring 1985): 35.
8. R. Woodruff and E. Cadotte, "Analyzing Market Opportunities for New Ventures," *Survey of Business* (Summer 1987): 15.
9. M. Porter and V. Millar, "How Information Gives You Competitive Advantage," *Harvard Business Review,* 63, no. 4 (1985): 149–159.
10. M. Porter, *Competitive Strategy,* New York: Free Press (1985): 169.
11. P. Drucker, "The Coming of the New Organization," *Harvard Business Review* (January-February 1988): 45–53.
12. Woodruff and Cadotte, "Analyzing Market Opportunities for New Ventures," 10–15.
13. M. J. Stahl and D. W. Grigsby, *Strategic Management for Decision Making,* Boston: PWS-Kent (1992): 95.
14. Ibid.
15. "Getting Personal: At Fidelity Investments, Computers Are Designed to Make the Company Seem More Human," *The Wall Street Journal* (April 6, 1992): R19.

16. "Office Automation: Making It Pay Off," *Business Week* (October 12, 1987): 134–146.
17. "Betting on the 21st Century Jet," *Fortune* (April 20, 1992): 102.
18. "Race for Computerized Booking Systems Is Heating Up Among European Airlines," *The Wall Street Journal* (December 1, 1988): B3.
19. "The New Realism in Office Systems," 128.
20. "Who's Winning the Information Revolution?" *Fortune* (November 30, 1992): 116.
21. Ibid., 110.
22. "Nightly Business Report," *Cable News Network* (May 19, 1993).
23. "The New Realism in Office Systems," 128.
24. Adapted from G. Dickson and J. Simmons, "The Behavioral Side of MIS," *Business Horizons* (August 1970): 59–71.

Managing Technology and Technological Change

Corning Laboratories

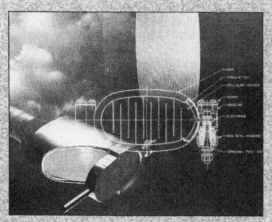

One of Corning's World Class Quality goals is to exceed expectations—the way a prototype Corning catalytic converter did when it reduced non-methane hydrocarbons and carbon monoxide to emission levels less than half of those mandated by California's stringent 1997 regulations. (Photo credit: Corning, Inc.)

Corning Inc., headquartered in Corning, New York, and formerly known as Corning Glass Works, is a name known in most kitchens in the United States. Its consumer products include housewares sold under the Pyrex, Corning Ware, Corelle, Visions, and Revere Ware names. But these well-known products are only part of Corning, as they account for only about 20 percent of sales. The firm has three other divisions, providing laboratory services (laboratory equipment, lenses for eye glasses, testing services, and industrial laboratory services), communications products (optical fibers and glass for computer terminals and televisions), and specialty materials (ceramics for auto pollution devices, headlamps, and technical ceramics). Since many of these products are based on technological expertise in ceramics and glass, Corning's management of technology and technological change to yield new products in less time than its competitors has always been important to the health of the firm.

In the early 1980s Corning's health was seriously in question and the engine of technological expertise and adaptation was laboring. Its profits were flat in a time when profits were being eroded by inflation, and the time Corning took to get new products to market left much to be desired.

As an example of the malaise inflicting Corning in that decade, Ralph Westwig's experiments in fiber-optic technology were hindered by a shortage of odd tools and spare parts. He felt that valuable research time was wasted because his superiors at Corning's research and development labs were acting penny-wise and pound-foolish. Such events are rare now that Corning chairman James R. Houghton's concept of Total Quality has been implemented. The Total Quality idea has led to the creation of "corrective action teams" to solve thorny problems. In 1986 Westwig and four other scientists formed the first such corrective action team in research and development. The team proposed buying $66,000 worth of supplies, including lasers and delicate lenses, that would reduce idle time during experiments for up to 40 researchers. Westwig calculated that in the next three years the investment netted Corning $1.2 million in higher productivity. "We were skeptical about this quality concept," says

continued

Westwig. "But when we saw that it worked, it gave us a warm feeling inside."

Corning considers its quality program to be a key element in its emergence as a leader in markets hotly contested by the Japanese, including fiber optics. In fact, quality programs have saved the labs $21 million over the past four years. New products are being pushed out faster than ever, and costs are coming down—part of the reason Corning's profit margin was greater than 9 percent in the early 1990s, up from less than 6 percent in the early 1980s. "They're one of the few companies outside Japan that successfully encourages a spirit of continuous improvement and innovation" among scientists, says Alan R. Fusfeld, a consultant in Framingham, Massachusetts, who worked with Corning during its TQ transformation in the mid-1980s. As a further testament, companies such as Westinghouse and Clorox have paid Corning to learn about its approach.

But what are they buying? Are the ideas of teams and TQ in research and development transferable to other organizations? Is teaming in R&D any different than in other parts of the organization?

For decades the tools, techniques, knowledge, and processes used to transform an organization's inputs into outputs changed slowly. However, in the past few decades the pace of change in science and engineering has exploded. This new technological knowledge has found its way into the internationally competitive marketplace. Technology is now being used as a competitive weapon to gain new customers.

CONCEPT OF TECHNOLOGY

In this chapter we are not trying to turn the reader into a scientist or engineer. Rather we are attempting to help the reader understand that technology is a tool that enables the manager to deliver greater value to customers. Those managers who find ways to use technology to yield greater value for customers will win increased market share and profits for their efforts.

Technology is the sum of knowledge, tools, techniques, and processes used to transform organizational inputs into outputs.[1] **Technological change** refers to changes in any of these technological factors.

The United States is the unquestioned global leader in the development of new technology. However, some international competitors, especially Japan, have been implementing new technology at an ever-increasing pace to yield new products for customers. Herein lies the challenge for managers in the 1990s: to implement new technology at a faster rate to yield new products for customers.

Management of Technology

The **management of technology** refers to how the organization uses technology to yield value to customers. As such, the management of technology (MOT) concerns itself not only with many strictly managerial tasks, but also with many technical subjects related to engineering and science. Management intersects with engineering and science to yield the management of technology.[2]

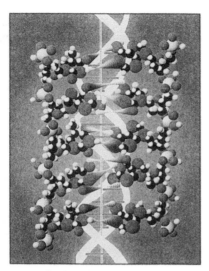

*New technology has allowed the pharma-
ceutical industry to invent drugs that
were previously not possible and deliver
new value to customers.* (Photo credit:
Comstock.)

For example, a research scientist at a pharmaceutical company like Merck may be extremely interested in the reaction of Alzheimer's disease to a new drug. The scientist may be pursuing the issue strictly from the science side of the issue. A manager at Merck involved with the same project may need to work through the maze of federal activities to win approval to distribute the new drug. The manager may also need to work with banks to gain financing for the new plant to produce the drug, with industrial engineers to design the production process, and with an advertising agency to launch the new product. Those managerial activities are referred to as the management of technology.

Processes

Processes are often an overlooked aspect of technology. A *process* is any group of activities that takes an input, adds value to it, and provides an output to an internal or external customer.[3] Thus a manager can change the technology and deliver more value to the customer by improving the process.

A simple change in process can often yield dramatic results. For example, the Capsugel division of Warner-Lambert makes hard gelatin capsules for the pharmaceutical industry. Capsugel had formerly relied on after-the-fact inspection to weed out defects. That process was costly, however, as it employed about 100 inspectors per manufacturing plant. The company changed the process by introducing statistical process control to spot the source of the defects at the point of production. The quality also improved, as the inspectors had not been able to catch all of the defects due to fatigue and eyesight limitations. In this case a change in manufacturing process that employed proven techniques lowered costs and improved quality.

D I V E R S I T Y   E X H I B I T

Du Pont's Policy of Exclusion from the Workplace

In January 1981 the *New York Times* reviewed a new and startling development in the workplaces of the nation. Some fertile women workers chose to undergo voluntary sterilization rather than give up high-paying jobs that involved exposure to chemicals potentially harmful to a developing fetus.

Some background information is necessary for understanding this issue. The causes of congenital (or "birth") defects in humans are not well understood. Four to six percent are known to be caused by specific drugs and environmental chemicals, but the causes of at least 65 to 70 percent are unknown. It is known, however, that of the 28,000 toxic substances listed by the National Institute of Occupational Safety and Health (NIOSH), 56 are known animal mutagens (that is, they cause chromosomal damage to either the ova or the sperm cells), and 471 are known animal teratogens (that is, they can damage the developing fetus). As the 1960s' thalidomide tragedy showed, a substance can be perfectly harmless to the mother, while at the same time having devastating effects on the developing fetus. (Doctors prescribed thalidomide for pregnant women as a tranquilizer, but found that the drug caused such fetal defects as severely shortened and often useless arms and legs.)

Exposure to mutagenic or teratogenic substances in the workplace is complicated by the fact that chemicals and other toxic substances usually do not occur singly, but in combination. Also, the average worker does not have knowledge of the chemical makeup of many products. Furthermore, the period of maximum hazard to the developing fetus occurs during the third and fourth weeks of pregnancy, which is often before the woman is even aware of her pregnancy. The U.S. government (FDA and EPA, in particular) requires animal testing of drugs to ensure that any new product to which pregnant women may be exposed is harmless to the fetus.

Industries such as chemical plants and zinc smelters with high concentrations of lead have coped with this potential threat to the fetus in various ways. The most common strategy is simply to make jobs that involve the risk of exposure "off limits" to women "of child-bearing potential." That is, fertile women in their late teens, twenties, thirties, and forties are banned from those particular positions. (Ironically, lead poses an equal danger to the male reproductive system.) Since a woman is assumed fertile until proven otherwise, this sweeping policy affects a large portion of the female workforce. This policy, entitled "protective exclusion," has aroused the ire of proponents of the women's movement and of civil libertarians, who see these policies as one more form of sex discrimination.

Charges of discrimination are made credible for several reasons. Jobs that *are* open to "women of child-bearing potential" are almost always lower-paying jobs. In addition, women's groups have noted a shortage of well-supported evidence about exposure to certain alleged toxic hazards and a general lack of consensus in government and industry about proper levels of unsafe exposure. The most significant charge of discrimination rests on evidence of the *male's* contribution to birth defects. As noted earlier, mutagenic substances affect the sperm as well as the egg. This can result in sterility for the man, but it also can produce mutated sperm and ultimately a malformed fetus. Thus any policy designed to protect the fetus must include considerations of both the sperm and egg that form it. This would logically include a more expansive protective policy than the mere exclusion of women from the workplace.

Du Pont de Nemours & Co., the largest chemical manufacturer in the United States, has been concerned about these issues since a high incidence of bladder tumors appeared at its large Chambers plant in southern New Jersey in the 1930s. Du Pont has issued perhaps the most explicit policy statement about hazards to women and fetuses. If a chemical is found to be or is suspected of being an "embryotoxin" (toxic to the fetus), the first step is to use engineering and administrative procedures to eliminate the risk or to reduce it to an acceptable level. Engineering

continued

procedures might, for example, involve special ventilation equipment, and administrative procedures might involve management of the length of exposure time or the required use of protective clothing. However, where no "acceptable exposure level" has been determined or where engineering and administrative procedures are inadequate to control exposure, the Du Pont policy reads: "Females of childbearing capacity shall be excluded from work areas."

Du Pont has rejected the suggestion that a woman be apprised of the health risk and sign a waiver if she chooses to accept the risk. The Du Pont position is that the exclusionary policy is to protect the fetus, not the woman. Bruce Karrh, medical director of Du Pont, holds that "the primary issue . . . is not whether the exclusion from the workplace is necessary to protect the adult female or male, but whether it is a necessary step to protect the embryo or fetus."

Du Pont holds that " . . . the waiver of subsequent claims by the female worker would be of no legal significance because the deformed fetus, if born, may have its own rights as a person which could not be waived by the mother." Women's groups continue, however, to view "protective exclusion" as sex discrimination, especially since there is growing evidence that the reproductive systems of men are also adversely affected by certain industrial chemicals.

The Coalition for the Reproductive Rights of Women, a group organized to fight discrimination against women of childbearing age, points out that the exclusionary protections are unusually broad, especially since not all women want or plan to have children. An attorney for the women's rights project of the American Civil Liberties Union has criticized the notion that women should be protected "against their wishes" and states that "we insist that the cost of safety cannot be equality. Another solution should be found."

Du Pont sees the sex of the excluded party as irrelevant, on grounds that the sole issue is that of protecting the susceptible fetus. The company also notes that implementation of [this policy] is far more costly to the company than a policy that would allow women to make their own choices. However, women's advocates take the view that

companies such as Du Pont are simply remiss in developing technological solutions for the control of embryotoxins. A common union complaint is that industry makes the worker safe for the workplace, even to the point of exclusion, rather than making the workplace safe for the worker. These women view with suspicion management contentions that acceptable levels of exposure cannot be achieved. Growing evidence that toxic substances pose a threat to the *future* fetus, as well as to the *existing* one, through mutation of the sperm and egg, indicates that this issue is not likely to prove amenable to simple solution.

All these issues are further complicated because information that a chemical may be embryotoxic often is not available well in advance of policy decisions. In the case of a chemical used by Du Pont in some resins and elastomers, Du Pont was informed by a supplier in March 1981 that it was possible teratogenic. The data were preliminary and needed corroboration by a study designed to show if teratogenicity occurs. Rather than wait for such a study to be completed, Du Pont immediately determined a level of exposure considered to pose "no risk." Du Pont then promptly advised all employees working with the chemical of the preliminary findings and determined that the jobs of about 50 women involved unacceptable levels of exposure. About one-half were found to be of childbearing capability and were excluded. All excluded women were moved to comparable positions without penalty in wages or benefits.

Du Pont's Haskell Laboratory simultaneously instituted an animal study to corroborate the preliminary work. The supplier's follow-up study and the Du Pont study both found no teratogenic effect in the animals studied. The supplier's earlier study results apparently contained experimental error. Du Pont notified its employees of the new findings and no longer excluded women of childbearing capability. Return preference was given to women formerly removed from these jobs. During this period, Du Pont made its plant physicians available for counseling employees and for consulting with the personal physicians of employees.

Source: Tom L. Beauchamp, *Case Studies in Business, Society, and Ethics,* 3rd ed., Prentice-Hall. Copyright Tom L. Beauchamp.

Knowledge and Techniques

Technology is more than tools, materials, and processes. All such technological dimensions are made through the application of knowledge and techniques. The knowledge and techniques of how to use the various technological tools, materials, and processes are crucial. The manager also must know how to combine them into a single system to deliver greater value to customers.

For example, high-strength composite materials are increasingly being used in aircraft design. However, the aircraft manufacturer must know how to manipulate the brittle materials and machine them into complex shapes. This knowledge of how to work these materials was associated with the greater use of high-performance materials in U.S. military aircraft than in Soviet military aircraft during the Cold War.

Tools

Tools and machinery are part of technology. Some firms design and manufacture their own tools. The Sonoco Products Company produces a broad line of industrial and consumer packaging such as paper and plastic sacks, plastic and paper composite cans, and tubes and cores for winding products. Sonoco manufactures much of the machinery used in the production process.

Computer Hardware and Software

As a technological advance, computers can be used as a particular kind of tool to improve the processes without changing the underlying tools, materials, and techniques. For example, computer-integrated manufacturing can produce, without any change in the tools, materials, and techniques, more uniform output than manually controlled manufacturing. **Computer-integrated manufacturing** is the extensive use of computers to plan and to control the entire manufacturing process. Indeed, computer-integrated manufacturing has been introduced into the home appliance industry to reduce the variation in production without changing the underlying system of production.

Rules of Competition in an Industry

Many firms use technology to improve their competitive positions in their industries. Managers can either develop the new technology or borrow it from others if it is not proprietary. **Proprietary technology** is technology held by one firm and not shared with other firms. Proprietary technology held by one firm in an industry can change the rules of competition in that industry. As one researcher noted, "Technology affects competitive advantage if it has a significant role in determining relative cost position or differentiation."[4]

For example, a chemical company that develops a new chemical process that lowers the cost of production by 35 percent can become the lowest-cost producer. Competitors in the industry have three choices: switch to a strategy in which they try to differentiate their products, exit the business, or suffer losses if they stay in the business.

CRITICAL THINKING QUESTIONS

1. Explain the concept of technology. Compare the technology in use in the tobacco industry with the technology in use in the banking industry.

2. Technology covers process, knowledge, tools, and techniques. In which of these areas is the idea of continuous improvement likely to have the greatest payoff?

CONTRIBUTION TO CUSTOMER VALUE

New technology is expensive in terms of the money involved and the disruption to the organization resulting from its introduction. Personnel must be retrained, equipment needs to be replaced or modified, and productive output is often disrupted. Therefore managers should not introduce new technology just for the sake of having the latest technological toys in the industry.

New technology should be introduced only if it enables the firm to produce additional value for its customers. Whether the increased value is in the form of reduced cycle time, lower cost, or higher quality, technology is a means to improved customer value.

Product /Market /Industry Life Cycle

To understand how the introduction of new or modified technology adds value to customers, it is useful to review the life-cycle concept of a product. This concept also applies to entire markets and industries. The life-cycle concept shows that products, industries, and entire markets develop, grow rapidly, mature, and decline in a somewhat predictable fashion over time.[5] If sales are graphed as a function of time, the resulting pattern is a lazy-S curve, as shown in Figure 17.1.

In the introduction/development phase, the product or service is initially offered to customers. Sales are slowly built up as more customers become aware of the new product or service and make initial purchases of it.

After some demand for the new product or service has been established, sales take off in an accelerated, exponential growth rate. Increasingly large numbers of new customers demand the new product or service for the first time. Such explosive sales and growing profits for the original firm offering the new product or service attract other firms into the market.

As initial demand by customers for the product or service is satisfied in the marketplace, sales become replacement sales. This is the maturity phase. In this stage further sales gains for one firm come at the expense of another firm rather than from first-time customers.

As new technology and resulting other new products or services makes the original product or service obsolete, or as substitute products or services arrive, sales decline. Some firms leave the industry. Some firms stay in the industry and "milk" the product for profitability with little new investment.

Record players followed this life-cycle pattern. Cassette tape recorders and players have been following the pattern and are replacing record players. And today compact disks are replacing cassette tapes in many markets.

FIGURE 17.1   *Product/Market/Industry Life Cycle*

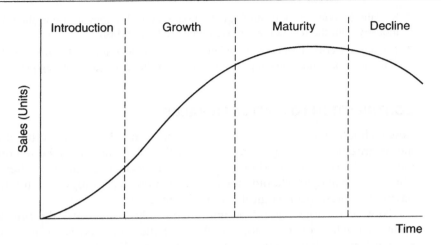

Continuous improvement of products can extend the maturity phase of the cycle. By improving and adding new value to the product or service, the firm can extend the time until customers switch to other products or services. This continuous improvement tactic is counter to the old tactic of "milking" the product for profitability with little new investment.

Short Product Development Cycle Times

A way to offer value to customers is to offer the new product or service to customers earlier. In many markets today customers are demanding the latest in new technology in products and services without delay. By shortening product development cycle time, the firm is able to be the first to market with the new product or service. **Product development cycle time** is the time from conception of the idea for a new product, through the product development phase, until the new product is first offered to the customer.

In terms of Figure 17.1, the firm hopes to move the introduction back in time and to be the first firm to offer the new product or service to the market. In Figure 17.2 the dotted line indicates the result of a shortened product development cycle time that allows the firm to introduce the product earlier than its competitor. The solid line refers to the traditional product development cycle time of the competitor.

Good examples of shortened product development cycle times are found in the automobile industry. Figure 17.3 shows how Toyota's product development cycle time is three years, whereas the comparable time for some Detroit firms is five years. Since reduction in cycle time means close ties between new-product development and manufacturing, there are some manufacturing terms that need to be defined and that will be more fully described in Chapter 18, on operations management. A **just-in-time (JIT) inventory system** orders materials to arrive at the point of use exactly when they are needed. JIT is usually used in conjunction with computer-integrated manufacturing because of the precision needed for the JIT system to function.

FIGURE 17.2 *Short and Traditional Development Cycles*

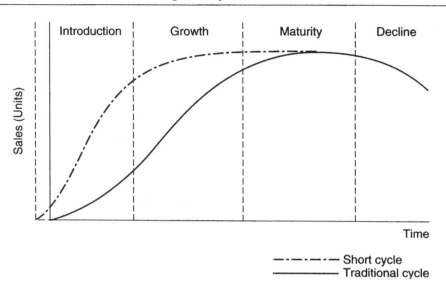

Flexible cells are adaptable groupings of people and machinery in the manufacturing process. **Inventory turns** refer to how many times in a given time period, like a year, the inventory is turned over or used up in the manufacturing process.

In Detroit the Chrysler Corporation has dramatically shortened its new-product development cycle time, having decreased its new-car development cycle time in the last five years from 54 months to 39 months.[6]

The cost of being late to market can be huge. Table 17.1 shows the cost of arriving late to market. Just a few months "slip" in the schedule can be costly.

Reduced Cost

An obvious area for the application of new technology is in cost reduction. Cost reduction may be the most frequently used factor to justify new technology. The steel industry in this country, for example, has been replacing obsolete open-hearth furnaces with basic oxygen furnaces. The new basic oxygen furnaces produce a ton of steel at much lower cost than the old open-hearth furnaces.

Variance Reduction and Quality Improvement

Another good reason to introduce new technology is to reduce the variance of production and thereby improve quality. Sometimes robots are used to yield consistent quality. Training in the use of statistical process control is a good example of the use of technology to improve quality and reduce variance.

CRITICAL THINKING QUESTIONS

1. Explain how technology contributes to customer value. Give an example from the health care and insurance industries.

FIGURE 17.3 *Fast-Cycle Capability*

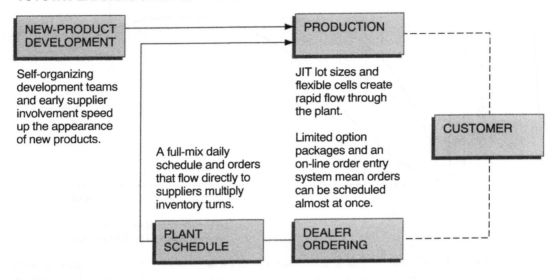

TOYOTA PERFORMS CRITICAL OPERATIONS FASTER...

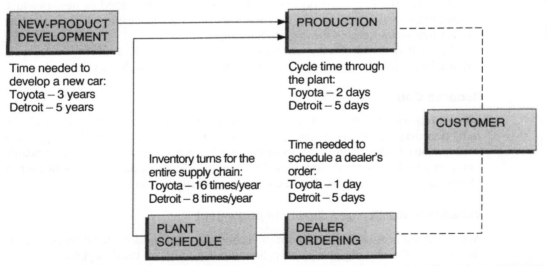

...SO IT CUTS TIME AT EVERY TURN.

2. New-product development cycle times are being viewed as a competitive battleground of the 1990s. Discuss the advantages and disadvantages of having the shortest cycle times and always being first to market.

TABLE 17.1   *Costs of Being Late to Market*

Number of Months Late to Market	Reduction in Gross Profit
6	33%
4	18
2	7
1	3

Source: Adapted from J. T. Vesey, "The New Competitors Think in Terms of 'Speed-to-Market,'" *SAM Advanced Management Journal* (Autumn 1991): 28.

RESEARCH AND DEVELOPMENT SPECTRUM

The discovery and implementation of new technology usually follows a certain life cycle. These phases in the life cycle are described as basic research, advanced research, product development, process improvement, and value engineering.[7]

Basic Research

Basic research is often referred to as pure or fundamental research. **Basic research** consists of scientific activities conducted for the sake of gaining new knowledge without any specific application in mind. For example, research into composite materials without anticipating their use in a specific product is a good example of basic research. Much basic research is conducted in colleges and universities. As industry is increasingly focusing its research and development on new products and services for customers, the trend is toward less basic research in industry.

Advanced Research

Advanced research, or applied research, is more practical than basic research and depends on the findings of basic research. **Advanced research** consists of the scientific activities conducted to advance the state of the art in a specific technical field with the objective of solving a problem. For example, research into carbon-based composite materials for future aircraft is a good example of advanced research. Advanced research is more structured than basic research, and the output of advanced research is expected to have practical applications.

Product Development

Once the knowledge has been developed and the state of the art has been advanced through the basic and advanced research phases, it is time to translate the knowledge into new products. **Product development** consists of the activities that translate the results of research into a new or an improved product.

For example, application of the knowledge gained from research into composite materials to the design of a lightweight, high-strength wing on a military fighter plane is product development. Product development is so important to the technological

QUALITY EXHIBIT

The Man Who Keeps the Juices Flowing at the Skunk Works: Sherm Mullin

A backstage hero of the recent Persian Gulf War, Sherm Mullin, 55, has one of the world's most secret jobs. He's president of the so-called Skunk Works—officially Lockheed Advanced Development Co.—that created such warplanes as the F-117A Stealth fighter. "A little-known fact of the war," says Mullin, "is that Stealth fighters faced significant numbers of Russian-built surface-to-air missiles, particularly around Baghdad. What's gratifying is that every plane and every person in them is coming home—the objective of Stealth."

In another critical role, Mullin led development of the Advanced Tactical Fighter that in April 1991 won the Pentagon's nod. Lockheed, in partnership with Boeing and General Dynamics, beat out Northrop and McDonnell Douglas to build that fighter in a $60 billion program. Says Mullin: "This is the plane that can extend U.S. air supremacy into the 21st century."

A tough manager, Mullin was lent by the Skunk Works to inject a creative approach into the Advanced Tactical Fighter program. He greeted his new team members with a briefing slide that said, simply, "Lead, follow, or get the hell out of the way." Later, Mullin exhorted his staff to keep that fighter on schedule with a memo he entitled "The Coming Fury"—meaning of course, his fury if the plane lagged.

Abhorrent of bureaucracy, Mullin deliberately put the Stealth fighter into production before the aircraft was perfected. "We delivered several airplanes to the Air Force when we were still in the early phases of flight testing," he explains. As a result, the program was driven by the demands of fighter pilots rather than engineers. Another advantage, says Mullin: "The kinds of missions flown in Iraq were being practiced in 1982, when we delivered the first plane."

Mullin, who became president of the Skunk Works late last year upon the retirement of famed

Just as this stealth fighter changed the rules of combat, so too can new technology change the rules of competition in industry. (Photo credit: AP/World Wide Photos.)

aircraft designer Ben Rich, maintains that its methods for building fabulous new flying machines have broader applications. "Even though the work we do is secret," he says, "how we do it is not secret at all." In essence, he picks small teams of highly motivated people, gives them very austere budgets, and puts them in isolation to keep senior management off their backs. "You don't let anyone in, and you give them the freedom to do their thing," he remarks. Most Skunk Works projects come in well under their budgets, although for a while the Stealth lagged behind a purposely demanding schedule. Explains Mullin: "That's the challenge—to do it faster and cheaper."

Surprisingly, the Skunk Works technique has few emulators. Says Mullin: "Most U.S. companies have huge amounts of bureaucracy. The illusion is that bureaucracy brings stability and control. The fact is that it brings inertia and slowness."

success of an organization that firms spend much more money on product development than on basic or applied research. It takes a particular kind of manager to develop the results of research into new products, as is shown in the quality exhibit.

FIGURE 17.4 *Life Cycle for Technological Innovation*

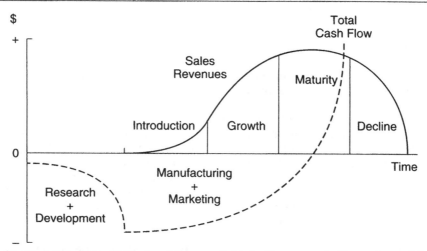

Source: Adapted from W. Boulton, "Resource Guide for Management of Innovation and Technology." A joint publication of the American Assembly of Collegiate Schools of Business, the National Consortium for Technology in Business, and the Thomas Walter Center for Technology Management at Auburn University (1993): 16.

Process Improvement

Process improvement refers to minor changes in the manufacturing process to increase yield, reduce cycle time, lower costs, or otherwise improve efficiency. Changing the way a manufacturing line is laid out is an example of process improvement. In the manufacture of hard gelatin capsules, Capsugel found that the number of defects could be reduced by uniformly heating the liquid gelatin in the manufacturing process. This minor process improvement helped to deliver higher-quality shipments to customers and lower the cost of quality.

Value Engineering

Value engineering refers to minor changes in a product to reduce costs. An example of value engineering is the substitution of a less costly component for a more expensive component in an assembly. In the manufacture of dishwashers, replacing copper tubing with plastic tubing is an illustration of value engineering.

Life Cycle for Technological Innovation

The various phases of the research and development spectrum yield a typical life cycle for technological innovations. Combined with the product life cycle shown in Figure 17.1, a complete technological life cycle from basic research through maturity of the product can be visualized. Figure 17.4 shows the complete life cycle for technological innovation. The chart shows why positive cash flow occurs so late in the life cycle. This presents another reason to shorten the product development cycle time and thereby recoup investments earlier.

QUALITY CASE

Back to the Corning Laboratories Case

Westinghouse and Clorox are companies that are paying Corning Inc. to learn about that company's approach to quality. What they are buying is a cross-functional teaming process that is the same in R&D as it is in manufacturing and marketing. Nearly 70 percent of Corning's 1,200 scientists and engineers belong to cross-functional quality teams. These teams probe issues ranging from improving cooperation among researchers, marketeers, financiers, and manufacturers to increasing external customer satisfaction.

Corning has also formalized an innovation process to improve product development. New products are subject to tough scrutiny at specified points in the development cycle, and weak ones are eliminated before too much is invested in them. Then project teams with representatives from research, development, manufacturing, finance, and marketing guide promising prototypes from the labs to the market. By focusing on the promising products, and by using the cross-functional teams to speed the development and initial manufacturing, the new-product development cycle time is reduced.

The innovation process helped Corning develop a new cranberry-colored version of Corning's Visions cookware in record time for the Christmas of 1991. The project did not start until June, and "doing it in five months"—the normal development time—"was not going to be good enough," says Gerald J. Fine, manager of consumer products development. To beat the normal time and make the product available for Christmas shoppers, about 30 team members worked concurrently on everything from ordering raw materials to advertising. They cut the development time to a manageable three months.

Innovation can occur at any stage of the life cycle. To keep innovative ideas flowing, Hoechst Celanese, a major worldwide chemicals firm, is concerned about the "not invented here (NIH)" syndrome: If the idea was not invented here, then it cannot be a good idea. To counter such NIH thinking, the Office of Innovation at Hoechst Celanese has published a list of NIH statements. Managers need to guard against the kind of thinking reflected in many of the following statements in their own thinking and that of other employees:

— Be Practical.
— That's Not Logical.
— It's Too Radical.
— It's against Policy.
— That's Not My Job.
— It Worries Our Lawyers.
— It Won't Work Here.
— We Tried That 10 Years Ago.
— Management Will Never Buy It.
— We Need to Be Careful with This.
— The Universal Idea Killer: SILENCE.[8]

FIGURE 17.5 *A Superior Product Development Process for an Innovative Product*

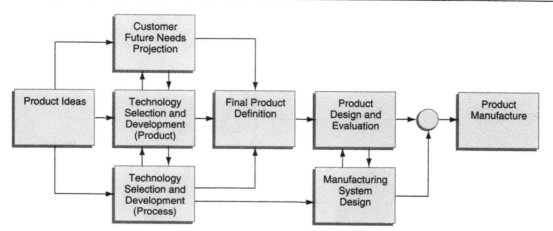

Source: C. Wilson and M. Kennedy, "Improving the Product Development Process," in M. Stahl and G. Bounds (eds.), *Competing Globally Through Customer Value: The Management of Strategic Suprasystems,* Quorum Books (1991): 433. Reprinted with permission of Greenwood Publishing Group, Inc., Westport, CT. Copyright © 1991 Greenwood Publishing Group, Inc.

CRITICAL THINKING QUESTIONS

1. What are the comparative advantages of industry and academia in basic research?

2. What are the comparative advantages of industry and academia in product development?

PRODUCT DEVELOPMENT

Product development is the phase of the technological life cycle where most of the organization's investments and activities in new technology occur. Of the many variables that should be considered in the development of new products, the most important is the link to customer value.

Link to Customer Value

As Figure 17.5 indicates, product development is tied to a projection of customer future needs and to the selection of technology for the product and the process. As this entire book stresses, satisfaction of customer needs is a prime function of management. Thus it follows that projection of future customer needs is the chief determinant in product development decisions. Needs must be projected into the future because of long lead times to develop both the technology and the product.

The product development cycle time for new automobiles is three or four years, depending on the manufacturer. To offer airbags or antilock brakes on new automobiles, the manufacturer must project the demand for those products three or four years into the future. After establishing these long-range projections, the manufacturer can decide to start development of such technological features.

We see, then, that technology should be selected for its contribution to customer value and that the selection of the product and process technology should be

FIGURE 17.6   *The New-Product Development System in Action*

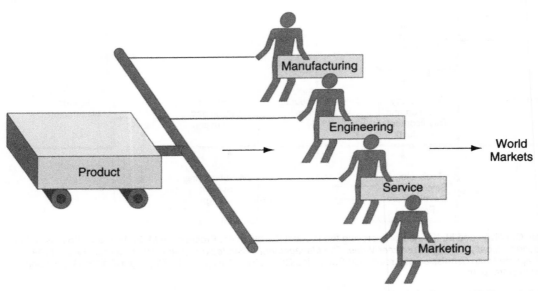

Source: C. Wilson and M. Kennedy, "Improving the Product Development Process," in M. Stahl and G. Bounds (eds.), *Competing Globally Through Customer Value: The Management of Strategic Suprasystems,* Quorum Books (1991): 436. Reprinted with permission of Greenwood Publishing Group, Inc., Westport, CT. Copyright © 1991 Greenwood Publishing Group, Inc.

tied to satisfying the projected customers' future needs. In a portable personal computer, for example, do customers prefer color displays or low price? The answer to such a question helps the manager select the product and process technology.

New-Product Development System

As we discussed in Chapter 8, one cross-functional system common to many organizations is the new-product development system. Figure 17.6 shows how the various functions in an organization can all pull together in the new-product development system based on Figure 17.5. Projection of customer needs is the yoke that unites the four functions of manufacturing, engineering, service, and marketing in pulling the new-product development wagon.

A projection of customers' future needs probably does not include their untimely deaths. Thus the product development system used with the Pinto automobile is worth comparing with the process described in Figure 17.5.

Technological Leadership

Some firms have a policy of being a technological leader. **Technological leadership** is being the first to market with new technology. By communicating that policy to customers, the firm is hoping that customers will know that the firm's products have the latest technology available. Being a technological leader can be very rewarding if cus-

E T H I C S   E X H I B I T

The Ford Pinto

The Ford Motor Company is the second-largest producer of automobiles. With annual sales of over 6 million cars and trucks worldwide, it has revenues of over $30 billion per year. In 1976 Ford's net worth was $7.7 billion and its income after taxes was over $983 million.

During the early 1960s Ford's market position was being dangerously eroded by competition from domestic and foreign subcompacts, especially Volkswagens. Lee Iacocca, president of Ford, was determined to regain Ford's share of the market by having a new subcompact, the Pinto, in production by 1970. Design on the subcompact automobile began in 1968. Iacocca conceived the project whose objective was to build a car at or below 2,000 pounds to sell for no more than $2,000. The feasibility study for the Pinto was conducted under the supervision of Robert Alexander, vice president of car engineering. Ford's Product Planning Committee—whose members included Iacocca, Alexander, and Harold MacDonald, Ford's group vice president of car engineering—approved the Pinto's concept and made the decision to go forward with the project. During the course of the project, regular product review meetings were held which were chaired by MacDonald and attended by Alexander. As the project approached actual production, the engineers responsible for the components of the project "signed off" to their immediate supervisors, who in turn "signed off" to their superiors and so on up the chain of command until the entire project was approved for public release by vice presidents Alexander and MacDonald and ultimately by Iacocca.

Although the normal preproduction testing and development of an automobile takes about 43 months, the Ford teams managed to bring the Pinto to the production stage in a little over 2 years. Because the Pinto was a rush project, styling preceded engineering and dictated engineering design to a greater degree than usual. Among other things, the Pinto's styling required that the gas tank be placed behind the rear axle, leaving only 9 or 10 inches of "crush space" between the rear axle and rear bumper. In addition, the differential housing had an exposed flange and a line of exposed bolt heads that were sufficient to puncture a gas tank driven forward against the differential upon rear impact.

Among the reports forwarded up the chain of command by Ford's engineers were several describing the results of crash tests conducted on early prototypes of the Pinto. These tests were later described in court as follows. These prototypes as well as two production Pintos were crash-tested by Ford to determine, among other things, the integrity of the fuel system in rear-end accidents. Prototypes struck from the rear with a moving barrier at 21 miles per hour caused the fuel tank to be driven forward and to be punctured, causing fuel leakage . . . A production Pinto crash-tested at 21 miles per hour into a fixed barrier caused the fuel neck to be torn from the gas tank and the tank to be punctured by a bolt head on the differential housing. In at least one test, spilled fuel entered the driver's compartment.

In a crash, stray sparks could ignite any spilling gasoline and engulf the car in flames. According to Harley Copp, then a Ford engineer and executive in charge of the crash-testing program, the test results were forwarded to the highest level of Ford's management. Other test results conducted by Ford showed that when rubber bladders were installed in the tank or when the fuel tank was installed above rather than behind the rear axle, test vehicles could pass the 20-mile-per-hour rear-impact test.

Nonetheless, the company went on with production of the Pinto as designed, since it met all applicable federal safety standards then in effect and was comparable in safety to other cars then being produced. Moreover, a later Ford company study released by J. C. Echold, director of automotive safety for Ford, claimed that an improved design that would have rendered the Pinto and other similar cars less likely to burst into flames
continued

on collision would not be cost-effective for society. Entitled "Fatalities Associated with Crash-Induced Fuel Leakage and Fires," the Ford study (which was intended to counter the prospect of stiffer government regulations on gasoline tank design) claimed that the costs of the design improvement ($11 per vehicle) far outweighed its social benefits. The total benefit was shown to be just under $50 million, while the associated cost was $137 million. Thus the cost was almost three times the benefits, even using a number of highly favorable benefit assumptions. The following benefits and costs are from a memorandum attached to a statement of J. C. Echold.

Benefits:

Savings	180 burn deaths, 180 serious burn injuries, 2,100 burned vehicles
Unit cost	$200,000 per death, $67,000 per injury, $700 per vehicle
Total benefits	(180 x $200,000) + (180 x $67,000) + (2,100 x $700) = $49.15 million

Costs:

Sales	11 million cars, 1.5 million light trucks
Unit cost	$11 per car, $11 per truck
Total costs	(11,000,000 x $11) + 1,500,000 x $11 = $137 million

Ford's estimate of the number of deaths, injuries, and vehicles that would be lost as a result of fires from fuel leakage were based on statistical studies. The $200,000 value attributed to the loss of life was based on a study of the National Highway Traffic Safety Administration, which broke down the estimated social costs of a death as follows:

Component	1971 Costs
Future productivity losses:	
Direct	$132,000
Indirect	41,300
Medical costs:	
Hospital	700
Other	425
Property damage	1,500
Insurance administration	4,700
Legal and court	3,000
Employer losses	1,000
Victim's pain and suffering	10,000
Funeral	900
Assets (lost consumption)	5,000
Miscellaneous accident costs	200
Total per Fatality	**$200,725**

At an April 1971 product review meeting chaired by MacDonald and attended by Alexander, those present received and discussed a report containing much the same materials as those later incorporated into the study entitled "Fatalities Associated with Crash-Induced Fuel Leakage and Fires."

continued

tomers like the latest technology. The technological leader frequently retains market share leadership because it has set the standard for the market. The policy can also be very risky if customers do not like the unproven technology. Porsche automobiles, for example, have usually had the latest technological innovations. Some customers buy their Porsches because they think they are buying something not found on other cars.

Technological Followership

Some firms have a policy of being a technological follower. They let other firms test the technology in the marketplace to determine if customers will buy it. **Technological**

On May 28, 1972, Lily Gray was driving a 6-month-old Pinto on Interstate 15 near San Bernardino, California. In the car with her was Richard Grimshaw, a 13-year-old boy. Gray was a unique person. She had adopted two girls, worked 40 hours a week (earning $20,000 a year), was den mother for all the teenagers in the neighborhood, sold refreshments at the Bobby Sox games, and had maintained a happy marriage of 22 years.

Gray stopped in San Bernardino for gasoline, got back onto the freeway (Interstate 15) and proceeded toward her destination at 60 to 65 miles per hour. As she approached the Route 30 off-ramp, where traffic was congested, she moved from the outer fast lane to the middle lane of the freeway. Shortly after this lane change, the Pinto suddenly stalled and coasted to a halt in the middle lane. A car traveling immediately behind the Pinto was able to swerve and pass it. But the driver of a 1962 Ford Galaxie was unable to avoid colliding with the Pinto. Before impact the Galaxie had been braked to a speed of from 28 to 37 miles per hour.

At the moment of impact, the Pinto caught fire and its interior burst into flames. The crash had driven the Pinto's gas tank forward and punctured it against the flange on the differential housing. Fuel spraying into the passenger compartment immediately ignited. By the time the Pinto came to rest, both occupants had suffered serious burns. When they tumbled from the Pinto, their clothing was almost completely burned off. Gray died a few days later. Although badly disfigured, Grimshaw managed to survive with severe burns over 90 percent of his body. He subsequently underwent over 70 painful operations and skin grafts and would have to undergo additional surgeries over the next 10 years. He lost portions of several fingers on his left hand and portions of his left ear, while his face required many skin grafts from various parts of his body.

As of 1978, at least 53 persons had died in accidents involving Pinto fires and many more had been severely burned.

Discussion Questions

1. Using the Ford figures given in the memorandum on page 490, calculate the probability that a vehicle would be involved in a burn death (that is, divide the number of burn deaths by the total number of cars and trucks sold). In your opinion, is there a limit to the amount that Ford should have been willing to invest in order to reduce this figure to zero? If your answer is yes, then determine from your answer what price you place on life and compare your price to the government's. If your answer is no, then discuss whether your answer implies that no matter how much it would take to make such cars, automakers should make cars completely accident-proof.

2. In your opinion, was the management of Ford morally responsible for Gray's "burn death"? Explain. Was there something wrong with the utilitarian analysis Ford management used? Explain. Would it have made any difference from a moral point of view if Ford management had informed its buyers of the risks of fire? Explain.

3. Suppose that you were on Mr. Echold's staff and before the Pinto reached the production stage you were assigned the task of writing an analysis of the overall desirability of producing and marketing the Pinto as planned. One part of your report is to be subtitled "ethical and social desirability." What would you write in this part?

Source: Manuel G. Velasquez, *Business Ethics: Concepts and Cases*, 2nd ed., © 1988, pp. 119–123. Reprinted by permission of Prentice-Hall, Englewood Cliffs, NJ.

followership is letting other firms introduce new technology into the marketplace first and then copying or modifying the proven technology. Being a technological follower can be less risky in terms of original financial outlay, but the policy usually means that the follower will not become market dominant. For example, IBM was not the first firm to offer personal computers in the early 1980s. It appears that IBM waited to see if customers were interested in the personal computers offered by Apple.

QUALITY CASE

Conclusion to the Corning Laboratories Case

Corning's quality process is not without unresolved issues. Some employees complain there's too much paperwork, especially surveys on how long it takes to do certain tasks. Given the importance of cycle time to the success of Corning, those measurements are critically important. Managers and Total Quality adherents at Sullivan Park, Corning's R&D home, keep track of 88 statistical measures of performance. In response, consultant Fusfeld remarked: "My biggest fear is that scientists will be overbureaucratized and overritualized."

So far, this fear has not been realized, even though quality has "become a way of life," says David A. Duke, vice chairman for technology at Corning. Indeed, James Houghton's idea of Total Quality to reduce cycle time in R&D and bring new products to market faster has turned out to be right. The firm has realized several new products in short order and has experienced growth in sales. Its fiber optics, automobile pollution control, and laboratory services businesses were all growing at 20 percent sales growth rates in 1993. These are all new product lines for a laboratory originally started in 1908 to develop new technology for glass.

DISCUSSION QUESTIONS

1. Explain how Corning's TQ concept is relevant to its laboratories.

2. Why are cross-functional teams relevant in research?

3. Why is cycle time so important in products developed from new technology?

Source: "Corning, Incorporated," *Standard & Poor's Reports* (June 9, 1993): 672; "Corning, Inc.," *Value Line Investment Survey* (April 30, 1993): 1001; "The Quality Imperative," *Business Week* (October 25, 1991): 158.

CRITICAL THINKING QUESTIONS

1. Discuss the product development process with its links to customer value and strategy.

2. Compare and contrast the advantages and disadvantages of technological leadership versus technological followership.

THE INTERNATIONAL DIMENSIONS OF TECHNOLOGY

Technology is increasingly being used by international competitors as a way to compete. The Japanese and the Germans, in particular, recognize the importance of investing in new technology to yield more value to customers.

Technology as an International Customer Strategy

A recent international survey shows that some leading economic powers, especially the Japanese, use technology as a way to provide customer value. The data in Figure 17.7 show that Japanese firms were more than twice as likely as U.S. firms to use technology to provide value to customers. "Japanese manufacturers place much more importance on flexibility by targeting variety, innovation, and technological superiority."[9]

FIGURE 17.7 *International Quality Study: Top-Line Findings*

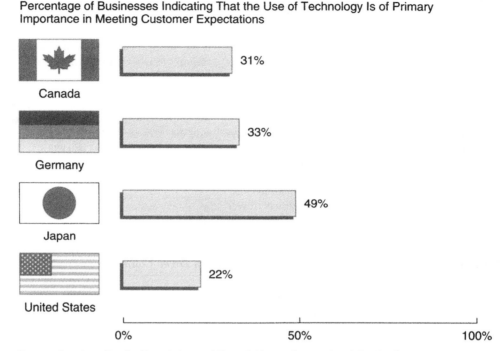

Percentage of Businesses Indicating That the Use of Technology Is of Primary
Importance in Meeting Customer Expectations

Canada — 31%
Germany — 33%
Japan — 49%
United States — 22%

Source: American Quality Foundation and Ernst & Young, "International Quality Study: The Definitive
Study of the Best International Quality Management Practices," Cleveland: Ernst & Young (1991): 23.

International Investment in Research and Development

Consistent with the strategy of using technology as an international competitive
weapon, Japan and Germany continue to invest in technology at a faster rate of
growth than does the United States. The data in Figure 17.8 show that both Japan
and Germany dramatically increased the rate of investment in R&D during the
1970s and the 1980s.

As a measure of that investment, Japanese firms continue to receive more patents in
this country than domestic firms. In 1992 Japanese firms headed the list of U.S. patent
awards for the seventh year in a row. Canon, Toshiba, Mitsubishi, and Hitachi held the
top four slots. In fifth place, General Electric was the highest ranking U.S. firm.[10]

CRITICAL THINKING QUESTIONS

1. Discuss the international competitive nature of technology.

2. Discuss the wage and employment implications for a country that elects to be a
technological follower.

INTERNATIONAL EXHIBIT

What Makes B &D Go

Black & Decker, in danger of falling over and slowly perishing when Far Eastern toolmakers (like Makita) started invading its markets in the late 1970s, is big and tough again. How did B&D do it? Lots of ways. Here's one:

It used to be that every B&D market—British, German, U.S., etc.—did its own designs. At one point, the company made 100 different motors worldwide for its power tools. Now it's down below 20 and aiming at 5.

The name of the game is fewer variations, fewer parts, fewer suppliers, fewer contracts, fewer production technologies, and so on—and at the same time, more and more product offerings brought to market in less and less time. In power tools, B&D launched 60 new or rejiggered products in two years, mostly the fast-growing cordless type. All are designed around a motor. So just plunk the new product's components down beside the right motor line, set up for assembly and pack, and off it goes to market.

Source: R. J. Schonberger, *Building a Chain of Customers: Linking Business Functions to Create the World Class Company,* New York: Free Press (1990): 219.

FIGURE 17.8 *Research and Development Spending in Three Countries*

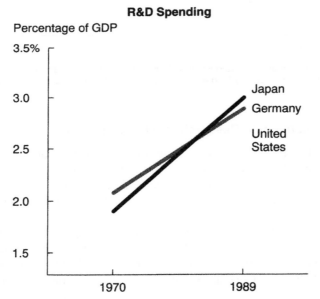

Source: "What the US. Can Do About R&D," *Fortune* (October 19, 1992): 75. © 1992 Time, Inc. All rights reserved.

SUMMARY

Technology refers to the knowledge, tools, techniques, and processes used to transform organizational inputs into outputs. Technological change refers to changes in any of these factors.

The management of technology is concerned with how the organization uses technology to yield greater value to the customer. Reduced cycle time, reduced cost, reduced variation, and quality improvement are all ways in which new technology adds value to customers. The product/market life cycle reflects how new technology is introduced, grows, and then declines in the marketplace.

The research and development spectrum, from basic research through advanced research and product development, helps explain the investments firms make in new technology before a payoff is realized.

Product development is the phase of the technological life cycle in which most of the organization's investments and activities in new technology pay off. Of the many variables that should be considered in the development of new products, the most important is the link to customer value. To communicate with customers, some firms have a policy of being technological leaders. Others choose to be technological followers.

New technology is a very active area in international competition. In terms of new patents and dollar investment in R&D, Japanese and German firms are investing at a higher rate of growth than U.S. firms. Such high levels of investment in technology are consistent with the strategy of using technology to deliver value to customers.

EXPERIENTIAL EXERCISE

Rip Van Winkle

Assume that you have been the general manager at the Personal Computer Company (PCC) for five years. You understand your customers (both corporate and individual) and their requirements for computing. Your firm translates their requirements into the latest designs, manufactures the computers, and markets them throughout the world. The technology of the computers themselves has been changing at a blistering pace, with some firms—those that have not been able to keep up—leaving the market. The manufacturing technology to produce computers—including clean rooms, robots, and worldwide sourcing of parts—has also been changing rapidly. PCC's market share had been growing because the firm has been able to anticipate customer requirements and to translate those requirements into new products faster than its competitors. Because of its speedy product development cycle, PCC has been able to ramp up manufacturing faster than its competitors, and with that manufacturing experience, it has lowered the cost of manufacturing faster than competitors. With its new products and lower costs, the firm's market share and profits have grown.

One day when you arrive for work, you are surprised to find that the firm looks very different. The manufacturing plant is laid out differently, different processes are being used, there are different people engaged in the manufacturing process, and the product is dramatically different. You start to ask questions and find to your amazement that like Rip Van Winkle, you have slept for 20 years.

Assignment

After reading the story, the class should divide into discussion groups of three or four students each. In this chapter technology was defined as the sum of the knowledge, tools, techniques, and processes used to transform organizational inputs into outputs. In each group specific attention should be paid to these elements of technology in answering the following questions:

1. What changes in each of the technological elements are forecasted to have taken place in the 20-year period?
2. What processes should managers use to anticipate and keep up with technological change?

CHAPTER CASE

OPCO

The data management division of OPCO, a communications company, decided to develop and sell a software accounting system that would process credit card transactions over its data network. To enter the business quickly, OPCO purchased a start-up firm with a system under development, and after several months of additional work at OPCO, the service was introduced to the market. The system did not operate properly, however, and was canceled. As suggested by the quotes below, the innovation encountered many problems. The quotes also suggest that the participants interpreted issues from narrow departmental perspectives. The business manager saw no need to talk with customers since he considered the market opportunity to be obvious. He now believes, however, that OPCO failed to position the product properly against its competitors.

In response to the interviewer's question, "Did you talk to customers?" the business manager replied, "No, because we knew that this was needed. We could see some competitors getting into the business ... Had we done some market research and defined needs more carefully, and figured out the dozens of pieces we would need for a full system, we'd be positioned with a much better strategy."

The technical director saw no "market" problems at all with the effort. He described design problems, however, that perhaps could have been resolved had a thorough analysis of users and how they operate been carried out: "There were no market problems with this product ... Our mistake was we didn't understand the application in total ... We had a difficult time trying to figure out the relationships between us here at the operating level and the retail establishments, and the relationships between them and their banks and credit card clearing houses.... There were a lot of players involved, which is different from [our regular product], where we interface with one customer at a time. It looks very nice theoretically, but the more relationships there are, the more complex the recovery."

The sales support person downplayed general positioning and technological design. Instead, he blamed OPCO's failure to specify which users in the market could best use the product: "I have never seen a definition for this service. There are no criteria on what makes a good or bad customer for this product ... One person here had a pretty good understanding of what kind of customer would benefit from a system like this. More people here should have known. We needed a brain transplant."

The innovators also followed established routines at OPCO to develop and launch this new service. These routines included project teams and matrices, structures that are recommended for innovation, but all participants noted how they did not work. The routines did not synthesize components of the innovation itself nor relevant knowledge, and they squashed interaction. According to the business manager, "We were not successful in fully integrating the new business within the organization. A new product is unique—it has different distribution, different billing, a myriad of things have to work out well. It is difficult for a small organization [referring to the business unit] to handle all these issues, so things fall apart. We didn't see the pitfalls."

The technical director stated: "At OPCO we tend to categorize people into roles, and give people only what they need to know ... There are little shadings of meaning that get lost in the requirements statement from marketing."

From the sales-support angle: "They [from the small company] were a very tight group, and they all talked to one another all the time. But when we brought them here they were dispersed into our matrix ..."

In hindsight at least, these innovators knew that they should link technological and market issues, but they had not done so.

Discussion Questions

1. Why is it important to understand customer requirements in the design of new products and services?

2. If a firm is the first to enter the market with new technology, will customers buy?

Source: Adapted from D. Dougherty, "Interpretive Barriers to Successful Product Innovation in Large Firms," *Organization Science* (May 1992): 180–181.

KEY TERMS

advanced research Scientific activities conducted to advance the state of the art in a specific technical field with the objective of solving a problem.

basic research Scientific activities conducted for the sake of gaining new knowledge without any specific application in mind.

computer-integrated manufacturing Extensive use of computers to plan and to control the entire manufacturing process.

flexible cells Adaptable groupings of people and machinery in the manufacturing process.

inventory turns Number of times in a given time period, such as a year, that inventory is turned over or used up in the manufacturing process.

just-in-time (JIT) inventory system System in which materials are ordered to arrive at the point of use exactly when they are needed.

management of technology How the organization uses technology to yield value to customers.

process improvement Minor changes in the manufacturing process to increase yield, reduce cycle time, lower costs, or otherwise improve efficiency.

product development Activities that translate the results of research into a new or improved product.

product development cycle time Time from conception of the idea for a new product, through the product development phase, until the new product is first offered to the customer.

proprietary technology Technology held by one firm and not shared with other firms.

technological change Change in any of the technological factors of knowledge, tools, techniques, or outputs.

technological followership Letting other firms introduce new technology into the marketplace first and then copying or modifying the proven technology.

technological leadership Being the first to market with new technology.

technology Sum of knowledge, tools, techniques, and processes used to transform organizational inputs into outputs.

value engineering Making minor changes in a product to reduce costs.

ENDNOTES

1. D. Rosseau and R. Cooke, "Technology and Structure," *Journal of Management* (1984): 345–361.
2. W. Boulton, "Resource Guide for Management of Innovation and Technology," St. Louis: Joint publication of the American Assembly of Collegiate Schools of Business, the National Consortium for Technology in Business, and the Thomas Walter Center for Technology Management at Auburn University (1993).
3. H. J. Harrington, *Business Process Improvement: The Breakthrough Strategy for Total Quality, Productivity, and Competitiveness,* New York: McGraw-Hill (1991): 9.
4. M. Porter, *Competitive Strategy,* New York: Free Press (1985): 169.
5. T. Levitt, "Exploit the Product Life Cycle," *Harvard Business Review* (November-December 1965): 81-94; C. R. Anderson and C. P. Zeithaml, "Stage of the Product Life Cycle, Business Strategy, and Business Performance," *Academy of Management Journal* (March 1984): 134–145.
6. "Chrysler on the Road to Recovery," *USA Today* (March 6, 1992): B1.
7. R. Burgelman and M. Madique, *Strategic Management of Technology and Innovation,* Chicago: Irwin (1988).
8. Hoechst Celanese Corp., Charlotte, NC (1993).
9. "Brace for Japan's Hot New Strategy," *Fortune* (September 21, 1992): 63.
10. "Business Bulletin," *The Wall Street Journal* (February 4, 1993): A1.

Operations Management for Control and Improvement

LEARNING OBJECTIVES

After reading this chapter, you should be able to accomplish the following:

- Describe the differences between operations management and manufacturing management.

- Explain the importance of product and service design to operations management.

- Discuss the link between customer-value strategy and products or services.

- Describe the differences among the traditional kinds of operations processes.

- Describe product or service planning, process technology selection, capacity planning, facility location planning, and layout planning as five elements in designing operations.

- Relate traditional inventory ideas with the idea of just-in-time inventory.

- Describe the importance of quality control in operations management.

- Explain the current thinking concerning purchasing and supplier relations for Total Quality in terms of the basis of the contract, number of suppliers, length of relationship, and acceptance sampling.

CHAPTER OUTLINE

Integrating Design and Production at Sundstrand

By integrating design and production, and by continually improving processes, Sundstrand has achieved remarkable reliability with its accelerometers. (Photo credit: Sundstrand Aerospace.)

"If it isn't broken, fix it anyway. Improve the process. We look at everything as a process." The speaker is Richard Baker, manager of continuous-improvement systems at Sundstrand Data Control Inc., manufacturer of instruments and avionics for the defense industry. The company has won awards from prime defense contractors, including General Dynamics, McDonnell Douglas, and Honeywell Space Systems.

The company claims remarkable production, cost, and quality improvements. Rework on some production lines is down by 66 percent, scrap cost cut by 60 percent, quality up by 50 percent, and cycle time down by 90 percent. Baker says that despite these advances, fully integrating the Total Quality philosophy with company culture could take another five years, and that the ongoing effort will never be complete. "We had a start, but we don't have a beginning or an end."

Production workers were especially proud of a magnet assembly, a delicate device the size of a quarter and loaded with integrated circuits. It is used in inertial navigation systems. Baker said, "We are about to knock the Japanese out of this market."

Manufacture of the magnet assembly is a complicated process, progressing through six rooms with workstations in each room. The workers in each room make up a work team. The process is called *kanban* and relies on simple visual cues from the previous step in the process to inform the work team when parts are needed. With this information the team can distribute the workload, since each team member is cross-trained to do all of the tasks necessary to move the item to the next step in the process.

Another simplification is a traffic light like the one seen at a street intersection, which hangs in the hallway where everyone in the work teams of a particular production line can see it. If the production process is flowing smoothly, the light turns green. If a problem occurs, the light turns yellow and then red. This is the cue for workers to scramble and find a solution for the problem causing the red light.

Sundstrand's TQM program also contains a component called *concurrent engineering*, an approach that integrates the engineers and design personnel from both design and production. The philosophy is reflected in the comment, "Eighty percent of the cost of our product is in the design process. To make it cheaper, you've got to design a part better."

Operations management may be even more important in service operations than in manufacturing because value is provided immediately to the customers. (Photo credit: Mark Antman/The Image Works.)

IMPORTANCE OF OPERATIONS TO CUSTOMER VALUE

Whether hard-goods manufacturing of a durable item like an automobile or an aircraft, or service operations in a hotel or bank, operations management is at the core of many organizations.

Operations, Manufacturing, and Service Management

Operations management is the process of managing the production of goods and services. Thus *operations* is a broad term that encompasses both hard-goods manufacturing management and service management.

 Manufacturing management is the process of managing the production of tangible goods but not of services. Whether automobiles, motorcycles, soft drinks, apparel, or chemicals, there is tangible output in manufacturing.

 Service management is the process of producing nontangibles that require customer involvement and that are consumed at the point of delivery. Whether NationsBank, Fidelity Investments, McDonald's, UPS, or the British Royal Mail, service organizations deliver their nontangible services at the point of production. As services consume a growing part of our economy, the broader term of *operations management* is preferable and is used throughout this chapter.

 In the school of intense international competition and the school of demanding customers, many firms have learned that work gets done horizontally. In the spirit of Total Quality, many have recognized the importance of integrating processes across design, operations, and quality control. (See Figure 17.5 on page 487 for the impor-

FIGURE 18.1 *The Operations Management System*

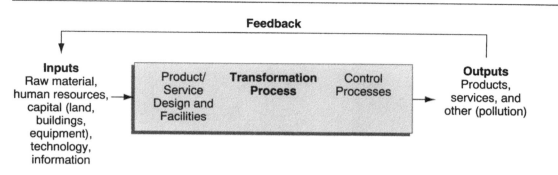

The product or service has the attributes that deliver the value to the customers. The product or service is the means of transmitting that value. That is why it is so important for an organization to be in control of its operations. If the orga-

tance of product design to manufacturing.) These topics, which are important enough to warrant separate chapters in this text, need to be fully integrated in operations management to deliver superior value to customers.

Today many firms recognize the critical importance of operations management to the ability of the firm to provide consistent value to customers. However, in the mid-1980s, prior to the widespread adoption of Total Quality, there was a disturbing trend in U.S. industry to deemphasize the importance of operations management. The term *hollow corporation* arose to describe a firm that did not manage its own operations. Many U.S. manufacturers were exiting manufacturing and turning themselves into marketers for foreign producers.[1] Fortunately for the sake of U.S. industry, that trend was reversed.

The experience at Xerox of almost giving up its business to the Japanese helped to halt the growth of the hollow corporation model. In describing Xerox's near bankruptcy, the former chairman of Xerox, David Kearns, offered a "handbook for decline." The list of what not to do included "Chapter Four: Deemphasize Manufacturing. Don't pay too much attention to how the product is made, to improvements in the manufacturing process, or to the relationship among design, development, engineering, and production. Keep anyone with manufacturing experience well away from the executive suite. The true secret of success is to completely get out of the business of producing things yourself."[2]

Translating Customer-Value Strategy into Products and Services

Under the banner of Total Quality and customer-value strategy, firms take responsibility for providing value to their customers. To make that value real and tangible, firms must be involved in some kind of operations. Whether these operations involve tangible products or intangible services, the operations translate the raw inputs into outputs with value for the customers. Figure 18.1 illustrates such a transformation function.

The product or service has the attributes that deliver the value to the customers. The product or service is the means of transmitting that value. That is why it is so important for an organization to be in control of its operations. If the orga-

FIGURE 18.2 *Operations in Two Different Electronics Firms*

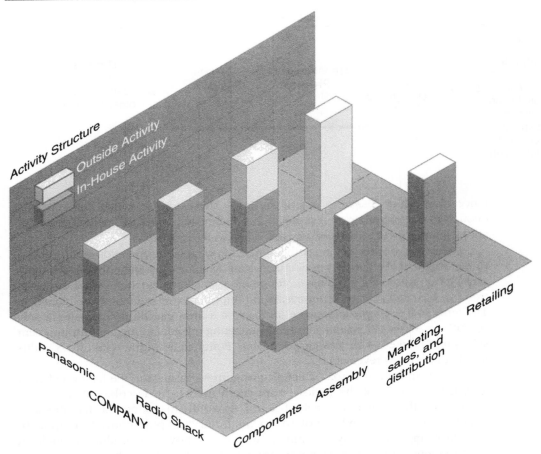

Source: W. Ebeling and T. Doorley, "A Strategic Approach to Acquisitions," *Journal of Business Strategy* (1983): 44–55.

nization has delegated control to others, then the organization is not in control of those processes that deliver value.

Radio Shack has become primarily a retailer. Its chief operations are in its retail stores and do not include much manufacturing activity. In contrast, Panasonic's operations are primarily in manufacturing, with little activity in retailing. Figure 18.2 shows the difference for the two organizations. Although the two organizations differ in terms of principal operations, each organization is in control of its principal operations that deliver value to its customers.

Alternatively, in the early 1980s Chrysler was at the brink of bankruptcy. The firm left to others almost all of the design and manufacturing operations that it had specialized in, and became an assembler and retailer of Japanese cars. It nearly lost control of its destiny as it became a hollow corporation.

FIGURE 18.3 *Process Reengineering*

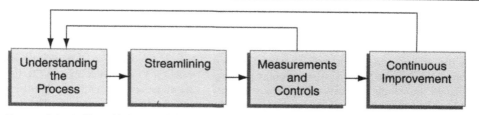

Source: Adapted from H. James Harrington, *Business Process Improvement: The Breakthrough Strategy for Total Quality, Productivity, and Competitiveness*, New York: McGraw-Hill (1991): 23.

The Importance of Control and Improvement

Today customers demand the delivery of consistent quality. Variance in defects, in delivery time, or in any other characteristic of a product or service is not tolerated in a competitive marketplace where the customer has alternatives. Thus the Capsugel Division of the pharmaceutical firm Warner-Lambert describes quality in terms of consistency among batches of capsules it delivers to its customers.[3]

This topic of quality control is so important to customers, and to the managers who are charged with delivering value to customers, that we have devoted an entire chapter to the subject. Chapter 15 presents a detailed analysis of quality control, which is an integral part of operations management. Operations managers should decide how to maintain control of quality if they hope to retain customers for the products or services resulting from their operations.

Process Reengineering

As we discussed in Chapter 1, a *process* is a group of activities that takes an input, adds value to it, and provides an output to an internal or external customer.[4] Processes are increasingly being seen as the way to organize in firms, rather than by function, as was traditionally done. One of the biggest advantages of concentrating on processes, rather than on functions, is that processes enable the organization to focus on the customer. Viewing the materials transformation process in terms of those activities tied to transforming materials into something of value for the customer is a process view. Such a view examines inventory in terms of customer value, not internal economics. Such a view can be the basis of reengineering processes. Figure 18.3 presents one view of process reengineering.

Process reengineering is the continuous improvement of the process by which a product or service is created and distributed. Process reengineering means the perpetual search for ways to improve procedures and methods for producing and distributing products and services.

Product Operations versus Service Operations

Many of the steps in product operations are identical to those in service operations. There are common concepts of plant layout, purchase of materials from suppliers, and training of employees in both product and service operations.

Q U A L I T Y   E X H I B I T

Circuit City Stores

In the coming decade it will be important for companies to plan their systems around gaining detailed knowledge of customers. Richard Sharp, CEO of Circuit City, the rapidly growing American home electronics and appliances chain, predicts that his operation will be setting up computerized files containing a complete profile of each customer. In addition to providing basic information about the customer and speeding up service and repair, the system would identify Circuit City's best customers and give them priority service. If its database showed that the customer bought a TV one year and a VCR the next, Circuit City might send him a flyer advertising video cameras. As Sharp has put it, "The winners of the 1990s will be those who can boost service and cut prices at the same time." One way of doing that will be to develop efficient systems for describing and targeting customers.

Source: Adapted from W. A. Band, *Creating Value for Customers*, New York: Wiley (1991): 25.

The biggest distinction between product and service operations is that services are consumed by the customer at the point of generation. Therefore there is no inventory function for finished goods. In a bank, for example, loans are generated at the point of servicing the customer; they are not held in inventory. Haircuts are not held in inventory in a barbershop. As the quality exhibit shows, retail stores like Circuit City do not manufacture the items in their stores, but they must determine their customers' needs just as a manufacturer should.

CRITICAL THINKING QUESTIONS

1. Compare and contrast the requirements of management in service management and in manufacturing management.
2. How is the customer-value strategy of the firm related to its products and services?

TRADITIONAL PROCESS DISTINCTIONS

There are three kinds of processes used in operations management, classified according to the number of products or services produced. Figure 18.4 describes the three kinds of processes in terms of the number of products or services involved: (1) unique production and batch processing, (2) flexible and rigid mass production, and (3) continuous process production.

Unique Production and Batch Processing

In **unique production** only one item is made. A good example would be a large construction project such as a football stadium. The stadium is unique and the planning and production processes are unique to that project.

FIGURE 18.4 *Processes and Number of Products*

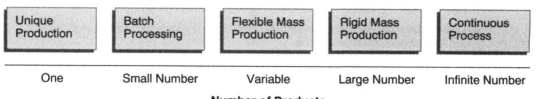

In **batch processing** a few items are made at a time. A textile company, for example, usually dyes fabric in batches to preserve color consistency. A batch of fabric for navy knit shirts may be dyed at one time, and a batch of fabric for pastel shorts may be dyed at another time.

Flexible and Rigid Mass Production

In **flexible mass production** the system is capable of producing a range of quantities because it has the capability for rapid changeover. The key concepts are flexibility and variable lot sizes. **Lot size** is the number of identical items produced before a changeover is made to other products. As customers demand more specialization in products and services, flexible mass production with smaller average lot sizes is one of the strongest trends in operations management in the 1990s.[5] Flexible mass production is finding its way into the automobile industry. Automobiles are being produced in smaller lot sizes today than ten years ago, since customers are demanding more tailored products.

Rigid mass production is usually referred to simply as mass production. **Rigid mass production** is the production of a large number of the same item. Many attribute the idea of mass production to Henry Ford, who popularized it in the manufacture of the Model T Ford. In order to keep the system running smoothly with only one item, he allegedly remarked that the customer could have any color desired as long as it was black. At the time many customers were demanding cheap cars and Ford's nondifferentiated mass production system was a way to deliver, even if all the cars were black. Today customers are demanding more differentiation in a number of different industries.

Continuous Process Production

As we learned in Chapter 8, *continuous process production* is the round-the-clock production of a near infinite amount of a nondifferentiated, commodity-like item. Continuous process production is found often in the chemical industry, where the process must be run nonstop so that the equipment does not corrode or the chemicals solidify in the equipment. A fertilizer plant that makes vegetable fertilizer, for example, may run the process nonstop so that the equipment does not corrode or the product does not harden at some intermediate stage. Electric power generation is another example of continuous process production.

CRITICAL THINKING QUESTIONS

1. Describe the consistency between flexible mass production and Total Quality.

2. Discuss the relative importance of continuous improvement in continuous process production and batch processing.

DESIGNING PRODUCTS AND SERVICES

The design of products and services is the first step to ensure manufacturability for quality and customer value. In Chapter 17 we reviewed product design as a crucial way to exploit new technology in delivering value to customers. Figure 17.5 (page 487) illustrates the driving force of customer needs in product design and the relationship with manufacturing system design. Many firms that in the past had tried to produce products with inferior designs today recognize that quality starts with simultaneous superior design of the product and of the process to manufacture it. To achieve its goal of Six Sigma quality—that is, less than 3.4 defects per million—Motorola is focusing on the design of the product and of the manufacturing process.

Defining Customer Requirements

The first step in superior product and service design is to define customer requirements. In Chapter 7 we identified customer requirements as the starting point of the entire TQ process. In Chapter 17 we saw that the product design process begins with customer requirements. By definition, no product can be a quality product if it does not meet customer requirements. The most perfectly manufactured horse-drawn wagon is of little use in an era when people buy and drive automobiles.

Quality Function Deployment

Quality function deployment (QFD) is a special design tool to explicitly consider customer-value requirements in the design process. As we saw in Chapter 7, QFD is a customer-driven system that attempts to achieve early coupling between the requirements of the customer, marketing, and design engineering.[6] QFD actually considers a product as a collection of attributes to fulfill customer-value requirements.

In designing a new car using the QFD process, the designers would start by listing the dimensions of value required by the customer. Characteristics such as price, fuel economy, size, safety, and other dimensions important to the customer should be listed. The design task is then to translate the characteristics into a car. The process is different from that used by General Motors in the mid-1980s when GM designed a platform, or size of, car and by modifying just a little sheet metal and ornamentation tried to sell the car under different nameplates at differing prices. In the late 1980s the Oldsmobile Cutlass, the Pontiac Grand Am, and the Buick Skylark were essentially the same car. Is it any surprise that sales plummeted because customers did not perceive that they were getting much additional value from the Oldsmobile and Buick relative to the lower-priced Pontiac?

An excellent example of using customer-value requirements to drive design is Gillette's Sensor for Women razor. In a survey of what women wanted from a razor, many women complained about the cuts and nicks associated with many razors. To minimize those cuts, Gillette produced a radical design. "A flat, wafer-shaped handle aligns the razor directly with the shaver's hand, giving more control in hard-to-see places."[7] Since the new design offered value to customers that was not found in competing designs, the Sensor for Women razor garnered a 60 percent market share in its first year on the market.

Value Engineering

Value engineering is an attempt to make a product cheaper with minor improvements. In the quest for lower manufacturing cost, a manager must be careful that the quality of the product is not sacrificed. The manager should return to the first step in quality function deployment and review the customer requirements before changing the design of a product.

Design for Manufacturability and Quality (*Poka Yoke*)

Just as consideration of customer requirements should be the first step in product design, the design of the manufacturing process to ensure quality is also important. Many Japanese firms use the term **Poka Yoke** to mean design for quality in manufacturing. Under Poka Yoke a product is designed to reduce the number of parts so that the parts can be assembled in only one way. Parts are made so that they do not fit together if they are not assembled correctly. Rather than inspecting for a defect after it has occurred, this fail-safe approach prevents a defect from happening.

Cadillac, for example, cut the number of parts in its 1992 Seville Touring Sedan by 20 percent. Thus the assembly is less prone to worker error, is easier to build, and has fewer defects. Specifically, Cadillac halved the number of parts in the rear bumper, bringing it to 63. That reduced the assembly time by 57 percent, to less than 8 minutes, with an estimated annual labor savings of $462,000.[8]

CRITICAL THINKING QUESTIONS

1. Why is product design so critical to operations management?
2. Describe the dangers of process design being done separately from the service design for a financial services firm.

DESIGNING OPERATIONS

Figure 17.5 (page 487), which presents a superior product development process for an innovative product, shows the importance of simultaneous product *and* process design for the manufacturing of the product, known as **concurrent engineering.** Designing operations is a broader term than designing the manufacturing system, as the former includes service operations as well as product manufacturing.

Product or Service Planning (What Is to Be Produced?)

As shown in Figure 17.5, one of the first decisions in designing operations is to determine the products or services to be produced. This decision derives from a projection of customer needs in the future when the product or service will be available. As we learned earlier, quality function deployment is used to translate customer needs into the design of the product.

Process Technology Selection (How Will It Be Produced?)

There are at least three rules to be followed in selecting the technology for the operations process.[9]

The first rule in selecting technology for the process is to select only well-defined technology. Experimentation with a new technology can produce poor-quality products or delay the production process while the bugs are ironed out. As it experimented with a new production technology for making plastic car doors, for example, the Saturn Corporation was forced to delay the production of cars for the market.

The second rule is to automate only after the processes are stable. It makes no sense to use robots for spray painting if the quality of the paint is suspect. There is a temptation to automate to keep current with competitors' use of technology. **Computer-aided manufacturing (CAM)** uses some robots and computers in the manufacturing process. CAM can be contrasted with *computer-integrated manufacturing (CIM)*, which is the extensive use of computers to plan and control the entire manufacturing process. To be sure, CAM can consistently produce the same output. But if the process and the technology are not stable, CAM can also consistently make errors. For example, if the robot has not been properly programmed to spray the correct intensity, or if lumpy paint has been placed in the system, the robot will consistently produce poor results.

The third rule is to select a process technology that will permit critical manufacturing processes to be performed internally. Those operations that are critical need to be under the control of the organization. Restaurants almost always cook their own food, for example. Subcontracting the food preparation could jeopardize the quality of the food.

Sometimes even if these three rules are followed, the selected technology is still problematic, as the following ethics exhibit illustrates.

Capacity Planning (How Many?)

Capacity planning is the determination of how many units or how much volume an organization wants to be capable of producing. A hospital, for example, needs to decide how many patients it can accommodate, and a hotel needs to decide how many guests it can lodge at one time.

In general, an organization can expand capacity by expanding plant and equipment. It can also hire more workers, add a shift, or ask current workers to work overtime. Or it can expand capacity by becoming more efficient through the implementation of Total Quality Management.

E T H I C S   E X H I B I T

Asarco and Jobs

With its 571-foot smokestack, the Asarco copper smelter in Tacoma, Washington, had long been notorious for its contributions to the ripe "aroma of Tacoma." But the unpleasant odor was not the only thing the company contributed to the city's air. The smelter processed copper from ore with a high arsenic content, and some of this arsenic was vented into the air through the smokestack. Even though in the preceding decade the company had invested $40 million to reduce its arsenic emissions, in 1983 the Environmental Protection Agency (EPA), the federal agency charged with enforcing the nation's environmental laws, announced that the plant was still spewing 115 tons of arsenic into the air every year. A new court ruling on federal regulations would require a reduction of at least 25 percent. The arsenic, according to the EPA, was a carcinogenic for which there probably was no safe "threshold": Even a tiny amount might cause cancer in some people. The arsenic emitted from the smelter was estimated to be producing about four cases of lung cancer a year. The new standard would require the company to spend $4.5 million more on pollution control equipment that would reduce emissions of arsenic to a level that would produce about one case of lung cancer per year. In a statement issued at the time, Asarco officials announced that they intended to adhere to the new regulations and that the company was willing to spend the money required to bring its emissions into line with the new, court-mandated standards.

The EPA also announced that it might even require Asarco to reduce its arsenic emissions to zero. But according to its calculations, reducing the emissions to a level that would completely eliminate all risk of cancer would require such an investment in pollution control that the smelter would no longer be economically viable. Since the smelter employed about 570 people and pumped about $20 million per year into the local economy, closing the smelter would have a substantial negative impact on Tacoma residents. However, the EPA announcement continued, in accord with a new policy of involving the public in its enforcement activities, it would give Tacoma residents an opportunity, during hearings that would be held over the next several months, to voice their opinion on whether the EPA should require the smelter to completely eliminate its arsenic emissions, even though this would force the smelter to close down. Tacoma thus had a choice: Either it could choose to lose one additional resident per year to death by cancer or it could choose to lose 570 jobs and $20 million annually.

Opinions on the terrible choice posed by the EPA announcement varied widely. Tacoma's

continued

Facility Location Planning (Who and Where?)

There is a saying in real estate that the three most important characteristics of real estate are location, location, and location. This may also be true with regard to facility location for a service organization, because services are consumed by the customer at the point of service generation. The service facility needs to be visible and accessible to the customer.

Manufacturing facility location is not quite so critical as service facility location. However, a manufacturing firm usually determines location on the basis of availability and cost of an educated workforce, proximity of raw materials, proximity of key suppliers, and centrality of a transportation network. It appears that these criteria were important in BMW's decision to locate a manufacturing plant in South Carolina in 1993.

young mothers, like Ann Leask, 30, were frightened by the high arsenic levels that researchers had found in their children's hair: "[Cancer] is such an ugly way to die," she said as her eyes filled with tears. "It scares me to death to think we might have to contend with that with [our son] Ryan." Workers, such as Bill Powers, were skeptical of the EPA's estimates of the health risks involved: "I think it's a lot of baloney!"

Ralph L. Henneback, chairman of Asarco, argued that the risk estimates of the EPA were exaggerated: "We are convinced, based on studies of lung cancer incidence, that the risk of contracting lung cancer is no greater in Tacoma than in any other urban area .... The proposed arsenic standards, it seems to me, reflect the realization that government regulators do not have at their disposal the means to protect us from all risks ....The best we can do is reduce these risks to the lowest practicable level through the use of the best available technology. In cooperation with EPA we have been doing just that at our Tacoma plant and are well along on the installation of the technology specified in the proposed EPA arsenic regulations."

The EPA admitted that some uncertainties surrounded their estimate of the health risks of the airborne arsenic. Doctor Sam Milham, head of the epidemiology section of the Washington State Department of Social and Health Services, said that his own studies of lung cancer had failed to show any increase in the health risks of people living downwind from the smelter. EPA officials in Seattle themselves said that their data might be unreliable.

The newly appointed head of the EPA, William D. Ruckelshaus, defended his new policy of giving local communities a voice in determining whether an estimated (but uncertain) risk was acceptable: "For me to sit here in Washington and tell the people of Tacoma what is an acceptable risk would be at best arrogant and at worst inexcusable."

Discussion Questions

1. What level of pollution prevention do you think the Tacoma Asarco plant managers should have installed? Justify your position in terms of the utilitarian, rights, and justice perspectives that you believe apply to the case.

2. Discuss the ethics of the EPA policy to allow the local community to decide whether or not to have the Tacoma plant shut down. In your judgment is it possible for the community to make a "free" decision in such a matter? If the EPA reserved this decision to itself, how should it have decided? Explain your answer. Explain how a process of "hearings" differs from a process of voting. In your judgment are hearings an appropriate method for determining whether the members of a community consent to a policy?

3. If you were a member of the Tacoma community, what would you have wanted the Asarco plant to do? Why?

Source: Manuel G. Velasquez, *Business Ethics: Concepts and Cases*, 2nd ed., © 1988, pp. 263–265. Reprinted by permission of Prentice–Hall, Englewood Cliffs, NJ.

Layout Planning (How Does Work Flow?)

Layout planning is deciding how to arrange the physical configuration or the layout of facilities. A good layout minimizes rerouting, materials handling, and worker fatigue and thus also contributes to quality goals. There are three broad classes of layouts: process layouts, product layouts, and fixed-position layouts.

In a **process layout** machines and resources that perform the same task are grouped together. The route that a particular product or service takes through the layout may differ as a function of the product or service. A machine shop and parts of a hospital are two examples of process layouts. In the machine shop all the grinders are placed together. In the hospital all the X-ray machines are together. Process layouts are meant to increase efficiency through specialization and

QUALITY CASE

Back to the Sundstrand Case

The "traffic light system" at Sundstrand is a method pioneered by Shigeo Shingo and frequently called the *Shingo* method. Another company, a manufacturer in high-tech electronics, justifies the method by giving two basic reasons for the use of traffic lights:

1. They are a great visual communicator to all employees, telling us all the status of our production lines. No one need ask, "Gee, I wonder if Line 2 is running?"

2. They lend an air of urgency, reminding us all of the key thing that counts: on-time shipments of quality products to our customers! By indicating the problem and who is directly responsible for solving it, there is little left to chance in our drive to get the line going again!

A green light indicates a production line is running smoothly. There are no material, people, machine, or process problems at this time. Finished products are being produced on schedule.

A yellow light indicates a problem exists or is about to surface that is either impeding the scheduled flow of material or is about to. Yellow lights are indicative of things such as faulty machines requiring "baby-sitting," missing personnel (can't make schedule), parts requiring modification on the line, or potential missing parts that may cause a line shutdown in the immediate (two- to three-day) future.

A red light indicates a line is shut down, that is, no finished products are able to flow off this line. Typical causes of red lights are missing material, broken-down equipment, missing key personnel, irregular parts requiring excessive modification to work properly, and missing or dysfunctional tools.

economies of scale. However, high levels of specialization can cause poor coordination across the operations for the product in the machine shop or the patient in the hospital who ends up with the wrong X-ray.

In a **product layout** machines and tasks are laid out according to a set sequence of tasks in the production of a single standardized product or service. Such a layout is appropriate for repetitive operations in mass production with large quantities of a single product, such as in the manufacture of lawn mowers.

In a **fixed-position layout** a very large product stays in one place and the resources and tasks are brought to the product. Examples include shipbuilding and aircraft manufacturing. Because of the size of a Boeing 747, the fuselage remains stationary while workers, materials, and equipment are brought to it.

Job Design (Who Does What Task?)

There is a strong trend today toward reducing the layers of management in organizations and evolving to well-trained, cross-functional teams. This is certainly true in operations with the spread of self-managed work teams. Rather than the old way of designing highly specialized jobs with little coordination across jobs, the trend today is toward broader jobs performed by teams. Such a trend is associated with

D I V E R S I T Y   E X H I B I T

Brian Weber

The Kaiser Aluminum plant in Gramercy, Louisiana, opened in 1958. From the beginning, the Kaiser Gramercy plant had relatively few black workers. By 1965, although 39 percent of the local workforce was black, Kaiser had hired only 4.7 percent blacks. In 1970 a federal review of Kaiser employment practices at the Gramercy plant found that of 50 professional employees, none was black; of 132 supervisors, only one was black; and of 246 skilled craftworkers, none was black. A 1973 federal review found that although Kaiser had allowed several whites with no prior craft experience to transfer into the skilled craft positions, blacks were not transferred unless they possessed at least five years of prior craft experience. Since blacks were largely excluded from the crafts unions, they were rarely able to acquire such experience. As a result only 2 percent of the skilled craftworkers at Gramercy were black. A third federal review in 1975 found that 2.2 percent of Kaiser Gramercy's 290 craftworkers were black; that of 72 professional employees only 7 percent were black; and that of 11 draftsmen none was black. Moreover, although the local labor market in 1975 was still 39 percent black, the Kaiser Gramercy plant's overall workforce was only 13.3 percent black. Only the lowest-paying category of jobs—unskilled laborers—included a large proportion (35.5 percent) of blacks, a proportion that was brought about by implementing a 1968 policy of hiring one black unskilled worker for every white unskilled worker.

By 1974 Kaiser was being pressured by federal agencies to increase the number of blacks in its better-paying, skilled crafts positions. Moreover, the U.S. Steelworkers Union was simultaneously pressing Kaiser to institute a program for training its own workers in the crafts, instead of hiring all its craftsworkers from outside the company. As a response to both of these pressures, Kaiser agreed in 1974 to set up a training program that was intended to qualify its *own* workers (both white and black) for crafts positions, and that was also intended to eliminate the manifest racial imbalance in its crafts positions. According to the agreement with the union, Kaiser workers would be trained for crafts positions, in order of seniority, at Kaiser's own expense ($15,000–$20,000 per year per trainee). One-half of the slots in the crafts training program would be reserved for blacks until the percentage of black skilled craftworkers in the

continued

increased quality, productivity, and employee motivation. The Saturn Corporation, for example, prides itself on such an approach to job design and the resultant worker commitment and involvement.

CRITICAL THINKING QUESTIONS

1. Describe the importance of process technology selection in designing operations.

2. Compare the relative importance of facility location planning in service operations and in manufacturing.

Gramercy plant approximated the percentage of blacks in the local labor force. Openings in the program would be filled by alternating between the most senior qualified white employee and the most senior qualified black employee.

During the first year of the program, 13 workers were selected for the training program: 7 blacks and 6 whites. Brian Weber, a young white worker who had applied to the program was not among those selected. Brian, a talkative, likable southerner and father of three, had been working as a blue-collar lab analyst in the Gramercy plant. His position was rated as "semiskilled." He wanted very much to qualify for one of the skilled jobs. Upon investigation Brian found that he had several months more seniority than two of the black workers who had been admitted into the training program. Forty-three other white workers who were also rejected had even more seniority than Brian. Junior black employees were thus receiving training in preference to more senior white employees. Brian later found that none of the black workers who had been admitted to the program had themselves been the subject of any prior employment discrimination by Kaiser.

Discussion Questions

1. In your judgment was the Kaiser plant practicing discrimination? If you believe that it was, explain what kind of discrimination was involved and identify the evidence for your answer. If you believe Kaiser was not being discriminatory, prepare responses to the strongest objections to your own view. Was Kaiser management morally responsible for the situation in its plant? Why?

2. In your judgment did the management of Kaiser act rightly when it implemented its preferential treatment program? Explain your answer in terms of the ethical principles that you think are involved. Does the fact that none of the black workers had themselves been subject to any prior employment discrimination by Kaiser absolve Kaiser from any ethical duty to rectify the racial imbalance in its workforce? What policies would you have recommended for Kaiser?

3. Was Brian Weber treated fairly or unfairly? Explain your answer on the basis of the moral principles that you think are involved. What is the value of seniority relative to equality of opportunity? As a manager, how would you have dealt with Brian and others who felt as he did? Should seniority serve as a basis for deciding who gets trained for a job? What kinds of qualifications do you believe should be taken into account?

Source: Manuel G. Velasquez, *Business Ethics: Concepts and Cases,* 2nd ed., © 1988, pp. 343-344. Reprinted by permission of Prentice–Hall, Englewood Cliffs, NJ.

OPERATIONS SCHEDULING AND INVENTORY CONTROL

There are a number of traditional operations scheduling and inventory control techniques that have been widely used in spite of some of their drawbacks. Scheduling and inventory are treated together because the two are intimately related. Scheduling suggests when to order inventory, and the kind of scheduling system can influence how much inventory is needed as a buffer.

Gantt Charts

Gantt charts, or **milestone charts,** depict a schedule as a series of events to be completed. Unfortunately, the milestones are usually laid out in serial fashion without showing interdependencies among the events. This can encourage functional thinking and detract from cross-functional system thinking. Serial processing also stretches out the time required to complete a project.

Program Evaluation and Review Technique (PERT)

Program evaluation and review technique (PERT) is a planning and scheduling technique based on a network of activities and their relationships. PERT is useful for large projects that have not been done before and in which it is especially important to understand the interrelationships among activities. Because a large PERT program can be complicated to update, some believe that the primary benefit of PERT is in planning and understanding the interrelationships among activities.

The author worked on a large PERT program in the early 1970s for the design, development, testing, production, and launch of a communications satellite. The development of the PERT project required planning and communication among the various program participants from different organizations. That PERT program was particularly complicated to update as it had over 10,000 events and required a computer for updating.

The longest path through a PERT project is referred to as the critical path. The **critical path method (CPM)** is a modification of PERT that focuses on the critical path. In the satellite example above, the critical path included the design and testing of the communications module. With that understanding, the program manager could devote extra resources and attention to those activities on the critical path.

Inventory and Total Quality

There is a new view of inventory that treats inventory as waste and a barrier to improvement. Inventory is costly. It ties up capital that could be employed elsewhere. It is difficult to spot areas for continuous improvement in the presence of large inventories, because the inventories mask the problem. How can the manager find the source of a defect if the affected batch of inventory is mixed with other batches? "Inventory makes it possible to live with machine breakdowns, unreliable vendors, inaccurate inventory records, unpredictable yields, long and unpredictable lead times in processing customers' orders, poor quality, and poor scheduling."[10] With all those problems submerged under large inventory, it is easy to see why some are viewing large inventories as evil. Suffice it to say, "less is better" is an idea to be applied to inventory.

Economic Order Quantities

Recognizing that less inventory is better than more inventory, the manager must balance ordering costs and holding costs. An **economic order quantity (EOQ)** is an amount of inventory ordered that minimizes the total of holding and ordering costs. The EOQ is getting smaller in many industries as suppliers, with a just-in-time system, have been reducing ordering costs through computerized links to customers.

Material Requirements Planning

Material requirements planning (MRP) is an operations planning and control system that schedules the exact quantities of parts and materials required to produce the finished product. MRP deals primarily with inventory of parts and materials.

By lowering variability, computer-controlled operations can reduce cost, reduce delivery time, and increase accuracy. (Photo credit: Bill Barley/Superstock.)

Manufacturing resource planning (MRP II) is an extension of material requirements planning to control most resources of the organization, including cash and human resources as well as inventory, in overall operations. A drawback of both MRP and MRP II is that they are patterned on a push inventory system with its inherent problems, as we shall describe in the following section.

Just-in-Time Inventory and Production

As a modification of a television commercial for a wine, some firms state that they will neither order nor produce an item before its time. A **just-in-time (JIT) inventory system** orders materials to arrive at the point of use exactly when they are needed. The result is that the inventory level approaches zero. Thus the inventory holding cost approaches zero. A JIT system works only in cases where the process is in control, the managers know exactly when to order, and the orders arrive as scheduled with no variance. Such a finely tuned operations system works like clockwork when all the parts are coordinated, but if one part of the system introduces variance, the system shuts down quickly.

The Saturn Corporation works with a well-tuned JIT system. When there was a strike at a parts supplier in 1992, the production system at Saturn ground to a halt in a few days. Saturn had no buffer inventory. To its credit, rather than laying off employees when there was no production, Saturn used the down time for training.

Sometimes JIT systems are referred to as *zero inventory* or *Japanese kanban* inventory systems. A JIT system is also referred to as a **demand pull inventory system** because each workstation or worker produces its output only when the next workstation or worker up the line says it is ready to receive more input. This contrasts with a **push inventory system,** in which large numbers of parts are made independent of when the next workstation or worker can use them. The result is batches of unused inventory throughout the plant. Perhaps the most notorious push inventory system example was the Chrysler inventory system of the late 1970s. The company produced cars to inventory independent of whether the cars were selling. Chrysler was forced to rent warehousing space in abandoned fields to store unbought cars so they could sit there and rust. It is easy to understand why push inventory systems are seldom used today.

CRITICAL THINKING QUESTIONS

1. How do traditional inventory ideas contrast with the idea of just-in-time inventory?

2. What is the role of quality control in operations management?

PURCHASING AND SUPPLIER RELATIONS FOR TOTAL QUALITY

There has been a change in TQ organizations concerning relationships with suppliers. Part of the reason for the change is the Japanese concept of *keiretsu*. **Keiretsu** emphasizes long-term relationships with a few key suppliers over short-term relationships with many suppliers. This pattern is especially apparent in the operations management area.

Low-Bid Contracting versus Partnering

In the past a primary way to deal with suppliers was through low-bid contracting. Whichever supplier bid the lowest, that was the supplier who received this year's contract. Unfortunately, that form of contracting encouraged any supplier who needed the business to shave a little off the bid to get the work. Sometimes, to get the contract with a low bid, the supplier cut down on quality in an attempt to hold down costs rather than improve the system of production to lower costs and defects. This old way of contracting resulted in large numbers of suppliers with high turnover in supplier relationships.

Partly due to the Japanese idea of *keiretsu,* many firms today are establishing long-term relationships with suppliers. Rather than reject a good supplier because some other supplier bid a few percentage points lower on a new contract, customers are staying with suppliers as partners and working with them for long-term cost reduction and quality enhancement. This partnering even includes training of the supplier by the customer, especially in improvement of quality management systems. The Caterpillar Quality Institute and Motorola University both conduct substantial supplier training.

Large Number of Suppliers versus Single Suppliers

At many firms a partnering relationship with suppliers is reducing the number of suppliers. Based on a relationship of trust and long-term mutual interest, many

FIGURE 18.5 *Diminishing Suppliers*

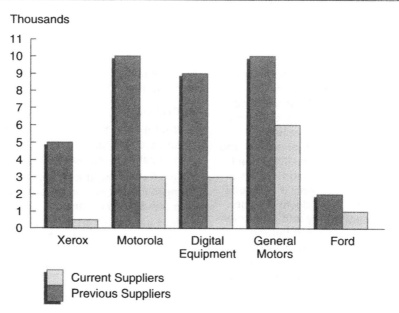

Source: *The Wall Street Journal* (August 16, 1991), B1. Reprinted by permission of The Wall Street Journal, © 1991 Dow Jones and Company, Inc. All rights reserved worldwide.

customer firms are now willing to invest in a few key suppliers rather than requiring several suppliers to constantly bid against each other. The trust and mutual interest also result in longer-term relationships with a few key suppliers, replacing the short-term relationships of the past that resulted from constant low bidding. Figure 18.5 shows how the number of suppliers has shrunk recently at a number of firms.

Acceptance Sampling versus No Incoming Inspection

In the low-bid, competitive mentality of the past, it was assumed that the supplier would not be responsible for the quality of the supplied parts. Therefore it was necessary for the customer to inspect incoming shipments from the supplier for defects to determine if the shipment was good enough. **Acceptance sampling** refers to making a decision to accept or reject a shipment based on the percentage or number of defects in an inspected sample from the shipment.

Today, rather than inspect the product, many customers are certifying the operations process of the supplier. Once the supplier's process has been certified, the customer can eliminate incoming inspection. This facilitates a just-in-time system in which the incoming parts are immediately integrated into the customer's operations. Many firms operating this way have a formal designation for qualified suppliers.

QUALITY CASE

Conclusion to the Sundstrand Case

In all cases at Sundstrand, it is the responsibility of the line manager and his or her personnel to operate the traffic light to indicate that a production problem exists. Since the objective is continuous improvement, it behooves the operator to turn on yellow and red lights for progressively smaller impact reasons. To quote Shigeo Shingo, who pioneered the traffic light method, "It is a poor supervisor who never shuts down his line, for he is not exposing quality and productivity problems. His product is not getting better. Likewise, it is a poor supervisor who continuously shuts down his line for the same reason. For he is continuously exposing the same problem over and over with no permanent solution."

DISCUSSION QUESTIONS

1. What do you think of the statement, "If it isn't broken, fix it anyway"? What are the implications—good or not so good?

2. To what extent, if any, can the remarkable improvement at Sundstrand be attributed to the *Shingo* method?

3. How would you go about integrating design and production?

Source: Joel E. Ross, *Total Quality Management*, Delray Beach, FL: St. Lucie Press (1993): 184, 185.

CRITICAL THINKING QUESTIONS

1. Describe the risks of a just-in-time inventory system with unionized suppliers.

2. What is the role of suppliers in a Total Quality environment?

SUMMARY

Operations management is the process of managing the production of goods and services. Many firms today recognize the critical importance of operations management to the ability of the firm to provide consistent value to customers. Products or services are viewed as mechanisms to deliver value to customers. Quality function deployment is a tool to recognize explicitly the importance of customer criteria in the design of products or services.

Operations managers today recognize the importance of process control. Stable, in-control processes yield products and services of consistent quality. Process reengineering is the continuous improvement of the process by which a product or service is created and distributed.

Rigid mass production is the production of a large number of the same item. In flexible mass production the system is capable of producing a variable number of different items. Today customers are demanding variety in products and services, which results in smaller lot sizes for the operations manager. As lot sizes become smaller, flexible mass production will become increasingly popular.

In designing operations, the manager must select a process technology. An increasing number of firms are recognizing that proven, well-defined technologies yield products and services of consistent quality. Capacity planning refers to the determination of how many units or how much volume the organization wants to be capable of producing. Facility location planning, layout planning, and job design are all aspects of designing the firm's operations.

Ever since the start of the industrial revolution in the late eighteenth century, managers have worried about the optimal level of inventory. Historically, many operations managers wanted large inventories to serve as buffers against unforeseen problems. Today managers recognize that a just-in-time approach, with the delivery of parts just as they are needed for further processing, is the most efficient way to conduct operations. This leads to a near-zero inventory level and exposes quality problems as they occur.

Suppliers and vendors occupy a new and prominent position of importance in a Total Quality era. Because of customer demands for no defects and a JIT approach, firms are entering into long-term partnerships with a few key suppliers. By certifying the suppliers' quality management processes, many firms are eliminating incoming inspection for suppliers. This contrasts with the traditional purchasing method based on low-bid contracting that resulted in a continual turnover of suppliers and in inconsistent quality.

EXPERIENTIAL EXERCISE

The Safety Inspection

You're surprised and just a little nervous to be asked to accompany an Occupational Safety and Health Administration (OSHA) compliance officer and the plant manager through the assembly area of your department. The OSHA visit and the request were totally unexpected.

As you walk through the assembly area, you are pleased to note the orderly and efficient arrangement of the assembly tables. In one of the material bins, you notice that several random pieces of tubing are protruding about eight inches beyond the rack. You recall that someone had tripped over such a piece of protruding tubing a few weeks ago. Almost at the same time, you see that one of the engineers has removed a portion of the protective rail around a heavy-duty source of power. It had been removed to facilitate an experiment with a new process, and evidently somebody has forgotten to replace it.

Discussion Questions

1. Should you point out the two possible safety violations or remain silent? Discuss.
2. What do you think will happen to your company as a result of this negligence?
3. How could these two safety problems have been avoided?

Source: R. Fulmer, *Supervision: Principles of Professional Management,* Encino, CA: Glencoe (1976): 151.

EXPERIENTIAL AND INTERNATIONAL EXERCISE

Choosing a Supplier

This exercise will give you the opportunity to assess a variety of options that might be available to a small company seeking international sources of supply. This exercise takes about 30 minutes of class time; no outside preparation is necessary.

You represent a small North American company that wants to purchase supplies from a less developed country. Your company supplies fishnets and other fishing supplies to Great Lakes commercial fishermen. Mr. Perch, the president, started the company after several years as a commercial fisherman.

Mr. Perch recently visited a trade show where he had the opportunity to observe some nets manufactured in Korea. The price of these nets compared favorably with those made in North America—$4/sq. ft. versus $12/sq. ft. The Koreans have not exported nets to the United States or Canada; thus Mr. Perch sees an opportunity to gain a price advantage over the competition. He orders a small quantity of the nets on a trial basis; this involves considerable effort in terms of arranging letters of credit, transportation, clearing customs, and so on—but it seems well worth the effort if a cheap source of supply is the result.

The Korean company is excited about the prospect of a possible export market. Market research suggests that there is a large potential market for the products in the United States and Canada and that they enjoy a considerable cost advantage over competitors from North America.

The trial shipment arrives in North America and Mr. Perch finds that the nets are unsuitable for use in freshwater lakes—they were designed for use in the ocean. Mr. Perch is upset and angry; he contacts the Korean company to express his misgivings. In the meantime, he becomes aware of a variety of other potential sources of the supply, including the Philippines, Indonesia, and various Caribbean islands.

The Korean company is confused by this turn of events. The company is interested in pursuing this export opportunity but does not have the expertise necessary to manufacture nets that are appropriate for freshwater fishing. The Korean government is also interested in the export opportunity and has indicated a willingness to provide export incentives for the company.

The class is divided into an even number of small groups. Half of the groups represent the North American company; half represent the South Korean company. Each group discusses the situation within its small group and decides on an appropriate course of action; each group then meets with a counterpart group—one representing the North American company, one the South Korean—to decide on a detailed agreement. A spokesperson for the joint groups is chosen to report the details of the agreement to the class.

Each group wants to maximize the benefits from its perspective; at the same time the groups are seeking a win–win solution that will be satisfactory to all parties.

You should consider the following issues:

— Continuity of supply

— Quality assurance and warranty

— Transaction currency and method of payment

— Exclusivity

— Credit and financing

CHAPTER CASE

How Velcro Got Hooked on Quality

The phone call came out of the blue one morning in August 1985. It was from our Detroit sales manager, who told me that General Motors was dropping us from its highest supplier quality rating to the next to lowest level, four (on a one to five scale). We had 90 days to set up and start a program of total quality control at our old U.S. plant in Manchester, New Hampshire, or face the loss of not only an important customer but also of our most promising growth market.

At the time we came under pressure from General Motors, we had 23 quality control people in the plant. (Now we have 12.) To the machine operators, quality was their responsibility—that is, someone else's. The quality control people were stationed at certain points, and they would inspect on a sample basis and say whether the particular run was good or bad. What was bad was thrown out. Nobody changed the process; there was no pressure on anybody to make a change. Many manufacturing people were extremely reluctant to take charge of quality; that was for the end of the line, when somebody else sorts out the errors.

To assume that the production employees were causing the waste would have been a mistake, and to beat on them about it without giving them the tools to deal with the problem would have been a bigger mistake. They would only have been afraid to report it. That's the fear element Deming talks about. The waste is going out in a dumpster during the third shift, and management thinks it's running at minimal waste until it takes inventory. We knew we had to invest in operator training, in more attention paid to operators, in machine repair and redesign, and in measurement and reporting techniques that tracked results, focused on responsibilities, and established up-and-down communication.

Part of the reason for the lack of pressure for change was the supervisors. We'd hear comments like "My boss won't let me shut the machine down. We make junk on my shift, but he doesn't care. He just says we've got to get *x* yards of material out. I show him the material, and he says, 'Run it anyway.'" The supervisors were a big barrier to making the operators responsible for quality.

The extensive use of computers in manufacturing for planning and control regulates the variability in the manufacturing processes through real-time SPC. (Photo credit: Bachman/The Image Works.)

The SPC system we installed went a long way toward pinpointing where in the production process we needed improvement. The charting mechanism of SPC also put pressure on the people on the line who had difficulty with the idea that quality and quantity aren't mutually exclusive expectations. The operators used to protest, "I see what you're saying, but I know that when I speed up the machine, it makes more mistakes." Gradually we pulled the quality control people out of stations early in the process, then we pulled them out of points later in the process. The number of mistakes declined.

Discussion Questions

1. Unless threatened with losing a major customer as in this case, why should an organization work to improve its quality?

2. Discuss the roles of managers, workers, and quality control inspectors in quality improvement.

Source: Reprinted by permission of *Harvard Business Review*. An excerpt from "How Velcro Got Hooked on Quality" by K. Theodor Krantz (September/October 1989). Copyright © 1989 by the President and Fellows of Harvard College. All rights reserved.

KEY TERMS

acceptance sampling   Making a decision to accept or reject a shipment based on the percentage or number of defects in an inspected sample from the shipment.

batch processing   Production in which only a few items are made at a time.

capacity planning   Determination of how many units or how much volume an organization wants to be capable of producing.

computer-aided manufacturing (CAM)   Use of some robots and computers in the manufacturing process.

concurrent engineering   Simultaneous product and process design for the manufacturing of the product.

critical path method (CPM)   Modification of PERT that focuses on the critical path.

demand pull inventory system   Inventory system in which each workstation or worker produces its output only when the next workstation or worker up the line says it is ready to receive more input.

economic order quantity (EOQ)   Amount of inventory ordered that minimizes the total of holding and ordering costs.

fixed-position layout   Layout in which a very large product stays in one place and the resources and tasks are brought to the product.

flexible mass production   Production in which the system is capable of producing a range of quantities because it has the capability for rapid changeover.

Gantt charts (milestone charts)   Charts that depict a schedule as a series of events to be completed.

just-in-time (JIT) inventory system   Inventory system that orders materials to arrive at the point of use exactly when they are needed.

keiretsu   Japanese concept that emphasizes long-term relationships with a few key suppliers over short-term relationships with many suppliers.

layout planning   Deciding how to arrange the physical configuration or the layout of facilities.

lot size   Number of identical items produced before a changeover is made to other products.

manufacturing management   Process of managing the production of tangible goods but not of services.

manufacturing resource planning (MRP II)   Extension of material requirements planning to control most resources of the organization, including cash and human resources as well as inventory, in overall operations.

material requirements planning (MRP)   Operations planning and control system that schedules the exact quantities of parts and materials required to produce the finished product.

operations management   Process of managing the production of goods and services.

Poka Yoke   Japanese term meaning design for quality in manufacturing.

process layout   Layout in which machines and resources that perform the same task are grouped together.

process reengineering   Continuous improvement of the process by which a product or service is created and distributed.

product layout   Layout in which machines and tasks are laid out according to a set sequence of tasks in the production of a single standardized product or service.

program evaluation and review technique (PERT)   Planning and scheduling technique based on a network of activities and their relationships.

push inventory system   Inventory system in which large numbers of parts are made independent of when the next workstation or worker can use them.

rigid mass production   Production of a large number of the same item.

service management   Process of producing nontangibles that require customer involvement and that are consumed at the point of delivery.

unique production   Production in which only one item is made.

value engineering   Attempt to make a product cheaper with minor improvements.

ENDNOTES

1. "The Hollow Corporation: The Decline of Manufacturing Threatens the Entire U.S. Economy," *Business Week* (March 3, 1986): 57.

2. D. T. Kearns and D. A. Nadler, *Prophets in the Dark*, New York: Harper Business (1992): 271.

3. W. Judge, M. Stahl, R. Scott, and R. Millender, "Long-Term Quality Improvement and Cost Reduction at Capsugel/Warner-Lambert," in M. Stahl and G. Bounds, *Competing Globally Through Customer Value*, Westport, CT: Quorum Books (1991): 703–709.

4. H. J. Harrington, *Business Process Improvement: The Breakthrough Strategy for Total Quality, Productivity, and Competitiveness*, New York: McGraw-Hill (1991): 9.

5. "Brace for Japan's Hot New Strategy," *Fortune* (September 21, 1992): 74.

6. W. A. Band, *Creating Value for Customers*, New York: Wiley (1991): 168–169.

7. "A New Equal Right: The Close Shave," *Business Week* (March 29, 1993): 58–59.

8. "The Quality Imperative," *Business Week* (October 25, 1991): 73, 95.

9. C. Wilson and M. Kennedy, "Improving the Product Development Process," in M. Stahl and G. Bounds (eds.), *Competing Globally Through Customer Value*, Westport, CT: Quorum Books (1991): 446–447.

10. K. Gilbert, "The Production and Inventory Control System," in M. Stahl and G. Bounds (eds.), *Competing Globally Through Customer Value*, Westport, CT: Quorum Books (1991): 533.

SUBJECT INDEX

Printed and bound by CPI Group (UK) Ltd, Croydon, CR0 4YY

09/06/2025

14686070-0004